seventh edition

The
St. Martin's
Handbook

Andrea A. Lunsford
Stanford University

A section for multilingual writers and a section on genre with

Paul Kei Matsuda
Arizona State University

Christine M. Tardy
DePaul University

A section on academic and professional writing with

Lisa Ede
Oregon State University

Bedford/St. Martin's
Boston ♦ New York

For Bedford/St. Martin's

Executive Editor: Carolyn Lengel
Production Editor: Ryan Sullivan
Senior Production Supervisor: Nancy Myers
Marketing Manager: Marjorie Adler
Art Director: Lucy Krikorian
Text Design: Anne Carter
Copy Editor: Wendy Polhemus-Annibell
Indexer: Kirsten Kite
Photo Research: Connie Gardner and Kristin Bowen
Cover Design: Donna Lee Dennison
Composition: Graphic World Inc.
Printing and Binding: RR Donnelley and Sons

President: Joan E. Feinberg
Editorial Director: Denise B. Wydra
Editor in Chief: Karen S. Henry
Director of Development: Erica T. Appel
Director of Marketing: Karen R. Soeltz
Director of Production: Susan W. Brown
Associate Director, Editorial Production: Elise S. Kaiser
Managing Editor: Shuli Traub

Library of Congress Control Number: 2010939977

Manufactured in the United States of America.

6   5   4   3   2   1
f   e   d   c   b

For information, write: Bedford/St. Martin's, 75 Arlington Street, Boston, MA 02116   (617-399-4000)

ISBN: 978-0-312-60293-2 (paperback)
ISBN: 978-0-312-60292-5 (hardcover)

Acknowledgments

Acknowledgments and copyrights appear at the back of the book on pages 918–19, which constitute an extension of the copyright page.

Preface

For decades now, it seems, I have been saying, "These are exciting times for writers and teachers of writing." And they have been exciting. But today, the word *exciting* scarcely begins to convey the wealth of opportunities — and challenges — ahead. Student writers are engaging with new media writing, creating arguments not simply as academic essays but as documentaries, videos, podcasts, visual collages, and much, much more. Centers and studios devoted to new literacies and new media writing are springing up, as colleges and universities try to catch up with what students are already doing. And writing teachers are working with a whole new range of media and genres as well, learning how to teach and assess the products of "new literacies" — while still holding on to the best of the "old" literacy, with its emphasis on academic essays and traditional print texts.

Are student writers and their teachers up to the challenges and opportunities offered today? Absolutely. Research I have done shows that student writers are already far ahead of us in terms of engaging new literacies, that they are thinking in sophisticated ways about the world-wide audiences they may now address, and that they are keenly aware of the need to adjust their messages according to audience, purpose, and context. In such an atmosphere of excitement and change, taking a rhetorical perspective is particularly important. Why? Because a rhetorical perspective rejects either/or, right/wrong, black/white approaches to writing in favor of asking what choices will be most appropriate, effective, and ethical in any given writing situation, using any genre and any medium.

The St. Martin's Handbook has always taken such a perspective, and the numerous changes to the seventh edition reflect this tradition. Throughout, this book invites student writers to take each choice they make as an opportunity for critical engagement with ideas, audiences, texts, media, and genre. But as I've incorporated new material, I've been careful not to lose sight of the mission of any handbook: to be an accessible reference to students and instructors alike.

Research for *The St. Martin's Handbook*

From the beginning, *The St. Martin's Handbook* has been informed by research on student writing. The late Robert J. Connors and I first began work on *The St. Martin's Handbook* in 1983, when we realized that most college handbooks were based on research into student writing conducted almost fifty years earlier. Our own historical studies had convinced us that student writing and what teachers think of as "good" writing change over time, so we began by gathering a nationwide sample of more than twenty-one thousand marked student essays and carefully analyzing a stratified sample to identify the twenty surface errors most characteristic of contemporary student writing.

Our analysis of these student essays revealed the twenty errors that most troubled students and teachers in the 1980s (spelling was by far the most prevalent error then) as well as the organizational and other global issues of greatest concern to teachers. Our findings on the twenty most common errors led to sections in *The St. Martin's Handbook* that attempt to put error in its place, presenting the conventions of writing as rhetorical choices a writer must make rather than as a series of rules that writers must obey.

Every subsequent edition of *The St. Martin's Handbook* has been informed by research, from a national survey of student writers on how they are using technology, to a series of intensive interviews with students and focus group sessions with first-year writing instructors, to a nationwide study for which Karen Lunsford and I replicated the research Connors and I did twenty-five years ago. Our "Mistakes Are a Fact of Life: A National Comparative Study" appeared in the June 2008 issue of *College Composition and Communication.* In sum, this study found that students are writing much longer essays than they were twenty-five years ago; that they are tackling more cognitively demanding topics and assignments, usually focusing on argument; *and* that the ratio of errors per one hundred words has not gone up but has remained almost constant during the last one hundred years (according to every national study we could find). While students are not making more mistakes, however, we found that they are making different ones — especially having to do with the use of and documentation of sources. And, in an ironic note, we found that while spelling errors have decreased dramatically with the use of spell checkers, the number of "wrong word" mistakes has risen—partly because of spell checkers suggesting that wrong word! Finally, in the midst of national hand-wringing over the damages texting, chatting, and blogging are doing to writing, our study showed that students in first-year writing classes, at least, know perfectly well when to write "LOL" or "GTG" or a host of other shortcuts and when such Internet lingo is inappropriate for their audience, purpose, and context. (You can find articles detailing my research with Bob Connors and with Karen Lunsford in *From Theory to Practice: A Selection of Essays* by Andrea A. Lunsford, available free from Bedford/St. Martin's.)

These findings are borne out by a six-year longitudinal study of both in-class and out-of-class writing (in any medium or genre) I have conducted, analyzing the writing of 189 writers. Again I saw longer pieces of writing and more analytical topics along with extracurricular writing of all kinds, from blog postings and emails to multimedia presentations and even a three-hour "hip-hopera." These student writers were aware of themselves as writers and rhetors, conscious that they could reach worldwide audiences at the click of a mouse; intrigued by new concepts of textual ownership and knowledge production brought about by collaborative programs like Google docs and file sharing of all kinds; and convinced that good writing is, as they told me over and over, "writing that makes something happen in the world." They see writing, then, as active and performative, as something that gets up off the page or screen and marches out into the world to do some good. In addition, they report that their best breakthroughs in terms of writing development tend to occur during what researcher Paul Rogers calls "dialogic interaction." That is, they learned most and best from interactions with knowledgeable others, whether peers, parents, or instructors—in the kind of give-and-take during which they could talk through ideas and get immediate response.

So today, some twenty-five years after I began working on *The St. Martin's Handbook*, I am optimistic about students and student writing. That optimism and the findings of my most recent research inform this seventh edition of the text. As always, this book seeks to serve students as a ready reference that will help them make appropriate grammatical, syntactical, and rhetorical choices. Beyond this immediate goal, though, I hope to guide students in understanding and experiencing for themselves the multiple ways in which truly good writing always means more than just following the rules. Truly good writing, as the students in the longitudinal study of writing insisted, means applying those rules in specific rhetorical situations for specific purposes and with specific audiences in ways that will bring readers and writers, teachers and students, to spirited conversation as well as to mutual understanding and respect.

New to This Edition

Students today are writing more than ever to communicate with friends and reach a wider public. My research shows that students already are making rhetorically informed decisions in their everyday writing—so I developed new features for this edition of *The St. Martin's Handbook* that will help students put the skills they already have to use in academic writing.

A focus on bridging extracurricular and academic writing

The St. Martin's Handbook shows how students can use the rhetorical strategies that they employ in their extracurricular writing—including an intuitive understanding of audience and purpose—to create more effective academic writing.

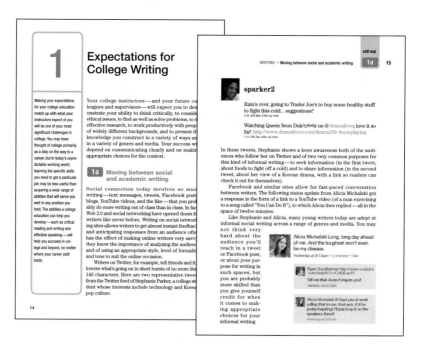

New attention to critical reading

A new chapter on critical reading highlights the wide range of texts students want, and are asked, to read today. Examples throughout the chapter analyze speeches, blogs, and photographs as well as literary works.

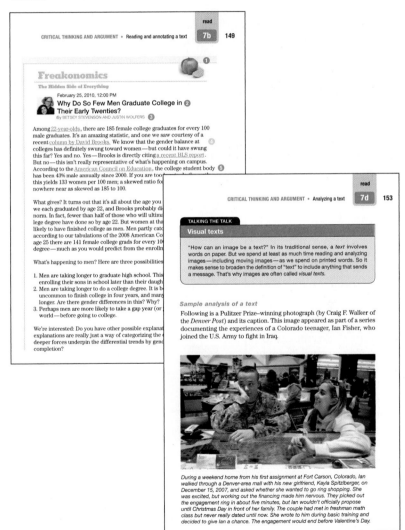

Detailed attention to multimodal writing

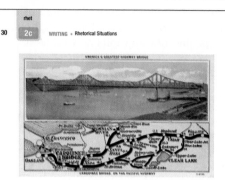

Images you choose to include in your writing can help establish credibility. But remember that images always have a point of view or perspective. The postcard seen here, for example, illustrates two physical perspectives—a photo of a bridge and a road map showing the bridge's location—as well as a time perspective—from 1927, when the bridge was new. This postcard, captioned "America's Greatest Highway Bridge," presents the construction of the bridge as a triumph of modern technology. So when you choose an image, think hard about how well it fits in with your topic and purpose attitude—and does that attitude serve the purp

3 Purposes for academic writing

Writing—even a simple note or text message multiple purposes, and academic work require your reasons for writing. On one level, you are credibility with your instructor, to demonstra thinker and an effective writer. On another leve to achieve goals of your own, to say as clearly what you think about a topic.

For example, if you are creating a project a pus, your purposes might include to inform y

- **Rhetorical advice on using media and images is integrated throughout the writing process.**

- **New tips from Paul Kei Matsuda (Arizona State University) and Christine Tardy (DePaul University) show how thinking carefully about genre helps shape texts.**

you need to make any other preparations to create a text that fulfills the demands of the genre?

2 Media

Much college writing is still done in print, but this tradition is changing. You may be asked to create multimodal writing using audio, video, images, and words—or some combination of these elements. As a result, you need to think about the medium where your writing will appear: in print on $8^1/_2'' \times 11''$ white paper? in print on a Web page? as an online audio or video essay? as a poster on campus? Make sure that you choose appropriate media for your topic, purpose, audience, and genre.

You may start off planning to work in print and then discover as you proceed that a different medium may offer more effective ways to communicate your point. One student, Will Rogers, who had been assigned to write an essay about something on campus that most students and faculty took for granted, focused on a giant crane being used in the construction of a new building complex. He did some research, finding out all he could about the crane and interviewing the crane's operator. That's when he got hooked: the operator was eighteen and had left his first year in college to take this job. The student carried out a series of interviews so that he could include the crane operator's own words. But he found the operator's story so compelling that he decided that it would work better—and be more powerful—in the medium of film. That way, viewers could actually see the crane operator and hear his voice as he described the decisions he had made. The result: a three-minute documentary called "Crane Man" for which he did all the writing, filming, and editing.

- **Expert advice helps students translate texts from one genre or medium to another, enhancing the publication and presentation skills that are increasingly important in today's multimodal classrooms. Model texts from a student writer show how a print essay becomes a multimedia presentation.**

To see an essay converted into a multimedia presentation, see pp. 467–78.

Translating work from one medium to another
You may be asked to create a work in one medium, such as print, and translate it to another, such as a multimedia presentation or scrapbook. Such translations may not be as straightforward as they seem. Just as filmmakers may omit content, streamline

More student writing in more genres

Work from more than thirty student writers appears in the book, with more models online. The variety of genres and media represented—from tweets and event promotions to multimedia presentations, literary analyses, and many more—reflects the writing students are doing today, both in and out of class.

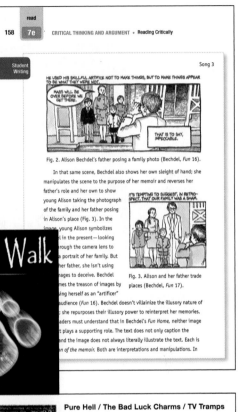

Student Writing

Song 3

HE USED HIS SKILLFUL ARTIFICE NOT TO MAKE THINGS, BUT TO MAKE THINGS APPEAR TO BE WHAT THEY WERE NOT.

MASS WILL BE OVER BEFORE WE GET THERE.

THAT IS TO SAY, IMPECCABLE.

Fig. 2. Alison Bechdel's father posing a family photo (Bechdel, *Fun* 16).

In that same scene, Bechdel also shows her own sleight of hand; she manipulates the scene to the purpose of her memoir and reverses her father's role and her own to show young Alison taking the photograph of the family and her father posing in Alison's place (Fig. 3). In the image, young Alison symbolizes ... l in the present—looking ... rough the camera lens to ... a portrait of her family. But ... her father, she isn't using ... ages to deceive. Bechdel ... mes the treason of images by ... sing herself as an "artificer" ... audience (*Fun* 16). Bechdel doesn't villainize the illusory nature of ... she repurposes their illusory power to reinterpret her memories. ... aders must understand that in Bechdel's *Fun Home*, neither image ... t plays a supporting role. The text does not only caption the ... and the image does not always literally illustrate the text. Each is ... n of the memoir. Both are interpretations and manipulations. In

IT'S TEMPTING TO SUGGEST, IN RETRO-SPECT, THAT OUR FAMILY WAS A SHAM.

Fig. 3. Alison and her father trade places (Bechdel, *Fun* 17).

Global AIDS Walk
— *A Call to Action* —

Fight
One a

April 27th 2003   10am   Freedom Plaz
The event will occur in 10 major U.S. cities. All proceeds will
HIV/AIDS clinics around the world through the Elizabeth Gla

REGISTER NOW at www.studentglo

Pure Hell / The Bad Luck Charms / TV Tramps
· Share · Public Event

Time:	Saturday, October 16 · 6:00pm - 9:30pm
Location:	Europa
Created By:	Scenic Nyc, Bryan Swirsky
More Info:	All Ages (16+ with government issued ID, under 16 w/ parent, guardian) $8 adv, $10 day of. !!! Early show.

+ Select Guests to Invite

Pure Hell, one of the earliest all-black American punk-rock bands, formed in Philadelphia, Pennsylvania, in 1974, as punk rock was taking off and developing a following in nearby New York City. Discovered by Johnny Thunders during the heyday of the New York Dolls, the band moved to New York. In 1978, they toured Europe and released their only single ("These Boots are Made for Walking" b/w "No Rules"). Live performances by Pure Hell have been compared to the MC5, Sex Pistols, Dead Boys, Germs, and fellow Afropunks the Bad Brains, who identi-fied Pure Hell as an influence. Their album (Noise Addiction), recorded in the late 1970s, was finally released this year. Pure Hell also has an unreleased album (The Black Box) produced in the mid 1990's by former members of L.A. Guns, Nine Inch Nails, and Lemmy Kilmister of Motorhead. Recent performances by Pure Hell in NYC showed that they still have what it takes!

New visual help with writing, research, and revision

An accessible, friendly design includes ample photographs and other illustrations that both show and tell students how to make good rhetorical choices.

- Color-coded source maps guide students in evaluating and citing print and electronic sources in MLA, APA, *Chicago*, and CSE styles.

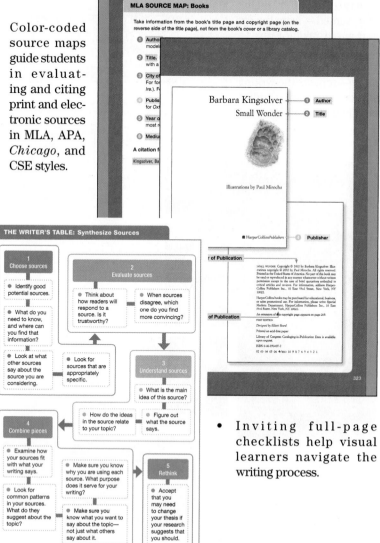

- Inviting full-page checklists help visual learners navigate the writing process.

Features of *The St. Martin's Handbook*

A FOCUS ON GOOD WRITING, NOT JUST CORRECTNESS. To write rhetorically effective texts, students must understand how to follow conventions that depend on their audience, situation, genre, medium, and discipline.

DETAILED COVERAGE OF CRITICAL THINKING AND ARGUMENT. Because first-year writing assignments continue to call for arguments, with or without multiple sources, *The St. Martin's Handbook* provides all the information student writers need to respond effectively to their writing assignments, including practical advice for analyzing and composing arguments as well as two complete student essays.

UP-TO-DATE ADVICE ON RESEARCH AND DOCUMENTATION. *The St. Martin's Handbook* includes thorough, up-to-date advice to help students do effective research in the library, online, and in the field, along with chapters on working with sources and avoiding plagiarism and full coverage of the latest guidelines for documenting sources in MLA, APA, *Chicago*, and CSE styles.

ESSENTIAL HELP FOR WRITING IN THE DISCIPLINES. Student writers will find strategies for understanding discipline-specific assignments, vocabulary, style, and use of evidence, along with complete student writing assignments by real students: research papers in MLA, APA, *Chicago*, and CSE styles; first-year writing assignments in the humanities, social sciences, and natural sciences; and business documents.

THOROUGH ATTENTION TO WRITING IN ANY MEDIUM. With advice on formal and informal online writing and on oral and multimedia presentations — and real-life student samples, including PowerPoint presentations, blogs, social networking posts, portfolio cover letters, and email — *The St. Martin's Handbook* shows students how writing in electronic and multimedia environments does (and doesn't) differ from writing for traditional print genres.

UNIQUE COVERAGE OF LANGUAGE. Practical advice helps students communicate effectively across languages and cultures — and shows how to use varieties of language both wisely and well. Extra help for multilingual writers appears in five chapters and in boxed tips throughout the book.

A USER-FRIENDLY INDEX. Entries include everyday words (such as *that* or *which*) as well as grammatical terms (such as *relative pronouns*), so students can find information even if they don't know grammatical terminology.

A Wide Array of Ancillaries

For a complete list of print and new media resources to accompany *The St. Martin's Handbook*, Seventh Edition, with download and ordering options, go to the catalog page: **bedfordstmartins.com/smhandbook/ catalog**.

Bedford/St. Martin's Research Pack
WITH CLOTHBOUND BOOK:
ISBN 978-0-312-55476-7
WITH PAPERBOUND BOOK:
ISBN 978-0-312-55478-1

Print resources

Instructor's Notes, Seventh Edition
ANDREA A. LUNSFORD AND ALYSSA O'BRIEN
ISBN 978-0-312-64526-7

The St. Martin's Pocket Guide to Research and Documentation, Fifth Edition
ANDREA A. LUNSFORD AND MARCIA MUTH
ISBN 978-0-312-66192-2

From Theory to Practice: A Selection of Essays, Third Edition
ANDREA A. LUNSFORD
ISBN 978-0-312-56729-3

The St. Martin's Sourcebook for Writing Tutors, Fourth Edition
CHRISTINA MURPHY AND STEVE SHERWOOD
ISBN 978-0-312-66191-5

The St. Martin's Guide to Teaching Writing, Sixth Edition
CHERYL GLENN AND MELISSA GOLDTHWAITE
ISBN 978-0-312-45133-2

Assigning, Responding, Evaluating, Fourth Edition
EDWARD M. WHITE
ISBN 978-0-312-43930-9

New media resources

Find details and ordering information at **bedfordstmartins.com/ smhandbook/catalog.**

CompClass for *The St. Martin's Handbook*

The St. Martin's Handbook book companion site

The St. Martin's e-Handbook

Re:Writing Plus: six collections of premium media for composition

Content for Course Management Systems, including Blackboard, WebCT, Desire2Learn, and Angel

Professional resources for instructors

For a broad range of free professional resources for composition instructors, go to **bedfordstmartins.com.**

Acknowledgments

The St. Martin's Handbook remains a collaborative effort in the best and richest sense of the word. For this edition, I am enormously indebted to Carolyn Lengel, whose meticulous care, tough-minded editing, great good humor, and sheer hard work are everywhere apparent. Carolyn is the consummate professional — and a very good friend. Also invaluable have been the contributions of Kristin Bowen, a friend, colleague, and terrific editor. I am also deeply indebted to friend and colleague Nick Carbone, whose extensive and detailed review of all material relating to online writing and research have been, simply, the sine qua non. As always, Nancy Perry, Denise Wydra, Joan Feinberg, Karen Henry, and Erica Appel have provided support, encouragement, and good advice, and my former editor Marilyn Moller continues to provide support and friendship.

Ryan Sullivan has managed the entire book from manuscript to bound book with skill and grace — and together with Shuli Traub and Nancy Myers has made an enormously complex project run smoothly. Wendy Polhemus-Annibell, the *Handbook's* multitalented copyeditor, edited the text efficiently and sensibly. Sarah Ferguson has deftly managed the many new media projects related to this book—and, amazingly, kept them all on track. Thanks also to editor Adam Whitehurst, who has offered advice on the media and research chapters and on the new media supplements and tutorials, and to Cecilia Seiter and Andrew Flynn, who have guided print ancillary development and worked on e-book and Web site content along with Nick McCarthy. For the truly snazzy cover and interior design, I am indebted to Donna Dennison, Anne Carter, Anna Palchik, and Lucy Krikorian. I am fortunate indeed to have had Karen Soeltz, Jane Helms, John Swanson, and Marjorie Adler as my marketing team; in my experience, they set the standard. And, as always, I am grateful to the entire Bedford/St. Martin's sales force, on whose wisdom and insights and energy I always depend.

Contributors

For this edition, I owe special thanks to Paul Kei Matsuda and Christine Tardy, who provided extremely helpful and innovative new coverage on genre. My friend and constant collaborator Lisa Ede has offered not only her ongoing support and sharp wit but also advice and counsel on the section on academic and professional writing. Special thanks also go to Christina Murphy and Steve Sherwood for their excellent new edition of the *Sourcebook for Writing Tutors*, to Alyssa O'Brien for her always brilliant work on the *Instructor's Notes*, to Mike Hennessy for his work on the preface to the *Instructor's Notes* and on the tutorial in the Handbook, and to Karen Lunsford, Paul Rogers, Jenn Fishman, Laurie Stapleton, Erin Krampetz, and Warren Liew, my partners in ongoing research on student writing.

As always, I am extremely fortunate to have had the contributions of very fine student writers, whose work appears throughout this text or on its companion Web site: Michelle Abbott, Carina Abernathy, Milena Ateyea, Julie Baird, Jennifer Bernal, Valerie Bredin, Taurean Brown, Tessa Cabello, Ben Canning, Leah Clendening, David Craig, Kelly Darr, Allyson Goldberg, Tara Gupta, Francisco Guzman, Joanna Hays, Dana Hornbeak, Ajani Husbands, Bory Kea, James Kung, Nastassia Lopez, Heather Mackintosh-Sims, Merlla McLaughlin, Alicia Michalski, Jenny Ming, Laura Montgomery, Elva Negrete, Katie Paarlberg, Shannan Palma, Stephanie Parker, Teal Pfeifer, Amrit K. Rao, Tawnya Redding, Heather Ricker, Amanda Rinder, Dawn Rodney, Rudy Rubio, Melissa Schraeder, Bonnie Sillay, Jessica Thrower, Dennis Tyler, and Caroline Warner.

I am especially grateful to Emily Lesk, whose imaginative and carefully researched essay appears in Chapters 2–6, and to Shuqiao Song, whose essay and multimedia presentation on Alison Bechdel's *Fun Home* enliven Chapters 7 and 22.

Advisory board

Many thanks to the astute members of our advisory board for their insights and thoughtful responses:

Mary Baumhover, Western New Mexico University
Darsie Bowden, DePaul University
Amy Childers, North Georgia College
Darren Defrain, Wichita State University
Christy Desmet, University of Georgia
Darrell Fike, Valdosta State University
Kathy Gillis, Texas Tech University
Monica Hatch, Southwestern Illinois College
Michael Keller, South Dakota State University
Susan Lang, Texas Tech University
Deb Miller, University of Georgia
Charlene Pate, Point Loma Nazarene
DaRelle Rollins, Hampton State University
Pat Sullivan, University of Arkansas–Fayetteville

Reviewers

For *The St. Martin's Handbook*, we have been blessed with a group of very special reviewers whose incisive comments, queries, criticisms, and suggestions have improved this book immeasurably:

Lena Andersson, Fulton-Montgomery Community College; Rhonda Armstrong, Newberry College; Mary Baumhover, Western New Mexico University; Tamar M. Boyadjian, University of California–Los Angeles; Edna C. Brown, Norfolk State University; Richard Carpenter, Valdosta State University; Rebecca Childs, Coastal Carolina University; Sarah V. Clere, Mount Olive College; Aaron S. Cohn, McKendree University; Rick Cole, Boston University; Renee Dechert, Northwest College; Scott Downing, DePaul University; Darrell Fike, Valdosta State University; Steven Gilbert, Newberry College; John

Goshert, Utah Valley University; Natalie Grinnell, Wofford College; Gary R. Hafer, Lycoming College; Karen Head, Georgia Tech; Fredric Jefferson Hendricks, Centenary College of Louisiana; Courtney Huntington, UNC Charlotte; Brandy L. James, University of West Georgia; Michael Keller, South Dakota State University; Lisa Drnec Kerr, Western New England College; Kathy L. Kufskie, Southwestern Illinois College; Carole Lane, University of Arkansas; Victoria-Sue Lombari, University of Arkansas; Marjorie Maddox-Hafer, Lock Haven University; Melinda Mahr, Washington University in St. Louis; Amy Childers Mansfield, North Georgia College & State University; Sean Alan Marsh, Southeastern Louisiana University; Paul Michael Mastrofrancesco, Washington University; Kacy McDonough, Tiffin University; Mitzi McFarland, University of West Georgia; Deborah Miller, University of Georgia; Molly Moran, University of Georgia; Stephanie S. Morgan, South College – Asheville; Samantha A. Morgan-Curtis, Tennessee State University; Roxanne F. Munch, Joliet Junior College; Alice Myatt, University of Mississippi; Kate Myers de Vega, Palm Beach Atlantic University; Harold Nelson, Minot State University; Lance Newman, Westminster College; Lisa M. Oldaker Palmer, Quinsigamond Community College; Matthew Parfitt, Boston University; David J. Peterson, University of Nebraska at Omaha; Cherri Randall, University of Pittsburgh; Gordon Rujanawech, California State University – Long Beach; Sara Schaff, University of Michigan; Lawrence Schwegler, University of Texas – San Antonio; Michael Shilling, University of Michigan; Mark Smith, Valdosta State University; Ann Spurlock, Mississippi State University; Peter Tatiner, Pace University; Alisa M. Thomas, Toccoa Falls College; Ruthe Thompson, Southwest Minnesota State University; Marjory Thrash, Pearl River Community College; Anne Thurmer, Winona State University; Bill D. Toth, Western New Mexico University; Linda P. Van Buskirk, Cornell University; Justin Williamson, Pearl River Community College; D'Anne Witkowski, University of Michigan; and Nolana Yip, Georgetown University.

Finally, I wish to offer very special thanks to the extraordinary community of teacher-researchers at the Bread Loaf Graduate School of English, whose responses to this text have helped to shape and refine its goals.

I could go on and on in praise of the support and help I have received, for I am fortunate to be part of a unique scholarly community, one characterized by compassion as well as passionate commitment to students and to learning. I remain grateful to be among you.

Andrea A. Lunsford

A Note to Students

The main goal of *The St. Martin's Handbook* is to help you become a competent and compelling writer—both throughout and beyond your college years.

This text encourages you to carefully analyze your own prose. Most chapters not only provide explanations and opportunities for practice but also ask you to apply the principles presented directly to your own writing. If you follow these directions, they will guide you in becoming a systematic self-critic—and a more effective writer. As your writing improves, so will your reading, your thinking, and your research.

I hope that this book will prove to be a useful reference. But in the long run, a book can be only a guide. You are the one who will put such guidance into practice as you work to become a precise, powerful, and persuasive writer. Why not get started on achieving that goal right now?

Andrea A. Lunsford

How to Use *The St. Martin's Handbook*

This book has been designed to be as easy as possible to use. Depending on what information or advice you're looking for, you may want to consult any or all of the following:

- **TABLES OF CONTENTS.** If you know what general topic you're looking for (such as using commas), the **Brief Contents** on the inside front cover will lead you to the chapter where you'll find that topic. If you're looking for a specific kind of information within a general topic (such as using commas in a series), the detailed **Contents** on the inside back cover or the even more detailed **Contents** following this introduction can lead you to this information.

- **INDEX.** The index covers everything in the book. It's especially useful for finding specific words you need help with (such as *that* or *which*) but don't know the exact technical term for (*relative pronouns*).

- **THE TOP TWENTY.** On pp. 1–12 you will find explanations and examples of the top twenty problems in the writing of U.S. college students today, with references to pages in the book where you can find additional information about avoiding and editing these problems.

- **DOCUMENTATION GUIDELINES.** For information on documenting sources, see the chapters on MLA (Chapter 16), APA (Chapter 17), *Chicago* (Chapter 18), and CSE (Chapter 19) styles.

- **REVISION SYMBOLS.** If your instructor uses revision symbols to mark up your drafts, consult the list of symbols at the back of the book and its cross-references to sections where you'll find more help.

- **GLOSSARIES.** The **Glossary of Terms** (p. 900) defines grammatical and writing-related terms; the **Glossary of Usage** (p. 910) gives help with troublesome words (such as *accept* and *except*).

Navigating Pages

1. **GUIDES AT THE TOP OF EVERY PAGE.** Headers tell you the title of the part and the chapter or section, the chapter number and section letter, and the page number. An abbreviated title on the tab allows quick flipping.

2. **BOXED TIPS THROUGHOUT THE BOOK.** Directories for boxes appear on pp. 949–50.

   - *"Talking the talk"* **boxes** help you understand academic language and concepts.
   - *"For multilingual writers"* **boxes** offer advice for those who speak, understand, or write languages in addition to English.
   - *"Considering disabilities"* **boxes** help you make your work accessible to readers with disabilities and point out strategies and resources for writers with disabilities.

3. **HAND-EDITED EXAMPLES.** Many examples are hand-edited in blue, allowing you to see the error and its revision at a glance. Pointers and boldface type make examples easy to spot.

4. **CROSS-REFERENCES.** Cross-references to the Book Companion Site appear in every chapter to direct you to online resources — from a tutorial on avoiding plagiarism to additional grammar exercises, model student writing, and more. Cross-references to other parts of the book appear in parentheses throughout.

5. **QUICK HELP BOXES.** Green boxes appear in most chapters to help you check your drafts with a critical eye and revise or edit as need be.

cap
50d 763

➊ MECHANICS • Unnecessary capitalization

English capitalization

Capitalization systems vary considerably among languages, and some languages (Arabic, Chinese, Hindi, and Hebrew, for example) do not use capital letters at all. English may be the only language to capitalize the first-person singular pronoun (*I*), but Dutch and German capitalize some forms of the second-person pronoun (*you*). German capitalizes all nouns; English used to capitalize more nouns than it does now (see, for instance, the Declaration of Independence).

➋

50d Unnecessary capitalization

Do not capitalize a compass direction unless the word designates a specific geographic region.

○ **Voters in the South and much of the West tend to favor socially conservative candidates.**

       west,
○ **John Muir headed ~~West,~~ motivated by the need to explore.** ➌
        ^

Do not capitalize a word indicating a family relationship unless the word is used as part of the name or as a substitute for the name.

○ **I could always tell when Mother was annoyed with Aunt Rose.**

bedfordstmartins.com/smhandbook
Exercise Central > Mechanics > Capital Letters
➍

QUICK HELP
➎
Editing for capitalization

- Capitalize the first word of each sentence. If you quote a poem, follow its original capitalization. (50a)

- Check to make sure you have appropriately capitalized proper nouns and proper adjectives. (50b)

- Review titles of people or of works to be sure you have capitalized them correctly. (50b and c)

- Double-check the capitalization of geographic directions (*north* or *North*?), family relationships (*dad* or *Dad*?), and seasons of the year (*winter*, not *Winter*). (50d)

A Tutorial on Using *The St. Martin's Handbook*, Seventh Edition

For this book to serve you well, you need to get to know it — to know what's inside and how to find it. The following tutorial is designed to help you familiarize yourself with *The St. Martin's Handbook*; the answers appear on pp. xxiv–xxv.

GETTING STARTED WITH *THE ST. MARTIN'S HANDBOOK*

1. Where will you find advice on revising a rough draft of an essay?
2. Where will you find quick information on identifying and fixing sentence fragments?
3. Where will you find guidelines on documenting electronic sources, such as information found on a Web site?
4. Where will you find advice for multilingual writers?

PLANNING AND DRAFTING

5. Where in the *Handbook* can you find general guidelines on planning and drafting an essay?
6. Where can you find information about how to make and support a claim?
7. Your instructor wants you to give an oral presentation based on a print essay you've written. Where would you find information in the *Handbook* about planning the presentation?

DOING RESEARCH

8. You have a topic but don't know where to begin your research. How can the *Handbook* help you narrow down your options?
9. You've found Web sites related to your topic, but you aren't sure how reliable they are. Where can you find help in evaluating them?
10. Your instructor asks you to become a more critical reader of the sources you have found for your writing project. What section of the *Handbook* will help you understand what to do?
11. You have misplaced the page number of a quotation from an essay you want to use in your final project. Can you omit it? Where can you find the answer in the *Handbook*?
12. Your instructor has asked you to use MLA style. How do you document information obtained from a DVD source?

EDITING

13. As you edit a final draft, you stop at the following sentence: *Winning may be the name of the game but it isn't a name I care for very much*. Should you put a comma before *but*? How and where do you find this answer?
14. You speak several languages, and you still confuse the English prepositions *in* and *on*. Where in the *Handbook* can you find help?
15. Your instructor has written *ref* next to this sentence: *Transmitting video signals by satellite is a way of overcoming the problem of scarce airwaves and limiting how they are used*. Where do you look in the *Handbook* for help responding to your instructor's comment?
16. You have spell-checked your document. Do you still need to proofread it? What information does the *Handbook* provide?

MEETING YOUR INSTRUCTORS' EXPECTATIONS

17. You have gotten a draft of your paper back from your instructor with the comment *underdeveloped*. How can the *Handbook* help you find out what you need to do to revise?
18. You want to let your instructor know that you will need to miss class the following day. What advice can the *Handbook* give you about sending a message to someone you don't know very well?
19. You turned in a revised draft, but your instructor says you have only corrected minor errors. Where can you find information on doing thorough revisions?
20. You have been asked to look at a classmate's electronic draft and make suggestions. How can you find out more about reviewing the work of your peers?

WRITING IN ANY DISCIPLINE

21. You have a take-home exam in political science. You've never before written a political science paper, so you're not sure how to proceed. Do political science papers follow any set format? Where in the *Handbook* can you look for help?
22. You need to write a lab report for your chemistry class. Is there a model in the *Handbook*?
23. For a literature course, you're writing an essay interpreting a poem by Emily Dickinson. Where can you find help in the *Handbook*?
24. You need to submit an electronic portfolio for your writing class. Where in the *Handbook* can you find information about what to include and how to present the work?

Answers to the tutorial

1. Chapter 4.
2. Chapter 37, on sentence fragments.
3. Chapter 16 covers documenting sources, including electronic sources, in MLA style; Chapters 17–19 cover documenting sources in APA, *Chicago*, and CSE styles, respectively.
4. Part 11 includes five chapters (Chapters 54–58) that cover language issues of special interest to students who speak languages in addition to English. Page 949 has a directory to all the materials in the *Handbook* for multilingual writers.
5. Chapter 3 offers guidelines on exploring, planning, and drafting.
6. Looking up *arguments* in the index leads you to section 8e on the elements that make up an argument and to Chapter 9, which explains how to construct an effective argument.
7. Looking in the directory of student writing points you toward the excerpts from a student presentation in 22c and to the sample PowerPoint presentation slides and script in 22d. Checking the table of contents would also direct you to Chapter 22, "Oral and Multimedia Presentations," which includes advice on turning a print text into a presentation.
8. Chapter 11, "Conducting Research," includes section 11b, "Using the library to get started."
9. Skimming the table of contents leads you to Chapter 12, on evaluating sources, and in particular to 12c, on evaluating usefulness and credibility, and to 12d, on reading sources critically.
10. Looking in the index under *reading* or *critical reading*—or checking the table of contents—should lead you to Chapter 7, "Reading Critically," which outlines steps in a critical reading process with examples for various kinds of texts.
11. Consulting the index under *acknowledging sources* takes you to Chapter 14, "Acknowledging Sources and Avoiding Plagiarism," where you will find that you must include all of the necessary elements of a citation. "The Top Twenty," on the orange pages before Chapter 1, points out that incomplete documentation is one of the three most common problems in student writing today.
12. The table of contents leads you to Chapter 16, which provides a full discussion of MLA documentation conventions. It also lists a directory to MLA style, which leads you to section 16d3 on documenting electronic sources.
13. You could turn directly to Chapter 44, on using commas, and look for examples of how to use commas in similar sentences. Looking at "The Top Twenty," on the orange pages before Chapter 1, will show you that omitting a comma in a compound sentence is one of the most common errors students make.
14. The table of contents tells you that Chapter 58 covers prepositions; 58a includes a set of strategies for using prepositions idiomatically, including several examples of sentences using *in* and *on*.
15. A list of revision symbols appears on p. 951 of the *Handbook*. Consulting this list tells you that *ref* refers to "unclear pronoun reference" and that this subject is discussed in Chapter 32.

16. Looking up *proofreading* in the index will take you to an entry on spell checkers and proofreading. The information in section 28e points out that spell checkers miss many kinds of mistakes—there is no substitute for careful proofreading!

17. Looking up *comments* in the index or skimming the table of contents will lead you to section 4d, which includes a chart on learning from instructor comments. Section 4e offers additional suggestions on using comments to revise your work.

18. A glance at the table of contents shows you that Chapter 20, "Formal and Informal Electronic Communication," offers guidelines for sending formal messages, such as an email to an instructor.

19. In the index, you'll find an entry for *reviewing* that directs you to a "Talking the Talk" box in Chapter 4. A directory to all the book's "Talking the Talk" boxes, which answer frequently asked questions about academic work, appears on p. 950.

20. Looking under *peer reviews* in the index, or scanning the table of contents, will lead you to section 4b, a detailed look at how to act as a peer reviewer—and how to react when your work is under review.

21. Part 12 covers academic and professional writing in general, and Chapter 61 covers social science subjects. Chapter 64 offers tips on take-home exams.

22. Consulting the student directory on p. 948 will lead you to a chemistry lab report in Chapter 62, on writing for the natural and applied sciences.

23. Chapter 60, on writing for the humanities, provides guidelines for close readings of literature and a student paper comparing two poems by E. E. Cummings. (On the book's Web site, you can also find a glossary of literary terms at **bedfordstmartins.com/smhandbook** under **Writing Resources**.)

24. Looking up *portfolios* in the index or skimming the table of contents will take you to Chapter 65, on planning a portfolio. In 65d, you will see an example of a student's portfolio home page.

Contents

The Top Twenty:
A Quick Guide
to Troubleshooting
Your Writing

Although many people think of correctness as absolute, based on unchanging rules, instructors and students know that there are rules, but they change with time. "Is it okay to use *I* in essays for this class?" asks one student. "My high school teacher wouldn't let us." In the past, use of first person was discouraged by instructors, sometimes even banned. But today, most fields accept such usage in moderation. Such examples show that rules clearly exist but that they are always shifting and that they thus need our ongoing attention.

The conventions involving surface errors—grammar, punctuation, word choice, and other small-scale matters—are a case in point. Surface errors don't always disturb readers. Whether your instructor marks an error in any particular assignment will depend on his or her judgment about how serious and distracting it is and what you should be giving priority to at the time. In addition, not all surface errors are consistently viewed as errors: some of the patterns identified in the research for this book are considered errors by some instructors but as stylistic options by others.

Shifting standards do not mean that there is no such thing as correctness in writing—only that *correctness always depends on some context.* Correctness is not so much a question of absolute right or wrong as of the way the choices a writer makes are perceived by readers. As writers, we all want to be considered competent and careful. We know that our readers judge us by our control of the conventions we have agreed to use, even if the conventions change from time to time.

To help you in producing writing that is conventionally correct, you should become familiar with the twenty most common error patterns among U.S. college students today, listed on the next page in order of frequency. These twenty errors are the ones most likely to result in negative responses from your instructors and other readers. A brief explanation and examples of each error are provided in the following sections, and each error pattern is cross-referenced to other places in this book where you can find more detailed information and additional examples.

The top twenty

1. Wrong word
2. Missing comma after an introductory element
3. Incomplete or missing documentation
4. Vague pronoun reference
5. Spelling (including homonyms)
6. Mechanical error with a quotation
7. Unnecessary comma
8. Unnecessary or missing capitalization
9. Missing word
10. Faulty sentence structure
11. Missing comma with a nonrestrictive element
12. Unnecessary shift in verb tense
13. Missing comma in a compound sentence
14. Unnecessary or missing apostrophe (including *its/it's*)
15. Fused (run-on) sentence
16. Comma splice
17. Lack of pronoun-antecedent agreement
18. Poorly integrated quotation
19. Unnecessary or missing hyphen
20. Sentence fragment

1 **Wrong word**

> precedence
> **Religious texts, for them, take ~~prescience~~ over other kinds of sources.**

Prescience means "foresight," and *precedence* means "priority of importance."

> allergy
> **The child suffered from a severe ~~allegory~~ to peanuts.**

Allegory, which refers to a symbolic meaning, is a spell checker's replacement for a misspelling of *allergy*.

▷ The panel discussed the ethical implications ~~on~~ *of* the situation.
   ^

Wrong-word errors can involve using a word with the wrong shade of meaning, a word with a completely wrong meaning, or a wrong preposition or word in an idiom. Selecting a word from a thesaurus without being certain of its meaning or allowing a spell checker to correct your spelling automatically can lead to wrong-word errors, so use these tools with care. If you have trouble with prepositions and idioms, memorize the standard usage. (See Chapter 27 on choosing the correct word, Chapter 28 on using spell checkers wisely, and Chapter 58 on using prepositions and idioms.)

2   Missing comma after an introductory element

▷ Determined to get the job done, we worked all weekend.
                              ^

▷ In German, nouns are always capitalized.
            ^

Readers usually need a small pause between an introductory word, phrase, or clause and the main part of the sentence, a pause most often signaled by a comma. Try to get into the habit of using a comma after every introductory element. When the introductory element is very short, you don't always need a comma after it. But you're never wrong if you do use a comma. (See 44a.)

3   Incomplete or missing documentation

▷ Satrapi says, "When we're afraid, we lose all sense of analysis and
                                    (263).
   reflection/"
            ^

The writer is citing a print source using MLA style and needs to include the page number where the quotation appears.

▷ According to one source, James Joyce wrote two of the five best
                        (Modern Library 100 Best).
   novels of all time/
                    ^

The writer must identify the source. Because *Modern Library 100 Best* is an online source, no page number is needed.

Be sure to cite each source as you refer to it in the text, and carefully follow the guidelines of the documentation style you are using to include all the information required (see Chapters 16–19). Omitting documentation can result in charges of plagiarism (see Chapter 14).

4 Vague pronoun reference

POSSIBLE REFERENCE TO MORE THAN ONE WORD

▶ Transmitting radio signals by satellite is a way of overcoming the
                                the airwaves
   problem of scarce airwaves and limiting how ~~they~~ are used.
                                           ^

Does *they* refer to the signals or the airwaves? The editing clarifies what is being limited.

REFERENCE IMPLIED BUT NOT STATED
                               a policy
▶ The company prohibited smoking, ~~which~~ many employees resented.
                                      ^

What does *which* refer to? The editing clarifies what employees resented.

A pronoun — a word such as *she, yourself, her, it, this, who,* or *which* — should refer clearly to the word or words it replaces (called the *antecedent*) elsewhere in the sentence or in a previous sentence. If more than one word could be the antecedent, or if no specific antecedent is present in the sentence, edit to make the meaning clear. (See 32f.)

5 Spelling (including homonyms)

                     bear
▶ No one came forward to ~~bare~~ witness to the crime.
                             ^

              Reagan
▶ Ronald ~~Regan~~ won the election in a landslide.
            ^

           Everywhere
▶ ~~Every where~~ we went, we saw crowds of tourists.
   ^

                        until
▶ The wolves stayed ~~untill~~ the pups were able to leave the den.
                         ^

The most common kinds of misspellings today are those that spell checkers cannot identify. The categories that spell checkers are most likely to miss include homonyms (words that sound alike but have different meanings); compound words incorrectly spelled as two separate words; and proper nouns, particularly names. Proofread carefully for errors that a spell checker cannot catch—and be sure to run the spell checker to catch other kinds of spelling mistakes. (See 28e.)

6   Mechanical error with a quotation

▷ "I grew up the victim of a disconcerting confusion,"/ Rodriguez says (249).

The comma should be placed *inside* the quotation marks.

▷ Captain Renault (Claude Rains) says that he is "shocked—shocked!

to find gambling going on in here" (*Casablanca*).

Both the beginning and the end of the quotation (from the film *Casablanca*) should be marked with quotation marks.

Follow conventions when using quotation marks with commas (44h), semicolons (45d), question marks (46b), and other punctuation (48e). Always use quotation marks in pairs, and follow the guidelines of your documentation style for block quotations and poetry (48a). Use quotation marks to mark titles of short works (48b), but use italics for titles of long works (52a).

7   Unnecessary comma

BEFORE CONJUNCTIONS IN COMPOUND CONSTRUCTIONS THAT ARE NOT COMPOUND SENTENCES

▷ This conclusion applies to the United States/ and to the rest of the world.

No comma is needed before *and* because it is joining two phrases that modify the same verb, *applies.*

WITH RESTRICTIVE ELEMENTS

▷ Many parents/ of gifted children/ do not want them to skip a grade.

No comma is needed to set off the restrictive phrase *of gifted children*; it is necessary to indicate which parents the sentence is talking about.

Do not use commas to set off restrictive elements—those necessary to the meaning of the words they modify. Do not use a comma before a coordinating conjunction (*and, but, for, nor, or, so, yet*) when the conjunction is not joining two parts of a compound sentence. Do not use a comma before the first or after the last item in a series, and do not use a comma between a subject and verb, between a verb and its object or complement, or between a preposition and its object. (See 44j.)

8 Unnecessary or missing capitalization

◉ Some ~~Traditional~~ ^{traditional} Chinese ~~Medicines~~ ^{medicines} containing ~~Ephedra~~ ^{ephedra} remain legal.

Capitalize proper nouns and proper adjectives, the first words of sentences, and important words in titles, along with certain words indicating directions and family relationships. Do not capitalize most other words, and proofread to make sure your word processor has not automatically added unnecessary capitalization (after an abbreviation ending with a period, for example). When in doubt, check a dictionary. (See Chapter 50.)

9 Missing word

◉ The site foreman discriminated ^{against} women and promoted men with less experience.

◉ Christopher's behavior becomes ^{so} bizarre that his family asks for help.

Be careful not to omit little words, including prepositions (58a), parts of two-part verbs (58b), and correlative conjunctions (29b7). Proofread carefully for any other omitted words, and be particularly careful not to omit words from quotations.

10 Faulty sentence structure

◉ ~~The information which~~ high ^{High} school athletes are presented with ~~mainly includes~~ information on what credits ^{they} needed to graduate,

and thinking about the college which athletes are trying to play for,
~~and thinking about the college~~ *colleges to try* ~~athletes are trying~~
how to
~~and~~ apply.
^

- People who use marijuana can build up a tolerance for it ~~will~~ want a
  and
  ^
  stronger drug.

When a sentence starts out with one kind of structure and then changes
to another kind, it confuses readers. If readers have trouble following the
meaning of your sentence, read the sentence aloud and make sure that
it contains a subject and a verb (29c). Look for mixed structures (39a),
subjects and predicates that do not make sense together (39b), and comparisons with unclear meanings (39e). When you join elements (such as
subjects or verb phrases) with a coordinating conjunction—*and, but,
for, nor, or, so,* or *yet*—make sure that the elements have parallel structures (35b).

11 Missing comma with a nonrestrictive element

- Marina, who was the president of the club, was first to speak.
  ^   ^

  The reader does not need the clause *who was the president of the club* to
  know the basic meaning of the sentence: Marina was first to speak.

A nonrestrictive element—one that is not essential to the basic meaning
of the sentence—could be removed, and the sentence would still make
sense. Use commas to set off any nonrestrictive parts of a sentence.
(See 44c.)

12 Unnecessary shift in verb tense

- A few countries produce almost all of the world's illegal drugs, but
  affects
  addiction ~~affected~~ many countries.
  ^

- Priya was watching the great blue heron. Then she ~~slips~~ and ~~falls~~
  slipped *fell*
  ^   ^
  into the swamp.

Verb tenses tell readers when actions take place: saying *Ron went to school* indicates a past action whereas saying *he will go* indicates a future action. Verbs that shift from one tense to another with no clear reason can confuse readers. (See 34a.)

13 Missing comma in a compound sentence

○ The words "I do" may sound simple, but they mean a life commitment.
^

○ Meredith waited for Samir, and her sister grew impatient.
^

Without the comma, a reader may think at first that Meredith waited for Samir and her sister.

A compound sentence consists of two or more parts that could each stand alone as a sentence. When the parts are joined by a coordinating conjunction—*and, but, so, yet, or, nor,* or *for*—use a comma before the conjunction to indicate a pause between the two thoughts. In very short sentences, the comma is optional if the sentence can be easily understood without it. Including the comma, however, will never be wrong. (See 44b.)

14 Unnecessary or missing apostrophe (including *its / it's*)

child's
○ Overambitious parents can be very harmful to a ~~childs~~ well-being.
^

Mets'
○ Johan Santana is one of the ~~Met's~~ most electrifying pitchers.
^

its   It's
○ The car is lying on ~~it's~~ side in the ditch. ~~Its~~ a white 2004 Passat.
^   ^

hers.
○ She passed the front runner, and the race was ~~her's.~~
^

To make a noun possessive, add either an apostrophe and an -s (*Ed's book*) or an apostrophe alone (*the boys' gym*). Do *not* use an apostrophe with the possessive pronouns *ours, yours, hers, its,* and *theirs*. Use *its* to mean *belonging to it*; use *it's* only when you mean *it is* or *it has*. (See Chapter 47.)

15 Fused (run-on) sentence

- The current was swift. ~~he~~ could not swim to shore.
  _{He}

- Klee's paintings seem simple, they are very sophisticated.
  _{but}

- ~~She~~ doubted the value of meditation, she decided to try it once.
  _{Although she}

A fused sentence (also called a run-on sentence) is created when clauses that could each stand alone as a sentence are joined with no punctuation or words to link them. Fused sentences must either be divided into separate sentences or joined by adding words, punctuation, or both. (See Chapter 36.)

16 Comma splice

- Westward migration had passed Wyoming by, even the discovery of gold in nearby Montana failed to attract settlers.

- I was strongly drawn to her, she had special qualities.
  _{for}

- We hated the meat loaf, the cafeteria served ~~it~~ every Friday.
  _{that}

A comma splice occurs when only a comma separates clauses that could each stand alone as a sentence. To correct a comma splice, you can insert a semicolon or period, connect the clauses clearly with a word such as *and* or *because*, or restructure the sentence. (See Chapter 36.)

17 Lack of pronoun-antecedent agreement

- Each of the puppies thrived in ~~their~~ new home.
  _{its}

Many indefinite pronouns, such as *everyone* and *each*, are always singular.

- Either Nirupa or Selena will be asked to give ~~their~~ speech to the graduates.
  _{her}

When antecedents are joined by *or* or *nor*, the pronoun must agree with the closer antecedent.

> *their*
> The team frequently changed ~~its~~ positions to get varied experience.

A collective noun can be either singular or plural, depending on whether the people are seen as a single unit or as multiple individuals.

> *or her*
> Every student must provide his own uniform.

With a singular antecedent that can refer to either a man or a woman, you can use *his or her*, *he or she*, and so on. You can also rewrite the sentence to make the antecedent and pronoun plural or to eliminate the pronoun altogether.

Pronouns must agree with their antecedents in gender (for example, using *he* or *him* to replace *Abraham Lincoln* and *she* or *her* to replace *Queen Elizabeth*) and in number. (See 32f.)

18 Poorly integrated quotation

> *showed how color affects taste:*
> A 1970s study of what makes food appetizing "Once it became apparent that the steak was actually blue and the fries were green, some people became ill" (Schlosser 565).

> *According to Lars Eighner,*
> "Dumpster diving has serious drawbacks as a way of life" (~~Eighner~~ 383). Finding edible food is especially tricky.

Quotations should fit smoothly into the surrounding sentence structure. They should be linked clearly to the writing around them (usually with a signal phrase) rather than dropped abruptly into the writing. (See 13b.)

19 Unnecessary or missing hyphen

> This paper looks at fictional and real-life examples.

A compound adjective modifying a following noun may require a hyphen.

○ **Some of the soldiers were only eleven/years/old.**

A complement that follows the noun it modifies should not be hyphenated.

○ **The buyers want to fix/up the house and resell it.**

A two-word verb should not be hyphenated.

A compound adjective that appears before a noun often needs a hyphen (53a). However, be careful not to hyphenate two-word verbs or word groups that serve as subject complements (53c).

20 Sentence fragment

NO SUBJECT

○ **Marie Antoinette spent huge sums of money on herself and her**
Her extravagance
favorites. ~~And~~ helped bring on the French Revolution.

NO COMPLETE VERB
was
○ **The old aluminum boat sitting on its trailer.**

Sitting cannot function alone as the verb of the sentence. The auxiliary verb *was* makes it a complete verb.

BEGINNING WITH A SUBORDINATING WORD
where
○ **We returned to the drugstore/, ~~Where~~ we waited for our buddies.**

A sentence fragment is part of a sentence that is written and punctuated as if it were a complete sentence. A fragment may lack a subject, a complete verb, or both. Fragments may also begin with a subordinating word (such as *because*) that makes the fragment depend on another sentence for its meaning. Reading your draft out loud, backwards, sentence by sentence, will help you spot sentence fragments easily. (See Chapter 37.)

QUICK HELP

Taking a writing inventory

One way to learn from your mistakes is to take a writing inventory. It can help you think critically and analytically about how to improve your writing skills.

1. Collect two or three pieces of your writing to which either your instructor or other students have responded.

2. Read through this writing, adding your own comments about its strengths and weaknesses. How do your comments compare with those of others?

3. Group all the comments into three categories—*broad content issues* (use of evidence and sources, attention to purpose and audience, overall impression), *organization and presentation* (overall and paragraph-level organization, sentence structure and style, formatting), and *surface errors* (problems with spelling, grammar, punctuation, and mechanics).

4. Make an inventory of your own strengths in each category.

5. Study your errors. Mark every instructor and peer comment that suggests or calls for an improvement and put them all in a list. Consult the relevant part of this handbook or speak with your instructor if you don't understand a comment.

6. Make a list of the top problem areas you need to work on. How can you make improvements? Then note at least two strengths that you can build on in your writing. Record your findings in a writing log that you can add to as the class proceeds.

Part 1

THE ART AND CRAFT OF WRITING

1 Expectations for College Writing

Making your expectations for your college education match up with what your instructors expect of you will be one of your most significant challenges in college. You may have thought of college primarily as a step on the way to a career, but in today's unpredictable working world, learning the specific skills you need to get a particular job may be less useful than acquiring a wide range of abilities that will serve you well in any position you hold. The abilities a college education can help you develop—such as critical reading and writing and effective speaking—will help you succeed in college and beyond, no matter where your career path leads.

Your college instructors—and your future colleagues and supervisors—will expect you to demonstrate your ability to think critically, to consider ethical issues, to find as well as solve problems, to do effective research, to work productively with people of widely different backgrounds, and to present the knowledge you construct in a variety of ways and in a variety of genres and media. Your success will depend on communicating clearly and on making appropriate choices for the context.

1a Moving between social and academic writing

Social connection today involves so much writing—text messages, tweets, Facebook posts, blogs, YouTube videos, and the like—that you probably do more writing out of class than in class. In fact, Web 2.0 and social networking have opened doors for writers like never before. Writing on social networking sites allows writers to get almost instant feedback, and anticipating responses from an audience often has the effect of making online writers very savvy: they know the importance of analyzing the audience and of using an appropriate style, level of formality, and tone to suit the online occasion.

Writers on Twitter, for example, tell friends and followers what's going on in short bursts of no more than 140 characters. Here are two representative tweets from the Twitter feed of Stephanie Parker, a college student whose interests include technology and Korean pop culture.

sparker2

Rain's over, going to Trader Joe's to buy some healthy stuff to fight this cold. . suggestions?
9:21 AM Mar 13th via web

Watching Queen Seon Duk/선덕여왕 on @dramafever, love it so far! http://www.dramafever.com/drama/56/ #nowplaying
1:16 AM Jan 10th via web

In these tweets, Stephanie shows a keen awareness both of the audiences who follow her on Twitter and of two very common purposes for this kind of informal writing — to seek information (in the first tweet, about foods to fight off a cold) and to share information (in the second tweet, about her view of a Korean drama, with a link so readers can check it out for themselves).

Facebook and similar sites allow for fast-paced conversation between writers. The following status update from Alicia Michalski got a response in the form of a link to a YouTube video (of a man exercising to a song called "You Can Do It"), to which Alicia then replied — all in the space of twelve minutes.

Like Stephanie and Alicia, many young writers today are adept at informal social writing across a range of genres and media. You may not think very hard about the audience you'll reach in a tweet or Facebook post, or about your purpose for writing in such spaces, but you are probably more skilled than you give yourself credit for when it comes to making appropriate choices for your informal writing.

Alicia Michalski Long, long day ahead of me. And the toughest won't even be my classes.
Yesterday at 8:14am • Comment • Like

 Ryan Sundheimer http://www.youtube.com/watch?v=rCvtldLxu1Y
Tell me that doesn't inspire you!
Yesterday at 8:23am

 Alicia Michalski If I had you at work yelling that to me, then yes, it'd be pretty inspiring! I'll just loop it on the speakers there!!
Yesterday at 8:26am

Of course, informal writing is not the only writing skill a student needs to master. You'll also need to move back and forth between informal social writing and formal academic writing, and to write across a whole range of genres and media. Look closely at your informal writing: What do you assume about your audience? What is your purpose? How do you achieve a particular tone? In short, why do you write the way you do in these situations? Analyzing the choices you make in a given writing context will help you develop the ability to make good choices in other contexts as well—an ability that will allow you to move between social and academic writing.

EXERCISE 1.1

Choose a sample of your own informal writing from a social networking site: a blog, posting, text message, or instant message, for example. Why did you write the post? What did you assume about your readers, and why? Why did you choose the words, images, links, or other parts of the text, and how do these choices contribute to the way the writing comes across to an audience? Does the writing do what you want it to do? Why, or why not?

1b Preparing to meet academic expectations

If you're like most students, you probably have less familiarity with academic writing contexts than you do with informal contexts. You may not have written anything much longer than five pages of formal academic writing before coming to college, and you may have done only the most minimal research. The contexts for your college writing will require you to face new challenges; you may be asked, for example, to create a persuasive Web site or to research, write, and deliver a multimedia presentation. You'll need to start by figuring out what your instructors expect from you. Different courses and disciplines will introduce different expectations about writing—a lab report in biology won't look much like a review of the literature in psychology. But widespread conventions across fields can help you prepare for many if not most academic situations.

1c Positioning yourself as an academic writer

Establishing authority

In the United States, most instructors expect student writers to begin to establish their own authority—to become constructive critics who can

Conventions

"Aren't conventions just rules with another name?" Not entirely. Conventions—agreed-on language practices of grammar, punctuation, and style—convey shorthand information from writer to reader. In college writing, you will generally want to follow the conventions of standard academic English unless you have a good reason to do otherwise. But unlike hard and fast rules, conventions are flexible; a convention appropriate for one time or situation may be inappropriate for another. You may also choose to ignore conventions at times to achieve a particular effect. (You might, for example, write a sentence fragment rather than a full sentence, such as the *Not entirely* at the beginning of this box.) As you become more experienced and confident in your writing, you will develop a sense of which conventions to apply in different writing situations.

analyze and interpret the work of others and can eventually create new knowledge based on their own thinking and on what others have said. But what does establishing your authority mean in practice?

- Assume that your opinions count (as long as they are informed rather than tossed out with little thought) and that your audience expects you to present them in a well-reasoned manner. In class discussion, for example, you can build authority by stating an opinion clearly and then backing it up with evidence.

- Draw conclusions based on what you have heard, observed, and read, and then offer those conclusions in a clear and straightforward way.

- Build your authority by citing the works of others, both from the reading you have done for class and from good points your instructor and classmates have made.

Being direct

Your instructors will often expect you to get to your main point quickly and to be direct throughout your project. Good academic writing prepares readers for what is coming next, provides definitions, and identifies clear topics and transitions. To achieve directness in your writing, try the following strategies:

- State your main point early and clearly; don't leave anything to the reader's imagination.

- Avoid overqualifying your statements. Instead of writing *I think the facts reveal*, come right out and say *The facts reveal*.

- Avoid digressions. If you use an anecdote or example from personal experience, be sure it relates directly to your main point.

- Make sure to use examples and concrete details to help support your main point.

- Make your transitions from point to point obvious and clear. The first sentence of a new paragraph should reach back to the paragraph before and then look forward to what is to come.

- If your project is long or complex, you may want to use brief summary statements between sections, but be careful to avoid unnecessary repetition.

Look at how one student, Killeen Hansen, opens an essay entitled "A Book Is a Book Is a Book":

> Think of a corkscrew: a generic corkscrew with a handle and a screw, meant to remove the cork from wine bottles. Would or could this corkscrew be a book? How would one read it? Where are the words? Most people would say no, the corkscrew cannot be a book. It has no pages, they might assert. Where is the story? But Lime Rock Press, a small publishing company specializing in miniature books, would disagree. Their "Corkscrew Book" is both a corkscrew *and* a book. A tiny leaflet with wine quotations from around the world slides inside the handle of the corkscrew. This corkscrew, against all expectations, is a book. It is an artist's book, a work of art presented in the form of a book.
>
> You may not have seen an artist's book, but you've certainly seen plenty of other books. Books, after all, are everywhere: on library shelves, on coffee tables at the dentist's office, or stuffed into the pocket of an airline seat. As the example of the artist's book demonstrates, the generic term *book*

Student Writing

can cover a very wide spectrum, from film script to e-book, from comic to corkscrew. Two distinct genres under the umbrella term of *book*—the artist's book and the graphic novel—can present information effectively, though in very different ways, through a combination of word, image, and form.

In this introduction, the writer presents herself as knowledgeable on the subject of artists' books: she builds her own authority through referring in vivid detail to a particular artist's book and the press that publishes it. She also makes a clear transition between the two paragraphs and then provides readers with her major point right away, stating the main goal of her essay at the end of the second paragraph. Thus she meets the expectations of her teachers by establishing her authority and by being direct.

1d Becoming an engaged reader

Your instructors expect you to be an actively engaged reader who can offer informed opinions in response to texts (see Chapter 7). Keep in mind that instructors are not asking you to be negative or combative; rather, they want to know that you are engaged with the text and with the class. Here are some expectations many college instructors have about what good reading requires you to do:

- Carefully note the name of the author or creator and the date and place of publication; these items can give you clues to purpose, audience, and context.

- Understand the overall content of a piece, and be able to summarize it in your own words.

- Formulate informed and critical questions about the text, and bring these questions up in class.

- Understand each sentence, and make direct connections among sentences and paragraphs. Keep track of repeated themes or images, and figure out how they contribute to the entire piece.

- Note the creator's attitude toward and assumptions about the subject. Then you can speculate on how the attitude and assumptions may have affected the creator's thinking.

- Distinguish between the creator's stance and how the creator reports on the stances of others. Keep an eye open for the key phrases a writer uses to signal an opposing argument: *while some have argued that, in the past,* and so on.

- Go beyond content to notice spatial and organizational patterns, use of sources, and choice of words and images.

1e   Writing academic work

Your instructors hold different expectations for the various kinds of formal academic writing you produce in college, especially as conventions vary from discipline to discipline, genre to genre, and medium to medium. But some general guidelines apply (see p. 21).

Beyond such guidelines, instructors hold additional expectations about organization, sentence structure, paragraph structure, idea development, use of evidence, and formatting for the kinds of texts you will produce in college. Research for this book confirms that readers depend on writers to organize and present their material—using sections, paragraphs, sentences, arguments, details, visuals, and source citations—in ways that aid understanding. Here are some things your writing needs to do to help establish your credibility and to help readers understand your point:

- Follow logical organizational patterns, and provide clear signals that help readers follow the overall thread of what you are trying to say (5d and 5e).

- Guide readers through your writing by using effective and varied sentences that link together smoothly (Chapters 40–43).

- Develop paragraphs or sections logically and completely, and make it easy for readers to understand how and why you are going from one paragraph or section to the next (5c1 and e).

- Use ample supporting evidence—good reasons, examples, illustrations, or other details—to demonstrate or support a clear, specific point. Choose evidence that helps readers understand your point and offers proof that what you are saying is sensible and worthy of attention (8e).

- Design and format the project appropriately for the audience and purpose you have in mind (Chapter 23).

Increasingly, your instructors may expect you to produce texts using a variety of media. You may be asked to create Web content; post

---

QUICK HELP

U.S. academic style

- Consider your purpose and audience carefully, making sure that your topic is appropriate to both. (Chapter 2)

- State your claim or thesis, and support it with examples, statistics, anecdotes, authorities, and visuals of various kinds. (Chapters 8 and 9)

- Carefully document all of your sources. (Chapters 16–19)

- Make explicit links between ideas. (5d and e)

- Consistently use the appropriate level of formality. (Chapters 26 and 27)

- Use conventional academic formats, such as research-based essays, literary analyses, lab reports, reviews of literature, and position papers. (Chapters 10–19 and 60–62)

- Use conventional grammar, spelling, punctuation, and mechanics. (Chapters 29–53)

- Use an easy-to-read type size and typeface, conventional margins, and double spacing. (Chapter 23)

---

your work to course management systems, lists, blogs, wikis, or social networking sites; and respond to the work of others on such sites. In addition, you will probably write email and text messages to your instructors and other students (see Chapter 20). You may use sound, video, or other multimedia content as part or all of the texts you create. As always, in writing such texts, remember to consider your audience and your context in deciding what is appropriate. Research for this book indicates that many student writers are already adept at making such calls: you probably know, for example, that using informal Internet abbreviations and emoticons in academic writing is seldom appropriate.

1f Preparing for college research

The reading and writing you do in college are part of what we broadly think of as research. In fact, much of the work you do in college may turn an informal search into various kinds of more formal research: an idea that comes to you over pizza, for example, may lead you to conduct a survey that in turn becomes an important piece of evidence in a research project for your sociology class, which may then become part of a multimedia presentation you give for a campus organization.

Many of your writing assignments will require extensive or formal research with a wide range of print, online, and media sources as well as information drawn from observations, interviews, or surveys. Even if you know a topic very well, your research will be an important tool for establishing credibility with your audience members and thus gaining their confidence in you as a writer. On many occasions, what you write will be only as good as the research on which it is based. (For more on research, see Chapters 10–15.)

THINKING CRITICALLY ABOUT YOUR EXPECTATIONS FOR COLLEGE WRITING

How do you define good college writing? Make a list of the characteristics you come up with. Then make a list of what you think your instructors' expectations are for good college writing, and note how they may differ from yours. (Research suggests that many students today define good writing as "writing that makes something happen in the world." Would that match your definition or that of your instructors?) What might account for the differences—and the similarities—in the definitions and lists? Do you need to alter your ideas about good college writing to meet your instructors' expectations? Why, or why not?

Rhetorical Situations

2

A writer has to analyze the rhetorical situation (sometimes called the writing situation) from all possible points of view, considering each element of the situation carefully. Of the many possible elements in a rhetorical situation, the most important are the topic and purpose; the audience being addressed; the speaker or writer; and the context, including time and space limitations, the medium and genre, the tone and style, and the level of language.

2a Making good choices for your situation

To communicate effectively, you need to make careful choices about all the elements of your rhetorical situation. It can be helpful to think of the situation in visual terms. Imagine the triangular representation of the rhetorical situation on p. 24 as dynamic, with all the angles intersecting with one another and with the context. All the pieces must fit together effectively; if the message is wrong for the audience—or wrong for you as the writer or speaker—then you may need to change the message, aim for a different audience, or perhaps both.

In addition to the key elements of audience, writer, and topic, this triangle includes three terms that are helpful in thinking through a rhetorical situation: *ethos* (the credibility of the writer or speaker), *pathos* (appeals to the emotions and values of the audience), and *logos* (appeals to reason or logic). Aristotle identified these terms some 2,500 years ago as basic appeals any speaker or writer could

What do a documented essay on stem-cell research, a letter to Visa disputing a charge on your bill, a tweet to other students in your sociology class, a comment on a blog post, and a Web site about energy conservation all have in common? To communicate successfully, the writers of all these texts must analyze their particular rhetorical situation and then respond to it in appropriate ways.

Writer
(Ethos)

Audience
(Pathos)

Topic
(Logos)

use. (For more on *ethos*, *pathos*, and *logos*, see Chapters 8–9.)

Informal and formal rhetorical situations

You may well be accustomed to writing in some rhetorical situations that you don't analyze closely. When you post something on a friend's Facebook wall, for example, you probably spend little time pondering what your friend values or finds amusing, how to phrase your words, which links or photos would best emphasize your point, or why you're taking the time to post.

However, academic and other formal rhetorical situations may seem considerably less familiar than the social writing you share with friends. Until you understand clearly what such situations demand of you, you should allow additional time to analyze the topic, purpose, audience, and other elements of your context with care.

Looking at the big picture

As the chart on the opposite page suggests, you'll benefit from thinking about audience, topic, and purpose together—as part of a whole—rather than as separate parts. Although one context may require you to begin by analyzing your audience, another may work better if you start by picking a topic or considering your purpose. The important point is that wherever you begin, you need to make all the elements of your rhetorical situation fit together into a comprehensible big picture.

2b Understanding academic assignments

Most formal on-the-job writing addresses specific purposes, audiences, and topics: a group of scientists produces a report on food additives for the federal government; an editorial assistant composes a memo for an editor summarizing the problems in a manuscript; a team of psychologists prepares video scripts to help companies deal with employee stress. These writers all have one thing in common: specific goals. They know why, for whom, and about what they are writing.

THE WRITER'S TABLE: Analyze the Rhetorical Situation

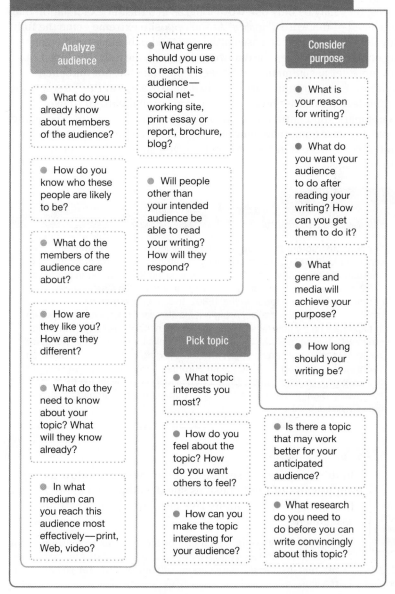

Analyze audience

- What do you already know about members of the audience?

- How do you know who these people are likely to be?

- What do the members of the audience care about?

- How are they like you? How are they different?

- What do they need to know about your topic? What will they know already?

- In what medium can you reach this audience most effectively—print, Web, video?

- What genre should you use to reach this audience—social networking site, print essay or report, brochure, blog?

- Will people other than your intended audience be able to read your writing? How will they respond?

Pick topic

- What topic interests you most?

- How do you feel about the topic? How do you want others to feel?

- How can you make the topic interesting for your audience?

- Is there a topic that may work better for your anticipated audience?

- What research do you need to do before you can write convincingly about this topic?

Consider purpose

- What is your reason for writing?

- What do you want your audience to do after reading your writing? How can you get them to do it?

- What genre and media will achieve your purpose?

- How long should your writing be?

College writing assignments, in contrast, may seem to appear out of the blue, with no specific purpose, audience, or topic. In extreme cases, they may be only one word long, as in a theater examination that consisted of the word *Tragedy*! At the opposite extreme come the fully developed, very specific cases often assigned in business and engineering courses. In between the one-word exam and the fully developed case, you may get assignments that specify purpose but not audience — to write an essay arguing for or against censorship on the Internet, for example. Or you may be given an organizational pattern to use — say, to compare and contrast two novels read in a course — but no specific topic. Because comprehending an assignment accurately and fully is crucial to your success in responding to it, you should always make every effort to do so.

TALKING THE TALK

Assignments

"How do instructors come up with these assignments?" Assignments, like other kinds of writing, reflect particular rhetorical contexts that vary from instructor to instructor, and they change over time. The assignment for an 1892 college writing contest was to write an essay "On Coal"; in research conducted for this textbook in the 1980s, the most common writing assignment was a personal narrative. Assignments also vary in response to changes in expectations for college students and in the needs of society. Competing effectively in today's workforce, for example, calls for high-level thinking, for being able to argue convincingly, and for knowing how to do the research necessary to support a claim. It's no surprise, then, that a recent study of first-year college writing in the United States found that by far the most common assignment today asks students to compose a researched argument. (See Chapters 8–9.)

Emily Lesk's assignment

For Emily Lesk's first draft, see 3g. For her final draft, see 4l.

In this and the next several chapters, you can follow the writing process of Emily Lesk as she developed an essay for her first-year English course. Her class was given the following assignment:

> Explore the ways in which one or more media (television, print advertising, and so on) have affected an aspect of American identity, and discuss the implications of your findings for you and your readers.

Emily saw that the assignment was broad enough to allow her to focus on something that interested her, and she knew that the key word *explore* invited her to examine—and analyze—an aspect of American identity that was of special interest to her. Her instructor said to assume that she and members of the class would be the primary audience for this essay. Emily felt comfortable having her instructor and classmates as the primary audience: she knew what their expectations were and how to meet those expectations. But Emily also hoped to post her essay on the class Web site, thus reaching a wider audience—in fact, her essay might be read by anyone with access to the Internet. With this broad and largely

---

QUICK HELP

Analyzing an academic assignment

- What exactly does the assignment ask you to do? Look for such words as *analyze, classify, compare, contrast, describe, discuss, define, explain,* and *survey.* Remember that the meaning of these words may differ among disciplines—*analyze* might mean one thing in literature, another in biology.

- What knowledge or information do you need? What kinds of research or exploration will you need to do, and where are you most likely to find the information you need? (3a7 and 3d)

- Do you need to find illustrations or other visuals? What purpose will they serve? (3d and e)

- How can you limit—or broaden—the topic or assignment to make it more interesting? Do you have interest in or knowledge about any particular aspect of the topic? Be sure to check with your instructor if you wish to redefine the assignment. (3b)

- What problem(s) does the topic suggest to you? How might the problem(s) give you an interesting angle on the topic? (2c)

- What are the assignment's specific requirements? Consider genre, length, format, organization, and deadline—all of which will help you know the scope expected. Your instructor is not likely to expect extensive library research for a paper due in twenty-four hours, for example. If no length is designated, ask for guidelines. (2b)

- What is your purpose? Do you need to demonstrate knowledge of certain material, or show your ability to express certain ideas clearly? (2c3)

- Who is the audience for this writing? Does the task imply that you will assume a particular readership besides your instructor? (2d)

unknown audience in mind, Emily determined to be as clear as possible and to take nothing for granted in terms of explaining her point of view and supporting her thesis.

EXERCISE 2.1

The following assignment was given to an introductory business class: "Discuss in an essay the contributions of the Apple and Microsoft companies to the personal computing industry." What would you need to know about the assignment in order to respond successfully? Using the questions in the Quick Help box on p. 27, analyze this assignment.

2c Thinking about topics and purposes

Whether you are writing in response to an academic assignment or for another reason, you will need to spend time thinking about the topic and purpose for your writing.

1 Choices about topics

When a topic is left open, many writers put off getting started because they can't decide what to write about. Experienced writers say that the best way to choose a topic is literally to let it choose you. The subjects that compel you—that confuse, puzzle, irritate, or in some way pose a problem for you—are likely to engage your interests and hence evoke your best writing. You can begin to identify a topic or problem by thinking through the following questions:

- What topics do you wish you knew more about?
- What topics are most likely to get you fired up?
- What about one of these topics is most confusing to you? most exciting? most irritating? most tantalizing?
- What person or group might this topic raise problems for?

Remember that regardless of the topic you choose, it must be manageable. To limit your topic to a manageable size, make the topic as explicit as possible (rather than "Politics in Modern Afghanistan," for example, narrow it to "The 2009 Presidential Election in Afghanistan"). For help with limiting a topic, see 10c.

2 Your rhetorical stance

"Where do you stand on that?" is a question often asked of political figures and other authorities. But writers must ask the question of themselves as well. Understanding where you stand on your topic—your *rhetorical stance*—has several advantages. It will help you examine where your opinions come from and thus help you address the topic fully; it will help you see how your stance might differ from the stances held by members of your audience; and it will help you establish your credibility with that audience. This part of your rhetorical stance—your *ethos* or credibility—helps determine how well your message will be received. To be credible, you will need to do your homework on your subject, present your information fairly and honestly, and be respectful of your audience.

A student writing a proposal for increased services for people with disabilities, for instance, knew that having a brother with Down syndrome gave her an intense interest that her audience might not have in this topic. She needed to work hard, then, to get her audience to understand—and share—her stance.

QUICK HELP

Examining your rhetorical stance

- What is your overall attitude toward the topic? How strong are your opinions?

- What social, political, religious, personal, or other influences have contributed to your attitude?

- How much do you know about the topic? What questions do you have about it?

- What interests you most about the topic? Why?

- What interests you least about it? Why?

- What seems important—or unimportant—about the topic?

- What preconceptions, if any, do you have about it?

- What do you expect to conclude about the topic?

- How will you establish your credibility (*ethos*)? That is, how will you show that you are knowledgeable and trustworthy?

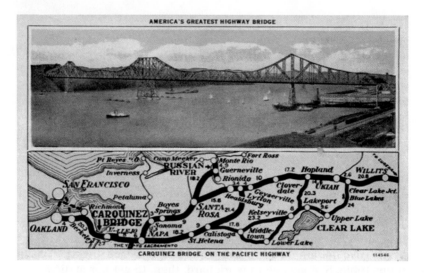

AMERICA'S GREATEST HIGHWAY BRIDGE

CARQUINEZ BRIDGE, ON THE PACIFIC HIGHWAY

Images you choose to include in your writing can help establish credibility. But remember that images always have a point of view or perspective. The postcard seen here, for example, illustrates two physical perspectives—a photo of a bridge and a road map showing the bridge's location—as well as a time perspective—from 1927, when the bridge was new. This postcard, captioned "America's Greatest Highway Bridge," presents the construction of the bridge as a triumph of modern technology. So when you choose an image, think hard about its perspective and about how well it fits in with your topic and purpose. Does the image have an attitude—and does that attitude serve the purpose of your writing?

3 Purposes for academic writing

Writing—even a simple note or text message—almost always involves multiple purposes, and academic work requires even more attention to your reasons for writing. On one level, you are writing to establish your credibility with your instructor, to demonstrate that you are a careful thinker and an effective writer. On another level, though, you are writing to achieve goals of your own, to say as clearly and forcefully as possible what you think about a topic.

For example, if you are creating a project about free speech on campus, your purposes might include to inform your readers, to persuade

---

QUICK HELP

Analyzing your purposes

- What is the primary purpose of the assignment—to entertain? to explain? to persuade? some other purpose? What does this purpose suggest about the best ways to achieve it? If you are unclear about the primary purpose, talk with your instructor. Are there any secondary purposes to keep in mind?

- What are the instructor's purposes in giving this assignment—to make sure you have read certain materials? to determine your understanding? to evaluate your thinking and writing? How can you fulfill these expectations?

- What are your goals in carrying out this assignment—to meet expectations? to learn? to communicate your ideas? How can you achieve these goals?

---

them to support or oppose speech codes, and even to clarify the issue in your own mind. If you are profiling your eccentric grandfather, you might be trying to amuse your readers and to pay tribute to someone who has been important in your life.

In ancient Rome, the great orator Cicero noted that a good speech generally fulfills one of three major purposes: to delight, to teach, or to move. Today, our purposes when we communicate with one another remain pretty much the same: we seek to *entertain* (delight), to *inform or explain* (teach), and to *persuade or convince* (move).

Most of the writing you do in college will address one or some of these purposes, and it is important for you to be able to recognize the overriding purpose of any piece of writing. If, for example, a history professor asks you to explain the events that led up to the 1964 Civil Rights Act (primary purpose: to explain), you should not write an impassioned argument on the need for the act (primary purpose: to persuade).

For most college writing, consider purpose in terms of the assignment, the instructor's expectations, and your own goals.

Emily Lesk's purposes

As she considered the assignment (see p. 26), Emily Lesk saw that her primary purpose was to explain the significance and implications of her topic to herself and her readers, but she recognized some other

For Emily
Lesk's first
draft, see 3g.
For her final
draft, see 4l.

purposes as well. Because this essay was assigned early in the term, she wanted to get off to a good start; thus, one of her purposes was to write as well as she could to demonstrate her ability to her classmates and instructor. In addition, she decided that she wanted to find out something new about herself and to use this knowledge to get her readers to think about themselves.

4 The decision to write

Because elements of the rhetorical situation, like your stance and purpose, are such important considerations in effective writing, you should start thinking about them at an early stage, as soon as you make the decision to write. In a general sense, of course, this decision is often made for you. Your editor sets a deadline for a newspaper story; your professor announces that a research project is due next month; your employer asks for a report before the next management meeting. But even in such situations, consciously deciding to write is important. Experienced writers report that making up their minds to begin a writing task represents a big step toward getting the job done.

EXERCISE 2.2

Think back to a recent writing assignment. What helped you finally decide to write? Once you made that decision, what exactly did you do to get going? In a paragraph or two, describe your situation and answer these questions. Then compare your description with those of two or three classmates.

2d Considering audiences

Every writer can benefit from thinking carefully about who the audience is, what the audience already knows or thinks, and what the audience needs and expects to find out. One of the characteristic traits of an effective writer is the ability to write for a variety of audiences, using language, style, and evidence appropriate to particular readers. The key word here is *appropriate*: just as a funeral director would hardly greet a bereaved family with "Hi, there! What can I sell you today?" neither would you be likely to sprinkle jokes through a presentation on child abuse written for a PTA. Such behavior would be wildly inappropriate given the nature of your audience.

1 Audiences for informal writing

For some informal writing — a MySpace message, for example — you know exactly who your audience is, and communicating appropriately may be a simple matter. It's still worth remembering that when you post informal writing in a public space — whether on a friend's Facebook page, in a blog's comment section, or on Twitter — you may not be aware of how large and varied your online audience can be. Can your friend's parents, or her potential employer, see your posts on her Facebook page? (The answer depends partly on her privacy settings.)

"On the Internet, nobody knows you're a dog."

Who's reading the blogs you comment on or following your tweets? For more on audiences for informal online writing, see 20b.

Peter Steiner's famous 1993 cartoon (shown here) asserted that claiming a different identity was easy online. However, as online privacy becomes less common — and as online writers become more likely to grant large audiences access to their thoughts, including everyone from old high school classmates and former coworkers to beer buddies and members of their church — maintaining distinct identities is more difficult. On the Internet today, some writers have suggested, *everyone* knows you're a dog, whether you want them to or not!

2 Audiences for formal and academic writing

Even if you write with intuitive ease in tweets and texts to friends, you may struggle when asked to write for an instructor or for a general audience. You may wonder, for example, why you need to define terms in your writing that your instructor has used in class, or what you can assume a general audience knows about your topic. When you are new to academic writing, making such assumptions can be tricky. If you can identify samples of writing that appeal to an audience similar to the one you are writing for, look for clues about what level of knowledge you can assume; if still in doubt, check with your instructor.

Members of your class will also usually be part of your audience, especially if you are responding to one another's drafts in peer review. You may also have a chance to identify an audience for your assignment—perhaps a business proposal addressed to a hypothetical manager or a Web presentation posted for an online audience that is potentially global. In each case, it pays to consider your audience(s) carefully.

Emily Lesk's audiences

For Emily Lesk's first draft, see 3g. For her final draft, see 4l.

In addition to her instructor, Emily Lesk's audience included the members of her writing class and her potential online readers. Emily saw that her classmates were mostly her age, that they came from diverse ethnic backgrounds, and that they came from many areas of the country. Her online readers could be almost anyone.

As you think about your audience, consider how you want them to respond to both the words and images you use. Remember that images can evoke strong responses, so choose them with special care. What audience(s), for example, can you imagine for this image from an early Ramones performance? How do you think different audiences might respond to this image?

3 Specific audiences

Thinking systematically about your audience can help you make decisions about a writing assignment. For example, it can help you decide what sort of organizational plan to follow, what information to include or exclude, and even what specific words to use. If you are writing

Analyzing your audience

- What person or group do you most want to reach? Is this audience already sympathetic to your views?

- How much do you know about your audience? In what ways may its members differ from you? from one another? Consider education, geographic region, age, gender, occupation, social class, ethnic and cultural heritage, politics, religion, marital status, sexual orientation, disabilities, and so on. (Chapter 25)

- What assumptions can you make about your audience members? What might they value—brevity, originality, conformity, honesty, wit, seriousness, thrift, generosity? What goals and aspirations do they have? Take special care to examine whether distant readers will understand references, allusions, and so on.

- What do members of the audience already know about your topic? Do you need to provide background information or define terms?

- What kind of information and evidence will the audience find most compelling—quotations from experts? personal experiences? photographs? statistics?

- What stance do your audience members have toward your topic? What are they likely to know about it? What views might they already hold?

- What is your relationship to the audience?

- What is your attitude toward the audience?

an article for a journal for nurses about a drug that prevents patients from developing infections from intravenous feeding tubes, you will not need to give much information about how such tubes work or to define many terms. But if you are writing about the same topic in a pamphlet for patients, you will have to give a great deal of background information and define (or avoid) technical terms.

EXERCISE 2.3

Describe one of your courses to three audiences: your best friend, your parents, and a group of high school students attending an open house at your college. Then describe the differences in content, organization, and wording that the differences in audience led you to make.

4 Appeals to your whole audience

All writers need to pay very careful attention to the ways in which their writing can either invite readers to be part of the audience or leave them out. Look at the following sentence: *As every schoolchild knows, the world is losing its rain forests at the rate of one acre per second.* The writer here gives a clear message about who is—and who is not—part of the audience: if you don't know this fact or suspect it may not be true, you are not invited to participate.

You can help make readers feel they are part of your audience. Be especially careful with the pronouns you use, the assumptions you make, and the kinds of support you offer for your ideas.

Using appropriate pronouns

The pronouns you use can include or exclude readers. When bell hooks says "The most powerful resource any of us can have as we study and teach in university settings is full understanding and appreciation of the richness, beauty, and primacy of our familial and community backgrounds," she uses "us" and "we" to connect with her audience—those who "study and teach in university settings." Using "us" and "we" to speak directly to your audience, however, can sometimes be dangerous: those who do not see themselves as fitting into the "we" group can feel left out—and they may resent it. So take special care with the pronouns you use to refer to your readers.

Avoiding unfounded assumptions

Be careful about any assumptions you make about your readers and their views, especially in the use of language that may unintentionally exclude readers. Use words like *naturally* and *of course* carefully, for what seems natural to you—that English should be the official U.S. language, for instance, or that smoking should be outlawed—may not seem at all natural to some members of your audience. Try to take nothing about your audience for granted.

Offering appropriate evidence

The evidence you offer in support of your arguments can help draw in your readers. A student writing about services for people with disabilities might ask readers who have no personal experience with the topic to imagine themselves in a wheelchair, trying to enter a building with steps

---

CONSIDERING DISABILITIES

Your whole audience

Remember that considering your whole audience means thinking about members with varying abilities and special needs. If you are writing to veterans in a VA hospital or to a senior citizens' group, for example, you can be sure that many audience members will be living with some form of disability. But it's very likely that any audience will include members with disabilities—from anorexia to dyslexia, multiple sclerosis, or attention deficit disorder—and that there may be significant differences within disabilities. Approximately 54 million Americans were living with a disability in the year 2000—an average of 1 in 5 Americans! All writers need to think carefully about how their words reach out and connect with such very diverse audiences.

---

but no ramp. Inviting them to be part of her audience would help them accept her ideas. On the other hand, inappropriate evidence can leave readers out. Complex statistical evidence might well appeal to public-policy planners but may bore or irritate ordinary citizens. (For more on building common ground with readers, see Chapter 25.)

2e Thinking about genres and media

You no doubt are familiar with the word *genre* in terms of movies (comedy, action, horror). But genre is also used to describe other forms of writing, such as research projects, personal narratives, and lab reports. Genre and media are not the same—the genre of a research project or promotional flyer might be created using either online or print media, for example—but some genres are tied closely to specific media, so the two categories are related.

1 Genres

A genre is a form of communication used for a particular purpose. An annotated bibliography, for example, lists and comments on potential sources for a research project. As an activity is repeatedly carried out in a particular form, certain aspects of the communication—such as the content, rhetorical strategies, and language forms—become conventional; the audience begins to expect those features in the genre.

Genre names

What does my instructor mean by "essay"? Writing assignments often mention a specific genre, such as *essay* or *report*, but genre names can be confusing. The same genre may work differently in different contexts, or people may use the same term in various ways. Depending on the field, an essay might be a personal narrative, a critical analysis, or even a journal article. Even when the name of the genre sounds familiar to you, look for specific instructions for each assignment or analyze examples provided by the instructor.

As an academic writer, you'll encounter genres both familiar and new. Even when a genre at first seems familiar, you may find new expectations or conventions at different levels of education, in different academic disciplines, or even in different classrooms, so you'll want to look closely at any genre you are considering for a writing project.

EXERCISE 2.4

Consider some of the genres that you have encountered as a student, jotting down answers to the following questions and bringing them to class for discussion.

1. What are some genres that you read but don't usually write?
2. What are some genres that you write for teachers?
3. What are some genres that you write to or with other students?
4. What are some genres that you will likely encounter in your major or in your career?
5. How are some of the genres you listed different from those you encountered in high school?

Analyzing genres

If you are asked to create your text in a particular genre, make sure you understand the conventional expectations — for style, appearance, organization, length, and so on. You may want to collect a range of sample texts so that you can get a sense of the variation within the genre. If you can't locate samples, ask your instructor or tutor for help.

QUESTIONS ABOUT GENRE CONVENTIONS

- What type of content or topics are usually found in this genre? What type of content is rare?

- How is the work generally organized? What appears first, next, and so on?

- How long is typical work in this genre? How long is each paragraph or unit?

- Can you identify a typical writing style? Is it formal, informal, personal, impersonal, objective, opinionated, or something else? What kinds of words or phrases help to create this style?

- What kind of sentence structure is common in this genre? Are sentences short, long, simple, complicated? Is passive voice common? Is the pronoun *I* used?

- Does the genre use technical terms (jargon)? If so, how common is it? Does the genre use slang or other common conversational expressions?

For examples of student work in various genres, see p. 948.

- What formatting and design choices (fonts, paragraphing, headings, layout, use of color) are customary? (See Chapter 23.)

- What medium is typically used for this genre? Are visual images or audio commonly used? If so, for what purposes?

- Who reads this genre, and why? Does the genre usually aim to inform, to persuade, to entertain, or to serve some other purpose?

- How much latitude do you have in ignoring or stretching some of the boundaries of the genre?

Preparing to work in a genre

Think carefully about what you'll need to do to write successfully in this genre. Plan ahead to allow the amount of time necessary for composing your text, and make sure that you understand limitations—such as delivery time (for a presentation) or bandwidth—for the length of the final product. Consider the media you will need to use (2e2), and make sure you have access to any technology required—and any training necessary to use it well. If the genre will require you to conduct interviews, seek permissions, or otherwise contact or collaborate with other people, allow time to find appropriate people and work with them effectively. Do you need to make any other preparations to create a text that fulfills the demands of the genre?

2 Media

Much college writing is still done in print, but this tradition is changing. You may be asked to create multimodal writing using audio, video, images, and words — or some combination of these elements. As a result, you need to think about the medium where your writing will appear: in print on $8^{1}/_{2}" \times 11"$ white paper? in print on a Web page? as an online audio or video essay? as a poster on campus? Make sure that you choose appropriate media for your topic, purpose, audience, and genre.

You may start off planning to work in print and then discover as you proceed that a different medium may offer more effective ways to

communicate your point. One student, Will Rogers, who had been assigned to write an essay about something on campus that most students and faculty took for granted, focused on a giant crane being used in the construction of a new building complex. He did some research, finding out all he could about the crane and interviewing the crane's operator. That's when he got hooked: the operator was eighteen and had left his first year in college to take this job. The student carried out a series of interviews so that he could include the crane operator's own words. But he found the operator's story so compelling that he decided that it would work better — and be more

powerful — in the medium of film. That way, viewers could actually see the crane operator and hear his voice as he described the decisions he had made. The result: a three-minute documentary called "Crane Man" for which he did all the writing, filming, and editing.

To see an essay converted into a multimedia presentation, see pp. 467–78.

Translating work from one medium to another

You may be asked to create a work in one medium, such as print, and translate it to another, such as a multimedia presentation or scrapbook. Such translations may not be as straightforward as they seem. Just as filmmakers may omit content, streamline plot, and conflate characters when they create a movie version of a book, developing a solid thesis and supporting it effectively may require different strategies if you are turning a text-based work into a video, a PowerPoint presentation, or some other highly visual form.

2f Considering language and style

Although most of your college writing will be done in standard academic English, some of it may demand that you use specialized occupational or professional varieties of English—those characteristic of medicine, say, or computer science or law or music. Similarly, you may wish to use regional, ethnic, or other varieties of English to connect with certain audiences or to catch the sound of someone's spoken words. You may even need to use words from a language other than English—in quoting someone, perhaps, or in using certain technical terms. In considering your use of language, think about what languages and varieties of English will be most appropriate for reaching your audience and accomplishing your purposes (see Chapter 26).

You will also want to think carefully about style: should you be casual and breezy, somewhat informal, formal, or extremely formal? The style you choose will call for certain kinds of sentence structures, organizational patterns, and word choices. And your style will be important in creating the tone you want, one that is appropriate to your assignment,

---

FOR MULTILINGUAL WRITERS
Bringing in other languages

If you are familiar with languages other than English, you may want or need to include words, phrases, or whole passages in another language. When you do so, consider whether your readers will understand that language and whether you need to provide a translation, as in this example from John (Fire) Lame Deer's "Talking to the Owls and Butterflies":

> Listen to the air. You can hear it, feel it, smell it, taste it.
>
> *Woniya waken*—the holy air—which renews all by its breath.
>
> *Woniya, woniya waken*—spirit, life, breath, renewal—it means all that.

In this instance, translation is necessary because the phrase that Lame Deer is discussing has multiple meanings in English. (See 26e for more on bringing in other languages.)

audience, topic, purpose, and genre.

Remember that visual elements can have as much influence on the tone of your writing as the words you choose. Visuals create associations in viewers' minds: one reader may react much more positively than another to this Wal-Mart logo, for example, based on experiences shopping there or views about the company's business practices.

Writers can, of course, influence how an image is perceived by carefully analyzing their audience and choosing visuals with a tone appropriate to the point they want to make. For example, in a serious academic essay about Albert Einstein's contributions to science, you would probably choose the first of the images below rather than the second—unless you were trying to make a point about Einstein's ability to poke fun at himself.

VISUALS THAT CONVEY DIFFERENT TONES

EXERCISE 2.5

Consider a writing assignment you are currently working on. What is its genre? What medium or media does it use? How would you describe the style and tone? Finally, what visuals are you going to include and how well do they work to create the appropriate style and tone?

THINKING CRITICALLY ABOUT RHETORICAL SITUATIONS

Reading with an Eye for Purpose, Audience, and Context

Advertisements provide good examples of writing that is tailored carefully for specific audiences. Find two ads for the same product in contexts that suggest that the ads aim to appeal to different audiences—for example, men and women. What differences do you see in the messages and photography? What conclusions can you draw about ways of appealing to specific audiences?

Thinking about Your Own Attention to Purpose, Audience, and Context

Analyze a text you have written or are working on right now for an academic course.

- Can you state its purpose(s) clearly and succinctly? If not, what can you do to clarify its purpose(s)?
- What other purposes for this piece of writing can you imagine? How would fulfilling some other purpose change the writing?
- Can you tell from reading the piece who the intended audience is? If so, what in your text clearly relates to that audience? If not, what can you add that will strengthen your appeal to this audience?
- What other audiences can you imagine? How would the writing change if you were to address a different audience? How would it change if you were writing to a largely unknown audience, such as people on the Web?
- What changes would you have to make to create the work in a different genre or medium?
- Does your writing follow the conventions of standard academic English—and if not, should you revise it so that it will? Note your conclusions about purpose and audience in your own writing.

3

Exploring, Planning, and Drafting

There are many productive ways to go about exploring, planning, and drafting. The goal is to find strategies that work well for you.

3a Exploring a topic

The point is so simple that it's easy to forget: you write best about topics you know well. One of the most important parts of the entire writing process, therefore, is choosing a topic that will engage your strengths and your interests, surveying what you know about it, and determining what you need to find out.

1 Brainstorming

Used widely in business and industry, brainstorming involves tossing out ideas — either orally or in writing — to discover new ways to approach a topic. You can brainstorm with others or by yourself.

1. Within five or ten minutes, list every word or phrase that comes to mind about the topic. Jot down key words and phrases, not sentences. No one has to understand the list but you. Don't worry about whether or not something will be useful — just list as much as you can in this brief span of time.

2. If little occurs to you, try calling out or writing down thoughts about the opposite side of your topic. If you are trying, for instance, to think of reasons to raise tuition and are coming up blank,

CONSIDERING DISABILITIES

Freespeaking

If you are better at talking out than writing out your ideas, try freespeaking. Begin by speaking into a recording device or into a computer with voice-recognition software, and just keep talking about your topic for at least seven to ten minutes. Say whatever comes to your mind, and don't stop talking. You can then listen to or read the results of your freespeaking and look for an idea to pursue at greater length.

try concentrating on reasons to reduce tuition. Once you start generating ideas in one direction, you'll find that you can usually move back to the other side fairly easily.

3. When the time is up, stop and read over the lists you've made. If anything else comes to mind, add it to the list. Then reread the list. Look for patterns of interesting ideas or for one central idea.

Emily Lesk's brainstorming

Emily Lesk, the student whose work appears in Chapters 2–4, did some brainstorming with her classmates on the general topic the class was working on: an aspect of American identity affected by one or more media. Here are some of the notes Emily made during the brainstorming session:

For Emily Lesk's first draft, see 3g. For her final draft, see 4l.

- *"American identity" — Don't Americans have more than one identity?*

- *Picking a kind of media could be hard. I like clever ads. Maybe advertising and its influence on us?*

- *Wartime advertising; recruiting ads that promote patriotic themes.*

- *Look at huge American companies like Wal-Mart and McDonald's and how their ads affect the way we view ourselves. Not sure what direction to take. . . .*

2 **Freewriting and looping**

Freewriting is a method of exploring a topic by writing about it for a period of time *without stopping.*

1. Write for ten minutes or so. Think about your topic, and let your mind wander freely. Write down everything that occurs to you — in

complete sentences as much as possible — but don't worry about spelling or grammar. If you get stuck, write anything. Just don't stop.

2. When the time is up, look at what you have written. Much of it will be unusable, but you may discover some important insights and ideas.

If you like, you can continue the process by looping: find the central or most intriguing thought from your freewriting, and summarize it in a single sentence. Freewrite for five more minutes on the summary sentence, and then find and summarize the central thought from the second "loop." Keep this process going until you discover a clear angle or something about the topic that you can pursue.

Emily Lesk's freewriting

Here is a portion of the freewriting Emily Lesk did to focus her ideas after the brainstorming session:

> Media and effect on American identity. What media do I want to write about? That would make a big difference — television, radio, Internet — they're all different ways of appealing to Americans. TV shows that say something about American identity? What about magazine or TV advertising? Advertising tells us a lot about what it means to be American. Think about what advertising tells us about American identity. What ads make me think "American"? And why?

Student Writing

③ Clustering

Clustering is a way of generating ideas using a visual scheme or chart. It is especially helpful for understanding the relationships among the parts of a broad topic and for developing subtopics. You may have a software program for clustering. If not, follow these steps:

1. Write your topic in the middle of a piece of paper, and circle it.

2. In a ring around the topic circle, write what you see as the main parts of the topic. Circle each part, and draw a line from it to the topic.

3. Think of more ideas, examples, facts, or other details relating to each main part. Write each of these near the appropriate part, circle each one, and draw a line from it to the part.

4. Repeat this process with each new circle until you can't think of any more details. Some trails may lead to dead ends, but you will still have many useful connections among ideas.

EMILY LESK'S CLUSTERING

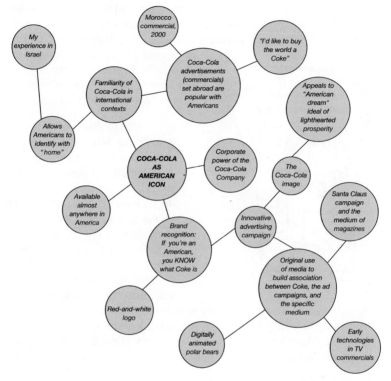

Emily Lesk's clustering

Later in her planning and exploring process, Emily Lesk decided to work on the topic of Coca-Cola advertising and American identity (pp. 51 and 54). After finding a large Coca-Cola advertising archive, she used clustering to help focus her emerging ideas. Her clustering appears above. (Remember that you may want to explore aspects of your ideas more than once — and exploring may be helpful at any stage as you plan and draft a piece of writing.)

4 Drawing or making word pictures

If you're someone who prefers visual thinking, you might either create a drawing about the topic or use figurative language—such as similes and metaphors—to describe what the topic resembles. Working with pictures or verbal imagery can sometimes also help illuminate the topic or uncover some of your unconscious ideas or preconceptions about it.

1. If you like to draw, try sketching your topic. What images do you come up with? What details of the drawing attract you most? What would you most like to expand on? A student planning to write an essay on her college experience began by thinking with pencils and pen in hand. Soon she found that she had drawn a vending machine several times, with different products and different ways of inserting money to extract them (one of her drawings appears here). Her sketches led her to think about what it might mean to see an education as a product. Even abstract doodling can lead you to important insights about the topic and to focus your topic productively.

2. Look for figurative language—metaphors and similes—that your topic resembles. Try jotting down three or four possibilities, beginning with "My subject is _____" or "My subject is like _____." A student working on the subject of genetically modified crops came up with this: "Genetically modified foods are like empty calories: they do more harm than good." This exercise made one thing clear to this student writer: she already had a very strong bias that she would need to watch out for while developing her topic.

Play around a bit with your topic. Ask, for instance, "If my topic were a food (or a song or a movie or a video game), what would it be, and why?" Or write a Facebook status update about your topic, or send a tweet to a friend saying—within 140 characters—why this topic appeals to you. Such exercises can get you out of the rut of everyday thinking and help you see your topic in a new light.

5 Keeping a journal

Writers often get their best ideas by jotting down or recording thoughts that come to them randomly. You can use a notebook, a computer, a phone — some writers even keep a marker and writing board on the shower wall so that they can write down the ideas that come to them while bathing! As you begin thinking about your assignment, taking time to write about or record what you know about your topic and what still puzzles you may lead you to a breakthrough or help you articulate your main idea.

6 Asking questions

Another basic strategy for exploring a topic and generating ideas is simply to ask and answer questions. Here are several widely used sets of questions to get you started, either on your own or with one or two others.

Questions to describe a topic

Originally developed by Aristotle, the following questions can help you explore a topic by carefully and systematically describing it:

- *What is it?* What are its characteristics, dimensions, features, and parts? What do your senses tell you about it?

- *What caused it?* What changes occurred to create your topic? How is it changing? How will it change?

- *What is it like or unlike?* What features differentiate your topic from others? What analogies can you make about your topic?

- *What larger system is the topic a part of?* How does your topic relate to this system?

- *What do people say about it?* What reactions does your topic arouse? What about the topic causes those reactions?

Questions to explain a topic

The well-known questions *who, what, when, where, why,* and *how,* widely used by news reporters, are especially helpful for explaining a topic.

- *Who* is doing it?
- *What* is at issue?
- *When* does it take place?

FOR MULTILINGUAL WRITERS

Using your native language to explore ideas

For generating and exploring ideas—the work of much brainstorming, free-writing, looping, clustering, and questioning—consider using your native language; it may help you come up with good ideas quickly and spontaneously. Later in the process of writing, you can choose the best of these ideas and begin working with them in English.

- *Where* is it taking place?
- *Why* does it occur?
- *How* is it done?

Questions to persuade

When your purpose is to persuade or convince, the following questions, developed by philosopher Stephen Toulmin, can help you think analytically about your topic (8e and 9i2):

- What *claim* are you making about your topic?
- What *good reasons* support your claim?
- What valid *underlying assumptions* support the reasons for your claim?
- What *backup evidence* can you find for your claim?
- What *refutations* of your claim should you anticipate?
- In what ways should you *qualify* your claim?

7 Consulting sources

At the library and on the Internet, browse for a topic you want to learn more about. If you have a short list of ideas, do a quick check of reference works to get overviews of the topics. You can begin with a general encyclopedia or a specialized reference work that focuses on a specific area, such as music or psychology (11b3). You can also use Wikipedia as a starting point: take a look at entries that relate to your topic, especially noting the sources they list. While you should never rely on Wikipedia alone, it is a highly accessible way to begin your research.

8 Collaborating

As you explore your topic, remember that you can gain valuable insights from others. Many writers say that they get their best ideas in conversation with other people. If you talk with friends or roommates about your topic, at the very least you will hear yourself describe the topic and your interest in it; this practice will almost certainly sharpen your understanding of what you are doing. You can also seek out Facebook groups, Web forums, or other networking sites as places to share your thinking on a topic and find inspiration.

3b Narrowing a topic

After exploring ideas, you may have found a topic that interests you and would also be interesting to your audience. The topic, however, may be too large to be manageable. If this is the case, narrow your topic to focus on a more workable idea. You might consider your personal connections to the topic and why it interests you, or think about the most controversial or intriguing aspects of the topic. (For help crafting a thesis from your narrowed topic, see 3c.)

Emily Lesk's work on narrowing her topic

Emily Lesk planned to discuss how advertising affects American identity, but she knew that her topic was far too broad. She began to think about possible types of advertising and then about products that are pitched as particularly "American" in their advertising. When she got stuck, she posted a Facebook status update asking her friends to "name products that seem super-American." She quickly got seventeen responses with answers ranging from Hummer and Winchester rifles to "soft toilet paper," Spam, Wheaties, and maple syrup. One friend identified Coca-Cola and Pepsi-Cola, two products that Emily associated with many memorable and well-documented advertising campaigns.

EXERCISE 3.1

Choose a topic that interests you, and explore it by using two of the strategies described in 3a. When you have generated some material, you might try comparing your results with those of other members of the class to see how effective or helpful each strategy was. If you have trouble choosing a topic, use one of the preliminary working theses in Exercise 3.2.

3c   Drafting a working thesis

A thesis states the main idea of a piece of writing. Most kinds of college writing contain a thesis statement, often near the beginning, which functions as a promise to readers, letting them know what the writer will discuss. Though you may not have a final thesis when you begin to write, you should establish a tentative working thesis early on in your writing process. The word *working* is important here because the working thesis may well change as you write. Even so, a working thesis focuses your thinking and research and helps keep you on track.

A working thesis should have two parts: a topic part, which states the topic, and a comment part, which makes an important point about the topic.

⌐————— TOPIC —————⌐ ⌐————— COMMENT —————⌐
○ **The current health care crisis arises from three major causes.**

A successful working thesis has three characteristics:

1. It is potentially *interesting* to the intended audience.
2. It is as *specific* as possible.
3. It limits the topic enough to make it *manageable*.

You can assess a working thesis by checking it against each of these characteristics, as in the following example:

PRELIMINARY WORKING THESIS

○ **Theories about global warming are being debated around the world.**

INTERESTING?	The topic itself holds interest, but it seems to have no real comment attached to it. The thesis merely states a bare fact, and the only place to go from here is to more bare facts.
SPECIFIC?	The thesis is not specific. Who is debating these theories? What is at issue in this debate?
MANAGEABLE?	The thesis is not manageable; it would require research on global warming in many countries.

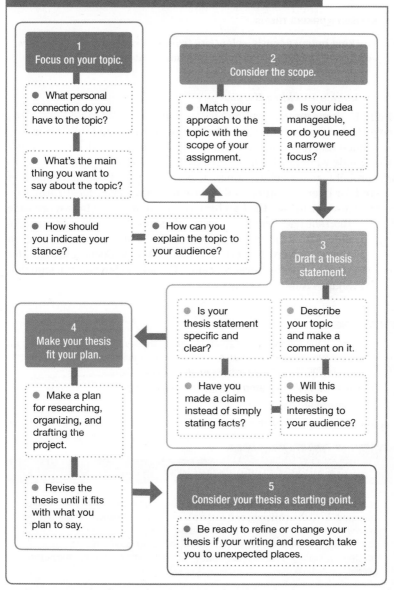

THE WRITER'S TABLE: Develop a Working Thesis

1 Focus on your topic.

- What personal connection do you have to the topic?
- What's the main thing you want to say about the topic?
- How should you indicate your stance?
- How can you explain the topic to your audience?

2 Consider the scope.

- Match your approach to the topic with the scope of your assignment.
- Is your idea manageable, or do you need a narrower focus?

3 Draft a thesis statement.

- Describe your topic and make a comment on it.
- Is your thesis statement specific and clear?
- Have you made a claim instead of simply stating facts?
- Will this thesis be interesting to your audience?

4 Make your thesis fit your plan.

- Make a plan for researching, organizing, and drafting the project.
- Revise the thesis until it fits with what you plan to say.

5 Consider your thesis a starting point.

- Be ready to refine or change your thesis if your writing and research take you to unexpected places.

ASSESSMENT   This thesis can be narrowed by the addition of a stronger comment and a sharper focus, as shown here:

REVISED WORKING THESIS

▷ **Working independently, scientists from several countries have now confirmed that global warming is demonstrably caused by humans.**

Emily Lesk's working thesis

Emily Lesk wrote this preliminary thesis: "Coca-Cola and Pepsi-Cola have shaped our national identity." When she analyzed this thesis, she concluded that it was indeed interesting; however, she decided that the two brands were not trying to do exactly the same thing, so her thesis was probably not specific enough. In addition, both Coke and Pepsi had existed for over a century, and she realized that just investigating the advertising for the two brands would probably take more time than she had available—so the thesis was probably not manageable. After talking with her instructor, Emily decided to focus on a single advertising icon, the world-famous Coca-Cola logo. Her revised working thesis became "Coca-Cola is a cultural icon that shapes American identity."

For Emily Lesk's first draft, see 3g. For her final draft, see 4l.

EXERCISE 3.2

Choose one of the following preliminary working theses, and after specifying an audience, evaluate the thesis in terms of its interest, specificity, and manageability. Revise the working thesis as necessary to meet these criteria.

1. The benefits of standardized testing are questionable.

2. Vaccinations are dangerous.

3. Too many American parents try to micromanage their children's college education.

FOR MULTILINGUAL WRITERS

Stating a thesis explicitly

In some cultures, stating the main point explicitly may be considered rude or inelegant. In U.S. academic and business practices, however, readers often expect the writer to make key points and positions explicit. Unless your main point is highly controversial or hard for the reader to accept (such as a rejection letter), state your main point early—before presenting the supporting details.

4. Many people are afraid to fly in a plane, although riding in a car is statistically more dangerous.
5. An educated public is the key to a successful democracy.

EXERCISE 3.3

Using the topic you chose in Exercise 3.1, write a preliminary working thesis. Evaluate the thesis in terms of its interest, specificity, and manageability. Revise it as necessary to create a satisfactory working thesis.

3d Gathering information

Writing often calls for research. An assignment may specify that you conduct research on your topic and cite your sources. Or you may find that you don't know enough about your topic to write about it effectively without doing research. Sometimes you need to do research at various stages of your writing process — early on, to help you understand or define your topic, and later on, to find additional examples and illustrations to support your thesis. Once you have developed a working thesis, consider what additional information you might need.

Basically, you can do three kinds of research to support your thesis: library research, which includes books, periodicals, and databases; online research, which gives you access to texts, visuals, and people on the Internet; and field research, which includes personal observation, interviews, surveys, and other means of gathering information directly. (For more information on conducting research, see Chapter 11.)

3e Organizing verbal and visual information

While you're finding information on your topic, think about how you will group or organize that information to make it accessible and persuasive to readers. At the simplest level, writers most often group information in their writing projects according to four principles — space, time, logic, and association.

1 Spatial organization

Organizing according to space directs readers' attention to where the various elements of something appear in physical space. Spatial organization of verbal texts allows the reader to "see" your information and to take a "virtual tour" beginning at one point and moving around in an organized manner—say, from near to far, left to right, or top to bottom. It can be especially useful in description. You might include a map or another graphic that would help readers visualize your description.

INFORMATION ORGANIZED SPATIALLY

This photo shows the spatial arrangement described, with the darkened side areas for spectators and the brightly lighted front of the room. The photograph and writing together help readers see the scene vividly.

The scene was being filmed in a windowless building with a corrugated tin roof. We entered through the single side door and sat in folding chairs on a platform along one wall, separated from the rest of the room by beaded red curtains. Behind us was darkness. On the far wall, neon lights glowed dimly, illuminating a few unoccupied barstools on the other side of the room. But the front of the room was ablaze with light. Purple and white flood-lights beamed down onto a circular dance floor, creating an almost supernatural glow. The film crew in the center of the room stood silhouetted against the light like an audience waiting for a show to begin.

2 Chronological (time) organization

The principle of time refers to *when* bits of information occur, usually chronologically. Chronological organization is the basic method used in cookbooks, lab reports, instruction manuals, and stories. Writers of these products organize information according to when it occurs in some process or sequence of events (narrative).

INFORMATION ORGANIZED CHRONOLOGICALLY

In July of 1877, Eadweard Muybridge photographed a horse in motion with a camera fast enough to capture clearly the split second when the horse's hooves were all off the ground—a moment never before caught on film. Throughout the fall of that year, newspapers were full of the news of Muybridge's achievement. His next goal was to photograph a sequence of such rapid images. In the summer of 1878, he set up a series of cameras along a track and snapped successive photos of a horse as it galloped past. Muybridge's technical achievement helped to pave the way for the first motion pictures a decade later.

This photo series shows the rapid passage of time, with each image capturing an instant too fast to see with the eye alone. The image and text together give readers a clear idea of Muybridge's achievement.

3 Logical organization

Organizing according to logic means relating pieces of information in ways that make sense. Following is an overview of some of the most commonly used logical patterns: *illustration, definition, division and classification, comparison and contrast, cause and effect, problem and solution, analogy,* and *narration.* The example that follows organizes information logically, according to the principle of division. For other examples of paragraphs organized according to these logical patterns, see 5c1.

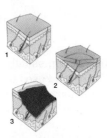

The images are logically arranged to show burns of increasing severity.

INFORMATION ORGANIZED LOGICALLY

Burns can be divided into three types or levels: (1) Superficial, or first-degree, burns damage the top layer of skin. They are red and painful. (2) Partial thickness, or second-degree, burns damage the outer layer of skin and the layer just below it. They are very painful and are characterized by blistering, swelling, and redness. (3) Full thickness, or third-degree, burns damage deep tissues. They appear charred and black. The burn area itself is numb, but the surrounding area is very painful.

Illustration

You will often gather examples to illustrate a point.

An essay discussing how one novelist influenced another might cite a number of examples from the second writer's books that echo themes or characters from the first writer's works. An appeal for donating money to the Red Cross might be organized in a series of examples of how donations are used, along with appropriate illustrations. For maximum effect, arrange your examples and accompanying visuals in order of increasing importance.

Definition

Often a topic can be developed by definition—by saying what something is (or is not) and perhaps by identifying the characteristics that distinguish it from things that are similar or in the same general category. A magazine article about poverty in the United States, for example, would have to define very carefully what level of income, assets, or other measure defines a person, family, or household as "poor." An essay about Pentecostalism for a religion class might explain what characteristics separate Pentecostalism from related religious movements.

Division and classification

Division means breaking a single topic into separate parts; classification means grouping many separate items of information about a topic according to their similarities. An essay about military recruiting policies might divide the military into different branches—army, navy, air force, and so on—and examine how each recruits volunteers. For a project on women's roles in the eighteenth century, you could organize your notes by classification: information related to women's education, occupations, legal status, and so on.

Comparison and contrast

Comparison focuses on the similarities between two things, whereas contrast highlights their differences, but the two are often used together. If you were asked to analyze two case studies in an advertising text (one on Budweiser ads and the other on ads for Ralph Lauren), you might well organize the response by presenting all the information on Budweiser advertising in one section and all on Ralph Lauren ads in another (block comparison) or by alternating between Budweiser and Ralph Lauren ads as you look at particular characteristics of each (alternating comparison).

Cause and effect

Cause-effect analysis may deal with causes, effects, or both. If you examine why something happens or happened, you are investigating causes. If you explain what has occurred or is likely to occur from a set of conditions, you are discussing effects. An environmental-impact study of the probable consequences of building a proposed dam, for instance, would focus on effects. On the other hand, a newspaper article on the breakdown of authority in inner-city schools might begin with the effects of the breakdown and trace them back to their causes.

Problem and solution

Moving from a problem to a solution is a natural way to organize certain kinds of information. For example, a student studying motorcycle parking on campus decided to organize his paper in just this way: he identified a problem (the need for more parking) and then offered two possible solutions, along with visuals to help readers imagine the solutions (his outline appears on p. 62). Many assignments in engineering, business, and economics call for a similar organizational strategy.

Analogy

An analogy establishes connections between two things or ideas. Analogies are particularly helpful in explaining something new in terms of something very familiar. Likening the human genome to a map, for example, helps explain the complicated concept of the genome to those unfamiliar with it.

Narration

Narration involves telling a story of some kind. You might, for example, tell the story of how deer ravaged your mother's garden as a way of showing why you support population control measures for wildlife. Narrating calls on the writer to set the story in a context readers can understand, providing any necessary background and descriptive details as well as chronological markers and transitions (*later that day, the following morning,* and so on) to guide readers through the story.

4 Associational organization

Some writers organize information through a series of associations that grow directly out of their own experiences and memories. In doing so, they may rely on a sensory memory, such as an aroma, a sound, or a scene. Thus, associational organization is common in personal narrative, where writers can use a chain of associations to render an experience vividly for readers.

INFORMATION ORGANIZED ASSOCIATIONALLY

Flying from San Francisco to Atlanta, I looked down to see the gentle roll of the Smoky Mountains begin to appear. Almost at once, I was back on my Granny's porch, sitting next to her drinking iced tea and eating peaches. Those peaches tasted good—picked ripe, skinned, and eaten with no regard for the sweet juice trickling everywhere. And on special occasions, we'd make ice cream, and Granny would empty a bowl brimming with chopped peaches into the creamy dish. Now—that was the life!

This image works by association, its old-fashioned look emphasizing the nostalgic charm of homemade ice cream and peaches.

5 Combined organizational patterns

In much of your writing, you will want to use two or more principles of organization. You might, for example, combine several passages of narration with vivid examples to make a striking comparison, as one student did in an essay about the dramatic differences between her life in her Zuñi community and her life as a teacher in Seattle. In addition, you may want to include not only visuals but sound and other multimedia effects as well.

FOR MULTILINGUAL WRITERS

Organizing information

You may know ways of organizing information that differ markedly from those discussed in 3e. A Navajo teacher notes, for example, that explicit linear organization, through chronology or other strictly logical patterns, doesn't ever sound quite right to her. As she puts it, "In traditional Navajo, it's considered rude to get right to the point. Polite conversation or writing between two engaged people always takes a while to get to the point." Although effective organization depends largely on the reader's expectations, it may sometimes make sense to deviate from those expectations. If you choose to organize your writing differently from what your teacher or classmates might expect, consider explaining the reason for your choice — for example, in a cover letter or a footnote.

Emily Lesk's organizational patterns

Emily Lesk begins the final draft of her essay (4l) with what she calls a "confession": *I don't drink Coke.* She follows this opening with an anecdote about a trip to Israel during which she nevertheless bought a T-shirt featuring the Coca-Cola logo. She goes on to explore what lies behind this purchase, relating it to the masterful advertising campaigns of the Coca-Cola Company and illustrating the way that the company's advertising "sells" a certain kind of American identity along with its products. She closes her draft by reflecting on the implications of this relationship between corporate advertising and national identity. Thus her essay, which begins with a personal experience, combines the patterns of narrative with cause-effect and comparison.

EXERCISE 3.4

Using the topic you chose in Exercise 3.1, identify the most effective means of organizing your information. Write a brief paragraph explaining why you chose this particular method (or these methods) of organization.

3f Planning

At this point, you will find it helpful to write out an organizational plan or outline. To do so, simply begin with your thesis; review your exploratory notes, research materials, and visual or multimedia sources; and then list all the examples and other good reasons you have to support the thesis. (For information on paragraph-level organization, see Chapter 5.)

Sample organizational plan

One informal way to organize your ideas is to figure out what belongs in your introduction, body paragraphs, and conclusion. A student who was writing about solutions to a problem used the following plan:

WORKING THESIS

▷ **Increased motorcycle use demands the reorganization of campus parking lots.**

INTRODUCTION

give background and overview (motorcycle use up dramatically), and use a photograph of overcrowding in a lot

state purpose — to fulfill promise of thesis by offering solutions

BODY

describe the current situation (tell of my research at area parking lots)

describe the problem in detail (report on statistics; cars vs. cycles), and include a graph representing findings

present two possible solutions (enlarge lots or reallocate space)

CONCLUSION

recommend against first solution because of cost and space

recommend second solution, and summarize benefits of it

Formal outline

Even if you have made an informal written plan before drafting, you may wish (or be required) to prepare a more formal outline, which can help you see exactly how the parts of your writing will fit together — how your ideas relate, where you need examples, and what the overall structure of your work will be. Even if your instructor doesn't ask you to make an outline or you prefer to use some other method of sketching out your plans, you may want to come back to an outline later: doing a retrospective outline — one you do after you've already drafted your project — is a great way to see whether you have any big logical gaps or whether parts of the essay are in the wrong place.

Most formal outlines follow a conventional format of numbered and lettered headings and subheadings, using roman numerals, capital letters, arabic numerals, and lowercase letters to show the levels of importance of the various ideas and their relationships. Each new level is indented to show its subordination to the preceding level.

Thesis statement

I. First main idea
   A. First subordinate idea
      1. First supporting detail or idea
      2. Second supporting detail or idea
      3. Third supporting detail
   B. Second subordinate idea
      1. First supporting detail or idea
      2. Second supporting detail or idea
II. Second main idea
   A. (continues as above)

Note that each level contains at least two parts, so there is no A without a B, no 1 without a 2. Comparable items are placed on the same level — the level marked by capital letters, for instance, or by arabic numerals. Keep in mind that headings should be stated in parallel form — either all sentences or all grammatically parallel topics.

Formal outlining requires a careful evaluation of your ideas, and this is precisely why it is valuable. (A full-sentence outline will reveal the relationships between ideas — or the lack of relationships — most clearly.) Remember, however, that an outline is at best a means to an end, not an end in itself. Whatever form your plan takes, you may want or need to change it along the way. (For an example of a formal outline, see 15e.)

A storyboard

The technique of storyboarding — working out a narrative or argument in visual form — can be a good way to come up with an organizational plan, especially if you are developing a Web site or other multimedia project. For such projects you can even find storyboard templates online to help you get started. For a typical college essay, however, you can

For a student's storyboard with sticky notes, see p. 298.

create your own storyboard by using note cards or sticky notes, taking advantage of different colors to keep track of threads of argument, subtopics, and so on. Remember that flexibility is a strong feature of storyboarding: you can move the cards and notes around, trying out different arrangements, until you find an organization that works well for your writing situation. Basic patterns for a storyboard include linear, hierarchical, and spoke-and-hub organization.

Use linear organization when you want most readers to move in a particular order through your material. An online report might use the following linear organization:

LINEAR ORGANIZATION

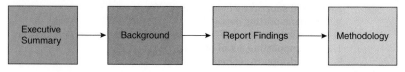

A hierarchy puts the most important material first, with subtopics branching out from the main idea. A Web site on dog bite prevention might be arranged like this:

HIERARCHICAL ORGANIZATION

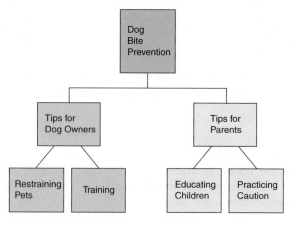

A spoke-and-hub organization allows readers to move from place to place in no particular order. Many portfolio Web sites are arranged this way:

SPOKE-AND-HUB ORGANIZATION

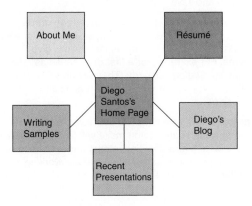

Whatever form your plan takes, you may want or need to change it along the way. Writing has a way of stimulating thought, and the process of drafting may generate new ideas. Or you may find that you need to reexamine some data or information or gather more material.

EXERCISE 3.5

Write out a plan for a piece of writing supporting the working thesis you developed for Exercise 3.3.

3g Drafting

In some sense, drafting begins the moment you start thinking about a topic. At some point, however, you attempt an actual written draft.

No matter how good your planning, investigating, and organizing have been, chances are you will need to return to these activities as you draft. This fact of life leads to the first principle of successful drafting: be flexible. If you see that your organizational plan is not working, do not hesitate to alter it. If some information now seems irrelevant, leave it out, even if you went to great lengths to obtain it. Throughout

QUICK HELP

Guidelines for drafting

- *Set up a computer folder or file for your essay.* Give the file a clear and relevant name, and save to it often.

- *Save and name your files to distinguish among drafts.* Since you will likely change your document over time, save a copy of each version. If you are sending a copy to classmates for review, give the file a new but related name. For example, for a first draft saved as *religion essay d1*, save a copy as *religion essay d2*. Then, when you receive responses, you can leave the copy of your first draft as is and make revisions on *religion essay d2*.

- *Track changes within a file to try out new versions.* Most writing software allows you to track changes you make within a draft, seeing how new material would look and deciding later whether to keep or discard the changes. This function is useful when you are working on a piece with another writer or when you aren't sure which version of your draft you like best.

- *Have all your information close at hand and arranged according to your organizational plan.* Stopping to search for a piece of information can break your concentration or distract you.

- *Keep track of any sources you plan to include.* Keep a working bibliography of sources you are using (12b), and make notes in your draft of any information that comes from your research. If you find useful information online, you can cut and paste it into a document to ensure that you have the information exactly as you found it; however, save it in a different color or with highlighting so that you don't mistakenly borrow writing that is not your own. (See Chapters 13 and 14.)

- *Try to write in stretches of at least thirty minutes.* Writing can provide momentum, and once you get going, the task becomes easier.

- *Don't let small questions bog you down.* Just make a note of them in brackets—or in all caps—or make a tentative decision and move on.

- *Remember that first drafts aren't perfect.* Concentrate on getting all your ideas written down, and don't worry about anything else.

- *Stop writing at a place where you know exactly what will come next.* Doing so will help you start easily when you return to the draft.

CONSIDERING DISABILITIES

A talking draft

Using a word processor with voice-recognition software will allow you to speak your ideas, which will then appear onscreen. A "talking" draft of this kind can be a very good way to get your initial draft done, especially if you have difficulty with the physical act of writing. If voice-recognition software isn't available, try to find another student who will work with you to produce talking drafts: as one of you talks, the other types in what is being said. Your school's office of disability services should be able to provide scribes or notetakers as well.

the drafting process, you may need to refer to points you have already written about. You may learn that you need to do more research, that your whole thesis must be reshaped, or that your topic is still too broad and should be narrowed further.

Emily Lesk's first draft

Here is Emily Lesk's first draft. She uses brackets and highlighting here to identify questions and sources she will need to cite.

All-Powerful Coke

I don't drink Coke. Call me picky for disliking the soda's saccharine aftertaste. 1 Call me cheap for choosing a water fountain over a twelve-ounce aluminum can that costs a dollar from a vending machine but only pennies to produce. Even call me unpatriotic for rejecting the potable god that over the last century has come to represent all the enjoyment and ease to be found in our American way of life. But don't call me a hypocrite when I admit that I still identify with Coke and the Coca-Cola culture.

I have a favorite T-shirt that says "Drink Coca-Cola Classic" in Hebrew. It's Israel's 2 standard tourist fare, like little nested dolls in Russia or painted horses in Scandinavia, and before setting foot in the Promised Land three years ago, I knew where I could find one. The T-shirt shop in the central block of a Jerusalem shopping center did offer other shirt designs ("Maccabee Beer" was a favorite), but that Coca-Cola shirt was what drew in most of the dollar-carrying tourists. I waited almost twenty minutes for mine, and I watched nearly everyone ahead of me say "the Coke shirt" (and "thanks" in Hebrew).

Student Writing

At the time, I never asked why I wanted the shirt. I do know, though, that the reason I wear it often, despite a hole in the right sleeve, has to do with its power as a conversation piece. Few people notice it without asking something like, "Does that say Coke?" I usually smile and nod. They mumble a compliment and we go our separate ways. But rarely does anyone want to know what language the world's most famous logo is written in. And why should they? Perhaps because Coca-Cola is a cultural icon that shapes American identity.

Throughout the company's history, marketing strategies have centered on putting Coca-Cola in scenes of the happy, carefree American life we never stop striving for. What 1950's teenage girl wouldn't long to see herself in the soda shop pictured in a Coca-Cola ad appearing in a 1958 issue of *Seventeen* magazine? A clean-cut, handsome man flirts with a pair of smiling girls as they laugh and drink Coca-Colas. And any girls who couldn't put themselves in that perfect, happy scene, could at least buy a Coke for consolation. The malt shop—complete with a soda jerk in a white jacket and paper hat—is a theme that, even today, remains a symbol of Americana. [Use ad? source is *'50s American Magazine Ads* edited by Ikuta.]

But while countless campaigns with this general strategy have together shaped the Coca-Cola image, presenting a product as key to a happy life represents a fairly typical approach to advertising everything from Fords to Tylenol. Coca-Cola's advertising is truly unique, however, for the original way the beverage giant has utilized specific advertising media—namely magazines and television—to drive home this message.

One of the earliest and best known examples of this strategy is artist Haddon Sundblom's masterpiece of Santa Claus. In December 1931, Coca-Cola introduced an advertising campaign featuring Sundblom's depiction of a jolly, Coke-drinking Santa whose face was modeled on Sundblom's own. [Cite "Haddon Sundblom & Coca-Cola" Web site.] [Look for a picture of this original Coke Santa.] But the success of Santa Claus goes far beyond Sundblom's magazine advertisements depicting a warm, happy grandfather figure delighting in an ice cold Coke after a tiring night of delivering presents. The way in which Coca-Cola advertisers presented that inviting image represents Coca-Cola's brilliant manipulation of the medium itself. [Need to cite Pendergrast book here.]

In today's world of CNN, e-journals, and Newsweek.com, it is often easy to forget how pervasive a medium the magazine was prior to the advent of television. Until the late 1950s, American households of diverse backgrounds and geographic locations subscribed loyally to general subject weeklies and monthlies such as *Life* and the *Saturday Evening Post*. These publications provided the primary source of news, entertainment, and other cultural information to families nationwide. This large and constant group of subscribers enabled Coca-Cola to build a perennial Christmastime advertising campaign that used an extremely limited number of ads ["designs" better word?] [add source], which Americans soon came to look forward to and seek out each holiday season. The marketing strategy was not to capture consumers with a few color drawings, but rather to make them wait eagerly by the mailbox each December so that they could flip through the *Saturday Evening Post* to find the latest scene featuring Santa gulping a Coke. For this strategy to be successful, the advertisements had to be seen by many, but also be just hard enough to come by to be exciting. What better location for this than the December issue of an immensely popular magazine?

There is no denying that this strategy worked brilliantly, as this inviting image of Santa Claus graduated from the pages of the *Saturday Evening Post* to become the central figure of the most celebrated and beloved season of the year. Travel to any strip mall in the United States during December (or even November—that's how much we love Christmas!) and you will no doubt run into Santa clones left and right, punched out of cardboard and sculpted in tinsel hung atop lampposts, all in Coca-Cola red and white. And while, in today's nonmagazine world, Coca-Cola must celebrate Christmas with specially designed diet Coke cans and television commercials, the Coca-Cola Santa Claus will forever epitomize the former power of magazine advertising in America. [Getting off track here?]   8

In other words, Coca-Cola has hammered itself into our perceptions—both conscious and subconscious—of an American cultural identity by equating itself with media that define American culture. When the omnipresent general magazine that marked the earlier part of the century fell by the wayside under television's power, Coke was there from the beginning. In its 1996 recap of the previous fifty years in industry history, the publication *Beverage Industry* [need to cite] cites Coca-Cola as a frontrunner in the very first form of television advertising: sponsorship of entire programs such as, in the case of Coke, *The Bob Dixon Show* and *The Adventures of Kit Carson*. Just as today we associate sports stadiums with their corporate sponsors, viewers of early television programs will forever equate them with Coke.   9

When networks switched from offering sponsorships to selling exclusive commercial time in short increments (a format modeled after magazine advertisements), Coca-Cola strove to distinguish itself again, this time by producing new formats and technologies for these commercials. [This sentence is way too long!] Early attempts at this—such as choppy "stop motion" animation, where photographs of objects such as Coke bottles move without the intervention of actors—attracted much attention, according to the Library of Congress Motion Picture Archives [need to cite]. Coca-Cola also experimented with color advertisements early enough that the excitement of color advertising technology drew additional attention to these commercials.   10

But the Coke advertising campaign that perhaps best illustrates the ability of   11
Coca-Cola advertisers to equate their product with a medium / technology [reword!]
did not appear until 1993. Who can forget the completely digitally animated polar
bears, that roll, swim, snuggle, slide, and gurgle about, in a computerized South [?]
Pole and finish off the playful experience with a swig of Coke? This campaign
captured America's attention and held it for six separate commercials, and not
because the bears are cute and cuddly. Their main draw — and the reason they remain
in our minds — was the groundbreaking technology used to create them. In 1993,
two years before the release of *Toy Story*, these were some of the very first widely
viewed digital films [cite Library of Congress here]. With these bears, as with other
campaigns, Coke didn't just utilize the latest technology — Coke introduced the latest
technology.

As a result of this brilliant advertising, a beverage which I do not even let enter   12
my mouth [reword!] is a significant part of my American cultural identity. That's
why I spent thirty Israeli shekels and twenty minutes in a tourist trap I would
ordinarily avoid buying my Hebrew Coca-Cola shirt. That shirt — along with the rest
of the Coca-Cola collectibles industry — demonstrates the power of [something
about Coke connecting itself with the American ideal of a life of diversion and
lightheartedness]. Seeing the logo that embodies all of this halfway around the
world gave me an opportunity to affirm a part of my American identity.

The red-and-white logo's ability to appeal to Americans even in such a foreign   13
context speaks to Coke advertisers' success at creating this association. A 1999
American television commercial described by the Library of Congress archive [need
to cite] as highly successful is set in Kenya, with dialogue in a local dialect and
English subtitles. In it, two Kenyan boys taste their first Cokes and comment that
the experience is much like the way they imagine kissing a girl will be. This image
appeals to Americans because it enables us to use the symbol of Coca-Cola to make
ourselves comfortable even in the most unfamiliar situations. And if that can't sell
your product, nothing can.

(For the works-cited page that Emily Lesk submitted with her final paper,
which includes the sources indicated in her notes in this draft, see 41.)

⊘   bedfordstmartins.com/smhandbook
    Student Writing > **Argument Writing**

EXERCISE 3.6

Write a draft from the plan you produced for Exercise 3.5.

THINKING CRITICALLY ABOUT YOUR WRITING PROCESS

Using the following guidelines, reflect on the process you went through as you prepared for and wrote your draft for Exercise 3.6. Make your answers an entry in your writing log if you are keeping one.

1. How did you arrive at your specific topic?
2. When did you first begin to think about the assignment?
3. What kinds of exploring or planning did you do? What kinds of research did you need to do?
4. How long did it take to complete your draft (including the time spent gathering information)?
5. Where did you write your draft? Briefly describe the setting.
6. How did awareness of your audience help shape your draft?
7. What have you learned from your draft about your own rhetorical stance on your topic?
8. What did you learn about your ideas for this topic by exploring, planning, and talking with others about it?
9. What do you see as the major strengths of your draft? What is your favorite sentence, and why?
10. What do you see as the major weaknesses of your draft? What are you most worried about, and why?
11. What would you like to change about your process of exploring, planning, and drafting?

4 Reviewing, Revising, and Editing

The ancient Roman poet Horace advised aspiring writers to get distance from their work by putting it away for nine years. Although impractical, to say the least, Horace's advice holds a germ of truth: putting the draft away even for just a short while will help clear your mind and give you some objectivity about your writing. Whether you are creating a wedding invitation, an email to a prospective employer, or a history essay, make time to review the work (by yourself or with others) and to revise, edit, and proofread.

Reviewing calls for reading your draft with a critical eye and asking others to look over your work. Revising involves reworking your draft on the basis of the review you and others have performed, making sure that the draft is clear and effective and includes all essential information. Editing involves fine-tuning your prose, attending to details of grammar, usage, punctuation, and spelling. Of course, you also need to format and proofread your writing carefully to make it completely ready for public presentation.

4a Rereading your draft

After giving yourself — and your draft — a rest, review the draft by rereading it carefully for meaning, recalling your purpose, reconsidering your rhetorical stance, considering your audience, and evaluating your organization and use of visuals.

1 Meaning

At this point, don't sweat the small stuff. Instead, concentrate on your message and on whether you have expressed it clearly. Note any places where the meaning seems unclear.

2 Purpose

Does your draft achieve its purpose? If you wrote for an assignment, make sure that you have produced what was asked for. If you set out to prove something, make sure you have succeeded. If you intended

> **TALKING THE TALK**
>
> ## Revision
>
> "I thought I had revised my assignment, but my instructor said I'd just corrected the typos." It's always a good idea to clarify what *revision* means with a particular instructor. Generally, though, when a writing teacher asks for a revision, minor corrections will not be enough. Plan to review your entire draft, looking first at the big picture—the thesis or overall argument—and be prepared to make major changes if necessary. Look for sentence-level errors and typos last, during the editing stage, since you may delete or change these as you revise.

to propose a solution to a problem, make sure you have set forth a well-supported solution rather than just an analysis of the problem.

3 Rhetorical stance

Take time to look at your draft with one central question in mind: where are you coming from in this draft? That is, articulate the rhetorical stance you take, and ask yourself what factors or influences have led you to that position. (For more on rhetorical stance, see 2c2.)

4 Audience

How appropriate is the essay for your audience? Think carefully about your audience members' experiences and expectations. Will they be interested in and able to follow your discussion? Is the language formal or informal enough for these readers? Have you defined any terms they may not know? What objections might they raise? (For more on audience, see 2d.)

When Emily Lesk reread her draft (3g), she noticed that she sounded a bit like a know-it-all, especially in the opening of her essay. She decided that her tone was inappropriate, perhaps because she was trying too hard to get her audience's attention, and that she needed to work on this problem in her revision.

EXERCISE 4.1

Take twenty to thirty minutes to look critically at the draft you prepared for Exercise 3.6. Reread it carefully, check to see how well the purpose is accomplished, and consider how appropriate the draft is for the audience. Then write a paragraph about how you would go about revising the draft.

EXERCISE 4.2

To prepare for a peer review, write a description of your purpose, rhetorical stance, and audience for your reviewer(s) to consider. For example, Emily Lesk might write, "I want to figure out why Coca-Cola seems so American and how the company achieves this effect. My audience is primarily college students like me, learning to analyze their own cultures. I want to sound knowledgeable, and I want this essay to be fun and interesting to read." This type of summary statement can help your reviewers keep your goals in mind as they give you feedback.

5 Organization

Look through your draft, paying attention to the way one idea flows into another. Note particularly the first sentence of each new paragraph, and ask yourself how it relates to the paragraph that came before. If you can't immediately see the connection, you probably need to strengthen the transition (see 5e).

Another good way to check your organization is to number the paragraphs in the draft, and then read through each one, jotting down the main idea or topic. Do the main ideas clearly relate to the thesis and to each other? Can you identify any confusing leaps from point to point? Have you left out any important points? Does any part of your essay go off track?

6 Genre and media

You decided to write in a particular genre, so think again about why you made that choice. Is writing in this genre the best way to achieve your purpose and reach your audience? Does the draft fulfill the requirements of the genre? Would any content in your draft be more effective presented in another medium—for example, as a print handout instead of a PowerPoint slide? Should you consider "translating" your work into another medium (22c and d)? Do you need to take any additional steps to make your work as effective as it can be in this medium?

Images and sound

Look closely at the images, audio, and video you have chosen to use. How do they contribute to your draft? Make sure that all visuals and media files are labeled with captions and sources, and remember to refer to visuals and media and to comment on their significance to the rest of your text. Would any information in your draft work better in visual than in verbal form?

4b Reviewing peer writers

If you are part of a peer-review group in your class, use these reviewers to your advantage — and do your best to help them when you review their work. (For more help with peer review, see the chart on p. 76.)

1 The role of the peer reviewer

The most helpful reviewers are interested in the topic and the writer's approach to it. They ask questions, make concrete suggestions, report on what is confusing and why, and offer encouragement. Good reviewers give writers a new way to see their drafts so that they can revise effectively. After reading an effective review, writers should feel confident about taking the next step in the writing process.

Peer review is difficult for two reasons. First, offering writers a way to imagine their next draft is just hard work. Unfortunately, there's no formula for giving good writing advice. But you can always do your best to offer your partner a careful, thoughtful response to the draft and a reasonable sketch of what the next version might contain. Second, peer review is challenging because your job as a peer reviewer is not to grade the draft or respond to it as an English instructor would. As a peer reviewer, you will have a chance to think alongside writers whose writing you may consider much better or far worse than your own. Don't dwell on these comparisons. Instead, remember that a thesis is well supported by purposefully arranged details, not by punctuation or impressive vocabulary. Your goal is to read the writer's draft closely enough to hear what he or she is trying to say and to suggest a few strategies for saying it better.

Being a peer reviewer should improve your own writing as you see how other writers approach the same assignment. So make it a point to tell writers what you learned from their drafts; as you express what you learned, you'll be more likely to remember their strategies. Also, you will likely begin reading your own texts in a new way. Although all writers have blind spots when reading their own work, you will gain a better sense of where readers expect cues and elaboration.

THE WRITER'S TABLE: Work with Peer Reviewers

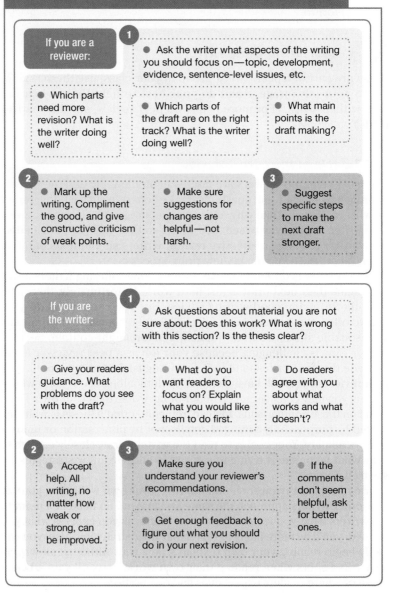

If you are a reviewer:

1
- Ask the writer what aspects of the writing you should focus on—topic, development, evidence, sentence-level issues, etc.

- Which parts need more revision? What is the writer doing well?

- Which parts of the draft are on the right track? What is the writer doing well?

- What main points is the draft making?

2
- Mark up the writing. Compliment the good, and give constructive criticism of weak points.

- Make sure suggestions for changes are helpful—not harsh.

3
- Suggest specific steps to make the next draft stronger.

If you are the writer:

1
- Ask questions about material you are not sure about: Does this work? What is wrong with this section? Is the thesis clear?

- Give your readers guidance. What problems do you see with the draft?

- What do you want readers to focus on? Explain what you would like them to do first.

- Do readers agree with you about what works and what doesn't?

2
- Accept help. All writing, no matter how weak or strong, can be improved.

3
- Make sure you understand your reviewer's recommendations.

- Get enough feedback to figure out what you should do in your next revision.

- If the comments don't seem helpful, ask for better ones.

FOR MULTILINGUAL WRITERS

Understanding peer reviews

If you are not used to giving or receiving criticisms directly, you may find it disturbing when some or most of your classmates take a questioning or even challenging stance toward your work. As long as the questions and suggestions are constructive, however, they are appropriate to peer-review collaboration. Your peers will expect you to join in the critical collaboration, too, so be sure to offer your questions, suggestions, and insights.

2 Tools for peer review

Before you get started with your first peer-review assignment, you should become familiar with the tools you can use for responding to a draft. Remember that one of your main goals as a peer reviewer is to help the writer see his or her draft differently. You want to *show* the writer what does and doesn't work about particular aspects of the draft. Visually marking the draft can help the writer know at a glance what revisions the reviewer suggests.

Marking up a print draft

If you are reviewing a hard copy of a draft, write compliments in the left margin and critiques, questions, and suggestions in the right margin. As long as you explain what your symbols mean, you can also use boxes, circles, single and double underlining, highlighting, or other visual annotations to point out patterns to the writer. If an idea is mentioned once in several paragraphs, for example, you can circle those sentences and suggest that the writer use them to form a new paragraph.

Marking up an electronic draft

If the draft comes to you as an electronic file, save the document in a peer-review folder under a name you will recognize. It's wise to include the writer's name, the assignment, the number of the draft, and your initials. For example, Ann G. Smith might name the file for the first draft of Javier Jabari's first essay *jabari essay1 d1 ags.doc.*

You can use the TRACK CHANGES function of your word-processing program to add comments and suggestions and to revise text. These suggestions and revisions appear in the document in a different color. Insert a

QUICK HELP

Guidelines for peer review

1. *Overall thoughts.* What are the main strengths and weaknesses of the draft? What might be confusing to readers? What is the single most important thing the writer says in the draft? What will readers want to know more about?

2. *Assignment.* Does the draft carry out the assignment? (4a2)

3. *Title and introduction.* Does the title tell readers what the draft is about? How does it catch their interest? Does the opening make readers want to continue? How else might the draft begin? (4h)

4. *Thesis and purpose.* Paraphrase the thesis as a promise: *In this paper, the writer will. . . .* Does the draft fulfill that promise? Why, or why not? Does it carry out the writer's purposes? (4a2 and 4c)

5. *Audience.* How does the draft interest and appeal to its intended audience? (4a4)

6. *Rhetorical stance.* Where does the writer stand? What words or phrases indicate the stance? What influences have likely contributed to that stance? (4a3)

7. *Major points.* List the main points, and review them one by one. Do any points need to be explained more or less fully? Do any seem confusing or boring? Should any points be eliminated or added? How well is each major point supported? (4f)

8. *Visuals.* Do the visuals, if any, add to the key points? Are they clearly referred to in the draft? Are they appropriately labeled? (4a6 and 4j)

9. *Organization and flow.* Is the writing easy to follow? Are the ideas presented in an order that will make sense to readers? Do effective transitions ease the flow between paragraphs and ideas? (4a5 and 4g)

10. *Paragraphs.* Which paragraphs are clearest and most interesting? Which paragraphs need further development, and how might they be improved? (4i1)

11. *Sentences.* Are any sentences particularly effective and well written? Are any sentences weak—confusing, awkward, or uninspired? Are the sentences varied in length and structure? Are the sentence openings varied? (4i2)

12. *Words*. Mark words that draw vivid pictures or provoke strong responses; then mark words that are weak, vague, or unclear. Do any words need to be defined? Are the verbs active and vivid? Are any words potentially offensive? (4i3)

13. *Tone*. What dominant impression does the draft create—serious, humorous, persuasive, something else? Where, specifically, does the writer's attitude come through most clearly? Is the tone appropriate to the topic and the audience? Is it consistent throughout? (4i4)

14. *Conclusion*. Does the draft conclude in a memorable way, or does it seem to end abruptly or trail off into vagueness? How else might it end? (4h3)

comment explaining each revision and suggesting how the writer can build on it in the next draft. (If your word processor doesn't have a COMMENT function, you can use footnotes for comments instead.)

You should also consider using highlighting. If you explain to the writer what the colors mean and use only a few colors, highlighting can make a powerful visual statement about what needs to be revised. Here is an example of a key for the writer:

Color	Revision Suggestion
Yellow	Read this sentence aloud, and then revise for clarity.
Green	This material seems out of place. Reorganize or delete?
Blue	This idea isn't clearly connected to your thesis. Cut?

3 The process of peer review

Whenever you respond to a piece of writing, think of the response you are giving—whether orally or in writing—as a letter to the writer of the draft. Your written response should usually have two parts: (1) a personal letter at the end of the draft or on a separate page, and (2) visual markings on the text.

Before you read the draft, ask the writer for any feedback instructions. Take the writer's requests seriously. If, for example, the writer asks you to look at specific aspects of his or her writing and to ignore others, be sure to respond to that request.

To begin your review, read straight through the essay or project and think how you would describe the writer's purpose, audience, stance, thesis, and support.

Beginning a letter to the writer

At the end of the draft, begin your letter by addressing the writer by name (*Dear Javier*). Summarize the main idea(s) of the piece of writing. You might begin your letter by writing *I think the main argument is* . . . or *In this draft, you promise to.* . . . Then outline the main points that support the thesis (3e and f). Once you prepare the outline, your most important work as a peer reviewer can begin. You need to think alongside the writer about how to support the thesis and arrange details most effectively for the audience. Ask yourself the following questions:

- If I heard this topic mentioned in another situation, what would I expect the conversation to include? Would any of those ideas strengthen this writing?

- If I had not read this draft, what order would I expect these ideas to follow?

- Are any ideas or connections missing?

In addition, consult the Quick Help box on p. 78 for guidelines for peer review to generate ideas for your response. Write your suggestions in the letter. You might use sentences like *I didn't understand* _____. *Could you explain it differently? I think* _____ *is your strongest point, and I recommend you move* _____. This portion of the letter will help the writer make the most significant changes to the argument and supporting evidence.

Marking up the draft

Next, as you reread the draft, use the mark-up strategies discussed earlier (4b2) to give the writer specific feedback. As you use these strategies, always think about how you would respond to the same

Compliments	Constructive Criticism
• I'd never thought of it that way. Really smart insight.	• Here I expected _____ instead of _____.
• Your strongest evidence is _____.	• I think you need more evidence to support your claim that _____.
• You got my attention here by _____.	• You might consider adding _____.
• This example is great because _____.	• What about _____? There are other perspectives on this topic.
• I like the way you use _____ to tie all these ideas together.	• I think you need to say this sooner.
• I like this sentence because _____.	• I had to read this sentence twice to get what you mean. Simplify it.
• I think this approach and your tone are perfect for the audience because _____.	• Your tone shifts here. Try to sound more _____.

mark-ups in your own draft. Avoid an overwhelming number of comments or changes, for example, and don't highlight too extensively. In addition, remember that your job in marking up the text is to point out the problems, not to solve them (though you should certainly offer suggestions).

Unlike in the personal letter, where you try to help the writer imagine the next draft, your comments, annotations, and other markings should respond to what is already written. Aim for a balance between compliments and constructive criticism. If you think the author has stated something well, comment on why you like it. If you have trouble understanding or following the writer's ideas, comment on what you think may be causing problems. The chart above provides several examples of ways to frame effective marginal comments.

Concluding the letter

After you have added all your mark-ups to the draft, conclude your letter by adding two or three brief paragraphs addressing the following points:

• *The strengths of the current draft.* Refer to the outline you developed and your compliments.

FOR MULTILINGUAL WRITERS

Reviewing a draft

Your knowledge of and experience with multiple languages or cultures may give you special insights that help you point out unclear or confusing ideas in your peers' work. Your peers may find questions or comments from your unique perspective helpful in expanding their ideas. Even if you are not used to speaking up in class, remember that you have a lot to offer!

- *Two or three things you think will significantly improve the draft's effectiveness.* Refer to your constructive criticism.

- *Areas on which the writer asked you to focus* (if any).

Read over your comments once more, checking your own tone and clarity. Close by signing your name. Save your response, and send it to the writer using the method recommended by your instructor.

4 Responses based on the stage of the draft

You may be asked to review your peers' work at any stage of the writing—after the first draft, during an intermediate stage, or when the paper is close to a final draft. Different stages in the writing process call for different strategies and areas of focus on the part of the peer reviewer.

Responding to early-stage drafts

Writers of early-stage drafts need direction and options, not editing that focuses on grammar or punctuation. Your goal as a peer reviewer of an early draft is to help the writer think of ways to expand on the ideas. Pose questions and offer examples that will help the writer think of new ways to approach the topic. Try to help the writer imagine what the final draft might be like.

Approach commenting on and marking up an early draft with three types of questions in mind:

- *Fit.* How does this draft fit the assignment? In what areas might the writer struggle to meet the criteria? How does this draft fit the audience? What else does the writer need to remember about the audience's expectations and needs?

- *Potential.* What ideas in this draft are worth developing more? What other ideas or details could inform the argument? Are there other viewpoints on this topic that the writer should explore?

- *Order.* Considering only the parts that are worth keeping, what sequence do you recommend? What new sections do you think need to be added?

Responding to intermediate-stage drafts

Writers of intermediate-stage drafts need to know where their claims lack sufficient evidence, what ideas confuse readers, and how their approach misses its target audience. They also need to know which parts of their drafts are clear and well written.

Approach commenting on and marking up an intermediate draft with these types of questions in mind:

- *Topic sentences and transitions.* Topic sentences introduce the idea of a paragraph, and transitions move the writing smoothly from one paragraph or section or idea to the next (5b, d, and e). How well does the draft prepare readers for the next set of ideas by explaining how they relate to the overall claim? Look for ideas or details that don't seem to fit into the overall structure. Is the idea or detail out of place because it is not well integrated into this paragraph? If so, recommend a revision or a new transition. Is it out of place because it doesn't support the overall claim? If so, recommend deletion.

- *Supporting details.* Well-developed paragraphs and arguments depend on supporting details (5c). Does the writer include an appropriate number and variety of details? Could the paragraph be improved by adding another example, a definition, a comparison or contrast, a cause-effect relationship, an analogy, a solution to a problem, or a personal narrative?

Responding to late-stage drafts

Writers of late-stage drafts need help with first and last impressions, sentence construction, word choice, tone, and format. Their next step is proofreading (4l), and your job as a peer reviewer is to call attention to the sorts of problems writers need to solve before submitting their final work. Your comments and markings should identify the overall strengths of the draft as well as one or two weaknesses that the writer can reasonably improve in a short amount of time.

FOR MULTILINGUAL WRITERS

Asking an experienced writer to review your draft

One good way to make sure that your writing is easy to follow is to have someone else read it. You might find it especially helpful to ask someone who is experienced in the kind of writing you are working on to read over your draft and to point out any words or patterns that are unclear or ineffective.

Reviews of Emily Lesk's draft

On the following page are the first three paragraphs of Emily Lesk's draft, as reviewed by two students, Beatrice Kim and Nastassia Lopez. Beatrice and Nastassia reviewed the draft separately and combined their comments on the draft they returned to Emily. They also decided to use highlighting for particular purposes: green for material they found particularly effective, yellow for language that seemed unclear, blue for material that could be expanded or made more detailed, and gray for material that could be deleted.

As this review shows, Nastassia and Bea agree on some of the major problems — and good points — in Emily's draft. The comments on the draft, however, reveal their different responses. You, too, will find that different readers do not always agree on what is effective or ineffective. In addition, you may find that you simply do not agree with their advice. In examining responses to your writing, you can often proceed efficiently by looking first for areas of agreement (*everyone was confused by this sentence — I'd better revise it*) or strong disagreement (*one person said my conclusion was "perfect," and someone else said it "didn't conclude" — better look carefully at that paragraph again*).

On p. 86 is the text of an email message Emily's two peer-review partners wrote to her, giving her some overall comments to accompany those they had written in the margins of her draft.

All-Powerful Coke

I don't drink Coke. Call me picky for disliking the soda's saccharine aftertaste. Call me cheap for choosing a water fountain over a twleve-ounce aluminum can that costs a dollar from a vending machine but only pennies to produce. Even call me unpatriotic for rejecting the potable god that over the last century has come to represent all the enjoyment and ease to be found in our American way of life. But don't call me a hypocrite when I admit that I still identify with Coke and the Coca-Cola culture.

I have a favorite T-shirt that says "Drink Coca-Cola Classic" in Hebrew. It's Israel's standard tourist fare, like little nested dolls in Russia or painted horses in Scandinavia, and before setting foot in the Promised Land three years ago. I knew where I could find one. The T-shirt shop in the central block of a Jerusalem shopping center did offer other shirt designs ("Maccabee Beer" was a favorite), but that Coca-Cola shirt was what drew in most of the dollar-carrying tourists. I waited almost twenty minutes for mine, and I watched nearly everyone ahead of me say "the Coke shirt" (and "thanks" in Hebrew).

At the time, I never asked why I wanted the shirt. I do know, though, that the reason I wear it often, despite a hole in the right sleeve, has to do with its power as a conversation piece. Few people notice it without asking something like, "Does that say Coke?" I usually smile and nod. They mumble a compliment and we go our separate ways. But rarely does anyone want to know what language the world's most famous logo is written in. And why should they? Perhaps because Coca-Cola is a cultural icon that shapes American identity.

Student Writing

Comment: I'm not sure your title says enough about what your essay will argue. NL

Comment: The opening sentence is a good attention-getter. Wonder what will come next? NL

Comment: The beginning seems pretty abrupt. BK

Comment: What does this mean?? Will other members of your audience know? BK

Comment: The style of repeating the phrase "call me" is good, but I don't think the first three "call me" statements have much to do with the rest of the paper. NL

Comment: It would be cool to show this. BK

Comment: Not sure you need all these details. Is any of it going to be important later? NL

Comment: one of what? a doll or horse? NL

Comment: Say it in Hebrew? BK

Comment: This transition works really well. I wasn't sure before about where this was going, but the beginning of the paragraph here starts to clue me in. NL

Comment: good detail! Lots of people can relate to a "conversation piece" shirt. NL

Comment: I like the question—but is your next sentence really the answer? NL

Comment: Is this the thesis? Kind of comes out of nowhere. BK

Hi Emily:

We're attaching your draft with our comments. Good luck on revising!

First, we think this is a great draft. You got us interested right away with the story about your T-shirt and we just wanted to keep on reading. So the introduction seems really good. But the introduction goes on for a while—several paragraphs, we think, and we were beginning to wonder what your point was and when you were going to get to it. And when you get to your thesis, could you make it a little more specific or say a little more about what it means that Coca-Cola is an icon that shapes identity? This last idea wasn't clear to us.

Your stance, though, is very clear, and we liked that you talked about how you were pulled into the whole Coke thing even though you don't particularly like the soda. Sometimes we got bogged down in a ton of details, though, and felt like maybe you were telling us too much.

We were impressed with some of the words you use—we had to look up what "potable" meant! But sometimes we weren't sure a word was the very best one—we marked some of these words on your draft for you.

See you in class.

Nastassia and Bea

P.S. Could you add a picture of your T-shirt? It would be cool to see what it looks like.

Emily also got advice from her instructor, who suggested that Emily do a careful outline of this draft to check for how one point led to another and to see if the draft stayed on track.

Based on her own review of her work as well as all of the responses she received, Emily decided to (1) make her thesis more explicit, (2) delete some extraneous information and examples, (3) integrate at least one more visual into her text, and (4) work especially hard on the tone and length of her introduction and on word choice.

4c Getting the most from peer reviewers' comments

Remember that your reviewers should be acting as coaches, not judges, and that their job is to help you improve your essay as much as possible. Listen to and read their comments carefully. If you don't understand a particular suggestion, ask for clarification, examples, and so on. Remember, too, that reviewers are commenting on your writing, not on *you*, so be open and responsive to what they recommend. But you are the final authority on your essay; you will decide which suggestions to follow and which to disregard. (See the chart on p. 90.)

4d Learning from instructor comments

Instructor comments on any work that you have done can help you identify mistakes, particularly ones that you make repeatedly, and can point you toward larger issues that prevent your writing from being as effective as it could be. Whether or not you will have an opportunity to revise a particular piece of writing, you should look closely at the comments from your instructor.

In responding to student writing, however, instructors sometimes use phrases or comments that are a kind of shorthand—comments that are perfectly clear to the instructor but may be less clear to the students reading them. The instructor comments in the following chart, culled from over a thousand first-year student essays, are among those that you may find most puzzling. If your paper includes a puzzling comment that is not listed here, be sure to ask your instructor what the comment means and how you can fix the problem.

Instructor Comment	Actions to Take in Response
"thesis not clear"	Make sure that you have a main point, and state it directly. (4f) The rest of the paper will need to support the main point, too—this problem cannot be corrected by adding a sentence or two.

Continued on p. 88

Instructor Comment	Actions to Take in Response
"trying to do too much" "covers too much ground"	Focus your main point more narrowly so that you can say everything that you need to in a project of the assigned length. You may need to cut back on some material and then expand what remains.
"hard to follow" "not logical" "incoherent" "jumps around" "parts not connected" "transition"	If overall organization is unclear, try mapping or outlining and rearranging your work. (15b2) See if transitions and signals (5d4) or additional explanation will solve the problem.
"too general" "vague"	Use concrete language and details, and make sure that you have something specific and interesting to say. (27c) If not, reconsider your topic.
"underdeveloped" "thin" "sparse"	Add examples and details, and be as specific as possible. (27c) You may need to do more research. (Chapters 10–12)
"what about the opposition?" "one-sided" "condescending" "overbearing"	Add information on why some people disagree with you, and represent their views fairly and completely before you refute them. Recognize that reasonable people may hold views that differ from yours. (9e3)
"repetitive" "you've already said this"	Revise any parts of your writing that repeat an argument, point, word, or phrase; avoid using the same evidence over and over.
"awk" "awkward"	Ask a peer or your instructor for suggestions about revising awkward sentences. (Chapters 34–39)
"syntax" "awkward syntax" "convoluted"	Read the sentence aloud to identify the problem; revise or replace the sentence. (Chapters 34–39)
"unclear"	Find another way to explain what you mean; add any background information or examples that your audience may need to follow your reasoning.
"tone too conversational" "not an academic voice" "too informal" "colloquial" "slang"	Look for overly informal words and phrasing you can revise. Consider your audience, and revise material that addresses or refers to that group too familiarly or informally. (Chapter 27)

Instructor Comment	Actions to Take in Response
"pompous" "stilted" "stiff"	Make sure you understand the connotations of the words you use, and revise any that contribute to a pompous, excessively old-fashioned, or inappropriate tone. (27a and b)
"set up quotation" "integrate quotation"	Read the sentence containing the quotation aloud; revise it if it does not make sense as a sentence. Introduce every quotation with information about the source. Explain each quotation's importance to your work. (Chapter 13)
"your words?" "source?" "cite"	Mark all quotations clearly. Cite paraphrases and summaries of others' ideas. Give credit for help from others, and remember that you are responsible for your own work. (Chapters 13 and 14)
"doc"	Check the citations to be sure that you include all of the required information, that you punctuate correctly, and that you omit information not required by the documentation style. (Chapters 16–19)

4e   Revising with peer and instructor comments

Approach comments from peer reviewers or from your instructor in several stages. First, read straight through the comments. Take a few minutes to digest the feedback and get some distance from your work (4a). Then make a revision plan — as elaborate or as simple as you want — that prioritizes the changes needed in your next draft. (See the chart on p. 90.)

If you have comments from more than one reviewer, you may want to begin by making two lists: (1) areas in which reviewers agree on needed changes, and (2) areas in which they disagree. You will then have to make choices about which advice to heed and which to ignore from both lists. Next, rank the suggestions you've chosen to address.

Focus on comments about your purpose, audience, stance, thesis, and support. Leave any changes to sentences, words, punctuation, and format for later in the process; your revision of bigger-picture issues comes first.

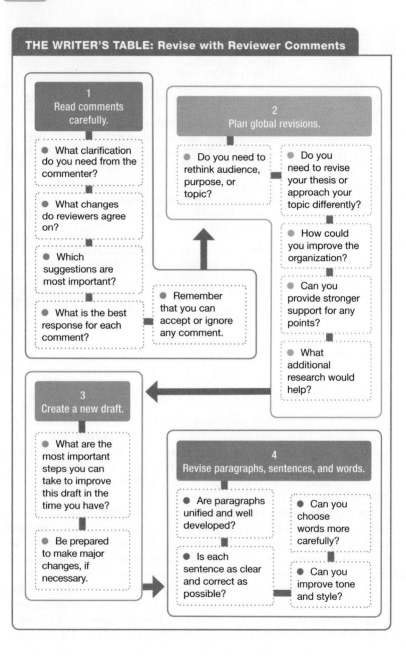

THE WRITER'S TABLE: Revise with Reviewer Comments

1 Read comments carefully.

- What clarification do you need from the commenter?
- What changes do reviewers agree on?
- Which suggestions are most important?
- What is the best response for each comment?

- Remember that you can accept or ignore any comment.

2 Plan global revisions.

- Do you need to rethink audience, purpose, or topic?
- Do you need to revise your thesis or approach your topic differently?
- How could you improve the organization?
- Can you provide stronger support for any points?
- What additional research would help?

3 Create a new draft.

- What are the most important steps you can take to improve this draft in the time you have?
- Be prepared to make major changes, if necessary.

4 Revise paragraphs, sentences, and words.

- Are paragraphs unified and well developed?
- Is each sentence as clear and correct as possible?
- Can you choose words more carefully?
- Can you improve tone and style?

Prepare a file for your revised draft. Use your previous draft as a starting point, renaming it to indicate that it is a revision. (For example, Javier Jabari might rename his file *jabari essay1 d2*, using his name, assignment number, and draft number.)

In the new file, make the changes you identified in your revision plan. Be prepared to revise heavily, if necessary; if comments suggest that your thesis isn't working, for example, you may need to change the topic or the entire direction of your text. Heavy revision is not a sign that there's something wrong with your writing; on the contrary, major revision is a common feature of serious, goal-oriented writing, as this image of a speech for President Obama (written by his speechwriter, with Obama's extensive handwritten changes) makes clear.

Once you are satisfied that your revisions adequately address major concerns, make corrections to sentences, words, and punctuation.

EXERCISE 4.3

Using the questions in the Quick Help box on pp. 78–79 as a guide, analyze the draft you wrote for Exercise 3.6.

4f Revising thesis and support

Once you have sufficient advice on your draft and have studied all the responses, reread the draft once more, paying special attention to your thesis and its support. Make sure your thesis sentence contains a clear statement of the topic and a comment explaining what is particularly significant or noteworthy about the topic (3c). As you read, ask yourself how each paragraph relates to or supports the thesis and how each sentence develops the paragraph topic. Such careful rereading can help you eliminate irrelevant material and identify sections needing further details or examples.

Be particularly careful to note what kinds of evidence, examples, or good reasons you offer in support of your major points. If some points are off topic, look back at your exploratory work (3a). Emily Lesk found, for example, that an entire paragraph in her draft (paragraph 8) did nothing to support her thesis. Thus she deleted the entire paragraph.

EXERCISE 4.4

After rereading the draft you wrote for Exercise 3.6, evaluate the revised working thesis you produced for Exercise 3.3. Then evaluate its support in the draft. Identify points that need further support, and list those things you must do to provide that support.

> bedfordstmartins.com/smhandbook
> **Student Writing** > **Argument Writing**

4g Rethinking organization

One good way to check the organization of a draft is to outline it. After numbering the paragraphs in the draft, read through each one, jotting down its main idea or topic. Then examine your outline, and ask yourself the following questions:

- What overall organizational strategies do you use? spatial? chronological? logical? associational?

- Do the main points clearly relate to the thesis and to one another? Are any of them irrelevant? Should any sections or paragraphs be moved to another part of the draft?

- Can you identify any confusing leaps from point to point? Do you need to provide additional or stronger transitions?

- Do you leave out any important points?

4h Revising title, introduction, and conclusion

Readers remember the first and last parts of a piece of writing better than anything else. For this reason, it is wise to pay careful attention to three important elements—the title, the introduction, and the conclusion.

1 Title

A good title gives readers information, draws them into the piece of writing, and may even indicate the writer's view of the topic. The title of Emily Lesk's draft, "All-Powerful Coke," did not provide the link Emily wanted to establish between Coca-Cola and American identity. During the review process, she titled her new draft "Red, White, and Everywhere." This title piques readers' curiosity and suggests that the familiar "red, white, and blue" would be linked to something that is everywhere.

2 Introduction

A good introduction accomplishes two important tasks: first, it attracts readers' interest, and, second, it presents the topic and makes some comment on it. It contains, in other words, a strong lead, or hook, and often an explicit thesis as well. Many introductions open with a general statement about the topic and then go into more detail, leading up to a specific thesis at the end. A writer can also begin an introduction effectively with a vivid statement of the problem that led to the thesis or with an intriguing quotation, an anecdote, a question, or a strong opinion. The rest of the introduction then moves from this beginning to a presentation of the topic and the thesis. (For more on introductions, see 5f1.)

In many cases, especially when a writer begins with a quotation or an anecdote, the introduction consists of two or three paragraphs: the first provides the hook, while the next paragraph or two explain the significance of the hook. Emily Lesk used this pattern in her introduction. Her first paragraph contains such a hook, which is followed by a two-paragraph narrative anecdote about a trip to Israel that links Coca-Cola advertising and Americans' sense of identifying with the product. After considering the responses of her peers and analyzing her opening, Emily decided that the introduction took too long to get to the point and that it didn't lead to a clearly articulated thesis. She decided to shorten the introduction and to make her thesis more explicit and detailed.

3 Conclusion

A good conclusion leaves readers satisfied that a full discussion has taken place. Many conclusions begin with a restatement of the thesis and end with more general statements that grow out of it: this pattern reverses the common general-to-specific pattern of the introduction. Writers also use other approaches to conclude effectively, including a provocative question, a quotation, a vivid image, a call for action, or a warning.

Emily Lesk's draft two-paragraph conclusion emphasizes the main point of her essay, that the Coke logo now represents America, but it then goes on to discuss the impact of such advertising in other countries, such as Kenya. On reflection, however, Emily decided to cut the paragraph on Kenya because it didn't really draw her essay to a close but rather went off in a different direction. (For more on conclusions, see 5f2.)

EXERCISE 4.5

Review Emily Lesk's draft (3g), and compose an alternative conclusion. Then write a paragraph commenting on the strengths and weaknesses of the two conclusions.

4i   Revising paragraphs, sentences, words, and tone

In addition to examining the larger issues of logic, organization, and development, effective writers look closely at the smaller elements: paragraphs, sentences, and words. Many writers, in fact, look forward to this part of revising and editing because its results are often dramatic. Turning a weak paragraph into a memorable one — or finding exactly the right word to express a thought — can yield great satisfaction and self-confidence.

1   Paragraphs

Paragraphing serves the reader by visually breaking up long expanses of writing and signaling a shift in focus. Readers expect a paragraph to develop an idea, a process that usually requires several sentences or more. These guidelines can help you revise your paragraphs:

- Look for the topic or main point of each paragraph, whether it is stated or implied. Does every sentence expand, support, or otherwise relate to the topic?

- Check to see how each paragraph is organized — spatially, chronologically, associationally, or by some logical relationship (3e). Is this organization appropriate to the topic of the paragraph?

- Note any paragraphs that have only a few sentences. Do these paragraphs sufficiently develop the topic of the paragraph?

For additional guidelines on editing paragraphs, see p. 108.

Paragraph 5 in Emily Lesk's draft (3g) contains only two sentences, and they don't lead directly into the next paragraph. In her revision, Emily lengthened (and strengthened) paragraph 5 by adding a sentence that points out the result of Coca-Cola's advertising campaign.

But while countless campaigns with this general strategy have together shaped the Coca-Cola image, presenting a product as key to a happy life represents a fairly typical approach to advertising everything from Fords to Tylenol. Coca-Cola's advertising is unique, however, for the original way the beverage giant has utilized specific advertising media — namely magazines and television — to drive home this message. As a result, Coca-Cola has come to be associated not only with the images of Americana portrayed in specific advertisements but also with the general forms of advertising media that dominate American culture.

EXERCISE 4.6

Choose two other paragraphs in Emily Lesk's draft in 3g, and evaluate them using the guidelines in the Quick Help box on pp. 78–79. Write a brief paragraph suggesting ways to improve the development or organization of these paragraphs.

2 Sentences

As with life, variety is the spice of sentences. You can add variety to your sentences by looking closely at their length, opening patterns, and structure. (See the guidelines for editing sentences in Chapter 42.)

Varying sentence length

Too many short sentences, especially one after another, can sound like a series of blasts on a car horn, whereas a steady stream of long sentences may tire or confuse readers. Most writers aim for some variety of length.

In looking at draft paragraph 9, Emily Lesk found that the sentences were all fairly long, from twenty-two to fifty words (see p. 69). In revising, she decided to shorten the second sentence, thereby inserting a short, easy-to-read sentence between two long sentences.

CONSIDERING DISABILITIES

Technology for revising

Many students with dyslexia and other language-processing disabilities can benefit from the use of assistive technologies. Today, reading and writing software offers active spell checking, word-predictor functions, audio and visual options, and help with mechanics, punctuation, and formatting. You may want to make these technologies a regular part of your revising process.

This is just one example of the media strategies Coca-Cola has used to encourage

us to equate Coke with the "happy life" element of American identity. As the

omnipresent magazine gave way to television, Coke was there from the beginning.

In its 1996 recap of the previous fifty years in industry history, the publication

Beverage Industry cites Coca-Cola as a frontrunner in the very first form of

television advertising: sponsorship of entire programs such as, in the case of

Coke. *The Bob Dixon Show* and *The Adventures of Kit Carson*. Just as we now

associate sports stadiums with their corporate sponsors, viewers of early

television programs will forever equate them with Coke.

> **Deleted:** In other words, Coca-Cola has hammered itself into our perceptions—both conscious and subconscious—of an American cultural identity by equating itself with media that define American culture.
>
> **Deleted:** When
>
> **Deleted:** general
>
> **Deleted:** that marked the earlier part of the century fell by the wayside under television's power.

Varying sentence openings

Most sentences in English follow subject-predicate order and hence open with the subject of an independent clause, as does the sentence you are now reading. But opening sentence after sentence this way results in a jerky, abrupt, or choppy rhythm. You can vary sentence openings by beginning with a dependent clause, a phrase, an adverb, a conjunctive adverb, or a coordinating conjunction (42b).

Emily Lesk's second paragraph (see p. 67) tells the story of how she got her Coke T-shirt in Israel. Before she revised her draft, every sentence in this paragraph opened with the subject. Emily deleted some examples and varied her sentence openings for a dramatic and easy-to-read paragraph.

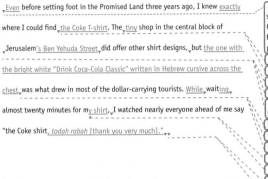

Even before setting foot in the Promised Land three years ago, I knew exactly

where I could find the Coke T-shirt. The tiny shop in the central block of

Jerusalem's Ben Yehuda Street, did offer other shirt designs, but the one with

the bright white "Drink Coca-Cola Classic" written in Hebrew cursive across the

chest, was what drew in most of the dollar-carrying tourists. While waiting

almost twenty minutes for my shirt, I watched nearly everyone ahead of me say

"the Coke shirt, *todah rabah* [thank you very much]."

Deleted: I have a favorite T-shirt that says "Drink Coca-Cola Classic" in Hebrew. It's Israel's standard tourist fare, like little nested dolls in Russia or painted horses in Scandinavia, and

Deleted: one

Deleted: T-shirt

Deleted: a

Deleted: shopping center

Deleted: ("Maccabee Beer" was a favorite).

Deleted: that Coca-Cola shirt

Deleted: I

Deleted: ed

Deleted: ine

Deleted: and

Deleted: "

Deleted: (and "thanks" in Hebrew).

Checking for sentences opening with it and there

As you go over the sentences of your draft, look especially at those beginning with *it* or *there*. Sometimes these words can create a special emphasis, as in "It was a dark and stormy night." But they can also cause problems. A reader doesn't know what *it* means, for instance, unless the writer has already pointed out exactly what the word stands for. A more subtle problem with these openings, however, is that they may allow a writer to avoid taking responsibility for a statement:

> The chancellor believes
> ◯ ~~It is believed~~ that fees must increase next semester.
>   ^

The original sentence avoids responsibility by failing to tell us who believes that fees must increase.

Varying sentence structure

Using only simple sentences can be very dull, but overusing compound sentences may result in a singsong or repetitive rhythm. At the same time, strings of complex sentences may sound, well, overly complex. Try to vary your sentence structure (see Chapter 42).

EXERCISE 4.7

Find a paragraph in your own writing that lacks variety in sentence length, sentence openings, or sentence structure. Then write a revised version.

3 Words

Perhaps even more than paragraphs and sentences, word choice—
or diction—offers writers an opportunity to put their personal stamp on
a piece of writing (see Chapter 27). The following questions will help you
become aware of the kinds of words you use:

- Do you use too many abstract and general nouns rather than concrete and specific ones? Saying that you bought a new car is much
  less memorable than saying you bought a new convertible or a new
  Mini Cooper (27c).

- Are there too many nouns in relation to the number of verbs? The
  effect of the *overuse* of *nouns* in *writing* is the *placing* of too much
  strain on the inadequate *number* of *verbs* and the resultant *prevention*
  of *movement* of the *thought.* In the preceding sentence, the verb *is*
  carries the entire weight of all those nouns (in italics). The result
  is a heavy, boring sentence. Why not say instead, *Overusing nouns
  places a big strain on the verbs and slows down the prose*?

- How many verbs are forms of *be—be, am, is, are, was, were, being,
  been*? If *be* verbs account for more than about a third of your total
  verbs, you are probably overusing them. (See 29b1 and Chapter 30.)

- Are most of your verbs *active* rather than passive? Although the
  passive voice has many uses (30g), your writing will generally be
  stronger and more energetic if you use active verbs.

- Are your words *appropriate*? Check to be sure they are not too
  fancy—or too casual (27a).

Emily Lesk made a number of changes in word choice. In the second paragraph, she decided to change *Promised Land* to *Israel* since
some of her readers might not regard these two as synonymous. She
also made her diction more lively, changing *from Fords to Tylenol* in
paragraph 5 to *from Allstate insurance to Ziploc bags* to take advantage of the A-to-Z reference.

4 Tone

Word choice is closely related to tone, the attitude that a writer's language carries toward the topic and the audience. In examining the tone
of your draft, think about the nature of the topic, your own attitude

toward it, and that of your intended audience. Check for connotations of words as well as for slang, jargon, emotional language, and your level of formality. Does your language create the tone you want to achieve (humorous, serious, impassioned, and so on)? Is that tone appropriate, given your audience and topic? (For more on creating an appropriate tone through word choice, see Chapter 27.)

Although Emily Lesk's peer reviewers liked the overall tone of her essay, one reviewer had found her opening sentence abrupt. To make her tone friendlier, she decided to preface *I don't drink Coke* with another clause, resulting in *America, I have a confession to make: I don't drink Coke.* Emily also shortened her first paragraph considerably, in part to eliminate the know-it-all attitude she herself had detected.

4j Checking visuals, media, and design

As you check what you've written about your topic, you also need to take a close look at the way your text looks and works.

- Do your reviewers think your visuals, audio, and video (if any) help you make your points? How can you make this content more effective?

- Do you use design effectively for your genre and medium? Is your text readable and inviting?

Emily Lesk's visuals

When Emily Lesk looked at her draft, she saw notes to herself about showing an early Coke ad and about looking for a picture of the original Coca-Cola Santa Claus. Since she was planning to post her essay on a class Web site that was open to the public, her instructor told her that she would need to obtain permission for these images. When she wrote to the owners of the copyright, however, she learned that she would have to pay a large fee to use the ad and the Santa picture on a public site. As a result, she looked for other images. Her mother had a button depicting one of Sundblom's Santas, so Emily took a photo of the button for her paper. Emily's peer reviewers had suggested that she include a photo of her T-shirt, so she took a photo of that as well for use in her text.

4k Editing

Because readers expect a final copy that is clean and correct in every way, you need to make time for careful final editing — checking your use of grammar, punctuation, mechanics, and spelling. If you have not run your spell checker yet, do so now, and check every word the spell checker flags. Remember, however, that spell checkers are limited and that relying too heavily on them can introduce new errors (28e1).

To improve your editing of future assignments, keep a personal checklist of the patterns of editing problems you find. Here again, your computer can help: if you notice that you often misuse a certain word, find every instance of that word, and then check the usage carefully.

An editing checklist

To begin a checklist, jot down all the errors or corrections marked on the last piece of writing you did. Then note the context in which each error appeared, and indicate what you should look for in the future. You can add to this inventory every time you write and edit a draft. Here is an example of one student's checklist:

ERRORS MARKED	IN CONTEXT	I NEED TO LOOK AT
fragment	starts with *when*	sentences beginning with *when*
missing comma	after *however*	sentences that include *however*
missing apostrophe	*company's*	all possessive nouns
tense shift	*go* for *went*	my use of the present tense
wrong word	*defiantly* for *definitely*	the spell checker's suggestions
incomplete documentation	no page number	the guidelines for documenting sources

This writer has begun to isolate patterns, such as her tendency to accept the spell checker's suggestions too readily.

EXERCISE 4.8

Using several essays you have written, establish your own editing checklist.

EXERCISE 4.9

Using the guidelines in 4a–j, reread the draft you wrote for Exercise 3.6 with an eye for revising. Try to do this at least one day after you completed the draft. List the things you need or want to address in your revision. At this point, you may want to exchange drafts with one or two classmates and share responses.

4l   Proofreading the final draft

Take time for one last, careful proofreading, which means reading to correct any typographical errors or other slips, such as inconsistencies in spelling and punctuation. Remember that running the spell checker, while necessary, is *not* the equivalent of thorough proofreading. To proofread most effectively, read through the copy aloud, making sure that you have used punctuation marks correctly and consistently, that all sentences are complete, and that no words are missing. Then go through the copy again, this time reading backward so that you can focus on each word and its spelling.

Student Writer

Emily Lesk

You have already seen and read about a number of the revisions Emily Lesk made to her first draft. On the following pages is the edited and proofread version she turned in to her instructor. If you compare her final draft with her first draft (3g), you will notice a number of additional changes she made in editing and proofreading. What corrections and improvements can you spot?

EXERCISE 4.10

Revise, edit, and proofread the draft you wrote for Exercise 3.6.

bedfordstmartins.com/smhandbook
Student Writing > Argument Writing

Emily Lesk
Professor Arraéz
Electric Rhetoric
November 15, 2010

Red, White, and Everywhere

America, I have a confession to make: I don't drink Coke. But don't call me a   1
hypocrite just because I am still the proud owner of a bright red shirt that advertises
it. Just call me an American.

Even before setting foot in Israel three years ago, I knew exactly where I could   2
find the Coke T-shirt. The tiny shop in the central block of Jerusalem's Ben Yehuda
Street did offer other designs, but the one with a bright white "Drink Coca-
Cola Classic" written in Hebrew cursive across the chest was what drew in
most of the dollar-carrying tourists. While waiting almost twenty minutes
for my shirt (depicted in Fig. 1), I watched nearly every customer ahead of
me ask for "the Coke shirt, *todah rabah* [thank you very much]."

At the time, I never thought it strange that I wanted one, too. After having   3
absorbed sixteen years of Coca-Cola propaganda through everything from NBC's
Saturday morning cartoon lineup to the concession stand at Camden Yards (the
Baltimore Orioles' ballpark), I associated the shirt with singing along to the "Just
for the Taste of It" jingle and with America's favorite pastime, not with a brown
fizzy beverage I refused to consume. When I later realized the immensity of Coke's
corporate power, I felt somewhat manipulated, but that didn't stop me from wearing
the shirt. I still don it often, despite the growing hole in the right sleeve, because of
its power as a conversation piece. Few Americans notice it without asking something
like "Does that say Coke?" I usually smile and nod. Then they mumble a one-word
compliment, and we go our separate ways. But rarely do they want to know what
language the internationally recognized logo is written in. And why should they?
They are interested in what they can relate to as Americans: a familiar red-and-white
logo, not a foreign language. Through
nearly a century of brilliant advertising
strategies, the Coca-Cola Company
has given Americans not only a thirst-
quenching beverage but a cultural icon that
we have come to claim as our own.

Throughout the company's history,   4
its marketing strategies have centered on
putting Coca-Cola in scenes of the happy,
carefree existence Americans are supposedly

Fig. 1. Hebrew Coca-Cola T-shirt.
Personal photograph by author.

striving for. What 1950s teenage girl, for example, wouldn't long to see herself in the Coca-Cola ad that appeared in a 1958 issue of *Seventeen* magazine? A clean-cut, handsome man flirts with a pair of smiling girls as they laugh and drink Cokes at a soda-shop counter. Even a girl who couldn't picture herself in that idealized role could at least buy a Coke for consolation. The malt shop, complete with a soda jerk in a white jacket and paper hat and a Coca-Cola fountain, is a theme that, even today, remains a piece of Americana (Ikuta 74).

But while countless campaigns with this general strategy have together shaped 5 the Coca-Cola image, presenting a product as key to a happy life is a fairly typical approach to advertising everything from Allstate insurance to Ziploc bags. Coca-Cola's advertising strategy is unique, however, for the original way the beverage giant has used the specific advertising media of magazines and television to drive home this message. As a result, Coca-Cola has become associated not only with the images of Americana portrayed in specific advertisements but also with the general forms of advertising media that dominate American culture.

Fig. 2. Coca-Cola Santa pin. Personal photograph by author.

One of the earliest and best-known 6 examples of this strategy is artist Haddon Sundblom's rendering of Santa Claus (see Fig. 2). Using the description of Santa in Clement Moore's poem "A Visit from St. Nicholas"—and his own rosy-cheeked face as a model—Sundblom contributed to the round, jolly image of this American icon, who just happens to delight in an ice-cold Coke after a tiring night of delivering presents ("Haddon Sundblom and Coca-Cola"). Coca-Cola utilized the concept of the magazine to present this inviting image in a brilliant manipulation of the medium (Pendergrast 181).

Today, it's easy to forget how pervasive a medium the magazine was before 7 television became readily available to all. Well into the 1960s, households of diverse backgrounds all across America subscribed loyally to general-subject weeklies and monthlies such as *Life* and the *Saturday Evening Post*, which provided news and entertainment to families nationwide. This large and constant group of subscribers enabled Coca-Cola to build an annual Christmastime campaign that used an extremely limited number of advertisements. According to the Coca-Cola Company's Web site, Sundblom created only around forty images of Santa Claus during the campaign's duration from 1931 to 1964 ("Coke Lore"). As a result, Americans soon began to seek out the ads each holiday season. The marketing strategy was to make consumers wait eagerly by the mailbox each December to see the latest *Saturday Evening Post* ad featuring Santa gulping a Coke. For this strategy to succeed, the advertisements had to be seen by many, but they also had to be just hard enough to come by to seem special. What better way to achieve these goals than to place an advertisement in the December issue of an immensely popular magazine?

Effective magazine advertising is just one example of the media strategies   8
Coca-Cola has used to encourage us to equate Coke with the "happy life" element of American identity. As the magazine gave way to television, Coke was there. In a 1996 recap of the previous fifty years in industry history, *Beverage Industry* cites Coca-Cola as a frontrunner in the very first form of television advertising: sponsorship of entire programs such as *The Bob Dixon Show* and *The Adventures of Kit Carson* ("Fabulous Fifties" 16). Just as we now associate sports stadiums with their corporate sponsors, viewers of early television programs will forever equate those programs with Coke.

When networks switched from offering sponsorships to selling exclusive   9
commercial time in short increments, Coca-Cola strove to distinguish itself once again, this time by experimenting with new formats and technologies for those commercials. Early attempts — such as choppy "stop motion" animation, where photographs of objects such as Coke bottles move without the intervention of actors — attracted much attention, according to the Library of Congress Motion Picture Archives Web site. Coca-Cola was also a pioneer in color television; after a series of experimental reels, the company produced its first color commercial in 1964 ("Highlights"). While the subject matter of these original commercials was not particularly memorable (Coca-Cola cans and bottles inside a refrigerator), the hype surrounding the use of new technologies helped draw attention to the product.

But the advertising campaign that perhaps best illustrates the ability of Coca-   10
Cola advertisers to tie their product to a groundbreaking technology did not appear until 1993. For the 1994 Winter Olympics, Coke created six television commercials featuring digitally animated polar bears rolling, swimming, snuggling, and sliding about in a computerized North Pole — and finishing off the playful experience with a swig of Coke. In 1993, two years before the release of *Toy Story*, these commercials were some of the very first widely viewed digital films ("Highlights"). As with Sundblom's Santa Clauses, television viewers looked forward to their next sighting of the cute, cuddly, cutting-edge bears, who created a natural association between Coca-Cola and digital animation. Once again, Coke didn't just use the latest technology — Coke defined it.

As a result of all of this brilliant advertising, a beverage I never even drink is [11]
a significant part of my American cultural identity. That's why I spent thirty Israeli
shekels and twenty minutes in a tourist trap I would ordinarily avoid buying my
Hebrew Coca-Cola shirt. That shirt, along with the rest of the enormous Coca-Cola
collectibles industry, demonstrates Coke's power to identify itself with the American
ideal of a lighthearted life of diversion and pleasure. Standing in line halfway around
the world for the logo that embodies these values gave me an opportunity to affirm a
part of my American identity.

Works Cited

Coca-Cola Santa pin. Personal photograph by the author. 9 Nov. 2010.

"Coke Lore." *The Coca-Cola Company: Heritage*. The Coca-Cola Company, 2006. Web. 3 Nov.
2010.

"The Fabulous Fifties." *Beverage Industry* 87.6 (1996): 16. *General OneFile*. Web. 2 Nov.
2010.

"Haddon Sundblom and Coca-Cola." *The History of Christmas*. 10 Holidays, 2004. Web. 2
Nov. 2010.

Hebrew Coca-Cola T-shirt. Personal photograph by the author. 8 Nov. 2010.

"Highlights in the History of Coca-Cola Television Advertising." *Fifty Years of Coca-Cola
Television Advertisements: Highlights from the Motion Picture Archives at the Library of
Congress*. Motion Picture, Broadcasting, and Recorded Sound Div., Lib. of Cong., 29
Nov. 2000. Web. 5 Nov. 2010.

Ikuta, Yasutoshi, ed. *'50s American Magazine Ads*. Tokyo: Graphic-Sha, 1987. Print.

Pendergrast, Mark. *For God, Country, and Coca-Cola: The Definitive History of the Great
American Soft Drink and the Company That Makes It*. 2nd ed. New York: Basic, 2000.
Print.

4m Reflecting on your writing

Research demonstrates a strong connection between careful reflection
and learning: thinking back on what you've learned and assessing it help
make that learning stick. As a result, first-year college writing courses
are increasingly encouraging students to take time for such reflection.
Whenever you finish a major piece of writing or a writing course, make
time to think back over the experience and see what lessons you can
learn from it.

- What lessons have you learned from writing—from an individual
  piece of writing or an entire course?

- From what you have learned, what can you apply to the work you will do for other classes?

- What about your writing do you feel most confident about — and why?

- What about your writing do you think needs additional work, and what plans do you have for improving?

- What confusions did you have while writing, and what did you do to resolve them?

- What major questions do you still have?

- How has writing helped you clarify your thinking, extend your knowledge, or deepen your understanding?

- Identify a favorite passage in your writing, and then try to articulate what you like about it. Can you apply what you learn from this analysis to other pieces of writing?

- How would you describe your development as a writer?

- What goals do you have for yourself as a writer?

THINKING CRITICALLY ABOUT YOUR REVIEWING AND REVISING PROCESS

1. How did you begin reviewing your draft?
2. What kinds of comments on or responses to your draft did you have? How helpful were they, and why?
3. How long did revising take? How many drafts did you produce?
4. What kinds of changes did you tend to make? in organization, paragraphs, sentence structure, wording, adding or deleting information? in the use of visuals?
5. What gave you the most trouble as you were revising?
6. What pleased you most? What is your very favorite sentence or passage in the draft, and why?
7. What would you most like to change about your process of revising, and how do you plan to go about doing so?

Developing Paragraphs

A paragraph is a group of sentences or a single sentence set off as a unit. All the sentences in a paragraph usually relate to one main idea, but within this general guideline, paragraph structure is highly flexible, allowing you to create many different effects.

Paragraphs serve as signposts—pointers that help guide readers through a piece of writing. A look at a periodical will show paragraphs working in particular ways: the first paragraph of an article may aim to get your attention and convince you to read on, while subsequent paragraphs may indicate a new point or a shift in focus or tone.

5a Creating strong paragraphs

Most readers of English come to any piece of writing with certain expectations about paragraphs:

- Paragraphs will begin and end with important information.
- The topic sentence will often let readers know what a paragraph is about.
- A paragraph will make sense as a whole; its words and sentences will be clearly related.
- A paragraph will relate to the paragraphs around it.

Let us look now at the elements in a well-written paragraph—one that is easy for readers to understand and follow.

> I never knew anyone who'd grown up in Jackson without being afraid of Mrs. Calloway, our librarian. She ran the Library absolutely by herself, from the desk where she sat with her back to the books and facing the stairs, her dragon eye on the front door, where who knew what kind of person might come in from the public? SILENCE in big black letters was on signs tacked up everywhere. She herself spoke in her normally commanding voice; every word could be heard all over the

¶

QUICK HELP

Editing the paragraphs in your writing

1. What is the topic sentence of each paragraph? Is it stated or implied? If stated, where in the paragraph does it fall? Should it come at some other point? Would any paragraph be improved by deleting or adding a topic sentence? (5b1)

2. Within each paragraph, how does each sentence relate to the main idea? (5b2)

3. How completely does each paragraph develop its topic? What details and methods of development are used? Are they effective? Do any paragraphs need more detail? What other methods of development might be used? (5c1)

4. Are paragraphs varied in length? Does any paragraph seem too long or too short? (5c2)

5. Is each paragraph organized in a way that is easy for readers to follow? Are sentences within each paragraph clearly linked? Do any of the transitional expressions try to create links between ideas that do not really exist? (5d)

6. Are the paragraphs clearly linked? Do more links need to be added? (5e)

7. How does the introductory paragraph catch readers' interest — with a quotation? an anecdote? a question? a strong opinion? How else might it open? (5f1)

8. How does the last paragraph draw the essay to a conclusion? What lasting impression will it leave with readers? How else might it conclude? (5f2)

Library above a steady seething sound coming from her electric fan; it was the only fan in the Library and stood on her desk, turned directly onto her streaming face.   —EUDORA WELTY, *One Writer's Beginnings*

This paragraph begins with a general statement of the main idea: that everyone who grew up in Jackson feared Mrs. Calloway. All the other sentences then give specific details about why she inspired such fear. This example demonstrates the three qualities essential to most academic paragraphs: unity, development, and coherence. It focuses on one

> **TALKING THE TALK**
>
> ### Paragraph length
>
> "How long should a paragraph be?" In college writing, paragraphs should address a specific topic or idea and develop that idea with examples and evidence. There is no set rule about how many sentences are required to make a complete paragraph. So write as many as you need—and no more.

main idea (unity); its main idea is supported with specifics (development); and its parts are clearly related (coherence).

5b   Writing unified paragraphs

An effective paragraph generally focuses on one main idea. A good way to achieve paragraph unity is to state the main idea clearly in one sentence—the topic sentence—and relate all other sentences in the paragraph to that idea. Like the thesis for an essay (3c), the topic sentence includes a topic and a comment on that topic. In the paragraph by Eudora Welty in 5a, the topic sentence opens the paragraph. Its topic is Mrs. Calloway; its comment, that those who grew up in Jackson were afraid of her.

1 Positioning a topic sentence

A topic sentence often appears at the beginning of a paragraph, but it can come at the end—or it may be implied rather than stated directly.

> **FOR MULTILINGUAL WRITERS**
>
> ### Being explicit
>
> In U.S. academic contexts, readers often expect paragraphs to be organized around a clearly defined topic and the relationship among ideas signaled by transitional devices (5d). Such step-by-step explicitness may strike you as unnecessary or ineffective, but it helps ensure that the reader understands your point.

Topic sentence at the beginning

If you want readers to see your point immediately, open with the topic sentence. This strategy can be particularly useful in letters of application (63b3) or in argumentative writing (Chapter 9). The following paragraph opens with a clear topic sentence (shown in italics), on which subsequent sentences build:

> *Our friendship was the source of much happiness and many memories.* We grooved to every new recording from Beyoncé. We sweated together in the sweltering summer sun, trying to win the championship for our softball team. I recall the taste of pepperoni pizza as we discussed the highlights of our team's victory. Once we even became attracted to the same person, but luckily we were able to share his friendship.

Topic sentence at the end

When specific details lead up to a generalization, putting the topic sentence at the end of the paragraph makes sense, as in the following paragraph about Alice Walker's "Everyday Use."

> During the visit, Dee takes the pictures, every one of them, including the one of the house that she used to live in and hate. She takes the churn top and dasher, both whittled out of a tree by one of Mama's uncles. She tries to take Grandma Dee's quilts. Mama and Maggie use these inherited items every day, not only appreciating their heritage but living it too. *Dee, on the other hand, wants these items only for decorative use, thus forsaking and ignoring their real heritage.*

Topic sentence at the beginning and end

Sometimes you will want to state a topic sentence at the beginning of a paragraph and then refer to it in a slightly different form at the end. Such an echo of the topic sentence adds emphasis to the main idea. In the following paragraph, the writer begins with a topic sentence announcing a problem:

> *Many of the difficulties we experience in relationships are caused by the unrealistic expectations we have of each other.* Think about it. Women are expected to feel comfortable doing most of the sacrificing. They are supposed to stay fine, firm, and forever twenty-two while doing double duty, in the home and in the workplace. The burden on men is no easier. They should be tall, handsome, and able to wine and dine the women. Many women go for the glitter and then expect these men to calm down once in a relationship and become faithful, sensitive, supportive, and loving. Let's face it. Both women and men have been unrealistic. *It's time we develop a new sensitiv-*

ity toward each other and ask ourselves what it is we need from each other that is realistic and fair.

The last sentence restates the topic sentence as a proposal for solving the problem. This approach is especially appropriate here, for the essay goes on to specify how the problem might be solved.

Topic sentence implied but not stated

Occasionally a paragraph's main idea is so obvious that it does not need to be stated explicitly in a topic sentence. Here is such a paragraph, from an essay about working as an airport cargo handler:

> In winter the warehouse is cold and damp. There is no heat. The large steel doors that line the warehouse walls stay open most of the day. In the cold months, wind, rain, and snow blow across the floor. In the summer the warehouse becomes an oven. Dust and sand from the runways mix with the toxic fumes of fork lifts, leaving a dry, stale taste in your mouth. The high windows above the doors are covered with a thick, black dirt that kills the sun. The men work in shadows with the constant roar of jet engines blowing dangerously in their ears. —PATRICK FENTON, "Confessions of a Working Stiff"

Here the implied topic sentence might be stated as *Working conditions in the warehouse are uncomfortable, dreary, and hazardous to one's health.* But the writer does not have to state this information explicitly because we can infer it easily from the specific details he provides.

Though implied topic sentences are common in descriptions, many instructors prefer explicit topic sentences in college writing.

EXERCISE 5.1

Choose an essay you have written, and identify the topic sentence of each paragraph, noting where in the paragraph the topic sentence appears or whether it is implied rather than stated. Experiment with one paragraph, positioning its topic sentence in at least two different places. What difference does the change make? If you have any implied topic sentences, try stating them explicitly. Does the paragraph become easier to read?

2 Relating each sentence to the main idea

Whether the main idea of a paragraph is stated in a topic sentence or is implied, each sentence in the paragraph should contribute to the main idea. Look, for example, at the following paragraph, which opens an essay about African American music:

> When I was a teenager, there were two distinct streams of popular music: one was black, and the other was white. The former could only be heard way at the end of the radio dial, while white music dominated everywhere else. This separation was a fact of life, the equivalent of blacks sitting in the back of the bus and "whites only" signs below the Mason-Dixon line. Satchmo might grin for days on "The Ed Sullivan Show" and certain historians hold forth ad nauseam on the black contribution to American music, but the truth was that our worlds rarely twined.
> —MARCIA GILLESPIE, "They're Playing My Music, but Burying My Dreams"

The first sentence announces the topic (there were two streams of popular music: black and white), and all of the other sentences back up this idea. The result is a unified paragraph.

EXERCISE 5.2

Choose one of the following topic sentences, and spend some time exploring the topic (3a). Then write a paragraph that includes the topic sentence. Make sure that each of the other sentences relates to it. Assume that the paragraph will be part of a letter you are writing to an acquaintance.

1. I found out quickly that college life was not quite what I had expected.
2. Being part of the "in crowd" used to be essential to me.
3. My work experience has taught me several important lessons.
4. Until recently, I never appreciated my parents fully.
5. One of my high school teachers helped prepare me for life as an adult.

EXERCISE 5.3

Choose an essay you have written recently, and examine the second, third, and fourth paragraphs. Does each have a topic sentence or strongly imply one? Do all the other sentences in the paragraph focus on its main idea? Would you now revise any of these paragraphs—and, if so, how?

5c Developing paragraphs

In addition to being unified, a paragraph should hold readers' interest and explore its topic fully, using whatever details, evidence, and examples are necessary. Without such development, a paragraph may seem lifeless and abstract.

Most good academic writing not only presents general ideas but also backs them up with specifics. This balance, the shifting between general and specific, is especially important at the paragraph level. If a paragraph contains nothing but details, readers may have trouble following the writer's meaning. If, on the other hand, a paragraph contains only general statements, readers may grow bored or may not be convinced.

A POORLY DEVELOPED PARAGRAPH

No such thing as human nature compels people to behave, think, or react in certain ways. From the time of our infancy to our death, we are constantly being taught by the society that surrounds us, the customs, norms, and mores of our distinct culture. Everything in culture is learned, not genetically transmitted.

This paragraph is boring. Although its main idea is clear, it fails to gain our interest or hold our attention because it lacks any examples or details. Now look at the paragraph revised to include needed specifics.

THE SAME PARAGRAPH, REVISED

A child in Los Angeles decorates a Christmas tree with shiny red ornaments and sparkling tinsel. A few weeks later, a child in Beijing celebrates the Chinese New Year with feasting, firecrackers, and gift money in lucky red envelopes. It is not by instinct that one child knows how to decorate the tree while the other knows how to celebrate the New Year. No such thing as human nature compels people to behave, think, or react in certain ways. Rather, from the time of our infancy to our death, we are constantly being taught by the society that surrounds us, the customs, norms, and mores of one or more distinct cultures. Everything in culture is learned, not genetically transmitted.

Though both paragraphs make the same point, the second one comes to life by bringing in specific details from life, including images that show what the paragraph describes.

Details in visual texts

Details are important in both written and visual texts. If you decide to use an image because of a particular detail, make sure your readers will notice what you want them to see. Crop out any unnecessary information, and clarify what's important about the image in your text or with a caption. The first image below shows the original photograph taken to illustrate a blog post about street food. The cropped second image, which appeared on the blog, makes the sandwich the center of the frame.

The herring at Jan's comes straight from the sea to your sandwich. If it were any fresher, it would still be swimming!

1 Logical patterns of development

The patterns shown in 3e3 for organizing essays can also help you develop paragraphs. These logical patterns include narration, description, illustration, definition, division and classification, comparison and contrast, cause and effect, process, problem and solution, analogy, and reiteration.

Narration

Narration tells a story in order to develop a main idea. Although writers usually arrange narrative paragraphs in chronological order, they sometimes use such variations as flashbacks and flash-forwards. Some narratives include dialogue; some gradually lead to a climax, the most dramatic point in the story. Here is one student's narrative paragraph that tells a personal story in order to support a point about the dangers of racing bicycles with flimsy alloy frames. Starting with a topic sentence, the paragraph proceeds chronologically and builds to a climax.

> People who have been exposed to the risk of dangerously designed bicycle frames have paid too high a price. I saw this danger myself in the 1984 Putney Race. An expensive Stowe-Shimano graphite frame failed, and the rider was catapulted onto Vermont pavement at fifty miles per hour. The pack of riders behind him was so dense that most other racers crashed

into a tangled, sliding heap. The aftermath: four hospitalizations. I got off with some stitches, a bad road rash, and severely pulled tendons. My Italian racing bike was pretzeled, and my racing was over for that summer. Others were not so lucky. An Olympic hopeful, Brian Stone of the Northstar team, woke up in a hospital bed to find that his cycling was over — and not just for that summer. His kneecap had been surgically removed. He couldn't even walk.

Description

Description uses specific details to create a clear impression. In the following descriptive paragraph, the writer includes details about an old schoolroom to convey the strong impression of a room where "time had taken its toll." Although a topic sentence may be unnecessary in such a paragraph (5b), sometimes a topic sentence at the beginning helps set the scene. Notice as well how the writer uses spatial organization (3e1), moving from the ceiling to the floor.

The professor's voice began to fade into the background as my eyes wandered around the classroom in the old administration building. The water-stained ceiling was cracked and peeling, and the splitting wooden beams played host to a variety of lead pipes and coils. My eyes followed these pipes down the walls and around corners until I eventually saw the electric outlets. I thought it was strange that they were exposed, not built in, until I realized that there probably had been no electricity when the building was built. Below the outlets the sunshine was falling in bright rays across the hardwood floor, and I noticed how smoothly the floor was worn. Time had taken its toll on this building.

Illustration

Illustration makes a point with concrete examples or good reasons. To support the topic sentence in the following illustration paragraph, Mari Sandoz uses one long example about her short hair and short stature.

A SINGLE EXAMPLE

The Indians made names for us children in their teasing way. Because our very busy mother kept my hair cut short, like my brothers', they called me Short Furred One, pointing to their hair and making the sign for short, the right hand with fingers pressed close together, held upward, back out, at the height intended. With me this was about two feet tall, the Indians laughing gently at my abashed face. I am told that I was given a pair of small moccasins that first time, to clear up my unhappiness at being picked out from the dusk behind the fire and my two unhappy shortcomings made conspicuous.   —MARI SANDOZ, "The Go-Along Ones"

In the following excerpt, John Rickford offers several reasons that underlie linguists' argument that Ebonics is not "poor grammar" but a legitimate and powerful dialect of English.

SEVERAL REASONS

Why do linguists see the issue so differently from most other people? A founding principle of our science is that we describe *how* people talk; we don't judge how language should or should not be used. A second principle is that all languages, if they have enough speakers, have dialects—regional or social varieties that develop when people are separated by geographic or social barriers. And a third principle, vital for understanding linguists' reactions to the Ebonics controversy, is that all languages and dialects are systematic and rule-governed. Every human language and dialect that we have studied to date—and we have studied thousands—obeys distinct rules of grammar and pronunciation.

—JOHN RICKFORD, "Suite for Ebony and Phonics"

Definition

You will often need to write an entire paragraph in order to define a word or concept. In many such instances, however, you will want to combine definition with other patterns of development. In the following paragraph, Timothy Tregarthen starts with a definition of economics and then uses examples to support it:

Economics is the study of how people choose among the alternatives available to them. It's the study of little choices ("Should I take the chocolate or the strawberry?") and big choices ("Should we require a reduction in energy consumption in order to protect the environment?"). It's the study of individual choices, choices by firms, and choices by governments. Life presents each of us with a wide range of alternative uses of our time and other resources; economists examine how we choose among those alternatives.   —TIMOTHY TREGARTHEN, *Economics*

Division and classification

Division breaks a single item into parts. Classification groups many separate items according to their similarities. A paragraph evaluating one history course might divide the course into several segments—textbooks, lectures, assignments—and examine each one in turn. A paragraph giving an overview of many history courses at your college might classify, or group, the courses in a number of ways—by time periods, by geographic areas, by the kinds of assignments demanded, by the number of students enrolled, or by some other criterion. In the following paragraph, note how Aaron Copland divides the listening process into three parts:

DIVISION

We all listen to music according to our separate capacities. But, for the sake of analysis, the whole listening process may become clearer if we break it up into its component parts, so to speak. In a certain sense, we all listen to music on three separate planes. For lack of a better terminology, one might name these (1) the sensuous plane, (2) the expressive plane, (3) the sheerly musical plane. The only advantage to be gained from mechanically splitting up the listening process into these hypothetical planes is the clearer view to be had of the way in which we listen.

—AARON COPLAND, *What to Listen for in Music*

In this paragraph, the writer classifies, or separates, fad dieters into two groups:

CLASSIFICATION

Two types of people are seduced by fad diets. Those who have always been overweight turn to them out of despair; they have tried everything, and yet nothing seems to work. The second group to succumb appear perfectly healthy but are baited by slogans such as "look good, feel good." These slogans prompt self-questioning and insecurity — do I really look good and feel good? — and, as a direct result, many healthy people fall prey to fad diets. With both types of people, however, the problems surrounding such diets are numerous and dangerous. In fact, these diets provide neither intelligent nor effective answers to weight control.

Comparison and contrast

Comparing two things means looking at their similarities; contrasting means focusing on the differences. You can structure paragraphs that compare and contrast in two different ways. One way is to present all the information about one item and then all the information about the other item (the block method). The other possibility is to switch back and forth between the two items, focusing on particular characteristics of each in turn (the alternating method).

BLOCK METHOD

You could tell the veterans from the rookies by the way they were dressed. The knowledgeable ones had their heads covered by kerchiefs, so that if they were hired, tobacco dust wouldn't get in their hair; they had on clean dresses that by now were faded and shapeless, so that if they were hired they wouldn't get tobacco dust and grime on their best clothes. Those who were trying for the first time had their hair freshly done and wore attractive dresses; they wanted to make a good impression. But the dresses couldn't be seen at the distance that many were standing from the employment office, and they were crumpled in the crush. —MARY MEBANE, "Summer Job"

ALTERNATING METHOD

Malcolm X emphasized the use of violence in his movement and employed the biblical principle of "an eye for an eye and a tooth for a tooth." King, on the other hand, felt that blacks should use nonviolent civil disobedience and employed the theme of "turning the other cheek," which Malcolm X rejected as "beggarly" and "feeble." The philosophy of Malcolm X was one of revenge, and often it broke the unity of black Americans. More radical blacks supported him, while more conservative ones supported King. King thought that blacks should transcend their humanity. In contrast, Malcolm X thought they should embrace it and reserve their love for one another, regarding whites as "devils" and the "enemy." King's politics were those of a rainbow, but Malcolm X's rainbow was insistently one color—black. The distance between Martin Luther King Jr.'s thinking and Malcolm X's was the distance between growing up in the seminary and growing up on the streets, between the American dream and the American reality.

EXERCISE 5.4

Outline the preceding paragraph on Martin Luther King Jr. and Malcolm X, noting its alternating pattern. Then rewrite the paragraph using block organization: the first part of the paragraph devoted to King, the second to Malcolm X. Finally, write a brief analysis of the two paragraphs, explaining which seems more coherent and easier to follow—and why.

Cause and effect

You can often develop paragraphs by detailing the causes of something or the effects that something brings about. The following paragraph discusses the causes that led pediatrician Phil Offit to study science and become a physician:

> To understand exactly why Offit became a scientist, you must go back more than half a century, to 1956. That was when doctors in Offit's hometown of Baltimore operated on one of his legs to correct a club foot, requiring him to spend three weeks recovering in a chronic care facility with 20 other children, all of whom had polio. Parents were allowed to visit just one hour a week, on Sundays. His father, a shirt salesman, came when he could. His mother, who was pregnant with his brother and hospitalized with appendicitis, was unable to visit at all. He was five years old. "It was a pretty lonely, isolating experience," Offit says. "But what was even worse was looking at these other children who were just horribly crippled and disfigured by polio." That memory, he says, was the first thing that drove him toward a career in pediatric infectious diseases.   —AMY WALLACE, "An Epidemic of Fear"

Process

You may need to develop a paragraph to explain a process—that is, to describe how something happens or is done: first one step, then the next, and then the next. Every time you give directions or write down a recipe, you are showing a process, usually in chronological order. In college writing, you will probably use process paragraphs most often to tell readers how a process occurs in general—for example, how the Electoral College works or how aerosol sprays destroy the ozone layer of the atmosphere.

> By the late 20s, most people notice the first signs of aging in their physical appearance. Slight losses of elasticity in facial skin produce the first wrinkles, usually in those areas most involved in their characteristic facial expressions. As the skin continues to lose elasticity and fat deposits build up, the face sags a bit with age. Indeed, some people have drooping eyelids,

sagging cheeks, and the hint of a double chin by age 40 (Whitbourne, 1985). Other parts of the body sag a bit as well, so as the years pass, adults need to exercise regularly if they want to maintain their muscle tone and body shape. Another harbinger of aging, the first gray hairs, is usually noticed in the 20s and can be explained by a reduction in the number of pigment-producing cells. Hair may become a bit less plentiful, too, because of hormonal changes and reduced blood supply to the skin.

—KATHLEEN STASSEN BERGER, *The Developing Person through the Life Span*

Problem and solution

A paragraph developed in the problem-solution pattern opens with a topic sentence that states a problem or asks a question about a problem; then it offers a solution or an answer to the question, as in the following example from a review of Ted Nordhaus and Michael Shellenberger's book *Break Through: From the Death of Environmentalism to the Politics of Possibility.*

Unfortunately, at the moment growth means burning more fossil fuel. . . . How can that fact be faced? How to have growth that Americans want, but without limits that they instinctively oppose, and still reduce carbon emissions? [Nordhaus and Shellenberger's] answer is: investments in new technology. Acknowledge that America "is great at imagining, experimenting, and inventing the future," and then start spending. They cite examples ranging from the nuclear weapons program to the invention of the Internet to show what government money can do, and argue that too many clean-energy advocates focus on caps instead.

—BILL MCKIBBEN, "Can Anyone Stop It?"

Analogy

Analogies (comparisons that explain an unfamiliar thing in terms of a familiar one) can also help develop paragraphs. In the following paragraph, the writer draws an unlikely analogy — between the human genome and a Thanksgiving dinner — to help readers understand what scientists know about the human genome:

Think of the human genome as the ingredients list for a massive Thanksgiving dinner. Scientists long have had a general understanding of how the feast is cooked. They knew where the ovens were. Now, they also have a list of every ingredient. Yet much remains to be discovered. In most cases, no one knows exactly which ingredients are necessary for making, for example, the pumpkin pie as opposed to the cornbread. Indeed, many, if not most, of the recipes that use the genomic ingredients are missing, and there's little understanding why small variations in the quality of the ingredients can "cook up" diseases in one person but not in another.

— *USA TODAY*, "Cracking of Life's Genetic Code Carries Weighty Potential"

Reiteration

Reiteration is a method of development you may recognize from political speeches or some styles of preaching. In this pattern, the writer states the main point of a paragraph and then restates it, hammering home the point and often building in intensity as well. In the following passage from Barack Obama's 2004 speech at the Democratic National Convention, Obama contrasts what he identifies as the ideas of "those who are preparing to divide us" with memorable references to common ground and unity, including repeated references to the United States as he builds to his climactic point:

Now even as we speak, there are those who are preparing to divide us — the spin masters, the negative ad peddlers who embrace the politics of anything goes. Well, I say to them tonight, there is not a liberal America and a conservative America — there is the United States of America. There is not a black America and a white America and Latino America and an Asian America — there's the United States of America. The pundits like to slice and dice our country into Red States and Blue States: Red States for Republicans, Blue States for Democrats. But I've got news for them, too. We worship an awesome God in the Blue States, and we don't like federal agents poking around in our libraries in the Red States. We coach Little League in the Blue States and yes, we've got some gay friends in the Red States. There are patriots who opposed the war in Iraq and there are patriots who supported the war in Iraq. We are one people, all of us pledging allegiance to the stars and stripes, all of us defending the United States of America.

— BARACK OBAMA

Combining patterns

Most paragraphs combine patterns of development. In the following paragraph, the writer begins with a topic sentence and then divides his topic (the accounting systems used by American companies) into two subtopics (the system used to summarize a company's overall financial state and the one used to measure internal transactions). Next he develops the second subtopic through illustration (the assessment of costs for a delivery truck shared by two departments) and cause and effect (the system produces some disadvantages).

> Most American companies have basically two accounting systems. One system summarizes the overall financial state to inform stockholders, bankers, and other outsiders. That system is not of interest here. The other system, called the managerial or cost accounting system, exists for an entirely different reason. It measures in detail all of the particulars of transactions between departments, divisions, and key individuals in the organization, for the purpose of untangling the interdependencies between people. When, for example, two departments share one truck for deliveries, the cost accounting system charges each department for part of the cost of maintaining the truck and driver, so that at the end of the year, the performance of each department can be individually assessed, and the better department's manager can receive a larger raise. Of course, all of this information processing costs money, and furthermore may lead to arguments between the departments over whether the costs charged to each are fair.
>
> —WILLIAM OUCHI, "Japanese and American Workers: Two Casts of Mind"

EXERCISE 5.5

Choose two of the following topics or two others that interest you, and brainstorm or freewrite about each one for ten minutes (3a1 and 3a2). Then use the information you have produced to determine what method(s) of development would be most appropriate for each topic.

1. the pleasure a hobby has given you
2. the different images of two noted athletes
3. how to prepare for a storm
4. why wearing a seat belt should (or should not) be mandatory
5. the best course you've ever taken

EXERCISE 5.6

Take an assignment you have written recently, and study the ways you developed each paragraph. For one of the paragraphs, write a brief evaluation of its development. How would you expand or otherwise improve the development?

2 Determining paragraph length

Though writers must keep their readers' expectations in mind, paragraph length is determined primarily by content and purpose. Paragraphs should develop an idea, create any desired effects (such as suspense or humor), and advance the larger piece of writing. Fulfilling these aims sometimes requires short paragraphs, sometimes long ones. For example, if you are writing a persuasive essay, you may put all your evidence into one long paragraph to create the impression of a solid, overwhelmingly convincing argument. In a narrative about an exciting event, on the other hand, you may use a series of short paragraphs to create suspense, to keep the reader rushing to each new paragraph to find out what happens next.

Remember that a new paragraph often signals a pause in thought. Just as timing is crucial in telling a joke, so the pause signaled by a paragraph helps readers anticipate what is to follow or gives them a moment to think about the previous paragraph.

Reasons to start a new paragraph

- to turn to a new idea
- to emphasize something (such as a point or an example)
- to change speakers (in dialogue)
- to lead readers to pause
- to take up a subtopic
- to start the conclusion

EXERCISE 5.7

Examine the paragraph breaks in something you have written recently. Explain briefly in writing why you decided on each of the breaks. Would you change any of them now? If so, how and why?

5d **Making paragraphs coherent**

A paragraph has coherence—or flows—if its details fit together clearly in a way that readers can easily follow. You can achieve paragraph coherence by organizing ideas, by repeating key terms or phrases, and by using parallel structures and transitional devices.

1 **Organization**

When you arrange information in a particular order, you help readers move from one point to another. There are a number of ways to organize details—you might use spatial, chronological, or associational order

(3e) or one or more logical patterns, such as illustration, definition, or comparison and contrast (5c). Two other patterns commonly used in paragraphs are general to specific and specific to general.

Paragraphs organized in a general-to-specific pattern usually open with a topic sentence that presents a general idea. The topic sentence is then followed by specific points that support the generalization. In the following paragraph, the topic sentence presents a general idea about the Black Death, which is then backed up by specific examples:

GENERAL TO SPECIFIC

A massive epidemic, the Black Death of the fourteenth century, brought loss of life in the tens of millions of people and catastrophic debilitation to commerce and agriculture across Eurasia and North Africa. The bubonic plague seems to have initially irrupted into Chinese populations beginning in the 1320s. It spread in many parts of China until the 1350s with great loss of life. At the same time, it appears to have been carried into Mongolia and across the steppes into Crimea. Two Central Asian areas, one inhabited by the Nestorian Christians and the other by the Uzbek Muslims, were devastated by the plague before it struck in Europe, Southwest Asia, and Northwest Africa. Travel along Chinese and Central Asian trade routes facilitated the spread of this deadly disease (see Map 21.1).

—LANNY B. FIELDS, RUSSELL J. BARBER, AND CHERYL A. RIGGS, *The Global Past*

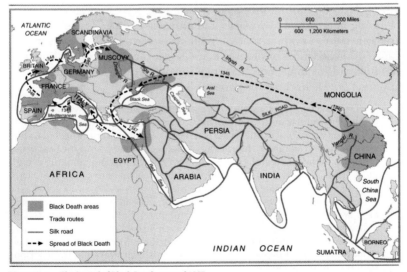

MAP 21.1 *The Spread of Black Death, around 1350.*

Paragraphs can also follow a specific-to-general organization, first providing a series of specific examples or details and then tying them together with a topic sentence that provides a conclusion. The following paragraph begins with specific details about two people's reactions to an event and ends with a topic sentence:

SPECIFIC TO GENERAL

I remember one afternoon as I was sitting on the steps of our monastery in Nepal. The monsoon storms had turned the courtyard into an expanse of muddy water and we had set out a path of bricks to serve as stepping-stones. A friend of mine came to the edge of the water, surveyed the scene with a look of disgust, and complained about every single brick as she made her way across. When she got to me, she rolled her eyes and said, "Yuck! What if I'd fallen into that filthy muck? Everything's so dirty in this country!" Since I knew her well, I prudently nodded, hoping to offer her some comfort through my mute sympathy. A few minutes later, Raphaèle, another friend of mine, came to the path through the swamp. "Hup, hup, hup!" she sang as she hopped, reaching dry land with the cry "What fun!" Her eyes sparkling with joy, she added: "The great thing about the monsoon is that there's no dust." Two people, two ways of looking at things; six billion human beings, six billion worlds. —MATTHIEU RICARD, *Happiness*

2 Repetition

A good way to build coherence in paragraphs is through repetition. Weaving in repeated key words and phrases — or pronouns that refer to them — not only links sentences but also alerts readers to the importance of those words or phrases in the larger piece of writing. Notice in the following example how the repetition of italicized key words and the pronoun *they* helps hold the paragraph together:

Over the centuries, *shopping* has changed in function as well as in style. Before the Industrial Revolution, most consumer goods were sold in open-air *markets, customers* who went into an actual *shop* were expected to *buy* something, and *shoppers* were always expected to *bargain* for the best possible price. In the nineteenth century, however, the development of the department *store* changed the relationship between buyers and sellers. Instead of visiting several *market* stalls or small *shops, customers* could now *buy* a variety of merchandise under the same roof; instead of feeling expected to *buy, they* were welcome just to look; and instead of *bargaining* with several merchants, *they* paid a fixed *price* for each *item.* In addition, *they* could return an *item* to the *store* and exchange it for a different one or get their money back. All of these changes helped transform *shopping* from serious requirement to psychological recreation.

3 Parallel structures

Parallel structures — structures that are grammatically similar — are another effective way to bring coherence to a paragraph. Readers are pulled along by the force of the parallel structures in the following example:

> William Faulkner's "Barn Burning" tells the story of a young boy trapped in a no-win situation. If he betrays his father, he loses his family. If he betrays justice, he becomes a fugitive. In trying to free himself from his trap, he does both.

For more on parallel structures, see Chapter 35.

4 Transitional devices

Transitional words and phrases, such as *after all, for example, indeed,* and *finally,* signal relationships between and among sentences and paragraphs. (For information on linking paragraphs together coherently, see 5e.) Transitions bring coherence to a paragraph by helping readers follow the progression of one idea to the next. To understand how important transitions are in guiding readers, try reading the following paragraph, from which all transitions have been removed:

A PARAGRAPH WITH NO TRANSITIONS

In "The Fly," Katherine Mansfield tries to show us the "real" personality of "the boss" beneath his exterior. The fly helps her to portray this real self. The boss goes through a range of emotions and feelings. He expresses these feelings to a small but determined fly, whom the reader realizes he unconsciously relates to his son. The author basically splits up the story into three parts, with the boss's emotions and actions changing quite measurably. With old Woodifield, with himself, and with the fly, we see the boss's manipulativeness. Our understanding of him as a hard and cruel man grows.

We can, if we work at it, figure out the relationship of these ideas to one another, for this paragraph is essentially unified by one major idea. But the lack of transitions results in an abrupt, choppy rhythm; the paragraph lurches from one detail to the next, dragging the confused reader behind. See how much easier the passage is to read and understand with transitions added.

THE SAME PARAGRAPH, WITH TRANSITIONS

In "The Fly," Katherine Mansfield tries to show us the "real" personality of "the boss" beneath his exterior. The fly *in the story's title* helps her to portray this real self. *In the course of the story,* the boss goes through a range of emotions and feelings. *At the end,* he *finally* expresses these feelings to a small but determined fly, whom the reader realizes he unconsciously relates to his son. *To accomplish her goal,* the author basically splits up the story into three parts, with the boss's emotions and actions changing quite measurably *throughout.* First with old Woodifield, *then* with himself, and *last* with the fly, we see the boss's manipulativeness. *With each part,* our understanding of him as a hard and cruel man grows.

Note that transitions can only clarify connections between thoughts; they cannot create connections. As a writer, you should not expect a transition to provide meaning.

5e Linking paragraphs together

The same methods that you use to link sentences and create coherent paragraphs can be used to link paragraphs themselves so that a whole piece of writing flows smoothly. You should include some reference to the previous paragraph, either explicit or implied, in each paragraph after the introduction. As with sentences, you can create this link by repeating or paraphrasing key words and phrases and by using parallel structures and transitional expressions.

Repeated key words

In fact, human offspring remain *dependent on their parents* longer than the young of any other species.

Children are *dependent on their parents* or other adults not only for their physical survival but also for their initiation into the uniquely human knowledge that is collectively called culture. . . .

Parallel structures

Kennedy made an effort to assure non-Catholics that he would respect the separation of church and state, and most of them did not seem to hold his religion against him in deciding how to vote. Since his election, *the church to which a candidate belongs* has become less important in presidential politics.

The region from which a candidate comes remains an important factor. . . .

Transitional expressions

While the Indian, in the character of Tonto, was more positively portrayed in *The Lone Ranger,* such a portrayal was more the exception than the norm.

Moreover, despite this brief glimpse of an Indian as an ever loyal side-kick, Tonto was never accorded the same stature as the man with the white horse and silver bullets. . . .

¶

Commonly used transitions

To signal sequence

again, also, and, and then, besides, finally, first . . . second . . . third, furthermore, last, moreover, next, still, too

To signal time

after a few days, after a while, afterward, as long as, as soon as, at last, at that time, before, earlier, immediately, in the meantime, in the past, lately, later, meanwhile, now, presently, simultaneously, since, so far, soon, then, thereafter, until, when

To signal comparison

again, also, in the same way, likewise, once more, similarly

To signal contrast

although, but, despite, even though, however, in contrast, in spite of, instead, nevertheless, nonetheless, on the contrary, on the one hand . . . on the other hand, regardless, still, though, yet

To signal examples

after all, even, for example, for instance, indeed, in fact, of course, specifically, such as, the following example, to illustrate

To signal cause and effect

accordingly, as a result, because, consequently, for this purpose, hence, so, then, therefore, thus, to this end

To signal place

above, adjacent to, below, beyond, closer to, elsewhere, far, farther on, here, near, nearby, opposite to, there, to the left, to the right

To signal concession

although it is true that, granted that, I admit that, it may appear that, naturally, of course

To signal summary, repetition, or conclusion

as a result, as has been noted, as I have said, as mentioned earlier, as we have seen, in any event, in conclusion, in other words, in short, on the whole, therefore, to summarize

¶

EXERCISE 5.8

Look at the essay you drafted for Exercise 3.6, and identify the ways your paragraphs are linked together. Identify each use of repetition, parallel structures, and transitional expressions, and then evaluate how effectively you have joined the paragraphs.

5f Writing special-purpose paragraphs

Some kinds of paragraphs deserve special attention: opening paragraphs, concluding paragraphs, transitional paragraphs, and dialogue paragraphs.

1 Opening paragraphs

Even a good piece of writing may remain unread if it has a weak opening paragraph. In addition to announcing your topic (usually in a thesis statement), an introductory paragraph must engage readers' interest and focus their attention on what is to follow. At their best, introductory paragraphs serve as hors d'oeuvres, whetting the appetite for the following courses.

One common kind of opening paragraph follows the general-to-specific pattern (5d1), in which the writer opens with a general statement and then gets more and more specific, ultimately concluding with the thesis.

> Throughout Western civilization, places such as the ancient Greek agora, the New England town hall, the local church, the coffeehouse, the village square, and even the street corner have been arenas for debate on public affairs and society. Out of thousands of such encounters, "public opinion" slowly formed and became the context in which politics was framed. Although the public sphere never included everyone, and by itself did not determine the outcome of all parliamentary actions, it contributed to the spirit of dissent found in a healthy representative democracy. Many of these public spaces remain, but they are no longer centers for political discussion and action. They have largely been replaced by television and other forms of media—forms that arguably isolate citizens from one another rather than bringing them together.   —MARK POSTER, "The Net as a Public Sphere"

In this paragraph, the opening sentence introduces a general subject—sites of public debate throughout history; subsequent sentences focus more specifically on political discussion; and the concluding sentence presents the thesis, which the rest of the essay will develop.

Other effective ways of opening an essay include quotations, anecdotes, questions, and strong opinions.

Opening with a quotation

There is a bumper sticker that reads, "Too bad ignorance isn't painful." I like that. But ignorance is. We just seldom attribute the pain to it or even recognize it when we see it. Take the postcard on my corkboard. It shows a young man in a very hip jacket smoking a cigarette. In the background is a high school with the American flag waving. The caption says, "Too cool for school. Yet too stupid for the real world." Out of the mouth of the young man is a bubble enclosing the words "Maybe I'll start a band." There could be a postcard showing a jock in a uniform saying, "I don't need school. I'm going to the NFL or NBA." Or one showing a young man or woman studying and a group of young people saying, "So you want to be white." Or something equally demeaning. We need to quit it.   —NIKKI GIOVANNI, "Racism 101"

Opening with an anecdote

I first met Angela Carter at a dinner in honor of the Chilean writer José Donoso at the home of Liz Calder, who then published all of us. My first novel was soon to be published; it was the time of Angela's darkest novel, "The Passion of New Eve." And I was a great fan. Mr. Donoso arrived looking like a Hispanic Buffalo Bill, complete with silver goatee, fringed jacket and cowboy boots, and proceeded, as I saw it, to patronize Angela terribly. His apparent ignorance of her work provoked me into a long expostulation in which I informed him that the woman he was talking to was the most brilliant writer in England. Angela liked that. By the end of the evening, we liked each other, too. That was almost 18 years ago. She was the first great writer I ever met, and she was one of the best, most loyal, most truth-telling, most inspiring friends anyone could ever have. I cannot bear it that she is dead.   —SALMAN RUSHDIE, "Angela Carter"

Opening with a question

When will international phone calls be free? Not anytime soon, bub. But when you eventually get your iPhone 4G, they should be included in your rate plan. Which is weird, because it's probably been a long time since you nervously eyed the clock while on the phone with your granny in Smallville. Long distance has been all-you-can-eat since cell phones and voice-over IP conquered the universe. But international telephony—whether landline, cellular, or Internet-based—is still a piggybank-rattling affair: Providers just can't offer dirt-cheap calls across borders.

—CLIFF KUANG, "Burning Question"

Opening with a strong opinion

Men need a men's movement about as much as women need chest hair. A brotherhood organized to counter feminists could be timely because—let's be honest—women are no more naturally inclined to equality and fairness than men are. They want power and dominion just as much as any group looking out for its own interests. Organizing to protect the welfare of males might make sense. Unfortunately, the current men's movement does not.

—JOHN RUSZKIEWICZ, *The Presence of Others*

2 Concluding paragraphs

A good conclusion wraps up a piece of writing in a satisfying and memorable way. It reminds readers of the thesis of the essay and leaves them feeling that their expectations have been met. The concluding paragraph is also your last opportunity to get your message across.

A common strategy for concluding uses the specific-to-general pattern (5d1), often beginning with a restatement of the thesis (but not word for word) and moving to more general statements. The following paragraph moves in such a way, opening with a final point of comparison between Generals Grant and Lee, specifying it in several sentences, and then ending with a much more general statement:

Lastly, and perhaps greatest of all, there was the ability, at the end, to turn quickly from war to peace once the fighting was over. Out of the way these two men behaved at Appomattox came the possibility of a peace of reconciliation. It was a possibility not wholly realized, in the years to come, but which did, in the end, help the two sections to become one nation again . . . after a war whose bitterness might have seemed to make such a reunion wholly impossible. No part of either man's life became him more than the part he played in this brief meeting in the McLean house at Appomattox. Their behavior there put all succeeding generations of Americans in their debt. Two great Americans, Grant and Lee—very different, yet under everything very much alike. Their encounter at Appomattox was one of the great moments of American history.

—BRUCE CATTON, "Grant and Lee: A Study in Contrasts"

Other effective strategies for concluding include questions, quotations, vivid images, calls for action, and warnings.

Concluding with a question

All so-called "permanent" antifreeze is basically the same. It is made from a liquid known as ethylene glycol, which has two amazing properties: It has a lower freezing point than water, and a higher boiling point than water. It does not break down (lose its properties), nor will it boil away. And every permanent antifreeze starts with it as a base. Also, just about every antifreeze has now got antileak ingredients, as well as antirust and anticorrosion ingredients. Now, let's suppose that, in formulating the product, one of the companies comes up with a solution that is pink in color, as opposed to all the others, which are blue. Presto — an exclusivity claim. "Nothing else looks like it, nothing else performs like it." Or how about, "Look at ours, and look at anyone else's. You can see the difference our exclusive formula makes." Granted, I'm exaggerating. But did I prove a point?

— PAUL STEVENS, "Weasel Words: God's Little Helpers"

Concluding with a quotation

Despite the celebrity that accrued to her and the air of awesomeness with which she was surrounded in her later years, Miss Keller retained an unaffected personality, certain that her optimistic attitude toward life was justified. "I believe that all through these dark and silent years God has been using my life for a purpose I do not know," she said. "But one day I shall understand and then I will be satisfied."

— ALDEN WHITMAN, "Helen Keller: June 27, 1880–June 1, 1968"

Concluding with a vivid image

At the time the Web was born, in the early 1990s, a popular trope was that a new generation of teenagers, reared in the conservative Reagan years, had turned out to be exceptionally bland. The members of "Generation X" were characterized as blank and inert. The anthropologist Steve Barnett saw in them the phenomenon of pattern exhaustion, in which a culture runs out of variations in their pottery and becomes less creative. A common rationalization in the fledgling world of digital culture back then was that we were entering a transitional lull before a creative storm — or were already in the eye of one. But we were not passing through a momentary calm. We had, rather, entered a persistent somnolence, and I have come to believe that we will escape it only when we kill the hive.

— JARON LANIER, *You Are Not a Gadget*

Concluding with a call for action

Do we have cause for hope? Many of my friends are pessimistic when they contemplate the world's growing population and human demands colliding with shrinking resources. But I draw hope from the knowledge that humanity's biggest problems today are ones entirely of our own making.

Asteroids hurtling at us beyond our control don't figure high on our list of imminent dangers. To save ourselves, we don't need new technology: we just need the political will to face up to our problems of population and the environment.   —JARED DIAMOND, "The Ends of the World as We Know Them"

Concluding with a warning

Because propaganda is so effective, it is important to track it down and understand how it is used. We may eventually agree with what the propagandist says because all propaganda isn't necessarily bad; some advertising, for instance, urges us not to drive drunk, to have regular dental checkups, to contribute to the United Way. Even so, we must be aware that propaganda is being used. Otherwise, we will have consented to handing over our independence, our decision-making ability, and our brains.

—ANN MCCLINTOCK, "Propaganda Techniques in Today's Advertising"

3 **Transitional paragraphs**

On some occasions, you may need to alert your readers to a major transition between ideas. To do so in a powerful way, you might use an entire short paragraph, as in the following example from a book on Web site design. The one-sentence transitional paragraph arrests our attention, announcing that the people who create Web sites expect certain responses from site users—but, as the next paragraph reveals, the users don't often behave the way a site's creator might hope.

When we're creating sites, we act as though people are going to pore over each page, reading our finely crafted text, figuring out how we've organized things, and weighing their options before deciding which link to click.

What they actually do most of the time (if we're lucky) is *glance* at each new page, scan *some* of the text, and click on the first link that catches their interest or vaguely resembles the thing they're looking for. There are usually large parts of the page that they don't even look at.

—STEVE KRUG, *Don't Make Me Think*

4 **Paragraphs to signal dialogue**

Dialogue can add life to almost any sort of writing. To set up written dialogue, simply start a new paragraph each time the speaker changes, no matter how short each bit of conversation is. Here is an example:

Whenever I brought a book to the job, I wrapped it in newspaper—a habit that was to persist for years in other cities and under other circumstances. But some of the white men pried into my packages when I was absent and they questioned me.

"Boy, what are you reading those books for?"

"Oh, I don't know, sir."

"That's deep stuff you're reading, boy."

"I'm just killing time, sir."

"You'll addle your brains if you don't watch out."

—RICHARD WRIGHT, *Black Boy*

THINKING CRITICALLY ABOUT PARAGRAPHS

Reading with an Eye for Paragraphs

Read something by a writer you admire. Find one or two paragraphs that impress you in some way, and analyze them, using the guidelines in the Quick Help box on p. 108. Try to decide what makes them effective paragraphs.

Thinking about Your Own Use of Paragraphs

Examine two or three paragraphs you have written, using the guidelines on p. 108, to evaluate the unity, coherence, and development of each one. Identify the topic of each paragraph, the topic sentence (if one is explicitly stated), any patterns of development, and any means used to create coherence. Decide whether or not each paragraph successfully guides your readers, and explain your reasons. Then choose one paragraph, and revise it.

6

Working with Others

The CEO of a successful software business tells an interesting story: twice a year, the company holds a staff retreat to devise a plan for attaining an important new goal or solving a major problem. What had this CEO learned at her first retreat? That effective collaboration was essential for all their improvements. In fact, she noted, no one person was ever the key to what the group had accomplished together.

In a memorable statement, philosopher Hannah Arendt confirms this discovery: "For excellence, the presence of others is always required."

The old maxim that two heads are better than one seems to be especially true in the twenty-first century. Online communication makes feedback more visible than ever; today's writers expect and want reactions to their posts, messages, and updates. And thanks to collaborative tools that allow writers anywhere in the world to work on a single document, working on a group project has never been more feasible. Still, successful collaboration requires special attention.

6a Collaborating in college

Although you will find yourself working together with many people on campus, your most immediate collaborators will probably be the members of your writing class. You can learn a great deal by comparing ideas with these classmates and by using them as a first audience for your writing (4b). As you talk and write, you will find the ideas they contribute making their way into your writing, and your ideas into theirs. In short, the texts you write are shaped in part by conversations with others. This exchange is one reason citing sources and help from others is so important (see Chapter 14).

In online communication, especially, the roles of "writer" and "reader" and "text" are often interchangeable, as readers become writers and then readers again, and texts constantly change as multiple voices contribute to them. An email message, for example, may carry with it a string of related messages that have accumulated as people have

> **TALKING THE TALK**
>
> ## Collaborating or cheating?
>
> "When is asking others for help and opinions acceptable, and when is it cheating?" In academic work, the difference between collaborating and cheating depends almost entirely on context. There will be times—during exams, for example—when instructors will expect you to work alone. At other times, working with others—for a team project, perhaps, or peer review—may be required, and getting others' opinions on your writing is always a good habit. You draw the line, however, at having another person do your work for you. Submitting material under your name that you did not write is unacceptable in college writing.

replied to one another. Or a document being drafted on Google Docs or another software program designed to facilitate collaboration will carry the voices of multiple authors. These examples paint a portrait of how meaning is made collaboratively.

6b Working on group projects

You may often be asked to work as part of a team to produce a group project—a print report, an oral presentation, or a Web document or site. Since group projects are collaborative from the outset, they require additional planning and coordination.

1 Project planning

Planning goes a long way toward making group collaboration work well. Although you will probably do much group work online, keep in mind that face-to-face meetings can accomplish things that virtual meetings cannot. Some guidelines for a successful group project appear in the Quick Help box on p. 139.

Many college instructors now routinely integrate online work into their classes. If your course has a Web site, it probably offers space for extending the collaborative work of the classroom. Your writing class may already have an email discussion list, chat space, blog, or wiki; if not, you may want to set up such a space for yourself and your collaborators. You may also want to use a space such as Google Docs to

CONSIDERING DISABILITIES

Accommodating group members' needs

When you are working with other members of your class to share files for peer review or other group activities, remember to consider differences group members may have. Think of such differences not only in terms of computer compatibility but also in terms of the sensory, physical, or learning abilities of yourself and your classmates. You may have colleagues who wish to receive files in a very large type size, for example, in order to read them with ease. Similarly, you may have a peer who prefers to share files early to read the material or avoid the stress of last-minute preparation. You may have a peer who uses a voice screen reader. Help your group get off to a good start by making a plan to accommodate everyone's needs.

create a collaborative project; if so, make sure that every member of your group knows where to find the project and has the appropriate level of access—the ability to edit, for example—to any document posted there.

2 Models for group collaboration

Experienced collaborative writers often use one of three models for setting up the project: an expertise model, a division-of-labor model, or a process model.

Expertise model. This model plays to the strengths of each team member. The person who knows the most about graphics and design, for example, takes on all jobs that require those skills, while the person who knows most about the topic takes the lead in drafting.

Division-of-labor model. In this model, each group member becomes an expert on one aspect of the project. For example, one person might agree to do Internet research, while another searches library resources, and still another conducts interviews. This model is particularly helpful if a project is large and time is short.

Process model. You can also divide up the project in terms of its chronology: one person gets the project going, presenting an outline for the group to consider and carrying out any initial research; then a second person takes over and begins a draft for the group to review; a third per-

Guidelines for group projects

1. Establish a regular meeting time and space (whether real or virtual), and exchange contact information.

2. During your first meeting, discuss the overall project and establish ground rules. For example, you might agree that everyone has a responsibility to participate and to meet deadlines, and that all members will be respectful toward others in the group.

3. Establish clear duties for each participant.

4. With final deadlines in mind, create an overall agenda to organize the project. At each group meeting, take turns writing up notes on what was discussed and review them at the end of the meeting.

5. Use group meetings to work together on difficult problems. If an assignment is complex, have each member explain one section to the others. Check with your instructor if part of the task is unclear or if members don't agree on what is required.

6. Express opinions politely. If disagreements arise, try paraphrasing to see if everyone is hearing the same thing.

7. Remember that the goal is not for everyone just to get along; constructive conflict is desirable. Get a spirited debate going, and discuss all the options.

8. If your project requires a group-written document, assign one member to get the writing project started. Set deadlines for each part of the project. Come to an agreement about how you will edit and change each other's contributions to avoid offending any member of the group.

9. Assess the group's effectiveness periodically. Should you make changes as you go forward? What has been accomplished? What has the group done best? What has it done less successfully? What has each member contributed? What have you learned about how to work more effectively with others on future projects?

son designs and illustrates the project; and another person takes the job of revising and editing. This model can work well if members are unable to participate equally throughout the entire project. Once the project is

FOR MULTILINGUAL WRITERS

Constructive criticism

When you collaborate with your peers, criticizing each other's work is often necessary, but different cultures have different ways of expressing criticisms that are appropriate. Observe how your peers communicate their suggestions and comments, and how others respond to them. If you feel uncomfortable with strong criticisms from peers, you can ask them to "put it more gently."

completely drafted, however, the whole group needs to work together to create a final version.

6c   Making presentations

Some collaborative projects may call for oral or multimedia presentations. If your group is to make such a presentation, follow these guidelines:

- Find out exactly how much time you will have for the presentation, and stick to that time limit.

- Divide the preparatory work fairly. For example, who will revise the written text for oral presentation? Who will prepare the slides or other visuals? Who will do the necessary research?

- Decide how each group member will contribute to the presentation. Make sure that everyone has an obvious role.

- Leave time for at least two practice sessions. During the first session, time yourselves carefully, and make a sound or video recording of the presentation. Then view or listen to the recording, and make any necessary adjustments. If you can't videotape your group presentation, then practice it in front of several friends: feedback is very important, so ask them to summarize what they got out of the presentation and to comment on how easy it was to understand the major points, how effective body language and eye contact were, and how well you used visual or multimedia support.

- If your presentation will be available online, remember that it's very hard to know who may see it. Try for a presentation that will be easily understood by people beyond your own class or university — or even your own culture. Also, remember that you *must* label all visuals and cite their sources.

- Make sure that your audience will be able to read any accompanying handouts, slides, or posters, and revise any that fail this test. Use your visuals as you rehearse, and try to do so in a room similar in size and lighting to the room in which you will make the presentation.

- After your presentation, try to have a debriefing with your instructor so that you can get pointers on improving future presentations.

For more on oral and multimedia presentations, see Chapter 22.

THINKING CRITICALLY ABOUT YOUR COLLABORATIVE WORK

Begin by making a list of all the ways in which you collaborate with others. Then reflect on the kinds of collaboration you find most effective. Finally, take an example of a recent collaboration you have been part of, and examine how well it worked by answering the following questions: What did I contribute to the collaboration? What worked well and did not work well? What could I have done to improve the collaboration?

CRITICAL
THINKING AND
ARGUMENT

Part 2

7

Reading Critically

Film critic Roger Ebert writes in a notebook as he watches movies, tearing out the pages as he fills them, until he "looks as though he's sitting on top of a cloud of paper," as an *Esquire* profile observed. According to writer Anatole Broyard, an effective reader "stomps around" in a text — highlighting, scribbling in the margins, jotting down questions and comments.

Reading critically means questioning and commenting thoughtfully on a text — whether an assignment for a psychology class, a graphic novel, a business email, or a YouTube video. Any method you use to keep track of your questions and make yourself concentrate on a text can help you become a better critical reader.

7a Previewing a text

Find out all you can about a text before beginning to look closely at it, considering its context, author, subject, genre, and design.

PREVIEWING THE CONTEXT

- Where have you encountered the work? Are you encountering it in its original context? For example, an essay in a collection of readings may have been previously published in a magazine; a speech you watch on YouTube may have been delivered to a live or televised audience; a painting on a museum wall may have been created for a wealthy patron in a distant country centuries earlier.

- What can you infer from the original or current context of the work about its intended audience and purpose?

LEARNING ABOUT THE AUTHOR OR CREATOR

- What information can you find about the author or creator of the text?

- What purpose, expertise, and possible agenda might you expect this person to have? Where do you think the author or creator is coming from in this text?

PREVIEWING THE SUBJECT

- What do you know about the subject of the text?

- What opinions do you have about the subject, and on what are your opinions based?

- What would you like to learn about the subject?

- What do you expect the main point to be? Why?

CONSIDERING THE TITLE, MEDIUM, GENRE, AND DESIGN

- What does the title (or caption or other heading) indicate?

- What do you know about the medium in which the work appears? Is it a text on the Web, a printed advertising brochure, a speech stored in iTunes, or an animated cartoon on television? What role does the medium play in achieving the purpose and connecting to the audience?

- What is the genre of the text — and what can it help illuminate about the intended audience or purpose? Why might the authors or creators have chosen this genre?

- How is the text presented? What do you notice about its formatting, use of color, visuals or illustrations, overall design, general appearance, and other design features?

TALKING THE TALK

Critical thinking

"Are criticizing and thinking critically the same thing?" *Criticize* can sometimes mean "find fault with," and you certainly do not have to be relentlessly negative when you think critically. Instead, critical thinking means, first and foremost, asking good questions — and not simply accepting what you see at face value. By asking not only what words and images mean, but also how meaning gets across, critical thinkers consider why an author makes a particular claim, what he or she may be leaving out or ignoring, and how to tell whether evidence is accurate and believable. If you're asking and answering questions like these, then you're thinking critically.

Sample preview of an assigned text

A student in a first-year composition class who had been asked to read and analyze Abraham Lincoln's Gettysburg Address made preview notes, a few of which are excerpted here.

CONTEXT: President Lincoln delivered the speech at a ceremony dedicating a national cemetery for Civil War soldiers. Crowds of people gathered in a field near Gettysburg, Pennsylvania, on November 19, 1863, to listen to him and other speakers. In July of that year, a Civil War battle that ended with 7,500 soldiers killed had taken place near where Lincoln spoke.

My textbook has the most famous version of the speech—but nobody knows for sure exactly what Lincoln said 150 years ago. There's obviously no audio recording of him giving the speech! Newspapers at the time reported what he said. The Library of Congress Web site has the first draft of the speech in Lincoln's handwriting.

Lincoln gave this speech in the middle of the war, dedicating a national cemetery, so it must have been a pretty solemn occasion. He probably wanted his audience to think about why the war was worth fighting. He probably also thought that some of the dead soldiers' families might be there listening — as well as people who had seen the battle or its aftermath. Did he think about the possibility that future generations would read and think about this speech?

AUTHOR: Abraham Lincoln, 16th US President, wrote / gave speech.
— Civil War began soon after he took office (1861) and ended soon after 2nd inauguration in March 1865.
— Assassinated April 14, 1865.
— Leader of Union cause, so probably very interested in showing why the United States needed to remain united.

EXERCISE 7.1

Following the guidelines in 7a, preview a text you have been assigned to read.

7b Reading and annotating a text

As you read a text for the first time, mark it up (if the medium allows you to do so) or take notes. Consider the text's content, author, intended audience, and genre and design.

READING FOR CONTENT

- What do you find confusing or unclear about the text? Where can you look for explanations or more information? Do you need background information in order to understand fully?

- What key terms and ideas—or key patterns—do you see? What key images stick in your mind?

- What sources or other works does this text cite, refer to, or allude to?

- How does the content fit with what you already know?

- Which points do you agree with? Which do you disagree with? Why?

READING FOR AUTHOR / CREATOR AND AUDIENCE

- Do the authors or creators present themselves as you anticipated in your preview?

- For what audience was this text created? Are you part of its intended audience?

- What underlying assumptions can you identify in the text?

- Are the medium and genre appropriate for the topic, audience, and purpose?

READING FOR DESIGN, COMPOSITION, AND STYLE

- Is the design appropriate for the subject and genre?

- Does the composition serve a purpose—for instance, does the layout help you see what is more and less important in the text?

- Do words, images, sound, and other media work together well?

- How would you describe the style of the text? What contributes to this impression—word choice? references to research or popular culture? formatting? color? something else?

Sample annotation of an assigned text

A student assigned to write about a posting on Freakonomics, a blog published on the *New York Times* Web site, annotated the text as shown.

1. Nice design for heading and image—from cover of <u>Freakonomics</u> book (written by someone else). How did the authors get involved with this blog?

2. Will the post answer the question in the title? (And why doesn't the title say "Graduate <u>from</u> College"?)

3. Link to other posts by this pair of bloggers, who both teach business at the University of Pennsylvania's Wharton School. They've only written a couple of posts here, but they have written a lot of other things together.

4. Another <u>New York Times</u> columnist gets credit for starting this discussion.

5. Links to other sources for the numbers they're citing. (Check the reliability of these reports.)

6. Evidence to prove that the small percentage of 22-year-old male grads can't be explained just by the ratio of female college students to male ones. So if that seemed like the easy answer to the title question, it isn't.

7. They talk about their own personal experiences and say that they are not "the norm." Most people take longer to finish college than these two did.

8. Three possible reasons for men being older than women when they graduate from college: older when they start school; take longer to finish a degree; take time off between high school and college. These reasons don't really answer the question in the title, though. Don't they all just raise more <u>why</u> questions? But starting a discussion is a good purpose for a blog post.

9. Authors ask for feedback—appropriate for a blog. Read the comments next!

Freakonomics

The Hidden Side of Everything

February 25, 2010, 12:00 PM

Why Do So Few Men Graduate College in Their Early Twenties?

By BETSEY STEVENSON AND JUSTIN WOLFERS

Among 22-year-olds, there are 185 female college graduates for every 100 male graduates. It's an amazing statistic, and one we saw courtesy of a recent column by David Brooks. We know that the gender balance at colleges has definitely swung toward women—but could it have swung this far? Yes and no. Yes—Brooks is directly citing a recent BLS report. But no—this isn't really representative of what's happening on campus. According to the American Council on Education, the college student body has been 43% male annually since 2000. If you are too lazy to do the math, this yields 133 women per 100 men; a skewed ratio for sure, but nowhere near as skewed as 185 to 100.

What gives? It turns out that it's all about the age you examine. While we each graduated by age 22, and Brooks probably did too, this isn't the norm. In fact, fewer than half of those who will ultimately complete a college degree have done so by age 22. But women at that age are twice as likely to have finished college as men. Men partly catch up by age 25, and according to our tabulations of the 2008 American Community Survey, by age 25 there are 141 female college grads for every 100 men with a college degree—much as you would predict from the enrollment data.

What's happening to men? Here are three possibilities:

1. Men are taking longer to graduate high school. This may reflect parents enrolling their sons in school later than their daughters.
2. Men are taking longer to do a college degree. It is becoming increasingly uncommon to finish college in four years, and many students take even longer. Are there gender differences in this? Why?
3. Perhaps men are more likely to take a gap year (or years)—seeing the world—before going to college.

We're interested: Do you have other possible explanations? These three explanations are really just a way of categorizing the differences—what deeper forces underpin the differential trends by gender in age to college completion?

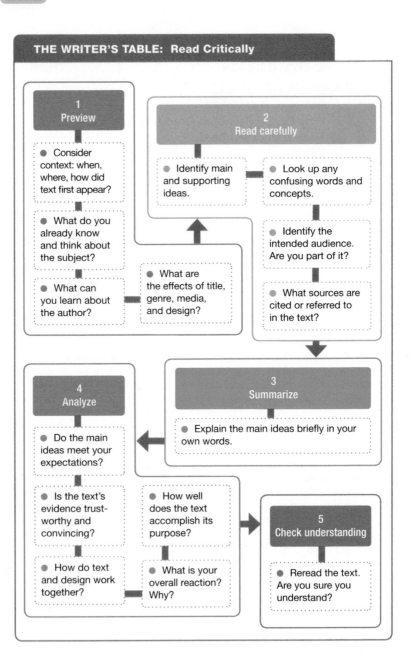

THE WRITER'S TABLE: Read Critically

1 Preview

- Consider context: when, where, how did text first appear?
- What do you already know and think about the subject?
- What can you learn about the author?
- What are the effects of title, genre, media, and design?

2 Read carefully

- Identify main and supporting ideas.
- Look up any confusing words and concepts.
- Identify the intended audience. Are you part of it?
- What sources are cited or referred to in the text?

3 Summarize

- Explain the main ideas briefly in your own words.

4 Analyze

- Do the main ideas meet your expectations?
- Is the text's evidence trustworthy and convincing?
- How well does the text accomplish its purpose?
- How do text and design work together?
- What is your overall reaction? Why?

5 Check understanding

- Reread the text. Are you sure you understand?

EXERCISE 7.2

Following is the full text of Abraham Lincoln's Gettysburg Address. Using the guide-lines in 7b, read and annotate Lincoln's speech.

> Four score and seven years ago our fathers brought forth on this continent a new nation, conceived in Liberty, and dedicated to the proposition that all men are created equal.
>
> Now we are engaged in a great civil war, testing whether that nation, or any nation so conceived and so dedicated, can long endure. We are met on a great battle-field of that war. We have come to dedicate a portion of that field, as a final resting place for those who here gave their lives that that nation might live. It is altogether fitting and proper that we should do this.
>
> But, in a larger sense, we can not dedicate—we can not consecrate—we can not hallow—this ground. The brave men, living and dead, who struggled here, have consecrated it, far above our poor power to add or detract. The world will little note, nor long remember what we say here, but it can never forget what they did here. It is for us the living, rather, to be dedicated here to the unfinished work which they who fought here have thus far so nobly advanced. It is rather for us to be here dedicated to the great task remaining before us—that from these honored dead we take increased devotion to that cause for which they gave the last full measure of devotion—that we here highly resolve that these dead shall not have died in vain—that this nation, under God, shall have a new birth of freedom—and that government of the people, by the people, for the people, shall not perish from the earth.   **—ABRAHAM LINCOLN,** *Gettysburg Address*

7c Summarizing a text

When you feel that you have read and understood the text, summarize the contents in your own words. A summary *briefly* captures the main ideas of a text and omits information that is less important. Try to iden-tify the key points in the text, find the essential evidence supporting those points, and explain the contents concisely and fairly, so that a reader unfamiliar with the original can make sense of it all. Deciding what to leave out can make summarizing a tricky task—but mastering this skill can serve you well in all the reading you do in your academic, professional, and civic life. (For more information on writing a summary, see 13d.)

Sample summary of an assigned text

A student summarized Betsey Stevenson and Justin Wolfers' *Freakonomics* blog post (7b) as shown on p. 152.

According to a recent study, there are 185 22-year-old female college graduates for every 100 22-year-old male college grads. For the past decade or more, females have outnumbered males in college, but not by such a big margin — there are about 133 women in college for every 100 college men. Why is the ratio so much bigger for 22-year-old graduates? This blog post says that 22-year-old women are "twice as likely to have finished college as men." Some suggestions offered to explain this surprising statistic are that perhaps parents enroll sons in school at older ages than daughters; perhaps men take longer to finish college once they start; and perhaps men take more time off between high school and college. But the writers note that they're really just listing categories of explanations, not answering the question: "Why do so many more 22-year-old women than 22-year-old men have college degrees?"

7d Analyzing a text

When you feel that you understand the meaning of the text, move on to your analysis by asking additional questions about the text.

ANALYZING IDEAS AND EXAMPLES

- What are the main points in this text? Are they implied or explicitly stated?
- Which points do you agree with? Which do you disagree with? Why?
- Does anything in the text surprise you? Why, or why not?
- What kind of examples does the text use? What other kinds of evidence does the text offer to back up the main points? Can you think of other examples or evidence that should have been included?
- Are viewpoints other than those of the author or creator included and treated fairly?
- How trustworthy are the sources the text cites or refers to?
- What assumptions does the text make? Are those assumptions valid? Why, or why not?

ANALYZING FOR OVERALL IMPRESSION

- Do the authors or creators achieve their purpose? Why, or why not?
- What intrigues, puzzles, or irritates you about the text? Why?
- What else would you like to know?

Visual texts

"How can an image be a text?" In its traditional sense, a *text* involves words on paper. But we spend at least as much time reading and analyzing images — including moving images — as we spend on printed words. So it makes sense to broaden the definition of "text" to include anything that sends a message. That's why images are often called *visual texts.*

Sample analysis of a text

Following is a Pulitzer Prize–winning photograph (by Craig F. Walker of the *Denver Post*) and its caption. This image appeared as part of a series documenting the experiences of a Colorado teenager, Ian Fisher, who joined the U.S. Army to fight in Iraq.

During a weekend home from his first assignment at Fort Carson, Colorado, Ian walked through a Denver-area mall with his new girlfriend, Kayla Spitzlberger, on December 15, 2007, and asked whether she wanted to go ring shopping. She was excited, but working out the financing made him nervous. They picked out the engagement ring in about five minutes, but Ian wouldn't officially propose until Christmas Day in front of her family. The couple had met in freshman math class but never really dated until now. She wrote to him during basic training and decided to give Ian a chance. The engagement would end before Valentine's Day.

A student's analysis of this photograph made the following points:

The couple are in the center of the photo — and at the center of our attention. But at this moment of choosing an engagement ring, they do not look "engaged" with each other. Kayla looks excited but uncertain, as if she knows that Ian feels doubts, but she hopes he will change his mind. She is looking right at him, with her body leaning toward him but her head leaning away: she looks very tentative. Ian is looking away from Kayla, and the expression on his face suggests that he's already having second thoughts about the expense of the ring (we see his wallet on the counter by his elbow) and perhaps even about asking Kayla to marry him. The accompanying caption helps us interpret the image, telling us about the couple's brief history together and noting that the engagement will last less than two months after this moment. But the message comes through pretty clearly without words.

Ian and Kayla look as if they're trying on roles in this photograph. She looks ready to take the plunge, and he is resisting. These attitudes conform to stereotypical gender roles for a man and woman considering marriage (or going shopping, for that matter). The woman is expected to want the marriage and the ring; the man knows that he shouldn't show too much enthusiasm about weddings and shopping. It's hard for the reader to tell whether Ian and Kayla really feel that they are making good or careful choices for their situation at this moment or whether they're just doing what they think they're supposed to do under the circumstances.

The reader also can't tell how the presence of the photographer, Craig F. Walker, affected the couple's actions. The photo is part of a series of images documenting Ian Fisher's life after joining the military, so Walker had probably spent a lot of time with Ian before this photo was taken. Did Ian want to give a particular impression of himself on this day? Were he and Kayla trying on "adult" roles in this situation? Were they feeling pressure to produce a memorable moment for the camera? And what was Walker thinking when he accompanied them to the mall and took this photograph? Did he foresee the end of their engagement when he captured this revealing moment? What was his agenda?

EXERCISE 7.3

Write a two- to three-paragraph analysis of a text you have read or seen.

THINKING CRITICALLY ABOUT READING

Choose a text you have been assigned to read for a class. Read it over carefully, annotating the material, and then write a one- or two-paragraph summary of the contents. Then analyze your summary. Did your annotations help you summarize? Why, or why not? Does your summary interpret the material or aim for an objective stance? What does your summary omit from the original material, and how did you decide what to leave out?

7e A student's critical reading of a text

Student Writer

Shuqiao Song

Following is an abridged version of a student essay by Shuqiao Song based on her critical reading of Alison Bechdel's graphic novel *Fun Home: A Family Tragicomic.* Shuqiao's critical reading involved looking closely at the words, at the images, and at how the words and images together create a very complex story.

bedfordstmartins.com/smhandbook
Student Writing > Writing in the Disciplines

For information on Shuqiao Song's PowerPoint presentation of this essay, see 22c.

Song 1

Shuqiao Song
Dr. Andrea Lunsford
English 87N
13 March 2009

Residents of a DysFUNctional HOME

In a recent online interview, comic artist Alison Bechdel remarked, "I love words, and I love pictures. But especially, I love them together—in a mystical way that I can't even explain" ("Stuck"). Indeed, in her graphic novel memoir, *Fun Home: A Family Tragicomic,* text and image work together in a mystical way: text *and* image. But that little conjunction *and* is a deceitfully simple demonstration of the relationship between the two. Using both image and text results not in a simple summation but in a strange relationship—as strange as the relationship between Alison Bechdel and her father. These strange pairings have an alluring quality that makes Bechdel's *Fun Home* compelling; for her, both text and image are necessary. As Bechdel tells and shows us, alone, words can fail; alone, images deceive. Yet her life story ties both concepts inextricably to her memories and revelations such that only the interplay of text and image offers the reader the rich complexity, honesty, and possibilities in Bechdel's quest to understand and find closure for the past.

The idea that *words are insufficient* is not new—certainly we have all felt moments when language simply fails us and we are at a loss for words—moments like being "left . . . wordless" by "the infinite gradations of color in a fine sunset" (Bechdel, *Fun* 150). In those wordless moments, we strain to express just what we mean. Writers are especially aware of what is lost between word and meaning; Bechdel's comment on the translation of Proust's *À la Recherche du Temps Perdu* is a telling example of the troubling gap:

> After Dad died, an updated translation of Proust came out.
> *Remembrance of Things Past* was re-titled In *Search of Lost Time*.
> The new title is a more literal translation of *À la Recherche du*

Temps Perdu, but it still doesn't capture the full resonance of *perdu.* This means not just lost, but ruined, undone, wasted, wrecked, and spoiled. (*Fun* 119)

Bechdel says of the new Proust title, "What's lost in translation is the complexity of loss itself"—the very struggles of loss that Bechdel must also confront (*Fun* 120). But how do we express something as complex as loss, if something is always lost between what we say and what we mean? Bechdel addresses the "complexity of loss" by trying to correlate herself with her father, attempting a "translation" of their lives (*Fun* 120).

René Magritte's painting *The Treason of Images* (Fig. 1), with text that translates as "This is not a pipe," reminds us to remain skeptical of images because *images can deceive.* This is a lesson that Alison Bechdel shows us again and again within her own story and images. Bechdel's father constructs a false image of himself and of his home and family.

Fig. 1. Magritte's *The Treason of Images*.

The elaborately restored house is the gilded, but tense, context of young Alison's familial relationships and a metaphor for her father's deceptions. "He used his skillful artifice not to make things, but to make things appear to be what they were not," Bechdel notes alongside an image of her father taking a photo of their family, shown in Fig. 2 (*Fun* 16). The scene represents the nature of her father's artifice; her father is *posing* a photo, an image of their family.

Song 3

Fig. 2. Alison Bechdel's father posing a family photo (Bechdel, *Fun* 16).

In that same scene, Bechdel also shows her own sleight of hand; she manipulates the scene to the purpose of her memoir and reverses her father's role and her own to show young Alison taking the photograph of the family and her father posing in Alison's place (Fig. 3). In the image, young Alison symbolizes Bechdel in the present—looking back through the camera lens to create a portrait of her family. But unlike her father, she isn't using false images to deceive. Bechdel overcomes the treason of images by confessing herself as an "artificer"

Fig. 3. Alison and her father trade places (Bechdel, *Fun* 17).

to her audience (*Fun* 16). Bechdel doesn't villainize the illusory nature of images; she repurposes their illusory power to reinterpret her memories.

Readers must understand that in Bechdel's *Fun Home,* neither image nor text plays a supporting role. The text does not only caption the image and the image does not always literally illustrate the text. Each is *a version of the memoir.* Both are interpretations and manipulations. In

Chapter 1, "Old Father, Old Artificer," Bechdel draws up a tableau of her family situation. Here is an excerpt with only the text narration:

> Daedalus, too, was indifferent to the human cost of his projects.
> He blithely betrayed the king, for example, when the queen asked
> him to build her a cow disguise so she could seduce the white
> bull. Indeed the result of that scheme—a half-bull, half-man
> monster—inspired Daedalus's greatest creation yet. He hid the
> minotaur in the labyrinth—a maze of passages and rooms opening
> endlessly into one another . . . and from which, as stray youths
> and maidens discovered to their peril . . . escape was impossible.
> Then there are those famous wings. Was Daedalus really stricken
> with grief when Icarus fell into the sea? Or just disappointed by the
> design failure? (*Fun* 11–12).

DAEDALUS, TOO, WAS INDIFFERENT TO THE HUMAN COST OF HIS PROJECTS.

DON'T HIT ME!

Fig. 4. Father as Daedalus
(Bechdel, *Fun* 11).

The text can stand alone as a story. However, a parallel story line is lost.

The images tell a story distinct from the text, yet the ties between image and text are not severed. In the first panel accompanying this story, Bechdel correlates her father with Daedalus (Fig. 4). Her father's household "projects" are accomplished at the "human cost" of cruelty to his children, as the father strikes Alison's brother and causes him to flee.

In the panel that introduces the "half-bull, half-man" minotaur, the reader shifts between the metaphors with surprising ease; now her father is the looming minotaur whose wrath Alison fears (Fig. 5). Alison's father morphs from Daedalus into "Daedalus's greatest creation," from father to

Student Writing

monster. The image evokes both the minotaur myth and Alison's genuine fear of her father's wrath.

In the next three panels (Fig. 6), Alison, too, flees. However, the text does not mesh exactly with what is seen within the frame: ". . . escape was impossible," Bechdel notes, but shows an image of young Alison escaping the house and evading the wrath of her father. Bechdel uses the Daedalus story—and Daedalus's relationship with Icarus—to explain her relationship with her father, but she complicates their relationship by casting both father and daughter as both Daedalus and Icarus. In the last two panels of this section, where Alison is seen first walking, then

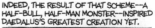

INDEED, THE RESULT OF THAT SCHEME--A HALF-BULL, HALF-MAN MONSTER--INSPIRED DAEDALUS'S GREATEST CREATION YET.

Fig. 5. Father as minotaur (Bechdel, *Fun* 12).

HE HID THE MINOTAUR IN THE LABYRINTH-- A MAZE OF PASSAGES AND ROOMS OPEN- ING ENDLESSLY INTO ONE ANOTHER...

...AND FROM WHICH, AS STRAY YOUTHS AND MAIDENS DISCOVERED TO THEIR PERIL...

...ESCAPE WAS IMPOSSIBLE.

Fig. 6. Alison flees the labyrinthine house (Bechdel, *Fun* 12).

Song 6   Student Writing

Fig. 7. Alison alone (Bechdel, *Fun* 12).

returning to the house, her now-dead father is implied to be the fallen Icarus while Alison, alone, suggests the bereaved or disappointed Daedalus (Fig. 7).

Finally, we can see how image and text function together. In *Fun Home,* Bechdel pushes the boundaries of the relationship between image and text. If the words and pictures matched exactly, the story would read like a children's book. However, text and image can't be so mismatched that meaning is completely incomprehensible. Bechdel crafts her story deliberately, leaving space for the reader to experience cognitive dissonance. The reader's need to create coherence from disparate text and image results in a more complex understanding of the story.

Through the strange but compelling pairings of image and text, the reader acquires a more thorough understanding of the strange and compelling relationship between father and daughter. Bechdel consistently informs the reader that *Fun Home* is her *interpretation* of the past. She understands that "[t]he memoir is in many ways a huge violation of [her] family" (Chute 1009). As an artist, her effort to lay to rest her anxieties about her past comes at the cost of publicizing her family's secrets. She does not let herself or the reader forget: "We really were a family, and we really did live in those period rooms" (*Fun* 17).

Song 7

Bechdel does not ignore the impact that her act of remembering has on
the present. In the end, her memoir is not so much an accurate record of
events as a monument to the incredible human ability to reappraise the
past. Bechdel's stories — told between the lines and entwined with stories
told within the frames — impel our heads and hearts. And if nothing else,
the painful confessions and wishful remembering of *Fun Home* provide a
proper tribute for her father and allow Alison Bechdel a sense, almost, of
closure.

Song 8

Works Cited

Bechdel, Alison. *Fun Home*. Boston: Houghton Mifflin, 2006.
    Print.

———. "Stuck in Vermont 109: Alison Bechdel." *YouTube*.
    YouTube 13 Dec. 2008. Web 6 Feb. 2009.

Chute, Hillary. "An Interview with Alison Bechdel." *MFS Modern
    Fiction Studies* 52.4 (2006): 1004-13. *Project Muse*. Web.
    30 Jan. 2009.

Magritte, René. *The Treason of Images*. 1929. Los Angeles
    County Museum of Art, Los Angeles. *LACMA Collections
    Online*. Web. 30 Jan. 2009.

Analyzing Arguments

8

In advertisements, news stories, textbooks, reports, and media of all kinds, language competes for your attention and argues for your agreement. Since argument so pervades your life, you need to be able to recognize and use it effectively — and to question your own arguments as well as those put forth by others.

8a Recognizing argument

In one important sense, all language use has an argumentative edge. When you greet friends warmly, you wish to convince them that you are genuinely glad to

How do you come to make up your mind about something? What causes you to give your assent to some ideas but not to others? And how do you seek — and sometimes gain — agreement from others?

The need to explore such questions has never been more pressing than it is today, as language intended to persuade — to gain your assent (and often your money, your vote, and even your soul) — surrounds you more than ever before.

QUICK HELP

Guidelines for analyzing an argument

Here are some questions that can help you judge the effectiveness of an argument:

- What conclusions about the argument can you reach by playing both the believing and the doubting game? (8b)

- What cultural contexts inform the argument, and what do they tell you about where the writer is coming from? (8b and c)

- What emotional, ethical, and logical appeals is the writer making in support of the argument? (8d)

- How has the writer established credibility to write about the topic? (8d)

- What is the claim (or arguable statement)? Is the claim qualified in any way? (8e)

- What reasons and assumptions support and underlie the claim? (8e)

- What additional evidence backs up the assumption and claim? How current and reliable are the sources? (8e)

- How does the writer use images, graphics, or other visuals to support the argument?

- What fallacies can you identify, and what effect do they have on the argument's persuasiveness? (8f)

- What is the overall impression you get from analyzing the argument? Are you convinced?

see them, that you value their presence. Even apparently objective news reporting has strong argumentative overtones. By putting a particular story on the front page, for example, a paper argues that this subject is more important than others; by using emotional language or by focusing on certain details, a newscaster tries to persuade the audience to view an event in a particular way. Consider the different ways reporters might describe the image on p. 163, such as *an outpouring of support for our troops* or *a pro-war rally*.

Emily Lesk's primary purpose in her essay "Red, White, and Everywhere" is to reflect on her own identification with one particular American icon, Coca-Cola (4l). But her essay clearly has an argumentative edge, asking readers to examine their own cultural identifications and to understand the power of advertising in creating and sustaining such identifications.

It's possible, then, to read any message or text, verbal or visual, as an argument, even if argument is not its primary purpose. In much academic writing, however, *argument* is more narrowly defined as a text that makes a claim (usually in the form of an arguable statement) and supports it fully.

8b Thinking critically about argument

Although critical thinking has a number of complex definitions, it is essentially the process by which you make sense of all the information around you. As such, critical thinking is a crucial component of argument, for it guides you in recognizing, formulating, and examining arguments.

Several elements of critical thinking are especially important.

Playing the believing—and the doubting—game. Critical thinkers are able to shift stances as they take in an argument, allowing them to gain different perspectives. One good way to begin is to play the *believing game*: that is, put yourself in the position of the person creating the argument, see the topic from that person's point of view as much as possible, and think carefully about how and why that person arrived at the claim(s). Once you have given the argument your sympathetic attention, play the *doubting game*: revisit the argument, looking skeptically at each claim and examining each piece of evidence to see how well (or if) it supports the claim. Eventually, this process of believing and doubting will become natural.

Asking pertinent questions. Concentrate on getting to the heart of the matter. Whether you are thinking about others' ideas or about your own, you will want to ask the following kinds of questions:

• What is the writer's agenda—his or her unstated purpose?

• Why does the writer hold these ideas or beliefs? What larger social, economic, political, or other conditions or factors may have influenced him or her?

• What does the writer want readers to do—and why?

• What are the writer's qualifications for making this argument?

• What reasons does the writer offer in support of his or her ideas? Are they good reasons?

- What are the writer's underlying values or unstated assumptions? Are they acceptable—and why, or why not?

- What sources does the writer rely on? How current and reliable are they? What agendas do these sources have? Are any perspectives left out?

- What objections might be made to the argument?

- What individual or group is responsible for publishing or promoting the argument? (See 12c.)

- Study the visual and audio aspects of arguments, including the use of color, graphics, and multimedia techniques. How do media and design appeal to the reader or listener? What do they contribute to the argument?

Getting information. To help you decide whether to accept an argument, often you will need to find more information on the topic as well as other perspectives.

Interpreting and assessing information. No information that comes to us in language or visuals is neutral; all of it has a perspective—a spin. Your job as a critical thinker is to identify the perspective and to assess it, examining its sources and finding out what you can about its context. Asking pertinent questions will help you examine the interpretations and conclusions drawn by others.

Making and assessing your own arguments. The ultimate goal of all critical thinking is to construct your own ideas and reach your own conclusions. These, too, you must question and assess. The rest of this chapter will guide you in the art of assessing arguments.

8c   Considering cultural contexts

If you want to understand as fully as possible the arguments of others, remember that writers come from an astonishing variety of cultural and linguistic backgrounds. Pay attention to clues to cultural context, and be open to the many ways of thinking you will encounter. In short, practice the believing game before you play the doubting game—especially when analyzing an argument influenced by a culture different from your own. In addition, remember that within any given culture there are great differences among individuals. So don't expect that every member of a culture will argue in any one way.

Above all, watch your own assumptions very closely as you read. Just because you assume that the use of statistics as support for your argument holds more water than, say, precedent drawn from religious belief, you can't assume that all writers agree with you. Take a writer's cultural beliefs into account before you begin to analyze an argument. (See Chapter 24.)

8d   Reading emotional, ethical, and logical appeals

Aristotle categorized argumentative appeals into three types: emotional appeals that speak to our hearts and values (known to the ancient Greeks as *pathos*), ethical appeals that appeal to character (*ethos*), and logical appeals that involve factual information and evidence (*logos*).

Emotional appeals

Emotional appeals stir our emotions and remind us of deeply held values. When politicians argue that the country needs more tax relief, they almost always use examples of one or more families they have met, stressing the concrete ways in which a tax cut would improve the quality of their lives. Doing so creates a strong emotional appeal. Some have criticized the use of emotional appeals in argument, claiming that they are a form of manipulation intended to mislead an audience. But emotional appeals are an important part of almost every argument. Critical readers are perfectly capable of "talking back" to such appeals by analyzing them, deciding which are acceptable and which are not.

The accompanying photo shows protesters rallying against a proposed California state law that would prohibit people from

openly displaying firearms. The protesters' signs read "Dictators prefer unarmed citizens" and "History shows tyrannical governments first disarm their citizens."

To what emotions are the protesters appealing? Do you find this appeal effective, manipulative, or both? Would you accept this argument?

Ethical appeals

Ethical appeals support the credibility, moral character, and goodwill of the argument's creator. These appeals are especially important for critical readers to recognize and evaluate. You may respect and admire cyclist Lance Armstrong, for example, but should his credibility as an athlete convince you to invest in mutual funds he promotes? To identify ethical appeals in arguments, ask yourself these questions: What is the creator of the argument doing to show that he or she is knowledgeable and credible about the subject—has really done the homework on it? What sort of character does he or she build, and how? More important, is that character trustworthy? What does the creator of the argument do to show that he or she has the best interests of an audience in mind? Do those best interests match your own, and, if not, how does that alter the effectiveness of the argument? Take a look at the following passage, which introduces an argument for viewing the Diné, or Navajo, people as a nation within a nation. As you read, try to identify the ethical appeals within the passage, paying special attention to the writer's identification of himself and the Diné people with the land.

> One of the most remarkable things about this republic is that there exists within its borders a parallel universe known as Dinetah, a nation of more than 155,000 souls who subscribe to a mind-set completely different from the modern American belief that everything in nature is there for the taking. Dinetah is the ancestral homeland of the Diné, more commonly called the Navajo, a misnomer perpetrated by the Spaniards, as are many of the names for the native tribes of the Southwest. An area larger than West Virginia that sprawls out of Arizona into New Mexico and Utah, Dinetah is bounded by four sacred mountains . . . and four sacred rivers (the Colorado, the Little Colorado, the San Juan, and the Rio Grande). It is some of the starkest, most magically open-to-the-sky country anywhere—a sagebrush steppe spotted with juniper and ancient, gnarled piñon trees, occasionally gashed by a yawning canyon or thrust up into a craggy, pine-clad mountain range, a magenta mesa, a blood-red cliff, a tiara of lucent, stress-fractured tan sandstone.
>
> "The land is our Bible," a Navajo woman named Sally once explained to me.   —ALEX SHOUMATOFF, "The Navajo Way"

Logical appeals

Logical appeals are viewed as especially trustworthy: "The facts don't lie," some say. Of course, facts are not the only type of logical appeals, which also include firsthand evidence drawn from observations, interviews, surveys and questionnaires, experiments, and personal experience; and secondhand evidence drawn from authorities, the testimony of others, statistics, and other print and online sources. Critical readers need to examine logical appeals just as carefully as emotional and ethical ones. What is the source of the logical appeal—and is that source trustworthy? Are all terms defined clearly? Has the logical evidence presented been taken out of context, and, if so, does that change the meaning of the data? Look, for example, at the following brief passage:

> [I]t is well for us to remember that, in an age of increasing illiteracy, 60 percent of the world's illiterates are women. Between 1960 and 1970, the number of illiterate men in the world rose by 8 million, while the number of illiterate women rose by 40 million.[1] And the number of illiterate women is increasing. —ADRIENNE RICH, "What Does a Woman Need to Know?"

As a critical reader, you would question these facts and hence check the footnote to discover the source, which in this case is the UN *Compendium of Social Statistics*. At this point, you might accept this document as authoritative—or you might look further into the United Nations' publications policy, especially to find out how that body defines *illiteracy*. You would also no doubt wonder why Rich chose the decade from 1960 to 1970 for her example and, as a result, check to see when this essay was written. As it turns out, the essay was written in 1979, so the most recent data available on literacy would have come from the decade of the sixties. That fact might make you question the timeliness of these statistics: Are they still meaningful more than thirty years later? Might the statistics today be even more alarming?

If you attend closely to the emotional, ethical, and logical appeals in any argument, you will be on your way to analyzing—and evaluating—it.

Analyzing appeals in a visual argument

The poster on p. 170, from TurnAround, an organization devoted to helping victims of domestic violence, is "intended to strike a chord with abusers as well as their victims." The dramatic combination of words and image builds on an analogy between a child and a target and makes strong emotional and ethical appeals.

The bull's-eye that draws your attention to the center of the poster is probably the first thing you notice when you look at the image. Then you may observe that the "target" is, in fact, a child's body; it also has arms, legs, and a head with wide, staring eyes. The heading at the upper left, "A child is not a target," reinforces the bull's-eye/child connection.

This poster's stark image and headline appeal to viewers' emotions, offering the uncomfortable reminder that children are often the victims of domestic violence. The design causes viewers to see a target first and only afterward recognize that the target is actually a child — an unsettling experience. But the poster also offers ethical appeals ("TurnAround can help") to show that the organization is credible and that it supports the worthwhile goal of ending "the cycle of domestic violence" by offering counseling and other support services. Finally, it uses the logical appeal of a statistic to support this ethical appeal, noting that TurnAround has served "more than 10,000 women, children and men each year" and giving specific information about where to get help.

FOR MULTILINGUAL WRITERS

Recognizing appeals in various settings

You may be familiar with emotional, ethical, or logical appeals that are not discussed in this chapter. If so, consider describing them — and how they work — to your class. Doing so would deepen the entire class's understanding of what appeals carry the most power in particular settings.

8e Identifying elements of an argument

According to philosopher Stephen Toulmin's framework for analyzing arguments, most arguments contain common features: a *claim* or *claims; reasons* for the claim; *assumptions* (whether stated or unstated) that underlie the argument; *evidence* (facts, authoritative opinion, examples, statistics, and so on); and *qualifiers* that limit the claim in some way. In the following discussion, we will examine each of these elements in more detail. The figure on the following page shows how these elements might be applied to an argument about sex education.

Claims

Claims (also referred to as arguable statements) are statements of fact, opinion, or belief that form the backbone of arguments. In longer essays, you may detect a series of linked claims or even several separate claims that you need to analyze before you agree to accept them. Claims worthy of arguing are those that are debatable: to say "Ten degrees Fahrenheit is cold" is a claim, but it is probably not debatable — unless you are describing northern Alaska, where ten degrees might seem balmy. If a

ELEMENTS OF A SAMPLE SEX-EDUCATION ARGUMENT

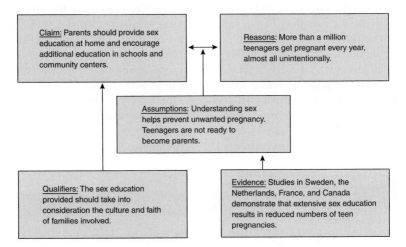

movie review you are reading has as its claim "Great movie!" is that claim debatable? Probably not if the reviewer is basing the claim solely on personal taste. But if the reviewer goes on to offer good reasons to admire the movie, along with strong evidence to support the reasons, he or she could present a debatable — and therefore arguable — claim.

Reasons

In fact, a claim is only as good as the reasons attached to it. An email to an instructor claiming that course portfolios should be graded pass or fail because the writer had a heavy course load is on very thin ice: critical readers will question whether that reason is sufficient to support the claim. As you analyze claims, look for reasons drawn from facts, from authorities, from personal experience, and from examples. Test each reason by asking how directly it supports the claim, how timely it is, and what counter-reasons you could offer to question it.

Assumptions

Putting a claim and reasons together often results in what Aristotle called an *enthymeme*, an argument that rests on an assumption the writer expects the audience to hold. These assumptions (which Toulmin calls *warrants*) that connect claim and reasons are often the hardest to detect in an argument, partly because they are often unstated, sometimes masking a weak link. As a result, it's especially important to identify the assumptions in arguments you are analyzing. Once the assumption is identified, you can test it against evidence and your own experience before accepting it. If a writer argues that grades for portfolios should be abolished because grading damages both teaching and learning, what is the assumption underlying this claim and reason? It is that *anything that prevents or hinders education should be abolished.* As a critical reader, remember that such assumptions are deeply affected by culture and belief: ask yourself, then, what cultural differences may be at work in your response to any argument.

Evidence

Evidence, what Toulmin calls *backing*, also calls for careful analysis in arguments. In an argument about abolishing grades, the writer may offer as evidence several key examples of the damage grading can cause; a statistical analysis of the correlation between grades and later success in life; a historical precedent from the centuries when grading was not used; or psychological studies of grade-related stress on undergraduate students. As a critical reader, you must evaluate each piece of evidence the writer offers, asking specifically how it relates to the claim, whether it is appropriate and timely, and whether it comes from a credible source.

Qualifiers

Qualifiers offer a way of limiting or narrowing a claim so that it is as precise as possible. Words or phrases that signal a qualification include *few, often, in these circumstances, rarely, typically,* and so on. Claims having no qualifiers can sometimes lead to overgeneralizations. For example, the statement *Grading damages learning* is less precise than *Grading can damage learning in some circumstances.* Look carefully for qualifiers in the arguments you analyze, since they will affect the strength and reach of the claim.

Analyzing elements of a visual argument

Visual arguments, too, can be analyzed using Toulmin's methods. Look at the accompanying advertising parody: it contains few words, yet it makes a subtle argument. A group of students discussed this advertisement, observing that the image intends to evoke a 1960s-era detergent commercial. They came up with several possible claims that the ad might be making.

POSSIBLE CLAIM	Pharmaceutical companies want to convince consumers that taking drugs to cure depression is no more serious than trying a new detergent.
POSSIBLE CLAIM	Consumers should beware of drug advertisements that make hard-to-prove claims aimed at getting customers to ask for a prescription
POSSIBLE CLAIM	Buying products will not lead to greater happiness.

All of these claims can be supported by the ad. If you were to choose the first claim, for instance, you might word a reason like this: *This parody of a Prozac ad looks like a detergent commercial from the 1960s, but the product is a chemical that promises to "wash your blues away."* With some research into the actual dangers and benefits of antidepressants, you might find evidence that ads for such drugs sometimes minimize their downside and exaggerate their promise. You might also note that the ad's design takes viewers back to a decades-old scene of domestic happiness, suggesting that Prozac could return its users to some mythically perfect time in the past—and you would be well on your way to an analysis of this visual argument.

8f Identifying fallacies

Fallacies have traditionally been viewed as serious flaws that damage the effectiveness of an argument. But arguments are ordinarily fairly complex in that they always occur in some specific rhetorical situation and in some particular place and time; thus what looks like a fallacy in one situation may appear quite different in another. The best advice is to learn to identify fallacies but to be cautious in jumping to quick conclusions about them. Rather than thinking of them as errors you can root out and use to discredit an arguer, you might think of them as barriers to common ground and understanding, since they so often shut off rather than engender debate. If a letter to the editor argues *If this newspaper thinks additional tax cuts are going to help the middle-class family, then this newspaper is run by imbeciles*, it clearly indulges in a fallacy—in this case, an argument ad hominem or argument against character. But the more important point is that this kind of argument shuts down debate: few are going to respond reasonably to being called imbeciles.

Verbal fallacies

AD HOMINEM

Ad hominem charges make a personal attack rather than focusing on the issue at hand.

▷ **Who cares what that fat loudmouth says about the health care system?**

GUILT BY ASSOCIATION

Guilt by association attacks someone's credibility by linking that person with a person or activity the audience considers bad, suspicious, or untrustworthy.

▷ **She does not deserve reelection; her husband had a gambling addiction.**

FALSE AUTHORITY

False authority is often used by advertisers who show famous actors or athletes testifying to the greatness of a product about which they may know very little.

▷ **He's today's greatest NASCAR driver—and he banks at National Mutual!**

BANDWAGON APPEAL

Bandwagon appeal suggests that a great movement is under way and the reader will be a fool or a traitor not to join it.

▷ **This new phone is everyone's must-have item. Where's yours?**

FLATTERY

Flattery tries to persuade readers by suggesting that they are thoughtful, intelligent, or perceptive enough to agree with the writer.

▶ **You have the taste to recognize the superlative artistry of Bling diamond jewelry.**

IN-CROWD APPEAL

In-crowd appeal, a special kind of flattery, invites readers to identify with an admired and select group.

▶ **Want to know a secret that more and more of Middletown's successful young professionals are finding out about? It's Mountainbrook Manor condominiums.**

VEILED THREAT

Veiled threats try to frighten readers into agreement by hinting that they will suffer adverse consequences if they don't agree.

▶ **If Public Service Electric Company does not get an immediate 15 percent rate increase, its services to you may be seriously affected.**

FALSE ANALOGY

False analogies make comparisons between two situations that are not alike in important respects.

▶ **The volleyball team's sudden descent in the rankings resembled the sinking of the *Titanic*.**

BEGGING THE QUESTION

Begging the question is a kind of circular argument that treats a debatable statement as if it had been proved true.

▶ **Television news covered that story well; I learned all I know about it by watching TV.**

POST HOC FALLACY

The post hoc fallacy (from the Latin *post hoc, ergo propter hoc*, which means "after this, therefore caused by this") assumes that just because B happened *after* A, it must have been *caused* by A.

▶ **We should not rebuild the town docks because every time we do, a big hurricane comes along and damages them.**

NON SEQUITUR

A non sequitur (Latin for "it does not follow") attempts to tie together two or more logically unrelated ideas as if they were related.

▶ **If we can send a spaceship to Mars, then we can discover a cure for cancer.**

EITHER-OR FALLACY

The either-or fallacy insists that a complex situation can have only two possible outcomes.

▶ **If we do not build the new highway, businesses downtown will be forced to close.**

HASTY GENERALIZATION

A hasty generalization bases a conclusion on too little evidence or on bad or misunderstood evidence.

▶ **I couldn't understand the lecture today, so I'm sure this course will be impossible.**

OVERSIMPLIFICATION

Oversimplification claims an overly direct relationship between a cause and an effect.

▶ **If we prohibit the sale of alcohol, we will get rid of binge drinking.**

STRAW MAN

A straw-man argument misrepresents the opposition by pretending that opponents agree with something that few reasonable people would support.

▶ **My opponent believes that we should offer therapy to the terrorists. I disagree.**

Visual fallacies

Fallacies can also take the form of misleading images. The sheer power of images can make them especially difficult to analyze — people tend to believe what they see. Nevertheless, photographs and other visuals can be manipulated to present a false impression.

MISLEADING PHOTOGRAPHS

Faked or altered photos have existed since the invention of photography. Below, for example, is a photograph of Joseph Stalin, the Soviet Union's leader from 1929 to 1953, with his commissar Nikolai Yezhov. Stalin and the commissar had a political disagreement that resulted in Yezhov's execution in 1940. The second image shows the same photo after Stalin had it doctored to rewrite history.

Today's technology makes such photo alterations easier than ever. But photographs need not be altered to try to fool viewers. Think of all the photos that make a politician look misleadingly bad or good. In these cases, you should closely examine the motives of those responsible for publishing the images.

MISLEADING CHARTS AND GRAPHS

Facts and statistics, too, can be presented in ways that mislead readers. For example, the following bar graph purports to deliver an argument about how differently Democrats, on the one hand, and Republicans and Independents, on the other, felt about an issue:

DATA PRESENTED MISLEADINGLY

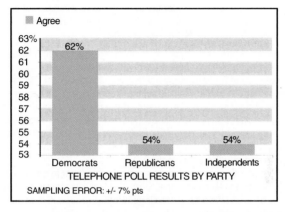

Look closely and you'll see a visual fallacy at work: the vertical axis starts not at zero but at 53 percent, so the visually large difference between the groups is misleading. In fact, a majority of all respondents agree about the issue, and only eight percentage points separate Democrats from Republicans and Independents (in a poll with a margin of error of $+/-$ seven percentage points). Here's how the graph would look if the vertical axis began at zero:

DATA PRESENTED MORE ACCURATELY

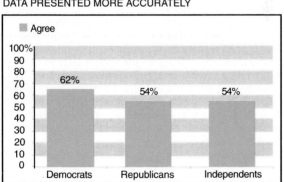

EXERCISE 8.1

Read the following brief essay by Derek Bok, which argues that college administrators should seek to educate and persuade rather than censor students who use speech or symbols that others find deeply offensive. Then carry out an analysis of the argument, beginning with identifying the audience and the author's purpose, and moving to identifying the claim, reason(s), assumption(s), evidence, and qualifiers (if any). As you work, be sure also to identify the emotional, ethical, and logical appeals as well as any fallacies put forward by Bok. You may want to compare your own analysis to the one written by Milena Ateyea in 8g.

> For several years, universities have been struggling with the problem of trying to reconcile the rights of free speech with the desire to avoid racial tension. In recent weeks, such a controversy has sprung up at Harvard. Two students hung Confederate flags in public view, upsetting students who equate the Confederacy with slavery. A third student tried to protest the flags by displaying a swastika.

> These incidents have provoked much discussion and disagreement. Some students have urged that Harvard require the removal of symbols that offend many members of the community. Others reply that such symbols are a form of free speech and should be protected.

> Different universities have resolved similar conflicts in different ways. Some have enacted codes to protect their communities from forms of speech that are deemed to be insensitive to the feelings of other groups. Some have refused to impose such restrictions.

> It is important to distinguish between the appropriateness of such communications and their status under the First Amendment. The fact that speech is protected by the First Amendment does not necessarily mean that it is right, proper, or civil. I am sure that the vast majority of Harvard students believe that hanging a Confederate flag in public view — or displaying a swastika in response — is insensitive and unwise because any satisfaction it gives to the students who display these symbols is far outweighed by the discomfort it causes to many others.

> I share this view and regret that the students involved saw fit to behave in this fashion. Whether or not they merely wished to manifest their pride in the South — or to demonstrate the insensitivity of hanging Confederate flags, by mounting another offensive symbol in return — they must have known that they would upset many fellow students and ignore the decent regard for the feelings of others so essential to building and preserving a strong and harmonious community.

> To disapprove of a particular form of communication, however, is not enough to justify prohibiting it. We are faced with a clear example of the conflict between our commitment to free speech and our desire to foster a community founded on mutual respect. Our society has wrestled with this problem for many years. Interpreting the First Amendment, the Supreme Court has clearly struck the balance in favor of free speech.

> While communities do have the right to regulate speech in order to uphold aesthetic standards (avoiding defacement of buildings) or to protect the public from disturbing noise, rules of this kind must be applied across the board and cannot be enforced selectively to prohibit certain kinds of messages but not others.

> Under the Supreme Court's rulings, as I read them, the display of swastikas or Confederate flags clearly falls within the protection of the free-speech clause of the First Amendment and cannot be forbidden simply because it offends the feelings of many members of the community. These rulings apply to all agencies of government, including public universities.

Although it is unclear to what extent the First Amendment is enforceable against private institutions, I have difficulty understanding why a university such as Harvard should have less free speech than the surrounding society—or than a public university.

One reason why the power of censorship is so dangerous is that it is extremely difficult to decide when a particular communication is offensive enough to warrant prohibition or to weigh the degree of offensiveness against the potential value of the communication. If we begin to forbid flags, it is only a short step to prohibiting offensive speakers.

I suspect that no community will become humane and caring by restricting what its members can say. The worst offenders will simply find other ways to irritate and insult.

In addition, once we start to declare certain things "offensive," with all the excitement and attention that will follow, I fear that much ingenuity will be exerted trying to test the limits, much time will be expended trying to draw tenuous distinctions, and the resulting publicity will eventually attract more attention to the offensive material than would ever have occurred otherwise.

Rather than prohibit such communications, with all the resulting risks, it would be better to ignore them, since students would then have little reason to create such displays and would soon abandon them. If this response is not possible—and one can understand why—the wisest course is to speak with those who perform insensitive acts and try to help them understand the effects of their actions on others.

Appropriate officials and faculty members should take the lead, as the Harvard House Masters have already done in this case. In talking with students, they should seek to educate and persuade, rather than resort to ridicule or intimidation, recognizing that only persuasion is likely to produce a lasting, beneficial effect. Through such effects, I believe that we act in the manner most consistent with our ideals as an educational institution and most calculated to help us create a truly understanding, supportive community.

—DEREK BOK, "Protecting Freedom of Expression at Harvard"

8g A student's rhetorical analysis of an argument

Student Writer

Milena Ateyea

For a class assignment, Milena Ateyea was asked to analyze Derek Bok's essay by focusing on the author's use of emotional, ethical, and logical appeals. Her rhetorical analysis follows.

Provocative title suggests mixed response to Bok

Connects article to her own experience to build credibility (ethical appeal)

Brief overview of Bok's argument

Identifies Bok's central claim

Links Bok's claim to strategies he uses to support it

Direct quotations show appeals to emotion through vivid description

Bok establishes common ground between two positions

Emphasizes Bok's credibility (ethical appeal)

A Curse and a Blessing

In 1991, when Derek Bok's essay "Protecting Freedom of Expression at Harvard" was first published in the *Boston Globe*, I had just come to America to escape the oppressive Communist regime in Bulgaria. Perhaps my background explains why I support Bok's argument that we should not put arbitrary limits on freedom of expression. Bok wrote the essay in response to a public display of Confederate flags and a swastika at Harvard, a situation that created a heated controversy among the students. As Bok notes, universities have struggled to achieve a balance between maintaining students' right of free speech and avoiding racist attacks. When choices must be made, however, Bok argues for preserving freedom of expression.

In order to support his claim and bridge the controversy, Bok uses a variety of rhetorical strategies. The author first immerses the reader in the controversy by vividly describing the incident: two Harvard students had hung Confederate flags in public view, thereby "upsetting students who equate the Confederacy with slavery" (51). Another student, protesting the flags, decided to display an even more offensive symbol—the swastika. These actions provoked heated discussions among students. Some students believed that school officials should remove the offensive symbols, whereas others suggested that the symbols "are a form of free speech and should be protected" (51). Bok establishes common ground between the factions: he regrets the actions of the offenders but does not believe we should prohibit such actions just because we disagree with them.

The author earns the reader's respect because of his knowledge and through his logical presentation of the issue. In partial support of his position, Bok refers to U.S. Supreme Court rulings, which remind us that "the display of swastikas or Confederate flags clearly falls within the protection of the free-speech clause of the First Amendment" (52). The

author also emphasizes the danger of the slippery slope of censorship
when he warns the reader, "If we begin to forbid flags, it is only a short
step to prohibiting offensive speakers" (52). Overall, however, Bok's work
lacks the kinds of evidence that statistics, interviews with students, and
other representative examples of controversial conduct could provide.
Thus, his essay may not be strong enough to persuade all readers to make
the leap from this specific situation to his general conclusion.

Throughout, Bok's personal feelings are implied but not stated
directly. As a lawyer who was president of Harvard for twenty years, Bok
knows how to present his opinions respectfully without offending the
feelings of the students. However, qualifying phrases like "I suspect that"
and "Under the Supreme Court's rulings, as I read them" could weaken
the effectiveness of his position. Furthermore, Bok's attempt to be fair
to all seems to dilute the strength of his proposed solution. He suggests
that one should either ignore the insensitive deeds in the hope that
students might change their behavior, or talk to the offending students to
help them comprehend how their behavior is affecting other students.

Nevertheless, although Bok's proposed solution to the controversy
does not appear at first reading to be very strong, it may ultimately be
effective. There is enough flexibility in his approach to withstand various
tests, and Bok's solution is general enough that it can change with the
times and adapt to community standards.

In writing this essay, Bok faced a challenging task: to write a short
response to a specific situation that represents a very broad and controversial
issue. Some people may find that freedom of expression is both a curse and
a blessing because of the difficulties it creates. As one who has lived under a
regime that permitted very limited, censored expression, I am all too aware
that I could not have written this response in 1991 in Bulgaria. As a result, I
feel, like Derek Bok, that freedom of expression is a blessing, in spite of any
temporary problems associated with it.

Links Bok's credibility to use of logical appeals

Comments critically on kinds of evidence Bok's argument lacks

Reiterates Bok's credibility

Identifies qualifying phrases that may weaken claim

Analyzes weaknesses of Bok's proposed solution

Raises possibility that Bok's imperfect solution may work

Summarizes Bok's task

Ties conclusion back to title

Returns to experience with censorship, which argues for accepting Bok's solution

Student Writing

Work Cited

Bok, Derek. "Protecting Freedom of Expression at Harvard."
    Rpt. in *Current Issues and Enduring Questions*. Ed.
    Sylvan Barnet and Hugo Bedau. 6th ed. Boston:
    Bedford, 2002. 51–52. *Boston Globe* 25 May 1991.
    Print.

EXERCISE 8.2

Working with one or two classmates, analyze a brief argumentative text—an essay, an advertisement, or an editorial cartoon—by playing the believing and doubting game; identifying emotional, ethical, and logical appeals; and listing claims, reasons, assumptions, evidence, and qualifiers. Then work together to create a collaborative critical response to the text you've chosen.

THINKING CRITICALLY ABOUT ANALYZING ARGUMENTS

In the following brief review for *Rolling Stone*, music critic James Hunter recaps five CDs that reissue ten Merle Haggard albums from early in the country star's career. What central claim(s) does Hunter make? What emotional, ethical, and logical appeals does he present in support of his claim (including in the headline and the image of Haggard accompanying the review), and how effective are these appeals?

Outlaw Classics: The Albums That Kept Nashville Real in the Sixties and Seventies

[Review of *Merle Haggard* (Capitol Nashville/EMI)]

By James Hunter

Merle Haggard wasn't the first outsider to rebuke Nashville prissiness in the Sixties—Johnny Cash, who arrived from Sun Records in Memphis, deserves that honor—but Hag was the most down-to-earth soul that the Music City had seen for some time when he loped onto the scene in the mid- to late Sixties. An ex-con from California with Oklahoma roots, he sang eloquently about booze and prison life. His beginnings were in honky-tonk Bakersfield, where he learned first-class musical directness from guys like the great Buck Owens and Wynn Stewart.

More than an Okie from Muskogee: Hag in the late Sixties

For years, Haggard's Sixties and early-Seventies work has been represented chiefly on compilations. This bunch of reissues restores ten of those albums, all with interesting bonus tracks; four of the ten albums have never appeared before on CD. Each showcases Haggard's awesome gifts and inextricable orneriness: There is no Tennessee gothic or flashy Texas ego to this outsider; Haggard was more about subtlety and West Coast calm. A hummable, elastic honky-tonk tune can convey everything he wants to say. His melodies carry a broad range of topics, from cranky love songs ("I'm Gonna Break Every Heart I Can") to prison tunes ("Bring Me Back Home") to perfectly wrought whiskey-and-wine songs, to looks back at his parents' lives. Sometimes, as on the scarily good "I Can't Be Myself," Haggard seems to want to jump out of his own skin; other times, as on "I Threw Away the Rose," he's as centered in his own smooth, crusty tenor as any singer has ever been. In all cases, Haggard sounds like country's coolest customer.

These reissues underscore how Haggard's music far exceeds "Okie from Muskogee," the anti-hippie 1969 smash that made him internationally famous. Cash rocked country up and then went on to become his world's black-clad cultural ambassador. George Jones showed how the field needs at least one opera star, and Willie Nelson yoked local songwriting to American poetry. Haggard proved how crucial it was for a country guy to say what was on his mind—and because he was such a sublime recording artist, he was able to make it stick, right from the start.

9 Constructing Arguments

Chances are, you've been making convincing arguments since early childhood, and those around you slowly learned to respond to these arguments. But family members and friends are not always easy to convince — and the job of making effective arguments to those you don't know presents even more challenges. It is especially difficult to argue with people who are thousands of miles away and are encountering your argument only in cyberspace.

You respond to arguments all the time. When you see a stop sign and come to a halt, you've accepted the argument that stopping at such signs is a sensible thing to do. Unfortunately, constructing an effective argument of your own is not as easy as putting up a stop sign. Creating a thorough and convincing argument requires careful reasoning and appropriate attention to your audience and purpose.

9a Arguing for a purpose

Since all language is in some sense argumentative, the purposes of argument vary widely. For many years, however, traditional notions of argument tended to highlight one purpose — winning. Although winning is still one important purpose of argument, studies of the argument strategies of people from groups historically excluded from public debate — including women and people of color — have demonstrated that it is by no means the only purpose. Nor is winning always going to be *your* purpose. For instance, if you are trying to decide whether to major in business or in chemistry, you may want to consider, or "argue," all sides of the issue. Your purpose is hardly to win out over someone else; instead, it is to understand your choices in order to make a wise decision.

To win

The most traditional purpose of academic argument, arguing *to win*, is used in campus debating societies, in political debates, in trials, and often in busi-

QUICK HELP

Checklist for constructing an argument

- What is the purpose of your argument—to convince others? to make a good decision? to change yourself? (9a)

- Is the point you want to make arguable? (9b)

- Have you formulated a clear claim and given good reasons for it? (9c and d)

- Have you formulated a strong working thesis, and have you qualified it sufficiently? (9c)

- How have you established your own credibility in the argument? (9e)

- Have you considered, and addressed, counterarguments? (9e3)

- How have you incorporated logical appeals into your argument? (9f)

- How have you used emotional appeals in your argument? (9g)

- How have you used sources in your argument, and how effectively are they integrated into your argument? (9h)

- Is your argument clearly organized? (9i)

- What design elements have you considered in composing your argument? How effective is your design? (9j)

ness. The writer or speaker aims to present a position that prevails over or defeats the positions of others. Presidential debates and trials, for example, focus most often not on changing the opponent's mind but on defeating him or her in order to appeal to someone else — the voting public, the judge, and so on.

To convince

More often than not, out-and-out defeat of another is not only unrealistic but also undesirable. Rather, the goal is *to convince* other persons that they should change their minds about an issue. A writer must provide reasons so compelling that the audience willingly agrees with the writer's conclusion. Such is the goal of advocates of assisted suicide: they well know that they cannot realistically hope to defeat or conquer those who oppose such acts. Rather, they understand that they must provide reasons compelling enough to change people's minds.

TALKING THE TALK

Arguments

"Argument seems so negative—I don't want to attack anybody or contradict what someone else says." In some times and places—law courts, for example—argument may call for attacking the credibility of the opponent. Or you may have used the word *argument* in childhood to describe a conversation in which you voiced nothing more than "I did not!" or "You did too!" But in college writing, you have a chance to reject this narrow definition and to use argument in a much broader way. Instead of attacking or contradicting, you will be expected to explore ideas and to work toward convincing yourself as well as others that these ideas are valuable.

To reach a decision or explore an issue

Often, a writer must enter into conversation with others and collaborate in seeking the best possible understanding of a problem, exploring all possible approaches and choosing the best alternative. Argument *to decide or explore* does not seek to conquer or control others or even to convince. Your purpose in many situations—from trying to decide which laptop to buy to exploring with your family the best way to care for an elderly relative—will be to share information and perspectives in order to make informed political, professional, and personal choices.

To change yourself

Sometimes you will find yourself arguing primarily with yourself, and those arguments often take the form of intense meditations on a theme, or even of prayer. In such cases, you may be hoping *to transform something in yourself* or to reach peace of mind on a troubling subject. If you know a familiar mantra or prayer, for example, think of what it "argues" for and how it uses quiet meditation to help achieve that goal.

9b Determining whether a statement can be argued

An early step in an argument intended to convince or decide is to make a statement about a topic and then check to see that the statement can, in fact, be argued. An arguable statement has three characteristics:

1. It attempts to convince readers of something, change their minds about something, or urge them to do something — or it explores a topic in order to make a wise decision.

2. It addresses a problem for which no easily acceptable solution exists or asks a question to which no absolute answer exists.

3. It presents a position that readers might realistically have varying perspectives on.

> ARGUABLE STATEMENT   Advertising in women's magazines contributes to the poor self-image that most young women have.

This statement seeks to convince, addresses a problem — poor self-image among young women — that has no clear-cut solution, and takes a position many could disagree with.

> UNARGUABLE   Women's magazines earn millions of dollars
> STATEMENT   every year from advertising.

This statement does not present a position; it states a fact that can easily be verified and thus offers a poor basis for argument.

EXERCISE 9.1

Using the three characteristics just listed, decide which of the following statements are arguable and which are not.

1. *The Dark Knight* was the best movie of the last decade.

2. The climate of the earth is gradually getting warmer.

3. The United States must further reduce social spending in order to balance the budget.

4. Shakespeare died in 1616.

5. President Roosevelt knew that the Japanese were planning to bomb Pearl Harbor in December 1941.

6. Water boils at 212 degrees Fahrenheit.

7. Van Gogh's paintings are the work of a madman.

8. The incidence of breast cancer has risen in the last ten years.

9. The Federal Emergency Management Agency's response to disasters must be radically improved.

10. A fifty-five-mile-per-hour speed limit lowers accident rates.

> bedfordstmartins.com/smhandbook
> **Exercise Central > Critical Thinking and Argument**

9c   Formulating a working thesis

Once you have an arguable statement, you need to develop it into a working thesis (3c). One way to do so — often called the Toulmin system — is to identify the elements of an argument (8e and 9i2), which include the following: the claim or arguable statement; one or more reasons for the claim; and assumptions — sometimes unstated — that underlie the claim and reasons. Let's apply these elements to a specific topic — the use of pesticides.

Begin with an arguable statement (or initial claim). The following statement is arguable because it aims to convince, it addresses an issue with no one identifiable answer, and it can realistically be disputed.

ARGUABLE STATEMENT (OR INITIAL CLAIM)	Pesticides should be banned.

Attach a good reason. Although the preceding statement does make a claim — that pesticides should be banned — it offers no reason for doing so. To turn a claim into a working thesis for an argument, you need to include at least one good reason to support the arguable statement.

REASON	They endanger the lives of farmworkers.
WORKING THESIS (CLAIM WITH REASON ATTACHED)	Because they endanger the lives of farmworkers, pesticides should be banned.

Develop or identify assumptions underlying the claim and reasons. Once you have a working thesis, examine your assumptions to help test your reasoning and strengthen your argument. Begin by identifying underlying assumptions that support the working thesis.

WORKING THESIS	Because they endanger the lives of farmworkers, pesticides should be banned.
ASSUMPTION 1	Workers have a right to a safe working environment.
ASSUMPTION 2	Substances that endanger the lives of workers deserve to be banned.

Once you have a working thesis, you may want to use qualifiers to make it more precise and thus less susceptible to criticism. The preceding thesis might be qualified in this way:

▶ **Because they *often* endanger the lives of farmworkers, *most* pesticides should be banned.**

EXERCISE 9.2

Using two arguable statements from Exercise 9.1 or two that you create, formulate two working theses, identifying the claim, reason(s), and assumption(s) for each.

EXERCISE 9.3

Formulate an arguable statement, and create a working thesis, for two of the following general topics.

1. the Palestinian-Israeli conflict
2. sex education in public schools
3. lowering college tuition
4. reinstatement of a U.S. military draft
5. music downloading

EXERCISE 9.4

Working with two other members of your class, find two current advertisements you consider particularly eye-catching and persuasive. Then work out what central claim each ad is making, and identify reasons and assumptions in support of the claim. Finally, prepare a brief collaborative report of your findings for the class.

9d   Finding good reasons

In his *Rhetoric*, Aristotle discusses various ways one can support a claim. Torture, he notes, makes for a very convincing argument but not one that reasonable people will resort to. In effecting real changes in minds and hearts, we need instead to rely on *good reasons* — reasons that establish our credibility, that appeal to logic, and that appeal to emotion. You can use these appeals to analyze the arguments of others (8d) as well as to construct arguments of your own.

9e   Making ethical appeals

To make your argument convincing, you must first gain the respect and trust of your readers, or establish your credibility with them. The ancient Greeks called this particular kind of character appeal *ethos*, and we refer to it as an ethical appeal (8d). You can establish credibility by demonstrating your knowledge of the topic, by showing that you and your audience share at least some common ground, and by showing yourself to be fair and evenhanded. Visuals can strengthen your ability to make such ethical appeals.

1   Knowledge about the topic

A writer can establish credibility first by demonstrating his or her knowledge about the topic at hand. You can show that you have some personal experience with the subject: for example, if you are a former preschool teacher, you could mention your teaching background as part of an argument for increased funding of the Head Start program. In addition, showing that you have thought about and researched the subject carefully can help you establish a confident tone.

To determine whether you can effectively present yourself as knowledgeable enough to argue about an issue, consider the following questions:

- Can you provide information about your topic from sources other than your own knowledge?

- How reliable are your sources?

- Do any sources contradict one another? If so, can you account for or resolve the contradictions?

- If you have personal experience relating to the issue, would telling about this experience help support your claim?

These questions may help you see what other work you need to do to establish credibility: perhaps you should do more research, resolve contradictions, refocus your working thesis, or even change your topic.

2 Common ground

Many arguments between people or groups are doomed to end without resolution because the two sides occupy no common ground, no starting point of agreement. They are, to use an informal phrase, coming from completely different places. Such has often been the case, for example, in India-Pakistan talks, in which the beginning positions of each party have directly conflicted with those of the other side, leaving no room for a settlement that appeases both nations.

Lack of common ground also dooms many arguments that take place in our everyday lives. If you and your roommate cannot agree on how often to clean your apartment, for instance, the difficulty may well be that your definition of a clean apartment conflicts radically with your roommate's. You may find, in fact, that you will not be able to resolve such issues until you can establish common definitions, ones that can turn futile quarrels into constructive arguments. (For more on establishing common ground, see Chapter 25.)

Common ground is just as important in written arguments as it is in diplomatic negotiations or personal disputes. The following questions can help you find common ground in presenting an argument:

- What are the differing perspectives on this issue?

- What common ground can you find — aspects of the issue on which all sides agree?

- How can you express such agreement clearly to all sides?

- How can you discover — and consider — opinions on this issue that differ from your own?

- How can you use language — occupational, regional, or ethnic varieties of English or languages other than English (26c–e) — to establish common ground with those you address?

If you turn to Teal Pfeifer's essay in 9k, you will see that she attempts to establish common ground by assuming that all her readers are concerned about the health and well-being of young

For Teal Pfeifer's essay, see pp. 213–18.

women—and by explaining that she, like most women, cannot conform to a magazine's ideal of beauty.

3 Fairness toward counterarguments

In arguing a position, writers must demonstrate fairness toward opposing arguments, sometimes called counterarguments (9i2). Audiences are more inclined to give credibility to writers who seem to be fairly considering and representing their opponents' views than to those who seem to be ignoring or distorting such views. Part of your job as an effective writer, then, might involve anticipating possible counterarguments to your writing and establishing yourself as open-minded and evenhanded. The following questions can help you discover ways of doing so:

- How can you show that you are taking into account all significant points of view?

- How can you demonstrate that you understand and sympathize with points of view other than your own?

- What can you do to show that you have considered evidence carefully, even when it does not support your position?

Some writers, instead of demonstrating fairness, may make unjustified attacks on an opponent's credibility. Such attacks, which are known as fallacies (8f), should be avoided in your writing.

4 Visuals that make ethical appeals

In arguments and other kinds of writing, visuals can combine with text to help present a writer or an organization as trustworthy and credible. Like businesses, many institutions and individuals are using logos and other

SUSTAINABLE FOOD LABORATORY

images to brand themselves as they wish the public to see them. The Sustainable Food Laboratory logo, seen here, suggests that the organization is concerned about both food production and the environment.

Similarly, the PowerPoint slide from a presentation on the

Sustainable Food Laboratory explains one of the organization's goals in visual and verbal terms that viewers are likely to find highly credible — and that is far more persuasive than a bullet point providing the same information.

The ability of farmers and farm workers to earn a decent living.

Visuals that make ethical appeals add to your credibility and fairness as a writer. Just as you probably consider the impression your Facebook profile photo makes on your audience, you should think about what kind of case you're making for yourself when you choose images and design elements for your argument.

EXERCISE 9.5

List the ways in which the Sustainable Food Laboratory's logo and/or the presentation slide demonstrate knowledge, establish common ground, and show fairness. Do you think the visuals are helpful in convincing you of the organization's credibility? Why, or why not?

EXERCISE 9.6

Using a working thesis you drafted for Exercise 9.2 or 9.3, write a paragraph or two describing how you would go about establishing your credibility in arguing that thesis.

9f Making logical appeals

While the character a writer presents in writing always exerts a strong appeal (or lack of appeal) in an argument, credibility alone cannot and should not carry the full burden of convincing readers. Indeed, many are inclined to think that the logic of the argument — the reasoning behind it — is as important as its ethos. Logical appeals (8d), known to the ancient Greeks as *logos*, can thus be very effective; particularly useful types of logical appeals include examples, precedents, and narratives; authority and testimony; causes and effects; and inductive and deductive reasoning. In addition, visuals can help you enhance your logical appeals.

1 Examples, precedents, and narratives

Just as a picture can sometimes be worth a thousand words, so can a well-conceived example be extremely valuable in arguing a point. Examples are used most often to support generalizations or to bring abstractions to life. In an argument about American mass media and body image, for instance, you might make the general statement that popular media send the message that a woman must be thin to be attractive; you might then illustrate your generalization with these examples:

> At the supermarket checkout, a tabloid publishes unflattering photographs of a young singer and comments on her apparent weight gain in shocked captions that ask "What happened?!?" Another praises a starlet for quickly shedding "ugly pounds" after the recent birth of a child. The cover of *Cosmopolitan* features a glamorously made-up and airbrushed actress in an outfit that reveals her remarkably tiny waist and flat stomach. Every woman in every advertisement in the magazine is thin — and the context makes it clear that we're supposed to think that she is beautiful.

The generalization would mean far less without the examples.

Examples can also help us understand abstractions. Poverty, for instance, may be difficult for us to think about in the abstract, but a description of several residents of a poverty-stricken community, vying for low-paying jobs, visiting local food pantries and soup kitchens, or facing homelessness, speaks directly to our understanding.

Precedents are particular kinds of examples taken from the past. The most common use of precedent occurs in law, where an attorney may ask for a certain ruling based on a similar earlier case. Precedent appears in everyday arguments as well. If, as part of a proposal for increasing lighting in the library garage, you point out that the university has increased lighting in four other garages in the past year, you are arguing on the basis of precedent.

In research writing (see Chapters 10–19), you must identify your sources for any examples or precedents not based on your own knowledge.

The following questions can help you check any use of example or precedent:

- How representative are the examples?
- Are they sufficient in strength or number to lead to a generalization?
- In what ways do they support your point?
- How closely does the precedent relate to the point you're trying to make? Are the situations really similar?

- How timely is the precedent? (What would have been applicable in 1920 is not necessarily applicable today.)

Because storytelling is universal, narratives can be very persuasive in helping readers understand and accept the logic of an argument. Narratives that use video and audio to capture the faces and voices of the people involved are often particularly compelling. In *As We Sow*, a documentary arguing against corporate pork production methods, the farmers shown here tell stories of their struggle to continue raising animals as their families have for generations.

Stories drawn from your own experience can appeal particularly to readers, for they not only help make your point in true-to-life, human terms but also help readers know you better and therefore identify with you more closely. In arguing for a stronger government campaign against smoking, for example, former President Clinton often drew on personal stories of his own family's experience with lung cancer.

When you include stories in an argument, ask yourself the following questions:

- Does the narrative support your thesis?

- Will the story's significance to the argument be clear to your readers?

- Is the story one of several good reasons or pieces of evidence—or does it have to carry the main burden of the argument?

In general, do not rely solely on the power of stories to carry your argument, since readers usually expect writers to state and argue their reasons more directly and abstractly as well. An additional danger if you use only your own experiences is that you can seem focused too much on yourself (and perhaps not enough on your readers).

As you develop your own arguments, keep in mind that while narratives can provide effective logical support, they may be used equally effectively for ethical or emotional appeals as well.

FOR MULTILINGUAL WRITERS

Counting your own experience

You may have learned that stories based on your own personal experience don't count in academic arguments. If so, reconsider this advice, for showing an audience that you have personal experience with a topic can carry strong persuasive appeal with many English-speaking audiences. As with all evidence used in an argument, however, narratives based on your own experience must be pertinent to the topic, understandable to the audience, and clearly related to your purpose.

---

2 Authority and testimony

Another way to support an argument logically is to cite an authority. For nearly fifty years, the use of authority has figured prominently in the controversy over smoking. Since the U.S. surgeon general's 1964 announcement that smoking is hazardous to health, millions of Americans have quit smoking, largely persuaded by the authority of the scientists offering the evidence.

But as with other strategies for building support for an argumentative claim, citing authorities demands careful consideration. Ask yourself the following questions to be sure you are using authorities effectively:

- Is the authority timely? (The argument that the United States should pursue a policy just because it was supported by Thomas Jefferson will probably fail because Jefferson's time was so radically different from ours.)

- Is the authority qualified to judge the topic at hand? (To cite a movie star in an essay on linguistics, an appeal to false authority, would not strengthen your argument [8f].)

- Is the authority likely to be known and respected by readers? (To cite an unfamiliar authority without some identification will lessen the impact of the evidence.)

- Are the authority's credentials clearly stated and verifiable? (Especially with Web-based sources, it is crucial to know whose authority guarantees the reliability of the information.)

Authorities are commonly cited in research writing (see Chapters 10–19), which often relies on the findings of other people. In addition, you may cite authorities in an assignment that asks you to review the literature of any field.

Testimony — the evidence an authority presents in support of a claim — is a feature of much contemporary argument. If testimony is timely, accurate, representative, and provided by a respected authority, then it, like authority itself, can add powerful support to an argument. In an essay for a literature class, for example, you might argue that a new edition of a literary work will open up many new areas of interpretation. You could strengthen this argument by adding a quotation from the author's biographer, noting that the new edition carries out the author's intentions much more closely than the previous edition did.

In research writing (Chapters 10–19), you should cite your sources for authority and testimony not based on your own knowledge.

FOR MULTILINGUAL WRITERS

Bringing in other voices

Sometimes quoting authorities will prompt you to use language other than standard academic English. For instance, if you're writing about political relations between Mexico and the United States, you might quote a leader of a Mexican American organization; using that person's own words — which may be partly or entirely in Spanish or a regional variety of English — can carry extra power, calling up a voice from a pertinent community. See Chapter 26 for advice about using varieties of English and other languages.

---

3 Causes and effects

Showing that one event is the cause — or the effect — of another can sometimes help support an argument. Suppose you are trying to explain, in a petition to change your grade in a course, why you were unable to take the final examination. In such a case, you would probably try to trace the causes of your failure to appear (the death of your grandmother followed by the theft of your car, perhaps) so that the committee reading the petition would reconsider the effect (your not taking the examination).

Tracing causes often lays the groundwork for an argument, particularly if the effect of the causes is one we would like to change. In an environmental science class, for example, a student may argue that a national law regulating smokestack emissions from utility plants is needed because (1) acid rain on the East Coast originates from emissions at utility plants in the Midwest, (2) acid rain kills trees and other vegetation, (3) utility lobbyists have prevented midwestern states from passing strict laws controlling emissions from such plants, and (4) in the absence of such laws, acid rain will destroy most eastern forests by 2020. In this case, the first point is that the emissions cause acid rain; the second, that acid rain causes destruction in eastern forests; and the third, that states have not acted to break the cause-effect relationship established by the first two points. The fourth point ties all of the previous points together to provide an overall argument from effect: unless a national law is passed, most eastern forests are doomed.

In fact, a cause-effect relationship is often extremely difficult to establish. Scientists and politicians continue to disagree, for example, over the extent to which acid rain is responsible for the so-called dieback of many eastern forests. If you can show strong evidence that a cause produces an effect, though, you will have a powerful argument at your disposal.

4 Inductive and deductive reasoning

Traditionally, logical arguments are classified as using either inductive or deductive reasoning, but in practice, the two types of reasoning usually appear together. Inductive reasoning is the process of making a generalization based on a number of specific instances. If you find you are ill on ten occasions after eating seafood, for example, you will likely draw the inductive generalization that seafood makes you ill. It may not be an absolute certainty that seafood was the culprit, but the probability lies in that direction.

Deductive reasoning, on the other hand, reaches a conclusion by assuming a general principle (known as a major premise) and then applying that principle to a specific case (the minor premise). In practice, this general principle is usually derived from induction. The inductive generalization *Seafood makes me ill,* for instance, could serve as the major premise for the deductive argument *Since all seafood makes me ill, the shrimp on this buffet is certain to make me ill.*

Deductive arguments have traditionally been analyzed as syllogisms— three-part statements containing a major premise, a minor premise, and a conclusion.

MAJOR PREMISE	All people die.
MINOR PREMISE	I am a person.
CONCLUSION	I will die.

Syllogisms, however, are too rigid and absolute to serve in arguments about questions that have no absolute answers, and they often lack any appeal to an audience. Aristotle's simpler alternative, the enthymeme (8e), calls on the audience to supply the implied major premise. Consider the following example:

> Since violent video games can be addictive and cause psychological harm, players and their parents must carefully evaluate such games and monitor their use.

You can analyze this enthymeme by restating it in the form of two premises and a conclusion.

MAJOR PREMISE	Games that cause harm to players should be evaluated and monitored.
MINOR PREMISE	Violent video games cause addiction and psychological harm to players.
CONCLUSION	These games should be evaluated and monitored.

Note that the major premise is one the writer can count on an audience agreeing with or supplying: safety and common sense demand that potentially harmful games should be used with great care. As such, this premise is *assumed* rather than stated in the enthymeme. By implicitly asking the audience to supply this premise to the argument, the writer engages the audience's participation.

Note that a deductive conclusion is only as strong as the premises on which it is based. The citizen who argues that *Ed is a crook and shouldn't be elected to public office* is arguing deductively, based on an implied major premise: *No crook should be elected to public office.* Most people would agree with this major premise. So the issue in this argument rests on the minor premise that Ed is a crook. Satisfactory proof of that premise will make us likely to accept the deductive conclusion that Ed shouldn't be elected.

At other times, the unstated premise may be more problematic. The person who says *Don't bother to ask for Ramon's help with physics—he's a jock* is arguing deductively on the basis of an implied major premise: *Jocks don't know anything about physics.* In this case, careful listeners would demand proof of the unstated premise. Because bigoted or prejudiced statements often rest on this kind of reasoning— a type of fallacy (8f)—writers should be particularly alert to it.

A helpful variation on the syllogism and the enthymeme is the Toulmin system (8e, 9c, and 9i2), which looks for claims, reasons, and assumptions rather than major and minor premises.

CLAIM	Violent video games should be carefully evaluated and their use monitored.
REASON(S)	Violent video games cause addiction and psychological harm to players.
ASSUMPTION	Games that cause harm to players should be evaluated and monitored.

Note that in this system the assumption—which may be unstated—serves the same function as the assumed major premise in an enthymeme.

EXERCISE 9.7

The following sentences contain deductive arguments based on implied major premises. Identify each of the implied premises.

1. The use of marijuana for medical purposes should be legal if it can improve a patient's condition and does not harm anyone.
2. Women soldiers should not serve in combat positions because doing so would expose them to a much higher risk of death.
3. Animals can't talk; therefore they can't feel pain as humans do.

5 Visuals that make logical appeals

Charts, graphs, tables, maps, photographs, and so on can be especially useful in arguments because they present factual information that can be taken in at a glance. For a report on minority-owned business enterprises, the U.S. Census Bureau used many charts and graphs, including the accompanying pie chart. In the same way, *Business Week* used a simple bar graph to carry a big message about equality of pay for men and

VISUALS THAT MAKE LOGICAL APPEALS

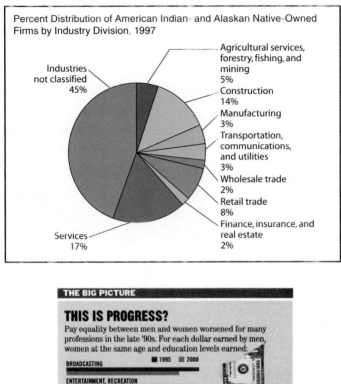

women. A quick glance will tell you how long it would take to explain all the information in these charts with words alone. In these instances, pictures can be worth a thousand words.

EXERCISE 9.8

Using a working thesis you drafted for Exercise 9.2 or 9.3, write a paragraph describing the logical appeals you would use to support the thesis.

9g Making emotional appeals

Most successful arguments appeal to our hearts as well as to our minds. Thus, good writers supplement appeals to logic and reason with emotional appeals to their readers. This principle was vividly demonstrated by the devastating earthquake in Haiti in 2010. Facts and figures — logical appeals — convinced us that the problem was real and serious. What elicited an outpouring of support, however, was the arresting emotional power of stories and images of a flattened city, of people searching for family members, and  of doctors doing their best with very little medicine or equipment. An effective emotional appeal (*pathos*, to the ancient Greeks) can be made with description and concrete language, with figurative language, and with visuals — as well as by shaping an appeal to a particular audience.

1 Description and concrete language

Like photographs, vivid, detailed description can bring a moving immediacy to any argument. A student may amass facts and figures, including diagrams and maps, to illustrate the problem of wheelchair access to the library. Her first draft may be packed with information. But only when the student asks a friend who uses a wheelchair to accompany her to the library does the student writer discover the concrete details necessary to move readers.

The heart of effective description is concrete or specific language (27c). Although the student could have written that her friend "had trouble entering the library," such a general statement would not appeal to readers' emotions. Instead, she uses concrete details: "Maria inched her heavy wheelchair up the narrow, steep entrance ramp, her arms straining to pull up the last twenty feet, her face pinched with the sheer effort."

2 Figurative language

Figurative language, or figures of speech (27d), paint detailed pictures that build understanding. They do so by relating something new or unfamiliar to something the audience knows well and by making striking comparisons between something you are writing about and something else that helps a reader visualize, identify with, or understand it.

Figures of speech include metaphors, similes, and analogies. Metaphors compare two things directly: *Richard the Lion-Hearted; old age is the evening of life; the defensive players are pit bulls on pork chops.* Similes make comparisons using *like* or *as: Richard was as brave as a lion; old age is like the evening of life; the defensive players are like pit bulls on pork chops.* Analogies are extended metaphors or similes that compare an unfamiliar concept or process to a more familiar one to help the reader understand the unfamiliar concept.

> I see the Internet as a city struggling to be built, its laws only now being formulated, its notions of social order arising out of the needs of its citizens and the demands of their environment. Like any city, the Net has its charlatans and its thieves as well as its poets, engineers, and philosophers. . . . Our experience of the Internet will be determined by how we master its core competencies. They are the design principles that are shaping the electronic city.
> —PAUL GILSTER, *Digital Literacy*

A student arguing for a more streamlined course-registration process may find good use for an analogy, saying that the current process makes students feel like laboratory rats in a maze. This analogy, which suggests manipulation, frustration, and a clinical coldness, creates a vivid description and adds emotional appeal to the argument. For the analogy to work effectively, however, the student would have to show that the current registration process has a number of similarities to a laboratory maze, such as confused students wandering through complex bureaucratic channels and into dead ends.

Visuals can also create vivid comparisons. The panels on p. 206 come from a cartoon from Tom Tomorrow's comic strip, *This Modern World*, called "If Real Life Were More Like the Internet." Tomorrow, whose work appears regularly on Salon.com as well as in print, suggests in these panels that online content has value, just as real-life products and services do — and that those who create such content should be able to earn a living from it. Tomorrow adds emotional weight to the comparison by making the cartoon characters who want free content seem selfish and blind to the needs of those who serve them.

As you use analogies or other figurative language to bring emotion into an argument, be careful not to overdo it. Emotional appeals that are unfair or overly dramatic — known as fallacies (8f) — may serve only to cloud your readers' judgment and ultimately diminish your argument.

3 Shaping your appeal to your audience

As with appeals to credibility and logic, appealing to emotions is effective only insofar as it moves your particular audience. A student arguing for increased lighting in campus parking garages, for instance, might consider the emotions such a discussion might raise (fear of attack, for example, or anger at being subjected to danger), decide which emotions the intended audience would be most responsive to, and then look for descriptive and figurative language or appropriate visuals to carry out such an appeal.

In a leaflet to be distributed on campus or in an online notice to a student list, for example, the writer might describe the scene in a dimly lit garage as a student parks her car and then has to walk to an exit alone down shadowy corridors. Or she might make a short video in the garage and post it with accompanying music from a horror film.

In a proposal to the university administration, on the other hand, the writer might describe past attacks on students in campus garages and the negative publicity and criticism these provoked. For the administration, the writer might compare the lighting in the garages to high-risk gambling, arguing that increased lighting would lower the odds of future attacks.

Notice that shaping your appeal to a specific audience calls on you to consider very carefully the language and images you use. The student arguing for better lighting in campus parking garages would probably stick to standard academic English in a proposal to the university administration but might well want to use more informal language and social media when writing for students.

4 Visuals that make emotional appeals

Visuals that make emotional appeals can add substance to an argument. Consider, for example, the accompanying photograph of coffins returning from Iraq. This image is undeniably powerful — but exactly what

argument does it make? For some viewers, such photographs could make an antiwar argument. But others may well see this image as arguing for other ideas, such as patriotism or respect for the sacrifices made by military troops.

You need to ensure that the visuals you choose to enhance the emotional appeal of your argument will have the intended effect on readers. Test any photos or other visuals you are thinking of using with several potential readers. While images of human suffering can create a vivid emotional appeal, photographs that are profoundly disturbing can backfire, making some readers feel manipulated and thus angry at the person making the argument.

EXERCISE 9.9

Make a list of common human emotions that might be attached to each of the following topics, and suggest appropriate ways to appeal to those emotions in a specific audience you choose to address.

1. banning drinking on campus
2. airport security
3. birth control
4. health care reform
5. steroid use among athletes

EXERCISE 9.10

Using a working thesis you formulated for Exercise 9.2 or 9.3, make a list of the emotional appeals most appropriate to your topic and audience. Then spend ten to fifteen minutes brainstorming, looking for descriptive and figurative language as well as images to carry out the appeals.

9h Using sources in an argument

In constructing a written argument, it is often essential to use sources. The key to persuading people to accept your argument is good reasons; and even if your assignment doesn't specify that you must consult outside sources, they are often the most effective way of finding and establishing these reasons. Sources can help you to do the following:

• provide background information on your topic

• demonstrate your knowledge of the topic to readers

CONSIDERING DISABILITIES

Description

Remember that some members of your class or peer group may have difficulty seeing visual arguments or recognizing nuances of color or spacing. Be sure to provide verbal descriptions of visual images. In a video presentation, embed voice descriptions of the visual images for members of the class with visual impairments.

- cite authority and testimony in support of your thesis
- find opinions that differ from your own, which can help you sharpen your thinking, qualify your thesis if necessary, and demonstrate fairness to opposing arguments

For a thorough discussion of finding, gathering, and evaluating sources, see Chapters 10–15.

9i Organizing an argument

Once you have assembled good reasons and evidence in support of an argumentative thesis, you must organize your material to present the argument convincingly. Although there is no universally favored, one-size-fits-all organizational framework, you may find it useful to try one of the following patterns.

1 The classical system

In the classical system of argument — followed by ancient Greek and Roman orators and still in widespread use today, some twenty-five hundred years later — the speaker begins with an introduction, which states the thesis and then gives background information. Next come the different lines of argument and then the consideration of alternative arguments. A conclusion both sums up the argument and makes a final appeal to the audience. You can adapt this format to arguments in many genres and media.

1. Introduction
   - Gain readers' attention and interest.
   - Establish your qualifications to write about your topic.
   - Establish common ground with readers.
   - Demonstrate fairness.
   - State or imply your thesis.

2. Background
   - Present any necessary background information, including pertinent personal narrative.

3. Lines of argument
   - Present good reasons and evidence (including logical and emotional appeals) in support of your thesis.
   - Generally present reasons in order of importance.
   - Demonstrate ways your argument may be in readers' best interest.

4. Consideration of alternative arguments
   - Examine alternative points of view.
   - Note advantages and disadvantages of alternative views.
   - Explain why one view is better than others.

5. Conclusion
   - Summarize the argument if you choose.
   - Elaborate on the implication of your thesis.
   - Make clear what you want readers to think or do.
   - Make a strong ethical or emotional appeal.

2 Toulmin's elements of argument

This simplified and systematic form of argument developed by Stephen Toulmin (8e and 9c) can help you organize an argumentative essay:

1. Make your claim or (arguable statement).

   The federal government should ban smoking.

2. Qualify your claim, if necessary.

   The ban would be limited to public places.

3. Present good reasons to support your claim.

   Smoking causes serious diseases in smokers.

   Nonsmokers are endangered by secondhand smoke.

4. Explain the underlying assumptions that connect your claim and your reasons. Also provide additional explanations of any controversial assumptions.

ASSUMPTION	The Constitution was established to "promote the general welfare."
ASSUMPTION	Citizens are entitled to protection from harmful actions by others.
ADDITIONAL EXPLANATION	The federal government is supposed to serve the basic needs of the American people, including safeguarding their health.

5. Provide additional evidence to support your claim (facts, statistics, testimony, and other ethical, logical, or emotional appeals).

STATISTICS	Cite the incidence of deaths attributed to secondhand smoke.
FACTS	Cite lawsuits won against large tobacco companies.
FACTS	Cite bans on smoking already imposed in many municipalities and states.
AUTHORITY	Cite the surgeon general.
EMOTIONAL APPEAL	Show images or video of nonsmokers suffering from tobacco-related illnesses.

6. Acknowledge and respond to possible counterarguments.

COUNTER-ARGUMENTS	Smoking is legal. Smokers have rights, too.
RESPONSE	The suggested ban applies only to public places; smokers would be free to smoke in private. A nonsmoker's right not to have to inhale smoke in public places counts for more than a smoker's right to smoke.

7. State your conclusion in the strongest way possible.

9j Designing an argument

As you are well aware, most arguments today no longer appear in black and white or only in print form. Instead, most writers today create arguments that are carefully designed to make the best use of space, font style and type size, color, visuals, and technology. Chapter 23 provides extensive information on design issues, and it would be wise to consult that chapter as you design an argument. The following tips will get you thinking about how to produce and design an argument that will add to the ethical, logical, and emotional appeals you are making:

- Spend some time deciding on a distinct visual style for your argument, one that will appeal to your intended readers, set a clear voice or tone for your argument, and guide readers through your text.

- Check out any conventions that may be expected in the kind of argument you are writing. Look for examples of similar arguments, or ask your instructor for information about such conventions (2e).

- Consider the use of white space, titles, and headings and how each page will look. Choose titles, headings, and subheadings that will guide readers from point to point (23c). You may want to set off an especially important part of your argument (such as a list of essential evidence) in a box, carefully labeled.

- Make sure that your visual design is consistent. If you choose a particular color, font, or type style for a particular purpose, such as a second-level heading, make sure that you use the same color, font, or type style for that purpose throughout your paper.

- Be sure to choose readable fonts and font sizes (23b and c).

- Choose colors carefully, and make sure that you use color appropriately for the genre and medium.

- Place images close to the text they illustrate, and label each one clearly. Make sure that audio and video files appear in appropriate places and are identified for users.

- After you have a rough draft of your design, test it out on friends and classmates, asking them to describe how readable it is, how easy it is to follow, and what you need to change to make it more effective. Decide what adjustments you need to make — in format, spacing, alignment, use of color and fonts, and so on.

EXERCISE 9.11

Using the guidelines in this chapter, draft an argument in support of one of the working theses you formulated in Exercise 9.2 or 9.3.

THINKING CRITICALLY ABOUT CONSTRUCTING ARGUMENTS

Using the checklist on p. 187, analyze an argument you've recently written or the draft you wrote for Exercise 9.11. Decide what you need to do to revise your argument, and write out a brief plan for revision.

9k A student's argument essay

Student Writer

Teal Pfeifer

Asked to write an essay addressed to her classmates — one that makes an argumentative claim and supports it with good reasons and evidence — Teal Pfeifer argues that images in the media affect how women see themselves, and she offers a solution to the problem she has identified. Her essay has been annotated to point out the various parts of her argument as well as her use of good reasons, evidence, and appeals to logic and emotion.

bedfordstmartins.com/smhandbook
Student Writing > Argument Writing

Pfeifer 1

Teal Pfeifer

Professor Rashad

English 102

13 April 2010

Devastating Beauty

Collarbones, hipbones, cheekbones — so many bones. She looks
at the camera with sunken eyes, smiling, acting beautiful. Her dress is
Versace, or Gucci, or Dior, and it is revealing, revealing every bone and
joint in her thin, thin body. She looks fragile and beautiful, as if I could
snap her in two. I look at her and feel the soft cushion of flesh that
surrounds my own joints, my own shoulders and hips that are broad, my
own ribs surrounded by skin and muscle and fat. I am not nearly as fragile
or graceful or thin. I look away and wonder what kind of self-discipline it
takes to become beautiful like the model in my magazine.

By age seventeen a young woman has seen an average of 250,000
ads featuring a severely underweight woman whose body type is, for
the most part, unattainable by any means, including extreme ones such
as anorexia, bulimia, and drug use ("The Skinny"). The media promote
clothing, cigarettes, fragrances, and even food with images like these.
In a culture that has become increasingly visual, the images put out
for public consumption feature women that are a smaller size than ever
before. In 1950, the White Rock Mineral Water girl was 5'4" tall and
weighed 140 pounds; now she is 5'10" tall and weighs only 110 pounds,
signifying the growing deviation between the weight of models and that
of the normal female population (Pipher 184).

This media phenomenon has had a major effect on the female
population as a whole, both young and old. Five to ten million women
in America today suffer from an eating disorder related to poor self-
image, and yet advertisements continue to prey on insecurities fueled

---

Title uses
play on
words to
pique interest

Opening
uses emotional
appeals and
tries to estab-
lish common
ground with
readers

Presents
background
information
on the
problem
and cites
sources

Introduces
problem:
ads encour-
age women's
poor body
image

Pfeifer 2

by a woman's desire to be thin. Current research shows that "80 percent of American women are dissatisfied with their appearance" and that "45 percent of those are on a diet on any given day" ("Statistics"). Yet even the most stringent dieting will generally fail to create the paper-thin body so valued in the media, and continuing efforts to do so can lead to serious psychological problems such as depression.

Good reason for thesis: stringent dieting can cause psychological problems

While many women express dissatisfaction with their bodies, they are not the only victims of the emaciated images so frequently presented to them. Young girls are equally affected by these images, if not more so. Eighty percent of girls under age ten have already been on a diet and expressed the desire to be thinner and more beautiful (*Slim Hopes*). Thus, from a young age, beauty is equated with a specific size. The message girls get is an insidious one: in order to be your best self, you should wear size 0 or 1. The pressure only grows more intense as girls grow up. According to results from the Kaiser Family Foundation Survey "Reflections of Girls in the Media," 16 percent of ten- to seventeen-year-old girls reported that they had dieted or exercised to look like a TV character. Yet two-thirds of teenage girls acknowledged that these thin characters were not an accurate reflection of "real life" (qtd. in Dittrich, "Children").

Provides statistical evidence that problem extends across age groups

Uses logical appeals

It is tragic to see so much of the American population obsessed with weight and reaching an ideal that is, for the most part, ultimately unattainable. Equally troubling is the role magazines play in feeding this obsession. When a researcher asked female students from Stanford University to flip through several magazines containing images of glamorized, super-thin models (see Fig. 1), 68 percent of the women felt significantly worse about themselves after viewing the magazine models (qtd. in Dittrich, "Media"). Another study showed that looking at models on a long-term basis leads to stress, depression, guilt, and lowered self-worth (qtd. in Dittrich, "Media"). As Naomi Wolfe points out in *The Beauty Myth*,

Good reason for thesis: magazines feed obsession with dieting

Backs up reasons with research and expert opinion

Pfeifer 3

Fig. 1. Young woman reading magazine. Personal
photograph by author.

thinking obsessively about fat and dieting has actually been shown to
change thought patterns and brain chemistry.

*Considers and
rejects alter-
native solu-
tions*

How do we reject images that are so harmful to the women and
young girls who view them? Legislation regarding what can be printed
and distributed is not an option because of First Amendment rights.
Equally untenable is the idea of appealing to the industries that hire
emaciated models. As long as the beauty and clothing industries are
making a profit from the physically insecure girls and women who view
their ads, nothing will change.

*States working
thesis: a boy-
cott would
effectively
solve problem*

What, however, might happen if those females stopped buying the
magazines that print such destructive images? A boycott is the most
effective way to rid the print medium of emaciated models and eliminate
the harmful effects they cause. If women stopped buying magazines that
target them with such harmful advertising, magazines would be forced

to change the kinds of ads they print. Such a boycott would send a clear message: women and girls reject the victimization that takes place every time they look at a skeletally thin model and then feel worse about themselves. Consumers can ultimately control what is put on the market: if we don't buy, funding for such ads will dry up fast.

In the past, boycotts have been effective tools for social change. Rosa Parks, often identified as the mother of the modern-day civil rights movement, played a pivotal role in the Montgomery bus boycott in December 1955. When Parks refused to give up her seat to a white bus rider, she was arrested, and this incident inspired the boycott. For more than a year, the vast majority of African Americans in Montgomery chose to walk instead of ride the buses. Many of them were terrorized or harassed, but the boycott was eventually successful: segregation on buses was declared illegal by the U.S. Supreme Court.

Between 1965 and 1973, Cesar Chavez also used boycotts successfully to change wage policies and working conditions for millions of Mexicans and Mexican Americans who were being exploited by growers of grapes and lettuce. In his boycott efforts, Chavez moved on two fronts simultaneously: he asked the workers to withhold their labor, and he asked consumers to refrain from purchasing table grapes (and later, lettuce) in order to show their support for the workers. In this situation, not only did the boycott force an industry to improve existing conditions, but it also made the public aware of pressing labor issues. Thus a bond was formed between the workers and the community their labor was benefiting.

As a society, we have much to learn from boycotts of the past, and their lessons can help us confront contemporary social ills. As I have shown, body-image dissatisfaction and eating disorders are rising at an alarming rate among young girls and women in American society. This growing desire for an unrealistically thin body affects our minds and our

Good reason: boycotts have been effective

Presents a precedent/ example as evidence

Presents a second precedent/ example as evidence

Appeals directly to audience by using "we" in conclusion

Pfeifer 5

Reinforces
severity of
problem and
appeals to
emotion

spirits, especially when we are pummeled dozens of times a day with
glamorized images of emaciated and unhealthy women. The resulting
anorexia and bulimia that women suffer from are not only diseases
that can be cured; they are also ones that can be prevented — if women
will take a solid stand against such supporting advertisements and the
magazines that publish them. This is where power lies — in the hands

Restates
thesis as
a call to
action

of those who hand over the dollars that support the glorification of
unhealthy and unrealistic bodies. It is our choice to exert this power and
to reject magazines that promote such images.

Pfeifer 6

Works Cited

Dittrich, Liz. "About-Face Facts on the Children and the Media."
    About-Face. About-Face, 1996–2010. Web. 10 Mar. 2010.
————. "About-Face Facts on the Media." *About-Face*. About-Face,
    1996–2010. Web. 10 Mar. 2010.
Pipher, Mary. *Reviving Ophelia: Saving the Selves of Adolescent Girls*. New
    York: Ballantine, 1994. Print.
"The Skinny on Media and Weight." *Common Sense Media*. Common
    Sense Media Inc., 27 Sept. 2005. Web. 15 Mar. 2010.
Slim Hopes. Dir. Sut Jhally. Prod. Jean Kilbourne. Media Education
    Foundation, 1995. Videocassette.
"Statistics." *National Eating Disorders Association*. National Eating
    Disorders Association, 2005. Web. 14 Mar. 2010.
Wolfe, Naomi. *The Beauty Myth*. New York: Harper, 2002. Print.
Young woman reading magazine. Personal photograph by author.
    14 Mar. 2010.

RESEARCH AND DOCUMENTATION

10 Preparing for a Research Project

Your employer asks you to recommend the best software for a particular project. You want to plan a week at the beach during your spring break. Your instructor assigns a term paper about an early-twentieth-century jazz musician. You need to find an inexpensive source for your dog's heartworm medication. Each of these situations calls for research, for examining various kinds of sources. Once you begin to think about it, you'll find that many of your day-to-day activities call for research. It's no exaggeration to say that almost everyone today is a researcher.

Preparing to begin your research means taking a long look at what you already know, the best way to proceed, and the amount of time you have to find out what you need to know. For success in college and beyond, you need to understand how to start the process of academic research.

10a Considering the research process

If you have little experience doing research for academic projects, you may feel some anxiety about a major research assignment. But chances are you have more experience as a researcher than you realize. Techniques you may have used to find out about a subject that interests you — whether a baseball player's statistics, information about a new comic, or the best places to get coffee before class — can also serve you well in academic research.

- *You already know something about doing research.* You act as a researcher whenever you try to find out more about anything that interests you. If you are researching coffee options, you may look up information online about the trade practices of different coffee suppliers or talk with friends about coffee shops with the best atmosphere or the lowest prices; you may also perform taste-tests at all the coffee shops near your school to see which coffee you like best.

- *Research projects that interest you are easier and more enjoyable to complete.* Researchers usually seek out information and opinions for a reason. Your main purpose in college research may be to fulfill an assignment, but if you can also find a purpose with which you make a personal connection, your research task will be more rewarding.

- *Research rarely progresses in a neat line from start to finish.* When you begin any research, you don't know exactly what you will discover. You begin with a question that you may or may not be able to answer. Then your research may lead you to other sources. This additional research may narrow your idea — or may cause you to change directions entirely. If you set out to find information on the development of the multiplayer online game *World of Warcraft* and end up interested in how players work together to succeed in the game, your new purpose will require you to take another look at the kind of research you need to do.

- *Good research can make you a genuine expert.* If you approach your research seriously and follow all the leads that you can, you may eventually become an expert on a topic that interests you — a Korean soap opera, homeopathic allergy treatments, or low-cost early childhood services in your neighborhood.

College research may range from a couple of hours spent gathering background information on a topic for a brief essay to weeks or months of full-scale exploration for a term project. Chapters 10–15 provide guidelines to help you with research for writing. In addition, these chapters show examples of work by David Craig, a student whose complete research essay appears in Chapter 16.

10b Analyzing the assignment

For an introductory writing course, David Craig received the following assignment:

> Choose a subject of interest to you, and use it as the basis for a research essay of approximately 2,500 words that makes and substantiates a claim. You should use a minimum of five sources, including at least three scholarly sources.

1 The requirements and limits of the assignment

Before you begin any research assignment, make sure you understand the requirements and limits of the assignment.

TALKING THE TALK

Reaching an audience

"Isn't my audience just my teacher?" To write effectively, you must think of your writing as more than just an assignment you go through to get a grade. Recognize that you have something to say—and that in order to get others to pay attention, you have to think about who they are and how to reach them. Of course, your instructor is part of your audience. But who else will be interested in your topic and the unique perspective you bring to it? What does that audience need from you?

- How many sources should you use?
- Does your instructor require certain kinds of sources? If so, what kinds?
- Will you use images, sound, or video in your assignment?
- Should you work independently or collaborate with others on the project?
- What kind of documentation style does your instructor want you to use? (See Chapters 16–19.)
- Do you understand what your instructor expects you to do? If not, ask for clarification.

In response to questions, David Craig's instructor clarified that the audience for the project would be members of the writing class.

2 The rhetorical situation of the research project

Be sure to consider the rhetorical situation of any research project. Here are detailed elements of the rhetorical situation to think about.

Purpose

- Do you have a choice about the purpose of your assignment? If you can choose the purpose, what would you like to accomplish?
- What do you need to do in this project—explain a situation? weigh opposing viewpoints and make a claim about which is correct? convince the audience to do something? explore the causes or effects

of a particular phenomenon? Your purpose will affect the kinds of sources you need to find.

- If you have been assigned a specific research project, keep in mind the key words in that assignment. Does the assignment ask that you *describe, survey, analyze, persuade, explain, classify, compare,* or *contrast?* What do such words mean in this field (2b)?

Audience

- Who will be the audience for your research project (2d)?
- Who will be interested in the information you gather, and why? What will they want to know? What will they already know?
- What do you know about their backgrounds? What assumptions might they hold about the topic?
- If you will post your research online, how will that change your audience?
- What response do you want to elicit from them?
- What kinds of evidence will you need to convince them?
- What will your instructor expect?

Rhetorical stance

What is your attitude toward your topic? Are you curious about it? critical of it? Do you like it? dislike it? find it confusing? What influences have shaped your stance? (For more about rhetorical stance, see 2c2.)

Scope

How many and what kind(s) of sources should you use? What kind(s) of visuals — charts, maps, photographs, and so on — will you need to include? Will you also include sound or video clips? Will you do any field research — interviewing, surveying, or observing? (For more on kinds of sources, see 11a.)

Length

How long is your project supposed to be? The amount of research and writing time you will need for a five-page essay differs markedly from that for a fifteen-page essay.

Sunday	Monday	Tuesday	Wednesday	Thursday	Friday	Saturday
	Get assignment. **1**	Analyze assignment; choose topic. **2**	◎ **3**	Develop research question & hypothesis. **4**	**5**	Plan search strategy **6**
Set up research log. **7**	Find & evaluate sources; read, analyze, & take notes. **8**	**9**	Draft working thesis **10**	Locate or develop visuals. **11**	Start working bibliography. ○ **12**	Write explicit thesis; plan writing. **13**
Write first draft. **14**	**15**	**16**	**17**	Get reviewer opinions. Do more research if necessary. **18**	**19**	◑ **20**
Revise draft. **21**	**22**	**23**	Prepare list of works cited. **24**	**25**	Revise draft again. Double-check sources. **26**	○ **27**
Edit, spell check, & proof-read. **28**	FINAL PROJECT DUE. **29**	**30**	**31**			

Deadlines

When is the project due? Are any preliminary materials—a working bibliography, a thesis, an outline, a first draft—due before this date? Create a schedule for your project (a sample schedule is shown here).

3 The topic

If your assignment, like David Craig's, does not specify a topic, consider the following questions:

- What subjects do you already know something about? Which of them would you like to explore more fully?

- What subjects do you care about? What might you like to become an expert on?

- What subjects evoke a strong reaction from you — intense puzzlement, skepticism, affirmation?

Be sure to get responses about your possible topic from your instructor, classmates, and friends. Ask them whether they would be interested in reading about the topic, whether it seems manageable, and whether they know of any good sources for information on the topic.

David Craig hit on his topic one evening after spending several hours sending text messages. As usual, he exchanged texts and instant messages (IMs) with several friends. Like most of the people his age that he knew, David had considered texting and instant messaging (IMing) a regular part of his writing experience for years, so he expected his classmates to find the subject intriguing.

> For David Craig's research essay, see 16e.

EXERCISE 10.1

Using the questions in 10b3, come up with at least two topics you would like to carry out research on. Then write a brief response to some key questions about each topic: How much information do you think is available on this topic? What sources on this topic do you know about or have access to? Who would know about this topic — historians, doctors, filmmakers, psychologists, others?

10c Narrowing a topic

Any topic you choose to research must be manageable — it must suit the scope, audience, length, and time limits of your assignment. Making a topic manageable often requires narrowing it, but you may also need to find a particular slant and look for a question to guide your research. To arrive at such a question, you might first generate a series of questions about your topic. You can then evaluate them and choose one or two that are both interesting and manageable.

David Craig knew that he had to zero in on some aspect of texting or IMing and take a position on it. He considered researching "the prevalence of IMing worldwide," but he decided that was too vague and unmanageable. He spoke with two instructors about his topic, and both of them criticized messaging for its negative influence on students' writing. Intrigued by this reaction, David decided to focus on messaging language and its harmful effects on youth literacy.

10d Moving from research question to hypothesis

The result of the narrowing process is a research question that can be tentatively answered by a hypothesis, a statement of what you anticipate your research will show. Like a working thesis (3c, 9c), a hypothesis must be manageable, interesting, and specific. In addition, it must be arguable, a debatable proposition that you can prove or disprove with a reasonable amount of research evidence (9b). For example, a statement like this one is not arguable since it merely states a widely known fact: "Senator Joseph McCarthy attracted great attention with his anti-Communist crusade during the 1950s." On the other hand, this statement is an arguable hypothesis because evidence for or against it can be found: "Roy Cohn's biased research while he was an assistant to Senator Joseph McCarthy was partially responsible for McCarthy's anti-Communist crusade."

In moving from a general topic of interest, such as Senator Joseph McCarthy's anti-Communist crusade of the 1950s, to a useful hypothesis, such as the one in the previous paragraph, you first narrow the topic to a single manageable issue: Roy Cohn's role in the crusade, for instance. After background reading, you then raise a question about that issue ("To what extent did Cohn's research contribute to McCarthy's crusade?") and devise a possible answer, your hypothesis.

Here is how David Craig moved from general topic to hypothesis:

TOPIC	Messaging
NARROWED TOPIC	The language of messaging
ISSUE	The effect of messaging on youth literacy
RESEARCH QUESTION	How has the popularity of messaging affected literacy among today's youth?
HYPOTHESIS	Messaging seems to have a negative influence on the writing skills of young people.

David's hypothesis, which tentatively answers his research question, is precise enough to be supported or challenged by a manageable amount of research.

10e Determining what you know

Once you have formulated a hypothesis, determine what you already know about your topic. Here are some strategies for doing so:

- *Brainstorming.* Take five minutes to list everything you think of or wonder about your hypothesis (3a). You may find it helpful to do this with a group with other students.

- *Freewriting about your hypothesis.* For five minutes, write about every reason for believing your hypothesis is true. Then for another five minutes, write down every argument you can think of, no matter how weak, that someone opposed to your hypothesis might make.

- *Freewriting about your audience.* Write for five minutes about your readers, including your instructor. What do you think they currently believe about your topic? What sorts of evidence will convince them to accept your hypothesis? What sorts of sources will they respect?

- *Tapping your memory for sources.* List everything you can remember about *where* you learned about your topic: Web sites, email, books, magazines, courses, conversations, television. What you know comes from somewhere, and that "somewhere" can serve as a starting point for research.

EXERCISE 10.2

Using the tips provided in 10e, write down as much as you can about one of the topics you identified in Exercise 10.1. Then take some time to reread your notes, and jot down the questions you still need to answer as well as the sources you need to find.

10f Making a preliminary research plan

Once you've considered what you already know about your topic, you can develop a research plan. To do so, answer the following questions:

- What kinds of sources (books, journal articles, databases, Web sites, government documents, specialized reference works, images, videos, and so on) will you need to consult? How many sources should you consult? (For more on different kinds of sources, see Chapter 11.)

- How current do your sources need to be? (For topical issues, especially those related to science, current sources are usually most important. For historical subjects, older sources may offer the best information.)

- How can you determine the location and availability of the kinds of sources you need?

- Do you need to consult sources contemporary with an event or a person's life? If so, how will you get access to those sources?

One goal of your research plan is to begin building a strong working bibliography (see 12b). Carrying out systematic research and keeping careful notes on your sources will make developing your works-cited list or bibliography (Chapters 16–19) easier later on.

10g Keeping a research log

Keeping a research log will make the job of writing and documenting your sources more efficient and accurate. You can use your log to jot down ideas about your topic and possible sources — and to keep track of print and online materials. Whenever you record an online source in your log, include the URL.

Here are a few guidelines for setting up an electronic research log:

1. Create a new folder, and label it with a name that will be easy to identify, such as *Research Log for Project on Messaging*.

2. Within this folder, create subfolders that will help you manage your project. These might include *Project Deadlines, Notes on Hypothesis and Thesis, Working Bibliography, Background Information, Organizational Plan, Visuals, Drafts*, and so on.

You might prefer to begin a blog for your research project. You can use it to record your thoughts on the reading you are doing and, especially, add links from there to Web sites, documents, and articles you have found online. You might even find bloggers who are writing about your topic. If so, check them out carefully before citing them as sources for your research project. (For more on blogs, see 21b.)

If you prefer not to keep an electronic research log, set up a binder with dividers similar to the subfolders listed above. Whether your log is electronic or not, be sure to carefully distinguish the notes and comments you make from quoted passages you record.

CONSIDERING DISABILITIES

Dictation

If you have difficulty taking notes either on a computer or in a notebook, consider dictating your notes. You might dictate into a handheld recorder for later playback, into a word processor with voice-recognition capability, or into a phone for podcasting on a Web site.

10h Moving from hypothesis to working thesis

As you gather information and begin reading and evaluating sources, you will probably refine your research question and change your hypothesis significantly. Only after you have explored your hypothesis, tested it, and sharpened it by reading, writing, and talking with others does it become a working thesis.

David Craig, for instance, did quite a bit of research on messaging language, youth literacy, and the possible connection between the two. The more he read, the more he felt that the hypothesis suggested by his discussion with instructors—that messaging had contributed to a decline in youth literacy—did not hold up. Thus, he shifted his attention to the positive effects of texting and IMing on communication skills and developed the following working thesis: "Although some educators criticize messaging, it may aid literacy by encouraging young people to use words and to write—even if messaging requires a different kind of writing."

> For David Craig's research essay, see 16e.

In doing your own research, you may find that your interest shifts, that a whole line of inquiry is unproductive, or that your hypothesis is simply wrong. In each case, the process of research pushes you to learn more about your hypothesis, to make it more precise, to become an expert on your topic.

THINKING CRITICALLY ABOUT YOUR OWN RESEARCH

If you have done research for an essay or research project before, go back and evaluate the work you did as a researcher and as a writer in light of the principles developed in this chapter. What was the purpose of the research? Who was your audience? How did you narrow and focus your topic? What kinds of sources did you use? Did you use a research log? What about your research and your essay pleased you most? What pleased you least? What would you do differently if you were to revise the essay now?

Conducting Research

How would you find out where to get the best coffee in town? What would be the best sources for a Web project on a 1930s film star? Where would you get the most recent information about the economic impact of the 2010 Gulf oil spill? If you wanted to gauge the public reaction to Nixon's trip to China in 1972, where would you look first? When you need to answer questions like these, you conduct research.

Whether you are researching Heisenberg's uncertainty principle or haircuts, you need to be familiar with the kinds of sources you are likely to use, the searches you are likely to perform, and the three main types of research you will most often be doing: library, Internet, and field research.

11a Differentiating kinds of sources

Sources can include data from interviews and surveys, books and articles in print and online, Web sites, film, video, audio, images, and more. Consider these important differences among sources.

1 Primary and secondary sources

Primary sources provide firsthand knowledge; secondary sources report on or analyze the research of others. Primary sources are basic sources of raw information, including your own field research; films, works of art, or other objects you examine; literary works you read; and eyewitness accounts, photographs, news reports, and historical documents (such as letters and speeches). Secondary sources are descriptions or interpretations of primary sources, such as researchers' reports, reviews, biographies, and encyclopedia articles. Often what constitutes a primary or secondary source depends on the purpose of your research. A critic's review of a film, for instance, serves as a secondary source if you are writing about the film but as a primary source if you are studying the critic's writing.

Most research projects draw on both primary and secondary sources. A research-based essay on

230

the effects of steroid use on Major League Baseball, for example, might draw on primary sources, such as the players' testimony to Congress, as well as secondary sources, such as articles or books by baseball experts.

2 Scholarly and popular sources

While nonacademic sources like magazines and personal Web sites can help you get started on a research project, you will usually want to depend more heavily on authorities in a field, whose work generally appears in scholarly journals in print or online. The following list will help you distinguish scholarly and popular sources:

SCHOLARLY

POPULAR

SCHOLARLY	POPULAR
Title often contains the word *Journal*	*Journal* usually does not appear in title
Source available mainly through libraries and library databases	Source generally available outside of libraries (at newsstands or from a home Internet connection)
Few commercial advertisements	Many advertisements
Authors identified with academic credentials	Authors are usually journalists or reporters hired by the publication, not academics or experts
Summary or abstract appears on first page of article; articles are fairly long	No summary or abstract; articles are fairly short
Articles cite sources and provide bibliographies	Articles may include quotations but do not cite sources or provide bibliographies

3 Older and more current sources

Most projects can benefit from both older, historical sources and more current ones. Some older sources are classics in their fields, essential for understanding the scholarship that follows them. Others are simply dated, though even these works can be useful to researchers who want to see what people wrote and read about a topic in the past. Depending on your purpose, you may rely primarily on recent sources (for example, if you are writing about a new scientific discovery), primarily on historical sources (for instance, if your project discusses a nineteenth-century industrial accident), or on a mixture of both. Whether a source appeared hundreds of years ago or this morning, evaluate it carefully to determine how useful it will be for you (Chapter 12).

11b Using the library to get started

Even when you have a general idea of what kinds of sources exist and which kinds you need for your research project, you still have to locate these sources. Many beginning researchers are tempted to assume that all the information they could possibly need is readily available on the Internet from a home connection. However, it is a good idea to begin almost any research project with the sources available in your college library.

1 Reference librarians

You might start by getting to know one particularly valuable resource, your library staff — especially reference librarians. You can make an appointment to talk with a librarian about your research project and get specific recommendations about databases and other helpful places to begin your research. In addition, many libraries have online chat environments where students can ask questions about their research and have them answered, in real time, by a reference librarian. To get the most helpful advice, whether online or in person, pose *specific* questions — not "Where can I find information about computers?" but "Where can I find information on the history of messaging technologies?" If you are having difficulty asking precise questions, you probably need to do some background research on your topic and formulate a sharper hypothesis. A librarian may be helpful in this regard as well.

CONSIDERING DISABILITIES

Web site accessibility

While the Americans with Disabilities Act stipulates that all government Web sites must be accessible to those with disabilities, these rules have now been expanded to cover educational and other Web sites. If you encounter sites that are not accessible to you, ask a reference librarian to help you identify similar sites that may be more accessible. Also consider clicking on the CONTACT US button, if there is one, and letting the sponsors of the site know that some potential users can't get ready access to the information.

---

2 Catalogs and databases

Your library's computers hold many resources not available on the Web or not accessible to students except through the library's system. One of these resources is the library's own catalog of books and other holdings, but most college libraries also subscribe to a large number of databases—electronic collections of information, such as indexes to journal and magazine articles, texts of news stories and legal cases, lists of sources on particular topics, and compilations of statistics—that students can access for free. Many of these databases have been screened or compiled by editors, librarians, or other scholars. Your library may also have metasearch software that allows you to search several databases at once.

3 Reference works

Consulting general reference works is another good way to get started on a research project. These works are especially helpful for getting an overview of a topic, identifying subtopics, finding more specialized sources, and identifying useful keywords for electronic searches.

ENCYCLOPEDIAS

For general background on a subject, encyclopedias are a good place to begin, particularly because many include bibliographies that can point you to more specialized sources. A librarian can direct you to such reference works. Remember that encyclopedias will serve as a place to start your research—not as major sources for a research project.

TALKING THE TALK

Wikis as sources

"Why doesn't my instructor want me to use Wikipedia as a source?" Wikis are sites that users can add to and edit as they see fit; as a result, their contents are not always completely reliable for research. It's true that Wikipedia, a hugely popular site, has such a large and enthusiastic audience that editors and users are likely to catch mistakes and remove deliberately false information fairly quickly. But you can never be certain that a wiki entry has not been tampered with. The best advice is to use wikis as sources for preliminary research and then to make sure that you double-check any information you find there.

Specialized encyclopedias, on subjects from ancient history to world drama, provide more detailed articles by authorities in the field as well as extensive bibliographies.

BIOGRAPHICAL RESOURCES

The lives and historical settings of famous people are the topics of biographical dictionaries and indexes. Among the many bibliographical volumes available are the *African American Biographical Database, American Men and Women of Science, Contemporary Authors, Dictionary of American Biography, Dictionary of National Biography,* and *Who's Who.*

BIBLIOGRAPHIES

Bibliographies are collections of resources available on a subject—for example, Shakespeare or World War II. Bibliographies may be databases or bound collections, and they may list books alone, both books and articles, or media such as film or video. A bibliography may simply list or describe each resource it includes, or it may include analysis of the resources.

ALMANACS, YEARBOOKS, AND ATLASES

Almanacs and yearbooks contain statistical information and data on current events: *Facts on File Yearbook, Gallup Poll, Information Please Almanac, Statistical Abstracts of the United States* from the U.S. Census Bureau, and *World Almanac* are just a few options. An atlas includes maps and other geographical data.

11c Finding library resources

The library is one of a researcher's best friends, especially in an age of electronic communication. Your college library houses a great number of print materials and gives you access to electronic catalogs, indexes, and databases. But the library may seem daunting to you, especially on your first visit. Experienced student researchers will tell you that the best way to make the library a friend is to get to know it: a good starting place is its Web site, where you can find useful information, including its hours of operation, its floor plan, its collections, and so on; many libraries also have a virtual tour and other tutorials on their Web sites that give you a first-rate introduction to the available resources.

1 Search options

The most important tools your library offers are its online catalog and databases. Searching these tools will always be easier and more efficient if you use carefully chosen words to limit the scope of your research.

Subject word searching

Catalogs and databases usually index their contents not only by author and title, but also by subject headings — standardized words and phrases used to classify the subject matter of books and articles. (For books, most U.S. academic libraries use the *Library of Congress Subject Headings*, or LCSH, for this purpose.) When you search the catalog by subject, you need to use the exact subject words.

Keyword searching

Searches using keywords, on the other hand, make use of the computer's ability to look for any term in any field of the electronic record, including not just subject but also author, title, series, and notes. In article databases, a keyword search will look in abstracts and summaries of articles as well. Keyword searching is less restrictive, but it requires you to put some thought into choosing your search terms in order to get the best results.

Advanced searching

Many library catalogs and database search engines offer advanced search options (sometimes on a separate page) to help you combine keywords,

libr

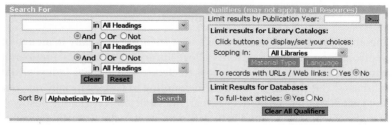

Advanced search page from a library catalog that incorporates Boolean operators

search for an exact phrase, or exclude items containing particular key-words. Often they limit your search in other ways as well, such as by date, language, country of origin, or location of the keyword within a site.

Many catalogs and databases offer a search option using the Boolean operators AND, OR, and NOT, and some allow you to use parentheses to refine your search or wildcards to expand it. Note that much Boolean decision making is done for you when you use an advanced search option (as on the advanced search page shown above). Note, too, that search engines vary in the exact terms and symbols they use to refine searches, so check before you search.

- AND *limits your search.* If you enter the terms *messaging* AND *language* AND *literacy*, the search engine will retrieve only those items that contain *all* the terms. Some search engines use a plus sign $(+)$ instead of AND.

- OR *expands your search.* If you enter the terms *messaging* OR *language*, the computer will retrieve every item that contains the term *messaging* and every item that contains the term *language*.

- NOT *limits your search.* If you enter the terms *messaging* NOT *language*, the search engine will retrieve every item that contains *messaging* except those that also contain the term *language*. Some search engines use a minus sign $(-)$ or AND NOT instead of NOT.

- *Parentheses customize your search.* Entering *messaging* AND (*literacy* OR *linguistics*), for example, will locate items that mention either of those terms in connection with messaging.

- *Wildcards expand your search.* Use a wildcard, usually an asterisk (*) or a question mark (?), to find related words that begin with the same letters. Entering *messag** will locate *message, messages,* and *messaging.*

- *Quotation marks narrow your search.* Most search engines interpret words within quotation marks as a phrase that must appear with the words in that exact order.

In one of his searches, David Craig used two keywords, *messaging* AND *linguistics*. He sometimes narrowed his search further by adding a third term, AND *students* or AND *literacy*. Since search engines don't pick up synonyms automatically, he might also have used the terms *messenger, language,* and *youth.*

For David Craig's research essay, see 16e.

2 Books

The library catalog lists all the library's books.

Catalog information

Library catalogs follow a standard pattern of organization, with each holding identified by three kinds of entries: one headed by the *author's name,* one by the *title,* and one or (usually) more by the *subject.* If you can't find a particular source under any of these headings, you can search the catalog by using a combination of subject headings and keywords. Such searches may turn up other useful titles as well.

Following are a search page, a page of results for noted linguist and author David Crystal, and a catalog entry for one of his books from a university library catalog. Many electronic catalogs indicate whether a book

Library catalog search page

Total number of items in catalog for author David Crystal

Items on this catalog page

Call number

Location

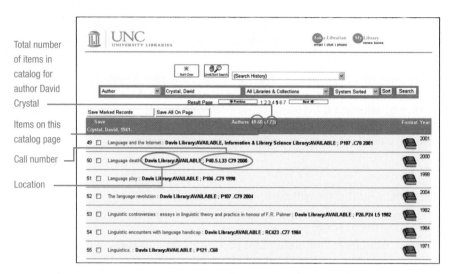

Results for author search in library catalog database

has been checked out and, if so, when it is due to be returned. Sometimes you must click on a link to check the availability of the book.

Catalog entries for books list not only the author, title, subject, and publication information but also a call number that indicates how the book is classified and where it is shelved. Like many online catalogs, the catalog in the preceding examples allows you to save the information about the book while you continue searching and then retrieve the call numbers for all of the books you want to find in one list. Once you have the call number for a book, look for a library map or shelving plan to tell you where the book is housed. Take the time to browse through the books near the call number you are looking for. Often you will find other books related to your topic in the immediate area.

Book indexes

Indexes can help you quickly locate complete bibliographic information on a book when you know only one piece of it—the author's last name, perhaps, or the title. Indexes such as *Books in Print, Cumulative Book Index,* and the electronic database WorldCat can also alert you to other

Catalog entry for a book chosen from author search

works by a particular author or on a particular subject. If you are looking for an older book, you may find the information you need in print
volumes rather than in an electronic database.

Review indexes

A review index will help you find reviews of books you are interested
in so that you can check the relevance of a source or get a thumbnail
sketch of its contents before you track it down. Review indexes include
Annual Bibliography of English Language and Literature (*ABELL*),
ARBA Online, *Book Review Digest, Book Review Index* (print only),
and *International Bibliography of Book Reviews.* For reviews more
than ten years old, you will generally need to consult the print version
of the index.

3 **Periodical articles**

Titles of periodicals held by a library appear in its catalog, but the titles of individual articles do not. To find the contents of periodicals, you will need to use an index source.

Periodical indexes

Periodical indexes are databases or print volumes that hold information about articles published in newspapers, magazines, and scholarly journals. Different indexes cover different groups of periodicals; articles written before 1990 may be indexed only in a print volume. Ask a reference librarian for guidance about the most likely index for the subject of your research.

Electronic periodical indexes come in different forms, with some offering the full text of articles and some offering abstracts (short summaries) of the articles. Be sure not to confuse an abstract with a complete article. Full-text databases can be extremely convenient—you can read and print out articles directly from the computer, without the extra step of tracking down the periodical in question. However, don't limit yourself to full-text databases, which may not contain graphics and images that appeared in the print version of the periodical—and which may not include the sources that would benefit your research most. Take advantage of databases that offer abstracts, which give you an overview of the article's contents that can help you decide whether you need to spend time finding and reading the full text.

GENERAL AND SPECIALIZED INDEXES

General indexes of periodicals list articles from general-interest magazines (such as *Newsweek*), newspapers, and perhaps some scholarly journals. General indexes are useful for finding current sources on a topic. Specialized indexes, which tend to include mainly scholarly periodicals, may focus on one discipline (as the education index ERIC does) or on a group of related disciplines (as Social Sciences Abstracts does). Ask a reference librarian for help choosing an appropriate index for your topic and purpose.

Locating indexed periodical articles

To locate an indexed article that seems promising for your research project, you can check the library catalog to see whether the periodical is available electronically and, if so, whether your library has access to it. Using the library computer network for access can help you avoid paying to view the text of the article that is available online only for subscribers or for a fee.

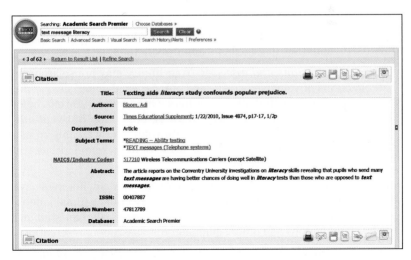

Results of a database search

Article page with abstract

If the periodical is not available electronically (some scholarly journals, for example, are not), the library catalog also will tell you whether a print version is available in your library's periodicals room. This room probably has recent issues of hundreds or even thousands of newspapers, magazines, and scholarly journals, and it may also contain bound volumes of past issues and microfilm copies of older newspapers.

David Craig's research on instant messaging required research on educators' opinions on this technology's effect on youth literacy. His search on the keywords *text message* and *literacy* gave him the results you see on p. 241. David clicked on an entry that looked like it might pertain to his subject. He was able to read an abstract, and, based on the summary, David thought the article would be helpful. He found the full text in his library's journals collection. Full articles are sometimes accessible in online databases, but you may have to consult your library's periodicals section for a hard copy of the article.

For David Craig's research essay, see 16e.

4 Bibliographies

Look at any bibliographies (lists of sources) in books or articles you are using for your research; they can lead you to other valuable resources. In addition, check with a reference librarian to find out whether your library has more extensive bibliographies devoted to the area of your research.

5 Other library resources

In addition to books and periodicals, libraries give you access to many other useful materials that might be appropriate for your research.

- *Special collections and archives.* Your library may house archives (collections of valuable papers) and other special materials that are often available to student researchers. One student, for example, learned that her university owned a vast collection of twentieth-century posters. With help from a librarian, she was able to use some of these posters as primary sources for her research project on German culture after World War II.

- *Audio, video, multimedia, and art collections.* Many libraries have areas devoted to media and art, where they collect films, videos, paintings, and sound recordings. Some libraries also let students check out laptops and other equipment for classroom presentations.

- *Government documents.* Many libraries have collections of historical documents produced by local or state government offices. Check with a librarian if government publications would be useful sources for your topic. You can also look at the online version of the U.S. Government Printing Office, known as GPO Access, for electronic versions of government publications from the past decade or so.

- *Interlibrary loans.* To borrow books, videos, or audio materials from another library, use an interlibrary loan. You can also request copies of journal articles from other libraries. Some loans—especially of books—can take time, so plan ahead.

11d Conducting Internet research

The Internet is many college students' favorite way of accessing information, and it's true that much information—including authoritative sources identical to those your library provides—can be found online, sometimes for free. However, information in library databases comes from identifiable and professionally edited sources; because no one is responsible for regulating information on the Web, you need to take special care to find out which information online is reliable and which is not. (See Chapter 12 for more on evaluating sources.)

1 Internet searches

Most search tools allow keyword searches as well as subject directory searches (11c1). With a search engine, you simply type in keywords and get results; some metasearch tools use several search engines at once and compile their findings. In a subject directory, on the other hand, you start with general categories and then click on increasingly narrow subcategories. At any point, you can switch to a keyword search to look for specific terms and topics.

If you decide to use a keyword search in an Internet search engine, you will need to choose keywords carefully in order to get a reasonable number of hits. For example, if you're searching for information on legal issues regarding the Internet and enter *Internet* and *law* as keywords in a Google search, you will get over three million possible sources—a number too huge to be helpful for a researcher. To be useful, then, the keywords you choose—names, titles, authors, concepts—need to lead you to more specific sources. Look for a search engine's search tips or advanced search options for help with refining and limiting a keyword search (11c1).

Google search yielding too many results

When David Craig typed in the keywords *text message language* for a search on Google, the search engine yielded more than 21 million hits. After browsing through the first two pages of results, he decided to change his keywords and try again.

Many people begin and end Internet searches with Google. However, every search tool has unique properties. If you try other search engines or a metasearch tool that searches multiple search engines simultaneously, you may find that one of them has capabilities that are particularly helpful for your purposes.

2 Bookmarking tools

Today's powerful bookmarking tools can help you browse, sort, and track resources online. Social bookmarking sites, such as Delicious and Digg, allow users to tag information and share it with others. Once you register on a social bookmarking site, you can tag an online resource with any words you choose. Users' tags are visible to all other users. If you find a helpful site, you can check to see how others have tagged it and quickly browse similar tags to find related information. You can sort and group information according to your tags. Fellow users whose tagged sites you like and trust can become part of your network so that you can follow their sites of interest.

Web browsers can also help you bookmark and return to online resources that you have found. However, unlike the bookmarking tools in a Web browser, which are tied to one machine, social bookmarking tools are available from any computer with an Internet connection.

3 Authoritative sources online

You can find many sources online that are authoritative and reliable. For example, the Internet enables you to enter virtual libraries that allow access to some collections in libraries other than your own.

Online collections housed in government sites can also be reliable and useful sources. The Library of Congress, the National Institutes of Health, and the U.S. Census Bureau are just a few of the government agencies with large online collections of articles. For current national news, consult online versions of reputable newspapers such as the *New York Times*, the *Washington Post*, the *Los Angeles Times*, or the *Chicago Tribune* or electronic sites for news services such as CNN and C-SPAN. You can also use a search tool like Yahoo!, which has a "News and Media" category you can click on from the main page.

Some scholarly journals (such as those from Berkeley Electronic Press) and general-interest magazines (including Slate and Salon) are published only on the Web, and many other publications, like *Newsweek*, the *New Yorker*, and the *New Republic*, make at least some of their contents available online for free.

11e Conducting field research

For many research projects, particularly those in the social sciences and business, you will need to collect field data. The "field" may be many things—a classroom, a church, a laboratory, or the corner grocery store. It may even be, as David Craig discovered, a collection of instant messages from the Internet. As a field researcher, then, you need to discover *where* you can find relevant information, *how* to gather it, and *who* might provide the best information.

If you decide to conduct field research, check with your instructor about whether your school has a review board that will need to approve your data-gathering plan.

1 Observation

"What," you might ask, "could be easier than observing something? You just choose a subject, look at it closely, and record what you see and hear." Yet trained observers tell us that making a faithful record of an observation requires intense concentration and mental agility.

Moreover, observation is never neutral. Just as a photographer has a particular angle on a subject, so an observer always has an angle on what he or she is looking at. If, for instance, you decide to conduct a formal observation of your writing class, the field notes you take will reflect your status as an insider. Consequently, you will need to check your observations to see what your participation in the class may have obscured or led you to take for granted. In other instances, when you are not an insider, you still need to aim for optimal objectivity, altering as little as possible the phenomena you are looking at.

Before you conduct any observation, decide exactly what you want to find out, and anticipate what you are likely to see. Are you going to observe an action repeated by many people (such as pedestrians crossing a street), a sequence of actions (such as a medical procedure), or the

---

QUICK HELP

Conducting an observation

1. Determine the purpose of the observation, and be sure it relates to your research question and hypothesis.

2. Brainstorm about what you are looking for, but don't be rigidly bound to your expectations (3a1).

3. If necessary, make appointments and gain permission to observe.

4. Develop an appropriate system for recording data. Consider using a "split" notebook or screen: on one side, record your observations directly; on the other, record your thoughts and interpretations.

5. Record the date, time, and place of the observation.

interactions of a group (such as a church congregation)? Also decide exactly what you want to record and how. In a grocery store, for instance, decide whether to observe shoppers or store employees and what you want to note about them—what they say, what they buy, how they are dressed, how they respond to one another, and so on.

2 Interviews

Some information is best obtained by interviewing—asking direct questions of other people. If you can talk with an expert in person, on the telephone, or online, you might get information you could not have obtained through any other kind of research. In addition to getting an expert opinion, you might ask for firsthand accounts or suggestions of other places to look or other people to consult.

Finding people to interview

Check first to see whether your research has generated the names of people you might contact directly. Next, brainstorm for names. In addition to authorities on your topic, consider people in your community— faculty members, war veterans, corporate executives, or others. Once

---

QUICK HELP

Conducting an interview

1. Determine your exact purpose, and be sure it relates to your research question and hypothesis.

2. Set up the interview well in advance. Specify how long it will take, and if you wish to record the session, ask permission to do so.

3. Prepare a written list of factual and open-ended questions. Brainstorming or freewriting can help you come up with questions (3a). Leave plenty of space for notes after each question. If the interview proceeds in a direction that seems fruitful, do not feel that you have to ask all of your prepared questions.

4. Record the subject, date, time, and place of the interview.

5. Even if you are taping, take notes. Ask your interviewee for permission to use video, audio, or quotations that will appear in print.

6. Thank those you interview, either in person or in a letter or email.

you identify some promising possibilities, write, telephone, or email them to see whether an interview might be arranged.

Composing questions

To prepare useful questions, you need to know your topic well, and you need to know a fair amount about your interviewee. You will probably want to ask several kinds of questions. Questions about facts and figures (*How many employees do you have?*) elicit specific answers and do not invite expansion or opinion. You can lead the interviewee to think out loud and to give additional details by asking open-ended questions: *How would you characterize the atmosphere at the company just before the union went on strike? How do you feel now about your decision to go to Canada in 1968 rather than be drafted?*

Avoid questions that encourage vague answers (*What do you think of youth today?*) or yes/no answers (*Should the laws governing corporate accounting practices be changed?*). Instead, ask questions that must be answered with supporting details (*Why should the laws governing corporate accounting practices be changed?*).

After discovering a language Web site called the Discouraging Word, David Craig decided to try to set up an interview with the site's owner, an English literature graduate student at the University of Chicago. Once the owner agreed to an online interview, David drafted a number of specific questions about messaging language and other kinds of writing. He eventually used a quotation from the interview in his essay to bolster his thesis.

For David Craig's research essay, see 16e.

3 Surveys

Although surveys can take the form of interviews, they usually depend on questionnaires. To do survey research, all you need is a representative sample of people and a questionnaire that will elicit the information you need.

How do you choose the people you will survey? In some cases, you might want to survey all members of a small group, such as everyone in one of your classes. More often, however, you'll aim for a random sample of a large group — the first-year class at your university, for example. While a true random sample is probably unattainable, you can aim for a good cross section by, say, emailing every fifth person in the class directory.

QUICK HELP

Designing a survey questionnaire

1. Write out your purpose, and review your research question and hypothesis to determine the kinds of questions to ask.

2. Figure out how to reach the respondents you need—via email or telephone or in person.

3. Draft potential questions, and make sure that each question calls for a short, specific answer.

4. Test the questions on several people, and revise questions that seem unfair, ambiguous, too hard to answer, or too time consuming.

5. For a questionnaire that is to be mailed or emailed, draft a cover letter explaining your purpose.

6. State a deadline for respondents to submit the questionnaire.

7. On the final version of the questionnaire, leave adequate space for answers.

8. Proofread the questionnaire carefully.

On any questionnaire, the questions should be clear and easy to understand and designed so that you will be able to analyze the answers easily. For example, questions that ask respondents to say yes or no or to rank items on a five-point scale are particularly easy to tabulate.

The parking facilities on our campus are adequate.

Strongly agree   Somewhat agree   Somewhat disagree   Strongly disagree   Don't know

As you design your questionnaire, think about ways your respondents might misunderstand you or your questions. Adding a category called "other" to a list of options you are asking people about, for example, allows them to fill in information you would not otherwise get.

Because tabulating the responses takes time and because people often resent answering long questionnaires, limit the number of questions to no more than twenty. After tabulating your results, put them in an easily readable format, such as a chart or spreadsheet.

4 **Data analysis, synthesis, and interpretation**

To make sense of the information you have gathered, first try to identify what you want to look at: kinds of language? comparisons between men's and women's responses? The point is to find a focus, since you can't pay equal attention to everything. This step is especially important in analyzing results from observations or survey questionnaires. If you need assistance, see if your instructor can recommend similar research so that you can see how it was analyzed.

Next, synthesize the data by looking for recurring words or ideas that fall into patterns. Establish a system for coding your information, labeling each pattern you identify — a *V* for every use of violent language you observed, for example, or a plus sign for every positive response on a questionnaire. If you ask a few classmates to review your notes or data, they may notice other patterns.

> For a student analysis of field research, see 61c.

Finally, interpret your data by summing up the meaning of what you have found. What is the significance of your findings? Be careful not to make large generalizations.

David Craig's field research — another approach

If interviews, observations, or opinion surveys aren't quite right for your purposes, consider trying a different kind of field research. A large part of David Craig's essay, for instance, rests on analyzing the data he collected on messaging language. To determine whether the phrases used in online discussions constitute a language, David obtained and analyzed actual IM conversations from U.S. residents aged twelve to seventeen. After examining over eleven thousand lines of text, David identified four kinds of messaging language and was able to use his field research to support his thesis.

> For David Craig's research essay, see 16e.

THINKING CRITICALLY ABOUT CONDUCTING RESEARCH

Begin to analyze the research project you are now working on by examining the ways in which you conducted your research: What use did you make of primary and secondary sources? What library, online, and field research did you carry out? What aspect of the research process was most satisfying? What was most disappointing or irritating? How could you do research more efficiently? Bring your answers to these questions to class.

Evaluating Sources and Taking Notes

The difference between a useful source and a poor one depends to a great extent on your topic, purpose, and audience. Once you've found good sources, you will need to take effective notes to use the insights you find to your greatest advantage.

12a Using sources to meet a need

Why do writers decide to use one source rather than another? Sources serve different purposes, so part of evaluating sources involves deciding what you need the source to provide for your research projects. You may need background information or context that your audience will need to follow your writing; explanations of concepts unfamiliar to your audience; verbal and visual emphasis for your points; authority or evidence for your claims, which can help you create your own authority; other perspectives on your topic; or counter-examples or counter-evidence that you need to consider.

As you begin to work with your sources, make notes in your research log about why you plan to use a particular source. You should also begin your working bibliography.

12b Keeping a working bibliography

A working bibliography is a list of sources that you may ultimately use for your project. As you find and begin to evaluate research sources — articles, books, Web sites, and so on — you should record source information for every source you think you

On almost any topic you can imagine (Why do mosquitos bite? Who reads fan fiction? What musicians influenced Sonic Youth?), it takes some research — some looking into sources, some gathering of data, and some careful thought about these sources — to answer the question. With most topics, in fact, your problem will not be so much finding sources as figuring out *which* sources to consult in the limited time you have available. Learning how to tell which sources are best for you allows you to use your time wisely.

might use. (Relevant information includes everything you need to find the source again and cite it correctly; the information you will need varies based on the type of source, whether you found it in a library or not, and whether you consulted it in print or online.) The emphasis here is on *working* because the list will probably include materials that end up not being useful. For this reason, you don't absolutely need to put all entries into the documentation style you will use (see Chapters 16–19). If you do follow the required documentation style, however, that part of your work will be done when you prepare the final draft.

The following chart will help you keep track of the sorts of information you should try to find:

Type of Source	Information to Collect (if applicable)
Print book	Library call number, author(s) or editor(s), title and subtitle, place of publication, publisher, year of publication, any other information (translator, edition, volume)
Part of a book	Call number, author(s) of part, title of part, author(s) or editor(s) of book, title of book, place of publication, publisher, year of publication, inclusive page numbers for part
Print periodical article	Call number of periodical, author(s) of article, title of article, name of periodical, volume number, issue number, date of issue, inclusive page numbers for article
Electronic source	Author(s), title of document, title of site, editor(s) of site, sponsor of site, publication information for print version of source, name of database or online service, date of electronic publication or last update, date you accessed the source, URL

For other kinds of sources (films, recordings, visuals), you should also list the information required by the documentation style you are using (see Chapters 16–19), and note where you found the information.

Annotated bibliography

You might wish to annotate your working bibliography to include your own description and comments as well as publishing information (whether or not annotations are required) because annotating can help you understand and remember what the source says. If your instructor requires an annotated bibliography, be sure to ask for the specific guidelines you are to follow in creating the bibliography and then follow them carefully.

TALKING THE TALK
Research with an open mind

"What's wrong with looking for sources that back up what I want to say?" When you start researching a topic, keep an open mind: investigate every important source, even if you think you won't agree with it. If all your sources take the same position you take, you may be doing some pretty selective searching—and you may be missing a big part of the picture. Who knows? You may change your position after learning more about the topic. Even if you don't, ignoring counterarguments and other points of view harms your credibility, suggesting that you haven't done your homework.

Although some annotations can be very detailed—summarizing and evaluating the main points in a source—most annotations students do on their own include fairly brief descriptions and comments.

ANNOTATED BIBLIOGRAPHY ENTRY

Gere, Anne Ruggles. "Kitchen Tables and Rented Rooms: The Extracurriculum of Composition." *Literacy: A Critical Sourcebook*. Ed. Ellen Cushman, Eugene R. Kintgen, Barry M. Kroll, and Mike Rose. Boston: Bedford, 2001. 275-89. Print. This history of writing instruction argues that people teach writing and learn to write—and always have—more often in informal places like kitchens than in traditional writing classrooms. Gere presents numerous examples and comments on their importance to the study of writing today.

bedfordstmartins.com/smhandbook
Student Writing > Researched Writing

12c Evaluating usefulness and credibility

Since you want the information and ideas you glean from sources to be reliable and persuasive, you must evaluate each potential source carefully. The following guidelines can help you assess the usefulness and credibility of sources you are considering:

- *Your purpose.* What will this source add to your research project? Does it help you support a major point, demonstrate that you have thoroughly researched your topic, or help establish your own credibility through its authority?

- *Relevance.* How closely related is the source to the narrowed topic you are pursuing? You may need to read beyond the title and opening paragraph to check for relevance.

- *Level of specialization and audience.* General sources can be helpful as you begin your research, but you may then need the authority or currency of more specialized sources. On the other hand, extremely specialized works may be very hard to understand. Who was the source originally written for — the general public? experts in the field? advocates or opponents? How does this fit with your concept of your own audience?

- *Credentials of the publisher or sponsor.* What can you learn about the publisher or sponsor of the source you are using? For example, is it a major newspaper known for integrity in reporting, or is it a tabloid? Is it a popular source, whether in print or electronic, or is it sponsored by a professional or governmental organization or academic institution (11a2)? If you're evaluating a book, is the publisher one you recognize or can find described on its own Web site? No hard and fast rules exist for deciding what kind of source to use. But knowing the sponsor's or publisher's credentials can help you determine whether a source is appropriate for your research project.

- *Credentials of the author.* As you do your research, note names that come up from one source to another, since these references may indicate that the author is influential in the field. An author's credentials may also be presented in the article, book, or Web site, or you can search the Internet for information about the author. In U.S. academic writing, experts and those with significant experience in a field have more authority on the subject than others.

- *Date of publication.* Recent sources are often more useful than older ones, particularly in the sciences or other fields that change rapidly. However, in some fields — such as the humanities — the most authoritative works may be older ones. The publication dates of Internet sites can often be difficult to pin down. And even for sites that include dates of posting, remember that the material posted may have been composed some time earlier. Sites that list recent updates may be more reliable.

- *Accuracy of the source.* How accurate and complete is the information in the source? How thorough is the bibliography or list of works cited that accompanies the source? Can you find other sources that corroborate what your source is saying?

- *Stance of the source.* Identify the source's point of view or rhetorical stance, and scrutinize it carefully. Does the source present facts, or does it interpret or evaluate them? If it presents facts, what is included and what is omitted, and why? If it interprets or evaluates information that is not disputed, the source's stance may be obvious, but at other times, you will need to think carefully about the source's goals (12d). What does the author or sponsoring group want? to convince you of an idea? sell you something? call you to action in some way?

- *Cross-references to the source.* Is the source cited in other works? If you see your source cited by others, notice how they cite it and what they say about it to find additional clues to its credibility.

For more on evaluating Web sources and periodical articles, see the Source Maps on pp. 256–59.

EXERCISE 12.1

Choose two sources that seem well suited to your topic, and evaluate their usefulness and credibility using the criteria presented in this chapter. If possible, analyze one print source and one electronic source. Bring the results of your analysis to class for discussion.

12d Reading and interpreting sources

For those sources that you want to analyze more closely, reading with a critical eye can make your research process more efficient. Use the following tips to guide your critical reading.

Your research question

As you read, keep your research question in mind, and ask yourself the following questions:

- How does this material address your research question and support your hypothesis?

SOURCE MAP: Evaluating Web Sources

Is the sponsor credible?

1. Who is the **sponsor or publisher** of the source? See what information you can get from the URL. The domain names for government sites may end in *.gov* or *.mil* and for educational sites in *.edu*. The ending *.org* may—but does not always—indicate a nonprofit organization. If you see a tilde (~) or percent sign (%) followed by a name, or if you see a word such as *users* or *members*, the page's creator may be an individual, not an institution. In addition, check the header and footer, where the sponsor may be identified. The page shown here, from the domain **niemanwatchdog.org**, is from a site sponsored by the nonprofit Nieman Foundation for Journalism at Harvard University.

2. Look for an ***About* page** or a link to a home page for background information on the sponsor. Is a mission statement included? What are the sponsoring organization's purpose and point of view? Does the mission statement seem balanced? What is the purpose of the site (to inform, to persuade, to advocate for a cause, to advertise, or something else)? Does the information on the site come directly from the sponsor, or is the material reprinted from another source? If it is reprinted, check the original.

Is the author credible?

3. What are the **author's credentials**? Look for information accompanying the material on the page. You can also run a search on the author to find out more. Does the author seem qualified to write about this topic?

Is the information credible and current?

4. When was the information **posted or last updated**? Is it recent enough to be useful?

5. Does the page document sources with **footnotes or links**? If so, do the sources seem credible and current? Does the author include any additional resources for further information? Look for ways to corroborate the information the author provides.

1 Sponsor or Publisher

4 Posted or Last Updated

2 *About* Page

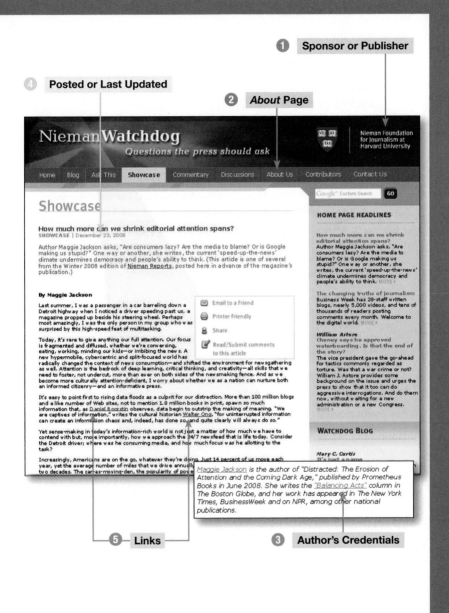

Nieman**Watchdog**
Questions the press should ask

Nieman Foundation
for Journalism at
Harvard University

Home | Blog | Ask This | **Showcase** | Commentary | Discussions | About Us | Contributors | Contact Us

Google™ Custom Search GO

Showcase

How much more can we shrink editorial attention spans?
SHOWCASE | December 23, 2008

Author Maggie Jackson asks, "Are consumers lazy? Are the media to blame? Or is Google making us stupid?" One way or another, she writes, the current 'speed-up-the-news' climate undermines democracy and people's ability to think. (This article is one of several from the Winter 2008 edition of <u>Nieman Reports</u>, posted here in advance of the magazine's publication.)

By Maggie Jackson

Last summer, I was a passenger in a car barreling down a Detroit highway when I noticed a driver speeding past us, a magazine propped up beside his steering wheel. Perhaps most amazingly, I was the only person in my group who was surprised by this high-speed feat of multitasking.

Today, it's rare to give anything our full attention. Our focus is fragmented and diffused, whether we're conversing, eating, working, minding our kids—or imbibing the news. A new hypermobile, cybercentric and split-focused world has radically changed the context of news consumption—and shifted the environment for newsgathering as well. Attention is the bedrock of deep learning, critical thinking, and creativity—all skills that we need to foster, not undercut, more than ever on both sides of the newsmaking fence. And as we become more culturally attention-deficient, I worry about whether we as a nation can nurture both an informed citizenry—and an informative press.

It's easy to point first to rising data floods as a culprit for our distraction. More than 100 million blogs and a like number of Web sites, not to mention 1.8 million books in print, spawn so much information that, as <u>Daniel Boorstin</u> observes, data begin to outstrip the making of meaning. "We are captives of information," writes the cultural historian <u>Walter Ong</u>, "for uninterrupted information can create an information chaos and, indeed, has done so, and quite clearly will always do so."

Yet sense-making in today's information-rich world is not just a matter of how much we have to contend with but, more importantly, how we approach the 24/7 newsfeed that is life today. Consider the Detroit driver; where was he consuming media, and how much focus was he allotting to the task?

Increasingly, Americans are on the go, whatever they're doing. Just 14 percent of us move each year, yet the average number of miles that we drive annually...two decades. The car-as-moving-den, the popularity of pow...

Email to a Friend
Printer Friendly
Share
Read/Submit comments to this article

HOME PAGE HEADLINES

How much more can we shrink editorial attention spans?
Author Maggie Jackson asks, "Are consumers lazy? Are the media to blame? Or is Google making us stupid?" One way or another, she writes, the current 'speed-up-the-news' climate undermines democracy and people's ability to think. MORE ›

The changing truths of journalism
Business Week has 28-staff written blogs, nearly 5,000 videos, and tens of thousands of readers posting comments every month. Welcome to the digital world. MORE ›

William Astore
Cheney says he approved waterboarding. Is that the end of the story?
The vice president gave the go-ahead for tactics commonly regarded as torture. Was that a war crime or not? William J. Astore provides some background on the issue and urges the press to show that it too can do aggressive interrogations. And do them now, without waiting for a new administration or a new Congress. MORE ›

WATCHDOG BLOG

Mary C. Curtis
It's just a name

<u>Maggie Jackson</u> is the author of "Distracted: The Erosion of Attention and the Coming Dark Age," published by Prometheus Books in June 2008. She writes the <u>"Balancing Acts"</u> column in The Boston Globe, and her work has appeared in The New York Times, BusinessWeek and on NPR, among other national publications.

5 Links

3 Author's Credentials

SOURCE MAP: Evaluating Articles

Determine the relevance of the source.

1 Look for an **abstract**, which provides a summary of the entire article. Is this source directly related to your research? Does it provide useful information and insights? Will your readers consider it persuasive support for your thesis?

Determine the credibility of the publication.

2 Consider the publication's **title**. Words in the title such as *Journal*, *Review*, and *Quarterly* may indicate that the periodical is a scholarly source. Most research projects rely on authorities in a particular field, whose work usually appears in scholarly journals. For more on distinguishing between scholarly and popular sources, see 11a2.

3 Try to determine the **publisher or sponsor**. This journal is published by Johns Hopkins University Press. Academic presses such as this one generally review articles carefully before publishing them and bear the authority of their academic sponsors.

Determine the credibility of the author.

4 Evaluate the **author's credentials**. In this case, they are given in a note, which indicates that the author is a college professor and has written at least two books on related topics.

Determine the currency of the article.

5 Look at the **publication date**, and think about whether your topic and your credibility depend on your use of very current sources.

Determine the accuracy of the article.

6 Look at the **sources cited** by the author of the article. Here, they are documented in footnotes. Ask yourself whether the works the author has cited seem credible and current. Are any of these works cited in other articles you've considered?

In addition, consider the following questions:

- What is the article's stance or point of view? What are the author's goals? What does the author want you to know or believe?

- How does this source fit in with your other sources? Does any of the information it provides contradict or challenge other sources?

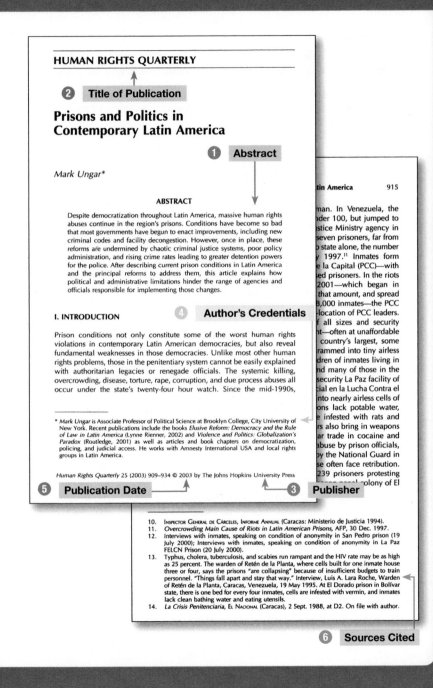

HUMAN RIGHTS QUARTERLY

② Title of Publication

Prisons and Politics in Contemporary Latin America

① Abstract

Mark Ungar*

ABSTRACT

Despite democratization throughout Latin America, massive human rights abuses continue in the region's prisons. Conditions have become so bad that most governments have begun to enact improvements, including new criminal codes and facility decongestion. However, once in place, these reforms are undermined by chaotic criminal justice systems, poor policy administration, and rising crime rates leading to greater detention powers for the police. After describing current prison conditions in Latin America and the principal reforms to address them, this article explains how political and administrative limitations hinder the range of agencies and officials responsible for implementing those changes.

I. INTRODUCTION

④ Author's Credentials

Prison conditions not only constitute some of the worst human rights violations in contemporary Latin American democracies, but also reveal fundamental weaknesses in those democracies. Unlike most other human rights problems, those in the penitentiary system cannot be easily explained with authoritarian legacies or renegade officials. The systemic killing, overcrowding, disease, torture, rape, corruption, and due process abuses all occur under the state's twenty-four hour watch. Since the mid-1990s,

* *Mark Ungar* is Associate Professor of Political Science at Brooklyn College, City University of New York. Recent publications include the books *Elusive Reform: Democracy and the Rule of Law in Latin America* (Lynne Rienner, 2002) and *Violence and Politics: Globalization's Paradox* (Routledge, 2001) as well as articles and book chapters on democratization, policing, and judicial access. He works with Amnesty International USA and local rights groups in Latin America.

Human Rights Quarterly 25 (2003) 909–934 © 2003 by The Johns Hopkins University Press

⑤ Publication Date —— **③ Publisher**

---

tin America   915

man. In Venezuela, the nder 100, but jumped to stice Ministry agency in seven prisoners, far from o state alone, the number y 1997.[11] Inmates form e la Capital (PCC)—with sed prisoners. In the riots 2001—which began in that amount, and spread 8,000 inmates—the PCC -location of PCC leaders. f all sizes and security nt—often at unaffordable country's largest, some rammed into tiny airless dren of inmates living in nd many of those in the security La Paz facility of cial en la Lucha Contra el nto nearly airless cells of ons lack potable water, e infested with rats and rs also bring in weapons ar trade in cocaine and abuse by prison officials, y the National Guard in se often face retribution. 239 prisoners protesting .... olony of El

10. INSPECTOR GENERAL DE CÁRCELES, INFORME ANUAL (Caracas: Ministerio de Justicia 1994).
11. *Overcrowding Main Cause of Riots in Latin American Prisons*, AFP, 30 Dec. 1997.
12. Interviews with inmates, speaking on condition of anonymity in San Pedro prison (19 July 2000); Interviews with inmates, speaking on condition of anonymity in La Paz FELCN Prison (20 July 2000).
13. Typhus, cholera, tuberculosis, and scabies run rampant and the HIV rate may be as high as 25 percent. The warden of Retén de la Planta, where cells built for one inmate house three or four, says the prisons "are collapsing" because of insufficient budgets to train personnel. "Things fall apart and stay that way." Interview, Luis A. Lara Roche, Warden of Retén de la Planta, Caracas, Venezuela, 19 May 1995. At El Dorado prison in Bolívar state, there is one bed for every four inmates, cells are infested with vermin, and inmates lack clean bathing water and eating utensils.
14. *La Crisis Penitenciaria*, EL NACIONAL (Caracas), 2 Sept. 1988, at D2. On file with author.

⑥ Sources Cited

QUICK HELP

Guidelines for examining potential sources

Looking quickly at the various parts of a source can provide useful information and help you decide whether to explore that particular source more thoroughly. You are already familiar with some of these basic elements: title and subtitle, title page and copyright page, home page, table of contents, index, footnotes, and bibliography. Be sure to check other items as well.

- *Abstracts*—concise summaries of articles and books—routinely precede journal articles and are often included in indexes and databases.

- A *preface* or *foreword* generally discusses the writer's purpose and thesis.

- *Subheadings* within the text can alert you to how much detail is given on a topic.

- A *conclusion* or *afterword* may summarize or draw the strands of an argument together.

- For an electronic source, click on some of the *links* to see if they're useful, and see if the overall *design* of the site is easy to navigate.

- What quotations from this source might help support your thesis?

- Does the source include counterarguments to your hypothesis that you will need to answer? If so, what answers can you provide?

The author's stance and tone

Even a seemingly factual report, such as an encyclopedia article, is filled with judgments, often unstated. Read with an eye for the author's overall rhetorical stance, or perspective, as well as for facts or explicit opinions. Also pay attention to the author's tone, the way his or her attitude toward the topic and audience is conveyed. The following questions can help:

- Is the author a strong advocate or opponent of something? a skeptical critic? a specialist in the field?

- Are there any clues to why the author takes this stance (2c2)? Is professional affiliation a factor?

- How does this stance affect the author's presentation and your reaction to it?

- What facts does the author include? Can you think of any important fact that is omitted?

- What is the author's tone? Is it cautious, angry, flippant, serious, impassioned? What words indicate this tone?

The author's argument and evidence

Every piece of writing takes a position. Even a scientific report implicitly "argues" that we should accept it and its data as reliable. As you read, look for the main point or the main argument the author is making. Try to identify the reasons the author gives to support his or her position. Then try to determine *why* the author takes this position. Consider these questions:

- What is the author's main point, and what evidence supports it?

- How persuasive is the evidence? Can you think of a way to refute it?

- Can you detect any questionable logic or fallacious thinking (8f)?

- Does this author disagree with arguments you have read elsewhere? If so, what causes the disagreements — differences about facts or about how to interpret facts?

For more on argument, see Chapters 7–9.

12e Synthesizing sources

When you read and interpret a source — for example, when you consider its purpose and relevance, its author's credentials, its accuracy, and the kind of argument it is making — you are analyzing the source. Analysis requires you to take apart something complex (such as an article in a scholarly journal) and look closely at the parts to understand the whole better. For academic writing you also need to *synthesize* — group similar pieces of information together and look for patterns — so you can put your sources (and your own knowledge and experience) together in an original argument. Synthesis is the flip side of analysis: you already understand the parts, so your job is to assemble them into a new whole.

To synthesize sources for a research project, try the following tips:

- *Read the material carefully.* For tips on reading with a critical eye, see Chapter 7.

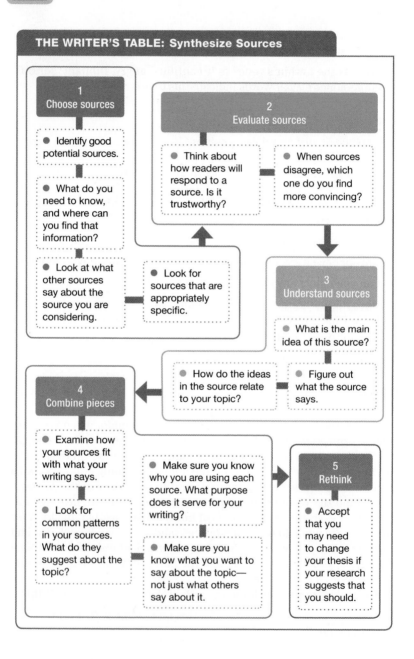

THE WRITER'S TABLE: Synthesize Sources

1 Choose sources

- Identify good potential sources.
- What do you need to know, and where can you find that information?
- Look at what other sources say about the source you are considering.

2 Evaluate sources

- Think about how readers will respond to a source. Is it trustworthy?
- When sources disagree, which one do you find more convincing?
- Look for sources that are appropriately specific.

3 Understand sources

- What is the main idea of this source?
- How do the ideas in the source relate to your topic?
- Figure out what the source says.

4 Combine pieces

- Examine how your sources fit with what your writing says.
- Look for common patterns in your sources. What do they suggest about the topic?
- Make sure you know why you are using each source. What purpose does it serve for your writing?
- Make sure you know what you want to say about the topic—not just what others say about it.

5 Rethink

- Accept that you may need to change your thesis if your research suggests that you should.

- *Determine the important ideas in each source.* Take notes on each source (12f). Identify and summarize the key ideas of each piece.

- *Formulate a position.* Review the key ideas of each source and figure out how they fit together. Look for patterns: discussions of causes and effects, specific parts of a larger issue, background information, and so on. Be sure to consider the complexity of the issue, and demonstrate that you have considered more than one perspective.

- *Summon evidence to support your position.* You might use para-phrases, summaries, or direct quotations from your sources as evidence (13b–d), or your personal experience or prior knowledge. Integrate quotations properly (see Chapter 13), and keep your ideas central to the piece of writing.

- *Deal with counterarguments.* You don't have to use every idea or every source available — some will be more useful than others. However, ignoring evidence that opposes your position makes your argument weaker. You should acknowledge the existence of valid opinions that differ from yours, and try to explain why they are incorrect or incomplete.

- *Combine your source materials effectively.* Be careful to avoid simply summarizing or listing your research. Think carefully about how the ideas in your reading support your argument. Try to weave the various sources together rather than discussing your sources one by one.

For more information on synthesis, see the chart on p. 262.

Excerpt from a student's synthesis project

Student Writer

Caroline Warner

Caroline Warner (whose real name and photo cannot be included in this book without jeopardizing her eligibility as a student athlete) wrote a research-based essay on "Hydration and Sports Drinks in Competitive Cycling." Caroline first investigated the problem of dehydration in various sports and then looked for information on the ways that competitive cyclists avoid dehydration during rides. In this excerpt from her final essay, she identifies important ideas from her research, formulates a position, and supports her argument, effectively synthesizing her sources.

Student Writing

Source identifies two main methods of hydration for athletes

There is little controversy as to the seriousness of dehydration. However, experts recommend varied methods for dealing with it. The *British Journal of Sports Medicine* outlines two general approaches. One method is for athletes to hydrate, using only water, whenever they are thirsty during exercise. The athlete, after his workout, is then free to use sports drinks for recovery and electrolyte replacement. While this method does result in some degree of dehydration, exercise-associated hyponatraemia (EAH) — overdrinking — is no longer a danger, and this method may better prepare athletes for any competitive situation in which they will not be able to rehydrate until after performing. This method has been adopted by USA Track & Field, as well as the International Marathon Medical Directors Association. The other approach to hydration maintains that an athlete should attempt to replace 100 percent of body weight lost during exercise. The athlete should drink every fifteen to twenty minutes, preferably consuming supplemental sodium like that found in sports drinks; the sodium allows the athlete to retain water and allows for better nervous system communication. In this scenario, the athlete does not wait to become thirsty (the assumption is that a thirsty athlete is already dehydrated); instead, he drinks small amounts consistently, and his body weight losses are less than 1 percent. This approach has been adopted by the American College of Sports Medicine as well as the National Athletic Trainers Association (Beltrami, Hew-Butler, & Noakes, 2008).

Summary of journal source

Reasons for cyclists' preference for second method

Evidence from cycling forums

Most cyclists are believers in the second method. In a sport that both requires alertness and demands performance for extended amounts of time, it makes sense to stay up on hydration. As for what to drink, online communities at both www.bikeforums.com and www.cyclingforums.com are filled with advocates for sports drinks rather than water. There is some debate over which drink is most effective — Heed, Cytomax, Pro-Opti, Aceelerade, GU_2O, and Gatorade are among the most popular — and over how much to use (many people dilute or mix their drinks), but everyone seems to advocate one drink or another. Arielle Filiberti, a three-time junior national champion cyclist and the favorite for women's U23s this year, says that her most horrific crash came at the end of a long ride when she ran out of both water and her preferred energy drink. Filiberti had been experiencing dizziness and light-headedness for some time, and as she was rounding a corner, she misjudged the turn and swung out too far into the road. She then swerved to avoid oncoming traffic, lost her balance, and skidded sideways off the road. Doctors found that Filiberti had lost about 3.5 percent of her body weight over a four-hour ride—almost five pounds of water. Furthermore, her reflexes were slow and she was unable to focus her eyes either close up or far away—a result of electrolyte and sodium loss. She was put on a saline drip and hospitalized overnight (personal interview). This kind of story is much more common than is safe or necessary. Thus for the competitive cyclist, it makes most sense to hydrate continuously through training.

Evidence from personal interview about need for cyclists to avoid dehydration

Note the way Caroline identifies important information from a journal and expands on the significance of the information in her discussion of sources from two well-known biking Web sites and a personal interview with a competitive cyclist. This synthesis supports her claim that continuous hydration with sports drinks is the best way for cyclists to combat the threat of dehydration. (Caroline's full essay, including a list of references, appears online.)

bedfordstmartins.com/smhandbook
Student Writing > Researched Writing

For more on synthesizing sources, see Chapter 13 and 15d.

12f Taking notes and annotating sources

Note-taking methods vary greatly from one researcher to another, so you may decide to use a computer file, a notebook, or index cards. Regardless of the method, however, you should (1) record enough information to help you recall the major points of the source; (2) put the information in the form in which you are most likely to incorporate it into your research essay, whether a summary, a paraphrase, or a quotation; and (3) note all the information you will need to cite the source accurately. The following example shows the major items a note should include:

ELEMENTS OF AN ACCURATE NOTE

Google docs **Child labor statistics**

File   Edit   View   Insert   Format   Table   Tools   Help

Styles   Verdana   **B** *I* U A   Link

Child labor statistics ❶

Arat, *Analyzing Child Labor*, p. 180 ❷

summary ❸
Difficult to gather accurate statistics
Between 200 and 500 million child laborers worldwide
95% are in the developing world
2 million in the US and UK

quotation ❸
"[O]ne in three children in Africa works, one in four in Asia, and one in five in Latin America."

❶ *Use a subject heading.* Label each note with a brief but descriptive subject heading so that you can group similar subtopics together.

❷ *Identify the source.* List the author's name and a shortened title of the source, and a page number, if available. Your working-bibliography entry (12b) for the source will contain the full bibliographic information, so you don't need to repeat it in each note.

❸ *Indicate whether the note is a direct quotation, paraphrase, or summary.* Make sure quotations are copied accurately. Put square brackets around any change you make, and use ellipses if you omit material.

Taking complete notes will help you digest the source information as you read and incorporate the material into your text without inadvertently plagiarizing the source (see Chapter 14). Be sure to reread each note carefully, and recheck it against the source to make sure quotations, statistics, and specific facts are accurate. (For more information on working with quotations, paraphrases, and summaries, see Chapter 13.)

1 Quotations

Some of the notes you take will contain quotations, which give the *exact words* of a source. Here, for example, is a note with a quotation that David Craig planned to use in his research paper:

Google docs **Comments from educators**

File Edit View Insert Format Table Tools Help

💾 🖨 ↶ ↷ 🖌 ▾ | Styles ▾ | Verdana ▾ | ▾ | **B** *I* <u>U</u> <u>A</u> ▾ ✎ ▾ | <u>Link</u>

Comments from educators **1**

Jennifer 8. Lee, "I Think, Therefore IM" **2**
New York Times **(Web)**

quotation: **3**
Melanie Weaver was stunned by some of the term papers she received from a 10th-grade class she recently taught as part of an internship. "They would be trying to make a point in a paper, they would put a smiley face in the end," says Ms. Weaver, who teaches at Alvernia College in Reading, Pa. "If they were presenting an argument and they needed to present an opposite view, they would put in a frown."

---

1 Subject heading

2 Author and short title of source (no page number for electronic source)

3 Direct quotation

QUICK HELP

Guidelines for quotations

- Copy quotations carefully, with punctuation, capitalization, and spelling *exactly* as in the original.

- Enclose the quotation in quotation marks; don't rely on your memory to distinguish your own words from those of the source.

- Use square brackets if you introduce words of your own into a quotation or make changes in it, and use ellipses if you omit material. If you later incorporate the quotation into your essay, copy it faithfully—brackets, ellipses, and all. (13b4)

- Record the author's name, the shortened title, and the page number(s) on which the quotation appears. If the note refers to more than one page, use a slash (/) within the quotation to indicate where one page ends and another begins. For sources without page numbers, record the paragraph or other section number(s), if any.

- Make sure you have a corresponding working-bibliography entry with complete source information. (12b)

- Label the note with a subject heading, and identify it as a quotation.

The above guidelines will help you take accurate notes not only of quotations but also of paraphrases and summaries.

2 Paraphrases

A paraphrase accurately states all the relevant information from a passage *in your own words and sentence structures*, without any additional comments or elaborations. A paraphrase is useful when the main points of a passage, their order, and at least some details are important but—unlike passages worth quoting—the particular wording is not. Unlike a summary, a paraphrase always restates *all* the main points of a passage in the same order and often in about the same number of words.

To paraphrase without plagiarizing inadvertently, do not simply substitute synonyms, and do not imitate an author's style. If you wish to cite some of an author's words within a paraphrase, enclose them in quotation marks. The following examples of paraphrases resemble the original either too little or too much:

ORIGINAL

Language play, the arguments suggest, will help the development of pronunciation ability through its focus on the properties of sounds and sound contrasts, such as rhyming. Playing with word endings and decoding the syntax of riddles will help the acquisition of grammar. Readiness to play with words and names, to exchange puns and to engage in nonsense talk, promotes links with semantic development. The kinds of dialogue interaction illustrated above are likely to have consequences for the development of conversational skills. And language play, by its nature, also contributes greatly to what in recent years has been called *metalinguistic awareness*, which is turning out to be of critical importance in the development of language skills in general and of literacy skills in particular.   —DAVID CRYSTAL, *Language Play* (180)

UNACCEPTABLE PARAPHRASE: STRAYING FROM THE AUTHOR'S IDEAS

Crystal argues that playing with language—creating rhymes, figuring out how riddles work, making puns, playing with names, using invented words, and so on—helps children figure out a great deal about language, from the basics of pronunciation and grammar to how to carry on a conversation. Increasing their understanding of how language works in turn helps them become more interested in learning new languages and in pursuing education (180).

This paraphrase starts off well enough, but it moves away from paraphrasing the original to inserting the writer's ideas; Crystal says nothing about learning new languages or pursuing education.

UNACCEPTABLE PARAPHRASE: USING THE AUTHOR'S WORDS

Crystal suggests that language play, including rhyme, helps children improve pronunciation ability, that looking at word endings and decoding the syntax of riddles allows them to understand grammar, and that other kinds of dialogue interaction teach conversation. Overall, language play may be of critical importance in the development of language and literacy skills (180).

Because the underlined phrases are either borrowed from the original without quotation marks or changed only superficially, this paraphrase plagiarizes.

UNACCEPTABLE PARAPHRASE: USING THE AUTHOR'S SENTENCE STRUCTURES

Language play, Crystal suggests, will improve pronunciation by zeroing in on sounds such as rhymes. Having fun with word endings and analyzing riddle structure will help a person acquire grammar. Being prepared to play with language, to use puns and talk nonsense, improves the ability to use semantics. These playful methods of communication are likely to influence a person's ability to talk to others. And language play inherently adds enormously to what has recently been known as *metalinguistic awareness*, a concept of great magnitude in developing speech abilities generally and literacy abilities particularly (180).

Although this paraphrase does not rely explicitly on the words of the original, it does follow the sentence structures too closely. Substituting synonyms for the major words in a paraphrase is not enough to avoid plagiarism. The paraphrase must represent your own interpretation of the material and thus must show your own thought patterns.

For David Craig's research essay, see 16e.

Here are two paraphrases of the same passage that express the author's ideas accurately and acceptably, the first completely in the writer's own words and the second, from David Craig's notes, including a quotation from the original.

ACCEPTABLE PARAPHRASE: IN THE STUDENT WRITER'S OWN WORDS

Crystal argues that playing with language—creating rhymes, figuring out riddles, making puns, playing with names, using invented words, and so on—helps children figure out a great deal, from the basics of pronunciation and grammar to how to carry on a conversation. This kind of play allows children to understand the overall concept of how language works, a concept that is key to learning to use—and read—language effectively (180).

QUICK HELP

Guidelines for paraphrases

- Include all main points and any important details from the original source, in the same order in which the author presents them.

- State the meaning in your own words and sentence structures (without looking at the original). If you want to include especially memorable language from the original, enclose it in quotation marks.

- Save your comments, elaborations, or reactions on another note.

- Record the author's name, the shortened title, and the page number(s) on which the original material appears. For sources without page numbers, record the paragraph or other section number(s), if any.

- Make sure you have a corresponding working-bibliography entry with complete source information. (12b)

- Label the note with a subject heading, and identify it as a paraphrase.

ACCEPTABLE PARAPHRASE: QUOTING SOME OF THE AUTHOR'S WORDS

Crystal argues that playing with language—creating rhymes, figuring out riddles, making puns, playing with names, using invented words, and so on—helps children figure out a great deal, from the basics of pronunciation and grammar to how to carry on a conversation. This kind of play allows children to understand the overall concept of how language works, or "metalinguistic awareness," a concept that Crystal sees as "of critical importance in the development of language skills in general and of literacy skills in particular" (180).

3 Summaries

A summary is a significantly shortened version of a passage or even of a whole chapter or work that captures main ideas *in your own words.* Unlike a paraphrase, a summary uses just enough information to record the main points you wish to emphasize. Your goal is to keep the summary as brief as possible, capturing only the main idea of the original and not distorting the author's meaning.

Here is David Craig's note recording a summary of the Crystal passage. The note states the author's main points selectively—without using his words.

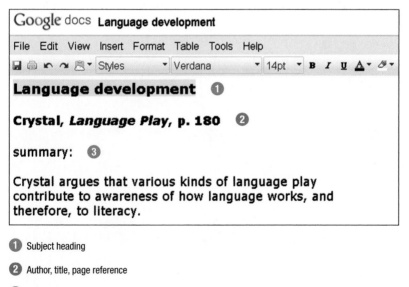

Google docs **Language development**

File   Edit   View   Insert   Format   Table   Tools   Help

Styles ▾   Verdana ▾   14pt ▾   **B** *I* <u>U</u> A▾ ✎▾

Language development ❶

Crystal, *Language Play*, p. 180 ❷

summary: ❸

Crystal argues that various kinds of language play contribute to awareness of how language works, and therefore, to literacy.

❶ Subject heading

❷ Author, title, page reference

❸ Summary of source

Summarizing short pieces

To summarize a short passage, read it carefully and, without looking at the text, write a one- or two-sentence summary.

Now read the brief article that follows, and then see a student's note summarizing it:

> One scientist hoarded a rare virus strain for more than a decade, refusing requests to let other researchers study it. Others refused to share biological materials like cloned genes unless they were included as authors of any resulting discoveries, a nice way to boost a résumé. Hundreds of biologists delay publishing their results by more than six months for reasons like applying for a patent or protecting their lead over competitors. The scientific ideal is openness and sharing—describing your experiments in enough detail that others can evaluate their accuracy, and giving even competitors samples of your cell lines and other material so they can replicate your experiment and thus check it—but "ideal" seems to be the operative word here. Now that genetics is big business, researchers are withholding data, refusing to share materials and delaying publication of results in order to commercialize them, finds a new study in the *Journal of the American Medical Association*. Of the 1,240 geneticists whom Eric G. Campbell and colleagues at the Institute for Health Policy at Massachusetts General Hospital surveyed, 47 percent had been denied information, data or materials in the last three years. "The geneticists told us that such denials were slowing research, preventing replication and causing them to abandon promising leads," says Campbell.
>
> —SHARON BEGLEY, "Science Failing to Share"

GENETICS AS BUSINESS
Begley, "Science," p. 10

In a perfect world, scientists would share findings freely. But the commercialization of genetics has led scientists to withhold information, sometimes for years, so that they can continue to make money from their research. This tactic has slowed scientific progress.
[SUMMARY]

QUICK HELP

Guidelines for summaries

- Include just enough information to recount the main points you wish to cite. A summary is usually far shorter than the original.

- Use your own words. If you include any language from the original, enclose it in quotation marks.

- Record the author's name, the shortened title, and the page number(s) on which the original material appears. For sources without page numbers, record the paragraph, screen, or other section number(s), if any.

- Make sure you have a corresponding working-bibliography entry with complete source information. (12b)

- Label the note with a subject heading, and identify it as a summary.

Summarizing longer pieces

To summarize a long passage or an entire chapter, skim the headings and topic sentences, and make notes of each; then write your summary in a paragraph or two. For a whole book, you may want to refer to the preface and introduction as well as chapter titles, headings, and topic sentences—and your summary may take a page or more. In general, try to identify the thesis or claim being made, and then look for the subtopics or supports for that claim.

4 Other kinds of notes

Many researchers take notes that don't fall into the categories of quotations, paraphrases, or summaries. Some take key-term notes, which might include the topic addressed in the source along with names or short statements—anything to jog their memories when they begin drafting. Others record personal or critical notes—questions, criticisms, or other ideas that come to mind as they read. In fact, an exciting part of research occurs when the materials you are reading spark new ideas in your mind, ideas that may become part of your thesis or argument. Don't let them get away. While you may later decide not to use these ideas, you need to make notes about them just in case.

You may adopt a system particular to your own research project. David Craig analyzed over eleven thousand lines of instant-message conversations as part of his study on messaging language and youth literacy. For each conversation, David kept a note on each occurrence of nonstandard English spellings and words and their frequencies. Since he was trying to categorize these occurrences as well as quantify them, David labeled each note with the type of change that he was noticing. By labeling these notes with subject headings, he could easily determine how often each type of change to the language appeared in his data. After he had taken notes, David sorted them to see how many related to the category of phonetic replacement; he then placed the notes in the order he planned to use them in his essay. In this case, David's notes not only helped him synthesize his data; they also made it easier for him to present the data in a clear, concise chart.

For David Craig's research essay, see 16e.

Researchers also take field notes, which record their firsthand observations or the results of their surveys or interviews (11e).

Whatever form your notes take, be sure to list the source's title, author, and page number(s) so that you can return to the material easily. In addition, check that you have carefully distinguished your own thoughts and comments from those of the source itself.

5 Annotations

Sometimes you may photocopy or print out a source you intend to use. In such cases, you can annotate the photocopies or printouts with your thoughts and questions and highlight interesting quotations and key terms.

If you take notes in a computer file, you may be able to copy online sources electronically, paste them into the file, and annotate them there. Try not to rely too heavily on copying or printing out whole pieces, however; you still need to read the material very carefully. Also resist the temptation to treat copied material as notes, an action that could lead to inadvertent plagiarizing. (In a computer file, using a different color for text pasted from a source will help prevent this problem.)

EXERCISE 12.2

Choose an online source you are sure you will use in your research project. Then download and print out the source, record all essential publication information for it, and annotate it as you read it.

THINKING CRITICALLY ABOUT YOUR EVALUATION OF SOURCES

Take a careful look at the sources you have gathered for your research project. How many make points that support your own point of view? How many provide counterarguments to your point of view? Which sources are you relying on most—and why? Which sources seem most credible to you—and why? Which sources, if any, are you suspicious of or worried about? Bring the results of this investigation to class for discussion.

13

Integrating Sources into Your Writing

The process of absorbing
your sources and then
integrating them gracefully
into your own writing is one
of the challenges but also
the pleasures of success-
ful research. As you work
with sources and make
plans to use them in your
own writing, they become
yours. When you integrate
sources appropriately into
your work, they don't take
over your writing or drown
out your voice. Instead, they
work in support of your own
good ideas.

Integrating sources successfully — whether you choose to quote from, paraphrase, or summarize them — is key to effective research-based writing.

13a Deciding whether to quote, paraphrase, or summarize

You tentatively decided to quote, paraphrase, or summarize material when you took notes on your sources (12f). As you choose which sources to use in your research project and how to use them, however, you may reevaluate those decisions. The guidelines on p. 277 can help you decide whether to quote, paraphrase, or summarize.

13b Working with quotations

Quoting involves using a source's exact words. You might use a direct quotation to catch readers' attention or make an introduction memorable. Quotations from respected authorities can help establish your credibility by showing that you've sought out experts in the field. In addition, quoting authors who disagree with your opinions helps demonstrate your fairness (9e3).

Finally, well-chosen quotations can broaden the appeal of your project by drawing on emotion as well as logic (8d and 9f–g). A student writing on the ethics of bullfighting, for example, might quote Ernest Hemingway's striking comment that "the formal bullfight is a tragedy, not a sport, and the bull is certain to be killed."

QUICK HELP

Deciding to quote, paraphrase, or summarize

Quote

- wording that is so memorable or powerful, or expresses a point so perfectly, that you cannot change it without weakening the meaning
- authors' opinions you wish to emphasize
- authors' words that show you are considering varying perspectives
- respected authorities whose opinions support your ideas
- authors whose opinions challenge or vary greatly from those of others in the field

Paraphrase

- passages in which the details, but not the exact words, are important to your point

Summarize

- long passages in which the main point is important to your point but the details are not

Although quotations can add interest and authenticity to an essay, be careful not to overuse them: your research paper is primarily your own work, meant to showcase your ideas and your argument.

1 Brief quotations

Short prose quotations should be run in with your text, enclosed in quotation marks that mark where someone else's words begin and end. When you include such quotations — or other source material — use both signal phrases and parenthetical references or notes, depending on the requirements of the documentation style you are using (see Chapters 16–19). Signal phrases (13b3) introduce the material, often including the author's name. Parenthetical references and notes direct your readers to full bibliographic entries included elsewhere in your text.

The following brief quotation follows Modern Language Association (MLA) style (16b):

In Miss Eckhart, Welty recognizes a character who shares with her "the love of her art and the love of giving it, the desire to give it until there is no more left" (10).

In this example, the signal phrase that introduces the quotation (*In Miss Eckhart, Welty recognizes*) includes the author's name, so MLA style requires only the page number for this print source in parentheses.

2 Long quotations

If you are following MLA style, set off a prose quotation longer than four lines. If you are following the style of the American Psychological Association (known as APA style), set off a quotation of more than forty words or more than one paragraph. If you are following *Chicago* style, set off a quotation of more than one hundred words or more than one paragraph. Begin such a quotation on a new line. For MLA style, indent every line one inch; for APA style, five to seven spaces; for *Chicago* style, indent the text or use a smaller font (check your instructor's preference). Quotation marks are unnecessary. Introduce long quotations with a signal phrase or a sentence followed by a colon.

The following long quotation follows MLA style:

> A good seating arrangement can prevent problems; however, "withitness," as defined by Woolfolk, works even better:
>
>> Withitness is the ability to communicate to students that you are aware of what is happening in the classroom, that you "don't miss anything." With-it teachers seem to have "eyes in the back of their heads." They avoid becoming too absorbed with a few students, since this allows the rest of the class to wander. (359)
>
> This technique works, however, only if students actually believe that their teacher will know everything that goes on.

Note that the parenthetical citation comes after the period at the end of the quotation and does not have a period after it.

Though long quotations are often necessary in research projects, use them cautiously. Too many of them may make your writing seem choppy—or suggest that you have not relied enough on your own thinking.

3 Signal phrases to integrate quotations

Carefully integrate quotations into your text so that they flow smoothly and clearly into the surrounding sentences. Use a signal phrase or signal verb, such as those underlined in the following examples or those in the Quick Help box on p. 279.

> As Eudora Welty notes, "learning stamps you with its moments. Childhood's learning," she continues, "is made up of moments. It isn't steady. It's a pulse" (9).

<u>Some instructors claim</u> that the new technology is a threat to the English language. "Abbreviations commonly used in online instant messages are creeping into formal essays that students write for credit," <u>said Debbie Frost,</u> who teaches language arts and social studies to sixth-graders ("Young Messagers").

Remember that the signal verb must be appropriate to the idea you are expressing. In the first example, the verb *notes* tells us that the writer probably agrees with what Welty is saying. If that were not the case, the writer might have chosen a different verb, such as *asserts* or *contends.* In the second example, from David Craig's essay, he uses the signal phrase *Some instructors claim* to indicate that other authorities might disagree with the teacher's opinion or that David himself does. If David supported the point, he might have used entirely different wording, such as *Many instructors agree.* Notice that these examples also use neutral signal verbs—*continues* and *said*—where appropriate. The signal verbs you choose allow you to characterize the author's viewpoint or perspective as well as your own, so choose them with care.

For David Craig's research essay, see 16e.

4 **Square brackets and ellipses to mark changes**

Sometimes you may wish to alter a direct quotation in some way—to make a verb tense fit smoothly into your text, to replace a pronoun with a noun, to eliminate unnecessary detail, to change a capital letter to

QUICK HELP

Signal verbs

acknowledges	concludes	emphasizes	replies
advises	concurs	expresses	reports
agrees	confirms	interprets	responds
allows	criticizes	lists	reveals
answers	declares	objects	says
asserts	describes	observes	states
believes	disagrees	offers	suggests
charges	discusses	opposes	thinks
claims	disputes	remarks	writes

lowercase or vice versa. Enclose any changed or added words or letters in square brackets (49b), and indicate any deletions with ellipsis points (49f). Do not use ellipses at the beginning or end of a quotation unless the last sentence as you cite it is incomplete.

Here is an example including the original passage and the quotation David Craig used in his research essay. Notice how he uses ellipses to mark omitted words and brackets to show additions or other changes.

ORIGINAL

> Even terms that cannot be expressed verbally are making their way into papers. Melanie Weaver was stunned by some of the term papers she received from a 10th-grade class she recently taught as part of an internship. "They would be trying to make a point in a paper, they would put a smiley face in the end," said Ms. Weaver, who teaches at Alvernia College in Reading, Pa. "If they were presenting an argument and they needed to present an opposite view, they would put a frown."   —JENNIFER 8. LEE, "I Think, Therefore IM"

DAVID CRAIG'S NOTE

> Echoing Frost's concerns is Melanie Weaver, a professor at Alvernia College, who taught a tenth-grade English class as an intern. In an interview with the *New York Times*, Weaver said, "[When t]hey would be trying to make a point in a paper, they would put a smiley face in the end [☺]. . . . If they were presenting an argument and they needed to present an opposite view, they would put a frown [☹]" (qtd. in Lee).

Here are two examples of quotations that have been altered with bracketed information or ellipsis points and then integrated smoothly into the surrounding text.

> "There is something wrong in the [Three Mile Island] area," one farmer told the Nuclear Regulatory Commission after the plant accident ("Legacy" 33).

The brackets indicate that this information was added by the writer and is not part of the original quotation.

> Economist John Kenneth Galbraith pointed out that "large corporations cannot afford to compete with one another. . . . In a truly competitive market someone loses" (qtd. in Key 17).

Whenever you change a quotation, be careful not to alter its meaning. In addition, use brackets and ellipses sparingly; too many of them make for difficult reading and might suggest that you have removed some of the context for the quotation.

FOR MULTILINGUAL WRITERS

Identifying sources

While some language communities and cultures expect audiences to recognize the sources of important documents and texts, thereby eliminating the need to cite them directly, conventions for writing in North America call for careful attribution of any quoted, paraphrased, or summarized material. When in doubt, explicitly identify your sources.

EXERCISE 13.1

Take a source-based piece of writing you have done recently or a research project you are working on now, and examine it to see how successfully you have integrated quotations. Have you used accurate signal verbs and introduced the sources of the quotations? Have you used square brackets and ellipses accurately to indicate changes in quotations?

13c Paraphrasing

Introduce paraphrases clearly in your text, usually with a signal phrase that includes the author of the source. Here are two passages — an original excerpt from a book and a student's integrated paraphrase of it into her text.

ORIGINAL

Understanding genderlects makes it possible to change — to try speaking differently — when you want to. But even if no one changes, understanding genderlects improves relationships. Once people realize that their partners have different conversational styles, they are inclined to accept differences without blaming themselves, their partners, or their relationships. The biggest mistake is believing there is one right way to listen, to talk, to have a conversation — or a relationship. Nothing hurts more than being told your intentions are bad when you know they are good, or being told you are doing something wrong when you know you're just doing it your way.

—DEBORAH TANNEN, *You Just Don't Understand:
Women and Men in Conversation* (298)

PARAPHRASE INTEGRATED INTO RESEARCH PROJECT

One observer of the battle of the sexes, linguistics professor Deborah Tannen, is trying to arrange a cease-fire. Tannen illustrates how communication between women and men breaks down and then suggests that an awareness of what she calls "genderlects" can help all speakers realize that there are many ways to communicate with others and that these differing styles of communication have their own validity. Understanding this crucial point can keep speakers from accusing each other of communicating poorly when they are in fact communicating differently (298).

In the preceding passage, notice how the student writer brings authority to the point she makes in the first sentence. She introduces the author by name and title and then paraphrases her work. Note also that a page number is included in parentheses at the end of the paraphrase.

In the following paraphrase, David Craig introduces an authoritative source for his information—the College Board—and then identifies the authors of the College Board's report in parentheses:

For David Craig's research essay, see 16e.

> The fact remains, however, that youth literacy seems to be declining. What, if not messaging, is the main cause of this phenomenon? According to the College Board, which collects data on several questions from its test takers, enrollment in English composition and grammar classes has decreased in the last decade by 14 percent (Carnahan and Coletti 11).

13d Summarizing

Summaries, too, need to be carefully integrated into your text. Indicate the source of a summary, including the author's name and the page number, if any. Here is how David Craig might have integrated his summary of the passage from David Crystal's book *Language Play* (you can see David's summary note on p. 271 and the entire Crystal passage on p. 269):

> David Crystal, an internationally recognized scholar of linguistics at the University of Wales, argues that various kinds of language play contribute to awareness of how language works and to literacy (180).

Note that in this hypothetical example David introduces his source (Crystal), establishes the source's expertise by identifying him as a recognized scholar in the field of linguistics, and uses the signal verb *argues* to characterize Crystal's passage as making a case, not simply offering information. Because his source is a print work, he also includes the page number in parentheses for the passage he has summarized.

Whenever you include summaries, paraphrases, or quotations in your own writing, it is crucially important that you identify the sources of the material; even unintentional failure to cite material that you drew from other sources constitutes plagiarism. Be especially careful with paraphrases and summaries, where there are no quotation marks to remind you that the material is not your own. For more information on acknowledging sources and avoiding plagiarism, see Chapter 14.

13e Working with visuals and media

Choose visuals and media wisely, whether you use video, audio, photographs, illustrations, charts and graphs, or other kinds of images. Integrate all visuals and media smoothly into your text.

1 Appropriate visuals and media

Choose visuals and media that will enhance your research project and pique the interest of your readers.

- *Does each visual or media file make a strong contribution to the written message?* Tangential or decorative visuals and media weaken the power of your writing.

- *Is each visual or media file appropriate and fair to your subject?* An obviously biased perspective may seem unfair or manipulative to your audience.

- *Is each visual or media file appropriate for and fair to your audience?* Visuals and media should appeal to various members of your likely audience.

Whenever you post documents containing visuals or media to the Web, make sure you check for copyright information. While it is considered "fair use" to use such materials in an essay or other project for a college class, once that project is published on the Web, you might infringe on copyright protections if you do not ask the copyright holder for permission to use the visual or media file. U.S. copyright law considers the reproduction of works for purposes of teaching and scholarship to be "fair use" not bound by copyright, but the law is open to multiple intepretations. If you have questions about whether your work might infringe on copyright, ask your instructor for help.

2 Integrated visuals and media

Like quotations, paraphrases, and summaries, visuals and media need to be introduced and commented on in some way.

- Refer to the visual, audio, or video in the text (*As Fig. 3 demonstrates . . .*) and position it as close as possible after the first reference.

- Explain or comment on the relevance of the visual or media file. This can be done after the insertion point.

- Check the documentation system you are using to make sure you label visuals and media appropriately; MLA, for instance, asks that you number and title tables and figures (*Table 1: Average Amount of Rainfall by Region*).

- If you are posting your document or essay on a Web site, make sure you have permission to use any visuals or media files that are covered by copyright.

For more on using visuals, see Chapters 2 and 23.

David Craig integrated a chart about SAT scores into his research essay (16e). The chart, which he found in a report published by the College Board, illustrated the point that youth literacy is declining. He

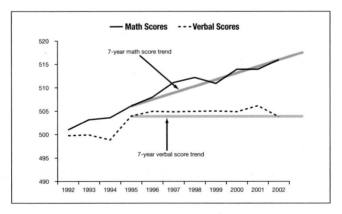

Fig. 1. Comparison of SAT math and verbal scores (1992-2002). Trend lines added. From Kristin Carnahan and Chiara Coletti, *Ten-Year Trend in SAT Scores Indicates Increased Emphasis on Math Is Yielding Results; Reading and Writing Are Causes for Concern* (New York: College Board, 2002; print; 9).

TALKING THE TALK

Saying something new

"What can I say about my topic that experts haven't already said?" All writers—no matter how experienced—face this problem. As you read more about your topic, you will soon see areas of disagreement among experts, who may not be as expert as they first appear. Notice what your sources say and, especially, what they don't say. Consider how your own interests and experiences give you a unique perspective on the topic. Slowly but surely you will identify a claim that you can make about the topic, one related to what others say but taking a new angle or adding something different to the discussion.

added his own trend lines to the chart to make the visual more effective. Following MLA style, David labeled the chart *Fig. 1* and included a descriptive title and source information. In the text of his paper, he included a reference to the chart and a detailed discussion of its data.

13f Checking for excessive use of source material

Your text needs to synthesize your research in support of your own argument; it should not be a patchwork of quotations, paraphrases, and summaries from other people. You need a rhetorical stance that represents you as the author. If you cite too many sources, your own voice will disappear, a problem the following passage demonstrates:

> The United States is one of the countries with the most rapid population growth. In fact, rapid population increase has been a "prominent feature of American life since the founding of the republic" (Day 31). In the past, the cause of the high rate of population growth was the combination of large-scale immigration and a high birth rate. As Day notes, "Two facts stand out in the demographic history of the United States: first, the single position as a receiver of immigrants; second, our high rate of growth from natural increase" (31).
>
> Nevertheless, American population density is not as high as in most European countries. Day points out that the Netherlands, with a density of 906 persons per square mile, is more crowded than even the most densely populated American states (33).

Most readers will think that the source, Day, is much too prominent here and that the author of the essay is only secondary. Using three different sources rather than one in this short passage also overwhelms the writer's voice; instead, the passage should advance the writer's own argument.

THINKING CRITICALLY ABOUT YOUR INTEGRATION OF SOURCES

From a research project you have finished or are drafting now, choose three passages that cite sources. Then examine how well these sources are integrated into your text. Consider how you can make that integration smoother, and try your hand at revising one of them.

Acknowledging Sources and Avoiding Plagiarism

In some ways, there really is nothing new under the sun, in writing and research as well as in life. Whatever writing you do has in some way been influenced by what you have already read and experienced and is part of a much larger conversation that includes other writers and thinkers. As a writer today, you need to understand the concept of intellectual property — those works protected by copyright or by alternatives such as a Creative Commons license — and how to acknowledge such works appropriately. It seems likely that an age of instant copying and linking will lead to revised understandings about who can "own" a text and for how long. But in college today, it is still important to cite the sources you use (whether written, oral, or visual) carefully and systematically and hence to avoid plagiarism, the use of someone else's words and ideas as if they were your own.

14a Understanding reasons to acknowledge sources

Acknowledging the sources you use offers a polite "thank you" for the work of others. In addition, the sources you acknowledge tell your reader that you have tried to gain expertise on your topic, that you are credible, and that you have been fair enough to consider several points of view. Similarly, your sources can help place your research in the context of other thinking. Most of all, you should acknowledge sources in order to help your readers follow your thoughts, understand how your ideas

Until about three hundred years ago, the idea that writers and speakers were all drawing on a large body of common information seemed perfectly natural: Shakespeare used stories that had been told by others and even parts of earlier texts in his work, and he didn't feel a need to provide citations for them. But as Western capitalism and the concept of individualism grew, so did the notion of *intellectual property rights*, which aimed to protect a writer's words as owned property. What started out as a limited time of protection (seven years) during which writers had exclusive ownership and use of the texts they wrote had by the end of the twentieth century expanded to life plus seventy years for an individual writer.

relate to the thoughts of others, and know where to go to find more information.

Acknowledging sources fully and generously, then, is a way to establish your trustworthiness as a researcher. Failure to credit sources can destroy both your own credibility and that of your research.

14b Knowing which sources to acknowledge

As you carry out research, you should understand the distinction between materials that require acknowledgment and those that do not.

1 Materials that do not require acknowledgment

Information does not need to be credited to a source if it is well known or if you gathered the data yourself.

- *Common knowledge.* If most readers know a fact, you probably do not need to cite a source for it. You do not need to credit a source to say that Barack Obama was elected in 2008, for example.

- *Facts available in a wide variety of sources.* If a number of encyclopedias, almanacs, reputable Web sites, or textbooks include a certain piece of information, you usually need not cite a specific source for it. For instance, you would not need to cite a source if you write that the Japanese bombed Pearl Harbor on December 7, 1941.

- *Findings from field research.* If you conduct observations or surveys, announce your findings as your own. Acknowledge people you interview as individuals rather than as part of a survey.

If you are not sure whether a fact, an observation, or a piece of information requires acknowledgment, err on the side of safety, and cite the source.

2 Materials that require acknowledgment

For material that does not fall under the preceding categories, credit sources as fully as possible. Follow the conventions of the citation style you are using (see Chapters 16–19), and include each source in a bibliography or list of works cited.

- *Quotations, paraphrases, and summaries.* Whenever you use another person's words, ideas, or opinions, credit the source. Even

QUICK HELP

Avoiding plagiarism

- Maintain an accurate and thorough working bibliography. (12b)

- Establish a consistent note-taking system, listing sources and page numbers and clearly identifying all quotations, paraphrases, summaries, statistics, and visuals. (12f)

- Identify all quotations with quotation marks—both in your notes and in your essay. (13b)

- Be sure your summaries and paraphrases use your own words and sentence structures. (13c and d)

- Give a citation or note for each quotation, paraphrase, summary, arguable assertion or opinion, statistic, and visual from a source, including an online source. (For material that needs citation, see 14b; for in-text documentation, see 16b, 17b, 18b, and 19b.)

- Prepare an accurate and complete list of sources cited according to the required documentation style. (See 16d, 17d, 18c, and 19c.)

- Plan ahead on writing assignments so that you can avoid the temptation to take shortcuts.

though the wording of a paraphrase or summary is your own, you should still acknowledge the source (12f and 13b–d).

- *Facts that aren't widely known or claims that are arguable.* If your readers would be unlikely to know a fact, or if an author presents as fact a claim that may or may not be true, cite the source. To claim, for instance, that Switzerland is amassing an offensive nuclear arsenal would demand the citation of a source because Switzerland has long been an officially neutral state. If you are not sure whether a fact will be familiar to your readers or whether a statement is arguable, go ahead and cite the source.

- *Images, statistics, charts, tables, graphs, and other visuals from any source.* Credit all visual and statistical material not derived from your own field research, even if you create your own graph or table from the data provided in a source.

- *Help provided by others.* If an instructor gave you a good idea or if friends responded to your draft or helped you conduct surveys, give credit — usually in a footnote that says something like "Thanks to Kiah Williams, who first suggested this connection."

Here is a quick-reference chart to guide you in deciding whether or not you need to acknowledge a source:

Need to acknowledge	Don't need to acknowledge
quotations	your own words, observations, surveys, and so on
paraphrases or summaries of a source	common knowledge
ideas you glean from a source	facts available in many sources
little-known or disputed facts	drawings or other visuals you create on your own
graphs, tables, and other statistical information from a source	
photographs, visuals, video, or sound taken from sources	
experiments conducted by others	
interviews that are not part of a survey	
organization or structure taken from a source	
help or advice from an instructor or another student	

14c Maintaining academic integrity and avoiding plagiarism

The principle of academic integrity in intellectual work allows you to trust the sources you use and to demonstrate that your own work is equally trustworthy. While there are many ways to damage your ethos and academic integrity, two that are especially important are the inaccurate or incomplete citation of sources — also called unintentional plagiarism — and plagiarism that is deliberately intended to pass off one writer's work as another's.

Whether intentional or not, plagiarism can bring serious consequences. At some colleges, students who plagiarize fail the course automatically; at others, they are expelled. Academics who plagiarize, even

---

FOR MULTILINGUAL WRITERS

Plagiarism as a cultural concept

Many cultures do not recognize Western notions of plagiarism, which rest on a belief that language and ideas can be owned by writers. Indeed, in many countries outside the United States, and even within some communities in the United States, using the words and ideas of others without attribution is considered a sign of deep respect as well as an indication of knowledge. In academic writing in the United States, however, you should credit all materials except those that are common knowledge, that are available in a wide variety of sources, or that are your own creations (photographs, drawings, and so on) or your own findings from field research.

---

inadvertently, have had their degrees revoked and their books withdrawn from publication. And outside academic life, eminent political, business, and scientific leaders have been stripped of candidacies, positions, and awards because of plagiarism.

1 Inaccurate or incomplete citation of sources

If your paraphrase is too close to the original wording or sentence structure of the source (even if you identify the source); if you do not identify the source of a quotation (even if you include the quotation marks); or if you fail to indicate clearly the source of an idea that you obviously did not come up with on your own, you may be accused of plagiarism even if your intent was not to plagiarize. Inaccurate or incomplete acknowledgment of sources often results either from carelessness or from not learning how to borrow material properly in the first place.

Academic integrity calls for you to be faithful not only to the letter of the material you are drawing on but also to its spirit: you need to honor the intention of the original source. For example, if your source says that an event *may* have happened in a particular way, then it isn't ethical to suggest that the source says that the event *absolutely* happened that way.

Because the costs of even unintentional plagiarism can be severe, it's important to understand how it can happen and how you can guard against it. In a January 2002 article published in *Time* magazine, historian Doris Kearns Goodwin explains how she made acknowledgment errors in one of her books. The book in question, nine hundred pages long and with thirty-five hundred footnotes, took Goodwin ten years to write. During this time, she says, she took most of her notes by hand, organized them, and later checked her sources to make sure all the material she was using was correctly cited. "Somehow in this process," Goodwin goes on to say, "a few books were not fully rechecked," and thus she omitted some acknowledgments and some quotation marks by mistake. Discovering such carelessness in her own work was very troubling to Goodwin since, as she puts it, "the writing of history is a rich process of building on the work of the past. . . . Through footnotes [and citations] you point the way to future historians."

Goodwin certainly paid a price for her carelessness: she had to leave Harvard's Board of Overseers and also resigned from the committee that awards Pulitzer Prizes. In addition, she was put on indefinite leave from a television program to which she had contributed regularly, was asked not to give a planned commencement address at the University of Delaware, and had to negotiate at least one settlement with a person whose work she had used without proper citation. Perhaps most seriously, this event called into question all of Goodwin's work.

As a writer of academic integrity, you will want to take responsibility for your research and for acknowledging all sources accurately. One easy way to keep track is to keep photocopies, printouts, or unaltered electronic copies of every source as you conduct your research; then you can identify needed quotations by highlighting them on each source.

2 Deliberate plagiarism

Deliberate plagiarism — handing in an essay written by a friend or purchased (or simply downloaded) from an essay-writing company; cutting and pasting passages directly from source materials without marking them with quotation marks and acknowledging your sources; failing to credit the source of an idea or concept in your text — is what most people think of when they hear the word *plagiarism*. This form of plagiarism is particularly troubling because it represents dishonesty and deception: those who intentionally plagiarize present the hard thinking and hard work of someone else as their own, and they deceive readers by claiming knowledge they don't really have.

Deliberate plagiarism is also fairly simple to spot: your instructor will be well acquainted with your writing and likely to notice any sudden shifts in the style or quality of your work. In addition, by typing a few words from an essay into a search engine, your instructor can identify "matches" very easily.

EXERCISE 14.1

Read the brief original passage that follows, and then look closely at the five attempts to quote or paraphrase it. Decide which attempts are acceptable and which plagiarize, prepare notes on what supports your decision in each case, and bring your notes to class for discussion.

> The strange thing about plagiarism is that it's almost always pointless. The writers who stand accused, from Laurence Sterne to Samuel Taylor Coleridge to Susan Sontag, tend to be more talented than the writers they lift from.
> —MALCOLM JONES, "Have You Read This Story Somewhere?"

1. According to Malcolm Jones, writers accused of plagiarism are always better writers than those they are supposed to have plagiarized.

2. According to Malcolm Jones, writers accused of plagiarism "tend to be more talented than the writers they lift from."

3. Plagiarism is usually pointless, says writer Malcolm Jones.

4. Those who stand accused of plagiarism, such as Senator Joseph Biden, tend to be better writers than those whose work they use.

5. According to Malcolm Jones, "plagiarism is . . . almost always pointless."

---

bedfordstmartins.com/smhandbook
Exercise Central > Research > Avoiding Plagiarism

14d Considering your intellectual property

Although you may not have thought much about it, all of your work in college—including all the research and writing you do, online and off—represents a growing bank of intellectual property. In fact, such original work is automatically copyrighted, even if it lacks the © symbol. But remember that the open source movement is gaining momentum and that sharing your ideas and writing freely with others is a way to perpetuate them and to gain an audience for your views.

For work that you want to protect, here are some tips for making sure that others respect your intellectual property just as you respect theirs:

- Realize that your email messages, blog postings, and posts to social networking sites and discussion groups are essentially public. If you don't want your thoughts and ideas repeated or forwarded, keep them offline. In addition, you may want to let your friends know specifically that you do not want your email messages passed on to any third parties. In turn, remember that you should not use material from email, discussion groups, or other online forums without first asking for permission.

- Be careful with your passwords and with discs or flash drives that contain your work. Use a secure storage method so that only you can give someone access to that work.

- Save all your drafts and notes so that you can show where your work has come from should anyone ask you.

14e Collaborating

With so much focus on plagiarism and with the advent of online paper mills, you may feel reluctant to share or discuss your work with anyone else. That would be a very unfortunate result, however, since much of our knowledge comes from talking with and learning from others. Indeed, many college projects now require some form of collaboration or teamwork, whether it involves commenting on someone else's draft, preparing a group presentation of research findings, or composing a text with many others on a wiki or on Google Docs.

Collaborative writing projects call for the same kind of acknowledgments you use in a paper or other project you prepare by yourself. In general, cite all sources used by the group, and acknowledge all assistance provided by others. In some cases, you may decide to do this in an endnote rather than in your bibliography or list of works cited.

THINKING CRITICALLY ABOUT YOUR OWN ACKNOWLEDGMENT OF SOURCES

Look at a recent piece of your writing that incorporates material from sources, and try to determine how completely and accurately you acknowledged them. Did you properly cite every quotation, paraphrase, and summary? every opinion or other idea from a source? every source you used to create visuals? Did you unintentionally plagiarize someone else's words or ideas? Make notes, and bring them to class for discussion.

Writing a Research Project

When you are working on an academic project, there comes a time to draw the strands of research together and articulate your conclusions in writing.

15a Refining your plans

You should by now have notes containing facts, opinions, paraphrases, summaries, quotations, and other material; you probably have some images or media to include as well. You may also have ideas about how to synthesize these many pieces of information. And you should have some sense of whether your hypothesis has sufficient support. Now is the time to reconsider your purpose, audience, stance, and working thesis.

- What is your central purpose? What other purposes, if any, do you have?

- What is your stance toward your topic (2c2)? Are you an advocate, a critic, a reporter, an observer (10b2)?

- What audience(s) are you addressing (2d and 10b2)?

- How much background information or context does your audience need?

- What supporting information will your readers find convincing — examples? quotations from authorities? statistics? graphs, charts, or other visuals? data from your field research?

- Should your tone be that of a colleague, an expert, a student?

Everyday decisions often call for research and writing. In trying to choose between two jobs in different towns, for example, one recent college graduate made a long list of questions to answer: Which company offered the best benefits? Which job location had the lower cost of living? How did the two locations compare in terms of schools, cultural opportunities, major league sports, and so on? After conducting careful research, he was able to send a letter of acceptance to one company and a letter of regret to the other.

- How can you establish common ground with your readers and show them that you have considered points of view other than your own? (See 9e and Chapter 25.)

- What is your working thesis trying to establish? Will your audience accept it?

1 From working thesis to explicit thesis

Writing out an explicit thesis statement allows you to articulate your major points and to see how well they carry out your purpose and appeal to your audience. Before you begin a full draft, then, try to develop your working thesis into an explicit statement.

David Craig, the student whose research we've been following throughout Part 3, developed the following explicit thesis statement (see Chapter 16):

> For David Craig's research essay, see 16e.

Instant messaging seems to be a positive force in the development of youth literacy because it promotes regular contact with words, the use of a written medium for communication, and the development of an alternative form of literacy.

FOR MULTILINGUAL WRITERS
Asking experienced writers to review a thesis

You might find it helpful to ask one or two classmates who have more experience with the particular type of academic writing to look at your explicit thesis. Ask if the thesis is as direct and clear as it can be, and revise accordingly.

2 Questions about your thesis

Although writing out an explicit thesis will often confirm your research, you may find that your hypothesis is invalid, inadequately supported, or insufficiently focused. In such cases, you need to rethink your original research question and perhaps do further research. To test your thesis, consider the following questions:

- How can you state your thesis more precisely or more clearly (3c)? Should the wording be more specific? Could you use more specific, concrete nouns (27c) or stronger verbs (43b)? Should you add qualifying adjectives or adverbs (Chapter 33)?

- In what ways will your thesis interest your audience? What can you do to increase that interest (2d)?

- Will your thesis be manageable, given your limits of time and knowledge? If not, what can you do to make it more manageable?

- What evidence from your research supports each aspect of your thesis? What additional evidence do you need?

EXERCISE 15.1

Take the thesis from your current research project, and test it against the questions provided in 15a2. Make revisions if your analysis reveals weaknesses in your thesis.

3 Planning design

As you move toward producing a draft, take some time to think about how you want your research project to look. What font will you use? Should you use color? Do you plan to insert text boxes and visuals? Will you need headings and subheadings? Will you incorporate audio, video, or other media? (For more on design, see Chapter 23.)

15b Organizing information

Experienced writers differ considerably in the ways they go about organizing ideas and information, and you will want to experiment until you find a method that works well for you. (For more on organizational strategies, see 3e.) This section will discuss two organizing strategies—grouping material by subject and outlining.

1 Subject groupings

You may find it useful to have physical notes to arrange—note cards or sticky notes, for example, or printouts of your slides or of notes you have been keeping online that you mark in some way to make the subject categories easy to identify. You can group the pieces around subject headings and reorder the parts until they seem to make sense. Shuqiao Song, the student who wrote the critical analysis in 7e, organized the plans for her PowerPoint presentation (22c) by moving sticky notes around on her window, as shown in her photo on p. 298.

Grouping your notes will help you see how well you can support your thesis and help you see if you have missed any essential points. Do

you need to omit any ideas or sources? Do you need to find additional evidence for a main or supporting point? Once you have gathered everything together and organized your materials, you can see how the many small pieces of your research fit together. Make sure that your evidence supports your explicit thesis; if not, you may need to revise it or do additional research — or both.

Once you have established initial groups, skim through the notes and look for ways to organize your draft. Figure out what background your audience needs, what points you need to make first, how much detail and support to offer for each point, and so on.

2 Outlines

You can use outlines in various ways and at various stages. Some writers group their notes, write a draft, and then outline the draft to study its tentative structure. Others develop an informal working outline from their notes and revise it as they go along. Still other writers prefer to plot out their organization early on in a formal outline. (For more on outlines, see 3f.)

David Craig drew up a working outline of his ideas while he was still doing research on his topic, thinking that this simple structure would help him focus on the information he still needed to find. Here is his informal outline:

Decline of youth literacy
    Lower test scores, other proof (statistics)
    How instant messaging fits in, examples from critics
My research
    Can I show that IM is a language?
    How widespread is it?
Comments from linguists — tie-in to IM language
What is the real cause of declining youth literacy?

For David Craig's research essay, see 16e.

Because he knew he was required to submit a formal outline with his essay, David Craig kept revising this informal outline as his research and writing progressed. He did not complete his formal outline until after his essay was drafted (see pp. 302–3). At that point, the formal outline helped him analyze and revise the draft.

15c Drafting

For most college research projects, drafting should begin *at least* two weeks before the instructor's deadline in case you need to gather more information or do more drafting. Set a deadline for having a complete draft, and structure your work with that date in mind. Gather your notes, outline, and sources, and read through them, getting involved in your topic. Most writers find that some sustained work (two or three hours at a time) pays off at this point. Begin drafting a section that you feel confident about. For example, if you are not sure how you want to introduce the draft but do know how you want to approach a particular point, begin with that, and return to the introduction later. The most important thing is to get started.

The drafting process varies considerably among researchers, and no one else can determine what will work best for you. The tips offered in 3g, however, can help. No matter what approach you take, remember to include sources (for quotations, paraphrases, summaries, and media) as you draft; doing so will save time later and help you produce your list of works cited.

1 Working title and introduction

The title and introduction (4h) play special roles, for they set the context for what is to come. Ideally, the title announces your subject in an intriguing or memorable way. To accomplish these goals, Emily Lesk (the student writer whose work we followed in Part 1) revised the title of her essay from "All-Powerful Coke" (p. 67) to "Red, White, and Everywhere" (4l). David Craig began with the title "Messaging and Texting," but he later added the more specific and intriguing subtitle "The Language of Youth Literacy."

The introduction should draw readers in and provide any background they will need to understand the discussion. Here are some tips for drafting an introduction to a research project:

- You may want to *open with a question*, especially your research question, or *with a strong or arresting statement* of some kind. Next, you might explain what you will do to answer the question or to elaborate on the statement. Then *end with your explicit thesis statement*—in essence, the answer to the question or the response to the strong statement.

- Help readers get their bearings by *forecasting your main points*.

- *Establish your own credibility* by revealing how you have become knowledgeable about your topic.

- A *quotation* can be a good attention-getter, but you may not want to open with a quotation from one source if doing so will give that source too much emphasis.

David Craig begins his essay with a strong statement (*The English language is under attack*) that immediately gets readers' attention. He then presents a brief overview of what the critics are saying about youth literacy and brings up messaging language—the general subject of his essay. In his second and third paragraphs, David helps establish his own credibility by including testimony from an educator, a definition of messaging, and an example from his own research. He then summarizes the criticism of messaging language, which leads naturally to his eventual thesis statement.

2 Conclusion

A good conclusion helps readers know what they have learned (4h and 5f). Its job is not to persuade (the body of the essay or project should already have done that) but to contribute to the overall effectiveness of your writing. The following strategies may be helpful:

- Refer to your thesis, and then expand to a more general conclusion that reminds readers of the significance of your discussion.

- If you have covered several main points, you may want to remind readers of them. Be careful, however, to provide more than a mere summary.

- Try to end with something that will have an impact—a provocative quotation or question, a vivid image, a call for action, or a warning. But guard against sounding preachy.

In his conclusion, David Craig briefly recaps his thesis and then summarizes the main point of his argument (p. 358). He ends with a strong assertion: *Although messaging may expose literacy problems, it does not create them.*

15d Incorporating source materials

When you reach the point of drafting your research project, a new task awaits: weaving your source materials into your writing. The challenge is to use your sources yet remain the author—to quote, paraphrase, and summarize other voices while remaining the major voice in your work.

Because learning how to effectively integrate source material is so important, Chapter 13 is devoted entirely to this process. Consult that chapter often as you draft.

15e Reviewing and getting responses to your draft

Because a research project involves a complex mix of your thoughts and materials from outside sources, it calls for an especially careful review. You should examine the draft yourself as well as seek the comments of other readers. Ask friends and classmates to read and respond to your draft, and get a response from your instructor if possible.

1 Your own review of your draft

As with most kinds of writing, taking a break after drafting is important so that when you reread the draft, you can bring a fresh eye to the task.

Questions for review

When you do return to the draft, read it straight through without stopping. Then read the draft again slowly, reconsidering your purpose, audience, stance, thesis, and support.

- From your reading of the draft, what do you now see as its *purpose?* How does this compare with your original purpose? Does the draft do what your assignment requires?

- What *audience* does your essay address?

- What is your *stance* toward the topic?

- What is your *thesis?* Is it clearly stated?

- What *evidence* supports your thesis? Is the evidence sufficient?

Answer these questions as best you can, since they are the starting point for revision. If you notice a problem but are unsure how to solve it, write down your concerns so that you can ask readers if they notice the same problem and have ideas about solving it.

Outline

You might find that outlining your draft (3f and 15b2) helps you analyze it at this point: an outline will reveal the bare bones of your argument and help you see what may be missing or out of place. Here is the formal outline that David Craig prepared after drafting his research paper on instant messaging.

> **Thesis statement:** Messaging seems to be a beneficial force in the development of youth literacy because it promotes regular contact with words, the use of a written medium for communication, and the development of an alternative form of literacy.
>
> I. Decline of youth literacy — overview
>
>   A. What many parents, librarians, educators believe
>
>   B. Messaging as possible cause
>
>   1. Definition of messaging
>
>   2. Example of IM conversation
>
>   3. Messaging as beneficial to youth literacy
>
> II. Two background issues
>
>   A. Current state of literacy
>
>   1. Decline in SAT scores
>
>   2. Decline in writing ability

For David Craig's research essay, see 16e.

     B. Prevalence of messaging
         1. Statistics indicating widespread usage
         2. Instant messagers and texters using new vocabulary
III. My field research to verify existence of messaging language
     A. Explanation of how research was done
     B. Results of research
         1. Four types of messaging language: phonetic replacements, acronyms, abbreviations, inanities
         2. Frequency of messaging language use
         3. Conclusions about vocabulary
IV. What critics of messaging say
     A. Many problems with student writing, such as incomplete sentences, grammar, and spelling
     B. Students using online abbreviations (smileys) in formal papers
V. What linguists and other supporters of messaging say
     A. Traditional literacy not harmed by messaging
     B. Messaging indicative of advanced literacy
         1. Crystal's explanation of metalinguistics and wordplay
         2. Human ability to write in many styles, messaging style being only one alternative
         3. Messaging helping students shift from language to language
VI. Other possible causes of decline in youth literacy
     A. Lower enrollment in English composition and grammar classes
     B. Messaging exposing literacy problems but not causing them

2 Peer responses

You should seek responses from friends and classmates as your draft evolves. Your reviewers will be best prepared to give you helpful advice and to ask questions specific to your project if they have background information about your writing task.

Tell your reviewers the purpose of your draft, the assignment's criteria, and your target audience. Ask them to explain their understanding of your stance on the topic. Also ask for feedback on your thesis and its support. If you are unsure about whether to include a particular point, how to use a certain quotation, or where to add more examples, ask your reviewers specifically what they think you should do. You should also ask them to identify any parts of your draft that confuse them. Even if you are writing to a target audience with more expertise in the topic than your peer reviewers, you should carefully consider revising the parts they identify as confusing: you may be making too many assumptions about what concepts need to be explained. (For more on peer review, see 4b.)

3 Reviews of others' research writing

When you are asked to respond to others' research writing, you may encounter arguments and ideas that are unfamiliar to you. It's tempting to assume that the writer has done a good job and that you are not the right person to give advice. Remember that your job as a peer reviewer is to note whether the writer's thesis, evidence, use of sources, and language are clear and effective.

The writer may direct your attention to specific parts of the draft; be sure to respond to these requests. If the writer does not have specific questions, try to restate the writer's stance, thesis, and key pieces of evidence in your own words. Seeing how someone else summarizes the draft will help the writer assess the effectiveness of the argument (4b). Next, report on what makes sense to you in the draft — and what does not. Pay special attention to these four aspects of the writing:

- *Thesis statement, topic sentences, and transitions.* Were you prepared for the main ideas of the paper and of each paragraph?

- *Organization.* Could you follow the writer's logic? Were the ideas ordered for maximum effect?

- *Amount and quality of evidence, including both visual and verbal sources.* Was there enough credible evidence from reputable sources to be convincing?

- *Sentences.* Could you easily read each sentence and understand its meaning?

The most important part of responding to research writing is deciding that you have something useful to say. Focus on how the text affects you. Even if the ideas are unfamiliar to you, you are not new to learning. If the draft is not helping you think carefully about the topic, identifying the sources of your confusion and doubt will help the writer revise. Many students report that thinking of this response as a letter written directly to the student writer (beginning the response with "Dear X" and concluding with something like "Good luck!") helps them focus on giving concrete criticism and helpful advice (4b3).

Guidelines for revising a research project

- *Take responses into account.* Look at specific problems that reviewers think you need to solve or strengths you might capitalize on. For example, if they showed great interest in one point but no interest in another, consider expanding the first and deleting the second.

- *Reconsider your original purpose, audience, and stance.* Have you achieved your purpose? If not, consider how you can. How well have you appealed to your readers? Make sure you satisfy any special concerns of your reviewers. If your rhetorical stance toward your topic has changed, does your draft need to change, too?

- *Assess your research.* Think about whether you have investigated the topic thoroughly and consulted materials with more than one point of view. Have you left out any important sources? Are the sources you use reliable and appropriate for your topic? Have you synthesized your research findings and drawn warranted conclusions?

- *Assess your use of visuals and media*, making sure that each one supports your argument, is clearly labeled, and is cited appropriately.

- *Gather additional material.* If you need to strengthen any points, first check your notes to see whether you already have the necessary information. In some instances, you may need to do more research.

- *Decide what changes you need to make.* List everything you must do to perfect your draft. With your deadline in mind, plan your revision.

- *Rewrite your draft.* Many writers prefer to revise first on paper rather than on a computer. However you revise, be sure to save copies of each draft. Begin with the major changes, such as adding content or reorganizing. Then turn to sentence-level problems and word choice. Can you sharpen the work's dominant impression?

- *Reevaluate the title, introduction, and conclusion.* Is your title specific and engaging? Does the introduction capture readers' attention and indicate what the work discusses? Does your conclusion help readers see the significance of your argument?

- *Check your documentation.* Make sure you've included a citation in your text for every quotation, paraphrase, summary, visual, and media file you incorporated, following your documentation style consistently.

- *Edit your draft.* Check grammar, usage, spelling, punctuation, and mechanics. Consider the advice of computer spell checkers (28e1) and grammar checkers carefully before accepting it.

15f Revising and editing

When you have considered your reviewers' responses and your own analysis, you can turn to revising and editing. See the box on p. 305 and sections 4e–4k for more information.

15g Preparing a list of sources

Once your final draft and source materials are in place, you are ready to prepare a list of sources. Follow the guidelines for your documentation style carefully (see Chapters 16–19), creating an entry for each source used. Double-check your work to make sure that you have listed every source mentioned in your draft and (unless you are listing all the sources you consulted) that you have not listed any sources not cited. Most word-processing programs can help you alphabetize and format lists of sources as well as prepare endnotes and footnotes.

15h Proofreading your final copy

Your final rough draft may look very rough indeed, so your next step is to create a final, perfectly clean copy. You will submit this version, which represents all your work and effort, to your instructor. At this point, run the spell checker but do not stop there. To make sure that this final version puts your best foot forward, proofread extremely carefully. It's best to work with a hard copy, since reading onscreen often leads to missed typos. Read the copy aloud for content and for the flow of the argument, making sure you haven't mistakenly deleted words, lines, or whole sections. Then read the copy backward from the last sentence to the first, looking for small mistakes such as punctuation problems or missing words. If you are keeping an editing inventory (4k), look for the types of editing problems you have had in the past.

Once you are sure your draft is free of errors, check the design one last time to be sure you are using effective margins, type size, color, boldface and italics, headings, and so on. You want your final copy to be as attractive and readable as possible (see Chapter 23).

After your manuscript preparation and proofreading are complete, celebrate your achievement: your research and hard work have produced a project that you can, and should, take pride in.

THINKING CRITICALLY ABOUT RESEARCH PROJECTS

Reflect on the research project you have completed. How did you go about organizing your information? What would you do to improve this process? What problems did you encounter in drafting? How did you solve these problems? How many quotations did you use, and how did you integrate them into your text? When and why did you use summaries and paraphrases? If you used visuals, how effective were they in supporting your points? What did you learn from revising?

16 MLA Style

The Modern Language Association (MLA) style of formatting manuscripts and documenting sources is widely used in literature, languages, and other fields in the humanities.

For more information on the Modern Language Association style, consult the *MLA Handbook for Writers of Research Papers*, Seventh Edition (2009).

16a Formatting MLA manuscripts

The MLA recommends the following format for the manuscript of a research-based essay or project. It's always a good idea, however, to check with your instructor about formatting issues before preparing your final draft.

For detailed guidelines on formatting a list of works cited, see 16d. For a sample student essay in MLA style, see 16e.

- *First page and title page.* The MLA does not require a title page. Type each of the following items on a separate line on the first page, beginning one inch from the top and flush with the left margin: your name, the instructor's name, the course name and number, and the date. Double-space between each item; then double-space again and center the title. Double-space between the title and the beginning of the text.

- *Margins and spacing.* Leave one-inch margins at the top and bottom and on both sides of each page. Double-space the entire text, including set-off quotations, notes, and the list of works cited. Indent the first line of a paragraph one-half inch.

- *Page numbers.* Include your last name and the page number on each page, one-half inch below the top and flush with the right margin.

- *Long quotations.* Set off a long quotation (more than four typed lines) in block format by starting it on a new line and indenting each line one inch from the left margin. Do not enclose the passage in quotation marks (48a1).

- *Headings.* MLA style allows, but does not require, headings. Many students and instructors find them helpful. (See 23c for guidelines on using headings and subheadings.)

- *Visuals.* Place tables, photographs, drawings, charts, graphs, and other figures as near as possible to the relevant text. (See 13e2 and 23d for guidelines on incorporating visuals into your text.) Tables should have a label and number (*Table 1*) and a clear caption. The label and caption should be aligned on the left, on separate lines. Give the source information below the table. All other visuals should be labeled *Figure* (abbreviated *Fig.*), numbered, and captioned. The label and caption should appear on the same line, followed by the source information (see 16d). Remember to refer to each visual in your text, indicating how it contributes to the point(s) you are making.

16b In-text citations

MLA style requires a citation in the text of an essay for every quotation, paraphrase, summary, or other material requiring documentation (see 14b). In-text citations document material from other sources with both signal phrases and parenthetical references. Parenthetical references should include the information your readers need to locate the full reference in the list of works cited at the end of the text (16d). An in-text citation in MLA style aims to give the reader two kinds of information: (1) it indicates *which source* on the works-cited page the writer is referring to, and (2) it explains *where in the source* the material quoted, paraphrased, or summarized can be found, if the source has page numbers or other numbered sections.

The basic MLA in-text citation includes the author's last name either in a signal phrase introducing the source material (see 13b3) or in parentheses at the end of the sentence. For print sources, it also includes the page number in parentheses at the end of the sentence.

Directory to MLA style for in-text citations

SAMPLE CITATION USING A SIGNAL PHRASE

In his discussion of Monty Python routines, Crystal notes that the group relished "breaking the normal rules" of language (107).

SAMPLE PARENTHETICAL CITATION

A noted linguist explains that Monty Python humor often relied on "bizarre linguistic interactions" (Crystal 108).

Note in the following examples where punctuation is placed in relation to the parentheses.

1. AUTHOR NAMED IN A SIGNAL PHRASE The MLA recommends using the author's name in a signal phrase to introduce the material and citing the page number(s), if any, in parentheses.

Lee claims that his comic-book creation, Thor, was "the first regularly published superhero to speak in a consistently archaic manner" (199).

2. AUTHOR NAMED IN A PARENTHETICAL REFERENCE When you do not mention the author in a signal phrase, include the author's last name

before the page number(s) in the parentheses. Use no punctuation between the author's name and the page number(s).

> The word *Bollywood* is sometimes considered an insult because it implies that Indian movies are merely "a derivative of the American film industry" (Chopra 9).

3. TWO OR THREE AUTHORS Use all the authors' last names in a signal phrase or in parentheses.

> Gortner, Hebrun, and Nicolson maintain that "opinion leaders" influence other people in an organization because they are respected, not because they hold high positions (175).

4. FOUR OR MORE AUTHORS Use the first author's name and *et al.* ("and others"), or to give credit to all authors, name all the authors in a signal phrase or in parentheses.

> Similarly, as Belenky et al. assert, examining the lives of women expands our understanding of human development (7).

> Similarly, as Belenky, Clinchy, Tarule, and Goldberger assert, examining the lives of women expands our understanding of human development (7).

5. ORGANIZATION AS AUTHOR Give the group's full name or a short-ened form of it in a signal phrase or in parentheses.

> Any study of social welfare involves a close analysis of "the impacts, the benefits, and the costs" of its policies (Social Research Corporation iii).

6. UNKNOWN AUTHOR Use the full title, if it is brief, in your text — or a shortened version of the title in parentheses.

> One analysis defines *hype* as "an artificially engendered atmosphere of hysteria" ("Today's Marketplace" 51).

7. AUTHOR OF TWO OR MORE WORKS CITED IN THE SAME PROJECT If your list of works cited has more than one work by the same author, include a shortened version of the title of the work you are citing in a signal phrase or in parentheses to prevent reader confusion.

> Gardner shows readers their own silliness in his description of a "pointless, ridiculous monster, crouched in the shadows, stinking of dead men, murdered children, and martyred cows" (*Grendel* 2).

8. TWO OR MORE AUTHORS WITH THE SAME LAST NAME Include the author's first *and* last names in a signal phrase or first initial and last name in a parenthetical reference.

> Children will learn to write if they are allowed to choose their own subjects, James Britton asserts, citing the Schools Council study of the 1960s (37-42).

9. INDIRECT SOURCE (AUTHOR QUOTING SOMEONE ELSE) Use the abbreviation *qtd. in* to indicate that you are quoting from someone else's report of a source.

> As Arthur Miller says, "When somebody is destroyed everybody finally contributes to it, but in Willy's case, the end product would be virtually the same" (qtd. in Martin and Meyer 375).

10. MULTIVOLUME WORK In a parenthetical reference, note the volume number first and then the page number(s), with a colon and one space between them.

> Modernist writers prized experimentation and gradually even sought to blur the line between poetry and prose, according to Forster (3: 150).

If you name only one volume of the work in your list of works cited, include only the page number in the parentheses.

11. LITERARY WORK Because literary works are often available in many different editions, cite the page number(s) from the edition you used followed by a semicolon; then give other identifying information that will lead readers to the passage in any edition. Indicate the act and/or scene in a play (*37; sc. 1*). For a novel, indicate the part or chapter (*175; ch. 4*).

> In utter despair, Dostoyevsky's character Mitya wonders aloud about the "terrible tragedies realism inflicts on people" (376; bk. 8, ch. 2).

For a poem, cite the part (if there is one) and line(s), separated by a period. If you are citing only line numbers, use the word *line(s)* in the first reference (*lines 33–34*).

> Whitman speculates, "All goes onward and outward, nothing collapses, / And to die is different from what anyone supposed, and luckier" (6.129-30).

For a verse play, give only the act, scene, and line numbers, separated by periods.

> The witches greet Banquo as "Lesser than Macbeth, and greater" (1.3.65).

12. WORK IN AN ANTHOLOGY OR COLLECTION For an essay, short story, or other piece of prose reprinted in an anthology, use the name of the author of the work, not the editor of the anthology, but use the page number(s) from the anthology.

> Narratives of captivity play a major role in early writing by women in the United States, as demonstrated by Silko (219).

13. SACRED TEXT To cite a sacred text such as the Qur'an or the Bible, give the title of the edition you used, the book, and the chapter and verse (or their equivalent), separated by a period. In your text, spell out the names of books. In parenthetical references, use abbreviations for books with names of five or more letters (*Gen.* for *Genesis*).

> He ignored the admonition "Pride goes before destruction, and a haughty spirit before a fall" (*New Oxford Annotated Bible*, Prov. 16.18).

14. ENCYCLOPEDIA OR DICTIONARY ENTRY An entry from a reference work — such as an encyclopedia or dictionary — without an author will appear on the works-cited list under the entry's title. Enclose the title in quotation marks and place it in parentheses. Omit the page number for reference works that arrange entries alphabetically.

> The term *prion* was coined by Stanley B. Prusiner from the words *proteinaceous* and *infectious* and a suffix meaning *particle*. ("Prion").

15. GOVERNMENT SOURCE WITH NO AUTHOR NAMED Because entries for sources authored by government agencies will appear on your list of works cited under the name of the country (see 16d, item 71), your in-text citation for such a source should include the name of the country as well as the name of the agency responsible for the source.

> To reduce the agricultural runoff into the Chesapeake Bay, the United States Environmental Protection Agency has argued that "[h]igh nutrient loading crops, such as corn and soybean, should be replaced with alternatives in environmentally sensitive areas" (2-26).

16. ELECTRONIC OR NONPRINT SOURCE Give enough information in a signal phrase or in parentheses for readers to locate the source in your list of works cited. Many works found online or in electronic databases lack stable page numbers; you can omit the page number in such cases. However, if you are citing a work with stable pagination, such as an article in PDF format, include the page number in parentheses.

> As a *Slate* analysis has noted, "Prominent sports psychologists get praised for their successes and don't get grief for their failures" (Engber).

The source, an article on a Web site, does not have stable pagination.

> According to Whitmarsh, the British military had experimented with using balloons for observation as far back as 1879 (328).

The source, an online PDF of a print article, includes stable page numbers.

If the source includes numbered sections, paragraphs, or screens, include the abbreviation (*sec.*), paragraph (*par.*), or screen (*scr.*) and the number in parentheses.

> Sherman notes that the "immediate, interactive, and on-the-spot" nature of Internet information can make nondigital media seem outdated (sec. 32).

17. ENTIRE WORK Include the reference in the text, without any page numbers.

> Jon Krakauer's *Into the Wild* both criticizes and admires the solitary impulses of its young hero, which end up killing him.

18. TWO OR MORE SOURCES IN ONE CITATION Separate the information with semicolons.

> Economists recommend that *employment* be redefined to include unpaid domestic labor (Clark 148; Nevins 39).

19. VISUAL INCLUDED IN THE TEXT When you include an image in your text, number it and include a parenthetical reference that precedes the image in your text *(see Fig. 2)*. Number figures (photos, drawings, cartoons, maps, graphs, and charts) and tables separately. Each visual should include a caption with the figure or table number and information about the source.

> This trend is illustrated in a chart distributed by the College Board as part of its 2002 analysis of aggregate SAT data (see Fig. 1).

Soon after the preceding sentence, readers find the following figure and caption (see 16e to read the research paper):

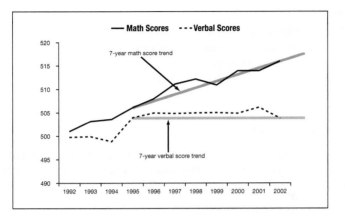

Fig. 1 Comparison of SAT math and verbal scores (1992-2002). Trend lines added. Kristin Carnahan and Chiara Coletti, *Ten-Year Trend in SAT Scores Indicates Increased Emphasis on Math Is Yielding Results; Reading and Writing Are Causes for Concern* (New York: College Board, 2002; print; 9).

An image that you create might appear with a caption like this:

Fig. 4. Young woman reading a magazine. Personal photograph by author.

16c Explanatory and bibliographic notes

MLA style recommends explanatory notes for information or commentary that would not readily fit into your text but is needed for clarification or further explanation. In addition, MLA style permits bibliographic notes for citing several sources for one point and for offering thanks to, information about, or evaluation of a source. Use superscript numbers in the text to refer readers to the notes, which may appear as endnotes (typed under the heading *Notes* on a separate page after the text but before the list of works cited) or as footnotes at the bottom of the page (typed four lines below the last text line).

SUPERSCRIPT NUMBER IN TEXT

Stewart emphasizes the existence of social contacts in Hawthorne's life so that the audience will accept a different Hawthorne, one more attuned to modern times than the figure in Woodberry.[3]

NOTE

[3] Woodberry does, however, show that Hawthorne *was* often an unsociable individual. He emphasizes the seclusion of Hawthorne's mother, who separated herself from her family after the death of her husband, often even taking meals alone (28). Woodberry seems to imply that Mrs. Hawthorne's isolation rubbed off onto her son.

16d List of works cited

A list of works cited is an alphabetical list of the sources you have referred to in your essay. (If your instructor asks you to list everything you have read as background, call the list *Works Consulted.*)

Guidelines for author listings

The list of works cited is arranged alphabetically. The in-text citations in your writing point readers toward particular sources on the list (16b).

NAME CITED IN SIGNAL PHRASE IN TEXT

Crystal explains. . . .

NAME IN PARENTHETICAL CITATION IN TEXT

. . . (Crystal 107).

BEGINNING OF ENTRY ON LIST OF WORKS CITED

Crystal, David.

Directory to MLA style for works-cited entries

Guidelines for author listings

Mahatma Gandhi, the Missing

continued

QUICK HELP

Formatting a list of works cited

- Start your list on a separate page after the text of your essay and any notes.

- Continue the consecutive numbering of pages.

- Center the heading *Works Cited* (not italicized or in quotation marks) one inch from the top of the page.

- Start each entry flush with the left margin; indent subsequent lines for the entry one-half inch. Double-space the entire list.

- List sources alphabetically by the first word. Start with the author's name, if available; if not, use the editor's name, if available. If no author or editor is given, start with the title.

- List the author's last name first, followed by a comma and the first name. If a source has multiple authors, subsequent authors' names appear first name first (see model 2).

- Italicize titles of books and long works, but put titles of articles and other short works in quotation marks.

- In general, use a period and a space after each element of the entry; look at the models in this chapter for information on punctuating particular kinds of entries.

- For a book, list the city of publication (add a country abbreviation for non-U.S. cities that may be unfamiliar). Follow it with a colon and a shortened form of the publisher's name—omit *Co.* or *Inc.*, shorten names such as *Simon & Schuster* to *Simon*, and abbreviate *University Press* to *UP*.

- List dates of periodical publication or of access to electronic items in day, month, year order, and abbreviate months except for May, June, and July.

- Give a medium, such as *Print* or *Web*, for each entry.

- List inclusive page numbers for a part of a larger work. For numbers 1–99, give all digits in the second number. For numbers larger than 99, give the last two digits of the second number (*115–18, 1378–79*) and any other digits that change in the second number (*296–301*).

Models 1–5 below explain how to arrange author names. The information that follows the name of the author depends on the type of work you are citing—a book (models 6–27); a print periodical (models 28–34); a written text from an electronic source, such as an article from a Web site or database (models 35–54); sources from art, film, radio, or other media, including online versions (models 55–69); and other kinds of sources (models 70–78). Consult the model that most closely resembles the kind of source you are using.

1. ONE AUTHOR Put the last name first, followed by a comma, the first name (and initial, if any), and a period.

Crystal, David.

2. MULTIPLE AUTHORS List the first author with the last name first (see model 1). Give the names of any other authors with the first name first. Separate authors' names with commas, and include the word *and* before the last person's name.

Martineau, Jane, Desmond Shawe-Taylor, and Jonathan Bate.

For four or more authors, either list all the names, or list the first author followed by a comma and *et al.* ("and others").

Lupton, Ellen, Jennifer Tobias, Alicia Imperiale, Grace Jeffers, and Randi Mates.

Lupton, Ellen, et al.

3. ORGANIZATION OR GROUP AUTHOR Give the name of the group, government agency, corporation, or other organization listed as the author.

Getty Trust.

United States. Government Accountability Office.

4. UNKNOWN AUTHOR When the author is not identified, begin the entry with the title, and alphabetize by the first important word. Italicize titles of books and long works, but put titles of articles and other short works in quotation marks.

"California Sues EPA over Emissions."

New Concise World Atlas.

5. TWO OR MORE WORKS BY THE SAME AUTHOR Arrange the entries alphabetically by title. Include the author's name in the first entry, but in subsequent entries, use three hyphens followed by a period. (For the basic format for citing a book, see model 6. For the basic format for citing an article from an online newspaper, see model 38.)

Chopra, Anupama. "Bollywood Princess, Hollywood Hopeful." *New York Times*. New York Times, 10 Feb. 2008. Web. 13 Feb. 2008.

---. *King of Bollywood: Shah Rukh Khan and the Seductive World of Indian Cinema*. New York: Warner, 2007. Print.

Note: Use three hyphens only when the work is by *exactly* the same author(s) as the previous entry.

1 Books

6. **BASIC FORMAT FOR A BOOK** Begin with the author name(s). (See models 1–5.) Then include the title and subtitle, the city of publication, the publisher, and the publication date. The source map on pp. 322–23 shows where to find this information in a typical book.

Crystal, David. *Language Play*. Chicago: U of Chicago P, 1998. Print.

Note: Place a period and a space after the name, title, and date. Place a colon after the city and a comma after the publisher, and shorten the publisher's name—omit *Co.* or *Inc.*, and abbreviate *University Press* to *UP*.

7. **AUTHOR AND EDITOR BOTH NAMED**

Bangs, Lester. *Psychotic Reactions and Carburetor Dung*. Ed. Greil Marcus. New York: Knopf, 1988. Print.

Note: To cite the editor's contribution instead, begin the entry with the editor's name.

Marcus, Greil, ed. *Psychotic Reactions and Carburetor Dung*. By Lester Bangs. New York: Knopf, 1988. Print.

8. **EDITOR, NO AUTHOR NAMED**

Wall, Cheryl A., ed. *Changing Our Own Words: Essays on Criticism, Theory, and Writing by Black Women*. New Brunswick: Rutgers UP, 1989. Print.

9. **ANTHOLOGY** Cite an entire anthology the same way you would cite a book with an editor and no named author (see model 8).

Walker, Dale L., ed. *Westward: A Fictional History of the American West*. New York: Forge, 2003. Print.

MLA SOURCE MAP: Books

Take information from the book's title page and copyright page (on the reverse side of the title page), not from the book's cover or a library catalog.

1. **Author.** List the last name first. End with a period. For variations, see models 2–5.

2. **Title.** Italicize the title and any subtitle; capitalize all major words. End with a period.

3. **City of publication.** If more than one city is given, use the first one listed. For foreign cities, add an abbreviation of the country or province (*Cork, Ire.*). Follow it with a colon.

4. **Publisher.** Give a shortened version of the publisher's name (*Oxford UP* for *Oxford University Press*). Follow it with a comma.

5. **Year of publication.** If more than one copyright date is given, use the most recent one. End with a period.

6. **Medium of publication.** End with the medium (*Print*) followed by a period.

A citation for the book on p. 323 would look like this:

Kingsolver, Barbara. *Small Wonder*. New York: Harper, 2002. Print.

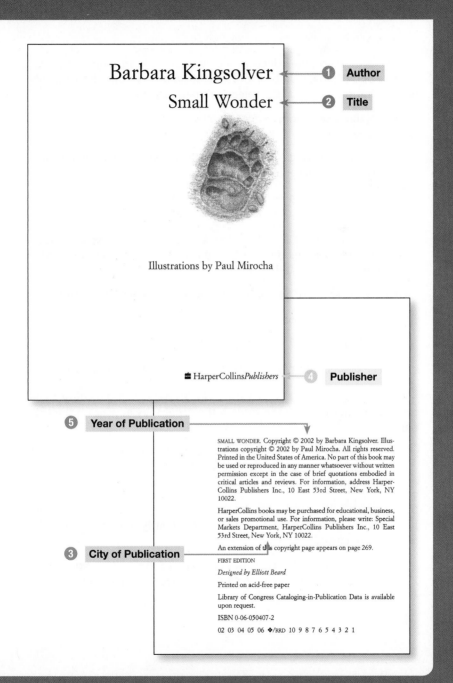

Barbara Kingsolver — **1** Author

Small Wonder — **2** Title

Illustrations by Paul Mirocha

HarperCollins*Publishers* — **4** Publisher

5 Year of Publication

SMALL WONDER. Copyright © 2002 by Barbara Kingsolver. Illustrations copyright © 2002 by Paul Mirocha. All rights reserved. Printed in the United States of America. No part of this book may be used or reproduced in any manner whatsoever without written permission except in the case of brief quotations embodied in critical articles and reviews. For information, address HarperCollins Publishers Inc., 10 East 53rd Street, New York, NY 10022.

HarperCollins books may be purchased for educational, business, or sales promotional use. For information, please write: Special Markets Department, HarperCollins Publishers Inc., 10 East 53rd Street, New York, NY 10022.

An extension of this copyright page appears on page 269.

FIRST EDITION

Designed by Elliott Beard

Printed on acid-free paper

Library of Congress Cataloging-in-Publication Data is available upon request.

ISBN 0-06-050407-2

02 03 04 05 06 ❖/RRD 10 9 8 7 6 5 4 3 2 1

3 City of Publication

10. WORK IN AN ANTHOLOGY OR CHAPTER IN A BOOK WITH AN EDITOR
List the author(s) of the selection or chapter; its title, in quotation marks; the title of the book, italicized; *Ed.* and the name(s) of the editor(s); publication information; and the selection's page numbers.

Komunyakaa, Yusef. "Facing It." *The Seagull Reader*. Ed. Joseph Kelly. New York: Norton, 2000. 126-27. Print.

Note: Use the following format to provide original publication information for a reprinted selection:

Byatt, A. S. "The Thing in the Forest." *New Yorker* 3 June 2002: 80-89. Rpt. in *The O. Henry Prize Stories 2003*. Ed. Laura Furman. New York: Anchor, 2003. 3-22. Print.

11. TWO OR MORE ITEMS FROM THE SAME ANTHOLOGY List the anthology as one entry (see model 9). Also list each selection separately with a cross-reference to the anthology.

Estleman, Loren D. "Big Tim Magoon and the Wild West." Walker 391-404. Print.

Salzer, Susan K. "Miss Libbie Tells All." Walker 199-212. Print.

12. TRANSLATION

Bolaño, Roberto. *2666*. Trans. Natasha Wimmer. New York: Farrar, 2008. Print.

13. BOOK WITH BOTH TRANSLATOR AND EDITOR List the editor's and translator's names after the title, in the order they appear on the title page.

Kant, Immanuel. *"Toward Perpetual Peace" and Other Writings on Politics, Peace, and History*. Ed. Pauline Kleingeld. Trans. David L. Colclasure. New Haven: Yale UP, 2006. Print.

14. TRANSLATION OF A SECTION OF A BOOK If different translators have worked on various parts of the book, identify the translator of the part you are citing.

García Lorca, Federico. "The Little Mad Boy." Trans. W. S. Merwin. *The Selected Poems of Federico García Lorca*. Ed. Francisco García Lorca and Donald M. Allen. London: Penguin, 1969. Print.

15. TRANSLATION OF A BOOK BY AN UNKNOWN AUTHOR

Grettir's Saga. Trans. Denton Fox and Hermann Palsson. Toronto: U of Toronto P, 1974.
   Print.

16. BOOK IN A LANGUAGE OTHER THAN ENGLISH Include a translation
of the title in brackets, if necessary.

Bendetti, Mario. *La borra del café [The Coffee Grind]*. Buenos Aires: Sudamericana,
   2000. Print.

17. GRAPHIC NARRATIVE If the words and images are created by the
same person, cite a graphic narrative just as you would a book (model 6).

Bechdel, Alison. *Fun Home: A Family Tragicomic*. New York: Houghton, 2006. Print.

If the work is a collaboration, indicate the author or illustrator who is
most important to your research before the title of the work. List other

---

QUICK HELP

Combining parts of models

What should you do if your source doesn't match the model exactly? Suppose,
for instance, that your source is a translated essay that appears in the fifth
edition of an anthology.

- Identify a basic model to follow. If you decide that your source looks most
  like an essay in an anthology, you would start with a citation that looks like
  model 10.

- Look for models that show the additional elements in your source. For
  this example, you would need to add elements of model 14 (for the translation) and model 18 (for an edition other than the first).

- Add new elements from other models to your basic model in the order
  indicated.

- If you still aren't sure how to arrange the pieces to create a combination
  model, check the *MLA Handbook* or ask your instructor.

contributors after the title, in the order of their appearance on the title page. Label each person's contribution to the work.

> Stavans, Ilan, writer. *Latino USA: A Cartoon History*. Illus. Lalo Arcaraz. New York: Basic, 2000. Print.

18. EDITION OTHER THAN THE FIRST

> Walker, John A. *Art in the Age of Mass Media*. 3rd ed. London: Pluto, 2001. Print.

19. ONE VOLUME OF A MULTIVOLUME WORK Give the number of the volume cited after the title. Including the total number of volumes after the medium is optional.

> Ch'oe, Yong-Ho, Peter Lee, and William Theodore De Barry, eds. *Sources of Korean Tradition*. Vol. 2. New York: Columbia UP, 2000. Print. 2 vols.

20. TWO OR MORE VOLUMES OF A MULTIVOLUME WORK

> Ch'oe, Yong-Ho, Peter Lee, and William Theodore De Barry, eds. *Sources of Korean Tradition*. 2 vols. New York: Columbia UP, 2000. Print.

21. PREFACE, FOREWORD, INTRODUCTION, OR AFTERWORD After the writer's name, describe the contribution. After the title, indicate the book's author (with *By*) or editor (with *Ed.*).

> Atwan, Robert. Foreword. *The Best American Essays 2002*. Ed. Stephen Jay Gould. Boston: Houghton, 2002. viii-xii. Print.

> Moore, Thurston. Introduction. *Confusion Is Next: The Sonic Youth Story*. By Alec Foege. New York: St. Martin's, 1994. xi. Print.

22. ENTRY IN A REFERENCE BOOK For a well-known encyclopedia, note the edition (if identified) and year of publication. If the entries are alphabetized, omit publication information and page number.

> Judge, Erica. "Foreign-Language Daily Newspapers in New York City." *The Encyclopedia of New York City*. Ed. Kenneth T. Jackson. New Haven: Yale UP, 1995.

> Kettering, Alison McNeil. "Art Nouveau." *World Book Encyclopedia*. 2002 ed. Print.

23. BOOK THAT IS PART OF A SERIES Cite the series name (and number, if any) from the title page.

> Nichanian, Marc, and Vartan Matiossian, eds. *Yeghishe Charents: Poet of the Revolution*. Costa Mesa: Mazda, 2003. Print. Armenian Studies Ser. 5.

24. REPUBLICATION (MODERN EDITION OF AN OLDER BOOK) Indicate the original publication date after the title.

> Austen, Jane. *Sense and Sensibility*. 1813. New York: Dover, 1966. Print.

25. PUBLISHER'S IMPRINT If the title page gives a publisher's imprint, hyphenate the imprint and the publisher's name.

> Hornby, Nick. *About a Boy*. New York: Riverhead-Penguin Putnam, 1998. Print.

26. BOOK WITH A TITLE WITHIN THE TITLE Do not italicize a book title within a title. For an article title within a title, italicize as usual and place the article title in quotation marks.

> Mullaney, Julie. *Arundhati Roy's* The God of Small Things: *A Reader's Guide*. New York: Continuum, 2002. Print.

> Rhynes, Martha. *"I, Too, Sing America": The Story of Langston Hughes*. Greensboro: Morgan, 2002. Print.

27. SACRED TEXT To cite individual published editions of sacred books, begin the entry with the title. If you are not citing a particular edition, do not include sacred texts in the list of works cited.

> *Qur'an: The Final Testament (Authorized English Version) with Arabic Text*. Trans. Rashad Khalifa. Fremont: Universal Unity, 2000. Print.

2 Print periodicals

Begin with the author name(s). (See models 1–5.) Then include the article title, the title of the periodical, the date or volume information, and the page numbers. The source map on pp. 328–30 shows where to find this information in a sample periodical.

28. ARTICLE IN A JOURNAL Follow the journal title with the volume number, a period, the issue number (if given), and the year (in parentheses).

> Gigante, Denise. "The Monster in the Rainbow: Keats and the Science of Life." *PMLA* 117.3 (2002): 433-48. Print.

1. **Author.** List the last name first. End with a period. For variations, see models 2–5.

2. **Article title.** Put the title and any subtitle in quotation marks; capitalize all major words. Place a period inside the closing quotation mark.

3. **Periodical title.** Italicize the title; capitalize all major words. Omit any initial *A*, *An*, or *The*.

4. **Volume and issue / Date of publication.** For journals, give the volume number and issue number (if any), separated by a period; then list the year in parentheses and follow it with a colon. For magazines, list the day (if given), month, and year.

5. **Page numbers.** List inclusive page numbers. If the article skips pages, put the first page number and a plus sign. End with a period.

6. **Medium.** Give the medium (*Print*). End with a period.

A citation for the journal article on p. 329 would look like this:

Marcoplos, Lucas. "Drafting Away from It All." *Southern Cultures* 12.1 (2006): 33-41. Print.

A citation for the magazine article on p. 330 would look like this:

Quart, Alissa. "Lost Media, Found Media: Snapshots from the Future of Writing." *Columbia Journalism Review* May/June 2008: 30-34. Print.

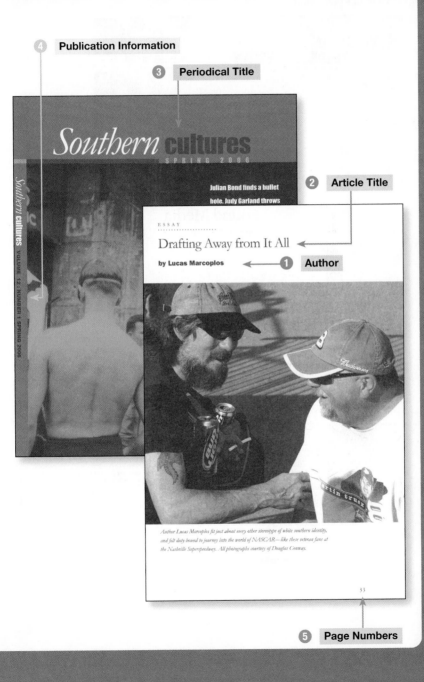

4 Publication Information

3 Periodical Title

Southern **cultures**
SPRING 2006

Julian Bond finds a bullet
hole. Judy Garland throws

Southern **cultures** VOLUME 12 : NUMBER 1 SPRING 2006

2 Article Title

ESSAY

Drafting Away from It All

by Lucas Marcoplos

1 Author

*Author Lucas Marcoplos fit just about every other stereotype of white southern identity,
and felt duty-bound to journey into the world of NASCAR—like these veteran fans at
the Nashville Superspeedway. All photographs courtesy of Douglas Conway.*

33

5 Page Numbers

4 Date of Publication

COLUMBIA
JOURNALISM
REVIEW

May / June 2008 • cjr.org

3 Periodical Title

The Futur[e...]
Writi[ng]

Nonfiction's disqui[...]
ALISSA QUART

Kindle isn't it, but [...]
EZRA KLEIN

UNDER THE SHI[...]
A reporter recalls [...]
that got him throu[gh...]
CAMERON MCWHIRT[ER]

LOVE THY NEIGH[BOR]
The religion beat i[...]
TIM TOWNSEND

2 Article Title

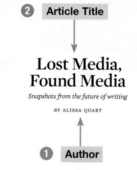

Lost Media,
Found Media

Snapshots from the future of writing

BY ALISSA QUART

1 Author

If there were an ashram for people who worship contemplative long-form journalism, it would be the Nieman Conference on Narrative Journalism. This March, at the Sheraton Boston Hotel, hundreds of journalists, authors, students, and aspirants came for the weekend event. Seated on metal chairs in large conference rooms, we learned about muscular storytelling (the Q-shaped narrative structure—who knew?). We sipped cups of coffee and ate bagels and heard about reporting history through letters and public documents and how to evoke empathy for our subjects, particularly our most marginal ones. As we listened to reporters discussing great feats—exposing Walter Reed's fetid living quarters for wounded soldiers, for instance—we also renewed our pride in our profession. In short, the conference exemplified the best of the older media models, the ones that have so recently fallen into economic turmoil.

Yet even at the weekend's strongest lectures on interview techniques or the long-form profile, we couldn't ignore the digital elephant in the room. We all knew as writers that the kinds of pieces we were discussing require months of work to be both deep and refined, and that we were all hard-pressed for the time and the money to do that. It was always hard for nonfiction writers, but something seems to have changed. For those of us who believed in the value of the journalism and literary nonfiction of the past, we had become like the people at the ashram after the guru has died.

Right now, journalism is more or less divided into two camps, which I will call Lost Media and Found Media. I went to the Nieman conference partially because I wanted to see how the forces creating this new division are affecting and afflicting the Lost Media world that I love best, not on the institutional level, but for reporters and writers themselves. This world includes people who write for all the newspapers and magazines that are currently struggling with layoffs, speedups, hiring freezes, buyouts, the death or shrinkage of film- and book-review sections, limits on expensive investigative work, the erasure of foreign bureaus, and the general narrowing of institutional ambition. It includes freelance writers competing with hordes of ever-younger competitors willing to write and publish online for free, the fade-out of established journalistic career paths, and, perhaps most crucially, a muddied sense of the meritorious, as blogs level and scramble the value and status of print publications, and of professional writers. The glamour and influence once associated with a magazine elite seem to have faded, becoming a sort of pastiche of winsome articles about yearning and boxers and dinners at Elaine's.

Found Media-ites, meanwhile, are the bloggers, the contributors to Huffington Post-type sites that aggregate blogs, as well as other work that somebody else paid for, and the new nonprofits and pay-per-article schemes that aim to save journalism from 20 percent profit-margin demands. Although these elements are often disparate, together they compose the new media landscape. In economic terms, I mean all the outlets for nonfiction writing that seem to be thriving in the new era or striving to fill niches that Lost Media is giving up in a new order. Stylistically, Found Media tends to feel spontaneous, almost accidental. It's a domain dominated by the young, where writers get points not for following traditions or burnishing them but for amateur and hybrid vigor, for creating their own venues and their own genres. It is about public expression and community—not quite John Dewey's Great Community, which the critic Eric Alterman alluded to in a recent *New Yorker* article on newspapers, but rather a fractured form of Dewey's ideal: call it Great Communities.

To be a Found Media journalist or pundit, one need not be elite, expert, or trained; one must simply produce punchy intellectual property that is in conversation with groups of

30 MAY/JUNE 2008

Illustration by Tomer Hanuka

5 Page Numbers

Formatting periodical entries

- Put titles of articles from periodicals in quotation marks. Place the period inside the closing quotation mark.

- Give the title of the periodical as it appears on the magazine's or journal's cover or newspaper's front page; omit any initial *A*, *An*, or *The*. Italicize the title.

- For journals, include the volume number, a period, the issue number, if given, and the year in parentheses.

- For magazines and newspapers, give the date in this order: day (if given), month, year. Abbreviate months except for May, June, and July.

- List inclusive page numbers if the article appears on consecutive pages. If it skips pages, give only the first page number and a plus sign.

- If you read the article in a print publication, end with the medium *Print* and a period. If you accessed the article electronically, consult models 35–38 to see what additional information you will need to include; then give the medium *Web*, a period, and the date you accessed the source.

29. ARTICLE IN A MAGAZINE Provide the date from the magazine cover instead of volume or issue numbers.

Surowiecki, James. "The Stimulus Strategy." *New Yorker* 25 Feb. 2008: 29. Print.

Taubin, Amy. "All Talk?" *Film Comment* Nov.-Dec. 2007: 45-47. Print.

30. ARTICLE IN A NEWSPAPER Include the edition (if listed) and the section number or letter (if listed).

Bernstein, Nina. "On Lucille Avenue, the Immigration Debate." *New York Times* 26 June 2006, late ed.: A1+. Print.

Note: For locally published newspapers, add the city in brackets after the name if it is not part of the name: *Globe and Mail [Toronto]*.

31. ARTICLE THAT SKIPS PAGES When an article skips pages, give only the first page number and a plus sign.

Tyrnauer, Matthew. "Empire by Martha." *Vanity Fair* Sept. 2002: 364+. Print.

QUICK HELP

Citing electronic sources

The entry for an electronic source may include up to six basic elements.

- *Author*. For variations on author, see models 1–5.

- *Title*. Italicize the titles of books or entire sites. Put shorter titles in quotation marks. Capitalize all important words.

- *Print publication information*. For an online book, journal article, or work from a database that provides information about the work's publication in print, include the volume and issue number with the year in parentheses, then a colon and the inclusive page numbers, or *n. pag.* if no page numbers are listed. (For articles taken from online newspapers and magazines, however, omit the print publication information.)

- *Electronic publication information*. For a work from a Web site, including online magazines and newspapers, list all of the following that you can find: the title of the site, italicized; the site's editor(s), if given, preceded by *Ed.*; and the name of any sponsor. (The sponsor's name usually appears at the bottom of the home page.) Then add the date of electronic publication or latest update. For a work from a database such as InfoTrac or LexisNexis, give the name of the database, italicized.

- *Medium of publication*. List the medium (*Web*).

- *Date of access*. Give the most recent date you accessed the source.

The *MLA Handbook* does not usually require a URL. If you think your readers will have difficulty finding the source without one, put it after the period following the date of access, inside angle brackets. Put a period after the closing bracket.

---

32. EDITORIAL OR LETTER TO THE EDITOR Include the writer's name, if given, and the title, if any, followed by a label for the work.

"California Dreaming" Editorial. *Nation* 25 Feb. 2008: 4. Print.

Galbraith, James K. "JFK's Plans to Withdraw." Letter. *New York Review of Books* 6 Dec. 2007: 77-78. Print.

33. REVIEW

Franklin, Nancy. "Teen Spirit." Rev. of *Glee*, by Ryan Murphy, Brad Falchuk, and Ian Brennan. *New Yorker* 10 May 2010: 72-73. Print.

Schwarz, Benjamin. Rev. of *The Second World War: A Short History*, by R.A.C. Parker. *Atlantic Monthly* May 2002: 110-11. Print.

34. UNSIGNED ARTICLE

"Performance of the Week." *Time* 6 Oct. 2003: 18. Print.

3 Electronic sources

Electronic sources such as Web sites differ from print sources in the ease with which they can be—and frequently are—changed, updated, or even eliminated. In addition, the various electronic media do not organize their works the same way. The most commonly cited electronic sources are documents from Web sites and databases.

35. WORK FROM A DATABASE The basic format for citing a work from a database appears in the source map on pp. 334–35.

For a periodical article that you access in an online database, including a work you find in a library subscription service such as Academic Search Premier, begin with the author's name (if given); the title of the work, in quotation marks; and publication information for the print version of the work (see models 28–34). Include the page numbers from the print version; if no page numbers are available, use *n. pag.* Then give the name of the online database, italicized; the medium (*Web*); and your most recent date of access.

Collins, Ross F. "Cattle Barons and Ink Slingers: How Cow Country Journalists Created a Great American Myth." *American Journalism* 24.3 (2007); 7-29. *Communication and Mass Media Complete.* Web. 7 Feb. 2010.

36. ARTICLE IN AN ONLINE JOURNAL Cite an online journal article as you would a print journal article (see model 28). If an online article does not have page numbers, use *n. pag.* End with the medium consulted (*Web*) and the date of access.

Gallagher, Brian. "Greta Garbo Is Sad: Some Historical Reflections on the Paradoxes of Stardom in the American Film Industry, 1910-1960." *Images: A Journal of Film and Popular Culture* 3 (1997): n. pag. Web. 7 Aug. 2009.

37. ARTICLE IN AN ONLINE MAGAZINE See model 29 for print publication information if the article also appears in print. After the name of the magazine, give the sponsor of the Web site, followed by a comma and the date of publication. Then give the medium (*Web*) and the date of access.

Shapiro, Walter. "The Quest for Universal Healthcare." *Salon.* Salon Media Group, Inc., 21 Feb. 2008. Web. 2 Mar. 2008.

MLA SOURCE MAP: Articles from databases

Library subscriptions—such as EBSCOhost and Academic Search Premier—provide access to huge databases of articles.

1. **Author.** List the last name first. End with a period. For variations, see models 2–5.

2. **Article title.** Enclose the title and any subtitle in quotation marks.

3. **Periodical title.** Italicize it. Exclude any initial *A*, *An*, or *The*.

4. **Print publication information.** List the volume and issue number, if any; the date of publication, including the day (if given), month, and year, in that order; and the inclusive page numbers. If an article has no page numbers, write *n. pag.*

5. **Database name.** Italicize the name of the database.

6. **Medium.** For an online database, use *Web*.

7. **Date of access.** Give the day, month, and year, then a period.

A citation for the article on p. 335 would look like this:

Arnett, Robert P. "*Casino Royale* and Franchise Remix: James Bond as

Superhero." *Film Criticism* 33.3 (2009): 1-16. *Academic Search Premier.*

Web. 16 May 2010.

③ **Periodical Title**

② **Article Title**

Title:	**Casino Royale and Franchise Remix: James Bond as Superhero.**
Authors:	Arnett, Robert P.1 ← ① **Author**
Source:	Film Criticism; Spring2009, Vol. 33 Issue 3, p1-16, 16p
Document Type:	Article
Subject Terms:	*JAMES Bond films ④ **Print Publication Information** *FILM genres *BOND, James (Fictitious character) *SUPERHERO films
Reviews & Products:	CASINO Royale (Film)
People:	CRAIG, Daniel
Abstract:	The article discusses the role of the film "Casino Royale" in remixing the James Bond franchise. The author believes that the remixed Bond franchise has shifted its genre to a superhero franchise. When Sony acquired MGM in 2004, part of its plans is to transform the 007 franchise at par with "Spiderman." The remixed franchise re-aligns its franchise criteria with those established by superhero films. The author cites "Casino Royale's" narrative structure as an example of the success of the film as franchise remixed for the future. The portrayal of Bond as a superhero by actor Daniel Craig is discussed.
Author Affiliations:	1Associate professor, Department of Communication and Theatre Arts, Old Dominion University
ISSN:	01635069
Accession Number:	47966995
Database:	Academic Search Premier

⑤ **Database Name**

38. ARTICLE IN AN ONLINE NEWSPAPER After the name of the newspaper, give the publisher, publication date, medium (*Web*), and access date.

> Bustillo, Miguel, and Carol J. Williams. "Old Guard in Cuba Keeps Reins." *Los Angeles Times*. Los Angeles Times, 25 Feb. 2008. Web. 26 Feb. 2010.

39. ONLINE BOOK Provide information as for a print book (see models 6–27); then give the electronic publication information, the medium, and the date of access.

> Euripides. *The Trojan Women*. Trans. Gilbert Murray. New York: Oxford UP, 1915. *Internet Sacred Text Archive*. Web. 12 Oct. 2010.

Note: Cite a part of an online book as you would a part of a print book (see models 10 and 21). Give the print (if any) and electronic publication information, the medium (*Web*), and the date of access.

> Riis, Jacob. "The Genesis of the Gang." *The Battle with the Slum*. New York: Macmillan, 1902. *Bartleby.com: Great Books Online*. 2000. Web. 31 Mar. 2010.

40. ONLINE POEM Include the poet's name, the title of the poem, and the print publication information (if any). End with electronic publication information, the medium (*Web*), and the date of access.

> Dickinson, Emily. "The Grass." *Poems: Emily Dickinson*. Boston, 1891. *University of Michigan Humanities Text Initiative: American Verse Project*. Web. 6 Jan. 2010.

41. ONLINE EDITORIAL OR LETTER Include the word *Editorial* or *Letter* after the author (if given) and title (if any). End with the periodical name, the sponsor of the Web site, the date of electronic publication, the medium, and the access date.

> "The Funding Gap." Editorial. *Washington Post*. Washington Post, 5 Nov. 2003. Web. 19 Oct. 2009.

> Moore, Paula. "Go Vegetarian." Letter. *New York Times*. New York Times, 25 Feb. 2008. Web. 25 Feb. 2010.

42. ONLINE REVIEW Cite an online review as you would a print review (see model 33). End with the name of the Web site, the sponsor, the date of electronic publication, the medium, and the date of access.

> O'Hehir, Andrew. "Parody or Party?" Rev. of *Iron Man 2*, dir. Jon Favreau. *Salon*. Salon Media Group, 7 May 2010. Web. 24 May 2010.

43. ENTRY IN AN ONLINE REFERENCE WORK Cite the entry as you would an entry from a print reference work (see model 22). Follow with the name of the Web site, the sponsor, date of publication, medium, and date of access.

"Tour de France." *Encyclopaedia Britannica Online.* Encyclopaedia Britannica, 2006.
    Web. 21 May 2006.

44. WORK FROM A WEB SITE For basic information on citing a work from a Web site, see the source map on pp. 338–39. Include all of the following elements that are available: the author; the title of the document, in quotation marks; the name of the Web site, italicized; the name of the publisher or sponsor (if none is available, use *N.p.*); the date of publication (if not available, use *n.d.*); the medium consulted (*Web*); and the date of access.

"America: A Center-Left Nation." *Media Matters for America.* Media Matters for
    America, 27 May 2009. Web. 31 May 2009.

Stauder, Ellen Keck. "Darkness Audible: Negative Capability and Mark Doty's 'Nocturne
    in Black and Gold.'" *Romantic Circles Praxis Series.* U of Maryland, 2003. Web. 28
    Sept. 2003.

45. ENTIRE WEB SITE Follow the guidelines for a specific work from the Web, beginning with the name of the author, editor, compiler, or director (if any), followed by the title of the Web site, italicized; the name of the sponsor or publisher (if none, use *N.p.*); the date of publication or last update; the medium of publication (*Web*); and the date of access.

Bernstein, Charles, Kenneth Goldsmith, Martin Spinelli, and Patrick Durgin, eds.
    Electronic Poetry Corner. SUNY Buffalo, 2003. Web. 26 Sept. 2006.

Weather.com. Weather Channel Interactive, 2010. Web. 13 Mar. 2010.

For a personal Web site, include the name of the person who created the site; the title, in quotation marks if it is part of a larger work or italicized if it is not, or (if there is no title) a description such as *Home page*, not italicized; the name of the larger site, if different from the personal site's title; the publisher or sponsor of the site (if none, use *N.p.*); the date of the last update; the medium of publication (*Web*); and the date of access.

Ede, Lisa. Home Page. *Oregon State.* Oregon State U, 2010. Web. 17 May 2010.

MLA SOURCE MAP: Works from Web sites

You may need to browse other parts of a site to find some of the following elements, and some sites may omit elements. Uncover as much information as you can.

1 **Author.** List the last name first. End with a period. If no author is given, begin with the title. For variations, see models 2–5.

2 **Title of work.** Enclose the title and any subtitle of the work in quotation marks.

3 **Title of Web site.** Give the title of the entire Web site, italicized.

4 **Publisher or sponsor.** Look for the sponsor's name at the bottom of the home page. If no information is available, write *N.p.* Follow it with a comma.

5 **Date of publication or latest update.** Give the most recent date, followed by a period. If no date is available, use *n.d.*

6 **Medium.** Use *Web* and follow it with a period.

7 **Date of access.** Give the date you accessed the work. End with a period.

A citation for the work on p. 339 would look like this:

Tønnesson, Øyvind. "Mahatma Gandhi, the Missing Laureate." *Nobelprize.org.*

Nobel Foundation, 1 Dec. 1999. Web. 4 May 2005.

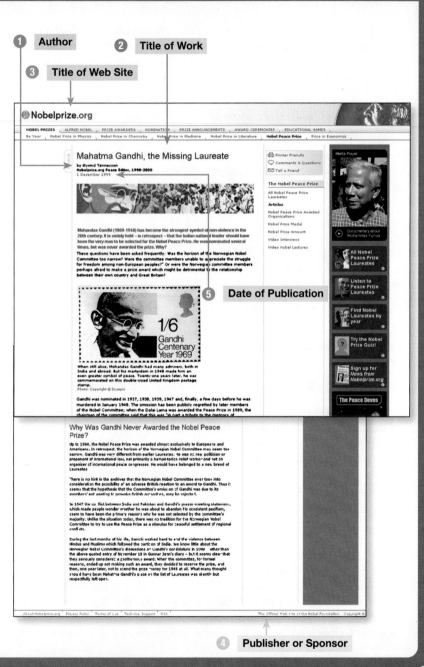

1 Author

2 Title of Work

3 Title of Web Site

5 Date of Publication

4 Publisher or Sponsor

Nobelprize.org

NOBEL PRIZES   ALFRED NOBEL   PRIZE AWARDERS   NOMINATION   PRIZE ANNOUNCEMENTS   AWARD CEREMONIES   EDUCATIONAL GAMES
By Year   Nobel Prize in Physics   Nobel Prize in Chemistry   Nobel Prize in Medicine   Nobel Prize in Literature   Nobel Peace Prize   Prize in Economics

Mahatma Gandhi, the Missing Laureate

by Øyvind Tønnesson
Nobelprize.org Peace Editor, 1998-2000
1 December 1999

Printer Friendly
Comments & Questions
Tell a Friend

The Nobel Peace Prize

All Nobel Peace Prize Laureates

Articles

Nobel Peace Prize Awarded Organizations

Nobel Prize Medal

Nobel Prize Amount

Video Interviews

Video Nobel Lectures

Mohandas Gandhi (1869-1948) has become the strongest symbol of non-violence in the 20th century. It is widely held – in retrospect – that the Indian national leader should have been the very man to be selected for the Nobel Peace Prize. He was nominated several times, but was never awarded the prize. Why?

These questions have been asked frequently: Was the horizon of the Norwegian Nobel Committee too narrow? Were the committee members unable to appreciate the struggle for freedom among non-European peoples?" Or were the Norwegian committee members perhaps afraid to make a prize award which might be detrimental to the relationship between their own country and Great Britain?

When still alive, Mohandas Gandhi had many admirers, both in India and abroad. But his martyrdom in 1948 made him an even greater symbol of peace. Twenty-one years later, he was commemorated on this double-sized United Kingdom postage stamp.
Photo: Copyright © Scanpix

Gandhi was nominated in 1937, 1938, 1939, 1947 and, finally, a few days before he was murdered in January 1948. The omission has been publicly regretted by later members of the Nobel Committee; when the Dalai Lama was awarded the Peace Prize in 1989, the chairman of the committee said that this was "in part a tribute to the memory of

Media Player

Documentary about Muhammad Yunus

All Nobel Peace Prize Laureates

Listen to Peace Prize Laureates

Find Nobel Laureates by year

Try the Nobel Prize Quiz!

Sign up for News from Nobelprize.org

The Peace Doves

Why Was Gandhi Never Awarded the Nobel Peace Prize?

Up to 1960, the Nobel Peace Prize was awarded almost exclusively to Europeans and Americans. In retrospect, the horizon of the Norwegian Nobel Committee may seem too narrow. Gandhi was very different from earlier Laureates. He was no real politician or proponent of international law, not primarily a humanitarian relief worker and not an organiser of international peace congresses. He would have belonged to a new breed of Laureates

There is no hint in the archives that the Norwegian Nobel Committee ever took into consideration the possibility of an adverse British reaction to an award to Gandhi. Thus it seems that the hypothesis that the Committee's omission of Gandhi was due to its members' not wanting to provoke British authorities, may be rejected.

In 1947 the conflict between India and Pakistan and Gandhi's prayer-meeting statement, which made people wonder whether he was about to abandon his consistent pacifism, seem to have been the primary reason why he was not selected by the committee's majority. Unlike the situation today, there was no tradition for the Norwegian Nobel Committee to try to use the Peace Prize as a stimulus for peaceful settlement of regional conflicts.

During the last months of his life, Gandhi worked hard to end the violence between Hindus and Muslims which followed the partition of India. We know little about the Norwegian Nobel Committee's discussions on Gandhi's candidature in 1948 – other than the above quoted entry of November 18 in Gunnar Jahn's diary – but it seems clear that they seriously considered a posthumous award. When the committee, for formal reasons, ended up not making such an award, they decided to reserve the prize, and then, one year later, not to spend the prize money for 1948 at all. What many thought should have been Mahatma Gandhi's place on the list of Laureates was silently but respectfully left open.

46. ACADEMIC COURSE WEB SITE For a course site, include the name of the instructor, the title of the course in quotation marks, the title of the site in italics, the department (if relevant) and institution sponsoring the site, the medium consulted (*Web*), and the access information.

> Creekmur, Corey K., and Philip Lutgendorf. "Topics in Asian Cinema: Popular Hindi Cinema." *University of Iowa*. Depts. of English, Cinema, and Comparative Literature, U of Iowa. Web. 13 Mar. 2007.

For a department Web site, give the department name, the description *Dept. home page*, the institution (in italics), the site sponsor, the medium (*Web*), and the access information.

> English Dept. home page. *Amherst College*. Amherst Coll., n.d. Web. 5 Apr. 2010.

47. BLOG (WEB LOG) For an entire blog, give the author's name; the title of the blog, italicized; the sponsor or publisher of the blog (if there is none, use *N.p.*); the date of the most recent update; the medium (*Web*); and the date of access.

> *Little Green Footballs*. Little Green Footballs. 5 Mar. 2010. Web. 5 Mar. 2010.

Note: To cite a blogger who writes under a pseudonym, begin with the pseudonym and then put the writer's real name (if you know it) in square brackets.

> Atrios [Duncan Black]. *Eschaton*. N.p., 27 June 2010. Web. 27 June 2010.

48. POST OR COMMENT ON A BLOG Give the author's name; the title of the post or comment, in quotation marks (if there is no title, use the description *Web log post* or *Web log comment*, not italicized); the title of the blog, italicized; the sponsor of the blog (if there is none, use *N.p.*); the date of the most recent update; the medium (*Web*); and the date of access.

> Marcotte, Amanda. "Rights without Perfection." *Pandagon*. N.p., 16 May 2010. Web. 16 May 2010.

49. ENTRY IN A WIKI Because wiki content is collectively edited, do not include an author. Treat a wiki as you would a work from a Web site (see model 44). Include the title of the entry; the name of the wiki, italicized; the sponsor or publisher of the wiki (use *N.p.* if there is no sponsor); the date of the latest update; the medium (*Web*); and the date of access. Check with your instructor before using a wiki as a source.

"Fédération Internationale de Football Association." *Wikimedia*. Wikimedia Foundation, 27 June 2010. Web. 27 June 2010.

50. POSTING TO A DISCUSSION GROUP OR NEWSGROUP Begin with the author's name and the title of the posting in quotation marks (or the words *Online posting*). Follow with the name of the Web site, the sponsor or publisher of the site (use *N.p.* if there is no sponsor), the date of publication, the medium (*Web*), and the date of access.

Daly, Catherine. "Poetry Slams." *Poetics Discussion List*. SUNY Buffalo, 29 Aug. 2003. Web. 1 Oct. 2003.

51. POSTING OR MESSAGE ON A SOCIAL NETWORKING SITE To cite a message or posting on Facebook or another social networking site, include the writer's name, a description of the posting that mentions the recipient, the date it was written, and the medium of delivery. (The MLA does not provide guidelines for citing postings or messages on such sites; this model is based on the MLA's guidelines for citing email.)

Ferguson, Sarah. Message to the author. 6 Mar. 2008. Facebook message.

52. EMAIL Include the writer's name; the subject line, in quotation marks; *Message to* (not italicized or in quotation marks) followed by the recipient's name; the date of the message; and the medium of delivery (*E-mail*). (MLA style hyphenates *e-mail*.)

Harris, Jay. "Thoughts on Impromptu Stage Productions." Message to the author. 16 July 2006. E-mail.

53. COMPUTER SOFTWARE OR ONLINE GAME Include the author name (if given); the title, italicized; the version number (if given); the publisher or sponsor; and the publication date (or *n.d.* if no date is given). End with the medium and the date of access.

Web Cache Illuminator. Vers. 4.02. NorthStar Solutions, n.d. Web. 12 Nov. 2003.

54. CD-ROM OR DVD-ROM Include the medium.

Cambridge Advanced Learner's Dictionary. 3rd ed. Cambridge: Cambridge UP, 2008. CD-ROM.

Grand Theft Auto: San Andreas. New York: Rockstar Games, 2004. DVD-ROM.

4 Video and audio sources (including online versions)

55. FILM OR DVD If you cite a particular person's work, start with that name. If not, start with the title; then name the director, distributor, and year of release. Other contributors, such as writers or performers, may follow the director. If you cite a DVD instead of a theatrical release, include the original film release date and the label *DVD*. For material found on a Web site, give the name of the site or database, the medium (*Web*), and the access date.

> *Spirited Away*. Dir. Hayao Miyazaki. 2001. Walt Disney Video, 2003. DVD.

> *Inception*. Dir. Christopher Nolan. Perf. Leonardo DiCaprio. Warner
> Brothers, 2010. Film.

56. ONLINE VIDEO CLIP Cite an online video as you would a work from a Web site (see model 44).

> Weber, Jan. "As We Sow, Part 1: Where Are the Farmers?" *YouTube*. YouTube, 15 Mar.
> 2008. Web. 27 Sept. 2010.

57. TELEVISION OR RADIO PROGRAM In general, begin with the title of the program, italicized. Then list important contributors (narrator, writer, director, actors); the network; the local station and city, if any; the broadcast date; and the medium. To cite a particular person's work, begin with that name. To cite a particular episode from a series, begin with the episode title, in quotation marks.

> *The American Experience: Buffalo Bill*. Writ., dir., prod. Rob Rapley. PBS. WNET, New
> York, 25 Feb. 2008. Television.

QUICK HELP

Citing sources without models in MLA style

To cite a source for which you cannot find a model, collect as much information as you can find—about the creator, title, sponsor, date of posting or latest update, the date you accessed the site and its location—with the goal of helping your readers find the source for themselves, if possible. Then look at the models in this section to see which one most closely matches the type of source you are using.

In an academic writing project, before citing an electronic source for which you have no model, also be sure to ask your instructor for help.

"The Fleshy Part of the Thigh." *The Sopranos*. Writ. Diane Frolov and Andrew
Schneider. Dir. Alan Taylor. HBO, 2 Apr. 2006. Television.

Note: For a streaming version online, give the name of the Web site, italicized. Then give the publisher or sponsor, a comma, and the date posted.
End with the medium (*Web*) and the access date. (For downloaded versions, see models 64–65.)

Komando, Kim. "E-mail Hacking and the Law." *CBSRadio.com*. CBS Radio, Inc., 28 Oct.
2003. Web. 11 Nov. 2003.

58. BROADCAST INTERVIEW List the person interviewed and then the
title, if any. If the interview has no title, use the label *Interview* and name
the interviewer, if relevant. Then identify the source. To cite a broadcast
interview, end with information about the program, the date(s) the interview took place, and the medium.

Revkin, Andrew. Interview by Terry Gross. *Fresh Air*. Natl. Public Radio. WNYC, New
York, 14 June 2006. Radio.

Note: If you found an archived version online, provide the site's sponsor
(if known), the date of the interview, the medium (*Web*), and the access
date. For a podcast interview, see model 64.

Revkin, Andrew. Interview by Terry Gross. *Fresh Air*. *NPR.org*. NPR, 14 June 2006. Web.
12 Jan. 2009.

59. UNPUBLISHED OR PERSONAL INTERVIEW List the person interviewed; the label *Telephone interview, Personal interview*, or *E-mail
interview*; and the date the interview took place.

Freedman, Sasha. Personal interview. 10 Nov. 2010.

60. SOUND RECORDING List the name of the person or group you
wish to emphasize (such as the composer, conductor, or band); the title
of the recording or composition; the artist, if appropriate; the manufac-
turer; and the year of issue. Give the medium (such as *CD, MP3 file*, or
LP). If you are citing a particular song or selection, include its title, in
quotation marks, before the title of the recording.

Bach, Johann Sebastian. *Bach: Violin Concertos*. Perf. Itzhak Perlman and Pinchas
Zukerman. English Chamber Orchestra. EMI, 2002. CD.

Sonic Youth. "Incinerate." *Rather Ripped*. Geffen, 2006. MP3 file.

Note: If you are citing instrumental music that is identified only by form, number, and key, do not underline, italicize, or enclose it in quotation marks.

> Grieg, Edvard. Concerto in A minor, op. 16. Cond. Eugene Ormandy.
> Philadelphia Orch. RCA, 1989. LP.

61. MUSICAL COMPOSITION When you are not citing a specific published version, first give the composer's name, followed by the title.

> Mozart, Wolfgang Amadeus. *Don Giovanni,* K527.

> Mozart, Wolfgang Amadeus. Symphony no. 41 in C major, K551.

Note: Cite a published score as you would a book. If you include the date the composition was written, do so immediately after the title.

> Schoenberg, Arnold. *Chamber Symphony No. 1 for 15 Solo Instruments, Op. 9.* 1906.
> New York: Dover, 2002. Print.

62. LECTURE OR SPEECH List the speaker; title, in quotation marks; sponsoring institution or group; place; and date. If the speech is untitled, use a label such as *Lecture.*

> Colbert, Stephen. Speech. White House Correspondents' Association Dinner. *YouTube.*
> YouTube, 29 Apr. 2006. Web. 20 May 2010.

> Eugenides, Jeffrey. Portland Arts and Lectures. Arlene Schnitzer Concert Hall,
> Portland, OR. 30 Sept. 2003. Lecture.

63. LIVE PERFORMANCE List the title, appropriate names (such as writer or performer), the place, and the date. To cite a particular person's work, begin the entry with that name.

> *Anything Goes.* By Cole Porter. Perf. Klea Blackhurst. Shubert Theater, New Haven.
> 7 Oct. 2003. Performance.

64. PODCAST For a podcast you view or listen to online, include all of the following that are available: the speaker, the title of the podcast, the title of the program, the host or performers, the title of the site, the site's sponsor, the date of posting, the medium (*Web*), and the access date. (This model is based on MLA guidelines for a short work from a Web site. For a downloaded podcast, see model 65.)

"Seven Arrested in U.S. Terror Raid." *Morning Report*. Host Krishnan Guru-Murthy.
    4 Radio. Channel 4 News, 23 June 2006. Web. 27 June 2006.

65. DIGITAL FILE A citation for a file that you can download—one that
exists independently, not only on a Web site—begins with citation information required for the type of source (a photograph or sound recording, for
example). For the medium, indicate the type of file (*MP3 file, JPEG file*).

Officers' Winter Quarters, Army of Potomac, Brandy Station. Mar. 1864. Prints and
    Photographs Div., Lib. of Cong. TIFF file.

"Return to the Giant Pool of Money." *This American Life*. Narr. Ira Glass. NPR, 25 Sept.
    2009. MP3 file.

66. WORK OF ART OR PHOTOGRAPH List the artist or photographer;
the work's title, italicized; the date of composition (if unknown, use
n.d.); and the medium of composition (*Oil on canvas, Bronze*). Then
cite the name of the museum or other location and the city. To cite a
reproduction in a book, add the publication information. To cite artwork
found online, omit the medium of composition, and after the location,
add the title of the database or Web site, italicized; the medium consulted
(*Web*); and the date of access.

Chagall, Marc. *The Poet with the Birds*. 1911. Minneapolis Inst. of Arts. *artsmia.org*.
    Web. 6 Oct. 2010.

General William Palmer in Old Age. 1810. Oil on canvas. National Army Museum,
    London. *White Mughals: Love and Betrayal in Eighteenth-Century India*. William
    Dalrymple. New York: Penguin, 2002. 270. Print.

Kahlo, Frida. *Self-Portrait with Cropped Hair*. 1940. Oil on canvas. Museum of Mod. Art,
    New York.

67. MAP OR CHART Cite a map or chart as you would a book or a
short work within a longer work, and include the word *Map* or *Chart*
after the title. Add the medium of publication. For an online source, end
with the date of access.

"Australia." Map. *Perry-Castañeda Library Map Collection*. U of Texas, 1999. Web. 4 Nov.
    2003.

California. Map. Chicago: Rand, 2002. Print.

68. CARTOON OR COMIC STRIP List the artist's name; the title (if any) of the cartoon or comic strip, in quotation marks; the label *Cartoon* or *Comic strip*; and the usual publication information for a print periodical (see models 28–31) or a work from a Web site (model 44).

> Johnston, Lynn. "For Better or Worse." Comic strip. *FBorFW.com*. Lynn Johnston Publications, 30 June 2006. Web. 20 July 2006.

> Lewis, Eric. "The Unpublished Freud." Cartoon. *New Yorker* 11 Mar. 2002: 80. Print.

69. ADVERTISEMENT Include the label *Advertisement* after the name of the item or organization being advertised.

> Microsoft. Advertisement. *Harper's* Oct. 2003: 2-3. Print.

> Microsoft. Advertisement. *New York Times*. New York Times, 11 Nov. 2003. Web. 11 Nov. 2003.

5 **Other sources (including online versions)**

If an online version is not shown here, use the appropriate model for the source and then end with the medium and date of access.

70. REPORT OR PAMPHLET Follow the guidelines for a print book (models 6–27) or an online book (model 39).

> Allen, Katherine, and Lee Rainie. *Parents Online*. Washington: Pew Internet and Amer. Life Project, 2002. Print.

> Environmental Working Group. *Dead in the Water*. Washington: Environmental Working Group, 2006. Web. 24 Apr. 2010.

71. GOVERNMENT PUBLICATION Begin with the author, if identified. Otherwise, start with the name of the government, followed by the agency. For congressional documents, cite the number, session, and house of Congress (*S* for Senate, *H* for House of Representatives); the type (*Report, Resolution, Document*) in abbreviated form; and the number. End with the publication information. The print publisher is often the Government Printing Office (GPO). For online versions, follow the models for a work from a Web site (model 44) or an entire Web site (model 45).

> Gregg, Judd. *Report to Accompany the Genetic Information Act of 2003*. US 108th Cong., 1st sess. S. Rept. 108-22. Washington: GPO, 2003. Print.

> Kinsella, Kevin, and Victoria Velkoff. *An Aging World: 2001*. US Bureau of the Census. Washington: GPO, 2001. Print.

> United States. Environmental Protection Agency. Office of Emergency and Remedial Response. *This Is Superfund*. Jan. 2000. *Environmental Protection Agency*. Web. 16 Aug. 2002.

72. PUBLISHED PROCEEDINGS OF A CONFERENCE Cite proceedings as you would a book.

> Cleary, John, and Gary Gurtler, eds. *Proceedings of the Boston Area Colloquium in Ancient Philosophy 2002*. Boston: Brill Academic, 2003. Print.

73. DISSERTATION Enclose the title in quotation marks. Add the label *Diss.*, the school, and the year the work was accepted.

> Paris, Django. "Our Culture: Difference, Division, and Unity in Multicultural Youth Space." Diss. Stanford U, 2008. Print.

Note: Cite a published dissertation as a book, adding the identification *Diss.* and the university after the title.

74. DISSERTATION ABSTRACT Cite as you would an unpublished dissertation (see model 73). For the abstract of a dissertation using *Dissertation Abstracts International* (*DAI*), include the *DAI* volume, year, and page number.

> Huang-Tiller, Gillian C. "The Power of the Meta-Genre: Cultural, Sexual, and Racial Politics of the American Modernist Sonnet." Diss. U of Notre Dame, 2000. *DAI* 61 (2000): 1401. Print.

75. PUBLISHED INTERVIEW List the person interviewed; the title of the interview (if any) or the label *Interview* and the interviewer's name, if relevant. Then provide information about the source, following the appropriate model.

> Paretsky, Sarah. Interview. *Progressive*. Progressive Magazine, 14 Jan. 2008. Web. 12 Feb. 2010.

> Taylor, Max. "Max Taylor on Winning." *Time* 13 Nov. 2000: 66. Print.

76. UNPUBLISHED LETTER Cite a published letter as a work in an anthology (see model 10). If the letter is unpublished, follow this form:

> Anzaldúa, Gloria. Letter to the author. 10 Sept. 2002. MS.

77. MANUSCRIPT OR OTHER UNPUBLISHED WORK List the author's name; the title (if any) or a description of the material; the form of the material (such as *MS* for manuscript or *TS* for typescript) and any identifying numbers; and the name and location of the library or research institution housing the material, if applicable.

> Woolf, Virginia. "The Searchlight." N.d. TS. Ser. III, Box 4, Item 184. Papers of Virginia Woolf, 1902-1956. Smith Coll., Northampton.

78. LEGAL SOURCE To cite a court case, give the names of the first plaintiff and defendant, the case number, the name of the court, and the date of the decision. To cite an act, give the name of the act followed by its Public Law (*Pub. L.*) number, the date the act was enacted, and its Statutes at Large (*Stat.*) cataloging number.

> Eldred v. Ashcroft. No. 01-618. Supreme Ct. of the US. 15 Jan. 2003. Print.

> Museum and Library Services Act of 2003. Pub. L. 108-81. 25 Sept. 2003. Stat. 117.991. Print.

Note: You do not need an entry in the list of works cited when you cite articles of the U.S. Constitution and laws in the U.S. Code.

16e A student research essay, MLA style

Student Writer

David Craig

David Craig's final essay appears on the following pages. In preparing this essay, he followed the MLA guidelines described in this chapter. Note that the essay has been reproduced in a narrow format to allow for annotation.

bedfordstmartins.com/smhandbook
Student Writing > **Researched Writing**

Craig 1

1″

David Craig

Professor Turkman

English 219

8 December 2009

Texting and Messaging: The Language of Youth Literacy

The English language is under attack. At least, that is what many people seem to believe. From concerned parents to local librarians, everyone seems to have a negative comment on the state of youth literacy today. They fear that the current generation of grade school students will graduate with an extremely low level of literacy, and they point out that although language education hasn't changed, kids are having more trouble reading and writing than in the past. When asked about the cause of this situation, many adults pin the blame on technologies such as texting and instant messaging, arguing that electronic shortcuts create and compound undesirable reading and writing habits and discourage students from learning conventionally correct ways to use language. But although the arguments against messaging are passionate, evidence suggests that they may not hold up.

The disagreements about messaging shortcuts are profound, even among academics. John Briggs, an English professor at the University of California, Riverside, says, "Americans have always been informal, but now the informality of precollege culture is so ubiquitous that many students have no practice in using language in any formal setting at all" (qtd. in McCarroll). Such objections are not new; Sven Birkerts of Mount Holyoke College argued in 1999 that "[students] read more casually. They strip-mine what they read" online and consequently produce "quickly generated, casual prose" (qtd. in Leibowitz A67). However, academics are also among the defenders of texting and instant messaging (IM), with some suggesting that messaging may be a beneficial force in the development of youth literacy because it promotes regular contact with

Student
Writing
MLA

words and the use of a written medium for communication.

Instant messaging allows two individuals who are separated by any distance to engage in real-time, written communication. Although messaging relies on the written word, many messagers disregard standard writing conventions. For example, here is a snippet from an IM conversation between two teenage girls:[1]

> Teen One: sorry im talkinto like 10 ppl at a time
>
> Teen Two: u izzyful person
>
> Teen Two: kwel
>
> Teen One: hey i g2g

As this brief conversation shows, participants must use words to communicate via IMing, but their words do not have to be in standard English.

Regardless of one's views on messaging, the issue of youth literacy does demand attention because standardized test scores for language assessments, such as the verbal section of the College Board's SAT, have declined in recent years. This trend is illustrated in a chart distributed by the College Board as part of its 2002 analysis of aggregate SAT data (see Fig. 1).

The trend lines, which I added to the original chart, illustrate a significant pattern that may lead to the conclusion that youth literacy is on the decline. These lines display the seven-year paths (from 1995 to 2002) of math and verbal scores, respectively. Within this time period, the average SAT math score jumped more than ten points. The average verbal score, however, actually dropped a few points — and appears to be headed toward a further decline in the future. Corroborating this evidence is a report from the United States Department of Education's National Center

---

[1] This transcript of an IM conversation was collected on 20 Nov. 2009. The teenagers' names are concealed to protect privacy.

Definition and example of messaging

Writer considers argument that youth literacy is in decline

Figure explained in text and cited in parenthetical reference

Discussion of Figure 1

Explanatory note; see 16c

Craig 3

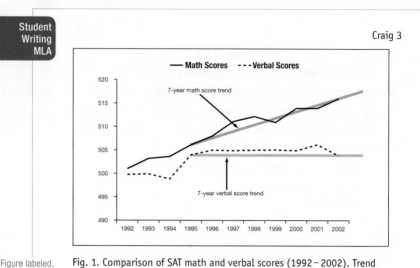

Fig. 1. Comparison of SAT math and verbal scores (1992 – 2002). Trend lines added. Source: Kristin Carnahan and Chiara Coletti, *Ten-Year Trend in SAT Scores Indicates Increased Emphasis on Math Is Yielding Results; Reading and Writing Are Causes for Concern* (New York: College Board, 2002; print; 9).

for Education Statistics. According to this agency's study, the percentage of twelfth graders whose writing ability was "at or above the basic level" of performance dropped from 78 to 74 percent between 1998 and 2002 (Persky, Daane, and Jin 21).

Based on the preceding statistics, parents and educators appear to be right about the decline in youth literacy. And this trend is occurring while electronic communication is on the rise. According to the Pew Internet & American Life Project, 81 percent of those aged 15-17 regularly send text messages (Lenhart, Madden, Macgill, and Smith 21).

In 2001, the most conservative estimate based on Pew numbers showed that American youths spent, at a minimum, nearly three million hours per

Craig 4

day on instant messaging services (Lenhart and Lewis 20). These numbers hold steady today, and they may even be expanding thanks to popular Web 2.0 sites—such as Facebook—that incorporate chat functions. What's more, young messagers seem to be using a new vocabulary.

In the interest of establishing the existence of a messaging language, I analyzed 11,341 lines of text from IM conversations between youths in my target demographic: U.S. residents aged twelve to seventeen. Young messagers voluntarily sent me chat logs, but they were unaware of the exact nature of my research. Once all of the logs had been gathered, I went through them, recording the number of times messaging language was used in place of conventional words and phrases. Then I generated graphs to display how often these replacements were used.

Writer's field research introduced

During the course of my study, I identified four types of messaging language: phonetic replacements, acronyms, abbreviations, and inanities. An example of phonetic replacement is using *ur* for *you are*. Another popular type of messaging language is the acronym; for a majority of the people in my study, the most common acronym was *lol*, a construction that means *laughing out loud*. Abbreviations are also common in messaging, but I discovered that typical IM abbreviations, such as *etc.*, are not new to the English language. Finally, I found a class of words that I call "inanities." These words include completely new words or expressions, combinations of several slang categories, or simply nonsensical variations of other words. My favorite from this category is *lolz*, an inanity that translates directly to *lol* yet includes a terminating *z* for no obvious reason.

Findings of field research presented

In the chat transcripts that I analyzed, the best display of typical messaging lingo came from the conversations between two thirteen-year-old Texan girls, who are avid IM users. Figure 2 is a graph showing how often they used certain phonetic replacements and abbreviations. On the

Figure introduced and explained

Student
Writing
MLA

Craig 5

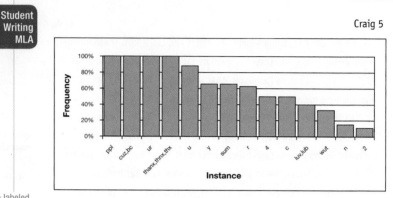

Fig. 2. Usage of phonetic replacements and abbreviations in messaging.

Figure labeled and titled

y-axis, frequency of replacement is plotted, a calculation that compares the number of times a word or phrase is used in messaging language with the total number of times that it is communicated in any form. On the *x*-axis, specific messaging words and phrases are listed.

Discussion of findings presented in Fig. 2

My research shows that the Texan girls use the first ten phonetic replacements or abbreviations at least 50 percent of the time in their normal messaging writing. For example, every time one of them writes *see*, there is a parallel time when *c* is used in its place. In light of this finding, it appears that the popular messaging culture contains at least some elements of its own language. It also seems that much of this language is new: no formal dictionary yet identifies the most common messaging words and phrases. Only in the heyday of the telegraph or on the rolls of a stenographer would you find a similar situation, but these "languages" were never a popular medium of youth communication. Instant messaging, however, is very popular among young people and continues to generate attention and debate in academic circles.

Craig 6

My research shows that messaging is certainly widespread, and it does seem to have its own particular vocabulary, yet these two factors alone do not mean it has a damaging influence on youth literacy. As noted earlier, however, some people claim that the new technology is a threat to the English language, as revealed in the following passage:

> Abbreviations commonly used in online instant messages are creeping into formal essays that students write for credit, said Debbie Frost, who teaches language arts and social studies to sixth-graders. . . . "You would be shocked at the writing I see. It's pretty scary. I don't get cohesive thoughts, I don't get sentences, they don't capitalize, and they have a lot of misspellings and bad grammar," she said. "With all those glaring mistakes, it's hard to see the content." ("Young Messagers")

Echoing Frost's concerns is Melanie Weaver, a professor at Alvernia College, who taught a tenth-grade English class as an intern. In an interview with the *New York Times*, she said, "[When t]hey would be trying to make a point in a paper, they would put a smiley face in the end [☺]. . . . If they were presenting an argument and they needed to present an opposite view, they would put a frown [☹]" (qtd. in Lee).

The critics of messaging are numerous. But if we look to the field of linguistics, a central concept — metalinguistics — challenges these criticisms and leads to a more reasonable conclusion — that messaging has no negative impact on a student's development of or proficiency with traditional literacy.

Scholars of metalinguistics offer support for the claim that messaging is not damaging to those who use it. As noted earlier, one of the most prominent components of messaging language is phonetic replacement, in which a word such as *everyone* becomes *every1*. This type of wordplay has a special importance in the development of an advanced literacy, and

Writer returns to opposition argument

Signal verb introduces quotation

Block quotation for a quotation more than four lines long

Parenthetical reference uses brief title, author unknown

Transition to support of thesis and refutation of critics

Student Writing MLA

Linguistic authority cited in support of thesis

for good reason. According to David Crystal, an internationally recognized scholar of linguistics at the University of Wales, as young children develop and learn how words string together to express ideas, they go through many phases of language play. The singsong rhymes and nonsensical chants of preschoolers are vital to their learning language, and a healthy appetite for such wordplay leads to a better command of language later in life (182).

As justification for his view of the connection between language play and advanced literacy, Crystal presents an argument for metalinguistic awareness. According to Crystal, *metalinguistics* refers to the ability to "step back" and use words to analyze how language works:

Ellipses and brackets indicate omissions and changes in quotation

> If we are good at stepping back, at thinking in a more abstract
> way about what we hear and what we say, then we are more likely
> to be good at acquiring those skills which depend on just such a
> stepping back in order to be successful—and this means, chiefly,
> reading and writing. . . . [T]he greater our ability to play with
> language, . . . the more advanced will be our command of language
> as a whole. (Crystal 181)

Writer links Crystal's views to thesis

If we accept the findings of linguists such as Crystal that metalinguistic awareness leads to increased literacy, then it seems reasonable to argue that the phonetic language of messaging can also lead to increased metalinguistic awareness and, therefore, increases in overall literacy. As instant messagers develop proficiency with a variety of phonetic replacements and other types of IM words, they should increase their subconscious knowledge of metalinguistics.

Another refutation of critics' assumptions

Metalinguistics also involves our ability to write in a variety of distinct styles and tones. Yet in the debate over messaging and literacy, many critics assume that either messaging or academic literacy will eventually win out in a person and that the two modes cannot exist side

Craig 8

by side. This assumption is, however, false. Human beings ordinarily develop a large range of language abilities, from the formal to the relaxed and from the mainstream to the subcultural. Mark Twain, for example, had an understanding of local speech that he employed when writing dialogue for *Huckleberry Finn*. Yet few people would argue that Twain's knowledge of this form of English had a negative impact on his ability to write in standard English.

However, just as Mark Twain used dialects carefully in dialogue, writers must pay careful attention to the kind of language they use in any setting. The owner of the language Web site *The Discouraging Word*, who is an anonymous English literature graduate student at the University of Chicago, backs up this idea in an e-mail to me:

> What is necessary, we feel, is that students learn how to shift
> between different styles of writing—that, in other words, the
> abbreviations and shortcuts of messaging should be used
> online . . . but that they should not be used in an essay submitted
> to a teacher. . . . Messaging might even be considered . . . a
> different way of reading and writing, one that requires specific and
> unique skills shared by certain communities.

The analytical ability that is necessary for writers to choose an appropriate tone and style in their writing is, of course, metalinguistic in nature because it involves the comparison of two or more language systems. Thus, youths who grasp multiple languages will have a greater natural understanding of metalinguistics. More specifically, young people who possess both messaging and traditional skills stand to be better off than their peers who have been trained only in traditional or conventional systems. Far from being hurt by their online pastime, instant messagers can be aided in standard writing by their experience with messaging language.

Example from well-known work of literature used as support

Email correspon-dence cited in support of claim

Writer synthesizes evidence for claim

Craig 9

Transition to
final point

Alternate
explanation for
decline in
literacy

The fact remains, however, that youth literacy seems to be declining. What, if not messaging, is the main cause of this phenomenon? According to the College Board, which collects data on several questions from its test takers, enrollment in English composition and grammar classes has decreased in the last decade by 14 percent (Carnahan and Coletti 11). The possibility of messaging causing a decline in literacy seems inadequate when statistics on English education for US youths provide other evidence of the possible causes. Simply put, schools in the United States are not teaching English as much as they used to. Rather than blaming texting and messaging language alone for the decline in literacy and test scores, we must also look toward our schools' lack of focus on the teaching of standard English skills.

Transition to
conclusion

Concluding
paragraph
sums up
argument and
reiterates
thesis

My findings indicate that the use of messaging poses virtually no threat to the development or maintenance of formal language skills among American youths aged twelve to seventeen. Diverse language skills tend to increase a person's metalinguistic awareness and, thereby, his or her ability to use language effectively to achieve a desired purpose in a particular situation. The current decline in youth literacy is not due to the rise of texting and messaging. Rather, fewer young students seem to be receiving an adequate education in the use of conventional English. Unfortunately, it may always be fashionable to blame new tools for old problems, but in the case of messaging, that blame is not warranted. Although messaging may expose literacy problems, it does not create them.

Craig 10

Works Cited

Carnahan, Kristin, and Chiara Coletti. *Ten-Year Trend in SAT Scores Indicates Increased Emphasis on Math Is Yielding Results: Reading and Writing Are Causes for Concern*. New York: College Board, 2002. Print.

Crystal, David. *Language Play*. Chicago: U of Chicago P, 1998. Print.

The Discouraging Word. "Re: Messaging and Literacy." E-mail to the author. 13 Nov. 2009. E-mail.

Lee, Jennifer 8. "I Think, Therefore IM." *New York Times*. New York Times, 19 Sept. 2002. Web. 14 Nov. 2009.

Leibowitz, Wendy R. "Technology Transforms Writing and the Teaching of Writing." *Chronicle of Higher Education* 26 Nov. 1999: A67-68. Print.

Lenhart, Amanda, and Oliver Lewis. *Teenage Life Online: The Rise of the Instant-Message Generation and the Internet's Impact on Friendships and Family Relationships*. Washington: Pew Internet & Amer. Life Project, 2001. Print.

Lenhart, Amanda, Mary Madden, Alexandra Rankin Macgill, and Aaron Smith. *Teens and Social Media*. Washington: Pew Internet & Amer. Life Project, 2007. Web. 8 Oct. 2009.

McCarroll, Christina. "Teens Ready to Prove Text-Messaging Skills Can Score SAT Points." *Christian Science Monitor* 11 Mar. 2005. Web. 12 Nov. 2009.

Persky, Hilary R., Mary C. Daane, and Ying Jin. *The Nation's Report Card: Writing 2002*. NCES 2003-529. Washington: GPO, 2003. Print.

"Young Messagers Ask: Why Spell It Out?" *Columbus Dispatch* 10 Nov. 2002: C1. *LexisNexis Academic*. Web. 14 Nov. 2009.

Heading centered
Report

Book

Email

Online newspaper article

Article in a newspaper

Works-cited entries double-spaced

First line of each entry flush with left margin; subsequent lines indented

Government document

Article from an online database

APA Style

The conventions of style vary according to what a discipline values and how it assigns credit for work in that field. Many fields in the social sciences ask students to follow the basic guidelines prescribed by the American Psychological Association (APA) for formatting manuscripts and documenting various kinds of sources.

For further reference on APA style, consult the *Publication Manual of the American Psychological Association*, Sixth Edition (2010).

17a Formatting APA manuscripts

The following formatting guidelines are adapted from the APA's recommendations for preparing manuscripts for publication in journals. However, check with your instructor before preparing your final draft.

For detailed guidelines on formatting a list of references, see 17d. For a sample student essay in APA style, see 17e.

- *Title page.* Center the title, and include your name, the course name and number, the instructor's name, and the date. In the top left corner, type the words *Running head:* and a short version of the title, using all capital letters (fifty characters or fewer, including spaces). In the top right corner, type the number *1.*

- *Margins and spacing.* Leave margins of at least one inch at the top and bottom and on both sides of the page. Do not justify the right margin. Double-space the entire text, including headings, set-off quotations, content notes, and the list of references. Indent the first line of each paragraph one-half inch (or five to seven spaces) from the left margin.

- *Short title and page numbers.* Type the short title flush left and the page number flush right at the top of each page, in the same position as on the title page.

- *Long quotations.* For a long, set-off quotation (one having more than forty words), indent it one-half inch (or five to seven spaces) from the left margin and do not use quotation marks. Place the page reference in parentheses one space after the final punctuation.

- *Abstract.* If your instructor asks for an abstract with your paper—a one-paragraph summary of your major thesis and supporting points—it should go on a separate page immediately after the title page. Center the word *Abstract* (not boldface) about an inch from the top of the page. Double-space the text of the abstract, and begin the first line flush with the left margin. APA recommends that an abstract not exceed 120 words.

- *Headings.* Headings (set in boldface) are used within the text of many APA-style papers. In papers with only one or two levels of headings, center the main headings; position the subheadings flush with the left margin. Capitalize all major words; however, do not capitalize articles, short prepositions, or coordinating conjunctions unless they are the first word or follow a colon.

- *Visuals.* Tables should be labeled *Table*, numbered, and captioned. All other visuals (charts, graphs, photographs, and drawings) should be labeled *Figure*, numbered, and captioned with a description and the source information. Remember to refer to each visual in your text, stating how it contributes to the point(s) you are making. Tables and figures should generally appear near the relevant text; check with your instructor for guidelines on placement of visuals.

Directory to APA style for in-text citations

17b In-text citations

APA style requires parenthetical references in the text to document quotations, paraphrases, summaries, and other material from a source. These citations correspond to full bibliographic entries in a list of references at the end of the text.

Note that APA style generally calls for using the past tense or present perfect tense for signal verbs: *Baker (2003) showed* or *Baker (2003) has shown*. Use the present tense only to discuss results (*the experiment demonstrates*) or widely accepted information (*researchers agree*).

An in-text citation in APA style always indicates *which source* on the references page the writer is referring to, and it explains *in what year* the material was published; for quoted material, the in-text citation also indicates *where* in the source the quotation can be found.

1. BASIC FORMAT FOR A QUOTATION Generally, use the author's name in a signal phrase to introduce the cited material, and place the date, in parentheses, immediately after the author's name. The page number, preceded by *p.*, appears in parentheses after the quotation.

> Gitlin (2001) pointed out that "political critics, convinced that the media are rigged against them, are often blind to other substantial reasons why their causes are unpersuasive" (p. 141).

If the author is not named in a signal phrase, place the author's name, the year, and the page number in parentheses after the quotation: (Gitlin, 2001, p. 141). For a long, set-off quotation (more than forty words), place the page reference in parentheses one space after the final quotation.

For electronic texts or other works without page numbers, you may use paragraph numbers, if the source includes them, preceded by the abbreviation *para.*

> Driver (2007) has noticed "an increasing focus on the role of land" in policy debates over the past decade (para. 1).

2. BASIC FORMAT FOR A PARAPHRASE OR SUMMARY Include the author's last name and the year as in model 1, but omit the page or paragraph number unless the reader will need it to find the material in a long work.

> Gitlin (2001) has argued that critics sometimes overestimate the influence of the media on modern life.

3. TWO AUTHORS Use both names in all citations. Use *and* in a signal phrase, but use an ampersand (&) in a parentheses.

Babcock and Laschever (2003) have suggested that many women do not negotiate their salaries and pay raises as vigorously as their male counterparts do.

A recent study has suggested that many women do not negotiate their salaries and pay raises as vigorously as their male counterparts do (Babcock & Laschever, 2003).

4. THREE TO FIVE AUTHORS List all the authors' names for the first reference.

Safer, Voccola, Hurd, and Goodwin (2003) reached somewhat different conclusions by designing a study that was less dependent on subjective judgment than were previous studies.

In subsequent references, use just the first author's name plus *et al.*

Based on the results, Safer et al. (2003) determined that the apes took significant steps toward self-expression.

5. SIX OR MORE AUTHORS Use only the first author's name and *et al.* in every citation.

As Soleim et al. (2002) demonstrated, advertising holds the potential for manipulating "free-willed" consumers.

6. CORPORATE OR GROUP AUTHOR If the name of the organization or corporation is long, spell it out the first time you use it, followed by an abbreviation in brackets. In later references, use the abbreviation only.

FIRST CITATION   (Centers for Disease Control and Prevention [CDC], 2006)

LATER CITATIONS   (CDC, 2006)

7. UNKNOWN AUTHOR Use the title or its first few words in a signal phrase or in parentheses. A book's title is italicized, as in the following example; an article's title is placed in quotation marks.

The employment profiles for this time period substantiated this trend (*Federal Employment,* 2001).

8. TWO OR MORE AUTHORS WITH THE SAME LAST NAME If your list of references includes works by different authors with the same last name, include the authors' initials in each citation.

S. Bartolomeo (2000) conducted the groundbreaking study on teenage childbearing.

9. TWO OR MORE WORKS BY AN AUTHOR IN A SINGLE YEAR Assign lowercase letters (*a*, *b*, and so on) alphabetically by title, and include the letters after the year.

Gordon (2004b) examined this trend in more detail.

10. TWO OR MORE SOURCES IN ONE PARENTHETICAL REFERENCE List sources by different authors in alphabetical order by authors' last names, separated by semicolons: (Cardone, 1998; Lai, 2002). List works by the same author in chronological order, separated by commas: (Lai, 2000, 2002).

11. INDIRECT SOURCE Use the phrase *as cited in* to indicate that you are reporting information from a secondary source. Name the original source in a signal phrase, but list the secondary source in your list of references.

Amartya Sen developed the influential concept that land reform was necessary for "promoting opportunity" among the poor (as cited in Driver, 2007, para. 2).

12. PERSONAL COMMUNICATION Cite any personal letters, email messages, electronic postings, telephone conversations, or interviews as shown. Do not include personal communications in the reference list.

R. Tobin (personal communication, November 4, 2006) supported his claims about music therapy with new evidence.

13. ELECTRONIC DOCUMENT Cite a Web or electronic document as you would a print source, using the author's name and date.

Link and Phelan (2005) argued for broader interventions in public health that would be accessible to anyone, regardless of individual wealth.

The APA recommends the following for electronic sources without names, dates, or page numbers:

AUTHOR UNKNOWN

Use a shortened form of the title in a signal phrase or in parentheses (see model 7). If an organization is the author, see model 6.

DATE UNKNOWN

Use the abbreviation *n.d.* (for "no date") in place of the year: (*Hopkins, n.d.*).

NO PAGE NUMBERS

Many works found online or in electronic databases lack stable page numbers. (Use the page numbers for an electronic work in a format, such as PDF, that has stable pagination.) If paragraph numbers are included in such a source, use the abbreviation *para.*: (*Giambetti, 2006, para. 7*). If no paragraph numbers are included but the source includes headings, give the heading and identify the paragraph in the section:

> Jacobs and Johnson (2007) have argued that "the South African media is still highly concentrated and not very diverse in terms of race and class" (South African Media after Apartheid, para. 3).

14. TABLE OR FIGURE REPRODUCED IN THE TEXT Number figures (graphs, charts, illustrations, and photographs) and tables separately.

For a table, place the label (*Table 1*) and an informative heading (*Hartman's Key Personality Traits*) above the table; below, provide information about its source.

Table 1

Hartman's Key Personality Traits

Trait category	Color			
	Red	Blue	White	Yellow
Motive	Power	Intimacy	Peace	Fun
Strengths	Loyal to tasks	Loyal to people	Tolerant	Positive
Limitations	Arrogant	Self-righteous	Timid	Uncommitted

Note: Adapted from *The Hartman Personality Profile*, by N. Hayden. Retrieved February 24, 2009, from http://students.cs.byu.edu/~nhayden/Code/index.php

For a figure, place the label (*Figure 3*) and a caption indicating the source below the image. If you do not cite the source of the table or figure elsewhere in your text, you do not need to include the source on your list of references.

17c Content notes

APA style allows you to use content notes, either at the bottom of the page or on a separate page at the end of the text, to expand or supplement your text. Indicate such notes in the text by superscript numerals (^{1}). Double-space all entries. Indent the first line of each note five spaces, but begin subsequent lines at the left margin.

SUPERSCRIPT NUMBER IN TEXT

The age of the children involved in the study was an important factor in the selection of items for the questionnaire.[1]

FOOTNOTE

[1]Marjorie Youngston Forman and William Cole of the Child Study Team provided great assistance in identifying appropriate items for the questionnaire.

Print periodicals

Electronic sources

Other sources (including online versions)

17d List of references

The alphabetical list of the sources cited in your document is called *References*. If your instructor asks that you list everything you have read—not just the sources you cite—call the list *Bibliography*.

All the entries in this section of the book use hanging indent format, in which the first line aligns on the left and the subsequent lines indent one-half inch or five spaces. This is the customary APA format.

Guidelines for author listings

List authors' last names first, and use only initials for first and middle names. The in-text citations in your text point readers toward particular sources in your list of references (see 17b).

NAME CITED IN SIGNAL PHRASE IN TEXT

Driver (2007) has noted . . .

NAME IN PARENTHETICAL CITATION IN TEXT

. . . (Driver, 2007).

QUICK HELP

Formatting a list of references

- Start your list on a separate page after the text of your document but before appendices or notes. Continue consecutive page numbers.

- Center the heading *References* one inch from the top of the page.

- Begin each entry flush with the left margin, but indent subsequent lines one-half inch or five spaces. Double-space the entire list.

- List sources alphabetically by authors' (or editors') last names. If no author is given, alphabetize the source by the first word of the title other than *A*, *An*, or *The*. If the list includes two or more works by the same author, list them in chronological order. (For two or more works by the same author published in the same year, see model 5.)

- Italicize titles and subtitles of books and periodicals. Do not italicize titles of articles, and do not enclose them in quotation marks.

- For titles of books and articles, capitalize only the first word of the title and the subtitle and any proper nouns or proper adjectives.

- For titles of periodicals, capitalize all major words.

- Follow the guidelines in 17d for punctuating an entry.

BEGINNING OF ENTRY IN LIST OF REFERENCES

Driver, T. (2007).

Models 1–5 below explain how to arrange author names. The information that follows the name of the author depends on the type of work you are citing—a book (models 6–15); a print periodical (models 16–23); an electronic source (models 24–35); or another kind of source (models 36–46).

1. ONE AUTHOR Give the last name, a comma, the initial(s), and the date in parentheses.

Zimbardo, P. G. (2009).

2. MULTIPLE AUTHORS List up to seven authors, last name first, with commas separating authors' names and an ampersand (&) before the last author's name.

Walsh, M. E., & Murphy, J. A. (2003).

Note: For a work with more than seven authors, list the first six, then an ellipsis (. . .), and then the final author's name.

QUICK HELP

Combining parts of models

What should you do if your source doesn't match the model exactly? Suppose, for instance, that your source is a translation of a republished book with an editor.

- Identify a basic model to follow. If you decide that your source looks most like a republished book, for example, start with a citation that looks like model 13.

- Look for models that show additional elements in your source. For this example, you would need elements of model 9 (for the translation) and model 7 (for the editor).

- Add new elements from other models to your basic model in the order that makes the most sense to you.

- If you still aren't sure how to arrange the pieces to create a combination model, check the APA manual or ask your instructor.

3. CORPORATE OR GROUP AUTHOR

Resources for Rehabilitation. (2003).

4. UNKNOWN AUTHOR Begin with the work's title. Italicize book titles, but do not italicize article titles or enclose them in quotation marks. Capitalize only the first word of the title and subtitle (if any) and proper nouns and proper adjectives.

Safe youth, safe schools. (2009).

5. TWO OR MORE WORKS BY THE SAME AUTHOR List two or more works by the same author in chronological order. Repeat the author's name in each entry.

Goodall, J. (1999).

Goodall, J. (2002).

If the works appeared in the same year, list them alphabetically by title, and assign lowercase letters (*a*, *b*, etc.) after the dates.

Shermer, M. (2002a). On estimating the lifetime of civilizations. *Scientific American, 287*(2), 33.

Shermer, M. (2002b). Readers who question evolution. *Scientific American, 287*(1), 37.

1 Books

6. BASIC FORMAT FOR A BOOK Begin with the author name(s). (See models 1–5.) Then include the publication year, title and subtitle, city of publication, country or state abbreviation, and publisher. The source map on pp. 372–73 shows where to find this information in a typical book.

Levick, S. E. (2003). *Clone being: Exploring the psychological and social dimensions.* Lanham, MD: Rowman & Littlefield.

7. EDITOR For a book with an editor but no author, list the source under the editor's name.

Dickens, J. (Ed.). (1995). *Family outing: A guide for parents of gays, lesbians and bisexuals.* London, England: Peter Owen.

To cite a book with an author and an editor, place the editor's name, with a comma and the abbreviation *Ed.*, in parentheses after the title.

Austin, J. (1995). *The province of jurisprudence determined.* (W. E. Rumble, Ed.). Cambridge, England: Cambridge University Press.

8. SELECTION IN A BOOK WITH AN EDITOR

Burke, W. W., & Nourmair, D. A. (2001). The role of personality assessment in organization development. In J. Waclawski & A. H. Church (Eds.), *Organization development: A data-driven approach to organizational change* (pp. 55–77). San Francisco, CA: Jossey-Bass.

9. TRANSLATION

Al-Farabi, A. N. (1998). *On the perfect state* (R. Walzer, Trans.). Chicago, IL: Kazi.

10. EDITION OTHER THAN THE FIRST

Moore, G. S. (2002). *Living with the earth: Concepts in environmental health science* (2nd ed.). New York, NY: Lewis.

11. MULTIVOLUME WORK

Barnes, J. (Ed.). (1995). *Complete works of Aristotle* (Vols. 1–2). Princeton, NJ: Princeton University Press.

Note: If you cite just one volume of a multivolume work, list that volume, not the complete span of volumes, in parentheses after the title.

12. ARTICLE IN A REFERENCE WORK

Dean, C. (1994). Jaws and teeth. In *The Cambridge encyclopedia of human evolution* (pp. 56–59). Cambridge, England: Cambridge University Press.

If no author is listed, begin with the title.

13. REPUBLISHED BOOK

Piaget, J. (1952). *The language and thought of the child.* London, England: Routledge & Kegan Paul. (Original work published 1932)

14. INTRODUCTION, PREFACE, FOREWORD, OR AFTERWORD

Klosterman, C. (2007). Introduction. In P. Shirley, *Can I keep my jersey?: 11 teams, 5 countries, and 4 years in my life as a basketball vagabond* (pp. v–vii). New York, NY: Villard-Random House.

APA SOURCE MAP: Books

Take information from the book's title page and copyright page (on the reverse side of the title page), not from the book's cover or a library catalog.

1. **Author.** List all authors' last names first, and use only initials for first and middle names. For more about citing authors, see models 1–5.

2. **Publication year.** Enclose the year of publication in parentheses.

3. **Title.** Italicize the title and any subtitle. Capitalize only the first word of the title and the subtitle and any proper nouns or proper adjectives.

4. **City and state of publication.** List the city of publication and the country or state abbreviation followed by a colon.

5. **Publisher.** Give the publisher's name, dropping any *Inc.*, *Co.*, or *Publishers*.

A citation for the book on p. 373 would look like this:

Tsutsui, W. (2004). *Godzilla on my mind: Fifty years of the king of monsters.* New York, NY: Palgrave Macmillan.

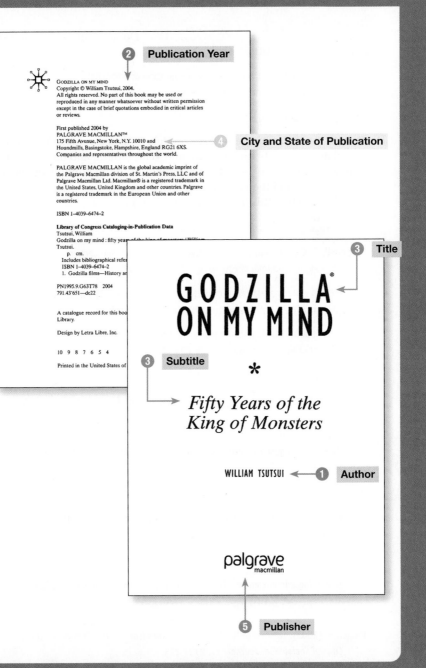

Publication Year

City and State of Publication

Title

Subtitle

Author

Publisher

First published 2004 by
PALGRAVE MACMILLAN™
175 Fifth Avenue, New York, N.Y. 10010 and
Houndmills, Basingstoke, Hampshire, England RG21 6XS.
Companies and representatives throughout the world.

PALGRAVE MACMILLAN is the global academic imprint of
the Palgrave Macmillan division of St. Martin's Press, LLC and of
Palgrave Macmillan Ltd. Macmillan® is a registered trademark in
the United States, United Kingdom and other countries. Palgrave
is a registered trademark in the European Union and other
countries.

ISBN 1–4039–6474–2

Library of Congress Cataloging-in-Publication Data
Tsutsui, William
Godzilla on my mind : fifty years of the king of monsters / William
Tsutsui.
    p.   cm.
  Includes bibliographical refer
  ISBN 1–4039–6474–2
  1. Godzilla films—History an

PN1995.9.G63T78   2004
791.43'651—dc22

A catalogue record for this boo
Library.

Design by Letra Libre, Inc.

10 9 8 7 6 5 4

Printed in the United States of

GODZILLA® ON MY MIND

*

*Fifty Years of the
King of Monsters*

WILLIAM TSUTSUI

palgrave
macmillan

15. BOOK WITH A TITLE WITHIN THE TITLE Do not italicize or enclose in quotation marks a title within a book title.

> Klarman, M. J. (2007). Brown v. Board of Education *and the civil rights movement.* New York, NY: Oxford University Press.

2 Print periodicals

Begin with the author name(s). (See models 1–5.) Then include the publication date (year only for journals, and year, month, and day for other periodicals); the article title; the periodical title; the volume and issue numbers, if any; and the page numbers. The source map on pp. 376–77 shows where to find this information in a sample periodical.

16. ARTICLE IN A JOURNAL PAGINATED BY VOLUME

> O'Connell, D. C., & Kowal, S. (2003). Psycholinguistics: A half century of monologism. *The American Journal of Psychology, 116,* 191–212.

17. ARTICLE IN A JOURNAL PAGINATED BY ISSUE If each issue begins with page 1, include the issue number after the volume number.

> Hall, R. E. (2000). Marriage as vehicle of racism among women of color. *Psychology: A Journal of Human Behavior, 37*(2), 29–40.

18. ARTICLE IN A MAGAZINE

> Ricciardi, S. (2003, August 5). Enabling the mobile work force. *PC Magazine, 22,* 46.

19. ARTICLE IN A NEWSPAPER

> Faler, B. (2003, August 29). Primary colors: Race and fundraising. *The Washington Post*, p. A5.

20. EDITORIAL OR LETTER TO THE EDITOR

> Zelneck, B. (2003, July 18). Serving the public at public universities [Letter to the editor]. *The Chronicle Review*, p. B18.

21. UNSIGNED ARTICLE

> Annual meeting announcement. (2003, March). *Cognitive Psychology, 46,* 227.

22. REVIEW

> Ringel, S. (2003). [Review of the book *Multiculturalism and the therapeutic process*]. *Clinical Social Work Journal, 31,* 212–213.

23. PUBLISHED INTERVIEW

Smith, H. (2002, October). [Interview with A. Thompson]. *The Sun*, pp. 4–7.

3 Electronic sources

Updated guidelines for citing electronic resources are maintained at the APA's Web site (www.apa.org).

24. ARTICLE FROM AN ONLINE PERIODICAL Give the author, date, title, and publication information as you would for a print document. Include both the volume and issue numbers for all journal articles. If the article has a digital object identifier (DOI), include it. If there is no DOI, include the URL for the periodical's home page or for the article (if the article is difficult to find from the home page). For newspaper articles accessible from a searchable Web site, give the site URL only.

Barringer, F. (2008, February 7). In many communities, it's not easy going green. *The New York Times*. Retrieved from http://www.nytimes.com

Cleary, J. M., & Crafti, N. (2007). Basic need satisfaction, emotional eating, and dietary restraint as risk factors for recurrent overeating in a community sample. *E-Journal of Applied Psychology 2*(3), 27–39. Retrieved from http://ojs.lib.swin .edu.au/index.php/ejap/article/view/90/116

25. ARTICLE FROM A DATABASE Give the author, date, title, and publication information as you would for a print document. Include both the volume and issue numbers for all journal articles. If the article has a DOI, include it. If there is no DOI, write *Retrieved from* and the URL of the journal's home page (not the URL of the database). The source map on pp. 380–81 shows where to find this information for a typical article from a database.

Hazleden, R. (2003, December). Love yourself: The relationship of the self with itself in popular self-help texts. *Journal of Sociology*, *39*(4), 413–428. Retrieved from http://jos.sagepub.com

Morley, N. J., Ball, L. J., & Ormerod, T. C. (2006). How the detection of insurance fraud succeeds and fails. *Psychology, Crime, & Law, 12*(2), 163–180. doi:10.1080/10683160512331316325

26. ABSTRACT FOR AN ONLINE ARTICLE

Gudjonsson, G. H., & Young, S. (2010). Does confabulation in memory predict suggestibility beyond IQ and memory? [Abstract]. *Personality & Individual Differences*, *49*(1), 65-67. doi: 10.1016/j.paid.2010.03.014

APA SOURCE MAP: Articles from periodicals

(1) Author. List all authors' last names first, and use only initials for first and middle names. For more about citing authors, see models 1–5.

(2) Publication date. Enclose the date in parentheses. For journals, use only the year. For magazines and newspapers, use the year, a comma, the month (spelled out), and the day, if given.

(3) Article title. Do not italicize or enclose article titles in quotation marks. Capitalize only the first word of the article title and subtitle and any proper nouns or proper adjectives.

(4) Periodical title. Italicize the periodical title (and subtitle, if any), and capitalize all major words.

(5) Volume and issue numbers. Follow the periodical title with a comma, and then give the volume number (italicized) and, without a space in between, the issue number (if given) in parentheses.

(6) Page numbers. Give the inclusive page numbers of the article. For newspapers only, include the abbreviation *p.* ("page") or *pp.* ("pages") before the page numbers. End the citation with a period.

A citation for the periodical article on p. 377 would look like this:

Etzioni, A. (2006). Leaving race behind: Our growing Hispanic population creates a golden

opportunity. *The American Scholar, 75*(2), 20–30.

The AMERICAN
SCHOLAR

4 ← Periodical Title

Spring 2006 | Vol. 75, No. 2 ← **5** Volume and Issue Numbers

2 Publication Date

The AMERICAN
SCHOLAR

3 Article Title

RICHA

Leaving Race Behind

Our growing Hispanic population creates a golden opportunity

AMITAI ETZIONI ← **1** Author

ANN BEA
EDWARD H
PHYLLIS RO

ALI
JOSEPH W. G
D

JO

For a subscription to THE AMERICAN S
$48 two years, $69 three years; for int
international subscriptions, add $15.
Newsstand Services. For more inform
advertising please contact: Linda Mil
THE AMERICAN SCHOLAR, a quarterly jo
Phi Beta Kappa Society, 1606 New
scholar@pbk.org. Manuscripts may be
AMERICAN SCHOLAR assumes no respon
Periodical postage paid at Washingto
P.O. Box 354, Mt. Morris, IL 61054-03
additional revenues, the Phi Beta Ka
deleted should send their name and

Some years ago the United States government asked me what my race was. I was reluctant to respond because my 50 years of practicing sociology—and some powerful personal experiences—have underscored for me what we all know to one degree or another, that racial divisions bedevil America, just as they do many other societies across the world. Not wanting to encourage these divisions, I refused to check off one of the specific racial options on the U.S. Census form and instead marked a box labeled "Other." I later found out that the federal government did not accept such an attempt to de-emphasize race, by me or by some 6.75 million other Americans who tried it. Instead the government assigned me to a racial category, one it chose for me. Learning this made me conjure up what I admit is a far-fetched association. I was in this place once before. When I was a Jewish child in Nazi Germany in the early 1930s, many Jews who saw themselves as good Germans wanted to "pass" as Aryans. But the Nazi regime would have none of it. Never mind, they told these Jews, *we determine* who is Jewish and who is not. A similar practice prevailed in the Old South, where if you had one drop of African blood you were a Negro, disregarding all other facts and considerations, including how you saw yourself.

You might suppose that in the years since my little Census-form protest

Amitai Etzioni is University Professor at George Washington University and the author of *The Monochrome Society*.

20 ← **6** Page Numbers

377

QUICK HELP

Citing electronic sources

When citing sources accessed online or from an electronic database, include as many of the following elements as you can find:

- *Author.* Give the author's name, if available.

- *Publication date.* Include the date of electronic publication or of the latest update, if available. When no publication date is available, use *n.d.* ("no date").

- *Title.* List the document title, neither italicized nor in quotation marks.

- *Print publication information.* For articles from online journals, magazines, or reference databases, give the publication title and other publishing information as you would for a print periodical (see models 16–23).

- *Retrieval information.* For a work from a database, do the following: if the article has a DOI (digital object identifier), include that number after the publication information; do not include the name of the database. If there is no DOI, write *Retrieved from* followed by the URL for the journal's home page (not the database URL). For a work found on a Web site, write *Retrieved from* and include the URL. If the work seems likely to be updated, include the retrieval date. If the URL is longer than one line, break it only before a punctuation mark; do not break *http://*.

27. DOCUMENT FROM A WEB SITE The APA refers to works that are not peer reviewed, such as reports, press releases, brochures, and presentation slides, as "gray literature." Include all of the following information that you can find: the author's name; the publication date (or *n.d.* if no date is available); the title of the document; the title of the site or larger work, if any; any publication information available in addition to the date; *Retrieved from* and the URL. Provide your date of access only if an update seems likely. The source map on pp. 382–83 shows where to find this information for an article from a Web site.

Behnke, P. C. (2006, February 22). The homeless are everyone's problem. *Authors' Den*. Retrieved from http://www.authorsden.com/visit/viewArticle.asp?id=21017

Hacker, J. S. (2006). The privatization of risk and the growing economic insecurity of Americans. *Items and Issues, 5*(4), 16–23. Retrieved from http://publications.ssrc.org/items/items5.4/Hacker.pdf

Citing sources without models in APA style

You may need to cite a source for which you cannot find a model in APA style. If so, collect as much information as you can find about the creator, title, sponsor, date, and so on, with the goal of helping readers find the source for themselves. Then look at the models in this section to see which one most closely matches the type of source you are using.

In an academic writing project, before citing an electronic source for which you have no model, also be sure to ask your instructor's advice.

> What parents should know about treatment of behavioral and emotional disorders in preschool children. (2006). *APA Online*. Retrieved from http://www.apa.org/releases/kidsmed.html

28. CHAPTER OR SECTION OF A WEB DOCUMENT Follow model 27. After the chapter or section title, type *In* and give the document title, with identifying information, if any, in parentheses. End with the date of access (if needed) and the URL.

> Salamon, Andrew. (n.d.). War in Europe. In *Childhood in times of war* (chap. 2). Retrieved April 11, 2008, from http://remember.org/jean

29. EMAIL MESSAGE OR REAL-TIME COMMUNICATION Because the APA stresses that any sources cited in your list of references be retrievable by your readers, you should not include entries for email messages, real-time communications (such as IMs), or any other postings that are not archived. Instead, cite these sources in your text as forms of personal communication (see p. 364).

30. ONLINE POSTING List an online posting in the references list only if you are able to retrieve the message from an archive. Provide the author's name, the date of posting, and the subject line. Include other identifying information in square brackets. End with the retrieval statement and the URL of the archived message.

> Troike, R. C. (2001, June 21). Buttercups and primroses [Electronic mailing list message]. Retrieved from http://listserv.linguistlist.org/archives/ads-l.html

> Wittenberg, E. (2001, July 11). Gender and the Internet [Newsgroup message]. Retrieved from news://comp.edu.composition

APA SOURCE MAP: Articles from databases

1 **Author.** Include the author's name as you would for a print source. List all authors' last names first, and use initials for first and middle names. For more about citing authors, see models 1–5.

2 **Publication date.** Enclose the date in parentheses. For journals, use only the year. For magazines and newspapers, use the year, a comma, the month, and the day if given.

3 **Article title.** Capitalize only the first word of the article title and the subtitle and any proper nouns or proper adjectives.

4 **Periodical title.** Italicize the periodical title.

5 **Print publication information.** For journals and magazines, give the volume number (italicized) and the issue number (in parentheses). For journals only, give the inclusive page numbers.

6 **Retrieval information.** If the article has a DOI (digital object identifier), include that number after the publication information; do not include the name of the database. If there is no DOI, write *Retrieved from* followed by the URL of the journal's home page (not the database URL).

A citation for the article on p. 381 would look like this:

Chory-Assad, R. M., & Tamborini, R. (2004). Television sitcom exposure and aggressive communication: A priming perspective. *North American Journal of Psychology, 6*(3), 415–422. Retrieved from http://www.najp.8m.com

3 Article Title

Print Publication Information **5**

1 Authors

Title:	**Television Sitcom Exposure and Aggressive Communication: A Priming Perspective.**
Authors:	Chory-Assad, Rebecca M.1 Tamborini, Ron2
Source:	North American Journal of Psychology; 2004, Vol. 6 Issue 3, p415-422, 8p
Document Type:	Article
Subject Terms:	*TELEVISION comedies *AGGRESSIVENESS *ATTITUDE (Psychology) *TELEVISION programs

2 Publication Date

Abstract: This study examined the relationship between exposure to verbally aggressive television sitcoms and aggressive communication, from a priming and cognitive neo-associationistic perspective. Participants reported their trait verbal aggressiveness and exposure to sitcoms approximately one month prior to their participation in the lab portion of the study. Once in the lab, participants evaluated four sitcoms and engaged in a question-response session that was observed and coded for aggression. Results indicated that increased exposure to television sitcoms was associated with lower levels of aggressive communication. Implications of these results for theory and research concerning the effects of exposure to aggression in a humorous context are discussed. [ABSTRACT FROM AUTHOR]

Author Affiliations:	1West Virginia University 2Michigan State University
Full Text Word Count:	2880
ISSN:	15277143
Accession Number:	15630823
Database:	Academic Search Premier

APA SOURCE MAP: Works from Web sites

1 **Author.** If one is given, include the author's name (see models 1–5). List last names first, and use only initials for first names. The site's sponsor may be the author. If no author is identified, begin the citation with the title of the document.

2 **Publication date.** Enclose the date of publication or latest update in parentheses. Use *n.d.* ("no date") when no publication date is available.

3 **Title of work.** Capitalize only the first word of the title and subtitle and any proper nouns or proper adjectives.

4 **Title of Web site.** Italicize the title. Capitalize all major words.

5 **Retrieval information.** Write *Retrieved from* and include the URL. If the work seems likely to be updated, include the retrieval date.

A citation for the Web document on p. 383 would look like this:

Alexander, M. (2001, August 22). Thirty years later, Stanford Prison Experiment lives on.

Stanford Report. Retrieved from http://news-service.stanford.edu/news/2001

/august22/prison2-822.html

Author ➊

➍ **Title of Web Site**

➎ **Retrieval Information**

➋ **Publication Date**

➌ **Title of Work**

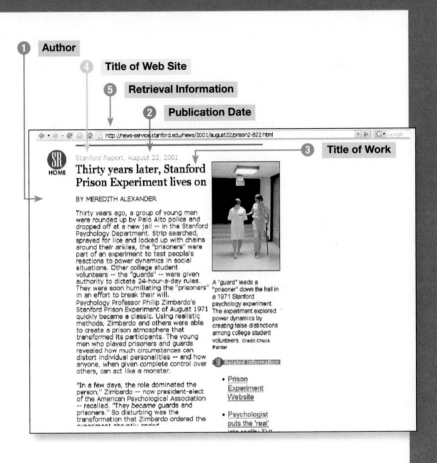

http://news-service.stanford.edu/news/2001/august22/prison2-822.html

Stanford Report, August 22, 2001

Thirty years later, Stanford Prison Experiment lives on

BY MEREDITH ALEXANDER

Thirty years ago, a group of young men were rounded up by Palo Alto police and dropped off at a new jail -- in the Stanford Psychology Department. Strip searched, sprayed for lice and locked up with chains around their ankles, the "prisoners" were part of an experiment to test people's reactions to power dynamics in social situations. Other college student volunteers -- the "guards" -- were given authority to dictate 24-hour-a-day rules. They were soon humiliating the "prisoners" in an effort to break their will. Psychology Professor Philip Zimbardo's Stanford Prison Experiment of August 1971 quickly became a classic. Using realistic methods, Zimbardo and others were able to create a prison atmosphere that transformed its participants. The young men who played prisoners and guards revealed how much circumstances can distort individual personalities -- and how anyone, when given complete control over others, can act like a monster.

"In a few days, the role dominated the person," Zimbardo -- now president-elect of the American Psychological Association -- recalled. "They *became* guards and prisoners." So disturbing was the transformation that Zimbardo ordered the experiment abruptly ended

A "guard" leads a "prisoner" down the hall in a 1971 Stanford psychology experiment. The experiment explored power dynamics by creating false distinctions among college student volunteers. Credit: Chuck Painter

Related Information

- Prison Experiment Website

- Psychologist puts the 'real' into reality TV/t

383

31. BLOG (WEB LOG) POST

Spaulding, P. (2010, April 27). Who believes in a real America? [Web log post].
Retrieved from http://pandagon.net/index.php/site/2010/04

32. WIKI ENTRY Use the date of posting, if there is one, or *n.d.* for "no date" if there is none. Include the retrieval date because wiki content can change frequently.

Happiness. (2007, June 14). Retrieved March 24, 2008, from PsychWiki:
http://www.psychwiki.com/wiki/Happiness

33. ONLINE AUDIO OR VIDEO FILE

Klusman, P. (2008, February 13). An engineer's guide to cats [Video file]. Retrieved
from http://www.youtube.com/watch?v=mHXBL6bzAR4

O'Brien, K. (2008, January 31). Developing countries [Audio file]. *KUSP's life in the
fast lane*. Retrieved from http://kusp.org/shows/fast.html

34. DATA SET

U.S. Department of Education, Institute of Education Sciences. (2009). *NAEP state
comparisons* [Data set]. Retrieved from http://nces.ed.gov/nationsreportcard
/statecomparisons/

35. COMPUTER SOFTWARE

PsychMate [Computer software]. (2003). Available from Psychology Software Tools:
http://pstnet.com/products/psychmate

4 Other sources (including online versions)

36. GOVERNMENT PUBLICATION

Office of the Federal Register. (2003). *The United States government manual
2003/2004*. Washington, DC: U.S. Government Printing Office.

Cite an online government document as you would a printed government work, adding the URL. If there is no date, use *n.d.*

U.S. Public Health Service. (1999). *The surgeon general's call to action to prevent
suicide*. Retrieved from http://www.mentalhealth.org/suicideprevention
/calltoaction.asp

37. DISSERTATION If you retrieved the dissertation from a database, give the database name and the accession number, if one is assigned.

Lengel, L. L. (1968). *The righteous cause: Some religious aspects of Kansas populism*. Retrieved from ProQuest Digital Dissertations. (6900033)

If you retrieve a dissertation from a Web site, give the type of dissertation, the institution, and year after the title, and provide a retrieval statement.

Meeks, M. G. (2006). *Between abolition and reform: First-year writing programs, e-literacies, and institutional change* (Doctoral dissertation, University of North Carolina). Retrieved from http://dc.lib.unc.edu/etd/

38. TECHNICAL OR RESEARCH REPORT Give the report number, if available, in parentheses after the title.

McCool, R., Fikes, R., & McGuinness, D. (2003). *Semantic Web tools for enhanced authoring* (Report No. KSL-03-07). Stanford, CA: Knowledge Systems Laboratory

39. CONFERENCE PROCEEDINGS

Robertson, S. P., Vatrapu, R. K., & Medina, R. (2009). YouTube and Facebook: Online video "friends" social networking. In *Conference proceedings: YouTube and the 2008 election cycle* (pp. 159–76). Amherst, MA: University of Massachusetts. Retrieved from http://scholarworks.umass.edu/jitpc2009

40. PAPER PRESENTED AT A MEETING OR SYMPOSIUM, UNPUBLISHED Cite the month of the meeting if it is available.

Jones, J. G. (1999, February). *Mental health intervention in mass casualty disasters*. Paper presented at the Rocky Mountain Region Disaster Mental Health Conference, Laramie, WY.

41. POSTER SESSION

Barnes Young, L. L. (2003, August). *Cognition, aging, and dementia*. Poster session presented at the 2003 Division 40 APA Convention, Toronto, Ontario, Canada.

42. FILM, VIDEO, OR DVD

Nolan, C. (Director). (2010). *Inception* [Motion picture]. United States: Warner Bros.

43. TELEVISION PROGRAM, SINGLE EPISODE

Imperioli, M. (Writer), & Buscemi, S. (Director). (2002). Everybody hurts [Television
series episode]. In D. Chase (Executive Producer), *The Sopranos*. New York, NY:
Home Box Office.

44. TELEVISION SERIES

Abrams, J. J., Lieber, J., & Lindelof, D. (2004). *Lost*. [Television series]. New York,
NY: WABC.

45. AUDIO PODCAST (DOWNLOADED AUDIO FILE)

Noguchi, Yugi. (2010, 24 May). BP hard to pin down on oil spill claims. [Audio
podcast]. *NPR morning edition*. Retrieved from http://www.npr.org

46. RECORDING

The Avalanches. (2001). Frontier psychiatrist. On *Since I left you* [CD]. Los Angeles,
CA: Elektra/Asylum Records.

17e A student research essay, APA style

Student Writer

Tawnya Redding

On the following pages is a paper by Tawnya
Redding that conforms to the APA guidelines
described in this chapter. Note that this essay has
been reproduced in a narrow format to allow for
annotation.

bedfordstmartins.com/smhandbook
Student Writing > Researched Writing

Running Head: MOOD MUSIC   1

Running head
(fifty charac-
ters or fewer)
appears flush
left on first line
of title page

Page number
appears flush
right on first
line of every
page

Mood Music: Music Preference and the Risk for Depression

and Suicide in Adolescents

Tawnya Redding

Psychology 480

Professor Ede

February 23, 2009

Title, name,
and affiliation
centered and
double-spaced

Annotations indicate effective choices or APA-style formatting.

MOOD MUSIC   2

Abstract

There has long been concern for the effects that certain genres of music (such as heavy metal and country) have on youth. While a correlational link between these genres and increased risk for depression and suicide in adolescents has been established, researchers have been unable to pinpoint what is responsible for this link, and a causal relationship has not been determined. This paper will begin by discussing correlational literature concerning music preference and increased risk for depression and suicide, as well as the possible reasons for this link. Finally, studies concerning the effects of music on mood will be discussed. This examination of the literature on music and increased risk for depression and suicide points out the limitations of previous research and suggests the need for new research establishing a causal relationship for this link as well as research into the specific factors that may contribute to an increased risk for depression and suicide in adolescents.

MOOD MUSIC   3

Mood Music: Music Preference and the Risk for Depression and Suicide in Adolescents

Music is a significant part of American culture. Since the explosion of rock and roll in the 1950s there has been a concern for the effects that music may have on listeners, and especially on young people. The genres most likely to come under suspicion in recent decades have included heavy metal, country, and blues. These genres have been suspected of having adverse effects on the mood and behavior of young listeners. But can music really alter the disposition and create self-destructive behaviors in listeners? And if so, which genres and aspects of those genres are responsible? The following review of the literature will establish the correlation between potentially problematic genres of music such as heavy metal and country and depression and suicide risk. First, correlational studies concerning music preference and suicide risk will be discussed, followed by a discussion of the literature concerning the possible reasons for this link. Finally, studies concerning the effects of music on mood will be discussed. Despite the link between genres such as heavy metal and country and suicide risk, previous research has been unable to establish the causal nature of this link.

The Correlation Between Music and Depression and Suicide Risk

Studies over the past two decades have set out to answer this question by examining the correlation between youth music preference and risk for depression and suicide. A large portion of these studies have focused on heavy metal and country music as the main genre culprits associated with youth suicidality and depression (Lacourse, Claes, & Villeneuve, 2001; Scheel & Westefeld, 1999; Stack & Gundlach, 1992). Stack and Gundlach (1992) examined the radio airtime devoted to country music in 49 metropolitan areas and found that the higher the percentages of country music airtime, the higher the incidence of suicides among whites. The reseachers hypothesized that themes in country music (such

Full title centered

Paragraphs indented

Background information about review supplied

Questions focus reader's attention

Boldface headings help organize review

Parenthetical references follow APA style

MOOD MUSIC   4

as alcohol abuse) promoted audience identification and reinforced a
preexisting suicidal mood, and that the themes associated with country
music were responsible for elevated suicide rates. Similarly, Scheel and
Westefeld (1999) found a correlation between heavy metal music listeners
and an increased risk for suicide, as did Lacourse et al. (2001).

Reasons for the Link: Characteristics of Those Who Listen to Problematic Music

Unfortunately, previous studies concerning music preference and
suicide risk have been unable to determine a causal relationship and have
focused mainly on establishing a correlation between suicide risk and music
preference. This leaves the question open as to whether an individual at risk
for depression and suicide is attracted to certain genres of music or whether
the music helps induce the mood — or both. Some studies have suggested
that music preference may simply be a reflection of other underlying
problems associated with increased risk for suicide (Lacourse et al., 2001;
Scheel & Westefeld, 1999). For example, in research done by Scheel and
Westefeld (1999), adolescents who listened to heavy metal were found
to have lower scores on the Reason for Living Inventory and several of its
subscales, a self-report measure designed to assess potential reasons for
not committing suicide. These adolescents were also found to have lower
scores on several subscales of the Reason for Living Inventory, including
responsibility to family along with survival and coping beliefs. Other risk
factors associated with suicide and suicidal behaviors include poor family
relationships, depression, alienation, anomie, and drug and alcohol abuse
(Lacourse et al., 2001). Lacourse et al. (2001) examined 275 adolescents in
the Montreal region with a preference for heavy metal and found that this
preference was not significantly related to suicide risk when other risk factors
were controlled for. This was also the conclusion of Scheel and Westefeld
(1999), in which music preference for heavy metal was thought to be a red

---

Discussion of correlation vs. causation points out limitations of previous studies

Alternative explanations considered

flag for suicide vulnerability, suggesting that the source of the problem may lie more in personal and familial characteristics.

George, Stickle, Rachid, and Wopnford (2007) further explored the correlation between suicide risk and music preference by attempting to identify the personality characteristics of those with a preference for different genres of music. A sample of 358 individuals was assessed for preference of 30 different styles of music along with a number of personality characteristics, including self-esteem, intelligence, spirituality, social skills, locus of control, openness, conscientiousness, extraversion, agreeableness, emotional stability, hostility, and depression (George et al., 2007). The thirty styles of music were then categorized into eight factors: rebellious (for example, punk and heavy metal), classical, rhythmic and intense (including hip-hop, rap, and pop), easy listening, fringe (for example, techno), contemporary Christian, jazz and blues, and traditional Christian. The results revealed an almost comprehensively negative personality profile for those who preferred to listen to the rebellious and rhythmic and intense categories, while those who preferred classical music tended to have a comprehensively positive profile. Like Scheel and Westefeld (1999) and Lacourse et al. (2001), this study also supports the theory that youth are drawn to certain genres of music based on already existing factors, whether they be related to personality or situational variables.

Reasons for the Link: Characteristics of Problematic Music

Another possible explanation is that the lyrics and themes of the music have an effect on listeners. In this scenario, music is thought to exacerbate an already depressed mood and hence contribute to an increased risk for suicide. This was the proposed reasoning behind higher suicide rates in whites in Stack and Gundlach's (1992) study linking country music to suicide risk. In this case, the themes associated with country music were thought to promote audience identification and

Transition links paragraphs

MOOD MUSIC   6

reinforce preexisting self-destructive behaviors (such as excessive alcohol
consumption). Stack (2000) also studied individuals with a musical
preference for blues to determine whether the genre's themes could
increase the level of suicide acceptability. The results demonstrated that
blues fans were no more accepting of suicide than nonfans, but that blues
listeners were found to have low religiosity levels, an important factor for

Need for more research indicated

suicide acceptability (Stack, 2000). Despite this link between possible
suicidal behavior and a preference for blues music, the actual suicide
behavior of blues fans has not been explored, and thus no concrete
associations can be made.

The Effect of Music on Mood

While studies examining the relationship between music genres

Discussion of previous research

such as heavy metal, country, and blues have been able to establish a
correlation between music preference and suicide risk, it is still unclear
from these studies what effect music has on the mood of the listener.
Previous research has suggested that some forms of music can both
improve and depress mood (Lai, 1999; Siedliecki & Good, 2006; Smith &
Noon, 1998). Lai (1999) found that changes in mood were more likely
to be found in an experimental group of depressed women versus a
control group. It was also found that both the experimental and control
groups showed significant increases in the tranquil mood state, but the
amount of change was not significant between the groups (Lai, 1999).
This study suggests that music can have a positive effect on depressed
individuals when they are allowed to choose the music they are listening
to. In a similar study, Siedliecki and Good (2006) found that music can
increase a listener's sense of power and decrease depression, pain,
and disability. Researchers randomly assigned 60 African American
and Caucasian participants with chronic nonmalignant pain to a
standard music group (offering them a choice of instrumental music

types — piano, jazz, orchestra, harp, and synthesizer), a patterning music group (asking them to choose music to ease muscle tension, to facilitate sleep, or to decrease anxiety), or a control group. There were no statistically significant differences between the two music groups. However, the music groups had significantly less pain, depression, and disability than the control group (Siedliecki & Good, 2006). On the other hand, Martin, Clark, and Pearce (1993) identified a subgroup of heavy metal fans who reported feeling worse after listening to their music of choice. Although this subgroup did exist, there was also evidence that listening to heavy metal results in more positive affect, and it was hypothesized that those who experience negative effects after listening to their preferred genre of heavy metal may be most at risk for suicidal behaviors (Martin et al., 1993).

Smith and Noon (1998) also determined that music can have a negative effect on mood. Six songs were selected for the particular theme they embodied: (1) vigorous, (2) fatigued, (3) angry, (4) depressed, (5) tense, and (6) all moods. The results indicated that selections 3 – 6 had significant effects on the mood of participants, with selection 6 (all moods) resulting in the greatest positive change in the mood and selection 5 (tense) resulting in the greatest negative change in mood. Selection 4 (depressed) was found to sap the vigor and increase anger / hostility in participants, while selection 5 (tense) significantly depressed participants and made them more anxious. Although this study did not specifically comment on the effects of different genres on mood, the results do indicate that certain themes can indeed depress mood. The participants for this study were undergraduate students who were not depressed, and thus it seems that certain types of music can have a negative effect on the mood of healthy individuals.

MOOD MUSIC 8

Is There Evidence for a Causal Relationship?

Despite the correlation between certain music genres (especially heavy metal) and increased risk for depression and suicidal behaviors in adolescents, it remains unclear whether these types of music can alter the mood of at-risk youth in a negative way. This view of the correlation between music and suicide risk is supported by a meta-analysis done by Baker and Bor (2008), in which the authors assert that most studies reject the notion that music is a causal factor and suggest that music preference is more indicative of emotional vulnerability. However, it is still unknown whether these genres can negatively alter mood at all, and if they can, whether the themes and lyrics associated with the music are responsible. Clearly, more research is needed to further examine this correlation, as a causal link between these genres of music and adolescent suicide risk has yet to be shown. However, even if the theory put forth by Baker and Bon and other researchers is true, it is still important to investigate the effects that music can have on those who may be at risk for suicide and depression. Even if music genres are not the ultimate cause of suicidal behavior, they may act as a catalyst that further pushes adolescents into a state of depression and increased risk for suicidal behavior.

Conclusion indicates need for further research

MOOD MUSIC 9

References

Baker, F., & Bor, W. (2008). Can music preference indicate mental health status in young people? *Australasian Psychiatry, 16*(4), 284–288. Retrieved from http://www3.interscience.wiley.com/journal/118565538/home

George, D., Stickle, K., Rachid, F., & Wopnford, A. (2007). The association between types of music enjoyed and cognitive, behavioral, and personality factors of those who listen. *Psychomusicology. 19*(2), 32–56.

Lacourse, E., Claes, M., & Villeneuve, M. (2001). Heavy metal music and adolescent suicidal risk. *Journal of Youth and Adolescence. 30*(3), 321–332.

Lai, Y. (1999). Effects of music listening on depressed women in Taiwan. *Issues in Mental Health Nursing, 20*, 229–246. doi: 10.1080/016128499248637

Martin, G., Clark, M., & Pearce, C. (1993). Adolescent suicide: Music preference as an indicator of vulnerability. *Journal of the American Academy of Child and Adolescent Psychiatry, 32*, 530–535.

Scheel, K., & Westefeld, J. (1999). Heavy metal music and adolescent suicidality: An empirical investigation. *Adolescence, 34*(134). 253–273.

Siedliecki, S., & Good, M. (2006). Effect of music on power, pain, depression and disability. *Journal of Advanced Nursing, 54*(5), 553–562. doi: 10.1111/j.1365-2648.2006.03860.x

Smith, J. L., & Noon, J. (1998). Objective measurement of mood change induced by contemporary music. *Journal of Psychiatric & Mental Health Nursing, 5*, 403–408.

Stack, S. (2000). Blues fans and suicide acceptability. *Death Studies, 24*, 223–231.

Stack, S., & Gundlach, J. (1992). The effect of country music on suicide. *Social Forces. 71*(1), 211–218. Retrieved from http://socialforces.unc.edu/

Student Writing APA

References begin on new page

Journal article from a database, no DOI

Print journal article

Journal article from a database with DOI

18

Chicago Style

One of the oldest formal documentation systems, *Chicago* style has long been used in history and some other fields in the humanities, as well as in publishing.

For further reference, consult *The Chicago Manual* or a volume intended specifically for student writers, Kate L. Turabian's *A Manual for Writers of Term Papers, Theses, and Dissertations,* Sixth Edition (1996).

The Sixteenth Edition of *The Chicago Manual of Style*, published in 2010, provides a complete guide to *Chicago* style. This chapter presents the notes and bibliography system. For easy reference, examples of notes and bibliographic references are shown together in 18c.

18a Formatting *Chicago* manuscripts

Chicago offers general guidelines for formatting a paper, but it does not specifically discuss student-paper formats. Your instructor may have other requirements, so check before preparing your final draft.

For detailed guidelines on formatting a bibliography, see 18b and 18c. For a sample student essay in *Chicago* style, see 18d.

- *Title page.* Center the full title of your paper, your name, the course name, the instructor's name, and the date submitted. Do not type a number on this page, but do count it; consequently, number the first page of text as page 2.

- *Margins and spacing.* Leave one-inch margins at the top, bottom, and sides of pages. Double-space the body of the text, including block quotations. Unless your instructor requests double-spacing throughout, single-space the notes and bibliographic entries, but double-space between entries.

- *Page numbers.* Number all pages (except the title page) in the upper right-hand corner. You may use a short title or your name before page numbers.

- *Long quotations.* Indent long quotations one-half inch from the left margin, and do not use quotation marks. In general, *Chicago* defines a long quotation as ten or more lines, though you may decide to set off shorter quotations for emphasis (see 48a).

- *Headings. Chicago* style allows, but does not require, headings. Many students and instructors find them helpful. (See 23c for guidelines on using headings and subheadings.)

- *Visuals.* Visuals (photographs, drawings, charts, graphs, and tables) should be placed as near as possible to the relevant text. Tables should be labeled *Table*, numbered, and captioned. All other visuals should be labeled *Figure* (abbreviated *Fig.*), numbered, and captioned. Remember to refer to each visual in your text, explaining how it contributes to the point(s) you are making.

18b In-text citations, notes, and bibliography

In *Chicago* style, use superscript numbers (^{1}) to mark citations in the text. Sequentially numbered citations throughout the text correspond to notes that contain either publication information about the source cited or explanatory or supplemental material not included in the main text. Place the superscript for each note near the cited material—at the end of the relevant quotation, sentence, clause, or phrase. Type the number after any punctuation mark except the dash, and leave no space between the superscript and the preceding letter or punctuation mark. When you use signal phrases to introduce quotations or other source material, note that *Chicago* style requires you to use the present tense (*citing Bebout's studies, Meier points out*).

The notes themselves can be footnotes (each typed at the bottom of the page on which the superscript for it appears in the text) or endnotes (all typed on a separate page at the end of the text under the heading *Notes*). Be sure to check your instructor's preference. The first line of each note is indented like a paragraph (one-half inch) and begins with a number followed by a period, one space, and the first word. All remaining lines of the entry are typed flush with the left margin. Footnotes and endnotes should be single-spaced, with a double space between notes, unless your instructor prefers that the notes also be double-spaced.

IN THE TEXT

Sweig argues that Castro and Che Guevara were not the only key players in the Cuban Revolution of the late 1950s.[19]

IN THE FIRST NOTE

19. Julia Sweig, *Inside the Cuban Revolution* (Cambridge, MA: Harvard University Press, 2002), 9.

After giving complete information the first time you cite a work, shorten any additional references to that work: list only the author's last name followed by a comma, a shortened version of the title, a comma, and the page number. If the reference is to the same source cited in the previous note, you can use the Latin abbreviation *Ibid.* (for "in the same place") instead of the name and title.

IN FIRST AND SUBSEQUENT NOTES

19. Julia Sweig, *Inside the Cuban Revolution* (Cambridge, MA: Harvard University Press, 2002), 9.

20. Ibid., 13.

21. Ferguson, "Comfort of Being Sad," 63.

22. Sweig, *Cuban Revolution*, 21.

The alphabetical list of the sources in your paper is usually titled *Bibliography* in *Chicago* style. You may instead use the title *Sources Consulted*, *Works Cited*, or *Selected Bibliography* if it better describes your list.

In the bibliographic entry for a source, include the same information as in the first note for that source, but omit the specific page reference. However, give the *first* author's last name first, followed by a comma and the first name; separate the main elements of the entry with periods rather than commas; and do not enclose the publication information for books in parentheses. Type the first line flush with the left margin, and indent the subsequent lines of each entry one-half inch.

IN THE BIBLIOGRAPHY

Sweig, Julia. *Inside the Cuban Revolution*. Cambridge, MA: Harvard University Press, 2002.

Start the bibliography on a separate page after the main text and any endnotes. Continue the consecutive numbering of pages. Center the title *Bibliography* (without underlining, italics, or quotation marks) one inch below the top of the page. List sources alphabetically by authors' last names or, if an author is unknown, by the first major word in the title. *The Chicago Manual of Style* recommends single-spacing the entries and double-spacing between entries, but some instructors may prefer that you double-space the entire list.

18c Notes and bibliographic entries

The following examples demonstrate how to format both notes and bibliographic entries according to *Chicago* style. The note, which is numbered, appears first; the bibliographic entry, which is not numbered, appears below the note.

Directory to *Chicago* style for notes and bibliographic entries

Print and online books

1. One author *400*
   SOURCE MAP *402–3*
2. Multiple authors *400*
3. Organization as author *401*
4. Unknown author *401*
5. Online book *401*
6. Electronic book (e-book) *401*
7. Edited book with no author *401*
8. Edited book with author *404*
9. Selection in an anthology or chapter in a book, with an editor *404*
10. Introduction, preface, foreword, or afterword *404*
11. Translation *404*
12. Edition other than the first *404*
13. Multivolume work *405*
14. Reference work *405*
15. Work with a title within the title *405*
16. Sacred text *405*
17. Source quoted in another source *406*

Print and online periodicals

18. Article in a print journal *406*
19. Article in an online journal *406*
20. Journal article from a database *406*
    SOURCE MAP *408–9*
21. Article in a print magazine *407*
22. Article in an online magazine *407*
23. Magazine article from a database *407*
24. Article in a newspaper *407*
25. Article in an online newspaper *410*
26. Newspaper article from a database *410*
27. Book review *410*

continued

Online sources

Other sources

1 Print and online books

For the basic format for citing a print book, see pp. 402–3. The note for a book typically includes four elements: author's name, title and subtitle, publication information, and page number(s) to which the note refers. The bibliographic entry usually includes the first three elements, but they are styled somewhat differently: commas separate major elements of a note, but a bibliographic entry uses periods.

1. ONE AUTHOR

1. Nell Irvin Painter, *The History of White People* (New York: W. W. Norton, 2010), 119.

Painter, Nell Irvin. *The History of White People.* New York: W. W. Norton, 2010.

2. MULTIPLE AUTHORS

2. Margaret Macmillan and Richard Holbrooke, *Paris 1919: Six Months That Changed the World* (New York: Random House, 2003), 384.

Macmillan, Margaret, and Richard Holbrooke. *Paris 1919: Six Months That Changed the World.* New York: Random House, 2003.

With more than three authors, you may give the first-listed author followed by *et al.* in the note. In the bibliography, list all the authors' names.

2. Stephen J. Blank et al., *Conflict, Culture, and History: Regional Dimensions* (Miami: University Press of the Pacific, 2002), 276.

Blank, Stephen J., Lawrence E. Grinter, Karl P. Magyar, Lewis B. Ware, and Bynum E. Weathers. *Conflict, Culture, and History: Regional Dimensions*. Miami: University Press of the Pacific, 2002.

3. ORGANIZATION AS AUTHOR

3. World Intellectual Property Organization, *Intellectual Property Profile of the Least Developed Countries* (Geneva: World Intellectual Property Organization, 2002), 43.

World Intellectual Property Organization. *Intellectual Property Profile of the Least Developed Countries*. Geneva: World Intellectual Property Organization, 2002.

4. UNKNOWN AUTHOR

4. *Broad Stripes and Bright Stars* (Kansas City, MO: Andrews McMeel, 2002), 10.

Broad Stripes and Bright Stars. Kansas City, MO: Andrews McMeel, 2002.

5. ONLINE BOOK

5. Dorothy Richardson, *Long Day: The Story of a New York Working Girl, as Told by Herself* (1906; UMDL Texts, 2010),159, http://quod.lib.umich.edu/cgi/t/text /text-idx?c=moa;idno=AFS7156.0001.001.

Richardson, Dorothy. *Long Day: The Story of a New York Working Girl, as Told by Herself*. 1906. UMDL Texts, 2010. http://quod.lib.umich.edu/cgi/t/text/text-idx?c=moa ;idno=AFS7156.0001.001.

6. ELECTRONIC BOOK (E-BOOK)

6. Manal M. Omar, *Barefoot in Baghdad* (Naperville, IL: Sourcebooks, 2010), Kindle edition, ch. 4.

Omar, Manal M. *Barefoot in Baghdad*. Naperville, IL: Sourcebooks, 2010. Kindle edition.

7. EDITED BOOK WITH NO AUTHOR

7. James H. Fetzer, ed., *The Great Zapruder Film Hoax: Deceit and Deception in the Death of JFK* (Chicago: Open Court, 2003), 56.

Fetzer, James H., ed. *The Great Zapruder Film Hoax: Deceit and Deception in the Death of JFK*. Chicago: Open Court, 2003.

CHICAGO SOURCE MAP: Books

Take information from the book's title page and copyright page (on the reverse side of the title page), not from the book's cover or a library catalog. Look carefully at the differences in punctuation between the note and the bibliographic entry.

1. **Author.** In a note, list author first name first. In a bibliographic entry, list the first author last name first. List other authors first name first.

2. **Title.** Italicize the title and subtitle and capitalize all major words.

3. **City of publication.** List the city (and country or state abbreviation for an unfamiliar city) followed by a colon. In a note only, city, publisher, and year appear in parentheses.

4. **Publisher.** Drop *Inc.*, *Co.*, *Publishing*, or *Publishers*. Follow with a comma.

5. **Publication year.** In a note, follow the year with the relevant page number. End with a period.

Citations for the book on p. 403 would look like this:

Endnote

1. Louis Menand, *The Metaphysical Club* (New York: Farrar, Straus and Giroux, 2001), 178.

Bibliographic entry

Menand, Louis. *The Metaphysical Club.* New York: Farrar, Straus and Giroux, 2001.

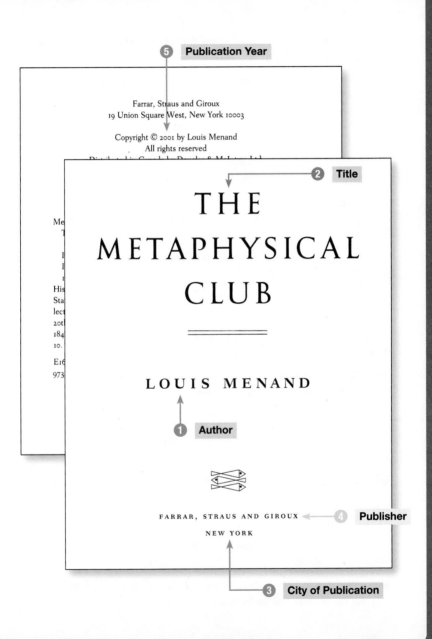

2 **Title**

THE
METAPHYSICAL
CLUB

LOUIS MENAND

1 **Author**

FARRAR, STRAUS AND GIROUX ⟵ 4 **Publisher**

NEW YORK

3 **City of Publication**

8. EDITED BOOK WITH AUTHOR

8. Leopold von Ranke, *The Theory and Practice of History*, ed. Georg G. Iggers (New York: Routledge, 2010), 135.

von Ranke, Leopold. *The Theory and Practice of History*. Edited by Georg G. Iggers. New York: Routledge, 2010.

9. SELECTION IN AN ANTHOLOGY OR CHAPTER IN A BOOK, WITH AN EDITOR

9. Denise Little, "Born in Blood," in *Alternate Gettysburgs,* ed. Brian Thomsen and Martin H. Greenberg (New York: Berkley Publishing Group, 2002), 245.

Give the inclusive page numbers of the selection or chapter in the bibliographic entry.

Little, Denise. "Born in Blood." In *Alternate Gettysburgs*. Edited by Brian Thomsen and Martin H. Greenberg, 242–55. New York: Berkley Publishing Group, 2002.

10. INTRODUCTION, PREFACE, FOREWORD, OR AFTERWORD

10. Robert B. Reich, introduction to *Making Work Pay: America after Welfare*, ed. Robert Kuttner (New York: New Press, 2002), xvi.

Reich, Robert B. Introduction to *Making Work Pay: America after Welfare*, vii–xvii. Edited by Robert Kuttner. New York: New Press, 2002.

11. TRANSLATION

11. Suetonius, *The Twelve Caesars,* trans. Robert Graves (London: Penguin Classics, 1989), 202.

Suetonius. *The Twelve Caesars*. Translated by Robert Graves. London: Penguin Classics, 1989.

12. EDITION OTHER THAN THE FIRST

12. Dee Brown, *Bury My Heart at Wounded Knee: An Indian History of the American West,* 4th ed. (New York: Owl Books, 2007), 12.

Brown, Dee. *Bury My Heart at Wounded Knee: An Indian History of the American West,* 4th ed. New York: Owl Books, 2007.

13. MULTIVOLUME WORK

13. John Watson, *Annals of Philadelphia and Pennsylvania in the Olden Time,* vol. 2 (Washington, DC: Ross & Perry, 2003), 514.

Watson, John. *Annals of Philadelphia and Pennsylvania in the Olden Time.* Vol. 2. Washington, DC: Ross & Perry, 2003.

14. REFERENCE WORK

In a note, use *s.v.*, the abbreviation for the Latin *sub verbo* ("under the word") to help your reader find the entry.

14. *Encyclopedia Britannica,* s.v. "carpetbagger."

Do not list reference works such as encyclopedias or dictionaries in your bibliography.

15. WORK WITH A TITLE WITHIN THE TITLE

Use quotation marks around any title within a book title.

15. John A. Alford, *A Companion to "Piers Plowman"* (Berkeley: University of California Press, 1988), 195.

Alford, John A. *A Companion to "Piers Plowman."* Berkeley: University of California Press, 1988.

16. SACRED TEXT

16. Luke 18:24–25 (New International Version)

16. Qur'an 7:40–41

Do not include a sacred text in the bibliography.

QUICK HELP

Citing sources without models in *Chicago* style

To cite a source for which you cannot find a model, collect as much information as you can find—about the creator, title, date of creation or update, and location of the source—with the goal of helping your readers find the source for themselves, if possible. Then look at the models in this section to see which one most closely matches the type of source you are using.

In an academic writing project, before citing an electronic source for which you have no model, also be sure to ask your instructor's advice.

17. SOURCE QUOTED IN ANOTHER SOURCE Identify both the original and the secondary source.

17. Frank D. Millet, "The Filipino Leaders," *Harper's Weekly*, March 11, 1899, quoted in Richard Slotkin, *Gunfighter Nation: The Myth of the Frontier in Twentieth-Century America* (New York: HarperCollins, 1992), 110.

Millet, Frank D. "The Filipino Leaders." *Harper's Weekly*, March 11, 1899. Quoted in Richard Slotkin, *Gunfighter Nation: The Myth of the Frontier in Twentieth-Century America* (New York: HarperCollins, 1992), 110.

2 Print and online periodicals

The note for an article in a periodical typically includes the author's name, the article title, and the periodical title. The format for other information, including the volume and issue numbers (if any), the date of publication, and the page number(s) to which the note refers, varies according to the type of periodical and whether you consulted it in print, on the Web, or in a database. In a bibliographic entry for a journal or magazine article from a database or a print periodical, also give the inclusive page numbers.

18. ARTICLE IN A PRINT JOURNAL

18. Karin Lützen, "The Female World: Viewed from Denmark," *Journal of Women's History* 12, no. 3 (2000): 36.

Lützen, Karin. "The Female World: Viewed from Denmark." *Journal of Women's History* 12, no. 3 (2000): 34–38.

19. ARTICLE IN AN ONLINE JOURNAL Give the DOI if there is one. If not, include the article URL. If page numbers are provided, include them as well.

19. Jeffrey J. Schott, "America, Europe, and the New Trade Order," *Business and Politics* 11, no. 3 (2009), doi:10.2202/1469-3569.1263.

Schott, Jeffrey J. "America, Europe, and the New Trade Order." *Business and Politics* 11, no. 3 (2009). doi:10.2202/1469-3569.1263.

20. JOURNAL ARTICLE FROM A DATABASE For basic information on citing a periodical article from a database in *Chicago* style, see the source map on pp. 408–9.

20. W. Trent Foley and Nicholas J. Higham, "Bede on the Britons," *Early Medieval Europe* 17, no. 2 (2009), 157, doi:10.1111/j.1468-0254.2009.00258.x.

Foley, W. Trent, and Nicholas J. Higham. "Bede on the Britons." *Early Medieval Europe* 17, no. 2 (2009). 154–85. doi:10.1111/j.1468-0254.2009.00258.x.

21. ARTICLE IN A PRINT MAGAZINE

21. Terry McDermott, "The Mastermind: Khalid Sheikh Mohammed and the Making of 9/11," *New Yorker*, September 13, 2010, 42.

McDermott, Terry. "The Mastermind: Khalid Sheikh Mohammed and the Making of 9/11." *New Yorker*, September 13, 2010, 38–51.

22. ARTICLE IN AN ONLINE MAGAZINE

22. Tracy Clark-Flory, "Educating Women Saves Kids' Lives," *Salon*, September 17, 2010, http://www.salon.com/life/broadsheet/2010/09/17/education_women /index.html.

Clark-Flory, Tracy. "Educating Women Saves Kids' Lives." *Salon*, September 17, 2010. http://www.salon.com/life/broadsheet/2010/09/17/education_women/index .html.

23. MAGAZINE ARTICLE FROM A DATABASE

23. Sami Yousafzai and Ron Moreau, "Twisting Arms in Afghanistan," *Newsweek*, November 9, 2009, 8, Academic Search Premier (44962900).

Yousafzai, Sami, and Ron Moreau. "Twisting Arms in Afghanistan." *Newsweek*, November 9, 2009. 8. Academic Search Premier (44962900).

24. ARTICLE IN A NEWSPAPER Do not include page numbers for a newspaper article, but you may include the section, if any.

24. Caroline E. Mayer, "Wireless Industry to Adopt Voluntary Standards," *Washington Post,* September 9, 2003, sec. E.

Mayer, Caroline E. "Wireless Industry to Adopt Voluntary Standards." *Washington Post*, September 9, 2003, sec. E.

If you provide complete documentation of a newspaper article in a note, you may not need to include it in the bibliography. Check your instructor's preference.

CHICAGO SOURCE MAP: Articles from databases

1. **Author.** In a note, list author first name first. In the bibliographic entry, list the first author last name first, comma, first name; list other authors first name first.

2. **Article title.** Enclose title and subtitle (if any) in quotation marks, and capitalize major words. In the notes section, put a comma before and after the title. In the bibliography, put a period before and after.

3. **Periodical title.** Italicize the title and subtitle, and capitalize all major words. For a magazine or newspaper, follow with a comma.

4. **Journal volume and issue numbers.** For journals, follow the title with the volume number, a comma, the abbreviation *no.*, and the issue number.

5. **Publication date.** For journals, enclose the publication year in parentheses and follow with a comma (in a note) or with a period (in a bibliography). For other periodicals, give the month and year or month, day, and year, followed by a comma.

6. **Retrieval information.** Provide the article's DOI, if one is given. If not, give the name of the database and an accession number, or a "stable or persistent" URL for the article in the database. Because you provide stable retrieval information, you do not need to identify the electronic format of the work (i.e., PDF, as in the example shown here). End with a period.

Citations for the journal article on p. 409 would look like this:

Endnote

1. Howard Schuman, Barry Schwartz, and Hannah D'Arcy, "Elite Revisionists and Popular Beliefs: Christopher Columbus, Hero or Villain?" *Public Opinion Quarterly* 69, no. 1 (2005), doi:10.1093/poq/nfi001.

Bibliographic entry

Schuman, Howard, Barry Schwartz, and Hannah D'Arcy. "Elite Revisionists and Popular Beliefs: Christopher Columbus, Hero or Villain?" *Public Opinion Quarterly* 69, no. 1 (2005). doi:10.1093/poq/nfi001.

3 Periodical Title   **4** Journal Volume and Issue Numbers

Public Opinion Quarterly, Vol. 69, No. 1, Spring 2005, pp. 2–29

5 Publication Date

ELITE REVISIONISTS AND POPULAR BELIEFS
CHRISTOPHER COLUMBUS, HERO OR VILLAIN?

HOWARD SCHUMAN
BARRY SCHWARTZ
HANNAH D'ARCY

1 Authors

2 Article Title

Abstract According to revisionist historians and American Indian activists, Christopher Columbus deserves condemnation for having brought slavery, disease, and death to America's indigenous peoples. We ask whether the general public's beliefs about Columbus show signs of reflecting these critical accounts, which increased markedly as the 1992 Quincentenary approached. Our national surveys, using several different question wordings, indicate that most Americans continue to admire Columbus because, as tradition puts it, "he discovered America," though only a small number of mainly older respondents speak of him in the heroic terms common in earlier years. At the same time, the percentage of Americans who reject traditional beliefs about Columbus is also small and is divided between those who simply acknowledge the priority of Indians as the "First Americans" and those who go further to view Columbus as a villain. The latter group of respondents, we find, show a critical stance toward modal American beliefs much more broadly.

We also analyze American history school textbooks for evidence of influence from revisionist writings, and we consider representations of Columbus in the mass media as well. Revisionist history can be seen as one consequence of the "minority rights revolution" that began after World War II and has achieved considerable success, but the endurance of Columbus's reputation—to a considerable extent even among the

HOWARD SCHUMAN is a research scientist and professor emeritus at the University of Michigan. BARRY SCHWARTZ is a professor emeritus at the University of Georgia. HANNAH D'ARCY is an independent statistical consultant who previously worked for the University of Michigan's Center for Statistical Consultation and Research. We thank Lawrence Bobo and Stanley Presser for stimulating us to do multiple validations, and we are grateful to the editor of *Public Opinion Quarterly* for recommendations that substantially improved our final presentation. In addition, we are much indebted for help during the course of the research to Virginia Hopcroft, Government Documents Librarian at Bowdoin College; Maria Krysan, University of Illinois at Chicago; Alyssa Miller, Evanston, Illinois; and Irina Poznansky, Departmental Librarian, Teachers College, Gottesman Libraries, Columbia University. Support for the research was drawn in part from a National Science Foundation grant (SES-0001844). Address correspondence to Howard Schuman; e-mail: hschuman@umich.edu.

doi:10.1093/poq/nfi001 **6** Retrieval Information

25. ARTICLE IN AN ONLINE NEWSPAPER If the URL for the article is very long, use the URL for the newspaper's home page.

25. Andrew C. Revkin, "Arctic Melt Unnerves the Experts," *New York Times*, October 2, 2007, http://www.nytimes.com/2007/10/02/science/earth/02arct.html.

Revkin, Andrew C. "Arctic Melt Unnerves the Experts." *New York Times*, October 2, 2007. http://www.nytimes.com/2007/10/02/science/earth/02arct.html.

26. NEWSPAPER ARTICLE FROM A DATABASE

26. Demetria Irwin, "A Hatchet, Not a Scalpel, for NYC Budget Cuts," *New York Amsterdam News*, November 13, 2008, Academic Search Premier (35778153).

Irwin, Demetria. "A Hatchet, Not a Scalpel, for NYC Budget Cuts." *New York Amsterdam News*, November 13, 2008. Academic Search Premier (35778153).

27. BOOK REVIEW After the information about the book under review, give publication information for the appropriate kind of source (see models 18–26).

27. Arnold Relman, "Health Care: The Disquieting Truth," review of *Tracking Medicine: A Researcher's Quest to Understand Health Care*, by John E. Wennberg, *New York Review of Books* 57, no. 14 (2010), 45.

Relman, Arnold. "Health Care: The Disquieting Truth." Review of *Tracking Medicine: A Researcher's Quest to Understand Health Care*, by John E. Wennberg. *New York Review of Books* 57, no. 14 (2010), 45–48.

3 Online sources

In general, include the author (if given); the title of a work from a Web site (in quotation marks); the name of the site (in italics, if the site is an online publication, but otherwise neither italicized nor in quotation marks); the sponsor of the site, if different from the name of the site or name of the author; the date of publication or most recent update; and a URL. If the online source does not indicate when it was published or last modified, or if your instructor requests an access date, place it before the URL.

28. WEB SITE

28. Rutgers School of Arts and Sciences, *The Rutgers Oral History Archive*, 2010, accessed September 17, 2010, http://oralhistory.rutgers.edu/.

Rutgers School of Arts and Sciences. *The Rutgers Oral History Archive*. 2010. Accessed September 17, 2010. http://oralhistory.rutgers.edu/.

29. WORK FROM A WEB SITE

29. Rose Cohen, "My First Job," *The Triangle Factory Fire*, Cornell University School of Industrial and Labor Relations, 2005, http://www.ilr.cornell.edu /trianglefire/texts/.

Cohen, Rose. "My First Job." *The Triangle Factory Fire*. Cornell University School of Industrial and Labor Relations. 2005. http://www.ilr.cornell.edu/trianglefire /texts/.

30. BLOG (WEB LOG) POST Treat a blog post as a short work from a Web site (see model 29).

30. Jai Arjun Singh, "On the Road in the USSR," *Jabberwock* (blog), November 29, 2007, http://jaiarjun.blogspot.com/2007/11/on-road-in-ussr.html.

Chicago recommends that blog posts appear in the notes section only, not in the bibliography, unless the blog is cited frequently. Check your instructor's preference. A bibliography reference to an entire blog would look like this:

Singh, Jai Arjun. *Jabberwock* (blog). http://jaiarjun.blogspot.com/.

31. EMAIL AND OTHER PERSONAL COMMUNICATIONS Cite email messages and other personal communications, such as letters and telephone calls, in the text or in a note only, not in the bibliography. (*Chicago* style recommends hyphenating *e-mail*.)

31. Kareem Adas, e-mail message to author, February 11, 2010.

32. PODCAST Treat a podcast as a short work from a Web site (see model 29) and give as much of the following information as you can find: the author or speaker, the title or a description of the podcast, the title of the site, the site sponsor (if different from the author or site name), the type of podcast or file format, the date of posting or access, and the URL.

32. Barack Obama, "Weekly Address: A Solar Recovery," *The White House,* podcast video, July 3, 2010, http://www.whitehouse.gov/photos-and-video/video /weekly-address-a-solar-recovery.

Obama, Barack. "Weekly Address: A Solar Recovery." *The White House*. Podcast video. July 3, 2010. http://www.whitehouse.gov/photos-and-video/video /weekly-address-a-solar-recovery.

33. ONLINE AUDIO OR VIDEO Treat an online audio or video source as a short work from a Web site (see model 29). If the source is downloadable, give the medium or file format before the URL (see model 32).

CHICAGO SOURCE MAP: Works from Web sites

1 **Author.** In a note, list author first name first. In a bibliographic entry, list the first author last name first, comma, first name; list additional authors first name first. Note that the host may serve as the author.

2 **Document title.** Enclose the title in quotation marks, and capitalize all major words. In a note, put a comma before and after the title. In the bibliography, put a period before and after.

3 **Title of Web site.** Capitalize all major words. If the site's title is analogous to a book or periodical title, italicize it. In the notes section, put a comma after the title. In the bibliography, put a period after the title.

4 **Sponsor of site.** If the sponsor is the same as the author or site title, you may omit it. End with a comma (in the note) or a period (in the bibliography entry).

5 **Date of publication or last modification.** If no date is available, or if your instructor requests it, include your date of access (with the word *accessed*).

6 **Retrieval information.** Give the URL for the Web site. If you are required to include a date of access, put the word *accessed* and the date in parentheses after the URL. End with a period.

Citations for the Web site on p. 413 would look like this:

Endnote

    1. Douglas Linder, "The Haymarket Riot Trial," *Famous Trials*, University of Missouri-Kansas City School of Law, 2006, http://www.law.umkc.edu/faculty/projects/FTrials /haymarket/haymarket.htm.

Bibliographic entry

Linder, Douglas. "The Haymarket Riot Trial." *Famous Trials*, University of Missouri-Kansas City School of Law. 2006, http://www.law.umkc.edu/faculty/projects/FTrials /haymarket/haymarket.htm.

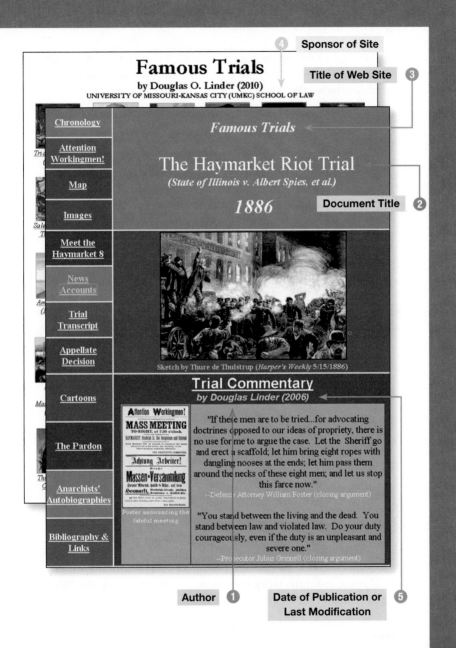

Sponsor of Site ④

Title of Web Site ③

Famous Trials
by Douglas O. Linder (2010)
UNIVERSITY OF MISSOURI-KANSAS CITY (UMKC) SCHOOL OF LAW

Chronology

Attention Workingmen!

Map

Images

Meet the Haymarket 8

News Accounts

Trial Transcript

Appellate Decision

Cartoons

The Pardon

Anarchists' Autobiographies

Bibliography & Links

Famous Trials

The Haymarket Riot Trial
(State of Illinois v. Albert Spies, et al.)

1886

Document Title ②

Sketch by Thure de Thulstrup (*Harper's Weekly* 5/15/1886)

Trial Commentary
by Douglas Linder (2006)

Attention Workingmen!
MASS MEETING
TO-NIGHT, at 7.30 o'clock.

Achtung Arbeiter!
Massen-Versammlung

Foster announcing the fateful meeting

"If these men are to be tried...for advocating doctrines opposed to our ideas of propriety, there is no use for me to argue the case. Let the Sheriff go and erect a scaffold; let him bring eight ropes with dangling nooses at the ends; let him pass them around the necks of these eight men; and let us stop this farce now."
--Defense Attorney William Foster (closing argument)

"You stand between the living and the dead. You stand between law and violated law. Do your duty courageously, even if the duty is an unpleasant and severe one."
--Prosecutor Julius Grinnell (closing argument)

Author ①

Date of Publication or Last Modification ⑤

413

33. Alyssa Katz, "Did the Mortgage Crisis Kill the American Dream?" YouTube video, 4:32, posted by NYCRadio, June 24, 2009, http://www.youtube.com/watch?v=uivtwjwd_Qw.

Katz, Alyssa. "Did the Mortgage Crisis Kill the American Dream?" YouTube video, 4:32. Posted by NYCRadio. June 24, 2009. http://www.youtube.com/watch?v=uivtwjwd_Qw.

4 Other sources

34. PUBLISHED OR BROADCAST INTERVIEW

34. Nina Totenberg, interview by Charlie Rose, *The Charlie Rose Show*, PBS, June 29, 2010.

Totenberg, Nina. Interview by Charlie Rose. *The Charlie Rose Show*. PBS, June 29, 2010.

Interviews you conduct are considered personal communications (see model 31).

35. VIDEO OR DVD

35. Edward Norton and Edward Furlong, *American History X*, directed by Tony Kaye (1998; Los Angeles: New Line Studios, 2002). DVD.

Norton, Edward, and Edward Furlong. *American History X*. Directed by Tony Kaye, 1998. Los Angeles: New Line Studios, 2002. DVD.

36. SOUND RECORDING

36. Paul Robeson, *The Collector's Paul Robeson*, recorded 1959, Monitor MCD-61580, 1989, compact disc.

Robeson, Paul. *The Collector's Paul Robeson*. Recorded 1959. Monitor MCD-61580, 1989, compact disc.

37. WORK OF ART Begin with the artist's name and the title of the work. If you viewed the work in person, give the medium, the date, and the name of the place where you saw it.

37. Mary Cassatt, *The Child's Bath*, oil on canvas, 1893, The Art Institute of Chicago, Chicago, IL.

Cassatt, Mary. *The Child's Bath*. Oil on canvas, 1893. The Art Institute of Chicago, Chicago, IL.

If you refer to a reproduction, give the publication information.

37. Mary Cassatt, *The Child's Bath,* oil on canvas, 1893, on *Art Access*, The Art Institute of Chicago, last modified August 2004, http://www.artic.edu/artaccess /AA_Impressionist/pages/IMP_6.shtml#.

Cassatt, Mary. *The Child's Bath*. Oil on canvas, 1893. On *Art Access*, The Art Institute of Chicago. Last modified August 2004. http://www.artic.edu/artaccess /AA_Impressionist/pages/IMP_6.shtml#.

38. PAMPHLET, REPORT, OR BROCHURE Information about the author or publisher may not be readily available, but give enough information to identify your source.

38. Jamie McCarthy, *Who Is David Irving?* (San Antonio, TX: Holocaust History Project, 1998).

McCarthy, Jamie. *Who Is David Irving?* San Antonio, TX: Holocaust History Project, 1998.

39. GOVERNMENT DOCUMENT

39. US House Committee on Ways and Means, *Report on Trade Mission to Sub-Saharan Africa*, 108th Cong., 1st sess. (Washington, DC: Government Printing Office, 2003), 28.

US House Committee on Ways and Means. *Report on Trade Mission to Sub-Saharan Africa*. 108th Cong., 1st sess. Washington, DC: Government Printing Office, 2003.

18d A student research essay, *Chicago* style

Student Writer

On the following pages is an essay by Amanda Rinder that conforms to the *Chicago* guidelines described in this chapter. Note that this essay has been reproduced in a narrow format to allow for annotation.

Amanda Rinder

Student
Writing
Chicago

Title
announces
topic clearly
and succinctly

Sweet Home Chicago: Preserving the Past,

Protecting the Future of the Windy City

Title and
writer's name
centered

Amanda Rinder

Course title,
instructor's
name, and
date centered
at bottom of
title page

Twentieth-Century U.S. History

Professor Goldberg

November 27, 2006

Annotations indicate effective choices or *Chicago*-style formatting.

Rinder 2

Only one city has the "Big Shoulders" described by Carl Sandburg: Chicago (fig. 1). So renowned are its skyscrapers and celebrated building style that an entire school of architecture is named for Chicago. Presently, however, the place that Frank Sinatra called "my kind of town" is beginning to lose sight of exactly what kind of town it is. Many of the buildings that give Chicago its distinctive character are being torn down in order to make room for new growth. Both preserving the classics and encouraging new creation are important; the combination of these elements gives Chicago architecture its unique flavor. Witold Rybczynski, a professor of urbanism at the University of Pennsylvania, told the *New York Times*, "Of all the cities we can think of . . . we associate Chicago with new things, with building new. Combining that with preservation is a difficult task, a tricky thing. It's hard to find the middle ground in Chicago."[1] Yet finding a middle ground is essential if the city is to retain the original character that sets it apart from the rest. In order to maintain Chicago's distinctive identity and its delicate balance between the old and

Paper refers to
each figure by
number

Double-spaced
text

Source cited
using super-
script numeral

Fig. 1. Chicago skyline, circa 1940s. (Postcard courtesy of Minnie Dangberg.)

Figure caption
includes num-
ber, short title,
and source

Rinder 3

Opening
paragraph
concludes
with thesis
statement

the new, the city government must provide a comprehensive urban plan
that not only directs growth, but calls for the preservation of landmarks
and historic districts as well.

Second para-
graph provides
background

Chicago's inclination toward unadorned, sturdy buildings began
in the late nineteenth century with the aptly named Chicago School, a
movement led by Louis Sullivan, John Wellborn Root, and Daniel Burnham
and based on Sullivan's adage, "Form follows function."[2] Burnham and
Root's Reliance Building (fig. 2) epitomizes this vision: simple, yet
possessing a unique angular beauty.[3] The early skyscraper, the very
symbol of the Chicago style, represents the triumph of function and utility
over sentiment, America over Europe, and perhaps even the frontier over
the civilization of the East Coast.[4] These ideals of the original Chicago
School were expanded upon by architects of the Second Chicago School.
Frank Lloyd Wright's legendary organic style and the famed glass and
steel constructions of Mies van der Rohe are often the first images that
spring to mind when one thinks of Chicago.

Clear transition
from previous
paragraph

Yet the architecture that is the city's defining attribute is being
threatened by the increasing tendency toward development. The root
of Chicago's preservation problem lies in the enormous drive toward
economic expansion and the potential in Chicago for such growth. The
highly competitive market for land in the city means that properties sell
for the highest price if the buildings on them can be obliterated to make
room for newer, larger developments. Because of this preference on the
part of potential buyers, the label "landmark" has become a stigma for
property owners. "In other cities, landmark status is sought after—in
Chicago, it's avoided at all costs," notes Alan J. Shannon of the *Chicago
Tribune*.[5] Even if owners wish to keep their property's original structure,
designation as a landmark is still undesirable as it limits the renovations
that can be made to a building and thus decreases its value. Essentially,
no building that has even been recommended for landmark status may

Signal verb
"notes"
introduces
quotation

Fig. 2. The Reliance Building. (Photo
courtesy of the Art Institute of Chicago.)

be touched without the approval of the Commission on Chicago Historical
and Architectural Landmarks, a restriction that considerably diminishes
the appeal of the real estate. "We live in a world where the owners say, 'If
you judge my property a landmark you are taking money away from me.'
And in Chicago the process is stacked in favor of the economics," says
former city Planning Commissioner David Mosena.[6]

Nowhere is this clash more apparent than on North Michigan
Avenue—Chicago's Magnificent Mile. The historic buildings along this
block are unquestionably some of the city's finest works. In addition,
the Mile is one of Chicago's most prosperous districts. The small-scale,
charming buildings envisioned by Arthur Rubloff, the real estate
developer who first conceived of the Magnificent Mile in the late 1940s,
could not accommodate the crowds. Numerous high-rises, constructed
to accommodate the masses that flock to Michigan Avenue, interrupt the

"Magnificent
Mile" illustrates
conflict
between devel-
opment and
preservation

Rinder 5

cohesion and unity envisioned by the original planners of the Magnificent Mile. In *Chicago's North Michigan Avenue*, John W. Stamper says that with the standard height for new buildings on the avenue currently at about sixty-five stories, the "pleasant shopping promenade" has become a "canyon-like corridor."[7]

Many agree that the individual style of Michigan Avenue is being lost. In 1995, the same year that the Landmarks Preservation Council of Illinois declared the section of Michigan Avenue from Oak Street to Roosevelt Road one of the state's ten most endangered historic sites, the annual sales of the Magnificent Mile ran around $1 billion and were increasing at an annual rate of about five to seven percent.[8] Clearly, the property's potential as part of a commercial hub is taking priority over its architectural and historic value. The future of this district rests on a precarious balance between Chicago's responsibility for its own heritage and Chicagoans' desire for economic gain.

Perhaps the best single example of the conflict between preservation and development in Chicago is the case of the McCarthy Building (fig. 3). Built in 1872, the McCarthy was designed by John M. Van Osdel, Chicago's first professional architect. Paul Gapp, a *Chicago Tribune* architecture critic, described it as "a stunningly appealing relic from Chicago's 19th century Renaissance era."[9] The McCarthy was made a landmark in 1984, but it wasn't long before developers recognized the potential of the property, situated on Block 37 of State Street, directly across from Marshall Field's. With plans for a $300 million retail and office complex already outlined, developers made a $12.3 million bid for the property, promising to preserve the McCarthy and integrate it into the complex. The city readily agreed. However, a series of modifications over the next two years completely transformed the original plan. With the old structure now useless to the project, developers made subsequent proposals to preserve just the facade, or even to move the entire McCarthy Building

Fig. 3. The McCarthy Building. (From the University of
Illinois at Chicago, *Chicago Imagebase*,
http://www.uic.edu/depts/ahaa/imagebase.)

Source of
image quoted
in figure
caption

to another location. When these propositions didn't work out, the
developers began offering to preserve other buildings in exchange for
permission to demolish the McCarthy. Gapp admitted that the city was
caught in a difficult situation: if it protected the McCarthy, it would be
impeding development in an important urban renewal area, and if it
allowed demolition, Chicago's landmark protection ordinance would be
completely devalued. He nonetheless urged city officials to choose the
"long view" and preserve the McCarthy.[10] However, the developers' offer to
buy and restore the Reliance Building, at a cost of between $7 million and
$11 million, and to contribute $4 million to other preservation efforts,
prevailed. In September 1987, the Chicago City Council voted to revoke
the McCarthy's landmark status.

Ironically, Chicago's rich architectural heritage may work against its
own preservation. With so many significant buildings, losing one does not
seem as critical as perhaps it should. The fact that Chicago boasts some
forty-five Mies buildings, seventy-five Frank Lloyd Wright buildings, and

Introduction
of counter-
evidence that
large number
of significant
buildings
diminishes
value of each

Rinder 7

numerous other buildings from the first and second Chicago Schools may inspire a nonchalant attitude toward preservation.[11]

The razing of the McCarthy Building in 1987 exposes the problems inherent in Chicago's landmark policy. But the real tragedy is that none of the plans for development of the property were ever carried out. Block 37 remains vacant to this day. Clearly, the city needs creative and vigilant urban planning.

Call for planning to address economic costs of preservation

To uphold Chicago's reputation as an architectural jewel, the city must manage development by easing the economic burdens that preservation entails. Some methods that have been suggested for this are property tax breaks for landmark owners and transferable development rights, which would give landmark owners bonuses for developing elsewhere. Overall, however, the city's planning and landmarks commissions simply need to become more involved, working closely with developers throughout the entire design process.

Example of successful planning introduced

The effectiveness of an earnest but open-minded approach to urban planning has already been proven in Chicago. Union Station (fig. 4) is one project that worked to the satisfaction of both developers and preservationists. Developers U.S. Equities Realty Inc. and Amtrak proposed replacing the four floors of outdated office space above the station with more practical high-rise towers. This offer allowed for the preservation of the Great Hall and other public spaces within the station itself. "We are preserving the best of the historical landmark . . . and at the same time creating an adaptive reuse that will bring back some of the old glory of the station," Cheryl Stein of U.S. Equities told the *Tribune*.[12] The city responded to this magnanimous offer in kind, upgrading zoning on the site to permit additional office space and working with developers to identify exactly which portions of the original structure needed to be preserved. Today, the sight of Union Station, revitalized and bustling, is proof of the sincere endeavors of developers and city planners alike.

Rinder 8

NEW UNION STATION, CHICAGO.

Fig. 4. Union Station, circa 1925. (Postcard courtesy of Minnie Dangberg.)

In the midst of abandonment and demolition, buildings such as
Union Station and the Reliance Building offer Chicago some hope for
a future that is as architecturally rich as its past. The key to achieving
this balance of preserving historic treasures and encouraging new
development is to view the city not so much as a product, but as a
process. Robert Bruegmann, author of *The Architects and the City*, defines
a city as "the ultimate human artifact, our most complex and prodigious
social creation, and the most tangible result of the actions over time
of all its citizens."[13] Nowhere is this sentiment more relevant than
in Chicago. Comprehensive urban planning will ensure that the city's
character, so closely tied to its architecture, is preserved.

Conclusion
offers hope of
a solution

Student
Writing
Chicago

Rinder 9

Notes

Newspaper
article in
database

1. Tracie Rozhon, "Chicago Girds for Big Battle over Its Skyline," *New York Times*, November 12, 2000, Academic Search Premier (28896783).

2. *Columbia Encyclopedia*, Sixth Ed., s.v. "Louis Sullivan."

3. David Garrard Lowe, *Lost Chicago* (New York: Watson-Guptill Publications, 2000), 123.

4. Daniel Bluestone, *Constructing Chicago* (New Haven: Yale University Press, 1991), 105.

Indirect source

5. Alan J. Shannon, "When Will It End?" *Chicago Tribune*, September 11, 1987, quoted in Karen J. Dilibert, *From Landmark to Landfill* (Chicago: Chicago Architectural Foundation, 2000), 11.

6. Steve Kerch, "Landmark Decisions," *Chicago Tribune*, March 18, 1990, sec. 16.

7. John W. Stamper, *Chicago's North Michigan Avenue* (Chicago: University of Chicago Press, 1991), 215.

Newspaper
article online

8. Alf Siewers, "Success Spoiling the Magnificent Mile?" *Chicago Sun-Times*, April 9, 1995, http://www.sun-times.com/.

9. Paul Gapp, "McCarthy Building Puts Landmark Law on a Collision Course with Developers," *Chicago Tribune*, April 20, 1986, quoted in Karen J. Dilibert, *From Landmark to Landfill* (Chicago: Chicago Architectural Foundation, 2000), 4.

Reference
to previous
source

10. Ibid.

11. Rozhon, "Chicago Girds for Big Battle."

Second refer-
ence to source

12. Kerch, "Landmark Decisions."

13. Robert Bruegmann, *The Architects and the City* (Chicago: University of Chicago Press, 1997), 443.

Rinder 10

Bibliography

Bluestone, Daniel. *Constructing Chicago*. New Haven: Yale University Press, 1991.

Bruegmann, Robert. *The Architects and the City*. Chicago: University of Chicago Press, 1997.

Dilibert, Karen J. *From Landmark to Landfill*. Chicago: Chicago Architectural Foundation, 2000.

Kerch, Steve. "Landmark Decisions." *Chicago Tribune*, March 18, 1990, sec. 16.

Lowe, David Garrard. *Lost Chicago*. New York: Watson-Guptill Publications, 2000.

Rozhon, Tracie. "Chicago Girds for Big Battle over Its Skyline." *New York Times*, November 12, 2000. Academic Search Premier (28896783).

Siewers, Alf. "Success Spoiling the Magnificent Mile?" *Chicago Sun-Times*, April 9, 1995. http://www.sun-times.com/.

Stamper, John W. *Chicago's North Michigan Avenue*. Chicago: University of Chicago Press, 1991.

Student Writing
Chicago

Bibliography starts on new page

Book

Pamphlet

Newspaper article

Article from database

Bibliography entries use hanging indent and are not numbered

19 CSE Style

Writers in the physical sciences, the life sciences, and mathematics use the documentation and format style of the Council of Science Editors (CSE). Guidelines for citing print and electronic sources can be found in *Scientific Style and Format: The CSE Manual for Authors, Editors, and Publishers*, Seventh Edition (2006).

19a Formatting CSE manuscripts

The CSE manual does not make recommendations for the basic format of a student paper, so check with your instructor about any specific guidelines you should follow. If your instructor does not require specific guidelines, use the formatting suggestions that follow.

For detailed guidelines on formatting a list of references, see 19c. For a sample student essay, see 19d.

- *Title page.* Center the title of your paper, your name, and other relevant information, such as the course name and number, the instructor's name, and the date submitted.

- *Margins and spacing.* Leave standard margins at the top and bottom and on both sides of each page. Double-space the text and list of references.

- *Page numbers.* Type a short version of the paper's title and the page number in the upper right-hand corner of each page.

- *Abstract.* CSE style often calls for a one-paragraph abstract (about one hundred words). The abstract should be on a separate page, right after the title page, with the title *Abstract* centered one inch from the top of the page.

- *Headings.* CSE style does not require headings, but it notes that they can help readers quickly find a specific section of a paper.

- *Tables and figures.* Tables and figures must be labeled *Table* or *Figure* and numbered separately, one sequence for tables and one for figures. Give each table and figure a short, informative title.

19b In-text citations

In CSE style, citations within an essay follow one of three formats.

- The *citation-sequence format* calls for a superscript number or a number in parentheses after any mention of a source. The sources are numbered in the order they appear. Each number refers to the same source every time it is used. The first source mentioned in the paper is numbered *1*, the second source is numbered *2*, and so on.

- The *citation-name format* also calls for a superscript number or a number in parentheses after any mention of a source. The numbers are added after the list of references is completed and alphabetized, so that the source numbered *1* is alphabetically first in the list of references, *2* is alphabetically second, and so on.

- The *name-year format* calls for the last name of the author and the year of publication in parentheses after any mention of a source. If the last name appears in a signal phrase, the name-year format allows for giving only the year of publication in parentheses.

Before deciding which system to use, check a current journal in the field or ask an instructor about the preferred style in a particular course or discipline.

1. IN-TEXT CITATION USING CITATION-SEQUENCE OR CITATION-NAME FORMAT

VonBergen[12] provides the most complete discussion of this phenomenon.

For the citation-sequence and citation-name formats, you would use the same superscript[(12)] for each subsequent citation of this work by VonBergen.

2. IN-TEXT CITATION USING NAME-YEAR FORMAT

VonBergen (2003) provides the most complete discussion of this phenomenon.

Hussar's two earlier studies of juvenile obesity (1995, 1999) examined only children with diabetes.

The classic examples of such investigations (Morrow 1968; Bridger et al. 1971; Franklin and Wayson 1972) still shape the assumptions of current studies.

19c List of references

The citations in the text of an essay correspond to items on a list titled *References*, which starts on a new page at the end of the essay. Continue to number the pages consecutively, center the title *References* one inch from the top of the page, and double-space before beginning the first entry.

The order of the entries depends on which CSE format you follow:

- *Citation-sequence format*: number and list the references in the order the references are first cited in the text.

- *Citation-name format*: list and number the references in alphabetical order.

- *Name-year format*: list the references, unnumbered, in alphabetical order.

In the following examples, you will see that the citation-sequence and citation-name formats call for listing the date after the publisher's name in references for books and after the periodical name in references for articles. The name-year format calls for listing the date immediately after the author's name in any kind of reference.

CSE style also specifies the treatment and placement of the following basic elements in the list of references:

- *Author.* List all authors last name first, and use only initials for first and middle names. Do not place a comma after the author's last name, and do not place periods after or spaces between the initials. Use a period after the last initial of the last author listed.

- *Title.* Do not italicize titles and subtitles of books and titles of periodicals. Do not enclose titles of articles in quotation marks. For books and articles, capitalize only the first word of the title and any proper nouns or proper adjectives. Abbreviate and capitalize all major words in a periodical title.

As you refer to these examples, pay attention to how publication information (publishers for books, details about periodicals for articles) and other specific elements are styled and punctuated.

Directory to CSE style for references

Books

Periodicals

Electronic sources

1 Books

For the basic format for citing a book, see the source map on pp. 432–33.

1. ONE AUTHOR

CITATION-SEQUENCE AND CITATION-NAME

1. Buchanan M. Nexus: small worlds and the groundbreaking theory of networks. New York: Norton; 2003.

NAME-YEAR

Buchanan M. 2003. Nexus: small worlds and the groundbreaking theory of networks. New York: Norton.

2. TWO OR MORE AUTHORS

CITATION-SEQUENCE AND CITATION-NAME

2. Wojciechowski BW, Rice NM. Experimental methods in kinetic studies. 2nd ed. St. Louis (MO): Elsevier Science; 2003.

NAME-YEAR

Wojciechowski BW, Rice NM. 2003. Experimental methods in kinetic studies. 2nd ed. St. Louis (MO): Elsevier Science.

3. ORGANIZATION AS AUTHOR

CITATION-SEQUENCE AND CITATION-NAME

3. World Health Organization. The world health report 2002: reducing risks, promoting healthy life. Geneva (Switzerland): The Organization; 2002.

Place the organization's abbreviation at the beginning of the name-year entry, and use the abbreviation in the corresponding in-text citation. Alphabetize the entry by the first word of the full name, not by the abbreviation.

NAME-YEAR

[WHO] World Health Organization. 2002. The world health report 2002: reducing risks, promoting healthy life. Geneva (Switzerland): The Organization.

4. BOOK PREPARED BY EDITOR(S)

CITATION-SEQUENCE AND CITATION-NAME

4. Torrence ME, Isaacson RE, editors. Microbial food safety in animal agriculture: current topics. Ames: Iowa State University Press; 2003.

NAME-YEAR

Torrence ME, Isaacson RE, editors. 2003. Microbial safety in animal agriculture: current topics. Ames: Iowa State University Press.

5. SECTION OF A BOOK WITH AN EDITOR

CITATION-SEQUENCE AND CITATION-NAME

5. Kawamura A. Plankton. In: Perrin MF, Wursig B, Thewissen JGM, editors. Encyclopedia of marine mammals. San Diego: Academic Press; 2002. p. 939–942.

NAME-YEAR

Kawamura A. 2002. Plankton. In: Perrin MF, Wursig B, Thewissen JGM, editors. Encyclopedia of marine mammals. San Diego: Academic Press. p. 939–942.

6. CHAPTER OF A BOOK

CITATION-SEQUENCE AND CITATION-NAME

6. Honigsbaum M. The fever trail: in search of the cure for malaria. New York: Picador; 2003. Chapter 2, The cure; p. 19–38.

NAME-YEAR

Honigsbaum M. 2003. The fever trail: in search of the cure for malaria. New York: Picador. Chapter 2, The cure; p. 19–38.

7. PAPER OR ABSTRACT IN CONFERENCE PROCEEDINGS

CITATION-SEQUENCE AND CITATION-NAME

7. Gutierrez AP. Integrating biological and environmental factors in crop system models [abstract]. In: Integrated Biological Systems Conference; 2003 Apr 14–16; San Antonio, TX. Beaumont (TX): Agroeconomics Research Group; 2003. p. 14–15.

CSE SOURCE MAP: Books

Note that, depending on whether you are using the citation-sequence or citation-name format or the name-year format, the date placement will vary.

1 **Author.** List authors' last names first, and use initials for first and middle names, with no periods or spaces. Use a period only after the last initial of the last author.

2,**6** **Publication year.** In name-year format, put the year of publication immediately after the author name(s). In citation-sequence or citation-name format, put the year of publication after the publisher's name.

3 **Title.** Do not italicize or put quotation marks around titles and subtitles of books. Capitalize only the first word of the title and any proper nouns or proper adjectives.

4 **City of publication.** List the city of publication (and the country or state abbreviation for unfamiliar cities) followed by a colon.

5 **Publisher.** Give the publisher's name. In citation-sequence or citation-name format, follow with a semicolon. In name-year format, follow with a period.

A citation for the book on p. 433 would look like this:

Citation-sequence or citation-name format

1. Wilson EO. The diversity of life. Cambridge: Belknap Press of Harvard University Press; 1992.

Name-year format

Wilson EO. 1992. The diversity of life. Cambridge: Belknap Press of Harvard University Press.

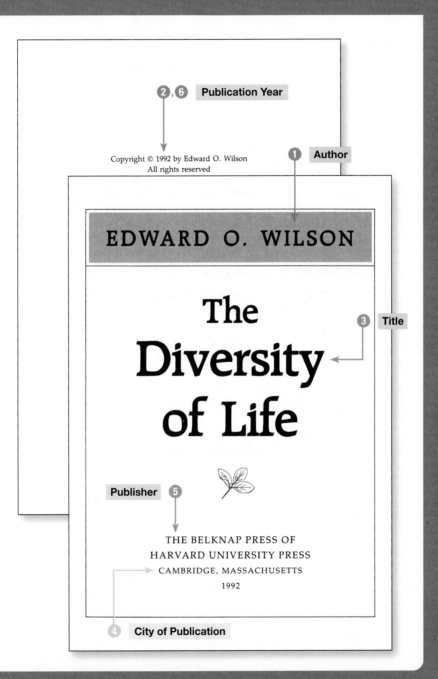

2,6 Publication Year

1 Author

EDWARD O. WILSON

The
Diversity ← **3** Title
of Life

Publisher **5**

THE BELKNAP PRESS OF
HARVARD UNIVERSITY PRESS
CAMBRIDGE, MASSACHUSETTS
1992

4 City of Publication

NAME-YEAR

Gutierrez AP. 2003. Integrating biological and environmental factors in crop system models [abstract]. In: Integrated Biological Systems Conference; 2003 Apr 14–16; San Antonio, TX. Beaumont (TX): Agroeconomics Research Group. p. 14–15.

2 Periodicals

For newspaper and magazine articles, include the section designation and column number, if any, in addition to the date and the inclusive page numbers. For rules on abbreviating journal titles, consult the CSE manual, or ask an instructor to suggest other examples.

8. ARTICLE IN A JOURNAL

CITATION-SEQUENCE AND CITATION-NAME

8. Mahmud K, Vance ML. Human growth hormone and aging. New Engl J Med. 2003;348(2):2256–2257.

NAME-YEAR

Mahmud K, Vance ML. 2003. Human growth hormone and aging. New Engl J Med. 348(2):2256–2257.

9. ARTICLE IN A WEEKLY JOURNAL

CITATION-SEQUENCE AND CITATION-NAME

9. Holden C. Future brightening for depression treatments. Science. 2003 Oct 31:810–813.

NAME-YEAR

Holden C. 2003. Future brightening for depression treatments. Science. Oct 31:810–813.

10. ARTICLE IN A MAGAZINE

CITATION-SEQUENCE AND CITATION-NAME

10. Livio M. Moving right along: the accelerating universe holds secrets to dark energy, the Big Bang, and the ultimate beauty of nature. Astronomy. 2002 Jul:34–39.

NAME-YEAR

Livio M. 2002 Jul. Moving right along: the accelerating universe holds secrets to dark energy, the Big Bang, and the ultimate beauty of nature. Astronomy. 34–39.

11. ARTICLE IN A NEWSPAPER

CITATION-SEQUENCE AND CITATION-NAME

11. Kolata G. Bone diagnosis gives new data but no answers. New York Times (National Ed.). 2003 Sep 28;Sect. 1:1 (col. 1).

NAME-YEAR

Kolata G. 2003 Sep 28. Bone diagnosis gives new data but no answers. New York Times (National Ed.). Sect. 1:1 (col. 1).

3 Electronic sources

These examples use the citation-sequence or citation-name system. To adapt them to the name-year system, delete the note number and place the update date immediately after the author's name.

The basic entry for most sources accessed through the Internet should include the following elements:

- *Author.* Give the author's name, if available, last name first, followed by the initial(s) and a period.

- *Title.* For book, journal, and article titles, follow the style for print materials. For all other types of electronic material, reproduce the title that appears on the screen.

- *Medium.* Indicate, in brackets, that the source is not in print format by using designations such as [Internet].

- *Place of publication.* The city usually should be followed by the two-letter abbreviation for the state. No state abbreviation is necessary for well-known cities such as New York, Chicago, Boston, and London or for a publisher whose location is part of its name (for example, University of Oklahoma Press). If the city is implied, put the city and state in brackets. If the city cannot be inferred, use the words *place unknown* in brackets.

- *Publisher.* For Web sites, pages on Web sites, and online databases, include the individual or organization that produces or sponsors

CSE SOURCE MAP: Articles from databases

Note that date placement will vary depending on whether you are using the citation-sequence or citation-name format or the name-year format.

1 **Author.** List all authors' last names first, and use only initials for first and middle names.

2, 5 **Publication date.** For name-year format, put publication date after author name(s). In citation-sequence or citation-name format, put it after periodical title. Use year only (for journals) or year month day (for other periodicals).

3 **Article title.** Capitalize first word and proper nouns/adjectives.

4 **Periodical title.** Capitalize major words. Abbreviate journal titles. Follow with [*Internet*] and a period.

6 **Date of access.** In brackets, write *cited* and year, month, and day. End with a semicolon.

7 **Publication information for article.** Give volume number, issue number (in parentheses), a colon, and page numbers. End with a period.

8 **Name of database.** End with a period.

9 **Publication information for database.** Include the city, the state abbreviation in parentheses, a colon, the publisher's name, and a period.

10 **Web address.** Write *Available from* and the brief URL.

11 **Document number.** Write *Document no.* and identifying number.

A citation for the article on p. 437 would look like this:

Citation-sequence or citation-name format

1. Miller AL. Epidemiology, etiology, and natural treatment of seasonal affective disorder. Altern Med Rev [Internet]. 2005 [cited 2010 25 May]; 10(1):5-13. Academic Search Premier. Ipswich (MA): EBSCO. Available from http://www.ebscohost.com Document No.: 16514813.

Name-year format

Miller AL. 2005. Epidemiology, etiology, and natural treatment of seasonal affective disorder. Altern Med Rev [Internet]. [cited 2010 25 May]; 10(1):5-13. Academic Search Premier. Ipswich (MA): EBSCO. Available from http://www.ebscohost.com Document No.: 16514813.

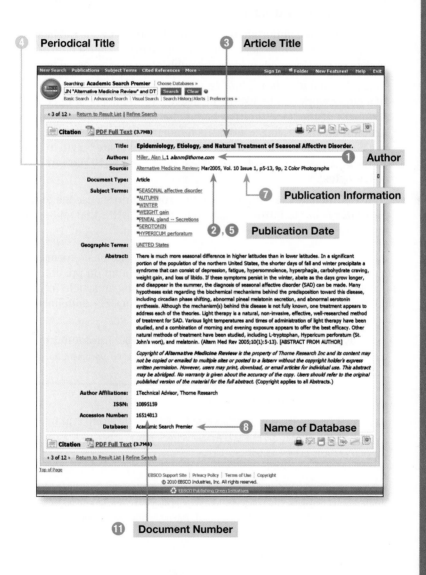

Periodical Title ④

Article Title ③

‹ 3 of 12 › | Return to Result List | Refine Search

📄 Citation 📄 PDF Full Text (3.7MB)

Title:	**Epidemiology, Etiology, and Natural Treatment of Seasonal Affective Disorder.**
Authors:	Miller, Alan L.1 *alanm@thorne.com* ① **Author**
Source:	Alternative Medicine Review; Mar2005, Vol. 10 Issue 1, p5-13, 9p, 2 Color Photographs
Document Type:	Article
Subject Terms:	*SEASONAL affective disorder*
	AUTUMN
	WINTER
	WEIGHT gain
	PINEAL gland -- Secretions
	SEROTONIN
	HYPERICUM perforatum
Geographic Terms:	UNITED States

⑦ **Publication Information**

②, ⑤ **Publication Date**

Abstract: There is much more seasonal difference in higher latitudes than in lower latitudes. In a significant portion of the population of the northern United States, the shorter days of fall and winter precipitate a syndrome that can consist of depression, fatigue, hypersomnolence, hyperphagia, carbohydrate craving, weight gain, and loss of libido. If these symptoms persist in the winter, abate as the days grow longer, and disappear in the summer, the diagnosis of seasonal affective disorder (SAD) can be made. Many hypotheses exist regarding the biochemical mechanisms behind the predisposition toward this disease, including circadian phase shifting, abnormal pineal melatonin secretion, and abnormal serotonin synthesis. Although the mechanism(s) behind this disease is not fully known, one treatment appears to address each of the theories. Light therapy is a natural, non-invasive, effective, well-researched method of treatment for SAD. Various light temperatures and times of administration of light therapy have been studied, and a combination of morning and evening exposure appears to offer the best efficacy. Other natural methods of treatment have been studied, including L-tryptophan, Hypericum perforatum (St. John's wort), and melatonin. (Altern Med Rev 2005;10(1):5-13). [ABSTRACT FROM AUTHOR]

Author Affiliations:	1Technical Advisor, Thorne Research
ISSN:	10895159
Accession Number:	16514813
Database:	Academic Search Premier ⑧ **Name of Database**

📄 Citation 📄 PDF Full Text (3.7MB)

‹ 3 of 12 › | Return to Result List | Refine Search

Top of Page

⑪ **Document Number**

the site. If no publisher can be determined, use the words *publisher unknown* in brackets. No publisher is necessary for online journals or journals accessed online.

- *Dates.* Cite three important dates if possible: the date the publication was placed on the Internet or the copyright date; the latest date of any update or revision; and the date the publication was accessed by you.

- *Page, document, volume, and issue numbers.* When citing a portion of a larger work or site, list the inclusive page numbers or document numbers of the specific item being cited. For journals or journal articles, include volume and issue numbers. If exact page numbers are not available, include in brackets the approximate length in computer screens, paragraphs, or bytes: [2 screens], [10 paragraphs], [332K bytes].

- *Address.* Include the URL or other electronic address; use the phrase *Available from:* to introduce the address. Only URLs that end with a slash are followed by a period.

12. MATERIAL FROM AN ONLINE DATABASE For the basic format for citing an article from a database, see the source map on pp. 436–37. (Because CSE does not provide guidelines for citing an article from an online database, this model has been adapted from CSE guidelines for citing an online journal article.)

12. Shilts E. Water wanderers. Can Geographic [Internet]. 2002 [cited 2010 Jan 27];122(3):72–77. Available from: http://www.ebscohost.com/ Document No.: 6626534.

13. ARTICLE IN AN ONLINE JOURNAL

13. Perez P, Calonge TM. Yeast protein kinase C. J Biochem [Internet]. 2002 Oct [cited 2008 Nov 3];132(4):513–517. Available from: http://edpex104.bcasj.or.jp /jb-pdf/132-4/jb132-4-513.pdf

14. ARTICLE IN AN ONLINE NEWSPAPER

14. Brody JE. Reasons, and remedies, for morning sickness. New York Times Online [Internet]. 2004 Apr 27 [cited 2009 Apr 30]. Available from: http://www.nytimes .com/2009/04/27/health/27BROD.html

15. ONLINE BOOK

15. Patrick TS, Allison JR, Krakow GA. Protected plants of Georgia [Internet]. Social Circle (GA): Georgia Department of Natural Resources; c1995 [cited 2010 Dec 3]. Available from: http://www.georgiawildlife.com/content/displaycontent .asp?txtDocument=89&txtPage=9

To cite a portion of an online book, give the name of the part after the publication information: *Chapter 6, Encouraging germination.* See model 6.

16. WEB SITE

16. Geology and public policy [Internet]. Boulder (CO): Geological Society of America; c2010 [updated 2010 Jun 3; cited 2010 Sep 19]. Available from: http://www.geosociety.org/geopolicy.htm

17. GOVERNMENT WEB SITE

17. Health disparities: reducing health disparities in cancer [Internet]. Atlanta (GA): Centers for Disease Control and Prevention (US); [updated 2010 Apr 5; cited 2010 May 1]. Available from: http://www.cdc.gov/cancer/healthdisparities/basic_info /disparities.htm

19d A student paper, CSE style

Student Writer

Tara Gupta

The following research proposal by Tara Gupta conforms to the citation-sequence format in the CSE guidelines described in this chapter. Note that these pages have been reproduced in a narrow format to allow for annotation.

Student Writing CSE

Specific and informative title

Field Measurements of
Photosynthesis and Transpiration
Rates in Dwarf Snapdragon
(*Chaenorrhinum minus* Lange):
An Investigation of Water Stress
Adaptations

Information centered on title page

Tara Gupta

Proposal for a
Summer Research
Fellowship
Colgate University
February 25, 2003

Annotations indicate effective choices or CSE-style formatting.

Water Stress Adaptations 2

Introduction

Dwarf snapdragon (*Chaenorrhinum minus*) is a weedy pioneer plant found growing in central New York during spring and summer. Interestingly, the distribution of this species has been limited almost exclusively to the cinder ballast of railroad tracks[1] and to sterile strips of land along highways[2]. In these harsh environments, characterized by intense sunlight and poor soil water retention, one would expect *C. minus* to exhibit anatomical features similar to those of xeromorphic plants (species adapted to arid habitats).

However, this is not the case. T. Gupta and R. Arnold (unpublished) have found that the leaves and stems of *C. minus* are not covered by a thick, waxy cuticle but rather with a thin cuticle that is less effective in inhibiting water loss through diffusion. The root system is not long and thick, capable of reaching deeper, moister soils; instead, it is thin and diffuse, permeating only the topmost (and driest) soil horizon. Moreover, in contrast to many xeromorphic plants, the stomata (pores regulating gas exchange) are not found in sunken crypts or cavities in the epidermis that retard water loss from transpiration.

Despite a lack of these morphological adaptations to water stress, *C. minus* continues to grow and reproduce when morning dew has been its only source of water for up to 5 weeks (2002 letter from R. Arnold to me). Such growth involves fixation of carbon by photosynthesis and requires that the stomata be open to admit sufficient carbon dioxide. Given the dry, sunny environment, the time required for adequate carbon fixation must also mean a significant loss of water through transpiration as open stomata exchange carbon dioxide with water. How does *C. minus* balance the need for carbon with the need to conserve water?

Purposes of the Proposed Study

The above observations have led me to an exploration of the extent to which *C. minus* is able to photosynthesize under conditions of

States pur-
poses and
scope of pro-
posed study

low water availability. It is my hypothesis that *C. minus* adapts to these conditions by photosynthesizing in the early morning and late afternoon, when leaf and air temperatures are lower and transpirational water loss is reduced. During the middle of the day, its photosynthetic rate may be very low, perhaps even zero, on hot, sunny afternoons. Similar diurnal changes in photosynthetic rate in response to midday water deficits have been described in crop plants[3,4]. There appear to be no comparable studies on noncrop species in their natural habitats.

Significance of
study noted

Thus, the research proposed here aims to help explain the apparent paradox of an organism that thrives in water-stressed conditions despite a lack of morphological adaptations. This summer's work will also serve as a basis for controlled experiments in a plant growth chamber on the individual effects of temperature, light intensity, soil water availability, and other environmental factors on photosynthesis and transpiration rates. These experiments are planned for the coming fall semester.

Relates
proposed
research proj-
ect to future
research

Methods and Timeline

Briefly
describes
methodology
to be used

Provides
timeline

Simultaneous measurements of photosynthesis and transpiration rates will indicate the balance *C. minus* has achieved in acquiring the energy it needs while retaining the water available to it. These measurements will be taken daily from June 22 to September 7, 2003, at field sites in the Hamilton, NY, area, using an LI-6220 portable photosynthesis system (LICOR, Inc., Lincoln, NE). Basic methodology and use of correction factors will be similar to that described in related studies[5-7]. Data will be collected at regular intervals throughout the daylight hours and will be related to measurements of ambient air temperature, leaf temperature, relative humidity, light intensity, wind velocity, and cloud cover.

Water Stress Adaptations 4

Budget

1	kg soda lime, 4-8 mesh	$70
	(for absorption of CO_2 in photosynthesis analyzer)	
1	kg anhydrous magnesium perchlorate	$130
	(used as desiccant for photosynthesis analyzer)	
	SigmaScan software (Jandel Scientific Software, Inc.)	$195
	(for measurement of leaf areas for which photosynthesis	
	and transpiration rates are to be determined)	
	Estimated 500 miles travel to field sites in own	$140
	car @ $0.28 / mile	
	CO_2 cylinder, 80 days rental @ $0.25 / day	$20
	(for calibration of photosynthesis analyzer)	
	TOTAL REQUEST	$555

Budget provides itemized details

Water Stress Adaptations 5

References

1. Wildrlechner MP. Historical and phenological observations of the spread of *Chaenorrhinum minus* across North America. Can J Bot. 1983;61(1):179–187.

Article from
government
Web site

2. Dwarf Snapdragon [Internet]. Olympia (WA): Washington State Noxious Weed Control Board; 2001 [updated 2001 Jul 7; cited 2003 Jan 25]. Available from: http://www.wa.gov/agr/weedboard/weed_info/dwarfsnapdragon.html

Article in
weekly journal

3. Boyer JS. Plant productivity and environment. Science. 1982 Nov 6:443–448.

4. Manhas JG, Sukumaran NP. Diurnal changes in net photosynthetic rate in potato in two environments. Potato Res. 1988;31:375–378.

Article in
journal

Includes all
published
works cited;
numbers cor-
respond to
order in which
sources are
first mentioned

5. Doley DG, Unwin GL, Yates DJ. Spatial and temporal distribution of photosynthesis and transpiration by single leaves in a rainforest tree, *Argyrodendron peralatum*. Aust J Plant Physiol. 1988;15(3):317–326.

6. Kallarackal J, Milburn JA, Baker DA. Water relations of the banana. III. Effects of controlled water stress on water potential, transpiration, photosynthesis and leaf growth. Aust J Plant Physiol. 1990;17(1):79–90.

7. Idso SB, Allen SG, Kimball BA, Choudhury BJ. Problems with porometry: measuring net photosynthesis by leaf chamber techniques. Agron. 1989;81(4):475–479.

Part 4

PRINT, ELECTRONIC, AND OTHER MEDIA

20 Formal and Informal Electronic Communication

As Clive Thompson noted in *Wired* magazine in 2009, "Before the Internet came along, most Americans never wrote anything, ever, that wasn't a school assignment. Unless they got a job that required producing text . . . , they'd leave school and virtually never construct a paragraph again." Times have indeed changed. Electronic tools have ensured that writing is not only important for school, but also essential for most jobs—and (thanks to texting, Twitter, Facebook, and so on) now a key part of social life for most people, a way to share information with everyone from close friends to total strangers.

Much of your communication today probably takes place electronically—via email, instant messaging, discussion forums, social sites, tweets, blogs, and so on. Computers and text-messaging devices allow people to remain in constant, and seemingly effortless, contact. Because electronic communication is so common, however, it's easy to fall into the habit of writing very informally. If you forget to adjust style and voice for different occasions and readers, you may undermine your own intentions.

Composing academic and professional messages

All writing requires you to consider your purpose and audience. Although email and online postings may seem much like informal online writing that you do every day, remember that people who do not know you may be getting an impression of you from such messages. Therefore, when you write a message to anyone you don't know well or to an authority figure such as an instructor or supervisor, follow the conventions of standard academic English (26b). Proofread to make sure that your message is clear and free of errors. Aim for a formal tone, and take particular care not to offend or irritate your reader.

Best practices for formal electronic messages

Email was once seen as highly informal, but many students today use it mainly for more formal purposes, particularly to communicate for work or for school. When writing most academic or professional emails, then, or when posting to a public discussion list that may be read by instructors (or by anyone you don't know), keep the following tips in mind.

- Use a subject line that states your purpose accurately and clearly. Remember to change the subject line if you are writing about something different from the original subject.

- Use a formal greeting and closing (*Dear Ms. Aulie* rather than *Hi*).

- Avoid insults (flaming), and remember that tone is difficult to convey in online messages: even if your intentions are good, readers may misinterpret humor.

- Avoid writing messages in ALL CAPS.

- Spell words conventionally instead of using texting shortcuts.

- Keep messages as concise as possible. Break long paragraphs into shorter paragraphs. For a very long message with several points, add headings.

For a student's email, see p. 448.

- Conclude your message with your name and email address.

- Before hitting SEND, make sure your message is addressed to the appropriate person.

- Use *Cc:* ("carbon copy") to copy someone other than the main recipient of your message.

- Ask for permission before forwarding a sensitive message from someone else.

- Make sure that the username on the email account you use for formal messages does not present a poor impression. If your username is *Party2Nite*, consider changing it, or use your school account for academic and professional communication.

Discussion lists and forums

A discussion forum or email discussion list allows you to participate in an ongoing electronic conversation. In an email discussion list, members post by writing an email message that is automatically copied and sent to other list subscribers; discussion forums, on the other hand, are usually conducted on a Web site or in a Web-based tool such as a course management system, and users must go to that site to join the discussion. In either case, as members post and respond to one another, the

A STUDENT'S FORMAL EMAIL MESSAGE

Subject:	Letter of Recommendation ①

Attach...: Recommender form.doc (23 KB); R.Rubio Global Leader appl.doc (23 KB); R.Rubio Resume.doc (23 KB); R.Rubio WC Seminar summ.doc (23 KB)   Attachment Options...

Dear Professor Lunsford, ②

I am writing with some great news: I am a finalist in the Global Leaders Program. The ③ program asks that I seek two letters of recommendation that will speak to the "specific qualities of the nominee."

I am attaching the recommender form that the program sent to me this week along with my application, a copy of my current résumé, and a summary of the work that I did in your Writing Center Seminar class. ④

If you will agree to write this letter of recommendation, I can pick it up from you, in a sealed envelope with your signature written across the back flap. The due date is June 1, 2010.

Thank you very much for considering this request, Professor Lunsford. I will be sure to keep you informed as I continue with the nomination process. ⑤

Sincerely yours,

Rudy

Rudy Rubio ⑥
r.rubio@stanford.edu

① *Subject heading* is clear and succinct.

② *Greeting* is appropriately formal.

③ *Short paragraphs* come to the point quickly.

④ Writer explains *attachments*.

⑤ *Polite, formal tone* is used throughout.

⑥ *Signature* includes full name and email address.

messages accumulate, creating a discussion thread that may be read by many people.

For a student's discussion posts, see p. 450.

When you participate in an academic or professional forum or list, you will generally want to use a polite and somewhat formal tone. Keep the following tips in mind:

- Avoid unnecessary criticism of others' spelling or other language errors. If a message is unclear, ask politely for a clarification. If you disagree with an assertion of fact, offer what you believe to be the correct information, but don't insult the writer.

- If you think you've been insulted (flamed), give the writer the benefit of the doubt. Replying with patience establishes your credibility and helps you appear mature and fair.

- For email discussion lists, decide whether to reply off-list to the sender of a message or to the whole group, and be careful to use REPLY or REPLY TO ALL accordingly to avoid potential embarrassment.

- Keep in mind that because many discussion forums and email lists are archived, more people than you think may be reading your messages.

20b Writing for less formal situations

Sometimes audiences expect informality. When you write in certain situations—Twitter posts, for example, and most text messages—you can play with (or ignore) the conventions you would probably follow in formal writing. But even when you write for sites that might seem to call for an informal tone, such as blogs and social networking spaces, be attuned to your audience's needs and your purpose for writing.

When writing for any public online writing space that allows users to say almost anything about themselves or to comment freely on the postings of others, bear in mind that anonymity sometimes makes online writers feel less inhibited than they would be in a real conversation. Don't say anything you want to remain private, and even if you disagree with another writer, avoid personal attacks.

Blogs

Some blogs resemble journals or diaries, giving personal perspectives on issues of importance in the life of the blogger. Other blogs

A STUDENT'S DISCUSSION-LIST POSTING

Subject: Class discussion of "self" ①

I've been thinking about our class discussion on the self. Carl Rogers theorized that people do things in line with their concept of themselves in order to avoid having to rework that self-concept. For instance, if I think of myself as an artist and not as a musician, even if I want to go to a concert, I might go to the art museum instead so that I don't have to change my view of myself. ②

We seem to feel as if we must fit one mold, and that mold blocks out other concepts of the self. How many families do you know where the parents proudly introduce a child as "the scientist (artist/musician/whatever) of the family"? And how does this inhibit other siblings who might also want to be scientists, artists, or musicians but fear taking over someone else's place?

Kristin C. ③

① *Subject line* provides specific information.

② *Tone* is engaged, friendly, and polite.

③ *Closing* includes first name and initial only; audience is a closed discussion list for a class.

A STUDENT'S DISCUSSION-LIST RESPONSE

Subject: RE: Class discussion of "self" ①

I think Kristin is right when she says that siblings may be inhibited from following up on an interest in science when parents introduce another child as "the scientist of the family." ②

But is that really an example of people doing things "in line with their concept of themselves in order to avoid having to rework that self-concept"? Maybe these siblings are trying to avoid conflict with their parents' idea of who they are and who their brothers and sisters are. If a child likes science but avoids becoming a scientist in order not to displace her brother as ③ "the scientist of the family," isn't she actually reworking her self-concept in order to keep peace in the family?

Yazmin G.

① *Opens* with a point of agreement.

② *Quotations* from earlier post clarify what is being discussed.

③ *Politely questions* conclusions of another writer.

may report on a particular topic, such as technology, travel, or politics. Some bloggers write short posts or comment on links to other sites; others write essay-length analyses of issues that interest them. There are as many varieties of blogs as there are reasons for writing them.

For a student's blog post, see 21b2.

Therefore, you won't find any hard and fast rules about how informal your tone should be when you write (or comment on) a blog post. Many bloggers adopt a conversational tone, but blogs aimed at a general audience tend to follow the conventions of standard edited English unless the writer wants to achieve a special effect. (For more on creating blogs, see 21b2.)

- When you create or contribute to a blog, consider how you want to represent yourself to readers. Will they expect humor, careful reasoning, personal anecdotes, expertise? What level of formality will produce the results you want from your audience?

- To comment on a blog, follow the same conventions you would for a discussion-list posting. Become familiar with the conversation before you add a comment of your own, and in general, avoid commenting on entries that are several days old.

Social networking sites

Social networking sites such as Facebook (1a) are the online versions of diaries, yearbooks signed by friends and acquaintances, and the like. Many users think of these online spaces as relatively private and safe, intended to be seen by only a few people. However, more people than you think may be reading posts and looking at images, video, and links on social networking sites. Think carefully about your privacy settings, and bear in mind that your circle of friends can include relatives and current or potential co-workers, employers, and instructors — people from all areas of your life.

For a student's Facebook posts, see 1a.

- Remember that even when you allow only friends to see what you post, you may still have a large potential audience — some of whom will expect more propriety than others. Don't post anything on such sites that you wish to remain private.

- If you post to a friend's social networking space, remember that people you may not know — including your friend's relatives and co-workers — can see your words and images.

Twitter and microblogging

Microblogging describes a blogging style that uses very short updates. A popular venue for microblogging is Twitter (1a), which limits post lengths to 140 characters and allows users to post updates from a cell phone. Twitter users can send a message (called a "tweet") to several people at once; you can tell anyone who is following your posts, for example, that you'll be at the coffee cart outside the library at noon.

For a student's tweets, see 1a.

- In tweets, brevity is more important than conventionally correct grammar and spelling. As always, remember your audience. Tweets and microblog posts do follow conventions (even though these don't always resemble the conventions for academic writing). Learn the current standards in the community you are trying to reach.

- Use punctuation appropriately to organize posts and help followers find information they want. For instance, to communicate with a particular group of followers, you can add the symbol # (called a *hashtag*) and an identifying label to your tweets to that group—so your Spanish 101 study group might use the tag *#span101* in messages to group members.

Text messages

Text messages are often the quickest way to convey brief information to another person. Like tweets, text messages must be very brief (usually 140 to 160 characters), so users often forgo traditional English grammar rules in order to accommodate the character limit. As with any writing, your job when texting is to meet your audience's expectations and accomplish your purpose. Most people receiving text messages expect shorthand substitutions (such as *u* for "you" and @ for "at"), but be cautious about using such shortcuts when you contact an employer or instructor. You may want to stick to a more formal method of contact (such as email)if your employer or instructor has not explicitly invited you to send text messages—or texted you first.

bedfordstmartins.com/smhandbook
Writing Resources > Working Online

THINKING CRITICALLY ABOUT FORMAL AND INFORMAL ELECTRONIC COMMUNICATION

For one day, make a note every time you write anything electronically—a text message or casual email, a Facebook status update, a blog comment, notes in a Word document for an upcoming assignment. At the end of the day, make an inventory of all your writing, and then stop to think critically about what you have written. What kinds of writing do you do most often? What purposes do you write for, and which audiences are you reaching (or trying to reach)? How does your writing differ from one audience to the next? How would you characterize the differences between your informal and more formal writing?

Online Texts

A text can be anything that you might "read"—not just words but also images, data, audio, video, or combinations of media. A print textbook, for example, has visuals as well as words. Texts that go online can become richer with the ability to include animations, video, audio, links, and interactive features. Some online texts are identical to their print versions, but many online texts—even e-books of print books—are taking on a life and form of their own. More and more online texts and online ways of writing simply have no print counterpart.

When you create an online text that involves some formality or complexity, you'll need to plan ahead. Take into account what you want your text to do and which features make sense for your writing situation.

21a Planning an online text

As with any writing you do, pay careful attention to your audience, purpose, topic, and rhetorical stance when planning an online text. You will also need to consider time and technical constraints in order to ensure that your project is manageable.

1 Rhetorical issues

Audience

Who is the audience for your text (2d)? Identifying your intended audience as clearly as possible will help you decide on appropriate tone, diction, graphic styles, level of detail, and many other factors. If your intended audience is limited to people you know—as in a wiki available only to students in a literature class, for example—you may be able to make assumptions about their background, knowledge, and likely responses to your text. If you are planning a text devoted to a particular topic, you may have some ideas about the type of audience you think you'll be able to attract. In any case, plan your text to appeal to the readers you expect and want to have — but remember that an online text may reach readers you could not have predicted would be part of your audience.

Purpose

Why are you creating this text (2c3)? How do you want readers to use it? Considering purpose helps you determine what features your online text will need to incorporate.

> **QUICK HELP**
>
> ## Guidelines for creating an online text
>
> - Consider audience, purpose, topic, and stance. How can your text appeal to the right readers? How will it accomplish its purpose? (21a1)
>
> - Be realistic about the time available for the project, and plan accordingly. (21a2)
>
> - Think about the various types of online texts you can create, and determine which suits your needs based on what you want or need to do and what your audience expects: text, images, audio, video, or a combination? the latest updates first, or an index page? collaborative writing? feedback on your writing? Choose appropriate tools for your project and skills. (21b)
>
> - Choose features that are appropriate for the type of text as well as for your purpose, audience, and topic. (21c)
>
> - Use contrast, proximity, repetition, and alignment to create an appealing design, or choose a template that follows basic design principles. (21d)
>
> - Pay attention to user feedback, and make appropriate adjustments.

Topic

Your topic choice depends on your purpose and audience, and the topic will affect the content and design of your project. For example, if you want to write about an unfolding political event or the latest Hong Kong film releases, you might create a blog; if you want to explore the works of your favorite 1940s detective writers or showcase photographs you have taken, you might choose a Web site. If you prefer to talk about or show information on your topic, you might consider creating a video or audio text that you can post to an existing site.

Rhetorical stance

How do you relate to your topic? Your rhetorical stance (2c2) determines how your audience will see you. Will you present yourself as an expert, a fan, a novice seeking input from others, or something else? What information will you need to provide about yourself to seem credible and persuasive to your audience in the stance you choose?

2 Time management

You already know that time management is crucial for your success in any writing situation. How well you can manage decisions will be affected both by your deadline and by how much time you can squeeze out of your other interests and responsibilities to meet that deadline. How much technical expertise do you have, and by how much will you need to learn in order to create your text? Allow enough time for that learning to take place. Also consider how much research you will have to do and how long you will need to find, prepare, and seek permission (if needed—see Chapter 14) for any images, sound, or video files you want to use.

21b Considering types of online texts

Decisions about the type of Web text you want to create should be based on your plans for the text (21a). Among the most common types of personal texts online are Web sites, blogs, wikis, and podcasts and streaming media.

1 Web pages

One of the most common formats for online texts is the Web page. The hypertext that makes up a Web site allows the writer to organize elements as a cluster of associations; links can take readers to other parts of the site or to other sites. (For more information on arranging pages of a site, see 3f.) An online text is dynamic and relatively easy to change in order to accommodate new information.

On p. 457 are an index page and an interior page from a personal Web site that serves as a portfolio for a musician and photographer with an interest in Indian films. The site includes text, photographs, and audio and video files. Heading styles and navigation remain constant throughout the site, even though content varies from one section to another.

PAGES FROM A WEB SITE

① *Header* identifies where the user is on the site.

② *Links* to broad categories of content appear below the header.

③ *Slideshow* on the site home page presents constantly changing photos by the site creator.

④ *Header design* is consistent from page to page.

⑤ *Navigation* at top shows pages in this section and highlights the current page.

⑥ *Images* are clearly identified.

2 Blogs

Blogs are often very similar to Web pages in appearance, and the similarities are becoming more pronounced. However, there are some key differences. Readers expect blog content to be refreshed frequently—more often than the contents of a Web page—so blog posts are often time-stamped, and the newest content appears first. Blogs often rely heavily on outside content and feature a writer's commentary on news, events, and topics of note, from politics and pop culture to knitting patterns. Many free hosting sites and available templates make blogs easy to create, empowering an increasing number of individual authors to make their thoughts available to a wide audience.

A student's blog post

Student Writer

Francisco Guzman

The following post comes from student Francisco Guzman's blog on technology, Teknix. In addition to offering analysis of new products and market trends, he also comments on others' writing on technology, as in this post.

TECHNOLOGY: FACILITATING MORE WORK

SATURDAY, FEBRUARY 27, 2010 AT 12:55PM

Technology has significantly increased the amount of information we have access to. In fact, Google's mission reads as follows: "to organize the world's information and make it universally accessible and useful." Nowadays, when one wants to find information on a certain topic, it's much easier to "Google it" instead of going to a public library, as some of us did when we were younger.

I came across an interesting piece posted by The New York Times' Freakonomics Blog entitled "Technology and Tenure." The basic premise of the paper is that since information is so easy to access, university professors should be expected to compile a greater amount of papers/books to be considered for tenure. I think this is a general trend that we see in our society. As technology continues to facilitate our way of life, more is expected of us. In many ways, this is defeating the purpose because we aren't expected to do any less than we were before. Take, for example, the word processor. Previously, the typewriter was revolutionary, but it always posed a problem when it came to correcting mistakes. With the word processor, it has been much easier to rectify mistakes and therefore we are expected to produce more pages than ever, whether it be in reports for school or work at the office.

What it has done is allow us to produce more sophisticated content, and maybe that's all that we should be aiming for - to progress as a society. Read the blog post when you get a chance. It's an interesting perspective.

Francisco Guzman | ◯ Post a Comment | ⬍ Share Article

1. *Title* indicates content of post (a blog may include writing on many topics).

2. Post appears with *time and date stamp*.

3. *Links* direct readers to content under discussion.

4. *Image* extends the idea under discussion and adds visual interest.

5. Each post invites *comments* from readers, pointing out the interactive nature of most blogs.

3 | Wikis

Wikis, such as Wikipedia, are collaborative online texts. They empower all users of the site to contribute content, although this content may be moderated before being posted. Wikis create communities where all content is peer-reviewed and evaluated by other members; they are powerful tools for sharing a lot of information because they draw on the collective knowledge of many contributors.

WIKI ARTICLE

1 Users can ask questions and post editing concerns on the *discussion* page.

2 Readers can also *edit* the page.

3 *Links* connect readers to related wiki content.

4 | Podcasts and streaming media

Today's technology makes it easy for users to record, edit, and upload audio and video files to the Web. Audio and video content can vary as widely as the content found in written-word media—audiobooks, video diaries, pop-culture mashups, radio shows, short documentaries, fiction films, and so on. Writers who create podcasts (which can be downloaded for playback) and streaming media (which can be played without

CONSIDERING DISABILITIES

Accessible Web texts

Much on the Web remains hard to access and read for persons with disabilities. For details on how to design accessible online texts, visit the Americans with Disabilities Act site at www.ada.gov. Here are a few of the ADA's design tips:

- Organize information simply and consistently, and make sure that important information is easy to find.

- Choose colors that create a sharp contrast for visibility. Do not rely on color alone to carry meaning; add words as well.

- Provide brief descriptions of all visuals to assist visually impaired readers using software that reads onscreen text aloud. If you use tables to convey data, identify the header cells in the rows and columns. Include a caption and summary with each table. Screen readers read from left to right, which will render the tables themselves meaningless.

- Give each link a descriptive name such as "Return to the home page."

- Provide alternative text for all pictures, photos, graphics, and decorative filters. If graphic material is important to the page, include an identifying tag or a title for each graphic. If the graphic is used for design or formatting, consider alternatives.

- Punctuate appropriately; screen readers pause for punctuation.

- For deaf or hearing-impaired readers, provide captions for any sound on your Web site. Do not rely on sound—even with captions—to carry the central or singular meaning of your text. Provide a transcript or other written text of a podcast or other audio file.

- For many readers, using a mouse may be problematic. If you are using a form or other interactive element, make sure it's possible to move from field to field in the form by using the TAB and ENTER keys.

- If, after your best efforts, the site cannot be made accessible, provide a text-only alternative and ensure that it is updated with the main page.

downloading) may produce episodic content united by a common host or theme.

Audio and video files can stand alone as online texts on sites such as YouTube, but they can also be embedded on a Web page or blog to add dimension to written-word texts.

21c Examining features of online texts

Choose the features that will enable your audience to get the most from your online text.

1 Text

Online readers generally prefer short, manageable chunks of text. If you are writing a long piece, consider breaking it up with headings and visuals. Include any introductory or transitional material that you need to help readers make sense of your content, captions for visuals, sound transcripts (if you include audio files), and so on. Be sure to obtain permission to use any material from another source (see Chapter 14) if your work will be available to the public.

2 Links

Links to external sites are one method of documenting sources online. You can link to content that helps to prove a point — complex explanations, supporting statistics, bibliographies, referenced Web sites, or additional readings, for example. Links also help readers navigate from one part of a text to another.

Each link should have a clear rhetorical purpose and be in an appropriate location. If, for example, you put a link in the middle of a paragraph, be aware that readers may go to the linked content before finishing what's before them — and if that link takes them to an external site, they may never come back! If it's important for users to read the whole paragraph, you may want to move the link to the end of it.

3 Visuals and multimedia

Integrate written words carefully with accompanying images. A compelling visual can help anchor readers on a page, but be careful not to use visuals for mere decoration.

- If you have not created a visual or video yourself, you will need to see if it is copyrighted and, if so, to ask permission to use it on a public Web site (see Chapter 14).

- Use white space (23b) to emphasize, to direct readers, and to keep your text from appearing uninvitingly dense.

4 Interactivity

Online texts are unique in their ability to include levels of interactivity. While wikis are full-scale collaborative efforts and frequently allow contribution from users, something as simple as a thumbs-up/thumbs-down or LIKE button allows users to register their reaction to a text. Online texts—from blogs and video channels to online newspaper articles—often incorporate polls, comments, and forums for discussing posts and contacting the writer.

21d Putting your text together

After you have thought through what you want your text to do and what features will best serve your purpose, integrate the parts into a unified whole.

Design

A good design helps attract the audience's interest and suggests that your site is worth looking at. As with any text you create, remember the following basic principles of good document design (23a2), first laid out by Robin Williams in *The Non-Designer's Design Book*:

- Differentiate parts of the page and text or visuals from the background (*contrast*).

- Arrange elements to line up with other elements for a clean look (*alignment*).

- Guide readers by using color, layout, and other elements consistently (*repetition*).

- Group related items together (*proximity*).

Many online writers use templates and other content-management tools to help them plan and build their texts. A template serves as a model, giving consistency to the sections of a text and making the text as a whole easier to follow. Basically, a template sets the background color, heading information, navigation buttons, typeface, contact information, and so on.

Ultimately, the organization and look of your text depend on what you are trying to achieve. You should make decisions about page length, color, visuals, multimedia, and interactive elements based on rhetorical choices (your audience, purpose, topic, and stance) and on practical constraints (the time and tools available). For more on design, see Chapter 23.

Structure and organization

Just as you might outline an essay, you should develop a clear structure for your Web text. Some types of texts are organized in standard ways—most blogs, for example, appear with the newest posts at the top. Others allow you to make choices about how to arrange materials. Choose a structure that makes sense for your purpose, audience, topic, and rhetorical stance. Arrange your text to allow readers to find what they are looking for as quickly and intuitively as possible. (For more on organizing and planning your text, see 3e and f.)

EXERCISE 21.1

Use a search engine to find a Web page, blog, or wiki entry that you haven't visited before but that addresses a topic you know something about. What is the purpose of the text? Who is its intended audience? What rhetorical stance does it take? What overall impression does the text create—and how?

THINKING CRITICALLY ABOUT ONLINE TEXTS

Take some time to reflect on an online text you have created, whether it's an assignment posted to a course Web site, a blog post or comment, or a YouTube video. Evaluate the work you've created. For what purpose did you create the text? Did you achieve your goals? What audience did you anticipate, and did that audience see your work? Who else saw it? What was your topic, and what stance did you take? Finally, what kind of feedback did you get? Conclude by drawing up a list of tips for making future online texts, noting what aspects of your text were successful and what you would do differently.

Oral and Multimedia Presentations

22

Successful presenters point to four elements crucial to their effectiveness:

- a thorough knowledge of the subject at hand
- careful attention to the interactive nature of speaking and thus to the needs of the audience
- careful integration of verbal and visual information
- practice, practice, and more practice

22a Joining class discussions

You may give some of the most important oral presentations of your college career when you participate in classroom discussions. The challenge is to contribute to such discussions without losing track of the overall conversation or aims of the class and without monopolizing the discussion. Especially if you are also taking notes, you may find yourself straining to manage all these tasks at once. Here are a few tips for making effective contributions to class discussions:

- Be prepared so that the comments you make will relate to the work of the class.
- Listen purposefully, jotting down related points and following the flow of the conversation.
- If you think you might lose track of your ideas while speaking, jot down key words to keep you on track.

When the Gallup Poll reports on what U.S. citizens say they fear most, the findings are always the same: public speaking is apparently even scarier than an attack from outer space. Nevertheless, many writing courses now require students not only to compose written texts, but also to give presentations in front of an audience. Perhaps it is not surprising, then, that students who use this handbook have consistently asked for information on giving oral presentations.

- Make your comments count by asking a key question to clarify a point, by taking the conversation in a more productive direction, or by analyzing or summarizing what has been said.

- Respond to questions or comments by others as specifically as possible (*The passage on p. 42 provides evidence to support your point* rather than *I agree*).

- Offer a brief analysis of a problem, issue, or text, one that leaves room for others to build on.

- If you have trouble participating frequently in class discussions, try making one comment a day. You might also speak with your instructor about ways to contribute to the conversation.

- Remember that there is no direct correlation between talking in class and being intellectually engaged: many students are participating actively, whether or not they are speaking.

FOR MULTILINGUAL WRITERS

Speaking up in class

Speaking up in class is viewed as inappropriate or even rude in some cultures. In the United States, however, doing so is expected and encouraged. Indeed, some instructors assign credit for such class participation.

22b Considering assignment, purpose, and audience for presentations

More and more students report that formal oral presentations are becoming part of their work both in and out of class. You will be wise to begin preparing for a presentation as soon as you get the assignment. Think about how much time you have to prepare; how long the presentation is to be; whether you will use written-out text or note cards; whether visual aids, handouts, or other materials are called for; and what equipment you will need. If you are making a group presentation, you will need time to divide duties and practice (6b2). Make sure that you understand the criteria for evaluation—how will the presentation be graded or assessed?

Consider the purpose of your presentation. Are you to lead a discussion? teach a lesson? give a report? engage a group in an activity? Also consider the audience (2d). If your instructor is a member of the

QUICK HELP

Guidelines for presentations

- How does your presentation accomplish the specifications of the assignment? (22b)

- How does your presentation appeal to your audience's experiences and interests? Does it achieve your purpose? (22b)

- How does the introduction get the audience's attention? Does it provide any necessary background information? (22c1)

- What organizational structure informs your presentation? (22c1)

- Check for signposts that can guide listeners. Are there explicit transitions? Do you repeat key words or ideas? (22c1)

- Have you used mostly straightforward sentences? Consider revising any long or complicated sentences to make your talk easier to follow. Check your words as well for too much abstraction. Substitute concrete words for abstract ones as often as you can. (22c1)

- Have you marked your presentation script or note cards for pauses and emphasis? Have you marked material that you can omit if you find yourself short of time? (22c1)

- Have you prepared all necessary visuals? If so, how do they contribute to your presentation? Are they large enough to be seen? Have you followed the principles of good design? (22c2 and 23a2)

- If you have not prepared visuals, can you identify any information that would be enhanced by them? (22c2 and 23d)

- Have you practiced your presentation so that you will appear confident and knowledgeable? (22c3 and e)

audience, what will he or she expect you to do — and do well? What do audience members know about your topic? What opinions do they already hold about it? What do they need to know to follow your presentation and perhaps accept your point of view? Finally, consider your own stance toward your topic and audience. Are you an expert? novice? well-informed observer? peer?

A student's analysis of a presentation assignment

Shuqiao Song's assignment for her writing class on graphic narratives had two major parts: she had to write a ten- to fifteen-page argument based on research on a graphic narrative, and then she had to turn that information into a script for a twelve-minute oral presentation accompanied by slides. After some brainstorming and talking with her instructor, Shuqiao chose her favorite graphic memoir, Alison Bechdel's *Fun Home*, as her topic.

As she thought about her assignment and topic, Shuqiao realized that she had more than one purpose. Certainly she wanted to do well on the assignment and receive a good grade. But she also wanted to convince her classmates that Bechdel's book was a complex and important one and that its power lay in the relationship of words and images. She also had to admit to at least one other purpose: it would be great to turn in a truly *impressive* performance. Her audience—the other students in the class—seemed smart, and some were apparently experienced presenters. Shuqiao knew she had her work cut out for her.

For Shuqiao Song's print essay, see 7e. For more on her presentation, see 22c.

22c Composing for oral presentations

Getting and keeping the attention of listeners may require you to use different strategies than the ones you generally employ when writing for a reading audience.

1 Writing to be heard—and remembered

To be *remembered* rather than simply heard, write a memorable introduction and conclusion, and use explicit structures, helpful signpost language, straightforward syntax, and concrete diction throughout the presentation.

A memorable introduction and conclusion

Remember that listeners, like readers, tend to remember beginnings and endings most readily, so work extra hard to make these elements memorable (4h). Consider, for example, using a startling statement, opinion, or question; a dramatic anecdote; a powerful quotation; or a vivid visual image. Shifting language, especially into a variety of language that your audience will identify with, is another effective way to catch their attention (see Chapter 26). Whenever you can link your subject to the experiences and interests of your audience, do so.

CONSIDERING DISABILITIES

Accessible presentations

Remember that some members of your audience may not be able to see your presentation or may have trouble hearing it, so do all you can to make your presentation accessible.

- Be sure to face any audience members who rely on lipreading to understand your words. For a large audience, request an ASL (American Sign Language) interpreter.

- Do not rely on color or graphics alone to get across information—some audience members may be unable to pick up these visual cues.

- For presentations you publish on the Web, provide brief textual descriptions of your visuals.

- If you use video, provide labels for captions to explain any sounds that won't be audible to some audience members, and embed spoken captions to explain images to those who cannot see them. Be sure that the equipment you'll be using is caption capable.

- Remember that students have very different learning styles and abilities. You may want to provide a written overview of your presentation or put the text of your presentation on slides or transparencies for those who learn better by reading *and* listening.

Shuqiao Song began her presentation this way:

> Welcome, everyone. I'm Shuqiao Song and I'm here today to talk about residents of a dys*FUNc*tional *HOME*.
>
> We meet these residents in a graphic memoir called *Fun Home*.

Student Writing

(Here, Shuqiao showed a three-second video clip of author Alison Bechdel saying, "I love words, and I love pictures. But especially, I love them together—in a mystical way that I can't even explain.")

> That was Alison Bechdel, author of *Fun Home*. In that clip, she conveniently introduces the topics of my presentation today: Words. Pictures. And the mystical way they work together.

Note that this presentation opened with a play on words ("dys*FUNc*tional *HOME*"), to which Shuqiao returned later on, and with a short, vivid video clip that perfectly summed up the main topic of the presentation. Also note the use of short sentences and fragments, special effects that act like drumbeats to get and hold the attention of the audience.

Explicit structure and signpost language

Organize your presentation clearly and carefully, and give an overview of your main points toward the beginning of your presentation. (You may wish to recall these points again toward the end of the talk.) Throughout your presentation, pause between major points, and use signpost language as you move from one topic to the next. Such signposts act as explicit transitions in your talk and should be clear and concrete: *The second crisis point in the breakup of the Soviet Union occurred hard on the heels of the first* instead of *The breakup of the Soviet Union came to another crisis point. . . .* In addition to such explicit transitions (5d4) as *next, on the contrary,* and *finally,* you can offer signposts to your listeners by carefully repeating key words and ideas as well as by sticking to concrete topic sentences to introduce each new idea.

At the end of Shuqiao's introduction, she set forth the structure of her presentation in a very clear, straightforward, and simple way to help her audience follow what came next:

> **Student Writing**
>
> So, to outline the rest of my presentation: first, I'll show how *text* is insufficient—but also why it is necessary to Bechdel's story. Second, I'll show how *images* can't be trusted, but again, why they are still necessary for Bechdel's purposes. Third and finally, I'll show how the interplay of text and image in *Fun Home* creates a more complex and comprehensive understanding of the story.

Syntax and diction

Avoid long, complicated sentences, and use straightforward sentence structure (subject-verb-object) as much as possible. Listeners prefer action verbs and concrete nouns to abstractions. You may need to deal with abstract ideas, but try to provide concrete examples for them (27c).

Shuqiao Song's presentation script included the following example:

> **Student Writing**
>
> Now, to argue my second point, I'll begin with an image. This is a René Magritte painting. The text means, *"This is not a pipe."* Is this some surrealist Jedi mind trick? Not really. Now listen to the title of the painting to grasp Magritte's point. The painting is called *The Treason of Images.* Here Magritte is showing us that "this is not a pipe" because it is an *image* of a pipe.

Ceci n'est pas une pipe.

Again, look at the short sentences, the vivid word choice ("surrealist Jedi mind trick") and the straightforward subject-verb-object syntax—all of which makes the passage easy on listeners.

Memorable language

Memorable presentations call on the power of figures of speech and other devices of language, such as careful repetition, parallelism, and climactic order.

You can see an example of careful repetition in the following passage from Shuqiao Song's presentation, in which the repeated words (*alone, text and image, strange relationship/strange pairings*) help to make her point that the combination of text and image is more compelling than either on its own:

> For Bechdel's purposes, words and images have to work together because alone, words can fail, and alone, images deceive. However, text and image are themselves necessary characters in Bechdel's story. The logical conclusion would then be to use both text and image together. Text *and* image. But *and* is too simple a word to explain the interaction between the two. A strange relationship emerges between image and text; as strange as the relationship between Alison Bechdel and her father. But these strange pairings have an alluring quality that makes Alison Bechdel's *Fun Home* compelling.

Student
Writing

Turning writing into a script for a presentation

Even though you will rely on some written material, you will need to adapt it for speech. Depending on the assignment, the audience, and your personal preferences, you may even speak from a full script. If so, double- or triple-space it, and use fairly large print so that it will be easy to read. Try to end each page with the end of a sentence so that you won't have to pause while you turn a page. In addition, you may decide to mark spots where you want to pause and to highlight words you want to emphasize.

Take a look at this paragraph from Shuqiao Song's written essay on *Fun Home*:

A PARAGRAPH FROM A WRITTEN ESSAY

Student Writing

Finally, we can see how image and text function together. On the one hand, image and text support each other in that each highlights the subtleties of the other; but on the other hand, the more interesting interaction comes when there is some degree of distance between what is written and what is depicted. In *Fun Home*, there is no one-to-one closure that mentally connects text and image. Rather, Bechdel pushes the boundaries of mental closure between image and text. If the words and pictures match exactly, making the same point, the story would read like a children's book, and that would be too simple for what Bechdel is trying to accomplish. However, text and image can't be so mismatched that meaning completely eludes the readers. Bechdel crafts her story deliberately, leaving just enough mental space for the reader to solve the rest of the puzzle and resolve the cognitive dissonance. The reader's mental closure, which brings coherence to the text and images and draws together loose ends, allows for a more complex and sophisticated understanding of the story.

Now look at how she revised that paragraph into a script for oral presentation:

A PARAGRAPH REVISED FOR A LISTENING AUDIENCE

Student Writing

Finally, image and text can work together. They support each other: each highlights the subtleties of the other. But they are even more interesting when there's a gap — some distance between the story the words tell and the story the pictures tell. In *Fun Home*, text and image are never perfectly correlated. After all, if the words and pictures matched up exactly, the story would read like a kids' book. That would be way too simple for Bechdel's purposes. But we wouldn't want a complete disconnect between words and images either, since we wouldn't be able to make sense of them.

Still, Bechdel certainly pushes the boundaries that would allow us to bring closure between image and text. So what's the take-home point here? That in Bechdel's *Fun Home*, image and text are not just supporting actors of each other. Instead, each offers a *version* of the story. It's for us — the readers. We take these paired versions and weave them into a really rich understanding of the story.

Note that the revised paragraph presents the same information, but this time it is written to be heard. The revision uses helpful signpost language, some repetition, simple syntax, and informal varieties of English to help listeners follow along and keep them interested.

Speaking from notes

If you decide to speak from notes rather than from a full script, here are some tips for doing so effectively:

- In general, use one note card for each point in your presentation, beginning with the introduction and ending with the conclusion.

- Number the cards so that you can quickly find the next part of your presentation if your cards are out of order.

- On each card, include the major point you want to make in large bold text. Include subpoints in a bulleted list below the main point, again printed large enough for you to see easily. You can use full sentences or phrases, as long as you include enough information to remind you of what you have planned to say.

- Include signpost language on each note so that you will be sure to use it to guide your listeners.

- Practice your presentation using the notes at least twice.

- Time your presentation very carefully so that you will be sure not to go overtime. If you think you may run out of time, use color or brackets to mark material in your notes that you can skip. If your presentation is too long, move past the marked material so that you can end with your planned conclusion.

The following note card for the introduction to a presentation reminds the student to emphasize her title and her three points about the origins of graphic novels. Notice how she has highlighted her signpost language as well as the card's number.

NOTECARD FOR AN ORAL PRESENTATION

[Card 3]

Overview of the rest of the presentation

- First, text is insufficient but necessary
- Second, images can't be trusted but are necessary
- Finally, interplay of text and image creates complex, comprehensive understanding

2 Using visuals

Visuals are often an integral part of an oral presentation, carrying a lot of the message the speaker wants to convey. So think of your visuals not as add-ons but as a major means of getting your points across. Many speakers use presentation software (such as PowerPoint or Prezi) to help keep themselves on track and to guide the audience. In addition, posters, flip charts, chalkboards, or interactive whiteboards can also help you make strong visual statements.

For her presentation, "Words, Images, and the Mystical Way They Work Together in Alison Bechdel's *Fun Home*," Shuqiao Song developed a series of very simple slides aimed at underscoring her points and keeping her audience focused on them. She began by introducing the work, showing the book cover on an otherwise black slide.

After Shuqiao's introduction of Bechdel and her book, Shuqiao provided the following overview of the presentation as she clicked through the slides that illustrated what she was doing:

> So let me tell you, quickly, what I'll be doing in the rest of this presentation:
>
> First, I'll show how text is *insufficient*, but also why it is *necessary* in Bechdel's story.

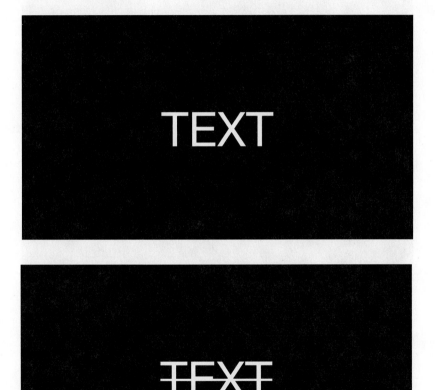

Second, I'll show how images can't be trusted yet why they are still necessary for Bechdel's purpose.

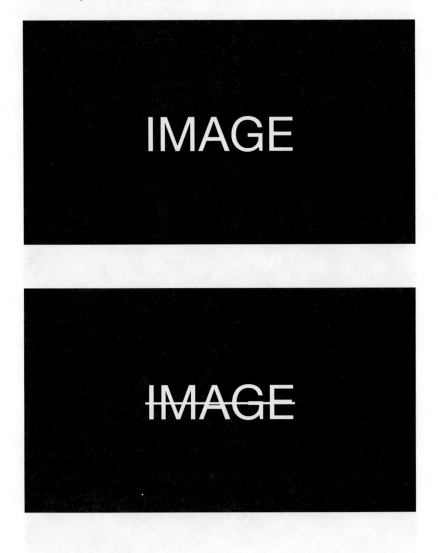

Third and finally, I'll show how the interplay of text and image in *Fun Home* works to create a more complex and comprehensive understanding of this magical story.

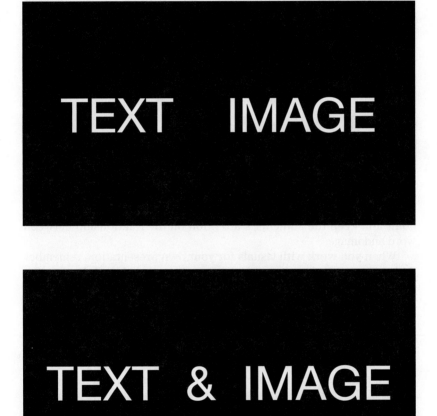

TEXT ? IMAGE

Each one of these slides—with a single word that is then crossed out or words that are resituated by & or *?*—serves to emphasize Shuqiao's point and keep the audience's attention on the relationship between word and image.

When you work with visuals for your own presentation, remember that they must be large enough to be easily seen and read. Be sure the information is simple, clear, and easy to understand. And remember *not* to read from your visuals or turn your back on your audience as you refer to them. Most important, make sure your visuals engage and help your listeners rather than distract them from your message. Try out each visual on your classmates, friends, or roommates: if they do not clearly grasp the meaning and purpose of the visual, scrap it and try again.

You may also want to prepare handouts for your audience: pertinent bibliographies, for example, or text too extensive to be presented otherwise. Unless the handouts include material you want your audience to use while you speak, distribute them at the end of the presentation.

3 Practicing the presentation

In oral presentations, as with many other things in life, practice makes perfect. Prepare a draft of your presentation, including visuals, far enough in advance to allow for several run-throughs. If possible, have yourself videotaped, and then examine the tape in detail. You can also make an audio recording or practice in front of a mirror or in front of friends. Do whatever works for you—just as long as you practice!

Make sure you can be heard clearly. If you are soft-spoken, concentrate on projecting your voice. If your voice tends to rise when you are in the spotlight, practice lowering your pitch. If you speak rapidly, practice slowing down and enunciating words clearly. Remember that tone of voice affects listeners, so aim for a tone that conveys interest in and commitment to your topic and listeners. If you practice with friends or classmates, ask them how well they can hear you and what advice they have for making your voice clearer and easier to listen to.

One student who taped her rehearsal found, to her great surprise, that she had used the word *like* thirty-two times in her eight-minute presentation, even though the word never appeared in her notes. In this case, it took a lot of practice to break the *like* habit.

Once you are comfortable giving the presentation, make sure you will stay within the allotted time. One good rule of thumb is to allow roughly two and a half minutes per double-spaced 8½" × 11" page of text (or one and a half minutes per note card). The only way to be sure about your time, however, is to time yourself as you practice. Knowing that your presentation is neither too short nor too long will help you relax and gain self-confidence; and when the members of your audience sense your self-confidence, they will become increasingly receptive to your message.

4 Making the presentation

Experienced speakers say they always expect to feel some anxiety before an oral presentation—and they develop strategies for dealing with it. In addition, they note that some nervousness can act to a speaker's advantage: adrenaline, after all, can help you perform well.

The best strategy seems to be to know your material. Having confidence in your own knowledge will go a long way toward making you a confident presenter. In addition to doing your homework, however, you may be able to use the following strategies to good advantage:

- Consider how you will dress and how you will move around. In each case, your choices should be appropriate for the situation. Most experienced speakers like to dress simply and comfortably for easy movement. But they are seldom overly casual — dressing up a little signals your pride in your appearance and your respect for your audience.

- Go over the scene of your presentation in your mind, and think it through completely, in order to feel more comfortable during it.
- Get some rest before the presentation, and avoid consuming an excessive amount of caffeine.
- Try to relax while you wait to begin. You might want to do some deep-breathing exercises.

If possible, stand up. Most speakers make a stronger impression standing than sitting. Move around the room if you are comfortable doing so. If you are more comfortable in one spot, then keep both feet flat on the floor. If you are behind a lectern, rest your hands lightly on it. Many speakers find that this stance keeps them from fidgeting.

Pause before you begin your presentation, concentrating on your opening lines. During your presentation, interact with your audience as much as possible. You can do so by facing the audience at all times and making eye contact as often as possible. You may want to choose two or three people to look at and "talk to," particularly if you are addressing a large group. Allow time for the audience to ask questions. Try to keep your answers short so that others may participate in the conversation. When you conclude, remember to thank your audience.

EXERCISE 22.1

Attend a lecture or presentation, and analyze its effectiveness. How does the speaker capture and hold your interest? What signpost language and other guides to listening can you detect? How well are visuals integrated into the presentation? How do the speaker's tone of voice, dress, and eye contact affect your understanding and appreciation (or lack of it)? What is most memorable about the presentation, and why? Bring your analysis to class and report your findings.

22d Giving multimedia presentations

Among the most popular forms of multimedia presentation are those that use presentation software.

1 Presentation software

Presentation software such as PowerPoint allows you to prepare slides you want to display and even to enhance the images with sound. Before you begin designing your presentation, make sure that the equipment you need will be available. As you design presentation slides, keep some simple principles in mind (for more on principles of visual design, see Chapter 23):

• Audiences can't read and listen to you at the same time, so make the slides support what you are saying as clearly and visually as possible. Sometimes just one or two words—or a visual without words—can back up what you are saying more effectively than a list of bullet points.

• Never simply read the text of your slides. Your audience can read faster than you can talk, and you are guaranteed to bore them with this technique.

• Use your media wisely, and respect your audience's time. If you feel that you need to include more than three or four bullet points (or more than fifty words of text) on a slide, you may be trying to convey information in a slideshow that would make more sense in a report. Rethink your presentation so that what you say and what you show work together to win over your audience.

• Use text on your slides to guide your audience—not as a teleprompter. Be familiar enough with your material so that you don't have to rely on your slides to know what comes next.

• Make sure any text you show is big enough to read, and create a clear contrast between text or illustration and background. In general, light backgrounds work better in a darkened room, and dark backgrounds in a lighted one.

• Be careful not to depend too heavily on slide templates. The choices of color, font, and layout offered by such templates may not always match your goals or fit with your topic.

• Choose visuals—photographs, graphs, and so on—that will reproduce sharply, and make sure they are large enough to be clearly visible.

• Make sure that sound or video clips are audible and that they relate directly to your topic. If you want to use sound as background, make sure it does not distract from what you are trying to say.

- Although there are no firm rules about how many slides you should use or how long each slide should be made visible, plan length and timing with your audience's needs and your purpose in mind.

A student's PowerPoint slides and script

Student Writer

Jennifer Bernal

Following are the full script and the PowerPoint slides prepared by student Jennifer Bernal for a class presentation. Her assignment was to analyze a graphic novel. Note that she cites the source of each image on the slide where it appears and that she includes a list of her sources on the final slide in the presentation.

Student Writing

[slide 1] Hello, I'm Jennifer Bernal. And I've been thinking about the voice of the child narrator in the graphic novel *Persepolis* by Marjane Satrapi, an autobiographical narrative of a young girl's coming of age in Iran during the Islamic revolution. My research questions seemed fitting for a child: what? how? why? What is the "child's voice"? How is it achieved? Why is it effective? The child's voice in this book is characterized by internal conflict: the character sometimes sounds like a child and sometimes like an adult. She truly is a child on the threshhold of adulthood. I'm going to show how Satrapi expresses the duality of this child's voice, not only through content but also through her visual style.

[slide 2] The main character, Marjane, faces a constant conflict between childhood and adulthood. But the struggle takes place not only between the child and the adults in her society but also between the child and the adult *within Marjane herself*. For example, Marjane is exposed to many ideas and experiences as she tries to understand the world around her. Here [first image] we see her surprising an adult by discussing Marx. But we also see her being a kid. Sometimes, like all children, she is unthinkingly cruel: here [second image] we see her upsetting another little girl with the horrifying (and, as it turns out, incorrect) "truth" about her father's absence.

[slide 3] In her review of *Persepolis* for the *Village Voice*, Joy Press says that "Satrapi's supernaive style . . . persuasively communicates confusion and horror through the eyes of a precocious preteen." It seems to me that this simple visual style is achieved through repetition and filtering. Let's take a look at this. [point to slide] First, there's *repetition* of elements. We often see the same images being used over and over. Sometimes [point to first image] the repetition suggests the sameness imposed by the repressive government. At other times similar images are repeated throughout the book for emphasis. For example [point to examples], on several occasions we see her raising her finger and speaking directly to the reader to make an emphatic point. The repetition throughout *Persepolis* makes it look and feel more like a children's book.

The Child's Voice through Visual Style: Repetition

Fig. 3 from Marjane Satrapi, *Persepolis* (New York: Pantheon, 2003) 96.

Figs. 4, 5, 6 - from Satrapi 19, 114, 117.

[slide 4] In addition to simplification through repetition, there's a second simplifying process, that of *filtering*. *Persepolis* is filled with violent elements. One good example is the torture and execution of guerrilla fighter Ahmadi. Marjane recounts, "In the end he was cut to pieces." The dismemberment is one of the most violent images that we see in the book. However, Satrapi's representation filters the horror. [point to illustration] This figure doesn't seem real—it looks neatly sectioned and hollow, like a doll. We see the image presented as a child might imagine it.

So, let me conclude by answering *why* Satrapi's visual voice is so effective. Remember, she is connecting to the world of childhood through comics. Her story seems very grim and adult—too grim for children. But it *is* a child's story, or rather the story of a character standing on the threshhold of the adult world. So the graphic novel is an ideal way to reveal both the conflicting aspects of the child's voice and the balance between these aspects. For the author to explain the child Marjane's particular, slightly uncomfortable vantage point, the in-between genre of the graphic novel is a perfect fit.

[slide 5] Thanks! Are there any questions?

Fig. 7 - from Marjane Satrapi, *Persepolis* (New York: Pantheon, 2003) 52.

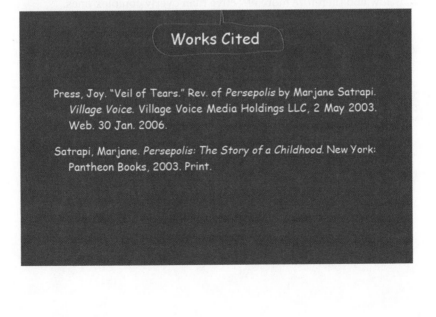

Works Cited

Press, Joy. "Veil of Tears." Rev. of *Persepolis* by Marjane Satrapi. *Village Voice*. Village Voice Media Holdings LLC, 2 May 2003. Web. 30 Jan. 2006.

Satrapi, Marjane. *Persepolis: The Story of a Childhood.* New York: Pantheon Books, 2003. Print.

2 Posters

Many college courses and conferences now call on students to make poster presentations. During the class or conference session, the presenter uses a poster board as background while talking through the presentation and answering questions. Follow these tips if you are preparing a poster presentation:

- Create a board that can be read from at least three feet away.

- Include a clear title (at least two inches high) at the top of the board.

- Include your name and other appropriate information: course title and number, name of instructor, conference title or session, and so on.

- Use a series of bullets or boxes to identify your major points and to lead the audience through the presentation.

- Include an arresting image or an important table or figure if it illustrates your points in a clear and memorable way.

- Consider using a provocative question toward the bottom of the poster to focus attention and anticipate your conclusion.

- Remember that simple, uncluttered posters are usually easier to follow and therefore more effective than overly complex ones.

- Practice the oral part of the presentation until you are comfortable referring to the poster while keeping your full attention on the audience.

22e Using Webcasts

This chapter on oral and multimedia presentations has thus far assumed that you will be speaking before an audience in the same room with you. Increasingly, however, you won't actually be in the same physical space as the audience for your presentations. Instead, you may make your presentation over the Web, speaking into a camera that captures your presentation (and perhaps your image) and relays it, via the Internet, to attendees who might be anywhere in the world.

As you learn to adapt to Webcast environments, most of the strategies that work in oral and multimedia presentations for an audience that is actually present will continue to serve you well. But there are some significant differences:

- Practice is even more important in Webcasts, since you need to make sure that you can immediately access everything you need online — a set of slides, for example, or a document or video clip, as well as any names, dates, or sources that you might be called on to provide during the Webcast.

- Because you cannot make eye contact with audience members, you should remember to look into the camera, if you are using one. If you are using a stationary Webcam, practice staying still enough to remain in the frame without looking stiff.

- Even though your audience may not be visible to you, assume that if you are on camera, the Web-based audience can see you quite well; if you slouch, they'll notice. Also assume that your microphone is always live — don't say anything that you don't want your audience to hear.

THINKING CRITICALLY ABOUT ORAL AND MULTIMEDIA PRESENTATIONS

Study the text of an oral or multimedia presentation you've prepared or given. Using the advice in this chapter, see how well your presentation appeals to your audience. Look in particular at how well you catch and hold their attention. How effective is your use of signpost language or other structures that help guide your listeners? How helpful are the visuals (PowerPoint slides, posters) in conveying your message? What would you do to improve this presentation?

23 Design for Writing

In the ancient Greek world, a speaker's delivery (known as *actio*) was an art every educated person needed to master; how a speaker delivered a speech — tone and volume of voice, use of gestures, and so on — had a great impact on how the speech would be received. Today, the technological revolution has dramatically affected the delivery of information, allowing writers to create and distribute increasingly complex texts.

Because visual and design elements such as headings, lists, fonts, images, and graphics can help you get and keep a reader's attention, they bring a whole new dimension to writing — what some call *visual rhetoric*.

23a Planning a visual structure

Effective writers consider the visual structure of any text they create. Their design decisions guide readers by making texts easier on the eyes and easier to understand.

1 Print and electronic options

One of your first design decisions will be choosing between print delivery and electronic delivery. In general, print documents are easily portable, easy to read without technical assistance, and relatively fast to produce. In addition, the tools for producing print texts are highly developed and stable. Electronic texts, on the other hand, can include sound, animation, and video; updates are easy to make; distribution is fast and efficient; and feedback can be swift. In many writing situations, the assignment will tell you whether to create a print document or an electronic text. Whether you are working to produce a text to be read in print or on a screen (or both), however, you should rely on some basic design principles.

2 Design principles

Designer Robin Williams, in her *Non-Designer's Design Book*, points out several very simple principles for designing effective texts — contrast, alignment, repetition, and proximity. These principles are illustrated in the examples shown below and on pp. 490–91.

Contrast

Contrast attracts your eye to elements on a page and guides you around it, helping you follow an argument or find information. You may achieve contrast through the use of color, icons, boldface or large type size, headings, and so on. Begin with a focus point — the dominant point, image, or words where you want your reader's eye to go first — and structure the flow of your visual information from this point.

CONTRAST

The National Geographic *Web site uses high-contrast yellow and white against a black background. This home page also features a high-contrast image of stars against blackness to draw the eye.*

Alignment

Alignment refers to the way visuals and text on a page are lined up, both horizontally and vertically. The overall guideline is not to mix alignments arbitrarily. That is, if you begin with a left alignment, stick with it for the major parts of your page. The result will be a cleaner and more organized look. In this book, for example, headings always align with the left margin. (See also the figure below.)

Repetition

Readers are guided by the repetition of key words and elements. Use a consistent design throughout your document for such elements as color, typeface, and images.

ALIGNMENT AND REPETITION

This iGoogle *home page aligns content under headings and repeats the color scheme and the design motif—a rounded box with a blue header bar—for every element the user adds.*

Proximity

Parts of a text that are closely related should appear together (*proximate* to one another). Your goal is to position related points, text, and visuals near one another and to use clear headings to identify these clusters, as the carbon-monoxide warning flyer on p. 491 does.

Consistent overall impression

Aim for a design that creates the appropriate overall impression or mood for your text. For an academic essay, you will probably make

PROXIMITY

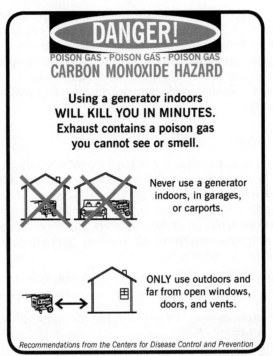

This flyer positions a statement about unsafe locations for a generator next to illustrations of those unsafe locations, crossed out in red; further down, a sentence about safe locations for a generator appears next to illustrations clarifying what the text specifies.

conservative choices that strike a serious scholarly note. In a newsletter for a campus group, you might choose attention-getting images.

23b Formatting

With so many options available, you should spend some time thinking about appropriate formatting elements for your text. Although the following guidelines often apply, remember that print documents, Web pages, slide shows, videos, and so on all have their own formatting conventions.

White space

Use white space, or negative space, to emphasize and direct readers to parts of the page. White space determines a page's density — the distance between information bits. You consider white space at the page level (margins), paragraph level (space between paragraphs), and sentence level (space between sentences). Within the page, you can also use white space around particular content, such as a graphic or list, to make it stand out.

Color

Decisions about color depend to a large extent not only on the kind of equipment you are using — and, for printing, who's paying for the color ink cartridges — but also on the purpose(s) of your document and its intended audience. As you design your documents, keep in mind that some colors can evoke powerful responses, so take care that the colors you use match the message you are sending. Here are some other tips about the effective use of color:

- Use color to draw attention to elements you want to emphasize: headings, bullets, text boxes, or parts of charts or graphs.

- Be consistent in your use of color; use the same color for all subheads, for example.

- For most documents, keep the number of colors fairly small; too many colors can create a jumbled or confused look.

- Avoid colors that clash or that are hard on the eyes.

Certain color combinations clash or are hard to read.

Other combinations are easier on the eyes.

- Make sure all color visuals and text are legible in the format where they will be read. What appears readable on the screen — where colors can be sharper — may be less legible in a printed document.

Paper

The quality of the paper affects the overall look and feel of print documents. Although inexpensive paper is fine for your earlier drafts, use

---

CONSIDERING DISABILITIES

Color for contrast

Remember when you are using color that not everyone will see it as you do. Some individuals do not perceive color at all; others perceive color in a variety of ways, especially colors like blue and green, which are close together on the color spectrum. When putting colors next to one another, then, use those on opposite sides of the color spectrum, such as purple and gold, in order to achieve high contrast. Doing so will allow readers to see the contrast, if not the nuances, of color.

8½" × 11" good-quality white bond paper for your final presentation. For résumés, you may wish to use parchment or cream-colored bond. For brochures and posters, colored paper may be appropriate as long as your text is still readable. Use the best-quality printer available to you for your final product.

Pagination

Your instructor may ask that you follow a particular pagination format for print texts (for MLA, APA, *Chicago*, and CSE styles, see Chapters 16–19); if not, beginning with the first page of text, place your last name and a number in the upper-right-hand corner of the page.

FOR MULTILINGUAL WRITERS

Reading patterns

In documents written in English and other Western languages, information tends to flow from left to right and top to bottom—since that is the way English texts are written. In some languages, which may be written from right to left or vertically, documents may be arranged from top right to bottom left. Understanding the reading patterns of the language you are working in will help you design your documents most effectively.

Type

Computers allow writers to choose among a great variety of type sizes and typefaces, or fonts. For most college writing, the easy-to-read 11- or 12-point type size is best.

This is 12-point Times New Roman
This is 11-point Times New Roman

A serif font, as is used in the main text of this book, is generally easier to read than a sans serif font. Although unusual fonts might seem attractive at first glance, readers may find such styles distracting and hard to read over long stretches of material.

Remember that typefaces help you create the tone of a document, so consider your audience and purpose when selecting type.

Different fonts convey different feelings.
Different fonts convey different feelings.
DIFFERENT FONTS CONVEY DIFFERENT FEELINGS.
Different fonts convey different feelings.

Most important, be consistent in the size and style of typeface you use, especially for the main part of your text. Unless you are striving for some special effect, shifting sizes and fonts within a document can give an appearance of disorderliness.

Spacing

Final drafts for most of your college writing should be double-spaced, with the first line of paragraphs indented one-half inch. Certain kinds of writing for certain disciplines may call for different spacing. Letters, memorandums, and online texts, for example, are usually single-spaced, with no paragraph indentation. Some long print reports may be printed with one-and-a-half-line spacing to save paper. Other kinds of documents, such as flyers and newsletters, may call for multiple columns. If in doubt, consult your instructor.

In general, leave one space after all punctuation except in the following cases:

- Leave no space before or after a dash (*Please respond—right away—to this message*).
- Leave no space before or after a hyphen (*a red-letter day*).
- Leave no space between punctuation marks ("*on my way,*").

Computers allow you to decide whether or not you want both side margins justified, or squared off—as they are on this page. Except in posters and other writing where you are trying to achieve a distinctive visual effect, you should always justify the left margin, though you may decide to indent lists and blocks of text that are set off. However, most readers—and many instructors—prefer the right margin to be "ragged," or unjustified.

23c Using headings

For brief essays and reports, you may need no headings at all. For longer documents, however, these devices call attention to the organization of the text and thus aid comprehension. Some kinds of reports use set headings (such as *Abstract* and *Summary*), which readers expect and writers therefore must provide; see 17e for an example. When you use headings, you need to decide on type size and style, wording, and placement.

Type size and style

This book, which is a long and complex document, uses various levels of headings. These levels of headings are distinguished by type sizes and fonts as well as by color.

In a college paper, you will usually distinguish levels of headings using only type—for example, all capitals for the first-level headings, capitals and lowercase boldface for the second level, capitals and lowercase italics for the third level, and so on.

FIRST-LEVEL HEADING
   Second-Level Heading
     Third-Level Heading

Consistent headings

Look for the most succinct and informative way to word headings. In general, state a topic in a single word, usually a noun (*Toxicity*); in a phrase, usually a noun phrase (*Levels of Toxicity*) or a gerund phrase (*Measuring Toxicity*); in a question that will be answered in the text (*How Can Toxicity Be Measured?*); or in an imperative that tells readers what steps to take (*Measure the Toxicity*). Whichever structure you choose, make sure you use it consistently for all headings of the same level.

Positioning

Be sure to position each level of heading consistently throughout the text. And remember not to put a heading at the very bottom of a page, since readers would have to turn to the next page to find the text that the heading is announcing.

23d Planning visuals

Creating a visual design is more likely than ever before to be a part of your process of planning for a completed writing project. Visuals can help make a point more vividly and succinctly than words alone. In some cases, visuals may even be your primary text.

Selecting visuals

Consider carefully what you want visuals to do for your writing before making your selections. What will your audience want or need you to show? Try to choose visuals that will enhance your credibility, allow you to make your point more emphatically, and clarify your overall text. (See the following table for advice on which visuals are best for particular situations.)

Effective visuals can come from many sources—your own drawings or photographs, charts or graphs you create on a computer, or materials created by others. If you are using a visual from another source, be sure to give appropriate credit and to get permission before using any visual that will be posted online or otherwise available to the public.

Identifying visuals in your writing

Position visuals alongside or after the text that refers to them. Number your visuals (number tables separately from other visuals), and give them informative titles. In some instances, you may need to provide captions to give readers additional data as source information.

Figure 1. College Enrollment for Men and Women by Age, 2007 (in millions)

Table 1. Word Choice by Race: *Seesaw* and *Teeter-totter*, Chicago, 1986

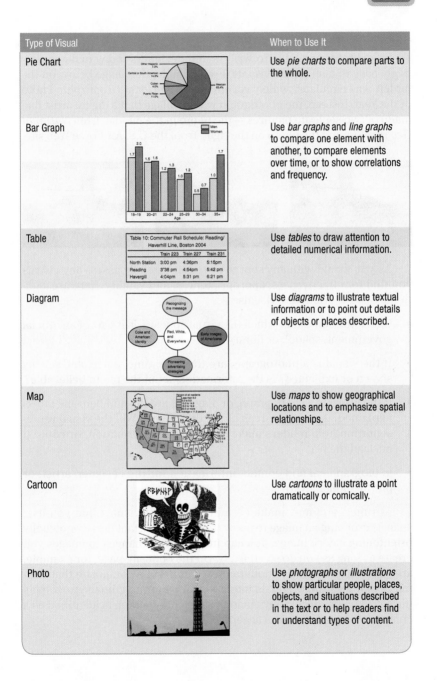

Type of Visual		When to Use It
Pie Chart		Use *pie charts* to compare parts to the whole.
Bar Graph		Use *bar graphs* and *line graphs* to compare one element with another, to compare elements over time, or to show correlations and frequency.
Table		Use *tables* to draw attention to detailed numerical information.
Diagram		Use *diagrams* to illustrate textual information or to point out details of objects or places described.
Map		Use *maps* to show geographical locations and to emphasize spatial relationships.
Cartoon		Use *cartoons* to illustrate a point dramatically or comically.
Photo		Use *photographs* or *illustrations* to show particular people, places, objects, and situations described in the text or to help readers find or understand types of content.

Analyzing and altering visuals

Technical tools available to writers and designers today make it relatively easy to manipulate visuals. For example, the image below on the far left was circulated widely via email as a *National Geographic* Photo of the Year. Instead, the photograph was a collage that a digital artist had made of two separate pictures—the photo in the middle, from *National Geographic*, and the photo on the right, from the U.S. Air Force Web site.

As you would with any source material, carefully assess any visuals you find for effectiveness, appropriateness, and validity. Here are additional tips for evaluating visuals:

- Check the context in which the visual appears. Is it part of an official government, school, or library site?

- If the visual is a photograph, are the date, time, place, and setting shown or explained? Is the information about the photo believable?

- If the visual is a chart, graph, or diagram, are the numbers and labels explained? Are the sources of the data given? Will the visual representation help readers make sense of the information, or could it mislead them?

- Is biographical and contact information for the designer, artist, or photographer given?

At times, you may make certain changes to visuals that you use, such as cropping an image to show the most important detail or digitally brightening a dark image. You can make digital changes to images you create as long as you do so ethically. On the opposite page, for example, are separate photos of a mountaintop cabin and a composite that digitally combines the originals into a single panoramic image to convey the setting more accurately. As long as the photograph is identified as a composite, the alteration is acceptable.

Combining photos can sometimes be an appropriate choice.

The composite photo conveys the setting more effectively than the individual images.

To ensure that alterations to images are ethical, follow these guidelines:

- Do not attempt to mislead readers. Show things as accurately as possible.
- If you make changes, tell your audience what you have done.
- Include all relevant information about the visual, including the source.

bedfordstmartins.com/smhandbook
Writing Resources > Design Tutorials

QUICK HELP

Using visuals effectively

- Use visual elements for a specific purpose in your text — to illustrate something, to help prove a point, or to guide readers, for example.

- Tell the audience explicitly what the visual demonstrates, especially if it presents complex information. Do not assume readers will "read" the visual the way you do; your commentary on it is important.

- Number and title all visuals. Number and label tables and figures separately.

- Refer to each visual before it appears.

- Follow established conventions for documenting visual sources, and ask permission for use if your work will become available to the public.

- Get responses to your visuals in an early draft. If readers can't follow them or are distracted by them, revise accordingly.

- If you crop, brighten, or otherwise alter visuals to include them in your writing, be sure to do so ethically.

EXERCISE 23.1

Take an essay or other writing assignment you have done recently, one that makes little use of visuals or the other design elements discussed in this chapter. Reevaluate the effectiveness of your text, and make a note of all the places where visuals and other design elements (color, different type size, and so on) would help you get your ideas across more effectively.

THINKING CRITICALLY ABOUT DESIGN FOR WRITING

Take a look at a piece of writing or a document you have recently completed. Using the advice in this chapter, assess your use of visual structure, consistent use of conventions for guiding readers through your text, and use of headings, color, font size, visuals, and other media. Then write a brief assessment of how well your text is designed and how you could improve it.

Part 5

EFFECTIVE
LANGUAGE

24 Writing to the World

People today often communicate instantaneously across vast distances and cultures. Businesspeople complete multinational transactions with the click of a mouse, students in Ohio take online classes at MIT or chat with hundreds of Facebook friends, and bloggers in Baghdad find readers in Atlanta.

Who will read what you write? What choices do you need to make in your writing to have the desired effect on your audience?

You will almost certainly find yourself writing to (or with) others throughout the country and across the globe, and students in your classes may well come from many countries and cultures. When the whole world can be your potential audience, it's time to step back and think about how to communicate successfully with such a diverse group—how to become a world writer.

24a Thinking about what seems "normal"

One good place to begin thinking about cross-cultural communication is with a hard look at your own assumptions about others. It's likely that your judgment on what's "normal" is based on assumptions you are not even aware of. But remember: behavior that is considered out of place in one context may appear perfectly normal in another. What's considered "normal" in a Facebook note or text message would be anything but in a request for an internship with a law firm. If you want to communicate with people across cultures, try to learn something about the norms in those cultures and, even more important, be aware of the norms that guide your own behavior.

Remember that most of us tend to see our own way as the "normal" or right way to do things. How do your own values and assumptions guide your thinking and behavior? Keep in mind that if your ways seem inherently right, then—even without

---

QUICK HELP

Communicating across cultures

- Recognize what you consider "normal." Examine your own customary behaviors and assumptions, and think about how they may affect what you think and say (and write). (24a)

- Listen closely to someone from another culture, and ask for clarification if necessary. Carefully define your terms. (24b)

- Think about your audience's expectations. (24c) How much authority should you have? Should you sound like an expert? a subordinate? something else? (24c1) What kind of evidence will count most with your audience? (24c2)

- Organize your writing with your audience's expectations in mind. How direct should you be? (24c3) If in doubt, use formal style. (24c4)

---

thinking about it — you may assume that other ways are somehow less than right.

- Know that most ways of communicating are influenced by cultural contexts and differ widely from one culture to the next.

- Pay close attention to the ways that people from cultures other than your own communicate, and be flexible.

- Perhaps most important, don't overgeneralize. Pay attention to and respect the differences among individual people within a given culture. Don't assume that all members of a community behave in just the same way or value exactly the same things.

- Remember that your audience may be made up of people from many backgrounds who have very different concepts about what is appropriate or "normal." So don't assume unanimity!

24b   Clarifying meaning

When an instructor called for "originality" in his students' essays, what did he mean? A Filipina student thought *originality* meant going to an original source and explaining it; a student from Massachusetts thought *originality* meant coming up with an idea entirely on her own. The professor, however, expected students to read multiple sources and develop a critical point of their own about those sources. In subsequent classes, this professor defined *originality* as he was using it in his classes, and he gave examples of student work he judged original.

This brief example points to the challenges all writers face in trying to communicate across space, across languages, across cultures. While there are no foolproof rules, here are some tips for communicating with people from cultures other than your own:

- Listen carefully. Don't hesitate to ask people to explain or even repeat a point if you're not absolutely sure you understand.

- Take care to be explicit about the meanings of the words you use.

- Invite response—ask whether you're making yourself clear. This kind of back-and-forth is particularly easy (and necessary) in email.

- Remember that sometimes a picture is worth a thousand words. A visual may help make your meaning absolutely clear.

24c Meeting audience expectations

When you do your best to meet an audience's expectations about how a text should work, your writing is more likely to have the desired effect. In practice, figuring out what audiences want, need, or expect can be difficult—especially when you are writing in public spaces online and your audiences can be composed of anyone, anywhere, with access to the Internet. If you do know something about your readers' expectations, use what you know to present your work effectively. If you know little about your potential audiences, however, err on the side of caution and carefully examine your assumptions about your readers.

1 Expectations about your authority as a writer

In the United States, students are often asked to establish authority in their writing—by drawing on certain kinds of personal experience, by reporting on research they or others have conducted, or by taking a position for which they can offer strong evidence and support. But this expectation about writerly authority is by no means universal. Indeed, some cultures view student writers as novices whose job is to reflect what they learn from their teachers—those who hold the most important knowledge, wisdom, and, hence, authority. One Japanese student, for example, said he was taught that it's rude to challenge a teacher: "Are you ever so smart that you should challenge the wisdom of the ages?"

As this student's comment reveals, a writer's tone also depends on his or her relationship with listeners and readers. In this student's case, the valued relationship is one of respect and deference, of what one Indonesian student called "good modesty." As a world writer, you need to remember that those you're addressing may hold a wide range of attitudes about authority.

- Whom are you addressing, and what is your relationship to him or her? (See 2d.)

- What knowledge are you expected to have? Is it appropriate for or expected of you to demonstrate that knowledge—and, if so, how?

- What is your goal—to answer a question? to make a point? to agree? something else? (See 2b and c.)

- What tone is appropriate? If in doubt, show respect: politeness is rarely if ever inappropriate. (See 4i.)

- What level of control do you have over your writing? In a report, you may have the final say. But if you are writing on a wiki, where you share control with others, sensitivity to communal standards is key.

2 Expectations about persuasive evidence

How do you decide what evidence will best support your ideas? The answer depends, in large part, on the audience you want to persuade. American academics generally give great weight to factual evidence. In doing research at a U.S. university, a Chinese student reports she was told by her instructors that "facts, and facts alone, provide the sure route to truth." While she learned to document her work in ways her U.S. professors found persuasive, she also continued to value the kinds of evidence often favored in China, especially those based on authority and on allusion.

Differing concepts of what counts as evidence can lead to arguments that go nowhere. Consider, for example, how rare it is for a believer in creationism to be persuaded by what the theory of evolution presents as evidence—or how rare for a supporter of evolutionary theory to be convinced by what creationists present as evidence. A person who regards biblical authority as the supreme evidence in any argument may never see eye to eye with a person who views religion and science as occupying separate spheres, each of which offers its own kind of truth. Think carefully about how you use evidence in writing, and pay attention to what counts as evidence to members of other groups you are trying to persuade.

- Should you rely on facts? concrete examples? firsthand experience? religious or philosophical texts? other sources?

- Should you include the testimony of experts? Which experts are valued most, and why?

- Should you use analogies as support? How much will they count?

- When does evidence from unedited Web sites such as blogs offer credible support, and when should you question or reject it?

- Once you determine what counts as evidence in your own thinking and writing, think about where you learned to use and value this kind of evidence. You can ask these same questions about the use of evidence by members of other cultures.

3 Expectations about organization

As you make choices about how to organize your writing, remember that cultural influences are at work here as well: the patterns that you find pleasing are likely to be ones that are deeply embedded in your own culture. For example, the organizational pattern favored by U.S. engineers, highly explicit and leaving little or nothing unsaid or unexplained, is probably familiar to most U.S. students: introduction and thesis, necessary background, overview of the parts to follow, systematic presentation of evidence, consideration of other viewpoints, and conclusion. If a piece of writing follows this pattern, American readers ordinarily find it "well organized" or "coherent."

In the United States, many audiences (especially those in the academic and business worlds) expect a writer to get to the point as directly as possible and to take on the major responsibility of articulating that point efficiently and unambiguously. But not all audiences have such expectations. For instance, a Chinese student with an excellent command of English found herself struggling in her American classes. Her writing, U.S. teachers said, was "vague," with too much "beating around the bush." As it turned out, her teachers in China had prized this kind of indirectness, expecting audiences to read between the lines. To be more explicit could send the message that readers aren't capable of such intellectual work.

When writing for audiences who may not share your expectations, then, think about how you can organize material to get your message across effectively. There are no hard and fast rules to help you organize your writing for effectiveness across cultures, but here are a few options to consider:

- Determine when to state your thesis—at the beginning? at the end? somewhere else? not at all?

- Consider whether the addition of tangential topics, what U.S. writers may think of as digressions, is a good idea, a requirement, or best avoided with your intended audience.

- Remember that electronic communication may call for certain ways of organizing. In messages or postings, you need to place the most important information first and be as succinct as possible. Or you may need to follow a template, as in submitting a résumé online.

4 Expectations about style

As with beauty, good style is most definitely in the eye of the beholder—and thus is always affected by language, culture, and rhetorical tradition. In fact, what constitutes effective style varies broadly across cultures and depends on the rhetorical situation—purpose, audience, and so on (see Chapter 2). Even so, there is one important style question to consider when writing across cultures: what level of formality is most appropriate? In most writing to a general audience in the United States, a fairly informal style is often acceptable, even appreciated. Many cultures, however, tend to value a more formal approach. When in doubt, it may be wise to err on the side of formality in writing to people from other cultures, especially to elders or to those in authority.

- Be careful to use proper titles:

    Dr. Atul Gawande   Professor Jaime Mejía

- Avoid slang and informal structures such as fragments.

- Do not use first names of people you do not know in correspondence (even in text messages) unless invited to do so. Note, however, that an invitation to use a first name could come indirectly; if someone signs a message to you with his or her first name, you are implicitly invited to use the first name as a term of address. (See Chapter 20 for more on electronic communication.)

- For business correspondence, use complete sentences and words; avoid contractions. Open with the salutation "Dear Mr./Ms. " or the person's title, if you know it. Write dates with the day before the month, and spell out the name of the month: *7 June 2010.*

Beyond formality, other stylistic preferences vary widely, and context matters. Long, complex sentences and ornate language may be exactly what some audiences are looking for. On Twitter, on the other hand, writers have to limit their message to 140 characters—so using abbreviated words, symbols, and fragments is expected, even desirable, there.

World writers, then, should take very little about language for granted. To be an effective world writer, aim to recognize and respect stylistic differences as you move from community to community and to meet expectations whenever you can.

THINKING CRITICALLY ABOUT ASSUMPTIONS IN YOUR WRITING

Choose one or two recent essays or other pieces of writing, and examine them carefully, noting what you assume about what counts as persuasive evidence, good organization, and effective style. How do you represent yourself in relation to your audience? What assumptions do you make about the audience and are such assumptions warranted? What other unstated assumptions about good writing can you identify?

Language That Builds Common Ground

25

Language that shows respect for differences and builds common ground can help persuade readers. Few absolute guidelines exist for using such language, but two general rules can help: consider the sensitivities and preferences of others, and watch for words that carry stereotypes and betray your assumptions, even though you have not directly stated them.

25a Avoiding stereotypes and generalizations

Kids like video games; U.S. citizens value individual freedom; people who drop out of high school do not get the best jobs. These broad statements contain stereotypes, standardized or fixed ideas about a group. To some extent, we all think in terms of stereotypes, and sometimes they can be helpful in making a generalization. Stereotyping any individual on the basis of generalizations about a group, however, can lead to inaccurate and even hurtful conclusions.

For example, an instructor who notes a fraternity member's absence from class on the morning after a big frat party and remarks, "Ah, he must be nursing a hangover," is stereotyping the student on the basis of assumptions about fraternity men. But such stereotyping may be far off the mark with this particular student—and with many other fraternity members. By indulging in it, this instructor may well be alienating some of her students and undermining her effectiveness as a teacher.

As a child, you may have heard people say "sticks and stones will break my bones, but words will never hurt me." But words can hurt; indeed, the words we select have the power to praise, delight, inspire—or offend and even destroy. That's why we refer to "a stinging rebuke" or "a cutting remark." Words that offend prevent others from identifying with you and thus damage your credibility.

QUICK HELP

Editing to build common ground

- What stereotypes and other assumptions might come between you and your readers? Look, for instance, for language implying approval or disapproval and for the ways you use *we*, *you*, and *they*. (25a)

- Avoid potentially sexist language, and omit irrelevant references to gender. Be careful not to assume gender based on occupation, and use gender-neutral nouns when you may be referring to either men or women (*firefighters* instead of *firemen*, for instance). Avoid using a masculine pronoun such as *he* or *him* to refer to a person who may be female. (25b)

- Make sure your references to race, religion, gender, sexual orientation, physical ability, age, and so on are relevant or necessary to your discussion. (25b–d)

- Are the terms you use to refer to groups accurate and acceptable? Pay attention to the terms that members of the group prefer. (25c and d)

Because stereotypes are often based on half-truths, misunderstandings, and hand-me-down prejudices, they can lead to intolerance, bias, and bigotry. But even positive stereotypes — for example, *Jewish doctors are the best* — or neutral ones — *college students like pizza* — can hurt, for they inevitably ignore the uniqueness of an individual.

Other kinds of unstated assumptions also destroy common ground by ignoring the differences between others and ourselves. For example, a student in a religion seminar who uses *we* to refer to Christians and *they* to refer to members of other religions had better be sure that everyone in the class is Christian, or some people present may feel left out of the discussion.

Sometimes assumptions even lead writers to call special attention to a group affiliation when it is not relevant to the point, as in a *woman bus driver* or a *white basketball player*. Decisions about whether to generalize about a group or to describe an individual as a member of a group are often difficult for writers. Think about how your language can build — rather than destroy — common ground.

25b Avoiding assumptions about gender

An elementary teacher in Toronto got tired of seeing hands go up every time the children sang the line in Canada's national anthem, "True patriot love in all thy sons command." "When do we get to the part about the daughters?" the children inevitably asked. The children's questions point to the ways in which gender-related words can subtly affect our thinking and behavior. For instance, many young women at one time were discouraged from pursuing careers in medicine at least partially because speakers commonly referred to hypothetical doctors as *he* (and labeled any woman who worked as a doctor a *woman doctor*, as if to say, "She's an exception; doctors are normally men"). Similarly, a label like *male nurse* may offend by reflecting stereotyped assumptions about proper roles for men. Equally problematic is the traditional use of *man* and *mankind* to refer to people of both sexes and the use of *he, him, his,* and *himself* to refer to people of unknown sex. Because such usage ignores half the human race, it hardly helps a writer build common ground.

Who is a nurse and who is a doctor? Be careful not to make assumptions based on gender stereotypes.

Revising sexist language

Sexist language, those words and phrases that stereotype or ignore members of either sex or that unnecessarily call attention to gender, can usually be revised fairly easily. There are several alternatives to using masculine pronouns to refer to persons of unknown sex. (See also 32g.)

One option is to recast the sentence using plural forms.

> Lawyers   they
> ◗ ~~A lawyer~~ must pass the bar exam before ~~he~~ can begin to practice.

Another option is to substitute *he or she, him or her,* and so on.

>   or she
> ◗ A lawyer must pass the bar exam before he can begin to practice.

Yet another way to revise the sentence is to eliminate the pronouns.

>   beginning
> ◗ A lawyer must pass the bar exam before ~~he can begin~~ to practice.

You should also try to eliminate words that make assumptions about gender or emphasize it for no good reason.

INSTEAD OF	TRY USING
anchorman, anchorwoman	anchor
businessman	businessperson, business executive
chairman, chairwoman	chair, chairperson
congressman	member of Congress, representative
fireman	firefighter
mailman	mail carrier
male secretary	secretary
man, mankind	humans, human beings, humanity, the human race, humankind
manpower	workers, personnel
mothering	parenting
policeman, policewoman	police officer
salesman	salesperson
woman engineer	engineer

EXERCISE 25.1

The following excerpt is taken from the 1948 edition of Dr. Benjamin Spock's *Baby and Child Care.* Read it carefully, noting any language we might now consider sexist. Then try bringing it up-to-date by revising the passage, substituting nonsexist language as necessary.

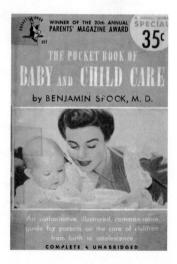

When you suggest something that doesn't appeal to your baby, he feels he *must* assert himself. His nature tells him to. He just says "no" in words or actions, even about things that he likes to do. The psychologists call it "negativism"; mothers call it "that terrible *no* stage." But stop and think what would happen to him if he never felt like saying "no." He'd become a robot, a mechanical man. You wouldn't be able to resist the temptation to boss him all the time, and he'd stop learning and developing. When he was old enough to go out into the world, to school and later to work, everybody else would take advantage of him, too. He'd never be good for anything.

bedfordstmartins.com/smhandbook
Exercise Central > Language > Common Ground

25c Avoiding assumptions about race and ethnicity

Generalizations about racial and ethnic groups can result in especially harmful stereotyping. To build common ground, then, avoid language that ignores differences not only among individual members of a race or ethnic group but also among subgroups. Writers must be aware, for instance, of the diverse places from which Americans of Spanish-speaking ancestry have come.

Using preferred terms

When writing about an ethnic or racial group, how can you refer to that group in terms that its members actually desire? Doing so is sometimes not an easy task, for terms can change often and vary widely.

The word *colored*, for example, was once widely used in the United States to refer to Americans of African ancestry. By the 1950s, the preferred term had become *Negro*. This changed in the 1960s, however, as *black* came to be preferred by most, though certainly not all, members of that community. Since the late 1980s, both *black*—sometimes capitalized (*Black*)—and *African American* have been widely used.

The word *Oriental*, once used to refer to people of East Asian descent, is now often considered offensive. At the University of California at Berkeley, the Oriental Languages Department is now known as the East Asian Languages Department. One advocate of the change explained that *Oriental* is appropriate for objects—like rugs—but not for people.

Once widely preferred, the term *Native American* is being challenged by those who argue that the most appropriate way to refer to indigenous peoples is by the specific name of the tribe or pueblo, such as *Chippewa* or *Diné*. Many indigenous peoples once referred to as *Eskimos* now prefer *Inuit* or a specific term such as *Tlingit*. It has also become fairly common for tribal groups to refer to themselves as *Indians* or *Indian tribes*.

Among Americans of Spanish-speaking descent, the preferred terms of reference are many: *Chicano/Chicana, Hispanic, Latin American, Latino/Latina, Mexican American, Dominican,* and *Puerto Rican,* to name but a few.

Clearly, then, ethnic terminology changes often enough to challenge the most careful writers — including writers who belong to the groups they are writing about. Consider your words carefully, seek information about ways members of groups refer to themselves (or ask about preferences), but don't expect one person to speak for all members of a group or expect unanimity on such terms. Finally, check any term you are unsure of in a current dictionary. *Random House Webster's College Dictionary* includes particularly helpful usage notes about racial and ethnic designations.

25d   Considering other kinds of difference

Gender, race, and ethnicity are among the most frequent challenges to a writer seeking to find common ground with readers, but you will face many others as well.

1   Age

Mention age if it is relevant, but be aware that age-related terms can carry derogatory connotations (*matronly, well-preserved,* and so on). Although describing Mr. Fry as *elderly but still active* may sound polite to you, chances are Mr. Fry would prefer being called *an active seventy-eight-year-old* — or just *a seventy-eight-year-old,* which eliminates the unstated assumption of surprise that he is active at his age.

2   Class

Take special care to examine your words for assumptions about class. In a *New York Times* column, for example, a young woman wrote about losing her high-paying professional job. Unable to find other "meaningful work," as she put it, she was forced to accept "absurd" jobs like cleaning houses and baby-sitting.

The column provoked a number of angry letters to the *Times,* including this one: "So the young and privileged are learning what we of the working classes have always understood too well: there is no entitlement in life. We have always taken the jobs you label 'absurd.' Our mothers are the women who clean your mothers' houses."

As a writer, then, do not assume that all your readers share your background or values—that your classmates all own cars, for instance. And avoid using any words—*redneck, old money,* and the like—that might alienate members of an audience.

3 Geographic area

Geography does not necessarily determine personality, politics, or life-style. New Englanders are not all thrifty and tight-lipped; people in "red states" may hold liberal social and political views; midwesterners are not always polite. Check your writing carefully to be sure it doesn't make such simplistic assumptions.

Check also that you use geographic terms accurately:

AMERICA, AMERICAN	Although many people use these words to refer to the United States alone, such usage will not necessarily be acceptable to people from Canada, Mexico, and Central or South America.
BRITISH, ENGLISH	Use *British* to refer to the island of Great Britain, which includes England, Scotland, and Wales, or to the United Kingdom of Great Britain and Northern Ireland. In general, do not use *English* for these broader senses.
ARAB	This term refers only to people of Arabic-speaking descent. Note that Iran is not an Arab nation; its people speak Farsi, not Arabic. Note also that *Arab* is not synonymous with *Muslim* or *Moslem* (a believer in Islam). Most (but not all) Arabs are Muslims, but many Muslims (those in Pakistan, for example) are not Arab.

4 Physical ability or health

When writing about a person with a serious illness or disability, ask yourself whether mentioning the disability is relevant to your discussion and whether the words you use carry negative connotations. You might choose, for example, to say someone *uses* a wheelchair rather than to say he or she is *confined to* one. Similarly, you might note a subtle but meaningful difference between calling someone *a person with AIDS* rather than *an AIDS victim.* Mentioning the person first and the

CONSIDERING DISABILITIES

Knowing your readers

The American Council on Education reports that nearly 10 percent of all first-year college students—some 155,000—identify themselves as having one or more disabilities. As this figure suggests, living with a disability is more the norm than many previously thought. And the actual figure may well be higher, since many students with disabilities do not identify themselves as disabled. Effective writers learn as much as possible about their readers so that they can find ways to build common ground.

disability second, such as referring to a *child with diabetes* rather than a *diabetic child* or a *diabetic*, is always a good idea. In addition, remember that people with disabilities may well resent the use of euphemisms like "physically challenged" because such terms can minimize the importance of a disability.

5 Religion

Religious stereotypes are very often inaccurate and unfair. For example, Roman Catholics hold a wide spectrum of views on abortion, Muslim women do not all wear veils, and many Baptists are not fundamentalists—so beware making generalizations based on religion. In fact, many people do not believe in or practice a religion at all, so be careful of such assumptions. As in other cases, do not use religious labels at all unless they are relevant.

6 Sexual orientation

If you wish to build common ground, do not assume that readers all share one sexual orientation—that everyone is attracted to the opposite sex, for example. As with any label, reference to sexual orientation should be governed by context. Someone writing about Representative Barney Frank's or Federal Reserve Chairman Ben Bernanke's economic views would probably have no reason to refer to either person's sexual orientation. On the other hand, someone writing about diversity in U.S. government might find it important to note that Frank has long made his homosexuality public.

THINKING CRITICALLY ABOUT HOW LANGUAGE CAN BUILD COMMON GROUND

Writer and filmmaker Ruth Ozeki has written widely on issues related to the environment. In this June 2009 posting from her blog, Ozeki appeals to readers to step back and cultivate silence as a necessary prelude to making difficult decisions. Who is the "we" that Ozeki addresses? What views and values do you think she expects her readers to share with her? Note the strategies the writer uses to establish common ground with readers in this paragraph.

> I'm more and more convinced that we need to cultivate mindful silence, and share it with others whenever possible, if we are going to be able to make the careful and difficult choices we will need to make in order to survive in a wired and warming world. This seems to me to be a key piece of activism and eco-pedagogy that we can all learn to cultivate. —RUTH OZEKI, Ozekiland (Weblog)

26 Language Variety

As a college student, you will be called on to think carefully about how to make appropriate choices. Since standard academic English will be the expected variety of English for most if not all your writing for your classes, you will want to use it effectively. But you may also choose to use another language or another variety of English for rhetorical purpose or special effect. Strong writers recognize these differences and learn to use all their languages and language varieties in the most appropriate ways.

26a Using varieties of language in academic writing

How do writers decide when to use another language or when to use a particular variety of English — when to insert eastern Tennessee dialect or African American vernacular patterns into a formal essay, for example? Even writers who are perfectly fluent in several languages must think carefully before switching linguistic gears. The key to shifting among varieties of English and among languages is appropriateness: you need to consider when such shifts will help you connect with your audience, get their attention, make a particular point, or represent the actual words of someone you are writing about.

Sometimes writers' choices are limited by various kinds of pressures. One example is the tendency of many to discriminate against those who fail to use an expected variety of English. Some listeners

When Pulitzer Prize–winning author Junot Díaz spoke to a group of first-year college students in California in 2008, he used colloquial English and Spanish, plus a few four-letter words — and the students loved every minute of it. When he was interviewed a month later on National Public Radio, however, Díaz addressed his nationwide audience in standard English.

Comedian Dave Chappelle has observed, "Every black American is bilingual. We speak street vernacular, and we speak job interview." Like Chappelle and Díaz, you probably already adjust the variety of English you use depending on how well — and how formally — you know the audience you are addressing. If you speak another language in addition to English, you may find yourself using different languages for different situations.

QUICK HELP

Using varieties of language effectively

Standard (26b) and nonstandard (26c and d) varieties of English, as well as other languages (26e), can all be used very effectively for the following purposes in your writing:

- to repeat someone's exact words
- to evoke a person, place, or activity
- to establish your credibility and build common ground
- to make a strong point
- to get your audience's attention

---

discriminate against speakers of so-called "nonstandard" varieties of English; in other communities, other audiences distrust speech that they consider "too proper." Used appropriately and wisely, however, all varieties of English can serve good purposes.

26b Using standard varieties of English

One variety of English, often referred to as "standard" or "standard academic," is taught prescriptively in schools, represented in this and most other textbooks, used in the national media, and written and spoken widely by those wielding the most social and economic power. As the language used in business and most public institutions, standard English is a variety you will want to be completely familiar with — while recognizing that it is only one of many effective and powerful varieties of our language.

Even standard English is hardly a monolith, however; the standard varies according to purpose and audience, from the very formal style used in most academic writing to the informal style characteristic of casual conversation. Thus there is usually more than one "standard" way to say or write something. Nevertheless, recognizable practices and conventions do exist, and they go by the shorthand name of standard English. (For more on academic conventions, see Chapter 1.)

> **FOR MULTILINGUAL WRITERS**
> ## Global varieties of English
>
> Like other world languages, English is used in many countries, so it has many global varieties. For example, British English differs somewhat from U.S. English in certain vocabulary (*bonnet for hood* of a car), syntax (*to hospital* rather than *to the hospital*), spelling (*centre* rather than *center*), and pronunciation. If you have learned a non-American variety of English, you will want to recognize, and to appreciate, the ways in which it differs from the variety widely used in U.S. academic settings.

26c Using varieties of English to evoke a place or community

> "Ever'body says words different," said Ivy. "Arkansas folks says 'em different from Oklahomy folks says 'em different. And we seen a lady from Massachusetts, an' she said 'em differentest of all. Couldn' hardly make out what she was sayin'."
> —JOHN STEINBECK, *The Grapes of Wrath*

Using the language of a local community is an effective way to evoke a character or place. Author and radio host Garrison Keillor, for example, peppers his tales of his native Minnesota with the homespun English spoken there: "I once was a tall dark heartbreaker who, when I slouched into a room, women jumped up and asked if they could get me something, and now they only smile and say, 'My mother is a big fan of yours. You sure are a day-brightener for her. You sure make her chuckle.'"

Weaving together regionalisms and standard English can also be effective in creating a sense of place. Here, an anthropologist writing about one Carolina community takes care to let the residents speak their minds—and in their own words:

> For Roadville, schooling is something most folks have not gotten enough of, but everybody believes will do something toward helping an individual "get on." In the words of one oldtime resident, "Folks that ain't got no schooling don't get to be nobody nowadays."
>
> —SHIRLEY BRICE HEATH, *Ways with Words*

Varieties of language can also help writers evoke other kinds of communities. In this panel from *One! Hundred! Demons!*, Lynda Barry uses playground language to present a vivid image of remembered childhood games. See how kids' use of slang ("Dag") and colloquialisms ("Whose up is it?") helps readers join in the experience.

26d Using varieties of English to build credibility with a community

Whether you are American Indian or trace your ancestry to Europe, Asia, Latin America, Africa, or elsewhere, your heritage lives on in the diversity of the English language.

See how one Hawaiian writer uses a local variety of English to paint a picture of young teens hearing a "chicken skin" story from their grandmother.

" — So, rather dan being rid of da shark, da people were stuck with many little ones, for dere mistake."

Then Grandma Wong wen' pause, for dramatic effect, I guess, and she wen' add, "Dis is one of dose times. Dis is da time of da mano." She wen' look at my kid brother 'Analu and said, "Da time of da sharks."

Those words ended another of Grandma's chicken skin stories. The stories she told us had been passed on to her by her grandmother, who had heard them from her grandmother. Always skipping a generation.

—RODNEY MORALES, "When the Shark Bites"

Notice how the narrator of the story uses both standard and nonstandard varieties of English—presenting information necessary to the story line mostly in standard English and using a local, ethnic variety to represent spoken language.

In a similar vein, Zora Neale Hurston's work often mixes African American vernacular with standard English.

> My grandmother worried about my forward ways a great deal. She had known slavery and to her my brazenness was unthinkable.
>
> "Git down offa dat gate-post! You li'l sow, you! Git down! Setting up dere looking dem white folks right in de face! They's gowine to lynch you, yet. And don't stand in dat doorway gazing out at 'em neither. Youse too brazen to live long."
>
> Nevertheless, I kept right on gazing at them, and "going a piece of the way" whenever I could make it.

—ZORA NEALE HURSTON, *Dust Tracks on a Road*

In each of these examples, one important reason for the shift from standard English is to demonstrate that the writer is a member of the community whose language he or she is representing and thus to build credibility with others in the community.

Take care, however, in using the language of communities other than your own. When used inappropriately, such language can have an opposite effect, perhaps destroying credibility and alienating your audience.

EXERCISE 26.1

Identify the purpose and audience for one of this chapter's examples of regional, ethnic, or communal varieties of English. Then rewrite the passage to remove all evidence of any variety of English other than the "standard." Compare your revised version with the original and with those produced by some of your classmates. What differences do you notice in tone (is it more formal? more distant? something else?) and in overall impression? Which version seems most appropriate for the intended audience and purpose? Which do you prefer, and why?

26e Using other languages

You might use a language other than English for the same reasons you might use different varieties of English: to represent the actual words of a speaker, to make a point, to connect with your audience, or to get their attention.

See how Gerald Haslam uses Spanish to capture his great-grandmother's words as well as to make a point about his relationship to her.

"*Expectoran su sangre!*" exclaimed Great-grandma when I showed her the small horned toad I had removed from my breast pocket. I turned toward my mother, who translated: "They spit blood."

"*De los ojos,*" Grandma added. "From their eyes," mother explained, herself uncomfortable in the presence of the small beast.

I grinned, "Awwwwwww."

But my Great-grandmother did not smile. "*Son muy tóxicos,*" she nodded with finality. Mother moved back an involuntary step, her hands suddenly busy at her breast. "Put that thing down," she ordered.

"His name's John," I said. **—GERALD HASLAM,** *California Childhood*

In the following passage, notice how the novelist Michele Herman uses Yiddish to evoke her grandmother's world:

> "Skip *shabes*?" Rivke chuckled. "I don't think this is possible. Once a week comes *shabes*. About this a person doesn't have a choice."
>
> "What I *mean*"—Myra's impatience was plain—"is skip the preparation. It's too much for you, it tires you out."
>
> "Ach," Rivke said. "Too much for me it isn't." This wasn't true. For some time she had felt that it really was too much for her. It was only for *shabes* that she cooked; the rest of the week she ate cold cereal, fruit, pot cheese, crackers.
>
> **—MICHELE HERMAN,** *Missing*

In this passage, Rivke's syntax—the inversion of word order (*Once a week comes* *shabes,* for example, and *Too much for me it isn't*)—reflects Yiddish rhythms. In addition, the use of the Yiddish *shabes* carries a strong association with a religious institution, one that would be lost if it were translated to "sabbath." It is not "sabbath" to Rivke; it is *shabes.*

In the following passage, a linguist uses Spanish—and English translations—in her discussion of literacy in a Mexican community in Chicago:

> *Gracia* (grace, wit) is used to refer to wittiness in talk; people who *tiene gracia* (have grace, are witty) are seen as clever and funny. Not everyone illustrates this quality, but those who do are obvious from the moment they speak. As one middle-aged male said,
>
> *. . . cuando ellos empiezan a hablar, desde el momento que los oyes hablar, tienen gracia. Entonces, la gente que tiene gracia, se va juntando gente a oírlos. Y hay gente más desabrida, diría yo. No tiene, no le quedan sus chistes. Aunque cuente uno una charrita . . . ya no te vas a reír igual.*
>
> (. . . when they start to speak, from the moment that you hear them speak, they are witty. So then, the people who are witty begin to have a listening crowd gather about them. And then there are people who are more boring, I would say. They don't have, their jokes just don't make it. Even though they may tell a joke . . . you're not going to laugh in the same manner.)
>
> **—MARCIA FARR,** "Essayist Literacy and Other Verbal Performances"

Here, Farr provides a translation of the Spanish, for she expects that many of her readers will not know Spanish. She evokes the language of the community she describes, however, by presenting the Spanish first.

In general, you should not assume that all your readers will understand another language. So, in most cases, including a translation (as Marcia Farr does) is appropriate. Occasionally, however, the words from the other language will be clear from the context (as is *shabes* in Michele Herman's passage). At other times, a writer might leave something untranslated to make a point—to let readers know what it's like not to understand, for example.

THINKING CRITICALLY ABOUT LANGUAGE VARIETY

The following description of a meal features English that is characteristic of the Florida backwoods in the 1930s. Using this passage as an example, write a description of a memorable event from your daily life. Try to include some informal dialogue. Then look at the language you used—do you use more than one variety of English? What effect does your use of language have on your description?

Jody heard nothing; saw nothing but his plate. He had never been so hungry in his life, and after a lean winter and a slow spring . . . his mother had cooked a supper good enough for the preacher. There were poke-greens with bits of white bacon buried in them; sandbuggers made of potato and onion and the cooter he had found crawling yesterday; sour orange biscuits and at his mother's elbow the sweet potato pone. He was torn between his desire for more biscuits and another sandbugger and the knowledge, born of painful experience, that if he ate them, he would suddenly have no room for pone. The choice was plain.

—MARJORIE KINNAN RAWLINGS, *The Yearling*

27

Word Choice

Deciding which word is the right word can be a challenge. English has borrowed and absorbed words from other languages for centuries, so it's not unusual to find many words that have similar but subtly different meanings—and choosing one instead of another can make a very different impression on the audience. For instance, the "pasta with marinara sauce" served in a restaurant may look and taste much like the "macaroni and gravy" served at an Italian American family dinner, but in each case the choice of words says something not only about the food but also about the people serving it—and about the people they expect to serve it to.

To choose the right words, you need to think about what is appropriate for your purpose, topic, and audience—the context for your writing. The perfect words for a band profile on MySpace, for example, will be very different from words that are precisely right for a news report or an oral presentation in a marketing class.

27a Choosing appropriate words for the context

A writer's tone and level of formality vary with context. In an email or letter to a friend or close associate, informal language is often expected and appropriate. But when you are addressing people you do not know well, as in most academic and professional writing, more formal language is likely to have a better effect on your audience. Compare these responses to a request for information about a job candidate:

EMAIL TO SOMEONE YOU KNOW WELL
Maisha is great—hire her if you can!

LETTER OF RECOMMENDATION TO SOMEONE YOU DO NOT KNOW
I am pleased to recommend Maisha Fisher. She will bring good ideas and extraordinary energy to your organization.

In deciding on the right words to use in a particular piece of writing, a writer needs to be aware of the possibilities and pitfalls of different kinds of

---

Editing for appropriate and precise language

- Check to see that your language reflects the appropriate level of formality and courtesy for your audience, purpose, and topic. If you use informal language (such as *yeah*), is it appropriate? (27a)

- Unless you are writing for a specialized audience that will understand technical jargon, either define the jargon or replace it with words that will be understood. (27a2)

- Revise any pompous language, inappropriate euphemisms, or double-speak. (27a3)

- Consider the connotations of words carefully. If you say someone is *pushy*, be sure you mean to be critical; otherwise, use a word like *assertive*. (27b)

- Be sure to use both general and specific words. If you are writing about the general category of "beds," for example, do you give enough concrete detail (*an antique four-poster bed*)? (27c)

- Look for clichés, and replace them with fresher language. (27d)

---

language, including slang and colloquial language; technical and occupational language; and pompous language, euphemisms, and double-speak.

1 Slang and colloquial language

Slang, or extremely informal language, is often confined to a relatively small group and usually becomes obsolete rather quickly, though some slang gains wide use (*duh, cool*). Colloquial language, such as *in a bind* or *snooze*, is slightly less informal, more widely used, and longer lasting than most slang.

Writers who use slang and colloquial language in the wrong context run the risk of not being understood or of not being taken seriously. If you are writing for a general audience about gun-control legislation, for example, and you use terms like *gat* or *Mac* to refer to types of weapons, some readers may not know what you mean, and others may be irritated by what they see as a frivolous reference to a deadly serious subject.

EXERCISE 27.1

Choose something or someone to describe—a favorite cousin, a stranger on the bus, an automobile, a musical instrument, whatever strikes your fancy. Describe your subject using colloquial language and slang. Then rewrite the description, this time using neither of these. Read the two passages aloud, and note what different effects each version creates.

2 | Technical and occupational language

Those who work—or play—in particular fields sometimes create their own technical language. Businesspeople talk about *e-tailers* and *upside movement*, biologists about *nucleotides* and *immunodestruction*, and baseball fans about *fielder's choices* and *suicide bunts*. If you use any technical or occupation-specific language, make sure that your audience will understand your terms, and replace or define those that they will not. Technical and occupational language can be divided into two overlapping categories: neologisms and jargon.

TALKING THE TALK

Texting abbreviations

"Can I use text-message slang when I contact my teacher?" In an IM chat or in a text message, abbreviations such as *u* for *you* are conventional usage, but using such shortcuts when communicating with an instructor can be a serious mistake. At least some of your instructors are likely to view these informal shortcuts as disrespectful, unprofessional, or simply sloppy writing. Unless your instructor has invited you to use text-message lingo, keep to the conventions of standard English for your college writing—even in email.

Neologisms

Defined as new words that have not yet found their way into dictionaries, neologisms are especially useful in rapidly changing fields, such as business and sciences. Terms like *nanotechnology* (coined in 1974 and popularized in the 1980s) and *vortal* (from "vertical portal"), for example, could not be easily replaced except by much more complex explanations. Some neologisms, however, do not meet a real need and are unlikely to have staying power. Before including a neologism in your writing, then, consider whether your audience will understand and appreciate it.

Jargon

Jargon is the special vocabulary of a trade or profession, enabling members to speak and write concisely to one another. Reserve jargon for an audience that will understand your terms. The example that follows, from a blog about fonts and typefaces, uses jargon appropriately for an interested and knowledgeable audience.

The Modern typeface classification is usually associated with Didones and display faces that often have too much contrast for text use. The Ingeborg family was designed with the intent of producing a Modern face that was readable at any size. Its roots might well be historic, but its approach is very contemporary. The three text weights (Regular, Bold, and Heavy) are functional and discreet while the Display weights (Fat and Block) catch the reader's eye with a dynamic form and a whole lot of ink on the paper. The family includes a boatload of extras like unicase alternates, swash caps, and a lined fill.

—FONTSHOP.COM Blog

Depending on the needs of the audience, jargon can be irritating and incomprehensible — or extremely helpful. Terms that begin as jargon for specialists (such as *asynchronous* or *vertical integration*) can quickly become part of the mainstream if they provide a useful shorthand for an otherwise lengthy explanation. Before you use technical jargon, remember your readers: if they will not understand the terms, or if you don't know them well enough to judge, then say what you need to say in everyday language.

3 Pompous language, euphemisms, and doublespeak

Stuffy or pompous language is unnecessarily formal for the purpose, audience, or topic. It gives writing an insincere or unintentionally humorous tone, making a writer's ideas seem insignificant or even unbelievable.

POMPOUS

Pursuant to the August 9 memorandum regarding petroleum supply exigencies, it is incumbent upon us to endeavor to make maximal utilization of telephonic communication in lieu of personal visitation.

REVISED

As noted in the August 9 memo, please make telephone calls rather than personal visits whenever possible because of the gasoline shortage.

As these examples illustrate, some writers use words in an attempt to sound expert or important, and these puffed-up words can easily backfire.

INSTEAD OF	TRY USING
ascertain	find out
commence	begin
finalize	finish or complete
functionality	function
impact (as a verb)	affect
methodology	method
operationalize	start; put into operation
optimal	best
parameters	boundaries
peruse	look at
ramp up	increase
utilize	use

Euphemisms are words and phrases that make unpleasant ideas seem less harsh. *Your position is being eliminated* seeks to soften the blow of being fired or laid off. Other euphemisms include *pass on* for *die* and *plus-sized* for *fat*. Although euphemisms can sometimes show that the writer is considerate of people's feelings, such language can also sound insincere or evasive — or can unintentionally insult by implying that the term or idea being avoided is something shameful.

Unlike euphemisms, *doublespeak*, a word coined from the *Newspeak* and *doublethink* of George Orwell's novel *1984*, is language used deliberately to hide or distort the truth. During cutbacks in the business world, companies may speak of layoffs as *employee repositioning* or *proactive downsizing*, and of unpaid time off as a *furlough*. Nevertheless, most people — and particularly those who have lost jobs or taken pay cuts — recognize these terms as doublespeak.

Avoiding fancy language

In writing standard academic English, which is fairly formal, students are often tempted to use many "big words" instead of simple language. Although learning impressive words can be a good way to expand your vocabulary, it is usually best to avoid flowery or fancy language in college writing. Academic writing at U.S. universities tends to value clear, concise prose.

EXERCISE 27.2

Revise each of these sentences to use formal language consistently. Example:

> Although   be enthusiastic   as soon as
> I can ~~get all enthused~~ about writing, ~~but~~ I sit down to write, ~~and~~ my
>   ^   ^   ^
>   blank.
> mind goes ~~right to sleep.~~
>   ^

1. In Shakespeare's *Othello*, Desdemona just lies down like some kind of wimp and accepts her death as inevitable.

2. The budget office doesn't want to cough up the cash to replace the drafty windows, but cranking up the heat in the building all winter doesn't come cheap.

3. Finding all that bling in King Tut's tomb was one of the biggest archeological scores of the twentieth century.

4. In unfamiliar settings or with people he did not know well, Duncan often came off as kind of snooty, but in reality he was scared to death.

5. My family lived in Trinidad for the first ten years of my life, and we went through a lot of bad stuff there, but when we came to the United States, we thought we finally had it made.

> bedfordstmartins.com/smhandbook
> **Exercise Central > Language > Word Choice**

27b   Using words with appropriate connotations

Thinking of a stone tossed into a pool and ripples spreading out from it can help you understand the distinction between *denotation*, the dictionary meaning of a word (the stone), and *connotation*, the associations that accompany the word (the ripples).

Words with similar denotations may have connotations that vary widely. The words *enthusiasm, passion,* and *obsession,* for instance, all have roughly the same dictionary meaning. But the associations called up by each word are quite different: an *enthusiasm* is a pleasurable and absorbing interest; a *passion* has a strong emotional component and may affect someone positively or negatively; an *obsession* is an unhealthy attachment that excludes other interests. *Pushy* and *assertive* also have similar denotations but different connotations—one negative, the other neutral or positive.

Take special care to use words with the appropriate connotations for your intended meaning. Note the differences in connotation among the following three statements:

▷ **The group Students Against Racism erected a temporary barrier on the campus oval. Members say it symbolizes "the many barriers to those discriminated against by university policies."**

▷ **Left-wing agitators planted an eyesore right on the oval to try to stampede the university into giving in to their every demand.**

▷ **Supporters of human rights for all students challenged the university's investment in racism by erecting a protest barrier on campus.**

The first statement is neutral, merely stating facts (and quoting the assertion about university policy to represent it as someone's words rather than as facts); the second, by using words with negative connotations (*agitators, eyesore, stampede*), is strongly critical; the third, by using words with positive connotations (*supporters of human rights*) and presenting assertions as facts (*the university's investment in racism*), gives a favorable slant to the group's actions. Political parties use words with loaded connotations regularly: during the health care reform debate in 2009–2010, for example, anti-reform groups used the term *death panels* to describe legislation that would reimburse doctors for optional consultations with patients about hospice care, living wills, and similar services.

EXERCISE 27.3

From the parentheses, choose the word with the denotation that makes most sense in the context of the sentence. Use a dictionary if necessary.

1. She listened (*apprehensively / attentively*) to the lecture and took notes.
2. The telemarketers were told to (*empathize / emphasize*) more expensive items.
3. The interns were (*conscientious / conscious*) workers who listened carefully and learned fast.

4. Franklin advised his readers to be frugal and (*industrial/industrious*).

5. All (*proceedings/proceeds*) from the bake sale went to the athletics program.

EXERCISE 27.4

Study the italicized words in each of the following passages, and decide what each word's connotations contribute to your understanding of the passage. Think of a synonym for each word, and see if you can decide what difference the new word would make on the effect of the passage.

1. If boxing is a sport, it is the most *tragic* of all sports because, more than any human activity, it consumes the very excellence it displays: Its very *drama* is this consumption.   —JOYCE CAROL OATES, "On Boxing"

2. Then one evening Miss Glory told me to serve the ladies on the porch. After I set the tray down and turned toward the kitchen, one of the women asked, "What's your name, *girl*?"   —MAYA ANGELOU, *I Know Why the Caged Bird Sings*

3. The Kiowas are a summer people; they *abide* the cold and keep to themselves; but when the season *turns* and the land becomes warm and *vital*, they cannot *hold still*.   —N. SCOTT MOMADAY, "The Way to Rainy Mountain"

> bedfordstmartins.com/smhandbook
> **Exercise Central** > **Language** > **Word Choice**

27c Balancing general and specific language

Effective writers move their prose along by balancing general words, which name or describe groups or classes of things, with specific words, which refer to individual items. Some general words are abstractions, referring to qualities or ideas, things that the five senses cannot perceive. Specific words are often concrete words, referring to things we can see, hear, touch, taste, or smell. We can seldom draw a clear-cut line between general or abstract words on the one hand and specific or concrete ones on the other. Instead, most words fall somewhere between these two extremes.

GENERAL	LESS GENERAL	SPECIFIC	MORE SPECIFIC
book	dictionary	abridged dictionary	my 2004 edition of *The American Heritage College Dictionary*

ABSTRACT	LESS ABSTRACT	CONCRETE	MORE CONCRETE
culture	visual art	painting	van Gogh's *Starry Night*

Passages that contain too many general terms or abstractions demand that readers supply the specific details with their imaginations, making such writing hard to read. But writing that is full of specifics can also be hard to follow if the main point is lost amid a flood of details. Strong writing usually provides readers both with a general idea or over-all picture and with specific examples or concrete details to fill in that picture. In the following passage, the author might have simply made a general statement—*their breakfast was always liberal and good*—or simply described the breakfast. Instead, he is both general and specific.

> There would be a brisk fire crackling in the hearth, the old smoke-gold of morning and the smell of fog, the crisp cheerful voices of the people and their ruddy competent morning look, and the cheerful smells of breakfast, which was always liberal and good, the best meal that they had: kidneys and ham and eggs and sausages and toast and marmalade and tea.

—THOMAS WOLFE, *Of Time and the River*

Here a student writer balances a general statement (*My next-door neighbor is a nuisance*) with specific details:

> My next-door neighbor is a nuisance, poking and prying into my life, constantly watching me as I enter and leave my house, complaining about the noise when I am having a good time, and telling my parents whenever she sees me kissing my date.

EXERCISE 27.5

Rewrite each of the following sentences to be more specific and concrete.

1. The entryway of the building was dirty.
2. The sounds at dawn are memorable.
3. Our holiday dinner tasted good.
4. The attendant came toward my car.
5. I woke up.

bedfordstmartins.com/smhandbook
Exercise Central > Language > Word Choice

27d Using figurative language

Figurative language, or figures of speech, can paint pictures in our minds, allowing us to "see" a point readily and clearly. For example, an economist might explain that if you earned one dollar per second, you would need nearly thirty-two years to become a billionaire. When scientists compare certain genetic variants to typographical errors, they too are giving us a picture to help us grasp a difficult concept. Far from being mere decoration, then, figurative language is crucial to understanding.

In important ways, all language is metaphoric, referring to something beyond the word itself for which the word is a symbol. Particularly helpful in building understanding are specific types of figurative language, including similes, metaphors, and analogies.

FOR MULTILINGUAL WRITERS

Mastering idioms

Why do you wear a diamond *on* your finger but *in* your ear? (See 58a.)

Similes

Similes use *like, as, as if,* or *as though* to make an explicit comparison between two things.

▷ **Rain slides slowly down the glass, as if the night is crying.**
                                                    —PATRICIA CORNWELL

▷ **You can tell the graphic-novels section in a bookstore from afar, by the young bodies sprawled around it like casualties of a localized disaster.**   —PETER SCHJELDAHL

Metaphors

Metaphors are implicit comparisons, omitting the *like, as, as if,* or *as though* of similes.

▷ **The Internet is the new town square.**   —JEB HENSARLING

Often, metaphors are more elaborate.

○ Black women are called, in the folklore that so aptly identifies one's status in society, "the mule of the world," because we have been handed the burdens that everyone else — everyone else — refused to carry.   —ALICE WALKER, *In Search of Our Mothers' Gardens*

Analogies

Analogies compare similar features of two dissimilar things; they explain something unfamiliar by relating it to something familiar. Analogies are often several sentences or paragraphs in length. In the first passage that follows, the writer draws an analogy between corporate pricing strategies and nuclear war:

○ One way to establish that peace-preserving threat of mutual assured destruction is to commit yourself beforehand, which helps explain why so many retailers promise to match any competitor's advertised price. Consumers view these guarantees as conducive to lower prices. But in fact offering a price-matching guarantee should make it less likely that competitors will slash prices, since they know that any cuts they make will immediately be matched. It's the retail version of the doomsday machine.   —JAMES SUROWIECKI

○ One Hundred and Twenty-fifth Street was to Harlem what the Mississippi was to the South, a long traveling river always going somewhere, carrying something.
                          —MAYA ANGELOU, *The Heart of a Woman*

Before you use an analogy, make sure that the two things you are comparing have enough points of similarity to justify the comparison.

Clichés and mixed metaphors

Just as effective figurative language can create the right impression, ineffective figures of speech — such as clichés and mixed metaphors — may wind up boring, irritating, or unintentionally amusing readers.

A cliché is a frequently used expression such as *busy as a bee* or *children are the future*. By definition, we use clichés all the time, especially in speech, and many serve usefully as shorthand for familiar ideas. If you use too many clichés in your writing, however, readers may conclude that what you are saying is not very new or interesting — or true. For example, if you write that a group of schoolgirls looked *pretty as a picture*, this cli-chéd simile may sound false or insincere. A more original figure of speech, such as *pretty as brand-new red shoes*, might be more effective.

Since people don't always agree on what is a cliché and what is a fresh image, how can you check your writing for clichés? Here is a rule to follow: if you can predict exactly what the upcoming word(s) in a phrase will be, it is probably a cliché.

Mixed metaphors are comparisons that are not consistent. Instead of creating a clear impression, they confuse the reader by pitting one image against another.

○ **The lectures were brilliant comets streaking through the night sky,**
dazzling   flashes
showering listeners with a torrential rain of insight.
^   ^

The images of streaking light and heavy precipitation are inconsistent; in the revised sentence, all of the images relate to light.

Allusions

Allusions are indirect references to cultural works, people, or events. When a sports commentator said, "If the Georgia Tech men have an Achilles heel, it is their inexperience, their youth," he alluded to the Greek myth in which the hero Achilles was fatally wounded in his single vulnerable spot, his heel.

You can draw allusions from history, literature, sacred texts, com-mon wisdom, or current events. Many movies and popular songs are full of allusions. The *Simpsons* episode called "Eternal Moonshine of the Simpson Mind," for example, alludes to the film *Eternal Sunshine of the Spotless Mind*. Remember, however, that allusions work only if your audience recognizes them.

Signifying

One distinctive use of figurative language found extensively in African American English is signifying, in which a speaker cleverly needles or insults the listener. In the following passage, two African American men (Grave Digger and Coffin Ed) signify on their white supervisor (Anderson), who ordered them to discover the originators of a riot:

> "I take it you've discovered who started the riot," Anderson said.
> "We knew who he was all along," Grave Digger said.

"It's just nothing we can do to him," Coffin Ed echoed.

"Why not, for God's sake?"

"He's dead," Coffin Ed said.

"Who?"

"Lincoln," Grave Digger said.

"He hadn't ought to have freed us if he didn't want to make provisions to feed us," Coffin Ed said. "Anyone could have told him that."

—CHESTER HIMES, *Hot Day, Hot Night*

Coffin Ed and Grave Digger demonstrate the major characteristics of effective signifying: indirection, ironic humor, fluid rhythm—and a surprising twist, the revelation that Abraham Lincoln caused the riot by ending slavery. This twist leaves the supervisor speechless—and gives Grave Digger and Coffin Ed the last word.

EXERCISE 27.6

Return to the description you wrote in Exercise 27.1. Note any words that carry strong connotations, and identify the concrete and abstract language as well as any use of figurative language. Revise any inappropriate language you find.

THINKING CRITICALLY ABOUT WORD CHOICE

Read the following brief poem. What dominant feeling or impression does the poem produce in you? Identify the specific words and phrases that help create that impression.

What happens to a dream deferred?

Does it dry up
Like a raisin in the sun?
Or fester like a sore—
And then run?
Does it stink like rotten meat?
Or crust and sugar over—
Like a syrupy sweet?

Maybe it just sags
Like a heavy load.

Or does it explode?

—LANGSTON HUGHES, "Harlem (A Dream Deferred)"

Dictionaries, Vocabulary, and Spelling

28

Expanding your vocabulary can expand your ability to reach a wide variety of audiences. To communicate effectively, pay careful attention to the meaning, and to the spelling, of the words you use.

28a Finding information in dictionaries

A good dictionary packs a surprising amount of information about words into a relatively small space, sometimes containing a dozen or more kinds of information about a word. Spelling, word division, pronunciation, part of speech, irregular forms (if any), the languages the word comes from, and its meanings are all discussed in most dictionary entries.

Usage notes and labels

Usage notes in dictionaries, such as the following note from *Merriam-Webster's Online Dictionary* about the nonstandard word *irregardless*, often provide extensive information about how a particular usage may affect readers:

> *Irregardless* originated in dialectal American speech in the early 20th century. Its fairly widespread use in speech called it to the attention of usage commentators as early as 1927. The most frequently repeated remark about it is that "there is no such word." There is such a word, however. It is still used primarily in speech, although it can be found from time to time in edited prose. Its reputation has not risen over the years, and it is still a long way from general acceptance. Use *regardless* instead.

Philosopher John Dewey wrote, "Everyone has experienced how learning an appropriate name for what was dim and vague cleared up and crystallized the whole matter." Think back to a time when you learned the word for something new. Before that time, this thing did not exist for you; yet curiously enough, once you knew its name, you began to see it all around you. Such is the power of vocabulary to enrich not only your personal language but your life as well.

Entries come from *The American Heritage Dictionary of the English Language*, Fourth Edition.

1. Spelling
2. Word division
3. Pronunciation
4. Part of speech / word forms
5. Word origin
6. Meanings
7. Examples
8. Usage notes
9. Field labels
10. Synonyms / antonyms
11. Related words
12. Idioms

Print dictionary entry

let•ter (lĕt´ər) *n.* **1a.** A written symbol or character representing a speech sound and being a component of an alphabet. **b.** A written symbol or character used in the graphemic representation of a word, such as the *h* in *Thames*. See Note at **Thames**. **2.** A written or printed communication directed to a person or organization. **3.** A certified document granting rights to its bearer. Often used in the plural. **4.** Literal meaning: *had to adhere to the letter of the law.* **5. letters** *(used with a sing. verb)* **a.** Literary culture; belles-lettres. **b.** Learning or knowledge, especially of literature. **c.** Literature or writing as a profession. **6.** *Printing* **a.** A piece of type that prints a single character. **b.** A specific style of type. **c.** The characters in one style of type. **7.** An emblem in the shape of the initial of a school awarded for outstanding performance, especially in varsity athletics. ❖ *v.* **-tered, -ter•ing, -ters** —*tr.* **1.** To write letters on. **2.** To write in letters. —*intr.* **1.** To write or form letters. **2.** To earn a school letter, as for outstanding athletic achievement: *She lettered in three collegiate sports.* —*idiom:* **to the letter** To the least detail; exactly: *followed instructions to the letter.* [Middle English, from Old French *lettre*, from Latin *littera*, perhaps from Etruscan, from Greek *diphtherā*, hide, leather, writing surface.] —**let´ter•er** *n.*

Synonyms *letter, epistle, missive, note* These nouns denote a written communication directed to another: *received a letter of complaint; read the Epistles of the New Testament; sent a missive of condolence; mailed a thank-you note.*

Online dictionary entry

letter ——————————————————————— ❶

SYLLABICATION: let·ter ——————————————————————————— ❷
PRONUNCIATION: ◁ lĕt´ər

NOUN: **1a.** A written symbol or character representing a speech sound and
being a component of an alphabet. **b.** A written symbol or character used

❸

❹ in the graphemic representation of a word, such as the *h* in *Thames.* See
Note at **Thames. 2.** A written or printed communication directed to a ——
person or organization. **3.** A certified document granting rights to its
bearer. Often used in the plural. **4.** Literal meaning: *had to adhere to the*
letter of the law. **5. letters** *(used with a sing. verb)* **a.** Literary culture;

❽ —— belles-lettres. **b.** Learning or knowledge, especially of literature.
c. Literature or writing as a profession. **6.** *Printing* **a.** A piece of type

❾ —— that prints a single character. **b.** A specific style of type. **c.** The characters in one style of type. **7.** An emblem in the shape of the initial of a
school awarded for outstanding performance, especially in varsity
athletics.

VERB: Inflected forms: **let·tered, let·ter·ing, let·ters** ————————————————
❻
TRANSITIVE **1.** To write letters on. **2.** To write in letters.
VERB: ❼
INTRANSITIVE **1.** To write or form letters. **2.** To earn a school letter, as for outstanding
VERB: athletic achievement: *She lettered in three collegiate sports.* ——————
❺
IDIOM: **to the letter** To the last detail; exactly: *followed instructions to the letter.* —
ETYMOLOGY: Middle English, from Old French *lettre,* from Latin *littera,* perhaps from
Etruscan, from Greek *diphtherā,* hide, leather, writing surface.
OTHER FORMS: **let´ter·er**—noun ——————————————————————— ⓫
SYNONYMS: *letter, epistle, missive, note* These nouns denote a written communica-
tion directed to another: *received a letter of complaint; the Epistles of*
❿ *the New Testament; a missive of condolence; a thank-you note.*
⓬

Many dictionaries include usage labels, which let readers know that some or all meanings of a particular word are nonstandard or inappropriate in certain contexts. An explanation of such labels usually occurs at the beginning of the dictionary. Here are some of the labels *Webster's New World Dictionary* uses:

1. *Archaic*: rarely used today except in specialized contexts

2. *Obsolete* or *obs.*: no longer used

3. *Colloquial* or *colloq.*: characteristic of conversation and informal writing

4. *Slang*: extremely informal

5. *Dialect*: used mostly in a particular geographic or linguistic area, often one that is specified, such as Scotland or New England

Many dictionaries also label words that are considered offensive and vulgar.

EXERCISE 28.1

Look up the spelling, syllable division, and pronunciation of the following words in your dictionary. Note any variants in spelling and pronunciation.

1. heinous
3. schedule
5. macabre

2. exigency
4. greasy
6. mature

EXERCISE 28.2

Look up the etymology of the following words in your dictionary.

1. rhetoric
3. tobacco
5. cinema

2. student
4. crib
6. okra

28b Using different kinds of dictionaries

Become familiar with the most common kinds of dictionaries.

1 Abridged dictionaries

Abridged, or abbreviated, dictionaries are popular with college writers and are widely available in print and online. Online versions are unbeat-

---

FOR MULTILINGUAL WRITERS

Using the dictionary to learn idioms

When you encounter an unfamiliar phrase that seems to involve an idiom, you might find help at the end of a word's dictionary definition, where idioms often are defined.

> **point** (point) *n.* 1. The sharp or tapered end of something. 2. An object having a sharp or tapered end, as a knife or needle. ***idioms*: beside the point.** Irrelevant. **to the point.** Pertinent.

For more help with idioms, see 58a.

---

able as a quick reference, but print versions may offer more information on usage.

Two college dictionaries that offer notably helpful usage notes are *Random House Webster's College Dictionary*, with usage notes and appendices that warn users about offensive or disparaging terms, and *The American Heritage College Dictionary*, which includes extensive notes on usage, including introductory essays in the form of a debate.

2 Unabridged dictionaries

Unabridged, or unabbreviated, dictionaries are the most complete and thorough dictionaries of English. Print versions may appear in multiple volumes, and access to online versions often requires a subscription. Libraries offer access to unabridged dictionaries.

Two especially important unabridged dictionaries are the *Oxford English Dictionary* and *Webster's Third New International Dictionary of the English Language*. The *OED* offers a full history of each English word: a record of its entry into the language and the development of the word's various meanings, with dated quotations in chronological order. *Webster's Third* aims to describe the way people actually use words today rather than to prescribe standards of correct and incorrect usage.

3 Specialized dictionaries

Sometimes you will need to turn to specialized dictionaries, especially if you are seeking more information on usage, synonyms, or slang. A librarian can help you find an appropriate resource in print or online.

- If you feel unsure of usage, you may want to consult a *dictionary of usage* that provides specialized information on the effects of using particular words.

- Each entry in a *dictionary of synonyms* or a *thesaurus* lists words that have similar meanings (synonyms). A thesaurus also provides words with opposing meanings (antonyms). Two words are rarely completely interchangeable, so use such resources carefully—as Mark Twain put it, the difference between the right word and the almost-right word is the difference between lightning and the lightning bug.

- *Dictionaries for specific disciplines* can give you information on usage in a particular discipline, such as law or medicine. Ask your instructor or a librarian for help finding standard references in a field that is new to you. (See also Chapter 59.)

- *Dictionaries of etymology, regional English, slang,* or *neologisms* can help if you need to investigate the origins of a word, look up a term used in only one area of the country, or understand a word that may be slang or jargon.

28c Building your vocabulary

At its largest, your vocabulary includes all the words whose meanings you either recognize or can deduce from context. This group of words, called your *processing vocabulary*, allows you to interpret the meanings of many passages whose words you might not use yourself. Your *producing* or *active vocabulary*, on the other hand, is more limited, made up of words you actually use in writing or speaking.

An important intellectual goal is to consciously strengthen your producing vocabulary—to begin to use in your own speech and writing more of the words you understand in context. To accomplish this goal, you must become an investigative reporter of your own language and the language of others.

The history of English

English, like one-third of all languages in the world, descends from Indo-European, a language spoken millennia ago. Scholars began to consider

Consulting a learner's dictionary

In addition to using a good college dictionary, you may want to invest in a dictionary intended especially for learners of English, such as the *Oxford Advanced Learner's Dictionary*. Such dictionaries provide information about count and noncount nouns, idioms and phrasal verbs, grammatical usage, and other topics important to learners of English. Bilingual dictionaries (such as English–Spanish) can be helpful for quick translations of common words but rarely give information about usage or related idioms. Many multilingual writers find it helpful to use multiple dictionaries to get a range of information about a word and its usage.

Indo-European a "common source" when they noted striking resemblances among words in a number of languages.

ENGLISH	LATIN	SPANISH	FRENCH	GREEK	GERMAN	DUTCH	HINDI
three	*tres*	*tres*	*trois*	*treis*	*drei*	*drie*	*teen*

A version of Indo-European was brought to Britain by the Germanic invasions following 449. This early language, called Anglo-Saxon or Old English, was influenced by Latin and Greek when Christianity was reintroduced into England beginning in 597, shaped by the Viking invasions in the late 700s, and transformed by French after the Norman Conquest (1066).

Although English continued to evolve after the conquest, educated people spoke not English but Latin and French, the languages of the church and court. In the late 1300s, Geoffrey Chaucer, writing *The Canterbury Tales* in the language of the common people, helped establish what is now called Middle English as the legal and literary language of Britain. With the advent of printing in the mid-1400s, that language became more accessible and standardized. By about 1600, it had essentially become the Modern English we use today.

This image of Chaucer appears in a manuscript of The Canterbury Tales.

In the past four hundred years, English has continued borrowing from many languages and, as a result, now has one of the world's largest vocabularies. Modern English, then, is a plant growing luxuriously in the soil of multiple language sources.

1 Word roots

As its name suggests, a root is a word from which other words grow, usually through the addition of prefixes or suffixes. From the Latin root *-dic-* or *-dict-* ("speak"), for instance, grows a whole range of words in English: *contradict, dictate, dictator, diction, dictionary, predict,* and others. Here are some other Latin (L) and Greek (G) roots and examples of words derived from them.

ROOT	MEANING	EXAMPLES
-audi- (L)	to hear	audience, audio
-bene- (L)	good, well	benevolent, benefit
-bio- (G)	life	biography, biosphere
-duc(t)- (L)	to lead or to make	ductile, reproduce
-gen- (G)	race, kind	genealogy, gene
-geo- (G)	earth	geography, geometry
-graph- (G)	to write	graphic, photography
-jur-, -jus- (L)	law	justice, jurisdiction
-log(o)- (G)	word, thought	biology, logical
-luc- (L)	light	lucid, translucent
-manu- (L)	hand	manufacture, manual
-mit-, -mis- (L)	to send	permit, transmission
-path- (G)	feel, suffer	empathy, pathetic
-phil- (G)	love	philosopher, bibliophile
-photo- (G)	light	photography, telephoto
-port- (L)	to carry	transport, portable
-psych- (G)	soul	psychology, psychopath
-scrib-, -script- (L)	to write	scribble, manuscript
-sent-, -sens- (L)	to feel	sensation, resent
-tele- (G)	far away	telegraph, telepathy
-tend- (L)	to stretch	extend, tendency
-terr- (L)	earth	inter, territorial

| -vac- (L) | empty | vacant, evacuation |
| -vid-, -vis- (L) | to see | video, envision, visit |

2 Prefixes

Originally individual words, prefixes are groups of letters added to the beginning of words or to roots to create new words. Prefixes modify or extend the meaning of the original word or root. Recognizing common prefixes can help you decipher the meaning of unfamiliar words.

Prefixes of negation or opposition

PREFIX	MEANING	EXAMPLES
a-, an-	without, not	amoral, anemia
anti-	against	antibody, antiphonal
contra-	against	contravene, contradict
de-	from, take away from	demerit, declaw
dis-	apart, away	disappear, discharge
il-, im-, in-, ir-	not	illegal, immature, indistinct, irreverent

PREFIX	MEANING	EXAMPLES
mal-	wrong	malevolent, malpractice
mis-	wrong, bad	misapply, misanthrope
non-	not	nonentity, nonsense
un-	not	unbreakable, unable

Prefixes of quantity

PREFIX	MEANING	EXAMPLES
bi-	two	bipolar, bilateral
milli-	thousand	millimeter, milligram
mono-	one, single	monotone, monologue
omni-	all	omniscient, omnipotent
semi-	half	semicolon, semiconductor
tri-	three	tripod, trimester
uni-	one	unitary, univocal

Prefixes of time and space

PREFIX	MEANING	EXAMPLES
ante-	before	antedate, antebellum
circum-	around	circumlocution, circumnavigate
co-, col-, com-, con-, cor-	with	coequal, collaborate, commiserate, contact, correspond
e-, ex-	out of	emit, extort, expunge
hyper-	over, more than	hypersonic, hypersensitive
hypo-	under, less than	hypodermic, hypoglycemia
inter-	between	intervene, international
mega-	enlarge, large	megalomania, megaphone
micro-	tiny	micrometer, microscopic
neo-	recent	neologism, neophyte
post-	after	postwar, postscript
pre-	before	previous, prepublication
pro-	before, onward	project, propel
re-	again, back	review, re-create
sub-	under, beneath	subhuman, submarine
super-	over, above	supercargo, superimpose
syn-	at the same time	synonym, synchronize
trans-	across, over	transport, transition

3 Suffixes

Like prefixes, suffixes modify and extend meanings. Suffixes, which are attached to the end of words or roots, often alter the grammatical function or part of speech of the original word—for example, turning the verb *create* into a noun, an adjective, or an adverb.

VERB	create
NOUNS	crea*tor*/crea*tion*/crea*tivity*/crea*ture*
ADJECTIVE	crea*tive*
ADVERB	creative*ly*

Noun suffixes

SUFFIX	MEANING	EXAMPLES
-acy	state or quality	democracy, privacy
-al	act of	dismissal, refusal
-ance, -ence	state or quality of	maintenance, eminence
-dom	place or state of being	freedom, kingdom
-er, -or	one who	trainer, investor
-ism	doctrine or belief characteristic of	liberalism, Taoism
-ist	one who	organist, physicist
-ity	quality of	veracity, opacity
-ment	condition of	payment, argument
-ness	state of being	watchfulness, cleanliness
-ship	position held	professorship, fellowship
-sion, -tion	state of being or action	digression, transition

Verb suffixes

SUFFIX	MEANING	EXAMPLES
-ate	cause to be	concentrate, regulate
-en	cause to be or become	enliven, blacken
-ify, -fy	make or cause to be	unify, terrify, amplify
-ize	cause to become	magnetize, civilize

Adjective suffixes

SUFFIX	MEANING	EXAMPLES
-able, -ible	capable of being	readable, edible
-al	pertaining to	regional, political
-esque	reminiscent of	picturesque, statuesque
-ful	having much of a quality	colorful, sorrowful
-ic	pertaining to	poetic, mythic
-ious, -ous	of or characterized by	famous, nutritious
-ish	having the quality of	prudish, clownish
-ive	having the nature of	festive, creative, massive
-less	without	endless, senseless

28d Understanding vocabulary in context

In addition to using prefixes and suffixes, you can increase your vocabulary by analyzing contexts and reading actively.

If a word is at first unfamiliar to you, look carefully at its context, paying attention to all the clues the context provides; often, you will be able to deduce the meaning. For instance, if the word *accouterments* is unfamiliar in the sentence *We stopped at a camping-supply store to pick up last-minute accouterments*, the context—*a camping-supply store* and *last-minute*—suggests strongly that *equipment* or some similar word fits the bill. And that is what *accouterments* means.

When you are studying a new field, you may encounter words that are completely unfamiliar to you or that have a different meaning in the field than they have in everyday use. You may want to keep a log of new vocabulary in your chosen field. (See also 27a2 and 59d.)

EXERCISE 28.3

Identify the contextual clues that help you understand any unfamiliar words in the following sentences. Then write paraphrases of three of the sentences.

1. Before Prohibition, the criminal fringe in the United States had been a self-effacing, scattered class with little popular support.

2. The judge failed to recuse himself from the trial, even though he had a vested interest in the case's outcome.

QUICK HELP

Building your vocabulary

- Keep a list of new words. Each time you come across a new word in a text, try to come up with a definition, and then check the dictionary to see how close you came. Copy the word's definition next to the word on your list.

- Practice naming the opposites of words. If you see *abbreviation*, for example, can you think of *enlargement* or *elaboration*?

- As you read, try to come up with better words than the authors have.

- While reading a work by a writer you admire, identify several words you like but do not yet use. Check the meanings of these words, and then try using them in your speech or writing.

3. The clownfish lives symbiotically among sea anemones: it is protected from predators by the anemones' poisonous tentacles, and it defends its territory by fighting off anemone-eaters.

4. Some have made the mistake of assuming that the new casinos will be a panacea for the state's financial problems.

5. Health officials warned the population of an extremely virulent strain of flu next season and urged those with compromised immune systems to be vaccinated.

28e   Checking spelling

Words work best for you, of course, when they are spelled correctly.

---

bedfordstmartins.com/smhandbook
Exercise Central > **Language** > **Vocabulary and Spelling**

---

1 Spell checkers

Research conducted for this textbook shows that spelling errors have changed dramatically in the past twenty-five years — and the reason is spell checkers. Although these programs have weeded out many once-common misspellings, spell checkers are not foolproof.

Common errors with spell checkers

Spell checkers still allow typical kinds of errors that you should look out for.

- *Homonyms.* Spell checkers cannot differentiate among words such as *affect* and *effect* that sound alike but are spelled differently (see p. 554 for a list of confusing homonyms). Proofread especially carefully for these words.

- *Proper nouns.* You can add names and other proper nouns to your spell checker's dictionary so that the spell checker will not flag these words as incorrect, but first be certain you have spelled the names correctly.

- *Compound words written as two words.* Spell checkers will not identify a problem, for example, when *nowhere* is incorrectly written as *no where*. When in doubt, check a dictionary.

TALKING THE TALK

Spell checkers and wrong-word errors

"Can I trust spell checkers to give me the correct alternative for a word that I have spelled wrong?" In a word, no. The spell checker may suggest bizarre substitutes for many proper names and specialized terms (even when you spell them correctly) and for certain typographical errors, thus introducing wrong words into your paper if you accept its suggestions automatically. For example, a student who had typed *fantic* instead of *frantic* found that the spell checker's first choice was to substitute *fanatic*—a replacement word that made no sense. Wrong-word errors are the most common surface error in college writing today (see p. 2), and spell checkers are partly to blame. So be careful not to take a spell checker's recommendation without paying careful attention to the replacement word.

- *Typos.* The spell checker will not flag *heat,* even if you meant to type *heart.* Careful proofreading is still essential.

Spell checker use

To make spell checkers work best for you, you need to learn to adapt them to your own needs.

- Always proofread carefully, even after you have used the spell checker. The more important the message or document, the more careful you should be about its accuracy and clarity.

- Use a dictionary to look up any word the spell checker highlights that you are not absolutely sure of.

- If your spell checker's dictionary allows you to add new words, enter any proper names, non-English words, or specialized language you use regularly and have trouble spelling. Be careful to enter the correct spelling!

- If you know that you mix up certain homonyms, such as *there* and *their,* check for them after running your spell checker.

- Remember that spell checkers are not usually sensitive to capitalization. If you write "the united states," the spell checker won't question it.

- Do *not* automatically accept the spell checker's suggestions: doing so can lead you to choose a word you really don't want.

EXERCISE 28.4

The following paragraph has been checked with a spell checker. Proofread carefully and correct any errors that the spell checker missed.

I see that you have send me a warning about a computer virus that can destroy my hard drive, mangle my soft ware, and generally reek havoc on my computer. How ever, you may not be aware oft he fact that warnings like this one are almost never real. When a message axes you to foreword it to every one in you're address book, you should know immediately that its a hoax. User who send false warnings about viruses to hundreds of there friends are not doing any one a favor; instead, they are simple slowing down traffic on line and creating problems that maybe worst then any technical difficulties cause by the virus—if the virus even exist. Please insure that warnings contain a grain of true before you past them on. If your worried that my computer might be in danger, set you mind at easy. I will except responsibility if the machine goes hay wire.

2 | **Homonyms**

English has many homonyms—words that sound alike but have different spellings and meanings. But a relatively small number of them, just eight groups, cause student writers frequent trouble (see the Quick Help box that follows). If you tend to confuse any of these words, create a special memory device to help you remember the differences: "the *weather* will determine *whether* I wear a jacket."

In addition, pay close attention to homonyms that may be spelled as one word or as two, depending on the meaning.

▶ **Of course, they did not wear *everyday* clothes *every day* of the year.**

▶ **Though we were *all ready* to dance, our dates had *already* departed.**

▶ **Sonya *may be* on time for the meeting, or *maybe* she'll be late.**

Other homonyms and frequently confused words can be found in the Glossary of Usage at the back of this book (see pp. 910–17).

EXERCISE 28.5

Choose the appropriate word in parentheses to fill each blank.

If _____ (*your/you're*) looking for summer fun, _____ (*accept/except*) the friendly _____ (*advice/advise*) of thousands of happy adventurers: spend three _____ (*weaks/weeks*) kayaking _____ (*thorough/threw/through*) the inside passage _____ (*to/too/two*) Alaska. For ten years, Outings, Inc., has _____

QUICK HELP

The most troublesome homonyms

accept (to take or receive)

except (to leave out)

affect (an emotion; to have an influence)

effect (a result; to cause to happen)

its (possessive form of *it*)

it's (contraction of *it is* or *it has*)

their (possessive form of *they*)

there (in that place)

they're (contraction of *they are*)

to (in the direction of)

too (in addition; excessive)

two (number between *one* and *three*)

weather (climatic conditions)

whether (if)

who's (contraction of *who is* or *who has*)

whose (possessive form of *who*)

your (possessive form of *you*)

you're (contraction of *you* are)

(*lead/led*) groups of novice kayakers _____ (*passed/past*) some of the most breathtaking scenery in North America. The group's goal is simple: to give participants the time of _____ (*their/there/they're*) lives and show them things they don't see _____ (*every day/everyday*). As one of last year's adventurers said, "_____ (*Its/It's*) a trip that is _____ (*already/all ready*) one of my favorite memories. It _____ (*affected/effected*) me powerfully."

bedfordstmartins.com/smhandbook
Exercise Central > Language > Vocabulary and Spelling

3 Spelling and pronunciation

Pronunciation often leads spellers astray. Not only do people who live in different regions pronounce words differently, but speakers also tend to blur letters or syllables. To link spelling and pronunciation, try to pronounce words mentally the way they look, including every letter and syllable (so that, for example, you hear the *b* at the end of *crumb*). Doing so will help you "see" words with unpronounced

letters or syllables, such as those listed here. The frequently unpronounced letters or syllables are italicized and underlined.

can*d*idate	forei*g*n	prob*a*bly
condem*n*	gover*n*ment	quan*t*ity
diff*e*rent	int*e*rest	rest*au*rant
drastica*l*ly	lib*r*ary	sep*a*rate (adjective)
enviro*n*ment	marr*i*age	su*r*prise
Feb*r*uary	mus*c*le	We*d*nesday

In English words, *a*, *i*, and *e* often sound alike in syllables that are
not stressed. Hearing the word *definite*, for instance, gives us few clues
as to whether the vowels in the second and third syllables should be *i*'s
or *a*'s. In this case, remembering the related word *finite* helps us know
that the *i*'s are correct. If you are puzzled about how to spell a word
with unstressed vowels, try to think of a related word, and then check
your dictionary. You can also use memory cues, or mnemonic devices,
to master words that tend to trip you up. Here are two memory cues one
student made up:

WORD	MISSPELLING	CUE
government	goverment	Government should serve those it *governs*.
separate	seperate	*Separate* rates two *a*'s.

28f Following spelling rules

Some general spelling rules can be of enormous help to writers.

1 *i* before *e*

Here is a slightly expanded version of the "*i* before *e*" rule:

i before *e* except after *c* or when pronounced "ay" as in *neighbor* and
weigh, or in *weird* exceptions like *either* and *species*

I BEFORE *E*	ach*ie*ve, br*ie*f, f*ie*ld, fr*ie*nd
EXCEPT AFTER *C*	c*ei*ling, conc*ei*vable, dec*ei*t, rec*ei*ve

---

FOR MULTILINGUAL WRITERS

American spellings

You have likely noticed that different varieties of English often use different spelling conventions. If you have learned a British form of English, for example, you will want to be aware of some of the more common spelling differences in American English. For example, words ending in *-yse or -ise* in British English (*analyse, criticise*) usually end in *-yze* or *-ize* in American English (*analyze, criticize*); words ending in *-our* in British English (*colour, labour*) usually end in *-or* in American English (*color, labor*); and words ending in *-re* in British English (*theatre, centre*) usually end in *-er* in American English (*theater, center*).

OR WHEN PRONOUNCED "AY"	*ei*ghth, n*ei*ghbor, r*ei*gn, w*ei*gh
OR IN WEIRD EXCEPTIONS	anc*ie*nt, for*ei*gn, h*ei*ght, le*i*sure, n*ei*ther, s*ei*ze

2 Prefixes

A prefix, added to the beginning of a word (28c2), does not change the spelling of the word it is added to, even when the last letter of the prefix and the first letter of the word are the same (*service, disservice; rate, overrate*). Some prefixes require the use of hyphens (see 53b).

3 Suffixes

A suffix, added to the end of a word (28c3), may change the spelling of the word it is added to.

Words ending in a silent e

In general, drop the final silent *e* on a word when you add a suffix that starts with a vowel. Keep the final silent *e* if the suffix starts with a consonant.

exercise, exercising	force, forceful
imagine, imaginable	state, stately
SOME EXCEPTIONS	argument, changeable, courageous, judgment, ninth, noticeable, truly

Words ending in -y

In general, when you add a suffix to words ending in *y*, change the *y*
to *i* if the *y* is preceded by a consonant. Keep the *y* if it is preceded by
a vowel, if the suffix begins with *i*, or if the *y* is part of a proper name.

bounty, bountiful	busy, busily	try, tried	fry, fries
employ, employed	Kennedy, Kennedyesque	dry, drying	

Words ending in a consonant

When a word ends in a consonant preceded by a single vowel, adding a
suffix beginning with a vowel requires you to double the final consonant
if the word contains only one syllable or ends in an accented syllable.

stop, stopping   occur, occurrence

Do not double the consonant if the accent shifts from the last to a previous syllable when the suffix is added (*prefer, preference*).

4 | Plurals

For most words, simply add *-s* to form a plural. For singular nouns ending in *s*, *ch*, *sh*, *x*, or *z*, add *-es*.

book, books	ibis, ibises	fox, foxes	flash, flashes
bus, buses	church, churches	buzz, buzzes	

Words ending in o

In general, add *-es* if the *o* is preceded by a consonant. Add *-s* if the *o* is
preceded by a vowel.

potato, potatoes	hero, heroes	veto, vetoes
rodeo, rodeos	patio, patios	zoo, zoos

EXCEPTIONS

memo, memos   piano, pianos   solo, solos

Words ending in y

For words ending in *y*, change *y* to *i* and add *-es* if the *y* is preceded by a consonant. (Do not change a *y* at the end of a proper name.)

theory, theories   bay, bays   O'Malley, O'Malleys

Compound words

For compound nouns written as one word, make the last part of the compound plural (*briefcases, mailboxes*). For compound nouns written as separate or hyphenated words, make the most important part plural.

brothers-in-law   lieutenant governors

THINKING CRITICALLY ABOUT DICTIONARIES, VOCABULARY, AND SPELLING

Reading with an Eye for Vocabulary

In his autobiography, Malcolm X says that he taught himself to write by reading and copying the dictionary. You can teach yourself to be a better writer by paying careful attention to the way other writers use words. Choose a writer whose work you admire, and read that author's work for at least thirty minutes, noting six or seven words that you would not ordinarily have thought to use. Do a little dictionary investigative work on these words, and bring your results to class for discussion.

Thinking about Your Own Vocabulary and Spelling

Read over a piece of your recent writing. Underline any words you think could be improved on, and come up with several possible substitutes. Then look for any words whose meanings are not absolutely clear to you, and check them in your dictionary. Finally, double-check spelling throughout. What do you notice about the words you use?

Part 6

SENTENCE
GRAMMAR

29

Grammatical Sentences

The grammar of our first language comes to us almost automatically. Listen in on a conversation between two four-year-olds.

AUDREY: **My new bike that Aunt Andrea got me has a red basket and a loud horn, and I love it.**
LILA: **Can I ride it?**
AUDREY: **Yes, as soon as I take a turn.**

This simple conversation features sophisticated grammar—the subordination of one clause to another, a compound object, and a number of adjectives—used effortlessly.

Grammatical correctness alone is not enough to ensure that a sentence is effective and artful—or that it serves an appropriate purpose in your writing. Understanding grammatical structures can, however, help you produce sentences that are appropriate and effective as well as grammatically correct.

29a The basic grammar of sentences

A sentence is a grammatically complete group of words that expresses a thought. To be grammatically complete, a sentence must contain both a subject, which identifies what the sentence is about, and a predicate, which says or asks something about the subject or tells the subject to do something.

SUBJECT	PREDICATE
I	have a dream.
The rain in Spain	stays mainly in the plain.
Rachel Maddow, who hosts a talk show on MSNBC,	owns no television.

Some sentences contain only a one-word predicate with an implied, or understood, subject (for example, *Stop!*). Most sentences, however, contain words that expand the basic subject and predicate. In the preceding example, for instance, the subject might have been simply *Rachel Maddow*; the words *who hosts a talk show on MSNBC,* say more about the subject. Similarly, the predicate of that sentence

560

TALKING THE TALK

Understanding grammatical terms

"I never learned any grammar." You may lack *conscious* knowledge of grammar and grammatical terms (and if so, you are not alone—American students today rarely study English grammar). But you probably understand the ideas that grammatical terms such as *auxiliary verb* and *direct object* represent, even if the terms themselves are unfamiliar. Brushing up on the terms commonly used to talk about grammar will make it easier for you and your instructor—as well as other readers and reviewers—to share a common language when you discuss the best ways to get your ideas across clearly and with few distractions.

could be *owns*; the words *no television* expand the predicate by telling us what she owns.

EXERCISE 29.1

Identify the subject and the predicate in each of the following sentences, underlining the subject once and the predicate twice. Example:

The roaring lion at the beginning of old MGM films is part of movie history.

1. Scientific experiments on human subjects are now carefully regulated.
2. Her first afternoon as a kindergarten teacher had left her exhausted.
3. The Croatian news media is almost entirely owned by the state.
4. Our office manager, a stern taskmaster with a fondness for Chanel suits, has been terrifying interns since 1992.
5. Reading edited prose shows writers how to communicate.
6. The security officer at the border questioned everyone suspiciously.
7. People in the nineteenth century communicated constantly through letters.
8. Disease killed off a large number of the tomato plants in the northeastern United States last year.
9. What do scientists know about dinosaurs?
10. The hula-hoop craze of the 1960s has made a comeback among adults looking for fun ways to exercise.

bedfordstmartins.com/smhandbook
Exercise Central > **Sentence Grammar** > **Grammatical Sentences**

SENTENCE MAP: Parts of Speech

1. Verbs show action, occurrence, or being.

Anita is running for mayor, and maybe she will win. Hey, who knows? This could finally be her big chance. She is honest—unlike the former mayor, who was caught in a financial scandal that made the newspapers shortly before he resigned.

> Verb phrases: *is running*—present progressive tense; *will win*—future tense; *could be*—present tense (*could* is a modal auxiliary); *was caught*—past tense of irregular verb *catch* (passive voice). Verbs: *knows*—present tense; *is*—present tense (irregular verb *be*); *had*—past tense of *have*; *made*—past tense of irregular verb *make*; *resigned*—past tense of regular verb *resign*.

2. Nouns name persons, places, things, or concepts.

Anita is running for mayor, and maybe she will win. Hey, who knows? This could finally be her big chance. She is honest—unlike the former mayor, who was caught in a financial scandal that made the newspapers shortly before he resigned.

> Proper noun: *Anita*—subject. Common nouns: *mayor* (first use)—object of preposition *for*; *chance*—subject complement; *mayor* (second use)—object of preposition *unlike*; *scandal*—object of preposition *in*; *newspapers*—direct object of verb.

3. Pronouns substitute for nouns.

Anita is running for mayor, and maybe she will win. Hey, who knows? This could finally be her big chance. She is honest—unlike the former mayor, who was caught in a financial scandal that made the newspapers shortly before he resigned.

> Personal pronouns: *she* (two uses) and *he*—subject. Interrogative pronoun: *who* (first use). Demonstrative pronoun: *this* (refers to the fact that Anita is running for mayor). Possessive pronoun: *her*. Relative pronouns: *who* (second use—refers to *the former mayor*) and *that* (refers to *a financial scandal*).

4. Adjectives modify nouns or pronouns.

Anita is running for mayor, and maybe she will win. Hey, who knows? This could finally be her big chance. She is honest—unlike the former mayor, who was caught in a financial scandal that made the newspapers shortly before he resigned.

> Articles: *the* (both uses); *a*. Subject complement: *honest*. Other adjectives: *big*—modifies *chance*; *former*—modifies *mayor*; *financial*—modifies *scandals*.

5. **Adverbs modify verbs, adjectives, other adverbs, or entire clauses.**

Anita is running for mayor, and *maybe* she will win. Hey, who knows? This could *finally* be her big chance. She is honest—unlike the former mayor, who was caught in a financial scandal that made the newspapers *shortly* before he resigned.

> *Maybe*—modifies the clause *he will win*; *finally*—modifies the verb phrase *could be*; *shortly*—modifies the clause *before he resigned.*

6. **Prepositions express relationships between nouns or pronouns and other words.**

Anita is running *for* mayor, and maybe she will win. Hey, who knows? This could finally be her big chance. She is honest—*unlike* the former mayor, who was caught *in* a financial scandal that made the newspapers shortly before he resigned.

> *For*—object is the noun *mayor*; *unlike*—object is the noun phrase *the former mayor*; *in*—object is the noun phrase *a financial scandal.*

7. **Conjunctions join words or groups of words.**

Anita is running for mayor, *and* maybe she will win. Hey, who knows? This could finally be her big chance. She is honest—unlike the former mayor, who was caught in a financial scandal that made the newspapers shortly *before* he resigned.

> Coordinating conjunction: *and.* Subordinating conjunction: *before.*

8. **Interjections express surprise or emotion and do not relate grammatically to other parts of speech.**

Anita is running for mayor, and maybe she will win. **Hey,** who knows? This could finally be her big chance. She is honest—unlike the former mayor, who was caught in a financial scandal that made the newspapers shortly before he resigned.

> Here is the paragraph again, with each of the eight parts of speech identified as above.

Anita is running for mayor, and maybe she will win. **Hey,** who knows? This could finally be her big chance. She is honest—unlike the former mayor, who was caught in a financial scandal that made the newspapers shortly before he resigned.

29b The parts of speech

The central elements of subjects and predicates are nouns and verbs.

```
┌──── SUBJECT ────┐ ┌──────── PREDICATE ────────┐
         NOUN   VERB
```
▷ **A solitary figure waited on the platform.**

Nouns and verbs are two of the grammatical categories called parts of speech. The other parts of speech are pronouns, adjectives, adverbs, prepositions, conjunctions, and interjections. Many English words can function as more than one part of speech. Take the word *book*: when you *book an airplane flight*, it is a verb; when you *take a good book to the beach*, it is a noun; and when you have *book knowledge*, it is an adjective.

1 Verbs

Verbs move the meaning of sentences along by showing action (*glance, speculate*), occurrence (*become, happen*), or being (*be, seem*). Verbs change form to show *time, person, number, voice,* and *mood* (30a, g–h and 31a).

TIME	we *work*, we *worked*
PERSON	I *work*, she *works*
NUMBER	one person *works*, two people *work*
VOICE	she *asks*, she *is asked*
MOOD	we *see*, if I *were to see*

Auxiliary verbs (or helping verbs) combine with main verbs to create verb phrases. Auxiliaries include the forms of *be, do,* and *have*, which are also used as main verbs, and *can, could, may, might, must, shall, should, will,* and *would* (30b).

▷ **I *could have danced* all night.**

▷ **She *would prefer* to learn Italian rather than Spanish.**

EXERCISE 29.2

Underline each verb or verb phrase in the following sentences. Example:

Drivers <u>should expect</u> weather-related delays.

1. The story was released to the press late on Friday evening.
2. Most athletes will be arriving well before the games.

3. Housing prices have fallen considerably in the past year.

4. No one spoke in the room where the students were taking the exam.

5. The suspect has been fingerprinted and is waiting for his lawyer.

bedfordstmartins.com/smhandbook
Exercise Central > Sentence Grammar > Grammatical Sentences

2 Nouns

Nouns name persons (*aviator, child*), places (*lake, library*), things (*truck, suitcase*), or concepts (*happiness, balance*). Proper nouns, which are capitalized, name specific persons, places, things, or concepts: *Bill, Iowa, Supreme Court, Buddhism*. Collective nouns (31d) name groups: *flock, jury*.

Most nouns change from singular (one) to plural (more than one) when you add -*s* or -*es*: *horse, horses; kiss, kisses*. Some nouns, however, have irregular plural forms: *woman, women; mouse, mice; deer, deer*. Noncount nouns (56a) cannot be made plural because they name things that cannot easily be counted: *dust, peace, prosperity*.

The possessive form of a noun shows ownership. Possessive forms add an apostrophe plus -*s* to most singular nouns or just an apostrophe to most plural nouns: *the horse's owner, the boys' department*.

Nouns are often preceded by the article (or determiner) *a, an*, or *the*: *a rocket, an astronaut, the launch* (56d).

FOR MULTILINGUAL WRITERS
Count and noncount nouns

Do people conduct *research or researches*? See 56a for a discussion of count and noncount nouns.

EXERCISE 29.3

Identify the nouns and the articles in each of the following sentences. Underline the nouns once and the articles twice. Example:

The Puritans hoped for a different king, but Charles II regained his father's throne.

1. After Halloween, the children got sick from eating too much candy.
2. Although June is technically the driest month, severe flooding has occurred in the late spring.
3. Baking is no longer a common activity in most households around the country.
4. A sudden frost turned the ground into a field of ice.
5. The cyclist swerved to avoid an oncoming car that had run a red light.

> bedfordstmartins.com/smhandbook
> **Exercise Central** > **Sentence Grammar** > **Grammatical Sentences**

3 Pronouns

Pronouns often take the place of nouns or other words functioning as nouns so that you do not have to repeat words that have already been mentioned. A word or word group that a pronoun replaces or refers to is called the *antecedent* of the pronoun (32f).

ANTECEDENT   PRONOUN
○ *Caitlin* **refused the invitation even though** *she* **wanted to go.**

Pronouns fall into several categories.

Personal pronouns

Personal pronouns refer to specific persons or things. Each can take several forms (*I, me, my, mine*) depending on its function in the sentence (32a).

I, me, you, he, she, him, her, it, we, they, them

○ **When Keisha saw the dogs again,** *she* **called** *them*, **and** *they* **ran to** *her*.

Possessive pronouns

Possessive pronouns are personal pronouns that indicate ownership (32a3 and 47a).

my, mine, your, yours, her, hers, his, its, our, ours, their, theirs

○ *My* **roommate lost** *her* **keys.**

Reflexive pronouns

Reflexive pronouns refer to the subject of the sentence or clause in which they appear. They end in *-self* or *-selves*.

myself, yourself, himself, herself, itself, oneself, ourselves, yourselves, themselves

○ **The seals sunned *themselves* on the warm rocks.**

Intensive pronouns

Intensive pronouns have the same form as reflexive pronouns. They emphasize a noun or another pronoun.

○ **He decided to paint the apartment *himself*.**

Indefinite pronouns

Indefinite pronouns do not refer to specific nouns, although they may refer to identifiable persons or things (31e and 32k). The following is a partial list:

all, another, anybody, both, each, either, everything, few, many, most, neither, none, no one, nothing, one, some, something

○ ***Everybody* screamed, and *someone* fainted, when the lights went out.**

Demonstrative pronouns

Demonstrative pronouns identify or point to specific nouns.

this, that, these, those

○ ***These* are Peter's books.**

Interrogative pronouns

Interrogative pronouns are used to ask questions.

who, which, what

○ ***Who* can help set up the chairs for the meeting?**

Relative pronouns

Relative pronouns introduce dependent clauses and relate the dependent clause to the rest of the sentence (29c4). The interrogative pronoun *who* and the relative pronouns *who* and *whoever* have different forms depending on how they are used in a sentence (32b).

> who, which, that, what, whoever, whichever, whatever

○ **Maya, *who* hires interns, is the manager *whom* you should contact.**

Reciprocal pronouns

Reciprocal pronouns refer to individual parts of a plural antecedent.

> each other, one another

○ **The business failed because the partners distrusted *each other*.**

EXERCISE 29.4

Identify the pronouns and any antecedents in each of the following sentences, underlining the pronouns once and any antecedents twice. Example:

> As identical <u>twins</u>, <u>they</u> really do understand <u>each other</u>.

1. He told the volunteers to help themselves to the leftovers.
2. There are two kinds of people: those who divide people into two kinds and those who don't.
3. Who is going to buy the jeans and wear them if the designer himself finds them uncomfortable?
4. Before an annual performance review, employees are asked to take a hard look at themselves and their work habits.
5. Forwarding an email warning about a computer virus to everyone in your address book is never a good idea.

○ bedfordstmartins.com/smhandbook
  Exercise Central > Sentence Grammar > Grammatical Sentences

---

4 Adjectives

Adjectives modify (limit the meaning of) nouns and pronouns, usually by describing, identifying, or quantifying those words (see Chapter 33). Adjectives that identify or quantify are sometimes called *determiners* (56c).

○ The *red* Corvette ran off the road. [describes]

○ *That* Corvette needs to be repaired. [identifies]

○ We saw *several other* Corvettes race by. [quantifies]

In addition to their basic forms, most descriptive adjectives have other forms that allow you to make comparisons: *small, smaller, smallest; foolish, more foolish, most foolish, less foolish, least foolish.*

○ This year's attendance was *smaller* than last year's.

Adjectives usually precede the words they modify, though they may follow linking verbs: *The car was defective.* Many pronouns (29b3) can function as identifying adjectives when they are followed by a noun.

○ *That* is a dangerous intersection. [pronoun]

○ *That* intersection is dangerous. [identifying adjective]

Other kinds of adjectives that identify or quantify are the articles *a, an,* and *the* (56d) and numbers (*three, sixty-fifth, five hundred*).

Proper adjectives, which are capitalized (50b), form from or relate to proper nouns (*Egyptian, Emersonian*).

5 Adverbs

Adverbs modify verbs, adjectives, other adverbs, or entire clauses (see Chapter 33). Many adverbs end in *-ly*, though some do not (*always, never, very, well*), and some words that end in *-ly* are not adverbs but adjectives (*friendly, lovely*). One of the most common adverbs is *not.*

○ Business writers *frequently* communicate with strangers. [modifies the verb *communicate*]

○ How can they attract customers in an *increasingly* difficult economy? [modifies the adjective *difficult*]

○ They must work *particularly* hard to avoid offending readers. [modifies the adverb *hard*]

○ *Obviously*, they weigh their words with special care. [modifies the independent clause that makes up the rest of the sentence]

Adverbs often answer the questions *when? where? why? how? to what extent?*

Many adverbs, like many adjectives, take different forms when making comparisons: *forcefully, more forcefully, most forcefully, less forcefully, least forcefully.*

▶ **Of all the candidates, she speaks the *most forcefully*.**

Conjunctive adverbs modify an entire clause and express the connection in meaning between that clause and the preceding clause (or sentence). Conjunctive adverbs include *however, furthermore, therefore,* and *likewise* (29b7).

EXERCISE 29.5

Identify the adjectives and adverbs in each of the following sentences, underlining the adjectives once and the adverbs twice. Remember that articles and some pronouns are used as adjectives. Example:

Inadvertently, the two agents misquoted their major client.

1. The small, frightened child firmly squeezed my hand and refused to take another step forward.
2. Meanwhile, she learned that the financial records had been completely false.
3. Koalas are generally quiet creatures that make loud grunting noises during mating season.
4. The huge red tomatoes looked lovely, but they tasted disappointingly like cardboard.
5. The youngest dancer in the troupe performed a brilliant solo.

> ⊙ bedfordstmartins.com/smhandbook
> **Exercise Central > Sentence Grammar > Grammatical Sentences**

6 Prepositions

Prepositions express relationships—in space, time, or other senses—between nouns or pronouns and other words in a sentence.

▶ **We did not want to leave *during* the game.**

▶ **The contestants waited nervously *for* the announcement.**

A prepositional phrase (see Chapter 58) begins with a preposition and ends with the noun or pronoun it connects to the rest of the sentence.

▶ Drive *across* the bridge and go *down* the avenue *past* three stoplights.

SOME COMMON PREPOSITIONS

about	at	down	near	since
above	before	during	of	through
across	behind	except	off	toward
after	below	for	on	under
against	beneath	from	onto	until
along	beside	in	out	up
among	between	inside	over	upon
around	beyond	into	past	with
as	by	like	regarding	without

SOME COMPOUND PREPOSITIONS

according to	except for	instead of
as well as	in addition to	next to
because of	in front of	out of
by way of	in place of	with regard to
due to	in spite of	

Research for this book shows that many writers—including native speakers of English—have trouble choosing appropriate prepositions. If you are not sure which preposition to use, consult your dictionary.

EXERCISE 29.6

Identify and underline the prepositions in the following sentences. Example:

<u>In</u> the dim interior <u>of</u> the hut crouched an old man.

1. The supervisor of the night shift requested that all available personnel work extra hours from October through December.
2. The hatchlings emerged from their shells, crawled across the sand, and swam into the sea.

3. Instead of creating a peaceful new beginning, the tribunal factions are constantly fighting among themselves.

4. After some hard thinking on a weeklong camping trip, I decided I would quit my job and join the Peace Corps for two years.

5. The nuclear power plant about ten miles from the city has the worst safety record of any plant in the country.

> → bedfordstmartins.com/smhandbook
> **Exercise Central > Sentence Grammar > Grammatical Sentences**

7 Conjunctions

Conjunctions connect words or groups of words to each other and tell something about the relationship between these words.

Coordinating conjunctions

Coordinating conjunctions (41a) join equivalent structures — two or more nouns, pronouns, verbs, adjectives, adverbs, prepositions, conjunctions, phrases, or clauses.

▷ A strong *but* warm breeze blew across the desert.

▷ Please print *or* type the information on the application form.

▷ Taiwo worked two shifts today, *so* she is tired tonight.

COORDINATING CONJUNCTIONS

and	but	for	nor	or	so	yet

Correlative conjunctions

Correlative conjunctions join equal elements, and they come in pairs.

▷ *Both* Bechtel *and* Kaiser submitted bids on the project.

▷ Maisha *not only* sent a card *but also* visited me in the hospital.

CORRELATIVE CONJUNCTIONS

both . . . and	just as . . . so	not only . . . but also
either . . . or	neither . . . nor	whether . . . or

Subordinating conjunctions

Subordinating conjunctions (41b) introduce adverb clauses and signal the relationship between the adverb clause and another clause, usually an independent clause. For instance, in the following sentence, the subordinating conjunction *while* signals a time relationship, letting us know that the two events in the sentence happened simultaneously:

▸ Sweat ran down my face *while* I frantically searched for my child.

SOME COMMON SUBORDINATING CONJUNCTIONS

after	if	unless
although	in order that	until
as	once	when
as if	since	where
because	so that	while
before	than	
even though	though	

Conjunctive adverbs

Conjunctive adverbs connect independent clauses and often act as transitional expressions (44e). As their name suggests, conjunctive adverbs can act as both adverbs and conjunctions because they modify the second clause in addition to connecting it to the preceding clause. Like many other adverbs yet unlike other conjunctions, they can move to different positions in a clause.

▸ The cider tasted bitter; *however*, each of us drank a tall glass of it.

▸ The cider tasted bitter; each of us, *however*, drank a tall glass of it.

SOME CONJUNCTIVE ADVERBS

also	indeed	now
anyway	instead	otherwise
besides	likewise	similarly
certainly	meanwhile	still
finally	moreover	then
furthermore	namely	therefore
however	nevertheless	thus
incidentally	next	undoubtedly

Independent clauses connected by a conjunctive adverb must be separated by a semicolon or a period, not just a comma (36c).

▶ **Some of these problems could occur at any company;** *still*, **many could happen only here.**

EXERCISE 29.7

Underline the coordinating, correlative, and subordinating conjunctions as well as the conjunctive adverbs in each of the following sentences. Example:

We used sleeping bags, <u>even though</u> the cabin had sheets <u>and</u> blankets.

1. After waiting for an hour and a half, both Jenny and I were disgruntled, so we went home.
2. The facilities were not only uncomfortable but also dangerous.
3. I usually get a bonus each January; however, sales were down this year, so the company did not give us any extra money.
4. Although I had completed a six-week training regimen of running, swimming, and cycling, I did not feel ready, so I withdrew from the competition.
5. Enrique was not qualified for the job because he knew one of the programming languages but not the other; still, the interview encouraged him.

> ↪ bedfordstmartins.com/smhandbook
> **Exercise Central > Sentence Grammar > Grammatical Sentences**

8 Interjections

Interjections express surprise or emotion: *oh, ouch, hey.* Interjections often stand alone. Even when they are included in a sentence, they do not relate grammatically to the rest of the sentence.

▶ *Hey*, **no one suggested that we would find an easy solution.**

29c The parts of a sentence

Knowing a word's part of speech helps you understand how to use it, but you also have to look at the part it plays in a particular sentence.

SUBJECT
▶ This *description* conveys the ecology of the Everglades.

DIRECT OBJECT
▶ I read a *description* of the ecology of the Everglades.

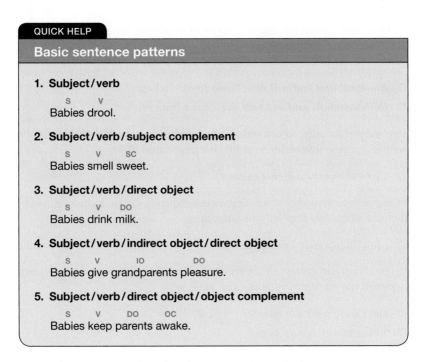

QUICK HELP

Basic sentence patterns

1. **Subject/verb**

   S   V
   Babies drool.

2. **Subject/verb/subject complement**

   S   V   SC
   Babies smell sweet.

3. **Subject/verb/direct object**

   S   V   DO
   Babies drink milk.

4. **Subject/verb/indirect object/direct object**

   S   V   IO   DO
   Babies give grandparents pleasure.

5. **Subject/verb/direct object/object complement**

   S   V   DO   OC
   Babies keep parents awake.

Description is a noun in both of these sentences, yet in the first it serves as the subject of the verb *conveys*, while in the second it serves as the direct object of the verb *read*.

[1] Subjects

The subject of a sentence identifies what the sentence is about. The simple subject consists of one or more nouns or pronouns; the complete subject consists of the simple subject (SS) with all its modifiers.

     SS
▷ *Baseball* **is a summer game.**

      ┌──── COMPLETE SUBJECT ────┐
                     SS
▷ *Sailing over the fence, the ball* **crashed through Mr. Wilson's window.**

      ┌──── COMPLETE SUBJECT ────┐
   SS
▷ *Those who sit in the bleachers* **have the most fun.**

A compound subject contains two or more simple subjects joined with a coordinating conjunction (*and, but, or*) or a correlative conjunction (*both ... and, either ... or, neither ... nor, not only ... but also*). (See 29b7.)

▷ ***Baseball and softball*** developed from cricket.

▷ ***Both baseball and softball developed*** from cricket.

The subject usually comes before the predicate, or verb, but sometimes writers reverse this order to achieve a particular effect.

▷ Up to the plate stepped *Casey.*

In imperative sentences, which express requests or commands, the subject *you* is usually implied but not stated.

▷ (*You*) Keep your eye on the ball.

In questions and certain other constructions, the subject usually appears between the auxiliary verb and the main verb.

▷ Did *Casey* save the game?

▷ Never have *I* felt so angry.

In sentences beginning with *there* or *here* followed by a form of the verb *be*, the subject always follows the verb. *There* and *here* are never the subject.

▷ There was no *joy* in Mudville.

EXERCISE 29.8

Identify the complete subject and the simple subject in each sentence. Underline the complete subject once and the simple subject twice. Example:

The tall, powerful woman defiantly blocked the doorway.

1. That container of fried rice has spent six weeks in the back of the refrigerator.
2. Did the new tour guide remember to stop in the ancient Greek gallery?
3. There was one student still taking the exam when the bell rang.
4. Japanese animation, with its cutting-edge graphics and futuristic plots, has earned many American admirers.

5. Sniffer dogs trained to detect drugs, blood, and explosives can help solve crimes and save lives.

 bedfordstmartins.com/smhandbook
Exercise Central > Sentence Grammar > Grammatical Sentences

2 Predicates

In addition to a subject, every sentence has a predicate, which asserts or asks something about the subject or tells the subject to do something. The key word of most predicates is a verb. The simple predicate of a sentence consists of the main verb and any auxiliaries; the complete predicate includes the simple predicate (SP) and any modifiers of the verb and any objects or complements and their modifiers.

▶ Both of us *are planning to major in history.*

A compound predicate contains two or more verbs that have the same subject, usually joined by a coordinating or a correlative conjunction.

▶ Omar *shut the book, put it back on the shelf, and sighed.*

On the basis of how they function in predicates, verbs can be divided into three categories: linking, transitive, and intransitive.

Linking verbs

A linking verb links, or joins, a subject with a subject complement (SC), a word or word group that identifies or describes the subject.

    S   V ┌──── SC ────┐
▶ Christine is an excellent teacher.

    S V ┌─ SC ─┐
▶ She is patient.

If it identifies the subject, the complement is a noun or pronoun (*an excellent teacher*). If it describes the subject, the complement is an adjective (*patient*).

The forms of *be*, when used as main verbs, are linking verbs (like *are* in this sentence). Other verbs, such as *appear, become, feel, grow, look, make, seem, smell,* and *sound,* can also function as linking verbs, depending on the sense of the sentence.

> ┌──────────── S ────────────┐ ┌──── V ────┐   SC
> ○ **The abandoned farmhouse had become dilapidated.**

Transitive verbs

A transitive verb expresses action that is directed toward a noun or pronoun, called the direct object of the verb.

>   S   V   ┌──── DO ────┐
> ○ **He peeled all the rutabagas.**

Here, the subject and verb do not express a complete thought. The direct object completes the thought by saying *what* he peeled.

A direct object may be followed by an object complement, a word or word group that describes or identifies it. Object complements may be adjectives, as in the next example, or nouns, as in the second example.

>   S V ┌──────────── DO ────────────┐ ┌──── OC ────┐
> ○ **I find cell-phone conversations in restaurants very annoying.**

>   S   V   DO   ┌──── OC ────┐
> ○ **Alana considers Keyshawn her best friend.**

A transitive verb may also be followed by an indirect object, which tells to whom or what, or for whom or what, the verb's action is done. You might say the indirect object is the recipient of the direct object.

> ┌──────────── S ────────────┐ V   IO ┌──── DO ────┐
> ○ **The sound of the traffic all night long gave me a splitting headache.**

Intransitive verbs

An intransitive verb expresses action that is not directed toward an object. Therefore, an intransitive verb does not have a direct object.

> ┌──── S ────┐   V
> ○ **The Red Sox persevered.**

> ┌──── S ────┐   V
> ○ **Their fans watched anxiously.**

The action of the verb *persevered* has no object (it makes no sense to ask, *persevered what?* or *persevered whom?*), and the action of the verb *watched* is directed toward an object that is implied but not expressed.

Some verbs that express action can be only transitive or only intransitive, but most can be used either way, with or without a direct object.

⊙ **A maid wearing a uniform opened the door.** [transitive]

⊙ **The door opened silently.** [intransitive]

EXERCISE 29.9

Underline the predicate in each of the following sentences. Then label each verb as linking (LV), transitive (TV), or intransitive (IV). Finally, label all subject and object complements and all direct and indirect objects. Example:

  We considered city life unbearable.

1. He is proud of his heritage.
2. The horrifying news story made me angry.
3. The old house looks deserted.
4. Rock and roll will never die.
5. Chloe's boss offered her a promotion.

> bedfordstmartins.com/smhandbook
> **Exercise Central > Sentence Grammar > Grammatical Sentences**

3 Phrases

A phrase is a group of words that lacks either a subject or a predicate or both.

⊙ **The new law will restrict smoking *in most public places*.**

The basic subject of this sentence is a noun phrase, *the new law*; the basic predicate is a verb phrase, *will restrict smoking*. The prepositional phrase *in most public places* functions here as an adverb, telling where smoking will be restricted.

This section will discuss the various kinds of phrases: noun, verb, prepositional, verbal, absolute, and appositive.

Noun phrases

Made up of a noun and all its modifiers, a noun phrase can function in a sentence as a subject, object, or complement.

⊙ *Delicious, gooey peanut butter* is surprisingly healthful. — SUBJECT

⊙ I craved a *green salad with plenty of fresh vegetables.* — OBJECT

⊙ A tuna sandwich is *a popular lunch.* — COMPLEMENT

Verb phrases

A main verb and its auxiliary verbs make up a verb phrase, which functions in a sentence in only one way: as a predicate.

⊙ Frank *can swim* for a long time.

⊙ His headaches *might have been caused* by tension.

Prepositional phrases

A prepositional phrase begins with a preposition and includes a noun or pronoun (the object of the preposition) and any modifiers of the object. Prepositional phrases usually function as adjectives or adverbs.

ADJECTIVE   Our house *in Maine* was a cabin.

ADVERB   *From Cadillac Mountain,* you can see the northern lights.

Verbal phrases

Verbals are verb forms that function not as verbs but as nouns, adjectives, or adverbs. There are three kinds of verbals: participles, gerunds, and infinitives.

PARTICIPLES AND PARTICIPIAL PHRASES

The present participle is the *-ing* form of a verb (*spinning*). The past participle of most verbs ends in *-ed* (*accepted*), but some verbs have an irregular past participle (*worn, frozen*). Participles function as adjectives (33a).

○ A kiss awakened the *dreaming* princess.

○ The cryptographers deciphered the *hidden* meaning in the message.

Participial phrases, which also act as adjectives, consist of a present or past participle and any modifiers, objects, or complements.

○ *Irritated by the delay,* Luisa complained.

○ A dog *howling at the moon* kept me awake.

GERUNDS AND GERUND PHRASES

The gerund has the same -*ing* form as the present participle but functions as a noun.

SUBJECT	*Writing* takes practice.
OBJECT	The organization promotes *recycling*.

Gerund phrases, which function as nouns, consist of a gerund and any modifiers, objects, or complements.

┌────────── SUBJECT ──────────┐
○ *Opening their eyes to the problem* was not easy.

┌────────── DIRECT OBJECT ──────────┐
○ They suddenly heard *a loud wailing from the sandbox*.

INFINITIVES AND INFINITIVE PHRASES

The infinitive is the *to* form of a verb (*to dream, to be*). An infinitive can function as a noun, an adjective, or an adverb.

NOUN	She wanted *to write*.
ADJECTIVE	They had no more time *to waste*.
ADVERB	The corporation was ready *to expand*.

Infinitive phrases, which also function as nouns, adjectives, or adverbs, consist of an infinitive and any modifiers, objects, or complements.

┌────────── NOUN / SC ──────────┐
○ My goal is *to be a biology teacher*.

○ A party would be a good way *to end the semester.* [labeled ADJECTIVE]

○ *To perfect a draft*, always proofread carefully. [labeled ADVERB]

Absolute phrases

An absolute phrase usually includes a noun or pronoun and a participle. It modifies an entire sentence rather than a particular word and is usually set off from the rest of the sentence with commas (44c).

○ I stood on the deck, *the wind whipping my hair.*

○ *My fears laid to rest*, I set off on my first solo flight.

When the participle is *being*, it is often omitted.

○ The ambassador, *her head (being) high*, walked out of the room.

Appositive phrases

An appositive phrase is a noun phrase that renames the noun or pronoun that immediately precedes it (44c3).

○ The report, *a hefty three-volume work*, included ninety recommendations.

○ We had a single desire, *to change the administration's policies.*

EXERCISE 29.10

Read the following sentences, and identify and label all of the prepositional, verbal, absolute, and appositive phrases. Notice that one kind of phrase may appear within another kind. Example:

[labeled ABSOLUTE, PREP]
His voice breaking with emotion, Ed thanked us for the award.

1. Chantelle, the motel clerk, hopes to be certified as a river guide.
2. Carpets made by hand are usually the most valuable.
3. My stomach doing flips, I answered the door.
4. Floating on my back, I ignored my practice requirements.
5. Driving across town during rush hour can take thirty minutes or more.

bedfordstmartins.com/smhandbook
Exercise Central > Sentence Grammar > Grammatical Sentences

4 Clauses

A clause is a group of words containing a subject and a predicate. There are two kinds of clauses: independent and dependent. Independent clauses (also known as main clauses) can stand alone as complete sentences.

- The window is open.

Pairs of independent clauses may be joined with a coordinating conjunction and a comma (29b7 and 44b).

- The window is open, *so* we'd better be quiet.

Like independent clauses, dependent clauses (also known as subordinate clauses) contain a subject and a predicate. They cannot stand alone as complete sentences, however, for they begin with a subordinating word—a subordinating conjunction (29b7) or a relative pronoun (29b3)—that connects them to an independent clause.

- *Because the window is open*, the room feels cool.

The subordinating conjunction *because* transforms the independent clause *the window is open* into a dependent clause. In doing so, it indicates a causal relationship between the two clauses.

Dependent clauses function as nouns, adjectives, or adverbs.

Noun clauses

Noun clauses, which can function as subjects, direct objects, subject complements, or objects of prepositions, are always contained within another clause. They usually begin with a relative pronoun (*that, which, what, who, whom, whose, whatever, whoever, whomever, whichever*) or with *when, where, whether, why,* or *how.*

- *That he had a college degree* was important to her.

  (S)

- She asked *where he went to college.*

  (DO)

⬭ The real question was *why she wanted to know.* [SC]

⬭ She was looking for *whatever information was available.* [OBJ OF PREP]

Notice that in each of these sentences the noun clause is an integral part of the independent clause that makes up the sentence; for example, in the second sentence the independent clause is not just *She asked* but *She asked where he went to college.*

Adjective clauses

Adjective clauses modify nouns and pronouns in another clause. Usually they immediately follow the words they modify.

⬭ The surgery, *which took three hours*, was a complete success.

⬭ It was performed by the surgeon *who had developed the procedure.*

⬭ The hospital was the one *where I was born.*

Sometimes the relative pronoun introducing an adjective clause may be omitted, as in the following example:

⬭ That is one book [*that*] *I intend to read.*

Adverb clauses

Adverb clauses modify verbs, adjectives, or other adverbs. They begin with a subordinating conjunction (29b7). Like adverbs, they usually tell when, where, why, how, or to what extent.

⬭ We hiked *where there were few other hikers.*

⬭ My backpack felt heavier *than it ever had.*

⬭ I climbed as swiftly *as I could under the weight of my backpack.*

EXERCISE 29.11

Identify the independent and dependent clauses and any subordinating conjunctions and relative pronouns in each of the following sentences. Example:

┌──────── DEPENDENT CLAUSE ────────┐ ┌──── INDEPENDENT CLAUSE ────┐
If I were going on a really long hike, I would carry a lightweight stove.

(If)is a subordinating conjunction.

1. The hockey game was postponed because one of the players collapsed on the bench.

2. She eventually discovered the secret admirer who had been leaving notes in her locker.

3. After completing three advanced drawing classes, Jason was admitted into the fine arts program, and he immediately rented a small studio space.

4. The test was easier than I had expected.

5. I could tell that it was going to rain, so I tried to get home quickly.

---

bedfordstmartins.com/smhandbook
Exercise Central > Sentence Grammar > Grammatical Sentences

EXERCISE 29.12

Expand each of the following sentences by adding at least one dependent clause to it. Be prepared to explain how your addition improves the sentence. Example:

As the earth continued to shake, the
~~The~~ books tumbled from the shelves.
^

1. The economy gradually began to recover.

2. Simone waited nervously by the phone.

3. New school safety rules were instituted this fall.

4. Rob always borrowed money from friends.

5. The crowd grew louder and more disorderly.

29d Types of sentences

Noticing how many and what types of clauses sentences contain and identifying whether they make a statement, ask a question, issue a command, or express an exclamation can help you analyze and assess your sentences as you write and revise.

1 Simple, compound, complex, and compound-complex sentences

Grammatically, sentences may be simple, compound, complex, or compound-complex.

Simple sentences

A simple sentence consists of one independent clause and no dependent clause. The subject or the predicate, or both, may be compound.

- **The trailer is surrounded by a wooden deck.**
- **Pompeii and Herculaneum disappeared under tons of lava and ash.**
- **At the country club, the head pro and his assistant give lessons, run the golf shop, and try to keep the members content.**

Compound sentences

A compound sentence consists of two or more independent clauses and no dependent clause. The clauses may be joined by a comma and a coordinating conjunction (29b7) or by a semicolon.

- **Occasionally a car goes up the dirt trail, and dust flies everywhere.**
- **Alberto is obsessed with soccer; he eats, breathes, and lives the game.**

Complex sentences

A complex sentence consists of one independent clause and at least one dependent clause.

┌──────── DEPENDENT CLAUSE ────────┐
- **Many people believe that anyone can earn a living.**

┌──────── DEPENDENT CLAUSE ────────┐
- **Those who do not like to get dirty should not go camping.**

┌──────── DEPENDENT CLAUSE ────────┐
- **As I awaited my interview, I sat with another candidate**

┌──── DEPENDENT CLAUSE ────┐
who smiled nervously.

Compound-complex sentences

A compound-complex sentence consists of two or more independent clauses and at least one dependent clause.

┌──── IND CLAUSE ────┐ ┌──── DEP CLAUSE ────┐
- **I complimented Joe when he finished the job, and**

┌──── IND CLAUSE ────┐
he seemed pleased.

┌──────── IND CLAUSE ────────┐ ┌──────── IND CLAUSE ────────┐
○ **The actors performed well, but the audience hated the play,**

┌──────── DEP CLAUSE ────────┐
which was confusing and far too long.

2 **Declarative, interrogative, imperative, and exclamatory sentences**

In terms of function, sentences can be declarative (making a statement), interrogative (asking a question), imperative (giving a command), or exclamatory (expressing strong feeling).

DECLARATIVE   He sings with the Grace Church Boys' Choir.

INTERROGATIVE   How long has he sung with them?

IMPERATIVE   Comb his hair before the performance starts.

EXCLAMATORY   What voices those boys have!

EXERCISE 29.13

Classify each of the following sentences as simple, compound, complex, or compound-complex. In addition, note any sentence that may be classified as interrogative, imperative, or exclamatory.

1. The boat rocked and lurched over the rough surf as the passengers groaned in agony.
2. Is this the coldest winter on record, or was last year even worse?
3. After waiting for over an hour, I was examined by the doctor for only three minutes!
4. Keeping in mind the terrain, the weather, and the length of the hike, decide what you need to take.
5. The former prisoner, who was cleared by DNA evidence, has lost six years of his life, and he needs a job right away.

○ bedfordstmartins.com/smhandbook
Exercise Central > Sentence Grammar > Grammatical Sentences

THINKING CRITICALLY ABOUT SENTENCES

The following sentences come from the openings of well-known works. Identify the independent and dependent clauses in each sentence. Then choose one sentence, and write a sentence of your own imitating its structure, clause for clause and phrase for phrase. Example:

Ten days after the war ended, my sister Laura drove a car off a bridge.
—MARGARET ATWOOD, *The Blind Assassin*

A few minutes before the detectives arrived, our friend Nastassia found a passageway behind the wall.

1. We observe today not a victory of party but a celebration of freedom, symbolizing an end as well as a beginning, signifying renewal as well as change.
—JOHN F. KENNEDY, *Inaugural Address*

2. Once in a long while, four times so far for me, my mother brings out the metal tube that holds her medical diploma.
—MAXINE HONG KINGSTON, "Photographs of My Parents"

Verbs

30

Used skillfully, verbs can be the heartbeat of prose, moving it along, enlivening it, carrying its action: As the little girl *skipped* in, she *bounced* a red rubber ball and *smiled* from ear to ear.

30a Verb forms

Except for *be*, all English verbs have five possible forms.

BASE FORM	PAST TENSE	PAST PARTICIPLE	PRESENT PARTICIPLE	-S FORM
talk	talked	talked	talking	talks
adore	adored	adored	adoring	adores

The base form is the one listed in the dictionary. For all verbs except *be*, use the base form to indicate an action or condition in the present when the subject is plural or when the subject is *I* or *you*.

○ **During the ritual, the women *go* into trances.**

Use the past tense to indicate an action or condition that occurred entirely in the past. For most verbs, the past tense is formed by adding *-ed* or *-d* to the base form. Some verbs, however, have irregular past-tense forms. *Be* has two past-tense forms, *was* and *were* (30a1).

○ **The Globe *was* the stage for many of Shakespeare's works.**

○ **In 1613, it *caught* fire and burned to the ground.**

Use the past participle to form perfect tenses and the passive voice (30g). A past participle usually has

Restaurant menus often spotlight verbs in action. One famous place in Boston, for instance, offers to bake, broil, wood-grill, pan-fry, deep-fry, poach, sauté, fricassée, blacken, or scallop any of the fish entrées on its menu. To someone ordering— or cooking—at this restaurant, the distinctions among the dishes lie entirely in the verbs.

the same form as the past tense, though some verbs have irregular past participles. (See 30c.)

- She *had accomplished* the impossible. [past perfect]
- No one *was injured* in the explosion. [passive voice]

The present participle is constructed by adding *-ing* to the base form. Use it with auxiliary verbs to indicate a continuing action or condition.

- Many students *are competing* in the race. [continuing action]

Present participles sometimes function as adjectives or nouns (gerunds), and past participles can also serve as adjectives; in such cases they are not verbs but verbals (29c3).

Except for *be* and *have*, the *-s* form consists of the base form plus *-s* or *-es*. This form indicates an action in the present for third-person singular subjects. All singular nouns; *he*, *she*, and *it*; and many other pronouns (such as *this* and *someone*) are third-person singular.

	SINGULAR	PLURAL
FIRST PERSON	I *wish*	we *wish*
SECOND PERSON	you *wish*	you *wish*
THIRD PERSON	he/she/it *wishes*	they *wish*
	Joe *wishes*	children *wish*
	someone *wishes*	many *wish*

The third-person singular form of *have* is *has*.

QUICK HELP

Editing for *-s* and *-es* endings

If you tend to leave off or misuse the *-s* and *-es* verb endings in academic writing, you should check for them systematically.

1. Underline every verb, and then circle all verbs in the present tense.
2. Find the subject of every verb you circled.
3. If the subject is a singular noun; *he, she,* or *it*; or a singular indefinite pronoun, be sure the verb ends in *-s* or *-es*. If the subject is not third-person singular, the verb should not have an *-s* or *-es* ending.
4. Be careful with auxiliary verbs such as *can* or *may* (57b). These auxiliaries are used with the base form, never with the *-s* or *-es* form.

1 Forms of *be*

Be has three forms in the present tense (*am, is, are*) and two in the past tense (*was, were*).

Present tense

	SINGULAR	PLURAL
FIRST PERSON	I *am*	we *are*
SECOND PERSON	you *are*	you *are*
THIRD PERSON	he/she/it *is*	they *are*
	Juan *is*	children *are*
	somebody *is*	many *are*

Past tense

	SINGULAR	PLURAL
FIRST PERSON	I *was*	we *were*
SECOND PERSON	you *were*	you *were*
THIRD PERSON	he/she/it *was*	they *were*
	Juan *was*	children *were*
	somebody *was*	many *were*

2 Absence of *be*; habitual *be*

○ **My sister at work. She be there every day 'til five.**

The preceding sentences illustrate common usages of *be*. The first sentence shows the absence of *be*; the second shows the use of "habitual *be*," indicating that something is always or almost always the case. (The same sentences rephrased in academic English would read, "My sister is at work. She is there every day until five.")

Many African American speakers regularly, effectively, and systematically use *be* in these ways. You may want to quote dialogue featuring these patterns in your own writing to evoke particular regions or communities (see Chapter 26) or to create a sense of everyday conversation. Most academic writing, however, calls for academic English.

30b Auxiliary verbs

Use auxiliary verbs with a base form, present participle, or past participle to create verb phrases. The base form or participle in a verb phrase is the main verb. The most common auxiliaries, forms of *be*, *do*, and *have*, indicate completed or continuing action, the passive voice, emphasis, questions, and negative statements.

○ We *have considered* all viewpoints. [completed action]
○ The college *is building* a new dormitory. [continuing action]
○ We *were warned* to stay away. [passive voice]
○ I *do respect* your viewpoint. [emphasis]
○ *Do* you *know* the answer? [question]
○ He *does* not *like* wearing a tie. [negative statement]

Modal auxiliaries—*can, could, might, may, must, ought to, shall, will, should, would*—indicate future action, possibility, necessity, obligation, and so on.

○ They *will explain* the procedure. [future action]
○ You *can see* three states from the top of the mountain. [possibility]
○ I *must try* harder to go to bed early. [necessity]
○ She *should visit* her parents more often. [obligation]

FOR MULTILINGUAL WRITERS

Modal auxiliaries

Why do we *not* say "Alice can to read Latin"? For a discussion of *can* and other modal auxiliaries, see 57b.

30c Regular and irregular verbs

A verb is regular when its past tense and past participle are formed by adding *-ed* or *-d* to the base form.

BASE FORM	PAST TENSE	PAST PARTICIPLE
love	loved	loved
honor	honored	honored
obey	obeyed	obeyed

> **QUICK HELP**
>
> ## Editing for *-ed* or *-d* endings
>
> Speakers who delete the *-ed* or *-d* endings in conversation may forget to include them in academic writing. If you tend to drop these endings, make a point of checking for them when proofreading. Underline all the verbs, and then underline a second time any that are past tense or past participles. Check each of these for an *-ed* or *-d* ending. Unless the verb is irregular (see the following list), it should end in *-ed* or *-d*.

Irregular verbs

A verb is irregular when it does not follow the *-ed* or *-d* pattern. If you are unsure about whether a verb is regular or irregular, or what the correct form is, consult the following list or a dictionary. Dictionaries list any irregular forms under the entry for the base form.

> **QUICK HELP**
>
> ## Some common irregular verbs
>
> | BASE FORM | PAST TENSE | PAST PARTICIPLE |
> |---|---|---|
> | arise | arose | arisen |
> | be | was/were | been |
> | bear | bore | borne, born |
> | beat | beat | beaten |
> | become | became | become |
> | begin | began | begun |
> | bite | bit | bitten, bit |
> | blow | blew | blown |
> | break | broke | broken |
> | bring | brought | brought |
> | broadcast | broadcast | broadcast |
> | build | built | built |
> | burn | burned, burnt | burned, burnt |
> | burst | burst | burst |
> | buy | bought | bought |
> | catch | caught | caught |
> | | | *(continued on next page)* |

(continued from p. 593)

BASE FORM	PAST TENSE	PAST PARTICIPLE
choose	chose	chosen
come	came	come
cost	cost	cost
cut	cut	cut
dig	dug	dug
dive	dived, dove	dived
do	did	done
draw	drew	drawn
dream	dreamed, dreamt	dreamed, dreamt
drink	drank	drunk
drive	drove	driven
eat	ate	eaten
fall	fell	fallen
feel	felt	felt
fight	fought	fought
find	found	found
fly	flew	flown
forget	forgot	forgotten, forgot
freeze	froze	frozen
get	got	gotten, got
give	gave	given
go	went	gone
grow	grew	grown
hang (suspend)[1]	hung	hung
have	had	had
hear	heard	heard
hide	hid	hidden
hit	hit	hit
keep	kept	kept
know	knew	known
lay	laid	laid

[1]*Hang* meaning "execute by hanging" is regular: *hang, hanged, hanged.*

BASE FORM	PAST TENSE	PAST PARTICIPLE
lead	led	led
leave	left	left
lend	lent	lent
let	let	let
lie (recline)[2]	lay	lain
lose	lost	lost
make	made	made
mean	meant	meant
meet	met	met
pay	paid	paid
prove	proved	proved, proven
put	put	put
read	read	read
ride	rode	ridden
ring	rang	rung
rise	rose	risen
run	ran	run
say	said	said
see	saw	seen
send	sent	sent
set	set	set
shake	shook	shaken
shoot	shot	shot
show	showed	showed, shown
shrink	shrank	shrunk
sing	sang	sung
sink	sank	sunk
sit	sat	sat
sleep	slept	slept
speak	spoke	spoken
spend	spent	spent
spread	spread	spread

(continued on next page)

---

[2]*Lie* meaning "tell a falsehood" is regular: *lie, lied, lied.*

(continued from p. 595)

BASE FORM	PAST TENSE	PAST PARTICIPLE
spring	sprang, sprung	sprung
stand	stood	stood
steal	stole	stolen
strike	struck	struck, stricken
swim	swam	swum
swing	swung	swung
take	took	taken
teach	taught	taught
tear	tore	torn
tell	told	told
think	thought	thought
throw	threw	thrown
wake	waked, woke	waked, woken
wear	wore	worn
win	won	won
wind	wound	wound
write	wrote	written

EXERCISE 30.1

Complete each of the following sentences by filling in each blank with the past tense or past participle of the verb listed in parentheses. Example:

They had already *eaten* (eat) the entrée; later they *ate* (eat) the dessert.

1. The babysitter _____ (let) the children play with my schoolbooks, and before I _____ (come) home, they had _____ (tear) out several pages.

2. After they had _____ (review) the evidence, the jury _____ (find) the defendant not guilty.

3. Hypnosis _____ (work) only on willing participants.

4. My parents _____ (plant) a tree for me in the town where I was born, but I have never _____ (go) back to see it.

5. Some residents _____ (know) that the levee was leaking long before the storms, but authorities _____ (ignore) the complaints.

6. I _____ (paint) a picture from a photograph my sister had _____ (take) at the beach.

7. When the buzzer sounded, the racers _____ (spring) into the water and _____ (swim) toward the far end of the pool.

8. We had _____ (assume) for some time that surgery was a possibility, and we had _____ (find) an excellent facility.

9. Once the storm had _____ (pass), we could see that the old oak tree had _____ (fall).

10. Some high-level employees _____ (decide) to speak publicly about the cover-up before the company's official story had _____ (be) released to the media.

> **bedfordstmartins.com/smhandbook**
> **Exercise Central > Sentence Grammar > Verbs**

30d *Lay* and *lie, sit* and *set, raise* and *rise*

Lay and *lie, sit* and *set,* and *raise* and *rise* cause problems for many writers because both verbs in each pair have similar-sounding forms and related meanings. In each pair, one of the verbs is transitive, meaning that it takes a direct object; the other is intransitive, meaning that it does not take an object. The best way to avoid confusing the two is to memorize their forms and meanings. All these verbs except *raise* are irregular.

BASE FORM	PAST TENSE	PAST PARTICIPLE	PRESENT PARTICIPLE	-S FORM
lie (recline)	lay	lain	lying	lies
lay (put)	laid	laid	laying	lays
sit (be seated)	sat	sat	sitting	sits
set (put)	set	set	setting	sets
rise (get up)	rose	risen	rising	rises
raise (lift)	raised	raised	raising	raises

Lie is intransitive and means "recline" or "be situated." *Lay* is transitive and means "put" or "place." This pair is especially confusing because *lay* is also the past-tense form of *lie.*

INTRANSITIVE   He *lay* on the floor when his back ached.

TRANSITIVE   I *laid* the cloth on the table.

Sit is intransitive and means "be seated." *Set* usually is transitive and means "put" or "place."

INTRANSITIVE   She *sat* in the rocking chair.

TRANSITIVE   We *set* the bookshelf in the hallway.

Rise is intransitive and means "get up" or "go up." *Raise* is transitive and means "lift" or "cause to go up."

INTRANSITIVE   He *rose* up in bed and glared at me.

TRANSITIVE   He *raised* his hand eagerly.

EXERCISE 30.2

Underline the appropriate verb form in each of the following sentences. Example:

The guests (*raised* / *rose*) their glasses to the happy couple.

1. That cat (*lies* / *lays*) on the sofa all morning.
2. The chef (*lay* / *laid*) his knives carefully on the counter.
3. The two-year-old walked carefully across the room and (*set* / *sat*) the glass vase on the table.
4. Grandpa used to love (*sitting* / *setting*) on the front porch and telling stories of his childhood.
5. Almost immediately, the dough (*sitting* / *setting*) by the warm oven began to (*raise* / *rise*).

⊙   bedfordstmartins.com/smhandbook
    Exercise Central > Sentence Grammar > Verbs

30e   Verb tenses

Tenses show when the action or condition expressed by a verb occurs. The three simple tenses are present tense, past tense, and future tense.

PRESENT TENSE   I *ask, write*

PAST TENSE   I *asked, wrote*

FUTURE TENSE   I *will ask, will write*

More complex aspects of time are expressed through progressive, perfect, and perfect progressive forms of the simple tenses. (Although this terminology sounds complicated, you regularly use all these forms.)

PRESENT PROGRESSIVE   she *is asking, is writing*

PAST PROGRESSIVE   she *was asking, was writing*

FUTURE PROGRESSIVE   she *will be asking, will be writing*

PRESENT PERFECT   she *has asked, has written*

PAST PERFECT   she *had asked, had written*

FUTURE PERFECT   she *will have asked, will have written*

PRESENT PERFECT
PROGRESSIVE   she *has been asking, has been writing*

PAST PERFECT
PROGRESSIVE   she *had been asking, had been writing*

FUTURE PERFECT
PROGRESSIVE   she *will have been asking, will have been writing*

The simple tenses locate an action only within the three basic time frames of present, past, and future. Progressive forms express continuing actions; perfect forms express actions completed before another action or time in the present, past, or future; perfect progressive forms express actions that continue up to some point in the present, past, or future.

1 Present-tense forms

The simple present indicates actions or conditions occurring now and those occurring habitually. The simple present can indicate a scheduled future event if the sentence explains when the event will take place.

- They *are* very angry about the decision.
- I *eat* breakfast every day at 8:00 AM.
- Love *conquers* all.
- Classes *begin* next week.

Write about general truths or scientific facts in the simple present, even when the predicate of the sentence is in the past tense.

makes
- Pasteur demonstrated that his boiling process ~~made~~ milk safe.
              ^

Use the simple present, not the past tense, when writing about action in literary works.

> _realizes_   _is_
> ● Ishmael slowly ~~realized~~ all that ~~was~~ at stake in the search for the
>   white whale.

In general, use the simple present when you are quoting, summarizing, or paraphrasing someone else's writing.

> _writes_
> ● Keith Walters ~~wrote~~ that the "reputed consequences and promised
>   blessings of literacy are legion."

But in an essay using APA (American Psychological Association) style (see Chapter 17), report your experiments or another researcher's work in the past tense (_wrote, noted_) or the present perfect (_has reported_).

> _noted_
> ● Comer (1995) ~~notes~~ that protesters who deprive themselves of food
>   are seen not as dysfunctional but rather as "caring, sacrificing, even
>   heroic" (p. 5).

Use the present progressive to indicate actions that are ongoing or continuous in the present. It typically describes an action that is happening now, in contrast to the simple present, which more often indicates habitual actions.

| PRESENT PROGRESSIVE | You _are driving_ too fast. |
| SIMPLE PRESENT | I always _drive_ carefully. |

With an appropriate expression of time, you can also use the present progressive to indicate a scheduled event in the future.

> ● We _are having_ friends over for dinner tomorrow night.

Use the present perfect to indicate actions begun in the past and either completed at some unspecified time in the past or continuing into the present.

> ● Uncontrolled logging _has destroyed_ many tropical forests.

Use the present perfect progressive to indicate actions begun in the past and continuing into the present.

▶ The two sides *have been trying* to settle the case out of court.

2 Past-tense forms

Use the simple past to indicate actions or conditions that occurred at a specific time and do not extend into the present.

▶ Germany *invaded* Poland on September 1, 1939.

Use the past progressive to indicate continuing actions in the past.

▶ Lenin *was living* in exile in Zurich when the tsar was overthrown.

Use the past perfect to indicate actions or conditions completed by a specific time in the past or before some other past action occurred.

▶ By the fourth century, Christianity *had become* the state religion.

Use the past perfect progressive to indicate continuing actions or conditions in the past that began before a specific time or before some other past action began.

▶ Carter *had been planning* a naval career until his father died.

3 Future-tense forms

Use the simple future to indicate actions or conditions that have not yet begun.

▶ The exhibition *will come* to Washington in September.

Use the future progressive to indicate continuing actions or conditions in the future.

▶ The loans *will be coming* due over the next two years.

Use the future perfect to indicate actions or conditions that will be completed by or before some specified time in the future.

▶ By next summer, she *will have published* the results of the study.

Use the future perfect progressive to indicate continuing actions or conditions that will be completed by some specified time in the future.

▷ **In May, I *will have been living* in Tucson for five years.**

EXERCISE 30.3

Complete each of the following sentences by filling in the blank with an appropriate form of the verb listed in parentheses. Since more than one form will sometimes be possible, be prepared to explain the reasons for your choices. Example:

The supply of a product _*rises*_ (rise) when the demand is great.

1. History _____ (show) that crime usually decreases as the economy improves.
2. Ever since the first nuclear power plants were built, opponents _____ (fear) disaster.
3. Thousands of Irish peasants _____ (emigrate) to America after the potato famine of the 1840s.
4. The soap opera *General Hospital* _____ (be) on the air since 1963.
5. Olivia _____ (direct) the play next year.
6. While they _____ (eat) in a neighborhood restaurant, they witnessed a minor accident.
7. By this time next week, each of your clients _____ (receive) an invitation to the opening.
8. By the time a child born today enters first grade, he or she _____ (watch) thousands of television commercials.
9. In one of the novel's most famous scenes, Huck _____ (express) his willingness to go to hell rather than report Jim as an escaped slave.
10. A cold typically _____ (last) for about a week and a half.

> bedfordstmartins.com/smhandbook
> **Exercise Central > Sentence Grammar > Verbs**

30f Verb tense sequence

Careful and accurate use of tenses is important to clear writing. Even the simplest narrative describes actions that take place at different times; when you use the appropriate tense for each action, readers can follow such time changes easily.

Editing verb tenses

Errors in verb tenses take several forms. If you have trouble with verb tenses, check for common errors as you proofread.

- Errors of verb form (30c): for example, writing *seen* for *saw*, which confuses the past participle and past-tense forms

- Omitted auxiliary verbs (30b and e): for example, using the simple past (*Uncle Charlie arrived*) when meaning requires the present perfect (*Uncle Charlie has arrived*)

- Nonstandard varieties of English in situations calling for academic English (see 30a2 and Chapter 26): for example, writing *they eat it all up* when the situation requires *they ate it all up*

The sequence of tenses shows the relationship between the tense of the verb in the independent clause of a sentence and the tense of a verb in a dependent clause or a verbal (29c4).

▶ By the time he *lent* her the money, she *had declared* bankruptcy.

1 Verb sequence with infinitives

Use the infinitive of a verb — *to* plus the base form (*to go, to be*) — to indicate actions occurring at the same time as or later than the action of the main verb in the clause.

▶ The child *waved to greet* the passing trains.

The waving and the greeting occurred at the same time in the past.

▶ Each couple *hopes to win* the dance contest.

The hoping is present; the winning is in the future.

Use *to have* plus the past participle (*to have asked*) to indicate that an action occurred before the action of the main verb.

▶ He *was reported to have left* his fortune to his cat.

The leaving of the fortune took place before the reporting.

2 **Verb sequence with participles**

Use the present participle (base form plus *-ing*) to indicate actions occurring at the same time as the action of the main verb.

> ○ *Seeking* **to relieve unemployment, Roosevelt established several public-works programs.**

Use the past participle or *having* plus the past participle to indicate action occurring before that of the main verb.

> ○ *Flown* **to the front, the troops** *joined* **their hard-pressed comrades.**
> ○ *Having changed* **his mind, he** *voted* **against the proposal.**

3 **Verb sequence and habitual actions**

In conversation, people often use *will* or *would* to describe habitual actions. In writing, however, stick to the present and past tenses for this purpose.

> ○ **When I have a deadline, I ~~will~~ work all night.**

> ○ **While we sat on the porch, the children ~~would play.~~** played.

EXERCISE 30.4

Edit each of the following sentences to create the appropriate sequence of tenses. Example:

> He needs to ~~send~~ have sent in his application before today.

1. When she saw *Chicago,* it had made her want to become an actress even more.
2. Leaving England in December, the settlers arrived in Virginia in May.
3. I hoped to make the football team, but injuries prevented me from trying out.
4. Working with great dedication as a summer intern at the magazine, Mohan called his former supervisor in the fall to ask about a permanent position.
5. As we waited for the bus, we would watch the taxis pass by.

○ bedfordstmartins.com/smhandbook
  Exercise Central > Sentence Grammar > Verbs

30g Voice

Voice tells whether the subject is acting (*he questions us*) or being acted upon (*he is questioned*). When the subject is acting, the verb is in the active voice; when the subject is being acted upon, the verb is in the passive voice (43b).

ACTIVE VOICE   The storm *uprooted* huge pine trees.

PASSIVE VOICE   Huge pine trees *were uprooted* by the storm.

The passive voice uses the appropriate form of the auxiliary verb *be* followed by the past participle of the main verb: *he is being questioned, he was questioned, he will be questioned, he has been questioned.*

Most contemporary writers use the active voice as much as possible because it livens up their prose. Passive-voice verbs often make a passage hard to understand and remember. In addition, writers sometimes use the passive voice to avoid taking responsibility for what they have written. A government official who admits that "mistakes were made" skirts the pressing question: made by whom?

QUICK HELP

Editing the verbs in your own writing

- Circle all forms of *be, do,* and *have* used as main verbs. Try in each case to substitute a stronger, more specific verb. (43a)

- Check verb endings that cause you trouble. (30c)

- Use the appropriate forms of *lay* and *lie, sit* and *set, raise* and *rise* for your meaning. (30d)

- If you have problems with verb tenses, use the guidelines on p. 603.

- If you are writing about a literary work, refer to the action in the work in the present tense. (30e1)

- Check all uses of the passive voice for appropriateness. (30g)

- Check all verbs used to introduce quotations, paraphrases, and summaries. If you rely on *say, write,* and other very general verbs, try substituting more vivid, specific verbs (*claim, insist, wonder,* for instance). (43a)

The passive voice can work to good advantage in some situations. Journalists often use the passive voice when the performer of an action is unknown or less important than the recipient.

○ DALLAS, Nov. 22—**President John Fitzgerald Kennedy was shot and killed by an assassin today.**   —TOM WICKER, *New York Times*

Wicker uses the passive voice with good reason: to focus on Kennedy, not on who killed him.

Much technical and scientific writing uses the passive voice to highlight what is being studied.

○ **The volunteers' food intake was closely monitored.**

To shift a sentence from the passive to the active voice (34c), make the performer of the action the subject of the sentence, and make the recipient of the action an object.

○ **His ~~acting career was destroyed by his~~ unprofessional behavior**
  destroyed his acting career.
on the set⋏

EXERCISE 30.5

Convert each sentence from active to passive voice or from passive to active, and note the differences in emphasis these changes make. Example:

The   *is advised by Machiavelli*
~~Machiavelli advises the~~ prince to gain the friendship of the people.
⋏   ⋏

1. The surfers were informed by the lifeguard of a shark sighting.
2. The cartoonist sketched a picture of Sam with huge ears and a pointy chin.
3. For months, the baby kangaroo is protected, fed, and taught how to survive by its mother.
4. The gifts were given out to the children by volunteers dressed as elves.
5. A new advertising company was chosen by the board members.

○ bedfordstmartins.com/smhandbook
  Exercise Central > **Sentence Grammar** > **Verbs**

30h Mood

The mood of a verb indicates the attitude of the writer. The indicative mood states facts and opinions or asks questions. The imperative mood gives commands and instructions. The subjunctive mood (used mainly in clauses beginning with *that* or *if*) expresses wishes or conditions that are contrary to fact.

INDICATIVE   I *did* the right thing.

IMPERATIVE   *Do* the right thing.

SUBJUNCTIVE   If I *had done* the right thing, I would not be in trouble now.

1 Subjunctive forms of verbs

The present subjunctive uses the base form, no matter what the subject of the verb is.

▷ **It is important that children *be* psychologically ready for a new sibling.**

The past subjunctive is the same as the simple past except for the verb *be*, which uses *were* for all subjects.

▷ **He spent money as if he *had* infinite credit.**

▷ **If the store *were* better located, it would attract more customers.**

2 Use of the subjunctive mood

Because the subjunctive can create a rather formal tone, many people today tend to substitute the indicative mood in informal conversation.

▷ **If I *was* a better swimmer, I would try out for the team.** [informal]

Nevertheless, formal writing still requires the use of the subjunctive in the following kinds of dependent clauses:

Clauses expressing a wish

▷ **He wished that his mother *were* still living nearby.**

As if *and* as though *clauses*

○ He started down the trail as if he *were* walking on ice.

That *clauses expressing a request or demand*

○ The job demands that the employee *be* in good physical condition.

If *clauses expressing a condition that does not exist*

○ If the sale of tobacco *were* banned, tobacco companies *would* suffer a great loss.

One common error is to use *would* in both clauses. Use the subjunctive in the *if* clause and *would* in the main clause.

> had
○ If I ~~would have~~ played harder, I would have won.
>   ^

FOR MULTILINGUAL WRITERS

Using the subjunctive

"If you were to practice writing every day, it would eventually seem much easier to you." For a discussion of this and other uses of the subjunctive, see 55f.

EXERCISE 30.6

Revise any of the following sentences that do not use the appropriate subjunctive verb forms required in formal writing. Example:

> were
I saw how carefully he moved, as if he ~~was~~ holding an infant.
>   ^

1. Josh kept spending money as if he was still earning high commissions.
2. Marvina wished that she was able to take her daughter along on the business trip.
3. Protesters demanded that the senator resign from her post.
4. If the vaccine was more readily available, the county health department would recommend that everyone receive the shot.
5. It is critical that the liquid remains at room temperature for at least seven hours.

→ bedfordstmartins.com/smhandbook
Exercise Central > Sentence Grammar > Verbs

THINKING CRITICALLY ABOUT VERBS

Reading with an Eye for Verbs

Some years ago a newspaper in San Francisco ran the headline "Giants Crush Cardinals, 3–1," provoking the following friendly advice from John Updike about the art of sports-headline verbs:

> The correct verb, San Francisco, is *whip*. Notice the vigor, force, and scorn obtained.... [These examples] may prove helpful: 3–1 — *whip*; 3–2 — *shade*; 2–1 — *edge*. 4–1 gets the coveted verb *vanquish*. Rule: Any three-run margin, *provided the winning total does not exceed ten*, may be described as a vanquishing.

Take the time to study a newspaper with an eye for its verbs. Copy down several examples of strong verbs as well as a few examples of weak or overused verbs. For the weak ones, try to come up with better choices.

Thinking about Your Own Use of Verbs

Writing that relies too heavily on the verbs *be, do,* and *have* almost always bores readers. Look at something you've written recently to see whether you rely too heavily on these verbs, and revise accordingly.

31 Subject-Verb Agreement

In everyday terms, the word *agreement* refers to an accord of some sort: you reach an agreement with your boss about salary; friends agree to go to a movie; the members of a family agree to share household chores; the United States and Russia negotiate an agreement about reducing nuclear arms. This meaning covers grammatical agreement as well.

In academic varieties of English, verbs must agree with their subjects in number (singular or plural) and in person (first, second, or third). In most sentences, making subjects and verbs agree is fairly simple; only a few subject-verb constructions cause confusion.

31a Verbs with third-person singular subjects

To make a verb in the present tense agree with a third-person singular subject, add *-s* or *-es* to the base form.

 A vegetarian diet *lowers* the risk of heart disease.

To make a verb in the present tense agree with any other subject, use the base form of the verb.

 I *miss* my family.

 They *live* in another state.

Have and *be* do not follow the *-s* or *-es* pattern with third-person singular subjects. *Have* changes to *has*; *be* has irregular forms in both the present and past tenses and in the first person as well as the third person. (See Chapter 30.)

 War *is* hell.

 The soldier *was* brave beyond the call of duty.

In some varieties of African American or regional English, third-person singular verb forms do not end

> **QUICK HELP**
>
> ## Editing for subject-verb agreement
>
> - Identify the subject that goes with each verb. Cover up any words between the subject and the verb to identify agreement problems more easily. (31b)
>
> - Check compound subjects. Those joined by *and* usually take a plural verb form. With those subjects joined by *or* or *nor*, however, the verb agrees with the part of the subject closest to the verb. (31c)
>
> - Check collective-noun subjects. These nouns take a singular verb form when they refer to a group as a single unit but a plural form when they refer to the multiple members of a group. (31d)
>
> - Check indefinite-pronoun subjects. Most take a singular verb form. *Both, few, many, others,* and *several* take a plural form; and *all, any, enough, more, most, none,* and *some* can be either singular or plural, depending on the noun they refer to. (31e)

with -*s* or -*es*: *She go to work every day.* In most academic writing, however, your audience will expect third-person singular verb forms to end in -*s* or -*es* (30a1 and 2).

31b Subjects and verbs separated by other words

Make sure the verb agrees with the subject and not with another noun that falls in between.

▶ A vase of flowers *makes* a room attractive.

▶ Many books on the best-seller list ~~has~~ little literary value.
    have

> The simple subject is *books,* not *list.*

Be careful when you use phrases beginning with *as well as, along with, in addition to, together with,* or similar prepositions. They do not make a singular subject plural.

▶ **The president, along with many senators,** *opposes* **the bill.**

> was
> ▶ A passenger, as well as the driver, ~~were~~ injured in the accident.
> ^

Though this sentence has a grammatically singular subject, it suggests the idea of a plural subject. The sentence makes better sense with a compound subject: *The driver and a passenger were injured in the accident.*

EXERCISE 31.1

Underline the appropriate verb form in each of the following sentences. Example:

The benefits of family planning (*is* / *are*) not apparent to many peasants.

1. Soldiers who are injured while fighting for their country (*deserves* / *deserve*) complete medical coverage.

2. The dog, followed by his owner, (*races* / *race*) wildly down the street every afternoon.

3. Just when I think I can go home, another pile of invoices (*appears* / *appear*) on my desk.

4. The pattern of secrecy and lies (*needs* / *need*) to stop in order for counseling to be successful.

5. A substance abuser often (*hides* / *hide*) the truth to cover up his or her addiction.

6. The police chief, in addition to several soldiers and two civilians, (*was* / *were*) injured in the explosion.

7. Garlic's therapeutic value as well as its flavor (*comes* / *come*) from sulfur compounds.

8. The fiber content of cereal (*contributes* / *contribute*) to its nutritional value.

9. The graphics on this computer game often (*causes* / *cause*) my system to crash.

10. Current research on AIDS, in spite of the best efforts of hundreds of scientists, (*leaves* / *leave*) serious questions unanswered.

bedfordstmartins.com/smhandbook
Exercise Central > **Sentence Grammar** > **Subject-Verb Agreement**

31c Verbs with compound subjects

Two or more subjects joined by *and* generally require a plural verb form.

▶ Tony and his friend *commute* from Louisville.

◐ A backpack, a canteen, and a rifle ~~was~~ ^{were} issued to each recruit.

When subjects joined by *and* are considered a single unit or refer to the same person or thing, they take a singular verb form.

◐ George W. Bush's older brother and political ally *was* the governor of Florida.

◐ Drinking and driving ~~remain~~ ^{remains} a major cause of highway fatalities.

In this sentence, *drinking and driving* is considered a single activity, and a singular verb is used.

If the word *each* or *every* precedes subjects joined by *and*, the verb form is singular.

◐ Each boy and girl *chooses* one gift to take home.

With subjects joined by *or* or *nor*, the verb agrees with the part closest to the verb.

◐ Neither my roommate nor my neighbors *like* my loud music.

◐ Either the witnesses or the defendant ~~are~~ ^{is} lying.

If you find this sentence awkward, put the plural noun closest to the verb: *Either the defendant or the witnesses <u>are</u> lying.*

31d Verbs with collective nouns or fractions

Collective nouns—such as *family, team, audience, group, jury, crowd, band, class,* and *committee*—refer to a group. Collective nouns can take either singular or plural verb forms, depending on whether they refer to the group as a single unit or to the multiple members of the group. The meaning of a sentence as a whole is your guide to whether a collective noun refers to a unit or to the multiple parts of a unit.

◐ After deliberating, the jury *reports* its verdict.

The jury acts as a single unit.

◑ The jury still *disagree* on a number of counts.

The members of the jury act as multiple individuals.

scatter
◑ The family of ducklings s̶c̶a̶t̶t̶e̶r̶s̶ when the cat approaches.
                            ^

Family here refers to the many ducks; they cannot scatter as one.

Treat fractions that refer to singular nouns as singular and those that refer to plural nouns as plural.

SINGULAR	Two-thirds of the park *has* burned.
PLURAL	Two-thirds of the students *were* commuters.

Treat phrases starting with *the number of* as singular and with *a number of* as plural.

SINGULAR	The number of applicants for the internship *was* unbelievable.
PLURAL	A number of applicants *were* put on the waiting list.

31e Verbs with indefinite-pronoun subjects

Indefinite pronouns do not refer to specific persons or things. Most take singular verb forms.

SOME COMMON INDEFINITE PRONOUNS

another	each	much	one
any	either	neither	other
anybody	everybody	nobody	somebody
anyone	everyone	no one	someone
anything	everything	nothing	something

◑ Of the two jobs, neither *holds* much appeal.

depicts
◑ Each of the plays d̶e̶p̶i̶c̶t̶ a hero undone by a tragic flaw.
                    ^

Both, few, many, others, and *several* are plural.

◑ Though many *apply*, few *are* chosen.

All, any, enough, more, most, none, and *some* can be singular or plural, depending on the noun they refer to.

○ **All of the cake *was* eaten.**

○ **All of the candidates *promise* to improve the schools.**

31f Verbs with antecedents of *who, which,* and *that*

When the relative pronouns *who, which,* and *that* are used as a subject, the verb agrees with the antecedent of the pronoun.

○ **Fear is an ingredient that *goes* into creating stereotypes.**

○ **Guilt and fear are ingredients that *go* into creating stereotypes.**

Problems often occur with the words *one of the.* In general, *one of the* takes a plural verb, while *only one of the* takes a singular verb.

○ **Carla is one of the employees who always ~~works~~ overtime.**
  ^work

> Some employees always work overtime. Carla is among them. Thus *who* refers to *employees,* and the verb is plural.

○ **Ming is the only one of the employees who always ~~work~~ overtime.**
  ^works

> Only one employee always works overtime, and that employee is Ming. Thus *one,* and not *employees,* is the antecedent of *who,* and the verb form is singular.

31g Linking verbs and their subjects

A linking verb should agree with its subject, which usually precedes the verb, not with the subject complement, which follows it (29c2).

○ **Three key treaties ~~is~~ the topic of my talk.**
  ^are

> The subject is *treaties,* not *topic.*

was
◯ Nero Wolfe's passion ~~were~~ orchids.
                                    ^

The subject is *passion,* not *orchids.*

31h Verbs with singular subjects ending in *-s*

Some words that end in *-s* appear plural but are singular and thus take singular verb forms.

strikes
◯ Measles still ~~strike~~ many Americans.
                      ^

Some nouns of this kind (such as *statistics* and *politics*) may be either singular or plural, depending on context.

SINGULAR   Statistics *is* a course I really dread.

PLURAL   The statistics in that study *are* highly questionable.

31i Verbs that appear before subjects

In English, verbs usually follow subjects. When this order is reversed, make the verb agree with the subject, not with a noun that happens to precede it.

stand
◯ Beside the barn ~~stands~~ silos filled with grain.
                        ^

The subject is *silos*; it is plural, so the verb must be *stand.*

In sentences beginning with *there is* or *there are* (or *there was* or *there were*), *there* serves only as an introductory word; the subject follows the verb.

◯ There *are* five basic positions in classical ballet.

The subject, *positions,* is plural, so the verb must also be plural.

31j Verbs with titles and words used as words

When the subject is the title of a book, film, or other work of art, the verb form is singular even if the title is plural in form.

○ *One Writer's Beginnings* **describes Eudora Welty's childhood.**

Similarly, a word referred to as a word requires a singular verb form even if the word itself is plural.

○ *Steroids* **is a little word that packs a big punch in the world of sports.**

EXERCISE 31.2

Revise any of the following sentences as necessary to establish subject-verb agreement. (Some of the sentences do not require any change.) Example:

> *darts*
> Into the shadows ~~dart~~ the frightened raccoon.
>   ^

1. Room and board are the most expensive part of my college education.
2. *Three Cups of Tea* tell the story of one man's mission to establish schools in poor, remote areas of Pakistan.
3. Hanging near the *Mona Lisa* is many more Renaissance paintings.
4. Most of the students oppose the shortened dining hall hours.
5. Each of the security workers are considered trained after viewing a twenty-minute videotape.
6. Neither his expensive clothes nor his charm were enough to get him the job.
7. The committee were expected to produce its annual report two weeks early.
8. My grandmother is the only one of my relatives who still goes to church.
9. Sweden was one of the few European countries that was neutral in 1943.
10. Economics involve the study of the distribution of goods and services.

⟳ bedfordstmartins.com/smhandbook
   Exercise Central > Sentence Grammar > Subject-Verb Agreement

THINKING CRITICALLY ABOUT SUBJECT-VERB AGREEMENT

Reading with an Eye for Subject-Verb Agreement

The following passage, from a 1990 essay questioning a "traditional" view of marriage, includes several instances of complicated subject-verb agreement. Note the rules governing subject-verb agreement in each case.

> Marriage seems to me more conflict-ridden than ever, and the divorce rate—with or without new babies in the house—remains constant. The fabric of men-and-women-as-they-once-were is so thin in places no amount of patching can weave that cloth together again. The longing for connection may be strong, but even stronger is the growing perception that only people who are real to themselves can connect. Two shall be as one is over, no matter how lonely we get.
>
> —VIVIAN GORNICK, "Who Says We Haven't Made a Revolution?"

Thinking about Your Own Use of Subject-Verb Agreement

Visiting relatives is / are treacherous. Either verb makes a grammatically acceptable sentence, yet the verbs result in two very different statements. Write a brief explanation of the two possible meanings. Then write a paragraph or two about visiting relatives. Using the information in this chapter, examine each subject and its verb. Do you maintain subject-verb agreement throughout? Revise to correct any errors you find. If you find any patterns, make a note to yourself of things to look for routinely as you revise your writing.

Pronouns

32

Pronouns "are tricky rather than difficult," says H. W. Fowler in *A Dictionary of Modern English Usage*. Pronouns pose several potential problems. Most pronouns have several forms (*I* versus *me*, for example), and a pronoun's form must match its function in the sentence (as *I* is used for a subject and *me* for an object). In addition, a pronoun stands in for another noun or pronoun called the *antecedent*, and making sure that the pronoun both agrees with its antecedent and refers clearly to the antecedent can indeed be tricky—but is essential for effective communication.

These directions show one reason why it's important to use pronouns clearly:

> *When you see a dirt road turning left off Winston Lane, follow it for two more miles.*

The word *it* could mean either the dirt road or Winston Lane. Pronouns can improve understanding, but only when they're used carefully and accurately.

32a Pronoun case

Most speakers of English know intuitively when to use *I*, *me*, or *my*. The choice reflects differences in case, the form a pronoun takes to indicate its function in a sentence. Pronouns functioning as subjects are in the subjective case; those functioning as objects are in the objective case; and those functioning as possessives are in the possessive case.

SUBJECTIVE PRONOUNS

I/we	you	he/she/it	they	who/whoever

OBJECTIVE PRONOUNS

me/us	you	him/her/it	them	whom/whomever

POSSESSIVE PRONOUNS

my/our	your	his/hers/its	their	whose
mine/ours	yours	his/hers/its	theirs	

Editing for case

- Are all pronouns after forms of the verb *be* in the subjective case in formal writing? (32a1)

- To check for correct use of *who* and *whom* (and *whoever* and *whomever*), try answering the question or rewriting the clause using *he* or *him*. If *he* is correct, use *who* or *whoever*; if *him*, use *whom* or *whomever*. (32b)

- In compound structures, make sure pronouns are in the same case they would be in if used alone (*Jake and she were living in Spain*). (32c)

- When a pronoun follows *than* or *as*, complete the sentence mentally to see whether the pronoun should be subjective or objective. (32d)

- Circle all the pronouns to see if you rely too heavily on any one pronoun or case, especially *I*. If you find that you do, try rewriting some sentences to change *I* to *me*, *she* to *her*, and so on.

1 **Pronouns as subjects**

Use a subjective pronoun as a subject of a clause, a subject complement, or an appositive renaming a subject or subject complement (29c).

SUBJECT OF A CLAUSE
They could either fight or face certain death with the lions.

Who is your closest friend?

Pedro told the story to Lizzie, *who* told all her friends.

SUBJECT COMPLEMENT
The person in charge was *she*.

APPOSITIVE RENAMING A SUBJECT OR SUBJECT COMPLEMENT
Three colleagues—Peter, John, and *she*—worked on the program.

Americans often use the objective case for subject complements, especially in conversation: *Who's there? It's me.* However, expect to use the subjective case in formal writing. If you find the subjective case stilted or awkward, try rewriting the sentence using the pronoun as the subject.

She was the
○ ~~The~~ first person to see Kishore after the awards. ~~was she.~~

2 Pronouns as objects

Use an objective pronoun as a direct or indirect object (of a verb or verbal), an object of a preposition, an appositive renaming an object, or when the pronoun is followed by an infinitive (29c2 and c3).

OBJECT OF A VERB OR VERBAL

The professor surprised *us* with a quiz. [direct object of *surprised*]

The grateful owner gave *him* a reward. [indirect object of *gave*]

The Parisians were wonderful about helping *me*. [direct object of gerund]

OBJECT OF A PREPOSITION

Several friends went with *him*.

APPOSITIVE RENAMING AN OBJECT

The committee elected two representatives, Sach and *me*.

PRONOUN FOLLOWED BY AN INFINITIVE

The students convinced *him* to vote for the school bond.

3 Pronouns as possessives

Use a possessive pronoun to show possession or ownership. Notice that there are two forms of possessive pronouns: those that function as adjectives (*my, your, his, her, its, our, their, whose*) and those that take the place of a noun (*mine, yours, his, hers, its, ours, theirs, whose*).

ADJECTIVE FORMS

People were buying *their* tickets weeks in advance of the show.

Whose fault was the accident?

NOUN FORMS

The responsibility is *hers*.

Whose is this blue backpack?

When a pronoun appears before a verbal (29c3) that ends in *-ing*, using a possessive pronoun leads to a different meaning than using an objective pronoun.

○ **I remember *his* singing.**

The possessive pronoun *his* makes *singing* the object of *remember*.

TALKING THE TALK

Correctness or stuffiness?

"I think *Everyone has their opinion* sounds better than *Everyone has his or her opinion*. And nobody says *whom*. Why should I write that way?" Over time, the conventions governing certain usages—such as *who* versus *whom*, or *their* versus *his* or *her* when it refers to an indefinite pronoun like *everyone* (32f and g)—have become much more relaxed. To many Americans, *Whom did you talk to?* and *No one finished his or her test*—both of which are technically "correct"—sound unpleasantly fussy. However, other people object to less formal constructions such as *Who did you talk to?* and *No one finished their test*; to them, such usages signal a lack of discrimination. Unfortunately, you can't please everyone. Use whatever you are most comfortable with in speaking but be more careful in formal writing. If you don't know whether your audience will prefer more or less formality, try recasting your sentence.

○ **I remember *him* singing.**

The pronoun *him* is the object of *remember*, and *singing* modifies *him*.

Choose the pronoun that makes sense for the meaning you want to convey.

32b *Who, whoever, whom,* and *whomever*

A common problem with pronoun case is deciding whether to use *who* or *whom*. Even when traditional grammar requires *whom*, many Americans use *who* instead, especially in speech. Nevertheless, you should understand the difference between *who* and *whom* so that you can make informed choices in situations such as formal college writing that may call for the use of *whom* (or *whomever*) in the objective case.

Two particular situations lead to confusion with *who* and *whom*: when they begin a question and when they introduce a dependent clause.

1 *Who* or *whom* in a question

You can determine whether to use *who* or *whom* at the beginning of a question by answering the question using a personal pronoun. If the answer is a subject pronoun, use *who*; if it is an object pronoun, use *whom*.

Who
○ ~~Whom~~ do you think wrote the story?
   ^

I think *she* wrote the story. *She* is subjective; so *who* is correct.

Whom
○ ~~Who~~ did you visit?
   ^

I visited them. *Them* is objective; so *whom* is correct.

2 *Who, whoever, whom,* or *whomever* in a dependent clause

The function a pronoun serves in a dependent clause determines whether you should choose *who* or *whom, whoever* or *whomever*—no matter how that clause functions in the sentence. If the pronoun acts as a subject or subject complement in the clause, use *who* or *whoever.* If the pronoun acts as an object, use *whom* or *whomever.*

                       whoever
○ The center is open to ~~whomever~~ wants to use it.
                          ^

Whoever is the subject of the clause *whoever wants to use it.* (The clause is the object of the preposition *to,* but the clause's function in the sentence does not affect the case of the pronoun.)

                           whom
○ The new president was not ~~who~~ she had expected.
                             ^

Whom is the object of the verb *had expected* in the clause *whom she had expected.*

If you are not sure which case to use, try separating the dependent clause from the rest of the sentence. Rewrite the clause as a new sentence, and substitute a personal pronoun for *who(ever)* or *whom(ever).* If the pronoun is in the subjective case, use *who* or *whoever;* if it is in the objective case, use *whom* or *whomever.*

⊙ **The minister grimaced at (*whoever/whomever*) made any noise.**

Isolate the clause *whoever/whomever made any noise.* Substituting a personal pronoun gives you *they made any noise.* *They* is in the subjective case; therefore, *The minister grimaced at <u>whoever</u> made any noise.*

⊙ **The minister smiled at (*whoever/whomever*) she greeted.**

Isolate and transpose the clause to get *she greeted whoever/whomever.* Substituting a personal pronoun gives you *she greeted them.* *Them* is in the objective case; therefore, *The minister smiled at <u>whomever</u> she greeted.*

⊙ **The minister grimaced at *whoever* ~~she thought~~ made any noise.**

Ignore such expressions as *he thinks* and *she says* when you isolate the clause.

EXERCISE 32.1

Insert *who, whoever, whom,* or *whomever* appropriately in the blank in each of the following sentences. Example:

She is someone __*who*__ will go far.

1. _____ did you say was our most likely suspect?
2. _____ the audience chooses will move up to the next level.
3. The awards banquet will recognize _____ made the honor roll.
4. Professor Quiñones asked _____ we wanted to collaborate with.
5. _____ received the highest score?

> bedfordstmartins.com/smhandbook
> Exercise Central > Sentence Grammar > Pronouns

32c Case in compound structures

When a pronoun is part of a compound structure, put it in the same case you would use if the pronoun were alone.

⊙ **Come to the park with José and ~~I~~.** *me.*

Eliminating the other part of the compound, *José and,* leaves *Come to the park with me.*

○ When ~~him~~ ^{he} and Zelda were first married, they lived in New York.

○ The next two speakers will be Philip and ~~her.~~ ^{she.}

○ The boss invited ~~she~~ ^{her} and her family to dinner.

○ This morning saw yet another conflict between my sister and ~~I.~~ ^{me.}

Pronoun case in a compound appositive (44c3) is determined by the word the appositive renames. If the word functions as a subject or subject complement, the pronoun should be subjective; if it functions as an object, the pronoun should be objective.

○ Both panelists—Tony and ~~me~~ ^I—were stumped.

> *Panelists* is the subject of the sentence, so the pronoun in the appositive *Tony and I* should be in the subjective case.

32d Case in elliptical constructions

In elliptical constructions, some words are left out but understood. A pronoun in an elliptical construction should be in the case it would be in if the construction were complete.

○ His brother has always been more athletic than *he* [is].

Sometimes the case depends on the meaning intended.

○ Willie likes Lily more than *she* [likes Lily].

> *She* is the subject of the implied clause *she likes Lily*.

○ Willie likes Lily more than [he likes] *her*.

> *Her* is the object of the verb *likes* in the implied clause *he likes her*.

32e *We* and *us* before a noun

If you are unsure about whether to use *we* or *us* before a noun, recast the sentence without the noun. Use whichever pronoun would be correct if the noun were omitted.

We
○ U̶s̶ fans never give up hope.

Fans is the subject, so the pronoun should be subjective.

us
○ The Rangers depend on w̶e̶ fans.

Fans is the object of a preposition, so the pronoun should be objective.

EXERCISE 32.2

Underline the appropriate pronoun from the pair in parentheses in each of the following sentences. Example:

The possibility of (*their* / *them*) succeeding never occurred to me.

1. Max has had more car accidents than Gabriella, but he still insists he is a better driver than (*she* / *her*).
2. Fixing the dock with Hank and (*they* / *them*) reminded me of our summers at the lake.
3. The coach gave honorable-mention ribbons to the two who didn't win any races—Aiden and (*I* / *me*).
4. There seemed to be no reason for (*them* / *their*) voluntarily studying on a Saturday night.
5. Tomorrow (*we* / *us*) recruits will have our first on-the-job test.

○ **bedfordstmartins.com/smhandbook**
Exercise Central > Sentence Grammar > Pronouns

32f **Pronoun-antecedent agreement**

The antecedent of the pronoun is the word the pronoun refers to. The antecedent usually appears before the pronoun—earlier in the sentence or in a previous sentence. Pronouns and antecedents are said to agree when they match up in person, number, and gender.

○ The conductor raised *her* baton, and the boys picked up *their* music.

1 Compound antecedents

Compound antecedents joined by *and* require plural pronouns.

▸ **My parents and I tried to resolve *our* disagreement.**

A compound antecedent preceded by *each* or *every*, however, takes a singular pronoun.

▸ **Every plant and animal has *its* own ecological niche.**

With a compound antecedent joined by *or* or *nor*, the pronoun agrees with the nearest antecedent. If the parts of the antecedent are of different genders or persons, however, this kind of sentence can be awkward.

AWKWARD   Neither Annie nor Barry got *his* work done.

REVISED   Annie didn't get *her* work done, and neither did Barry.

When a compound antecedent contains both singular and plural parts, the sentence may sound awkward unless the plural part comes last.

newspaper   radio stations   their

▸ **Neither the ~~radio stations~~ nor the ~~newspaper~~ would reveal ~~its~~ sources.**

2 Collective-noun antecedents

A collective-noun antecedent (*herd, team, audience*) that refers to a single unit requires a singular pronoun.

▸ **The audience fixed *its* attention on center stage.**

When such an antecedent refers to the multiple parts of the unit, however, it requires a plural pronoun.

▸ **The director chose this cast because *they* had experience in their roles.**

3 Indefinite-pronoun antecedents

Indefinite pronouns (31e) do not refer to specific persons or things. A pronoun whose antecedent is an indefinite pronoun should agree with it in number. Many indefinite pronouns are always singular (as with *one*);

Editing for pronoun-antecedent agreement

- Check all subjects joined by *and*, *or*, or *nor* to be sure they are treated as singular or plural, as appropriate. Recast any sentence in which agreement creates awkwardness. (32f1)

- Check all uses of *anyone*, *each*, *everybody*, *many*, and other indefinite pronouns (see list in 31e) to be sure they are treated as singular or plural, as appropriate. (32f3 and 32g)

- If you find *he*, *his*, or *him* used to refer to persons of either sex, revise the pronouns, or recast the sentences altogether. (32g)

a few are always plural (as with *many*). Some can be singular or plural depending on the context.

○ One of the ballerinas lost *her* balance.

○ Many in the audience jumped to *their* feet.

○ Some of the furniture was showing *its* age. [singular meaning for *some*]

○ Some of the farmers abandoned *their* land. [plural meaning for *some*]

32g Sexist pronouns

Indefinite pronouns (31e) often refer to antecedents that may be either male or female. Writers used to use a masculine pronoun, known as the generic *he*, in such cases. However, many people have pointed out that wording that ignores or excludes females should be avoided.

When an antecedent is a singular indefinite pronoun, some people avoid the generic *he* by using a plural pronoun.

○ Everybody had *their* own theories about Jennifer's resignation.

Although this usage is gaining acceptance, many readers still consider it incorrect. In formal writing, do not use a plural pronoun to refer to a grammatically singular indefinite pronoun.

○ Everybody had a theory about Jennifer's resignation.

> QUICK HELP

Editing out the generic use of *he*, *his*, or *him*

▶ **Every citizen should know *his* legal rights under the law.**

Here are three ways to express the same idea without *his*:

1. Revise to make the antecedent plural.

   All citizens should know their *legal rights.*

2. Revise the sentence altogether.

   Every citizen should have some knowledge of basic legal rights.

3. Use both masculine and feminine pronouns.

   Every citizen should know his or her *legal rights.*

The last option can be awkward when repeated several times in a passage.

EXERCISE 32.3

Revise the following sentences as needed to create pronoun-antecedent agreement and to eliminate the generic *he* and any awkward pronoun references. Some can be revised in more than one way. Example:

or her

Every graduate submitted his diploma card.
                              ^

All graduates   *their*   *cards.*
~~Every graduate~~ submitted ~~his~~ diploma ~~card.~~
^   ^   ^

1. While shopping for a new computer for school, I noticed that a laptop costs much less than they used to.
2. Congress usually resists a president's attempt to encroach on what they consider their authority.
3. Marco and Ellen were each given a chance to voice their opinion.
4. An emergency room doctor needs to be swift and decisive; he also needs to be calm and careful.
5. Every dog and cat has their own personality.

➡ bedfordstmartins.com/smhandbook
Exercise Central > **Sentence Grammar** > **Pronouns**

32h Ambiguous pronoun references

If a pronoun can refer to more than one antecedent, revise the sentence to make the meaning clear.

▷ **The car went over the bridge just before ~~it~~ fell into the water.**
    the bridge

What fell into the water — the car or the bridge? The revision makes the meaning clear by replacing the pronoun *it* with *the bridge*.

▷ **Kerry told Ellen, ~~she~~ should be ready soon.**
    "I"   "

Reporting Kerry's words directly, in quotation marks, eliminates the ambiguity.

If a pronoun and its antecedent are too far apart, you may need to replace the pronoun with the appropriate noun.

▷ **The right-to-life coalition believes that a *zygote*, an egg at the**

moment of fertilization, is as deserving of protection as is the born

human being and thus that abortion is as much murder as is the
                                                    the zygote
killing of a child. The coalition's focus is on what ~~it~~ will become as

much as on what it is now.

In the original, the pronoun *it* is too far away from the antecedent *zygote* in the first sentence, thus making the second sentence unclear to readers.

32i Vague use of *it, this, that,* and *which*

Writers often use *it, this, that,* or *which* as a shortcut for referring to something mentioned earlier. But such shortcuts can cause confusion. Make sure that these pronouns refer clearly to a specific antecedent.

▷ **When the senators realized the bill would be defeated, they tried to**
                                        The entire effort
postpone the vote but failed. ~~It~~ was a fiasco.

○ Nancy just found out that she won the lottery, ~~which~~ explains her

and her sudden wealth

resignation.

If a *that* or *which* clause refers to a specific noun, put the clause directly after the noun, if possible.

○ We worked all night on the float ~~for the Rose Parade~~ that our club

was going to sponsor/

for the Rose Parade.

Does *that* refer to the float or the parade? The editing makes the meaning clear.

32j   *Who* vs. *which* and *that* to refer to people

Use *who* to refer primarily to people or to animals with names. *Which* and *that* generally refer to animals or to things.

who

○ The veterinarian ~~that~~ operated saved my dog's life.

which

○ Cats, ~~who~~ are my favorite animals, often seem aloof.

32k   Indefinite use of *you*, *it*, and *they*

In conversation, we frequently use *you*, *it*, and *they* in an indefinite sense in such expressions as *you never know*; *it said in the paper*; and *on television, they said*. In college writing, however, use *you* only to mean "you, the reader," and *they* or *it* only to refer to a clear antecedent.

people

○ Commercials try to make ~~you~~ buy without thinking.

The

○ ~~On the~~ Weather Channel~~, it~~ reported that the earthquake

devastated parts of Pakistan.

Most restaurants in France

○ ~~In France, they~~ allow dogs. ~~in most restaurants.~~

32l Implied antecedents

Though an adjective or possessive may imply a noun antecedent, it does not serve as a clear antecedent.

>   her   Alexa
> ○ **In ~~Alexa's~~ formal complaint, ~~she~~ showed why the test question was**
>   ^   ^
>
> **wrong.**

EXERCISE 32.4

Revise each of the following items to clarify pronoun reference. Most of the items can be revised in more than one way. If a pronoun refers ambiguously to more than one possible antecedent, revise the sentence to reflect each possible meaning. Example:

> Miranda found Jane's keys after
> ~~After~~ Jane left/. ~~Miranda found her keys.~~
> ^   ^

> Miranda found her own keys after
> ~~After~~ Jane left/. ~~Miranda found her keys.~~
> ^   ^

1. All scholarship applicants must fill out a financial aid form, meet with the dean, and write a letter to the committee members. The deadline is October 24, so they should start the process as soon as possible.
2. Patients on medication may relate better to their therapists, be less vulnerable to what disturbs them, and be more responsive to them.
3. Ms. Dunbar wanted to speak to my mother before she spoke to me.
4. In Texas, you often hear about the influence of big oil corporations.
5. A small band of protestors picketed the new shopping center, which outraged many residents.

EXERCISE 32.5

Revise the following paragraph to establish a clear antecedent for every pronoun that needs one.

> In the summer of 2005, the NCAA banned the use of mascots that could be considered offensive to American Indians at any of their championship games. In order to understand this, it is important to consider that movies and television programs for years portrayed them as savage warriors that were feared and misunderstood. That is why some schools have chosen to use Indians as their mascot, a role typically played by wild animals or fictional beasts. You would not tolerate derogatory terms for other ethnic groups being used for school

---

QUICK HELP

Editing for clear pronoun reference

1. Identify a specific antecedent that each pronoun refers to. If you cannot find a specific antecedent, supply one. (32h, i, and k)

2. If the pronoun refers to more than one antecedent, revise the sentence. If the pronoun and its antecedent are so far apart that the reader cannot connect the two, replace the pronoun with the appropriate noun. (32h)

3. Be sure that any use of *you* refers to your specific reader or readers. (32k)

---

mascots. In the NCAA's new ruling, they ask schools to eliminate mascots that may be hurtful or offensive to America's Indian population.

---

bedfordstmartins.com/smhandbook
Exercise Central > Sentence Grammar > Pronouns

THINKING CRITICALLY ABOUT PRONOUNS

Reading with an Eye for Pronouns

Read the following passage from a brief review of *Harry Potter and the Goblet of Fire,* paying special attention to every pronoun: What antecedent does it refer to, and is the reference clear and direct? Does the use of any one pronoun case seem overused? Then go through and replace every pronoun with what it refers to, and read the two versions side by side to see the efficiency of good pronoun use.

Sexual attraction has entered the Harry Potter universe. Harry (Daniel Radcliffe) is now 14, and he's one of four contestants competing in the dangerous Tri-Wizard Tournament. The first event requires him to capture a golden egg that's guarded by a ferocious Hungarian flying dragon. Terrifying as this is, it pales in comparison with having to ask the beguiling Cho Chang (Katie Leung) to Hogwarts's Yule Ball. Now, *that* takes courage. . . .

The uncontestable triumph of "Goblet of Fire," however, is Brendan Gleeson's Alastor (Mad-Eye) Moody, the grizzled new Defense Against the Dark Arts professor. With a face like cracked pottery and a manner both menacing and mentoring, he becomes Harry's protector as he faces life-threatening tests. Gleeson, one of the screen's greatest character actors, steals every scene he's in—no small feat when you're up against Maggie Smith and Alan Rickman.

—DAVID ANSEN

Thinking about Your Own Use of Pronouns

Turn to a recent piece of your writing (something at least four pages long), and analyze your use of pronouns. Look carefully at the pronoun case you tend to use most; if it is first person, ask whether *I* is used too much. And if you find that you rely heavily on any one case (*you,* for example), decide whether your writing seems monotonous as a result. Take a look as well at whether you tend to use masculine pronouns exclusively to refer to people generally; if so, ask whether you would be more inclusive if you used both masculine and feminine pronouns or if you should revise to use plural pronouns that are not marked as either masculine or feminine (such as *we* or *they*). Finally, check to make sure that your pronouns and their antecedents agree and that the pronouns refer clearly and directly to antecedents.

Adjectives and Adverbs

33

Adjectives modify nouns and pronouns, answering the question *which? how many?* or *what kind?* Adverbs modify verbs, adjectives, other adverbs, or entire clauses; they answer the question *how? when? where?* or *to what extent?* Many adverbs are formed by adding *-ly* to adjectives (*slight, slightly*), but many are not (*outdoors, very*). And some words that end in *-ly* are adjectives (*lovely, homely*). To tell adjectives and adverbs apart, identify the word's function in the sentence.

33a Adjectives after linking verbs

When adjectives come after linking verbs, they usually describe the subject: *I am patient.* Note that in specific sentences, some verbs may or may not act as linking verbs — *look, appear, sound, feel, smell, taste, grow,* and *prove,* for instance. When a word following one of these verbs modifies the subject, use an adjective; when the word modifies the verb, use an adverb.

ADJECTIVE	Fluffy looked *angry.*
ADVERB	Fluffy looked *angrily* at the poodle.

Linking verbs suggest a state of being, not an action. In the preceding examples, *looked angry* suggests the state of being angry; *looked angrily* suggests an angry action.

As words that describe other words, adjectives and adverbs add liveliness and color to writing, helping writers show rather than just tell. In addition, adjectives and adverbs often provide indispensable meanings to the words they modify. In basketball, for example, there is an important difference between a *flagrant* foul and a *technical* foul, a layup and a *reverse* layup, or an *angry* coach and an *abusively angry* coach. In each instance, the modifiers are crucial to accurate communication.

QUICK HELP

Editing adjectives and adverbs

- Scrutinize each adjective and adverb. Consider synonyms for each one to see whether you have chosen the best word possible.

- See if a more specific noun would eliminate the need for an adjective (*mansion* rather than *enormous house*, for instance); do the same with verbs and adverbs.

- Consider adding an adjective or adverb that might make your writing more vivid or specific.

- Make sure all adjectives modify nouns or pronouns and all adverbs modify verbs, adjectives, or other adverbs. Check especially for proper use of *good* and *well*, *bad* and *badly*, *real* and *really*. (33b)

- Make sure all comparisons are complete. (33c4)

- If English is not your first language, check that adjectives are in the right order. (56e)

33b Adverb use

In everyday conversation, you will often hear (and perhaps use) adjectives in place of adverbs. When you write in standard academic English, however, use adverbs to modify verbs, adjectives, and other adverbs.

▷ You can feel the song's meter if you listen ~~careful~~. *carefully.*

▷ The audience was ~~real~~ disappointed by the show. *really*

Good *and* well, bad *and* badly

The modifiers *good*, *well*, *bad*, and *badly* cause problems for many writers because the distinctions between *good* and *well* and between *bad* and *badly* are often not observed in conversation. Problems also arise because *well* can function as either an adjective or an adverb. *Good* and *bad* are always adjectives, and both can be used after a linking verb. Do not use them to modify a verb, an adjective, or an adverb; use *well* or *badly* instead.

▶ The weather looks *good* today.

▶ We had a *bad* night with the new baby.

▶ He plays the trumpet ~~good~~ well and the trombone not ~~bad.~~ badly.

Badly is an adverb and can modify a verb, an adjective, or another adverb. Do not use it after a linking verb in formal writing; use *bad* instead.

▶ In her first recital, the soprano sang *badly*.

▶ I feel ~~badly~~ bad for the Cubs' fans.

As an adjective, *well* means "in good health"; as an adverb, it means "in a good manner" or "thoroughly."

ADJECTIVE   After a week of rest, Julio felt *well* again.

ADVERB   She plays *well* enough to make the team.

Right *smart,* wicked *fun*

Most regions have certain characteristic adjectives and adverbs. Some of the most colorful are intensifiers, adverbs meaning *very* or *absolutely.* In parts of the South, for example, and particularly in Appalachia, you are likely to hear the following: *He paid a right smart price for that car* or *She was plumb tuckered out.* In New England, you might hear *That party was wicked fun.* In each case, the adverb (*right, plumb, wicked*) acts to intensify the meaning of the adjective (*smart, tuckered out, fun*).

As with all language, use regional adjectives and adverbs only when they are appropriate (26d). In writing about a family member in Minnesota, for example, you might well quote her, bringing midwestern expressions into your writing. For most academic writing, however, you should use academic English.

EXERCISE 33.1

Revise the following sentences to correct adverb and adjective use. Then identify each adjective or adverb you have revised and the word each modifies. Example:

superbly

The attorney delivered a ~~superb~~ conceived summation.

1. Getting tickets at this late date is near impossible.
2. Derek apologized for behaving so immature on the football field.
3. Nora felt badly that the package would arrive one week later than promised.
4. It is real dangerous to hike those mountains in the winter.
5. He spoke confident about winning the race, but we doubted his abilities.
6. Paramedics rushed to help the victim, who was bleeding bad from the head.
7. The car ran good until the last two miles of the trip.
8. Arjun felt terrifically about his discussion with Professor Greene.
9. After we added cinnamon, the stew tasted really well.
10. Scientists measured the crater as accurate as possible.

> bedfordstmartins.com/smhandbook
> **Exercise Central > Sentence Grammar > Adjectives and Adverbs**

FOR MULTILINGUAL WRITERS

Adjectives with plural nouns

In Spanish, Russian, and many other languages, adjectives agree in number with the nouns they modify. In English, however, adjectives do not change number this way: *her kittens are cute* (not *cutes*).

33c Comparatives and superlatives

Most adjectives and adverbs have three forms: positive, comparative, and superlative.

POSITIVE	COMPARATIVE	SUPERLATIVE
large	larger	largest
early	earlier	earliest
careful	more careful	most careful
delicious	more delicious	most delicious

FOR MULTILINGUAL WRITERS

Adjective sequence

Should you write *these beautiful blue kitchen tiles* or *these blue beautiful kitchen tiles*? See 56e for guidelines on adjective sequence.

○ Canada is *larger* than the United States.

○ My son needs to be *more careful* with his money.

○ This is the *most delicious* coffee we have tried.

The comparative and superlative of most short (one-syllable and some two-syllable) adjectives are formed by adding *-er* and *-est*. With some two-syllable adjectives, longer adjectives, and most adverbs, use *more* and *most*: *scientific, more scientific, most scientific; elegantly, more elegantly, most elegantly.* If you are not sure whether a word has *-er* and *-est* forms, consult the dictionary entry for the simple form.

1 Irregular forms

Some adjectives and adverbs have irregular comparative and superlative forms.

POSITIVE	COMPARATIVE	SUPERLATIVE
good, well	better	best
bad, badly, ill	worse	worst
little (quantity)	less	least
many, some, much	more	most

2 Comparatives vs. superlatives

In academic writing, use the comparative to compare two things; use the superlative to compare three or more.

○ Rome is a much *older* city than New York.

○ Damascus is one of the ~~older~~ cities in the world.
  oldest

○ Which of the two candidates is the ~~strongest~~ for the job?
  stronger

3 Double comparatives and superlatives

Double comparatives and superlatives unnecessarily use both *more* or *most* and the *-er* or *-est* ending. Occasionally they can act to build a special emphasis, as in the title of Spike Lee's movie *Mo' Better Blues*. In college writing, however, make sure not to use *more* or *most* before adjectives or adverbs ending in *-er* or *-est*.

▷ Paris is the ~~most~~ loveliest city in the world.

4 Incomplete comparisons

Even if you think your audience will understand an implied comparison, you will be safer if you make sure that comparisons in formal writing are complete and clear (39e).

than those receiving a placebo.
▷ The patients taking the drug appeared healthier.

5 Absolute concepts

Some readers consider modifiers such as *perfect* and *unique* to be absolute concepts; according to this view, a construction such as *more unique* is illogical because a thing is either unique or it isn't, so modified forms of the concept don't make sense. However, many seemingly absolute words have multiple meanings, all of which are widely accepted as correct. For example, *unique* may mean *one of a kind* or *unequaled*, but it can also simply mean *distinctive* or *unusual*.

If you think your readers will object to a construction such as *more perfect* (which appears in the U.S. Constitution) or *somewhat unique* (which was used by J. D. Salinger), then avoid such uses.

6 Multiple negatives

Some speakers of English sometimes use more than one negative at a time (*I can't hardly see you*). Emphatic double negatives—and triple, quadruple, and more—appear in African American vernacular English (*Don't none of you know nothing at all*).

Even though double negatives occur in many varieties of English (and in many other languages), in academic or professional writing

adj/adv

you will play it safe if you avoid them—unless you are quoting regional dialogue or creating a special effect.

33d Nouns as modifiers

Sometimes a noun can function as an adjective by modifying another noun, as in *chicken soup* or *money supply*. If noun modifiers pile up, however, they can obscure meaning.

AWKWARD   The cold war–era Rosenberg espionage trial and execution continues to arouse controversy.

REVISED   The Rosenbergs' trial and execution for espionage during the cold war continues to arouse controversy.

EXERCISE 33.2

Revise each of the following sentences to use modifiers correctly, clearly, and effectively. Many of the sentences can be revised in more than one way. Example:

bill to approve a financial plan for the
He is sponsoring a housing project. ~~financial plan approval bill.~~

1. Alicia speaks both Russian and German, but she speaks Russian best.
2. The summers are more rainier in New York than they are in Seattle.
3. He glanced at the menu and ordered the expensivest wine on the list.
4. Most of the elderly are women because women tend to live longer.
5. Minneapolis is the largest of the Twin Cities.
6. She came up with the most silliest plan for revenge.
7. Our theater company has produced several of the famousest classical Greek plays.
8. The student cafeteria is operated by a college food service system chain.
9. It is safer to jog in daylight.
10. Evan argued that subtitled films are boringer to watch than films dubbed in English.

bedfordstmartins.com/smhandbook
Exercise Central > Sentence Grammar > Adjectives and Adverbs

THINKING CRITICALLY ABOUT ADJECTIVES AND ADVERBS

Reading with an Eye for Adjectives and Adverbs

Gwendolyn Brooks "describes the 'graceful life' as one where people glide over floors in softly glowing rooms, smile correctly over trays of silver, cinnamon, and cream, and retire in quiet elegance."

—MARY HELEN WASHINGTON, "Taming All That Anger Down"

Identify the adjectives and adverbs in the preceding passage, and comment on what they add to the writing. What would be lost if they were removed?

Thinking about Your Own Use of Adjectives and Adverbs

Take a few minutes to study something you can observe or examine closely. In a paragraph or two, describe your subject for someone who has never seen it. Using the guidelines in this chapter, check your use of adjectives and adverbs, and revise your paragraphs. How would you characterize your use of adjectives and adverbs?

SENTENCE CLARITY

Part 7

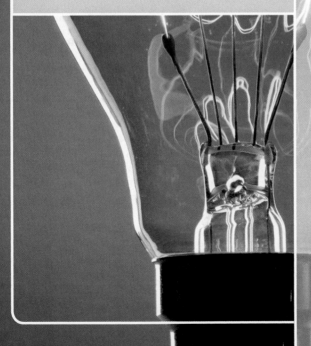

34 Confusing Shifts

Sometimes writers create deliberate shifts, as Dave Barry does in noting he "would have to say that the greatest single achievement of the American medical establishment is nasal spray." Barry's shift in tone from the serious (the American medical establishment) to the banal (nasal spray) makes readers laugh, as Barry intends.

A shift in writing is an abrupt change of some sort that results in inconsistency. Although writers sometimes deliberately make shifts for good reasons, unintentional shifts can be jolting and confusing to readers.

34a Revising shifts in tense

If the verbs in a passage refer to actions occurring at different times, they may require different tenses. Be careful, however, not to change tenses for no reason.

▷ A few countries produce almost all of the
world's illegal drugs, but addiction ~~affected~~ affects
many countries.

34b Revising shifts in mood

Be careful not to shift from one mood to another without good reason. The mood of a verb can be indicative (*he closes the door*), imperative (*close the door*), or subjunctive (*if the door were closed*). (See 30h.)

▷ Keep your eye on the ball, and ~~you should~~ bend your knees.

The writer's purpose is to give orders, but the original version shifts unnecessarily from the imperative to the indicative; the editing makes both verbs imperative.

34c Revising shifts in voice

Do not shift without reason between the active voice (*she sold it*) and the passive voice (*it was sold*). (See 30g.) Sometimes a shift in voice is justified, but often it only confuses readers.

> Two youths approached ~~me,~~ and ~~I was~~ asked for my wallet. *me*

The original sentence shifts from the active (*youths approached*) to the passive (*I was asked*), so it is unclear who asked for the wallet. Making both verbs active clears up the confusion.

34d Revising shifts in person and number

Unnecessary shifts in point of view between first person (*I, we*), second person (*you*), and third person (*he, she, it, one,* or *they*) or between singular and plural can be very confusing to readers.

> ~~One~~ can do well on this job if you budget your time. *You*

Is the writer making a general statement or giving advice to someone? Eliminating the shift eliminates this confusion.

Many shifts in number are actually problems with pronoun-antecedent agreement (32f).

INCONSISTENT	A *patient* should be able to talk to *their* doctor.
REVISED	*Patients* should be able to talk to *their* doctors.
REVISED	A *patient* should be able to talk to *his or her* doctor.

34e Revising shifts between direct and indirect discourse

When you quote someone's exact words, you are using direct discourse: *She said, "I'm an editor."* When you report what someone says without repeating the exact words, you are using indirect discourse: *She said she was an editor.* (See 57c.) Shifting between direct and indirect discourse in the same sentence can cause problems, especially when the sentence is a question.

>   *he*
> ◯ Viet asked what ^ could ~~he~~ do to help~~?~~ .

The editing eliminates an awkward shift by reporting Viet's question indirectly. The sentence could also be edited to quote Viet directly: *Viet asked, "What can I do to help?"*

EXERCISE 34.1

Revise the following sentences to eliminate unnecessary shifts in tense, mood, voice, or person and number and between direct and indirect discourse. Most of the items can be revised in more than one way. Examples:

> When a person goes to college, you face many new situations.
> When a <u>person</u> goes to college, <u>he or she</u> faces many new situations.
> When <u>people</u> go to college, <u>they</u> face many new situations.

1. The greed of the 1980s gave way to the occupational insecurity of the 1990s, which in turn gives way to reinforced family ties in the early 2000s.

2. The building inspector suggested that we apply for a construction permit and that we should check with his office again when the plans are complete.

3. The instructor grabbed her coat, wondered why was the substitute late, and ran out of the room.

4. Suddenly, we heard an explosion of wings off to our right, and you could see a hundred or more ducks lifting off from the water.

QUICK HELP

Editing for confusing shifts

- If you do not have a good reason for shifting from one verb tense to another, revise the shift. (34a)

- Make sure that any shifts in mood—perhaps from an indicative statement to an imperative—are necessary. (34b)

- Check for shifts from active voice (*She asks questions*) to passive voice (*Questions are asked*). Are they intentional—and if so, for what reason? (34c)

- Make sure you have good reasons for any shifts in person or number—from *we* to *you*, for example. (34d)

- Revise sentences that shift incorrectly between direct and indirect discourse. (34e)

- Check your writing for consistency in tone and diction. If your tone is serious, make sure it is consistently so. (34f)

5. In my previous job, I sold the most advertising spots and was given a sales excellence award.

6. A cloud of snow powder rose as skis and poles fly in every direction.

7. The flight attendant said, "Please turn off all electronic devices," but that we could use them again after takeoff.

8. The real estate market was softer than it had been for a decade, and a buyer could practically name their price.

9. When in Florence, be sure to see the city's famed cathedral, and many tourists also visit Michelangelo's statue David.

10. The freezing weather is threatening crops such as citrus fruits, which were sensitive to cold.

⊘ bedfordstmartins.com/smhandbook
    Exercise Central > Clarity > Shifts

34f   Revising shifts in tone and diction

Tone, a writer's attitude toward a topic or audience, is related to diction or word choice, and to overall formality or informality. Watch out for tone or diction shifts that could confuse readers and leave them wondering what your real attitude is. (See 4i4.)

INCONSISTENT TONE

The question of child care forces a society to make profound decisions about its economic values. Can most families with children actually live adequately on only one salary? If some conservatives had their way, June Cleaver would still be stuck in the kitchen baking cookies for Wally and the Beaver and waiting for Ward to bring home the bacon, except that with only one income, the Cleavers would be lucky to afford hot dogs.

In the preceding version, the first two sentences set a serious, formal tone as they discuss child care in fairly general, abstract terms. But in the third sentence, the writer shifts suddenly to sarcasm, to references

FOR MULTILINGUAL WRITERS

Shifts in speech

If Al said to Maria, "I will marry you," why did she then correctly tell her mom, "He said that he *would* marry me"? For guidelines on reporting speech, see 57c.

to television characters of an earlier era, and to informal language like *stuck* and *bring home the bacon*. Readers cannot tell whether the writer is presenting a serious analysis or preparing for a humorous satire. The revision makes the tone consistently formal.

REVISED

The question of child care forces a society to make profound decisions about its economic values. Can most families with young children actually live adequately on only one salary? Some conservatives believe that women with young children should not work outside the home, but many mothers are forced to do so for financial reasons.

THINKING CRITICALLY ABOUT SHIFTS

Reading with an Eye for Shifts

The following paragraph includes several necessary shifts in person and number. Read the paragraph carefully, marking all such shifts. Notice how careful the author must be as he shifts back and forth among pronouns.

It has been one of the great errors of our time to think that by thinking about thinking, and then talking about it, we could possibly straighten out and tidy up our minds. There is no delusion more damaging than to get the idea in your head that you understand the functioning of your own brain. Once you acquire such a notion, you run the danger of moving in to take charge, guiding your thoughts, shepherding your mind from place to place, controlling it, making lists of regulations. The human mind is not meant to be governed, certainly not by any book of rules yet written; it is supposed to run itself, and we are obliged to follow it along, trying to keep up with it as best we can. It is all very well to be aware of your awareness, even proud of it, but never try to operate it. You are not up to the job. — LEWIS THOMAS, "The Attic of the Brain"

Thinking about Any Shifts in Your Own Writing

Find an article about a well-known person you admire. Then write a paragraph or two about him or her, making a point of using both direct and indirect discourse. Using the information in 34e, check your writing for any inappropriate shifts between direct and indirect discourse, and revise as necessary.

Parallelism

35

Parallel grammatical structures are common not only in everyday expressions—*sink or swim*—but also in prose. Making similar structures parallel will help clarify your writing.

35a Making items in a series parallel

All items in a series should be in parallel form—all nouns, all prepositional phrases, all adverb clauses, and so on. Such parallelism makes a series both graceful and easy to follow.

- The quarter horse skipped, pranced, and sashayed.
  ~~was sashaying.~~
  ^

- The children ran down the hill, ~~raced over the~~ jumped
  lawn, and into the swimming pool.
  ^

- The duties of the job include baby-sitting, preparing
  house-cleaning, and ~~preparation of~~ meals.
  ^

Items in a list should be parallel.

- Kitchen rules: (1) Coffee to be made only by library staff. (2) Coffee service to be closed at 4:00 PM. (3) Doughnuts to be kept in cabinet.
  Coffee materials not to be handled by faculty.
  (4) ~~No faculty members should handle coffee~~
  ^
  ~~materials.~~

See how Jonathan Franzen uses parallelism in talking about a job:

Since I was paid better than the minimum wage, and *since* I enjoyed topological packing puzzles, and *since* the Geyers liked me and gave me lots of cake, it was remarkable *how* fiercely I hated the job—*how* I envied even those friends of mine who *manned* the deep-fry station at Long John Silver's or *cleaned* the oil traps at Kentucky Fried Chicken.

The parallelism indicated by the underscores brings a sense of orderliness to a long yet cohesive sentence.

Items on a formal outline and headings in a paper should be parallel. The headings in this chapter, for example, use parallel phrases.

35b Using parallel structures to pair ideas

Parallel structures can help you pair two ideas effectively. The more nearly parallel the two structures are, the stronger the connection between the ideas will be. Parallel structures are especially appropriate when two ideas are compared or contrasted.

○ **History became popular, and historians became alarmed.**
—WILL DURANT

○ **I type in one place, but I write all over the house.** —TONI MORRISON

To create an especially forceful impression, writers may construct a balanced sentence, one with two clauses that mirror each other.

○ **Mankind must put an end to war, or war will put an end to mankind.**
—JOHN F. KENNEDY

With coordinating conjunctions

When you link ideas with a coordinating conjunction—*and, but, or, nor, for, so, yet*—try to make the ideas parallel in structure.

○ **We performed *whenever folks would listen* and *wherever they would pay*.**

○ **Consult a friend in your class or** who is **good at math.**

With correlative conjunctions

Use the same structure after both parts of a correlative conjunction—*either . . . or, both . . . and, neither . . . nor, not . . . but, not only . . . but also, just as . . . so, whether . . . or.*

○ **The organization provided both *scholarships for young artists* and *grants for established ones*.**

> live in
> ◉ **I wanted not only to go away to school but also to New England.**
>   ^

The edited sentence is more balanced. Both parts of the correlative conjunction (*not only . . . but also*) precede a verb.

QUICK HELP

Editing for parallelism

- Look for any series of three or more items, and make all of the items parallel in structure. If you want to emphasize one particular item, try putting it at the end of the series. (35a and d)

- Be sure items in lists and headings are parallel in form. (35a)

- Check for sentences that compare, contrast, or otherwise pair two ideas. Often these ideas will appear on either side of *and, but, or, nor, for, so,* or *yet* or after each part of *either . . . or, both . . . and, neither . . . nor, not only . . . but also, just as . . . so,* or *whether . . . or.* Edit to make the two ideas parallel in structure. (35b)

- Check all parallel structures to be sure you have included all necessary words—articles, prepositions, the *to* of the infinitive, and so on. (35c)

EXERCISE 35.1

Complete the following sentences, using parallel words or phrases in each case. Example:

> The wise politician *promises the possible, faces the unavoidable,* and *accepts the inevitable.*

1. Before buying a used car, you should ____, ____, and ____.
2. Three activities I'd like to try are ____, ____, and ____.
3. Working in a restaurant taught me not only ____ but also ____.
4. We must either ____ or ____.
5. To pass the time in the waiting room, I ____, ____, and ____.

EXERCISE 35.2

Revise the following sentences as necessary to eliminate any errors in parallel structure.

> walking
> I enjoy skiing, playing the guitar, and I walk on the beach in warm weather.
>   ^

1. I remember watching it the first time, realizing I'd never seen anything like it, and immediately vowed never to miss an episode of *The Daily Show*.

2. A crowd stood outside the school and were watching as the graduates paraded by.

3. An effective Web site is well designed, provides useful information, and links are given to other relevant sites.

4. It is impossible to watch *The Office* and not seeing a little of yourself in one of the characters.

5. Lila was the winner not only of the pie-eating contest but also won the yodeling competition.

---

bedfordstmartins.com/smhandbook
Exercise Central > Clarity > Parallelism

35c Including all necessary words

In addition to making parallel elements grammatically similar, be careful to include all words—prepositions, articles, verb forms, and so on—that are necessary for clarity or grammar. (See also 39e.)

> We'll move to a city in the Southwest or ^in^ Mexico.

> To a city in Mexico or to Mexico in general? The editing makes the meaning clear.

> I had never before ^seen^ and would never again see such a sight.

> In the unedited version, *had . . . see* is not grammatically correct.

35d Using parallel structures for emphasis and effect

Parallel structures can help a writer emphasize a point, as Joan Didion does in this passage about people living in California's San Bernardino Valley in the late 1960s:

> Here is where the hot wind blows and the old ways do not seem relevant, where the divorce rate is double the national average and where one person in every thirty-eight lives in a trailer. Here is the last stop for all those who come from somewhere else, for all those who drifted away from the cold and

the past and the old ways. Here is where they are trying to find a new life style, trying to find it in the only places they know to look: the movies and the newspapers. —JOAN DIDION, "Some Dreamers of the Golden Dream"

The parallel phrases—*Here is, Here is*—introduce parallel details (*the hot wind* versus *the cold*; *the old ways* versus *a new life style*) that emphasize the emotional distance between *here* and the *somewhere else* that was once home for these new Californians.

THINKING CRITICALLY ABOUT PARALLELISM

Reading with an Eye for Parallelism

Read the following paragraph about a bareback rider practicing her circus act, and identify all the parallel structures. Consider what effect they create on you as a reader, and try to decide why the author chose to put his ideas in such overtly parallel form. Try imitating the next-to-last sentence, the one beginning *In a week or two.*

> The richness of the scene was in its plainness, its natural condition—of horse, of ring, of girl, even to the girl's bare feet that gripped the bare back of her proud and ridiculous mount. The enchantment grew not out of anything that happened or was performed but out of something that seemed to go round and around and around with the girl, attending her, a steady gleam in the shape of a circle—a ring of ambition, of happiness, of youth. (And the positive pleasures of equilibrium under difficulties.) In a week or two, all would be changed, all (or almost all) lost: the girl would wear makeup, the horse would wear gold, the ring would be painted, the bark would be clean for the feet of the horse, the girl's feet would be clean for the slippers that she'd wear. All, all would be lost.
> —E. B. WHITE, "The Ring of Time"

Thinking about Your Own Use of Parallelism

Read carefully several paragraphs from a draft you have recently written, noting any series of words, phrases, or clauses. Using the guidelines in this chapter, determine whether the series are parallel, and if not, revise them for parallelism. Then reread the paragraphs, looking for places where parallel structures would add emphasis or clarity, and revise accordingly. Can you draw any conclusions about your use of parallelism?

36

Comma Splices and Fused Sentences

A comma splice results from placing only a comma between two independent clauses. A related construction is a fused, or run-on, sentence, which results from joining two independent clauses with no punctuation or connecting word between them. You will seldom profit from using comma splices or fused sentences in academic writing. In fact, doing so will usually draw an instructor's criticism, so if you use a comma splice or fused sentence, be sure your instructor knows that you are doing so for special effect.

36a Separating the clauses into two sentences

The simplest way to revise comma splices or fused sentences is to separate them into two sentences.

COMMA SPLICE

My mother spends long hours every spring tilling the soil and moving manure/. this part of gardening is nauseating.

FUSED SENTENCE

My mother spends long hours every spring tilling the soil and moving manure. this part of gardening is nauseating.

If the two clauses are very short, making them two sentences may sound abrupt and terse, so some other method of revision is probably preferable.

36b Linking the clauses with a comma and a coordinating conjunction

If the ideas in the two clauses are closely related and equally important, you can join them with a comma and a coordinating conjunction: *and, but, or, nor, for, so,* or *yet.* (See Chapter 44.) The conjunction helps indicate what kind of link exists between the two clauses. For instance, *but* and *yet* signal opposition or contrast; *for* and *so* signal cause-effect relationships.

COMMA SPLICE	I got up feeling bad, ^{so} I took some aspirin.
FUSED SENTENCE	I should pay my tuition, ^{but} I need a new car.

QUICK HELP

Editing for comma splices and fused sentences

If you find no punctuation between two of your independent clauses—groups of words that can stand alone as sentences—you have identified a fused sentence. If you find two such clauses joined only by a comma, you have identified a comma splice. Revise comma splices and fused sentences with one of these methods.

1. Separate the clauses into two sentences. (36a)

▶ Education is an elusive idea, ^{It} it means different things

   to different people.

2. Link the clauses with a comma and a coordinating conjunction (*and, but, or, nor, for, so,* or *yet*). (36b)

▶ Education is an elusive idea, ^{for} it means different things

   to different people.

(continued on next page)

(continued from p. 655)

3. Link the clauses with a semicolon. (36c)

▷ Education is an elusive idea/; it means different things

  to different people.

If the clauses are linked with only a comma and a conjunctive adverb—a word like *however, then, therefore*—add a semicolon.

                                      indeed,
▷ Education is an elusive idea/; it means different

  things to different people.

4. Recast the two clauses as one independent clause. (36d)

      An elusive idea, education
▷ ~~Education is an elusive idea, it~~ means different things

  to different people.

5. Recast one independent clause as a dependent clause. (36e)

                              because
▷ Education is an elusive idea/ it means different things

  to different people.

6. In informal writing, link the clauses with a dash. (36f)

▷ Education is an elusive idea/—it means different things to

  different people.

36c   Linking the clauses with a semicolon

If the ideas in the two clauses are closely related and you want to give them equal emphasis, you can link them with a semicolon.

COMMA   This photograph is not at all realistic/; it uses
SPLICE
               dreamlike images to convey its message.

| FUSED SENTENCE | **The practice of journalism is changing dramatically; advances in technology have sped up news cycles.** |

Be careful when you link clauses with a conjunctive adverb or a transitional phrase. Precede such words and phrases with a semicolon (see Chapter 45), with a period, or with a comma combined with a coordinating conjunction (29b7).

| COMMA SPLICE | **Many developing countries have very high birthrates; therefore, most of their citizens are young.** |

| FUSED SENTENCE | **Many developing countries have very high birthrates. therefore, most of their citizens are young.** |

| FUSED SENTENCE | **Many developing countries have very high birthrates, *and* therefore, most of their citizens are young.** |

SOME CONJUNCTIVE ADVERBS AND TRANSITIONAL PHRASES

also	in contrast	next
anyway	indeed	now
besides	in fact	otherwise
certainly	instead	similarly
finally	likewise	still
furthermore	meanwhile	then
however	moreover	therefore
in addition	namely	thus
incidentally	nevertheless	undoubtedly

FOR MULTILINGUAL WRITERS

Sentence length

In U.S. academic contexts, readers sometimes find a series of short sentences "choppy" and undesirable. If you want to connect two independent clauses into one sentence, be sure to join them with a comma followed by a coordinating conjunction (*and*, *but*, *for*, *so*, *nor*, *or*, or *yet*) or with a semicolon. Doing so will help you avoid a comma-splice error. Another useful tip for writing in American English is to avoid writing several very long sentences in a row. If you find this pattern in your writing, try breaking it up by including a shorter sentence occasionally. See the tips in 42a and 42b for altering the sentence lengths and patterns in your writing.

36d   Recasting two clauses as one independent clause

Sometimes you can reduce two spliced or fused clauses to a single independent clause that is more direct and concise.

> COMMA SPLICE   A large part of my mail is advertisements, ~~most of the~~
> *and*
>
> ~~rest is~~ bills.

36e   Recasting one independent clause as a dependent clause

When one independent clause is more important than the other, try converting the less important one to a dependent clause.

> COMMA SPLICE   The arts and crafts movement, called for handmade
> *which reacted against mass production,*
>
> objects/. ~~it reacted against mass production.~~

In the revision, the writer chooses to emphasize the first clause, the one describing what the movement advocated, and to make the second clause, the one describing what it reacted against, into a dependent clause.

> FUSED SENTENCE   *Although*
> Zora Neale Hurston is regarded as one of America's
>
> major novelists, she died in obscurity.

In the revision, the writer chooses to emphasize the second clause and to make the first one into a dependent clause by adding the subordinating conjunction *although* (29b7).

36f Linking two independent clauses with a dash

In informal writing, you can use a dash to join two independent clauses, especially when the second clause elaborates on the first.

COMMA
SPLICE   **Exercise has become too much like work,/—it's a bad
            trend.**

EXERCISE 36.1

Using two of the methods in this chapter, revise each item to correct its comma splice or fused sentence. Use each of the methods at least once. Example:

so
I had misgivings about the marriage, I did not attend the ceremony.

Because
I had misgivings about the marriage, I did not attend the ceremony.

1. Many motorists are unaware of the dangers of texting while driving, lawmakers have taken the matter into their own hands.

2. The tallest human on record was Robert Wadlow he reached an amazing height of eight feet, eleven inches.

3. Some employers provide on-site care for the children of their employees, others reimburse workers for day-care costs.

4. The number of vaccine manufacturers has plummeted the industry has been hit with a flood of lawsuits.

5. Most crustaceans live in the ocean, some also live on land or in freshwater habitats.

6. She inherited some tribal customs from her grandmother, she knows the sewing technique called Seminole patchwork.

7. Don't throw your soda cans in the trash recycle them.

8. My West Indian neighbor has lived in New England for years, nevertheless, she always feels betrayed by winter.

9. The Hope diamond in the Smithsonian Institution is impressive in fact, it looks even larger in person than online.

10. You signed up for the course now you'll have to do the work.

EXERCISE 36.2

Revise the following paragraph, eliminating all comma splices by using a period or a semicolon. Then revise the paragraph again, this time using any of the other methods in this chapter. Comment on the two revisions. What differences in rhythm do you detect? Which version do you prefer, and why?

We may disagree on the causes of global warming, however, we cannot ignore that it is happening. Of course we still experience cold winters, on the other hand, average global temperatures have risen drastically for the last three decades. Polar ice caps are melting, as a result, sea levels are rising. Scientists predict more extreme weather in the coming decades, droughts will probably be more common, in addition, flooding and tropical storm activity may increase. Some experts fear that rising temperatures may cause large amounts of methane gases to be released, this could be disastrous for our atmosphere. Climate change may have human causes, it might be a natural occurrence, nevertheless, we must find ways to save our planet.

> bedfordstmartins.com/smhandbook
> **Exercise Central** > **Clarity** > **Comma Splices and Fused Sentences**

THINKING CRITICALLY ABOUT COMMA SPLICES AND FUSED SENTENCES

Reading with an Eye for Special Effects

Roger Angell is known as a careful and correct stylist, yet he often deviates from the "correct" to create special effects, as in this passage about pitcher David Cone:

> And then he won. Next time out, on August 10th, handed a seven-run lead against the A's, he gave up two runs over six innings, with eight strike-outs. He had tempo, he had poise. —ROGER ANGELL, "Before the Fall"

Angell uses a comma splice in the last sentence to emphasize parallel ideas; any conjunction, even *and*, would change the causal relationship he wishes to show. Because the splice is unexpected, it attracts just the attention that Angell wants for his statement.

Look through some stories or essays to find comma splices and fused sentences. Copy down one or two and enough of the surrounding text to show context, and comment in writing on the effects they create.

Thinking about Any Comma Splices and Fused Sentences in Your Own Writing

Go through some essays you have written, checking for comma splices and fused sentences. Revise any you find, using one of the methods in this chapter. Comment on your chosen methods.

Sentence Fragments

37

Sentence fragments are groups of words that are not sentences but are punctuated as sentences. Although you will often see and hear fragments, you will not want to use them in academic writing, where many readers will regard them as errors, unless you want to create a special effect.

37a Revising phrase fragments

Phrases are groups of words that lack a subject, a verb, or both (29c3). When phrases are punctuated like sentences, they become fragments. To revise such a fragment, attach it to an independent clause, or make it a separate sentence.

> NBC is broadcasting the debates*./* ~~With~~ *with*

> discussions afterward.

> The word group *with discussions afterward* is a prepositional phrase, not a sentence. The editing combines the phrase with an independent clause.

> The town's growth is controlled by zoning laws*./*,
> *a*
> A strict set of regulations for builders and
> corporations.

> *A strict set of regulations for builders and corporations* is an appositive phrase renaming the noun *zoning laws*. The editing attaches the fragment to the sentence containing that noun.

Sentence fragments are often used for special effect in advertisements:

Taste or nutrition? Convenience or savings? At Pop's, you don't have to choose. Get a healthy, mouth-watering breakfast for less than you probably pay for a cup of coffee — 24 hours a day. And we're right downtown, minutes from campus. *Ready when you are.* Breakfast is served!

The information in the italicized fragments would be less informal — and less memorable — as complete sentences.

○ **Kamika stayed out of school for three months**
    She wanted to
    after Linda was born. ~~To~~ recuperate and to take
                            ^
    care of the baby.

To recuperate and to take care of the baby includes verbals, not verbs. The revision—adding a subject (*she*) and a verb (*wanted*)—turns the fragment into a separate sentence.

Fragments beginning with transitions

If you introduce an example or explanation with a transition, such as one of the following, be certain you write a sentence, not a fragment.

again	but	instead
also	finally	like
and	for example	or
as a result	for instance	such as
besides	however	that is

                                                        such
○ **Barbara Ehrenreich has written on many subjects/, ~~Such~~ as under-**
                                                      ^
    employment and positive psychology.

In the original, the second word group is a phrase, not a sentence. The editing combines it with an independent clause.

QUICK HELP

Editing for sentence fragments

A group of words must meet the following three criteria to form a complete sentence. If it does not meet all three, it is considered a fragment in academic English. Revise a fragment by combining it with a nearby sentence or by rewriting it as a complete sentence.

1. A sentence must have a subject. (29a)

2. A sentence must have a verb, not just a verbal. A verbal needs an auxiliary verb in order to function as a sentence's verb. (29c3)

   VERBAL   The terrier *barking*.

   VERB   The terrier *is barking*.

3. Unless it is a question, a sentence must have at least one clause that does not begin with a subordinating word (29b7). Following are some common subordinating words:

although	if	when
as	since	where
because	that	whether
before	though	who
how	unless	why

37b Revising compound-predicate fragments

A compound predicate consists of two or more verbs, along with their modifiers and objects, that have the same subject. Fragments occur when one part of a compound predicate lacks a subject but is punctuated as a separate sentence. These fragments usually begin with *and, but,* or *or.* You can revise them by attaching them to the independent clause that contains the rest of the predicate.

▷ They sold their house. ~~And~~ *and* moved into an apartment.

EXERCISE 37.1

Revise each of the following items to eliminate any sentence fragments, either by combining fragments with independent clauses or by rewriting them as separate sentences. Example:

~~Zoe looked close to tears.~~ Standing with her head bowed. *Zoe looked close to tears.*

Zoe looked close to tears. ~~Standing~~ *She was standing* with her head bowed.

1. Long stretches of white beaches and shady palm trees. Give tourists the impression of an island paradise.

2. Forgetting to study for an exam. That is what many college students are afraid of.

3. Much of New Orleans is below sea level. Making it susceptible to flooding.

4. Uncle Ron forgot to bring his clarinet to the party. Fortunately for us.

5. Oscar night is an occasion for celebrating the film industry. And criticizing the fashion industry.

6. Diners in Creole restaurants might try shrimp gumbo. Or order turtle soup.

7. In the late 1940s, women began hosting Tupperware parties. Casual gatherings in which the hosts act as salespersons.

8. Attempting to lose ten pounds in less than a week. I ate only cottage cheese and grapefruit.

9. Our parents did not realize that we were hoarding our candy. Under our beds.

10. Thomas Edison was famous for his inventions. For example, the phonograph and the first practical lightbulb.

bedfordstmartins.com/smhandbook
Exercise Central > **Clarity** > **Sentence Fragments**

37c Revising dependent-clause fragments

Dependent clauses contain both a subject and a verb, but they cannot stand alone as sentences because they depend on an independent clause to complete their meaning. Dependent clauses usually begin with words such as *after, because, before, if, since, though, unless, until, when, where, while, who, which,* and *that* (29b7 and 29b3). You can usually combine dependent-clause fragments with a nearby independent clause.

> The team had a dismal record, ~~Which~~ *which* spurred the owner to fire the manager.

If you cannot smoothly attach a dependent clause to a nearby independent clause, try deleting the opening subordinating word and turning the dependent clause into a sentence.

> The majority of injuries in automobile accidents occur in two ways. ~~When an~~ *An* occupant either is hurt by something inside the car or is thrown from the car.

EXERCISE 37.2

Identify all the sentence fragments in the following items, and explain why each is grammatically incomplete. Then revise each one in at least two ways. Example:

Controlling my temper, ~~That~~ has been one of my goals this year.

One of my goals this year has been controlling
~~Controlling~~ my temper. ~~That has been one of my goals this year.~~

1. As soon as the seventy-five-year-old cellist walked onstage. The audience burst into applause.

2. The patient has only one intention. To smoke behind the doctor's back.

3. Some reality shows feature people working in dangerous situations. Such as fishing for Alaskan king crab or logging in swamps.

4. After writing and rewriting for almost three years. She finally felt that her novel was complete.

5. In the wake of the earthquake. Relief workers tried to provide food and shelter to victims.

6. Forster stopped writing novels after *A Passage to India*. Which is one of the greatest novels of the twentieth century.

7. Because only two students signed up. The class was canceled this semester.

8. I started running in April. And ran my first marathon in September.

9. We sat stunned as she delivered her monologue. A ten-minute speech about everything we had done to annoy her.

10. All primates have opposable thumbs. Which sets them apart from other mammals.

---

bedfordstmartins.com/smhandbook
Exercise Central > Clarity > Sentence Fragments

THINKING CRITICALLY ABOUT FRAGMENTS

Reading with an Eye for Fragments

Identify the fragments in the following passage. What effect does the writer achieve by using fragments rather than complete sentences?

> On Sundays, for religion, we went up on the hill. Skipping along the hexagon-shaped tile in Colonial Park. Darting up the steps to Edgecomb Avenue. Stopping in the candy store on St. Nicholas to load up. Leaning forward for leverage to finish the climb up to the church. I was always impressed by this particular house of the Lord.   —KEITH GILYARD, *Voices of the Self*

Thinking about Any Fragments in Your Own Writing

Read through some essays you have written. Using the guidelines on pages 662–63, see whether you find any sentence fragments. If so, do you recognize any patterns? Do you write fragments when you're attempting to add emphasis? Are they all dependent clauses? phrases? Note any patterns you discover, and make a point of routinely checking your writing for fragments. Finally, revise any fragments to form complete sentences.

38

Modifier Placement

Consider the following sign seen recently in a guidebook:

Visit the old Dutch cemetery where early settlers are buried from noon to five daily.

Does the cemetery really bury early settlers for five hours every day? Repositioning the modifier *from noon to five daily* eliminates the confusion and makes it clear when the cemetery is open: *From noon to five daily, visit the old Dutch cemetery where early settlers are buried.*

Modifiers describe or give more information about the words they modify. They enrich writing by making it more concrete or vivid, often adding important or even essential details. To be effective, modifiers should refer clearly to the words they modify and be placed close to those words.

38a Revising misplaced modifiers

Misplaced modifiers cause confusion because they are not close enough to the words they modify or because they seem to modify more than one thing.

○ ~~Clearly~~ I could hear the instructor lecturing. *clearly.*

The editing repositions the modifier *clearly* next to the word *lecturing*, which the writer wants to describe.

Phrases should usually be placed right before or after the words they modify.

○ She teaches a seminar this term ~~on voodoo~~ at *on voodoo*

Skyline College.

The voodoo is not at the college; the seminar is.

○ ~~Billowing from every window, we~~ saw clouds of *We*
smoke. *billowing from every window.*

People cannot billow from windows.

QUICK HELP

Editing for misplaced or dangling modifiers

1. Identify all the modifiers in each sentence, and draw an arrow from each modifier to the word it modifies.

2. If a modifier is far from the word it modifies, try to move the two closer together. (38a)

3. Does any modifier seem to refer to a word other than the one it is intended to modify? If so, move the modifier so that it refers clearly to only the intended word. (38a and b)

4. If you cannot find the word to which a modifier refers, revise the sentence: supply such a word, or revise the modifier itself so that it clearly refers to a word already in the sentence. (38c)

Although you have some flexibility in the placement of dependent clauses, try to position them close to what they modify.

After he lost the 1962 race,
◗ **Nixon said he would get out of politics.** ~~after he lost the 1962 race.~~

The unedited sentence implies that Nixon planned to lose the race.

EXERCISE 38.1

Revise each of the following sentences by moving any misplaced modifiers so that they clearly modify the words they should. Example:

When they propose sensible plans, politicians
~~Politicians~~ earn support from the people. ~~when they propose sensible plans.~~

1. The comedian had the audience doubled over with laughter relating her stories in a deadpan voice.

2. News reports can increase a listener's irrational fears that emphasize random crime or rare diseases.

3. Studying legal documents and court records from hundreds of years ago, ordinary people in the Middle Ages teach us about everyday life at that time.

4. Risking their lives in war zones, civilians learn about the conflict from the firsthand accounts of journalists abroad.

5. Melena saw lions in the wild on a safari in Africa last spring.

6. Doctors recommend a new test for cancer, which is painless.

7. Every afternoon I find flyers for free pizza left on my windshield.

8. Screeching strings told the audience that the killer was coming after the opening credits.

9. The coach awarded a medal to the most valuable player made of solid brass.

10. Hanging on by a thread, the five-year-old finally lost her tooth.

bedfordstmartins.com/smhandbook
Exercise Central > Clarity > Modifier Placement

Limiting modifiers

Be especially careful with the placement of limiting modifiers such as *almost, even, hardly, just, merely, nearly, only, scarcely,* and *simply.* In general, these modifiers should be placed right before or after the words they modify. Putting them in other positions may produce not just ambiguity but a completely different meaning.

AMBIGUOUS	The court *only* hears civil cases on Tuesdays.
CLEAR	The court hears *only* civil cases on Tuesdays.
CLEAR	The court hears civil cases on Tuesdays *only*.

In the first sentence, placing *only* before *hears* makes the meaning ambiguous. Does the writer mean that civil cases are the only cases heard on Tuesdays or that those are the only days when civil cases are heard?

> *almost*
> ● The city ~~almost~~ spent $20 million on the new stadium.
>   ^

The original sentence suggests the money was almost spent; moving *almost* makes clear that the amount spent was almost $20 million.

Squinting modifiers

If a modifier can refer to *either* the word before it *or* the word after it, it is a squinting modifier. Put the modifier where it clearly relates to only a single word.

| SQUINTING | Students who practice writing *often* will benefit. |

Does the writer mean that students often benefit from practice or that they benefit from practicing often?

REVISED   Students who *often* practice writing will benefit.

REVISED   Students who practice writing will *often* benefit.

EXERCISE 38.2

Revise each of the following sentences in at least two ways. Move the limiting or squinting modifier so that it unambiguously modifies one word or phrase in the sentence. Example:

completely
The course we hoped would engross us ~~completely~~ bored us.
                                     ^

completely.
The course we hoped would engross us ~~completely~~ bored us/
                                                          ^

1. The division that profited most deserves the prize.
2. The soldier was apparently injured by friendly fire.
3. The collector who owned the painting originally planned to leave it to a museum.
4. Alcoholics who try to quit drinking on their own frequently tend to relapse.
5. Ever since I was a child, I have only liked green peas with ham.

> **bedfordstmartins.com/smhandbook**
> **Exercise Central > Clarity > Modifier Placement**

38b Revising disruptive modifiers

Disruptive modifiers interrupt the connections between parts of a sentence, making it hard for readers to follow the progress of the thought. Most disruptive modifiers are adverbial clauses or phrases that appear between the parts of a verb phrase, between a subject and a verb, or between a verb and an object.

> *If they are cooked too long, vegetables will*
> **~~Vegetables will,~~ ~~if they are cooked too long,~~ lose most of their**
>   ^
> **nutritional value.**

Separating the parts of the verb phrase, *will* and *lose*, disrupts the flow of the sentence.

> *were discarded*
> **The books/ because they were no longer useful/. ~~were discarded.~~**
>   ^   ^

Separating the subject *books* from the verb *were discarded* is awkward.

a secondhand car
- He bought with his first paycheck. ~~a secondhand car.~~
  ^   ^

Separating the verb *bought* from the object *a secondhand car* makes it hard to follow the thought.

Modifiers splitting an infinitive

A modifier placed between the *to* and verb of an infinitive (*to boldly go*) is known as a split infinitive. Once considered a serious writing error, split infinitives are no longer taboo. Few readers will object to a split infinitive in a clear and understandable sentence.

- Students need to *really* know the material to pass the exam.

Sometimes, however, split infinitives are distracting to readers — especially when more than one word comes between the parts of the infinitive. In such cases, move the modifier before or after the infinitive, or reword the sentence, to remove the distracting interruption.

surrender
- Hitler expected the British to fairly quickly. ~~surrender.~~
  ^   ^

EXERCISE 38.3

Revise each of the following sentences by moving the disruptive modifier so that the sentence reads smoothly. Example:

During the recent economic depression, many
~~Many~~ unemployed college graduates ~~during the recent economic depression~~
^ attended graduate school.

1. Strong economic times have, statistics tell us, led to increases in the college dropout rate.

2. During finals an otherwise honest student, facing high levels of stress, may consider cheating to achieve a higher grade.

3. The director encouraged us to loudly and enthusiastically applaud after each scene.

4. Michael Jordan earned, at the pinnacle of his career, roughly $40 million a year in endorsements.

5. The stock exchange became, because of the sudden trading, a chaotic circus.

> bedfordstmartins.com/smhandbook
> **Exercise Central > Clarity > Modifier Placement**

38c   Revising dangling modifiers

Dangling modifiers *seem* to modify something that is implied but not actually present in the sentence. Dangling modifiers frequently appear at the beginnings or ends of sentences.

DANGLING   Driving nonstop, Salishan Lodge is two hours from Portland.

REVISED   Driving nonstop from Portland, you can reach Salishan Lodge in two hours.

REVISED   If you drive nonstop, Salishan Lodge is two hours from Portland.

The preceding revised sentences illustrate two ways to fix a dangling modifier. Often you need to add a subject that the modifier clearly refers to. Sometimes, however, you have to turn the dangling modifier itself into a phrase or clause.

our family gave
▷ Reluctantly, the hound ~~was given away~~ to a neighbor.

In the original sentence, was the dog reluctant, or was someone else who is not mentioned reluctant?

When he was
▷ ~~As~~ a young boy, his aunt told stories of her years as a country

doctor.

His aunt was never a young boy.

My
▷ ~~Thumbing through the magazine, my~~ eyes automatically noticed

as I was thumbing through the magazine.
the perfume ads./

Eyes cannot thumb through a magazine.

he was
▷ Although a reserved and private man, everyone enjoyed his

company.

The original clause does not refer to *everyone* or *his company*. It needs its own subject and verb.

EXERCISE 38.4

Revise each of the following sentences to correct the dangling phrase. Example:

a viewer gets

Watching television news, an impression ~~is given~~ of constant disaster.

1. No longer obsessed with being the first to report a story, information is now presented as entertainment.

2. Trying to attract younger viewers, news is blended with comedy on late-night talk shows.

3. Highlighting local events, important international news stories may get overlooked.

4. Chosen for their looks, the journalistic credentials of newscasters may be weak.

5. As an interactive medium, people can find information online that reinforces views they already hold.

> bedfordstmartins.com/smhandbook
> **Exercise Central > Clarity > Modifier Placement**

THINKING CRITICALLY ABOUT MODIFIERS

Reading with an Eye for Modifiers

Look at the limiting modifier italicized in the following passage. Identify which word or words it modifies. Then try moving the modifier to some other spot in the sentence, and consider how the meaning of the sentence changes as a result.

> It was, among other things, the sort of railroad you would occasionally ride *just* for the hell of it, a higher existence into which you would escape unconsciously and without hesitation.   —E. B. WHITE, "Progress and Change"

Thinking about Your Own Use of Modifiers

As you examine two pages of a draft, check for clear and effective modifiers. Can you identify any misplaced, disruptive, or dangling modifiers? Using the guidelines in this chapter, revise as need be. Then look for patterns—in the kinds of modifiers you use and in any problems you have placing them. Make a note of what you find.

Consistent and Complete Structures

39

Consistent, complete grammatical structures make information more accessible to readers. Learning to recognize and edit mixed and incomplete structures will help you avoid misunderstandings and communicate more clearly and effectively.

39a Revising faulty sentence structure

Faulty sentence structure poses problems for both writers and readers. A mixed structure results from beginning a sentence with one grammatical pattern and then switching to another one:

MIXED   The fact that I get up at 5:00 AM, a wake-up time that explains why I'm always tired in the evening.

The sentence starts out with a subject (*The fact*) followed by a dependent clause (*that I get up at 5:00 AM*). The sentence needs a predicate to complete the independent clause (29a and c), but instead it moves to another phrase (*a wake-up time*) followed by a dependent clause (*that explains why I'm always tired in the evening*), and what results is a fragment (Chapter 37).

REVISED   The fact that I get up at 5:00 AM explains why I'm always tired in the evening.

Deleting *a wake-up time that* changes the rest of the sentence into a predicate.

You hear inconsistent and incomplete structures all the time in conversation. For instance, during an interview with journalist Bill Moyers, Jon Stewart discussed the supposed objectivity of news reporting:

But news has never been objective. It's always . . . what does every newscast start with? "Our top stories tonight." That's a list. That's a subjective . . . some editor made a decision: "Here's our top stories. Number one: there's a fire in the Bronx."

Stewart is talking casually, so some of his sentences begin one way but then move in another direction. The mixed structures pose no problem for the listener, but sentences such as these can be confusing in writing.

REVISED   I get up at 5:00 AM, a wake-up time that explains why I'm always
           tired in the evening.

Deleting *The fact that* turns the beginning of the sentence into an independent clause.

Here is another example of a mixed structure:

◉ **Because hope was the only thing left when Pandora finally closed up**

the mythical box, ~~explains why~~ even today we never lose hope.
                  ^

The dependent clause beginning with *Because* is followed by a predicate (beginning with *explains*) without a subject. Deleting *explains why* changes the predicate into an independent clause.

QUICK HELP

Editing for consistency and completeness

- Check every confusing sentence to see whether it has a subject and a predicate. If not, revise as necessary. (39a) If you find both a subject and a predicate and you are still confused, see whether the subject and verb make sense together. If not, revise so that they do. (39b)

- Revise any *is when*, *is where*, and *the reason . . . is because* constructions. (39b)

◉ **Spamming is ~~where companies send~~ electronic junk mail.**
             ^

- Check all comparisons for completeness. (39e)

                          we like
◉ **We like Marian better than Margaret.**
                            ^

39b Matching subjects and predicates

Another kind of faulty sentence structure, called faulty predication, occurs when a subject and predicate do not fit together grammatically or simply do not make sense together. Many cases of faulty predication result from using forms of *be* when another verb would be stronger.

◉ **~~A characteristic that~~ I admire ~~is~~ a generous person.**

A person is not a characteristic.

> require that
> ○ The rules of the corporation ~~expect~~ employees ~~to~~ be on time.
>   ^

Rules cannot expect anything.

Is when, is where, *and* the reason . . . is because

Constructions using *is when, is where,* and *the reason . . . is because* are used frequently in informal contexts, but they may be inappropriate in academic writing because they use an adverb clause rather than a noun as a subject complement (29c4).

>   an unfair characterization of
> ○ A stereotype is ~~when someone characterizes~~ a group. ~~unfairly.~~
>   ^   ^
>   a place
> ○ A confluence is ~~where~~ two rivers join to form one.
>   ^

> ○ ~~The reason~~ I like to play soccer ~~is~~ because it provides aerobic
>
> exercise.

EXERCISE 39.1

Revise each of the following sentences in two ways to make its structures consistent in grammar and meaning. Example:

> Because
> ~~The fact that~~ our room was cold, we put a heater between our beds.
> ^
>   led us to
> The fact that our room was cold, we put a heater between our beds.
>   ^

1. To enroll in film school being my primary goal, so I am always saving my money and watching for scholarship opportunities.
2. The reason air-pollution standards should not be relaxed is because many people would suffer.
3. By turning off the water when you brush your teeth, saving up to eight gallons of water per day.
4. Irony is when you expect one thing and get something else.
5. The best meal I've ever eaten was sitting by a river eating bread and cheese from a farmers' market.

39c Completing elliptical constructions

Sometimes writers omit a word in a compound structure. They succeed with such an elliptical construction when the word omitted later in the compound is exactly the same as the word earlier in the compound.

> ○ **That bell belonged to the figure of Miss Duling as though it grew directly out of her right arm, as wings grew out of an angel or a tail [grew] out of the devil.** —EUDORA WELTY, *One Writer's Beginnings*

The omitted word, *grew*, is exactly the same verb that follows *it* and *wings* in the earlier parts of the compound. You should not omit a word that does not exactly match the word used in the other part(s) of the compound.

> is
> ○ **His skills are weak, and his performance ̬ only average.**

> The verb *is* does not match the verb in the other part of the compound (*are*), so the writer needs to include it.

39d Checking for missing words

The best way to catch inadvertent omissions is to proofread carefully, reading each sentence slowly — and aloud.

> at
> ○ **The new Web site makes it easier to look ̬ and choose from the**
>
> **company's inventory.**

39e Making complete comparisons

When you compare two or more things, the comparison must be complete, logically consistent, and clear.

FOR MULTILINGUAL WRITERS

Deciding which articles to use

Do you say "I'm working on *a* paper" or "I'm working on *the* paper"? Deciding when to use the articles *a*, *an*, and *the* can be challenging for multilingual writers since many languages have nothing directly comparable to them. See 56d for help using articles.

from my friends' parents.
▶ **I was embarrassed because my parents were so different.**
                                                         ^

Different from what? Adding *from my friends' parents* completes the comparison.

UNCLEAR   Aneil likes his brother more than his sister.

Does Aneil like his brother more than his sister does — or does he like his brother more than he likes his sister?

CLEAR   Aneil likes his brother more *than his sister does.*

CLEAR   Aneil likes his brother more *than he likes his sister.*

EXERCISE 39.2

Revise each of the following sentences to eliminate any inappropriate elliptical constructions; to make comparisons complete, logically consistent, and clear; and to supply any other omitted words that are necessary for meaning. Example:

                                        is
Most of the candidates are bright, and one brilliant.
                                            ^

1. Convection ovens cook more quickly and with less power.
2. Argentina and Peru were colonized by Spain, and Brazil by Portugal.
3. She argued that children are even more important for men than women.
4. Do you think the barbecue sauce in Memphis is better than North Carolina?
5. The equipment in our new warehouse is guaranteed to last longer than our current facility.

> bedfordstmartins.com/smhandbook
> **Exercise Central > Clarity > Consistent and Complete Structures**

THINKING CRITICALLY ABOUT CONSISTENCY AND COMPLETENESS

Read over three or four paragraphs from a draft or completed essay you have written recently. Check for mixed sentences and incomplete or missing structures. Revise the paragraphs to correct any problems you find. If you find any, do you recognize any patterns? If so, make a note of them for future reference.

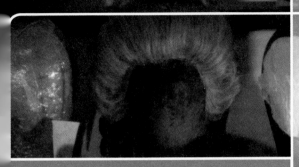

Part 8

SENTENCE STYLE

40 Concise Writing

Many examples of writing in the real world have to be extremely concise. Look, for example, at this set of instructions explaining the procedure for emergency evacuation on a commuter train:

Listen for directions from authorized personnel.

Remain inside train if possible. If not . . .

Go to next car through end doors. If unable . . .

Open side door and go out. If unable . . .

Go out emergency window.

You probably won't often need to instruct passengers how to leave a train safely, but you will want to write as clearly and concisely as you can in other contexts.

Making sure that your writing is as concise and to-the-point as possible is important not only in Twitter posts and text messages, with their strict character-length limits, but also in academic and professional writing. To make your formal writing more effective, use clear structures and choose words that convey exactly what you mean to say.

40a   Eliminating unnecessary words

Sometimes writers say that something is large *in size* or red *in color* or that two ingredients should be combined *together*. The italicized words are unnecessarily repetitive; delete such redundant words.

⊙ ~~Compulsory attendance~~ at assemblies is
   Attendance
   ^
   required.

⊙ Many different forms of hazing occur, such as

   physical ~~abuse~~ and mental abuse.

Deleting meaningless modifiers

Many modifiers are so overused that they have little meaning.

MEANINGLESS MODIFIERS

absolutely, awfully, definitely, fine, great, interesting, quite, really, very

Replacing wordy phrases

Wordy phrases can be reduced to a word or two with no loss in meaning.

WORDY	CONCISE
at all times	always
at that point in time	then
at the present time	now, today
due to the fact that	because
for the purpose of	for
in order to	to
in spite of the fact that	although
in the event that	if

QUICK HELP

Editing for conciseness

- Look for redundant words. If you are unsure about a word, read the sentence without it; if the meaning is not affected, leave the word out. (40a)

- Replace wordy phrases with a single word. Instead of *because of the fact that*, try *because*. (40a)

- Simplify grammatical structures whenever possible. For example, you might rewrite a sentence to make it more specific or combine two sentences that have the same subject or predicate. (40b)

- Identify all uses of *it is*, *there is*, and *there are*, and delete any that do not give your writing necessary emphasis. (40b1)

- Note noun phrases whose meaning could be expressed by a verb, and try revising using the verb. (40b2)

- Look for sentences that use the passive voice without a good reason. If the active voice would make the sentence livelier, clearer, or more concise, rewrite the sentence. (40c)

40b Simplifying sentence structure

Using simple grammatical structures will often strengthen your sentences considerably.

▶ Hurricane Katrina, ~~which was certainly~~ one of the most powerful
storms ever to hit the Gulf Coast, caused ^widespread^ damage. ~~to a very~~
~~wide area.~~

Deleting unnecessary words and replacing five words with one tightens the sentence and makes it easier to read.

▶ When ~~she was~~ questioned about her previous job, she
seemed nervous. ^and^ ~~She also~~ tried to change the subject.

Combining two sentences produces one concise sentence.

1 Unnecessary expletives

In general, do not use expletive constructions (*it seems, it is, there is, there are,* or similar phrases) unless you are introducing an idea to give it extra emphasis:

▶ It is for us, the living, to ensure that We the People shall become the
powerful. —JUNE JORDAN, "Inside America"

Here, *it is* slows down the opening of the sentence and sets up a formal rhythm that emphasizes what follows. Often, however, writers merely overuse expletives. Note how the following sentences are strengthened by deleting the expletives:

▶ ^Many^ ~~There are many~~ people ~~who~~ fear success because they do not
believe they deserve it.

▶ ^Presidential^ ~~It is necessary for presidential~~ candidates ~~to~~ ^must^ perform well on
television.

2 Wordy noun forms

Forming nouns from verbs, a process called *nominalization,* can help make prose more concise — for example, using *abolition* instead of *the process of abolishing* — but it can also make a sentence unnecessarily wordy and hard to read. Using noun phrases when verbs will do can bury the action of a sentence and force the writer to use weak verbs and too many prepositional phrases. Too often, writers use nominalization not to simplify a complex explanation but to make an idea sound more complex than it is.

> *assessing*
> The firm is now ~~engaged in an assessment of~~ its procedures for
>   ^
> *developing*
> ~~the development of~~ new products.
>   ^

The original sentence sounds pretentious, and the nominalization clouds the message. In contrast, the edited version is clear and forceful.

---

bedfordstmartins.com/smhandbook
Exercise Central > Sentence Style > Concise Writing

40c Using active and passive voice appropriately

In addition to choosing strong, precise verbs, you can help make your prose concise by using those verbs appropriately in active or passive voice (30g). Look at the following passage:

> [John F. Kennedy] died of a wound in the brain caused by a rifle bullet that was fired at him as he was riding through downtown Dallas in a motorcade.
>   Vice President Lyndon Baines Johnson, who was riding in the third car behind Mr. Kennedy's, was sworn in as the 36th President of the United States 99 minutes after Mr. Kennedy's death.
> —TOM WICKER, *New York Times*

As this passage indicates, the passive voice works effectively in certain situations: when the performer is unknown, unwilling to be identified, or less important than the recipient of the action. In general, however, try to use the active voice whenever possible. Because the passive voice diverts attention from the performer of an action and because it is usually wordier than the active voice, using it excessively makes for dull and difficult reading.

Edit an unnecessary passive construction to make it active.

> ◗ In ~~Gower's~~ research, ~~it was~~ found that pythons often dwell in trees.
>   *his*   *Gower*

EXERCISE 40.1

Look at the following sentences, which use the passive voice. Then rewrite each sentence in the active voice, and decide which version you prefer and why. Example:

> *I*   *you*
> ~~You are~~ hereby relieved of your duties. ~~by me.~~

1. Mistakes were made.
2. Musical legends such as Ray Charles, Billie Holiday, and Johnny Cash have all influenced Norah Jones.
3. Numerous reports of loud music from bars and shouting neighbors were taken by the city's new noise complaint hotline.
4. The violin solo was performed by an eight-year-old.
5. In a patient with celiac disease, intestinal damage can be caused by the body's immunological response to gluten.

> ⊙ bedfordstmartins.com/smhandbook
> **Exercise Central** > **Sentence Style** > **Active and Passive Voice**

EXERCISE 40.2

Revise the following paragraph to eliminate unnecessary words, nominalizations, expletives, and inappropriate use of the passive voice.

As dogs became tamed and domesticated by humans over many thousands of years, the canine species underwent an evolution into hundreds of breeds designed to perform particular, specific tasks, such as pulling sleds and guarding sheep. Over time, there was a decreased need for many breeds. For example, as humans evolved from hunter-gatherers into farmers, it was no longer at all necessary for them to own hunting dogs. Later, as farming societies became industrialized, there was a disappearance of herd animals, and fewer shepherds watching sheep meant that there were fewer sheepdogs. But by this time humans had grown accustomed to dogs' companionship, and breeding continued. Today, most dogs are kept by their owners simply as companions, but some dogs still do the work they were intentionally bred for, such as following a scent, guarding a home, or leading the blind.

THINKING CRITICALLY ABOUT CONCISE WRITING

Reading with an Eye for Conciseness

Bring two pieces of writing to class: one that is not just short, but concise—wasting no words but conveying its meaning clearly—and one that uses too many words to say too little. Bring both pieces to class to compare with those chosen by your classmates.

Thinking about Your Own Writing

Find two or three paragraphs you have written recently, and study them with an eye for empty words. Using 40a for guidance, eliminate meaningless words such as *quite* and *very*. Compare notes with one or two classmates to see what empty words, if any, you tend to use. Finally, make a note of the empty words you use, and try to avoid them in the future.

41 Coordination and Subordination

In speech, people tend to use *and* and *so* as all-purpose connectors.

He enjoys psychology, and the course requires a lot of work.

The meaning of this sentence may be perfectly clear in speech, which provides clues through voice, facial expressions, and gestures. But in writing, the sentence could have more than one meaning.

Although he enjoys psychology, the course requires a lot of work.

He enjoys psychology even though the course requires a lot of work.

Coordinating conjunctions like *and* give ideas equal weight, whereas subordinating conjunctions like *although* emphasize one idea over another.

41a Relating equal ideas with coordination

When used well, coordination relates separate but equal ideas. The element that links the ideas, usually a coordinating conjunction (*and, but, for, nor, or, so, yet*) or a semicolon, makes the precise relationship clear. The following sentences by N. Scott Momaday all use coordination, but the relationship between independent clauses differs in each sentence:

▷ **They acquired horses, and their ancient nomadic spirit was suddenly free of the ground.**

▷ **There is perfect freedom in the mountains, but it belongs to the eagle and the elk, the badger and the bear.**

▷ **No longer were they slaves to the simple necessity of survival; they were a lordly and dangerous society of fighters and thieves, hunters and priests of the sun.**

—N. SCOTT MOMADAY, *The Way to Rainy Mountain*

Coordination can help make explicit the relationship between two ideas.

▷ **Generations have now grown up with *The***

Simpsons **Bart, Lisa, and Maggie never get**

older, but today's college students may have been watching the show

since before they could talk.

Connecting these two sentences with a semicolon strengthens the connection between two closely related ideas.

When you connect ideas within a sentence, make sure the relationship between the ideas is clear.

but

▷ Watching television is a common way to spend leisure time, ~~and~~ it
                                                              ∧

makes viewers apathetic.

What does television's being a common form of leisure have to do with viewers' being apathetic? Changing *and* to *but* better relates the two ideas.

QUICK HELP

Editing for coordination and subordination

How do your ideas flow from one sentence to another? Do they connect smoothly and clearly? Are the more important ideas given more emphasis than the less important ones? These guidelines will help you edit with such questions in mind.

- Look for strings of short sentences that might be combined to join related ideas. (41a)

    but   *it*
  ▷ The report was short~~.~~, ~~It was~~ persuasive~~.~~; ~~It~~ changed my
          ∧   ∧
    mind.

- If you often link ideas with the conjunctions *and*, *but*, or *so*, are the linked ideas equally important? If not, edit to subordinate the less important ones. (41b)

- Are the most important ideas in independent clauses? If not, edit so that they are. (41b)

    Even though the
  ▷ ~~The~~ report was short, ~~even though~~ it changed my mind.
    ∧

Using coordination for special effect

Coordination can create special effects, as in a passage by Carl Sandburg describing the American reaction to Abraham Lincoln's assassination.

> Men tried to talk about it and the words failed and they came back to silence.
> To say nothing was best.
> Lincoln was dead.
> Was there anything more to say?
> Yes, they would go through the motions of grief and they would take part in a national funeral and a ceremony of humiliation and abasement and tears.
> But words were no help.
> Lincoln was dead. —CARL SANDBURG, *Abraham Lincoln: The War Years*

Together with the other short simple sentences, the coordinate clauses, phrases, and words in the first and fifth sentences create a powerful effect. Everything in the passage is grammatically equal, flattened out by the pain and shock of the death. In this way, the sentence structure and grammar mirror the dazed state of the populace. The short sentences and independent clauses are almost like sobs that illustrate the thought of the first sentence, that "the words failed."

EXERCISE 41.1

Using coordination to signal equal importance or to create special effects, combine and revise the following twelve short sentences into several longer and more effective ones. Add or delete words as necessary.

> The auditorium was filled with people. The sea of faces did not intimidate me. I had decided to appear in a musical with my local community theater group. There was no going back now. I reminded myself of how I had gotten here. It took hard work. I refused to doubt my abilities. Besides, the director and her staff had held auditions. I had read the heroine's part. I had sung a song. They had chosen me for the role. I was untrained. My skills as an actor would now be judged publicly. I felt ready to rise to the challenge.

bedfordstmartins.com/smhandbook
Exercise Central > Sentence Style > Coordination and Subordination

41b Emphasizing main ideas with subordination

Using subordination—putting less important ideas in dependent clauses or in phrases or words that serve as modifiers—allows you to emphasize the more important ideas in a sentence. The following sentence shows the subordinated point in italics:

▷ Mrs. Viola Cullinan was a plump woman *who lived in a three-bedroom house somewhere behind the post office.*

—MAYA ANGELOU, "My Name Is Margaret"

The dependent clause adds information about Mrs. Cullinan, but it is subordinate to the independent clause.

Notice that the choice of what to subordinate rests with the writer and depends on the intended meaning. Angelou might have given the same basic information differently.

▷ Mrs. Viola Cullinan, *a plump woman*, lived in a three-bedroom house somewhere behind the post office.

Subordinating the information about Mrs. Cullinan's size to that about her house would suggest a slightly different meaning, of course. As a writer, you must think carefully about what you want to emphasize and then subordinate information accordingly.

Subordination also helps establish logical relationships among ideas. These relationships are often specified by subordinating conjunctions—words such as *after*, *because*, and *so that*—and relative pronouns, words such as *which*, *who*, and *that*. Look, for example, at another sentence by Angelou. The subordinate clause is italicized, and the subordinating conjunction is underlined (29b7 and 29c4).

▷ She usually rested her smile until late afternoon <u>*when*</u> *her women friends dropped in and Miss Glory, the cook, served them cold drinks on the closed-in porch.*   —MAYA ANGELOU, "My Name Is Margaret"

Finally, subordination can help readers recognize your most important ideas. By subordinating some of the less important ideas in the following passage, the editing helps highlight the main idea:

◯ Many people check email in the evening, and so they turn on
the computer. ~~They~~ Though they may intend to respond only to urgent messages,
a friend sends a link to a blog post, ~~and~~ which they decide to read ~~it~~
for just a short while~~,~~ Eventually, ~~and~~ they get engrossed in Facebook, and they
end up spending the whole evening in front of the screen.

Like coordination, however, subordination can become excessive. When too many subordinate clauses are strung together, readers may have trouble keeping track of the main idea expressed in the independent clause.

TOO MUCH SUBORDINATION

◯ Philip II sent the Spanish Armada to conquer England, which was ruled by Elizabeth, who had executed Mary because she was plotting to overthrow Elizabeth, who was a Protestant, whereas Mary and Philip were Roman Catholics.

REVISED

◯ Philip II sent the Spanish Armada to conquer England, which was ruled by Elizabeth, a Protestant. She had executed Mary, a Roman Catholic like Philip, because Mary was plotting to overthrow her.

Putting the facts about Elizabeth executing Mary into an independent clause makes key information easier to recognize.

You can use a variety of grammatical structures—not only dependent clauses—to subordinate a less important element within a sentence:

◯ The parks report was persuasively written. It contained five typed pages. [no subordination]

◯ The parks report, *which contained five typed pages*, was persuasively written. [dependent clause]

◯ The parks report, *containing five typed pages*, was persuasively written. [participial phrase]

◯ The *five-page* parks report was persuasively written. [adjective]

◯ The parks report, *five typed pages*, was persuasively written. [appositive]

◯ The parks report, *its five pages neatly typed*, was persuasively written. [absolute]

EXERCISE 41.2

Combine each of the following sets of sentences into one sentence that uses subordination to signal the relationships among ideas. Example:

> I was looking through the cupboard.
> I noticed the cookies were gone.
> This snack is a favorite of my roommate.
>
> *While I was looking through the cupboard, I noticed that the cookies, one of my roommate's favorite snacks, were gone.*

1. The original *Star Trek* television show ran from 1966 to 1969.

   It was critically acclaimed.

   It had low ratings and was canceled by the network.

2. Athena was the goddess of wisdom.

   Ancient Greeks relied on Athena to protect the city of Athens.

   Athens was named in Athena's honor.

3. Harry Potter is a fictional wizard.

   He turns eleven years old.

   He is taken to Hogwarts School of Witchcraft and Wizardry.

4. Flappers seemed rebellious to their parents' generation.

   They broke with 1920s social conventions.

   They cut their hair short and smoked in public.

5. Skateboarding originated in Venice, California.

   The time was the mid-seventies.

   There was a drought.

   The swimming pools were empty.

bedfordstmartins.com/smhandbook

Exercise Central > Sentence Style > Coordination and Subordination

Using subordination for special effect

Some particularly fine examples of subordination come from Martin Luther King Jr. In the following passage, he piles up dependent clauses beginning with *when* to build up suspense for his main statement, given in the independent clause at the end:

> Perhaps it is easy for those who have never felt the stinging darts of segregation to say, "Wait." But *when* you have seen vicious mobs lynch your mothers and fathers at will and drown your sisters and brothers at whim; *when* you

have seen hate-filled policemen curse, kick, and even kill your black brothers and sisters; . . . *when* you have to concoct an answer for a five-year-old son who is asking: "Daddy, why do white people treat colored people so mean?"; *when* you take a cross-country drive and find it necessary to sleep night after night in the uncomfortable corners of your automobile because no motel will accept you; . . . *when* your first name becomes "nigger," your middle name becomes "boy" (however old you are) and your last name becomes "John," and your wife and mother are never given the respected title "Mrs."; . . . *when* you are forever fighting a degenerating sense of "nobodiness" — then you will understand why we find it difficult to wait.

—MARTIN LUTHER KING JR., "Letter from Birmingham Jail"

A dependent clause can also create an ironic effect if it somehow undercuts the independent clause. A master of this technique, Mark Twain once opened a paragraph with this sentence:

▶ Always obey your parents, *when they are present.*

—MARK TWAIN, "Advice to Youth"

THINKING CRITICALLY ABOUT COORDINATION AND SUBORDINATION

Reading with an Eye for Coordination and Subordination

Read over the first draft of "All-Powerful Coke" (see p. 67), paying special attention to the coordination and subordination. Do you notice any patterns—is there some of each? more of one than the other? Identify the coordination and subordination in one paragraph. Are they used appropriately? If not, revise the paragraph by following the guidelines in this chapter.

Thinking about Your Own Use of Coordination and Subordination

Analyze two paragraphs from one of your drafts. Do the independent clauses contain the main ideas? How many dependent clauses do you find? Should the ideas in the dependent clauses be subordinate to those in the independent clauses? Revise the paragraphs to use coordination and subordination effectively. What conclusions can you draw about your use of coordination and subordination?

Sentence Variety

42

Row upon row of trees identical in size and shape may appeal, at some level, to our sense of orderliness, but in spite of that appeal, the rows soon become boring. If variety is the spice of life, it is also the spice of sentence structure, where sameness can result in dull, listless prose.

42a Varying sentence length

Deciding how and when to vary sentence length is not always easy. Is there a "just right" length for a particular sentence or idea? The answer depends on, among other things, the writer's purpose, intended audience, and topic. A children's story, for instance, may call for mostly short sentences, whereas an article on nuclear disarmament may call for considerably longer ones.

Although a series of short or long sentences can sometimes be effective, alternating sentence length is usually the best approach in formal writing. For example, after one or more long sentences with complex ideas or images, the punch of a short sentence can be dramatic:

> The fire of, I think, five machine-guns was pouring upon us, and there was a series of heavy crashes caused by the Fascists flinging bombs over their own parapet in the most idiotic manner. It was intensely dark.
>
> —GEORGE ORWELL, *Homage to Catalonia*

In one college classroom, a peer-response group worked on an essay for almost an hour, but its overall effect still seemed boring. Finally, one student exclaimed, "These sentences all look the same!"

And they were: every sentence in the essay was about the same length, and every sentence started with the subject. The group went to work again, shortening some sentences and revising others to create new rhythms. With the resulting sentence variety, the essay took on new life; it flowed.

Similarly, try using a long sentence after several short ones.

 ***Sith.* What kind of a word is that? It sounds to me like the noise that emerges when you block one nostril and blow through the other, but to George Lucas it is a name that trumpets evil.** —ANTHONY LANE

EXERCISE 42.1

The following paragraph can be improved by varying sentence length. Read it aloud to get a sense of how it sounds. Then revise it, creating some short, emphatic sentences and combining other sentences to create more effective long sentences. Add words or change punctuation as you need to.

> Before planting a tree, a gardener needs to choose a good location and dig a deep enough hole. The location should have the right kind of soil, sufficient drainage, and enough light for the type of tree chosen. The hole should be slightly deeper than the root-ball and about twice as wide. The gardener must unwrap the root-ball, for even burlap, which is biodegradable, may be treated with chemicals that will eventually damage the roots. The roots may have grown into a compact ball if the tree has been in a pot for some time, and they should be separated or cut apart in this case. The gardener should set the root-ball into the hole and then begin to fill the hole with loose dirt. After filling the hole completely, he or she should make sure to water the tree thoroughly. New plantings require extra water and extra care for about three years before they are well rooted.

QUICK HELP

Editing for sentence variety

- Check sentence *length* by counting the words in each sentence. If the difference between the longest and the shortest sentences is fairly small—say, five words or fewer—try revising some sentences to create greater variety. Should two or more short sentences be combined because they deal with closely related ideas? Should a long sentence be split up because it contains too many important ideas? (42a)

- Look at sentence *openings.* If most sentences start with a subject, try recasting some to begin with a transition, a phrase, or a dependent clause. (42b)

- Vary *types* of sentences to make your writing more interesting. Do you use simple, compound, complex, and compound-complex sentences—or does one type predominate? Would a particular declarative sentence be more effective as a command or question or exclamation? Could you use a periodic or cumulative sentence for special effect? (42c)

42b Varying sentence openings

If sentence after sentence begins with a subject, a passage may become
monotonous or even hard to read.

▶ The way football and basketball are played is as interesting as the
    Because football   *each*
players. ~~Football~~ is a game of precision/. ~~Each~~ play is diagrammed
        ^   ^*however,*
to accomplish a certain goal. Basketball, is a game of endurance.
In fact, a   *the*
~~A~~ basketball game looks like a track meet/; ~~The~~ team that drops of
^   ^
exhaustion first loses.

The editing adds variety by using a subordinating word (*Because*) and transitions (*however* and *In fact*) and by linking sentences. Varying sentence openings prevents the passage from seeming to jerk or lurch along.

You can add variety to your sentence openings by using transitions, various kinds of phrases, and introductory dependent clauses.

1 Transitional expressions

See how transitions bring variety and clarity to this passage.

> In order to be alert Friday morning in New York, I planned to take the
> shuttle from Washington Thursday night. *On Thursday morning* it began
> to snow in Washington and to snow even harder in New York. *By mid-
> afternoon* I decided not to risk the shuttle and caught a train to New York.
> *Seven hours later* the train completed its three-hour trip. I arrived at Penn
> Station to find a city shut down by the worst blizzard since 1947.
>
> —LINDA ELLERBEE, "And So It Goes"

Here the transitional words establish chronology and help carry readers
smoothly through the paragraph. (For more on transitions, see 5d4.)

2 Phrases

Prepositional, verbal, and absolute phrases can also provide variety in
sentence openings.

PREPOSITIONAL PHRASES

Before dawn, tired commuters drink their first cups of coffee.

From a few scraps of wood in the Middle Ages to a precisely carved, electrified instrument in our times, the guitar has gone through uncounted changes.

VERBAL PHRASES

Frustrated by the delays, the driver shouted at his car radio.

To qualify for the finals, a speller must win a regional championship.

Having jumped the last hurdle, she sprinted toward the finish line.

ABSOLUTE PHRASES

Our hopes for victory shattered, we started home.

His nose against the window, Rover gazed hopefully at the street.

In general, use a comma after these phrases when they open a sentence (44a).

3 Dependent clauses

Dependent clauses are another way to open a sentence.

While the boss sat on his tractor, I was down in a ditch, pounding in stakes.

What they want is a place to call home.

In general, use a comma after an adverb clause that opens a sentence (44a).

42c Varying sentence types

In addition to using different lengths and openings, you can use different types of sentences. Sentences can be classified grammatically and functionally (as discussed in Chapter 29) as well as rhetorically.

1 Grammatical types

Grammatically, sentences fall into four categories—simple, compound, complex, and compound-complex—based on the number of independent and dependent clauses they contain (29d1). Varying your sentences among these grammatical types can help you create readable, effective prose.

2 Functional types

In terms of function, sentences are declarative (making a statement), interrogative (asking a question), imperative (giving a command), or exclamatory (expressing strong feeling). Most sentences are declarative, but occasionally a command, a question, or an exclamation may be appropriate.

COMMAND

Coal-burning plants undoubtedly harm the environment in various ways; for example, they contribute to acid rain. *But consider the alternatives.*

QUESTION

Why would sixteen middle-aged people try to backpack thirty-seven miles? At this point, I was not at all sure.

EXCLAMATION

Divorcés! They were everywhere! Sometimes he felt like a new member of an enormous club, the Divorcés of America, that he had never before even heard of.

3 Rhetorical types

By highlighting sentence endings and beginnings, periodic and cumulative sentences can create strong effects.

Periodic sentences

Periodic sentences postpone the main idea (usually in an independent clause) until the very end of the sentence. They are especially useful for creating tension or building toward a climactic, surprise, or inspirational ending.

> **Even though large tracts of Europe and many old and famous states have fallen or may fall into the grasp of the Gestapo and all the odious apparatus of Nazi rule,** *we shall not flag or fail.*
> —WINSTON CHURCHILL

Look at the following sentence and its revision to see how periodic order can provide emphasis:

ORIGINAL SENTENCE

The nations of the world have no alternative but coexistence because another world war would be unwinnable and because total destruction would certainly occur.

REVISED AS A PERIODIC SENTENCE

Because another world war would be unwinnable and because total destruction would certainly occur, the nations of the world have no alternative but coexistence.

Nothing is wrong with the first sentence. But to emphasize the idea in the independent clause—*no alternative but coexistence*—the writer chose to revise using the periodic pattern.

Cumulative sentences

Cumulative sentences, which begin with an independent clause and then add details in phrases and in dependent clauses (as does the preceding sentence labeled *original*), are far more common than periodic sentences. They are useful when you want to provide both immediate understanding of the main idea and a great deal of supporting detail.

▷ *I can still see her,* **a tiny nun with a sharp pink nose, confidently drawing a dead-straight horizontal line like a highway across the blackboard, flourishing her chalk at the end of it, her veil flapping out behind her as she turned back to class.** —KITTY BURNS FLOREY

▷ *Powther threw small secret appraising glances at the coffee cup,* **lipstick all around the edges, brown stains on the side where the coffee had dripped and spilled over, the saucer splotched with a whole series of dark brown rings.** —ANN PETRY, *The Narrows*

EXERCISE 42.2

Revise each of the following sentences twice, once as a periodic sentence and once as a cumulative sentence.

1. Obviously not understanding reporters, the politician did not know their names, did not answer their questions, and did not read their stories.

2. Able to think only of my mother's surgery the next morning, I could not even eat my dinner, much less get any sleep, nor could I do my homework.

bedfordstmartins.com/smhandbook
Exercise Central > Sentence Style > Sentence Variety

THINKING CRITICALLY ABOUT SENTENCE VARIETY

Reading with an Eye for Sentence Variety

Read something by an author you admire. Analyze two paragraphs for sentence length, opening, and type. Compare the sentence variety in these paragraphs with that in one of your paragraphs. What similarities or differences do you recognize, and what conclusions can you draw about sentence variety?

Thinking about Your Own Sentence Variety

Choose a piece of writing you have recently completed, and analyze two or three pages for sentence variety. Note sentence length, opening, and type (grammatical, functional, and rhetorical). Choose a passage you think can be improved for variety, and make those revisions.

43 Memorable Prose

How many times have you read or heard something so striking that you wanted immediately to share it with a friend? All of us recognize, and even quote, memorable words that have been written or spoken or sung — Monty Python's dead parrot sketch, perhaps, or passages from Martin Luther King Jr.'s "I Have a Dream" speech, or lyrics to an Aretha Franklin song. As writers, we can profit by examining — and using — some of the elements that help make such pieces memorable.

Great writers may have a genius for choosing the perfect words, but with practice, anyone can learn to write more memorable prose. When you notice a piece of writing that you admire — whether it's an advertisement, a magazine article, dialogue from a film, or a friend's Facebook status update — pay attention to what the writing does well and try to understand how it achieves its goals.

43a Writing emphatic sentences

When you speak, you achieve emphasis by raising your voice or stressing an important word or phrase. And much of the writing you see — in advertisements, on Web sites, in magazines — gains emphasis in similar fashion, with color or bold type, for instance. Even though academic writing can't always rely on such graphic devices, writers use other techniques to emphasize parts of their sentences.

1 Closing and opening positions for emphasis

When you read a sentence, you usually remember the ending. This part of the sentence moves the writing forward by providing new information, as in the following example:

▷ **Employers today expect college graduates to have *excellent writing skills*.**

A less emphatic but still important position in a sentence is the opening, which often connects the new sentence with what has come before.

○ **Today's employers want a college-educated workforce that can communicate well. *Excellent writing skills* are high on the list of qualifications.**

If you place relatively unimportant information in the memorable closing position of a sentence, you may undercut what you want to emphasize or give more emphasis to the closing words than you intend.

Last month, she $500,000.
○ **~~She gave $500,000 to~~ the school capital campaign ~~last month.~~**
   ^   ^

Moving *$500,000* to the end of the sentence emphasizes the amount.

QUICK HELP

Editing for memorable prose

- Identify the words you want to emphasize. If you've buried those words in the middle of a sentence, edit the sentence to change their position. The end and the beginning are generally the most emphatic. (43a1)

- Note any sentences that include a series of words, phrases, or clauses. Arrange the items in the series in climactic order, with the most important item last. (43a2)

- Underline all verbs, and look to see whether you rely too much on *be*, *do*, and *have*. If so, try to substitute more specific verbs. (43b)

---

2 **Climactic order**

Presenting ideas in climactic order means arranging them in order of increasing importance or drama so that your writing builds to a climax. By saving its most dramatic item for last, the following sentence makes its point forcefully:

○ **After they've finished with the pantry, the medicine cabinet, and the attic, [neat people] will throw out the red geranium (too many leaves), sell the dog (too many fleas), and send the children off to boarding school (too many scuffmarks on the hardwood floors).**
   —SUSANNE BRITT, "Neat People vs. Sloppy People"

The original version of the next sentence fails to achieve strong emphasis because its verbs are not sequenced in order of increasing power; the editing provides climactic order.

○ **Violent video games assault our eyes,** ~~offend our ears, and~~ **damage our brains.**
̬   ̬

~~and offend our ears.~~

EXERCISE 43.1

Revise each of the following sentences to highlight what you take to be the main or most important ideas. Example:

Theories about dinosaurs have run the gamut—simple lizards, fully adapted warm-blooded creatures/. ~~hybrids of cold-blooded capabilities.~~ *hybrids of cold-blooded capabilities,*

1. The president persuaded the American people, his staff, and Congress.
2. We can expect a decade of record-breaking tropical storms and hurricanes, if meteorologists are correct in their predictions.
3. From the sightseeing boat, we saw a whale dive toward us and then, before crashing its tail on the waves, lift itself out of the water.
4. I did not realize that living in the city would mean eating canned soup every night, selling my car, and losing half my closet space.
5. Jake experienced several side effects from the medication, including dizziness, severe abdominal pain, and dry mouth.

43b Choosing strong verbs

Verbs serve as the real workhorses of our language. Look, for instance, at the strong, precise verbs in the following passage:

○ **A fire engine, out for a trial spin, *roared* past Emerson's house, hot with readiness for public duty. Over the barn roofs the martens *dipped* and *chittered*. A swarthy daughter of an asparagus grower, in culottes, shirt, and bandanna, *pedalled* past on her bicycle.**

—E. B. WHITE, "Walden"

If White had used more general verbs—such as *drove*, *flew*, *called*, and *rode*—the passage would be much less effective. With White's verbs, however, readers can hear the roar of the fire engine, see the martens swooping downward and hear them chirping shrilly, and feel the young woman pushing on the pedals of her bicycle.

Some of the most common verbs in English—especially *be*, *do*, and *have*—carry little or no sense of specific action. Try not to overuse them in situations where precise verbs would be more effective. Look at how much stronger the following sentences become when precise verbs are used:

○ Malnutrition ~~is harmful to~~ children's development.
  ^ *stunts and distorts*

○ Sidewalk artists offered to ~~do~~ my portrait in ten minutes.
  ^ *sketch*

○ The young marines ~~had~~ basic training at Parris Island.
  ^ *sweated through*

43c Using special effects

Contemporary movies often succeed on the basis of their special effects. Similarly, special effects like repetition, antithesis, and inverted word order can animate your prose and help make it memorable.

1 Repetition for emphasis

Carefully used, repetition of sounds, words, phrases, or other grammatical constructions serves as a powerful stylistic device. Orators have long known its power. Here is a famous use of repetition from one of British Prime Minister Winston Churchill's addresses to the British people during World War II:

○ We shall not flag or fail, we shall go on to the end. We shall fight in France, we shall fight on the seas and oceans, we shall fight with growing confidence and growing strength in the air, we shall defend our island, whatever the cost may be; we shall fight on the beaches, . . . we shall fight in the fields and in the streets, . . . we shall never surrender.   —WINSTON CHURCHILL

In this passage, Churchill uses the constant hammering of *we shall* accompanied by the repetition of *f* sounds (*flag, fail, fight, France, confidence, defend, fields*) to strengthen his listeners' resolve.

Though you may not be a prime minister, you can use repetition to equally good effect. Here is another example:

○ **So my dream date turned into a nightmare. Where was the quiet, considerate, caring guy I thought I had met? In his place appeared this jerk. He strutted, he postured, he preened—and then he bragged, he bellowed, he practically brayed—just like the donkey he so much reminded me of.**

Be careful, however, to use repetition only for a deliberate purpose.

Multiple negatives

One common type of repetition is to use more than one negative term in a negative statement. In *I can't hardly see you*, for example, both *can't* and *hardly* carry negative meanings. Emphatic double negatives—and triple, quadruple, and more—are especially common in the South and among speakers of some African American varieties of English, who may say, for example, *Don't none of my people come from up North.*

Multiple negatives have a long history in English (and in other languages) and can be found in the works of Chaucer and Shakespeare. In the eighteenth century, however, in an effort to make English more logical, double negatives came to be labeled as incorrect. In college writing, you may well have reason to quote passages that include them (whether from Shakespeare, Toni Morrison, or your grandmother), but it is safer to avoid other uses of double negatives in academic writing.

EXERCISE 43.2

Go through the examples in 43c1, identifying the uses of repetition. Using one example as a model, write a passage of your own with effective repetition.

2 Antithesis to emphasize contrast

Antithesis is the use of parallel structures to highlight contrast or opposition (see Chapter 35). Like other uses of parallelism, antithesis provides a pleasing rhythm that calls readers' attention to the contrast, often in a startling or amusing way.

○ Love is an ideal thing, marriage a real thing.

○ The congregation didn't think much of the new preacher, and what
   the new preacher thought of the congregation she didn't wish to say.

○ It is a sin to believe evil of others—but it is not a mistake.

                                                            —H. L. MENCKEN

EXERCISE 43.3

Using one of the preceding examples as a guide, create a sentence of your own
that uses antithesis. You might begin by thinking of opposites you could build on:
hope/despair, good/evil, fire/ice. Or you might begin with a topic you want to write
about: success, greed, generosity, and so on.

3 Inverted word order

Writers may invert the usual word order, such as putting the verb before
the subject or the object before the subject and verb, to create surprise
or to emphasize a particular word or phrase.

   Out of the tree   two dead birds.
○ ~~Two dead birds~~ plummeted ~~out of the tree.~~
   ^   ^

   The inverted word order creates a more dramatic sentence by putting the
   emphasis at the end, on *two dead birds*.

As with any unusual sentence pattern, use inverted word order sparingly,
only to create occasional special effects.

○ Into this grey lake plopped the thought, I know this man, don't I?

                                                            —DORIS LESSING

○ In a hole in the ground there lived a hobbit.   —J. R. R. TOLKIEN

EXERCISE 43.4

Look at something you have written, and find a sentence that might be more effective with inverted word order. Experiment with the word order. Read the results
aloud, and compare the effects.

THINKING CRITICALLY ABOUT PROSE STYLE

Reading with an Eye for Prose Style

Chapters 40–43 present many elements that mark effective prose. One entertaining way to practice these elements is to imitate them. Choose a writer you admire. Reread (or listen to) this writer's work, getting a feel for the rhythms, the structures, the special effects. Make a list of the elements that contribute to the distinctive style. Then choose a well-known story, and retell it in that writer's style. Following is the opening of "The Three Little Pigs" as one student imagined Edgar Allan Poe might have told it.

> It began as a mere infatuation. I admired them from afar, with a longing that only a wolf may know. Soon, these feelings turned to torment. Were I even to set eyes upon their porcine forms, the bowels of my soul raged, as if goaded by some festering poison. As the chilling winds of November howled, my gullet yearned for them. I soon feasted only upon an earnest and consuming desire for the moment of their decease.

Thinking about Your Own Prose Style

Read over something you have written, looking for memorable sentences. If few sentences catch your eye, choose some that show promise—ones with strong verbs or a pleasing rhythm, perhaps. Using this chapter for guidance, try revising one or two sentences to make them more effective and memorable. Finally, note some ways in which your writing is effective and some strategies for making it more effective.

PUNCTUATION

Commas

It's hard to go through a day without encountering commas. Even the directions for making hot cereal depend on the careful placement of a comma: *Add Cream of Wheat slowly, stirring constantly.* Here the comma tells the cook to *add the cereal slowly.* If the comma came before the word *slowly*, however, the cook might add the cereal all at once and *stir slowly*—perhaps ending up with lumpy cereal.

Because the comma can play many roles in a sentence, comma use often doesn't follow hard and fast rules. Using commas effectively requires you to make decisions that involve audience, purpose, rhythm, and style—not just grammar.

44a Commas after introductory elements

A comma usually follows an introductory word, expression, phrase, or clause.

- However, health care costs keep rising.

- In the end, only you can decide.

- Wearing new running shoes, Logan prepared for the race.

- To win the contest, Connor needed skill and luck.

- Pencil poised in anticipation, Audrey waited for the drawing contest to begin.

- While her friends watched, Lila practiced her gymnastics routine.

Some writers omit the comma if the introductory element is short and does not seem to require a pause after it.

▶ *At the racetrack* **Henry lost nearly his entire paycheck.**

However, you will seldom be wrong if you use a comma after an introductory element. If the introductory element is followed by inverted word order, with the verb preceding the subject, do not use a comma unless misreading might occur.

▶ **From directly behind my seat/ came huge clouds of cigar smoke.**

▶ **Before he went, on came the rains.**

EXERCISE 44.1

In the following sentences, add any commas that are needed after the introductory element. Example:

> To find a good day-care provider, parents usually need both time and money.

1. After the concession speech the senator's supporters drifted out of the room.
2. To our surprise the charity auction raised enough money to build a new technology center.
3. Unaware that the microphone was on the candidate made an offensive comment.
4. Whenever someone rings the doorbell her dog goes berserk.
5. Therefore Sasha must take a summer course to receive her diploma.
6. With the fifth century came the fall of the Roman Empire.
7. A tray of shrimp in one hand and a pile of napkins in the other the waiter avoided me.
8. Toward the rapids floated an empty rubber raft.
9. When they woke up the exhausted campers no longer wanted to hike.
10. Tears in his eyes Keflezighi won the marathon.

Editing for commas

Research for this book shows that five of the most common errors in college writing involve commas. Check your writing for these errors:

- Check every sentence that doesn't begin with the subject to see whether it opens with an introductory element (a word, phrase, or clause that tells when, where, how, or why the main action of the sentence occurs). Use a comma to separate the introductory material from the main part of the sentence. (44a)

- Look at every sentence that contains one of the conjunctions *and*, *but*, *for*, *nor*, *or*, *so*, or *yet*. If the groups of words before and after the conjunction both function as complete sentences, you have a compound sentence. Use a comma before the conjunction. (44b)

- Look at each adjective clause beginning with *which*, *who*, *whom*, *whose*, *when*, or *where*, and at each phrase and appositive. Decide whether the element is essential to the meaning of the sentence. If the rest of the sentence would be unclear without it, you should not set off the element with commas. (44c)

- Identify all adjective clauses beginning with *that*, and make sure they are not set off with commas. (44c1 and 44j)

- Do not use commas to set off restrictive elements; between subjects and verbs, verbs and objects or complements, or prepositions and objects; to separate parts of compound constructions other than compound sentences; or before the first or after the last item in a series. (44j)

44b Commas in compound sentences

A comma usually precedes a coordinating conjunction (*and*, *but*, *for*, *nor*, *or*, *so*, or *yet*) that joins two independent clauses in a compound sentence.

▶ The title sounds impressive, but *administrative clerk* is just another word for *photocopier*.

▶ The show started at last, and the crowd grew quiet.

With very short clauses, writers sometimes omit the comma before *and* or *or*. You will never be wrong to include it, however.

○ **She saw her chance and she took it.**
○ **She saw her chance, and she took it.**

Always use the comma if there is any chance of misreading the sentence without it.

○ **The game ended in victory, and pandemonium erupted.**
    ^

You may want to use a semicolon rather than a comma when the clauses are long and complex or contain their own commas.

○ **When these early migrations took place, the ice was still confined
    to the lands in the far north; but eight hundred thousand years ago,
    when man was already established in the temperate latitudes, the ice
    moved southward until it covered large parts of Europe and Asia.**
                                        —ROBERT JASTROW, *Until the Sun Dies*

Be careful not to use *only* a comma between independent clauses. Doing so creates a comma splice (see Chapter 36). Either use a coordinating conjunction after the comma, or use a semicolon.

COMMA SPLICE   Luck isn't the only thing responsible for your new job,
               give yourself the credit you deserve.

REVISED   Luck isn't the only thing responsible for your new job, *so*
               give yourself the credit you deserve.

REVISED   Luck isn't the only thing responsible for your new job;
               give yourself the credit you deserve.

EXERCISE 44.2

Use a comma and a coordinating conjunction (*and*, *but*, *for*, *nor*, *or*, *so*, or *yet*) to combine each of the following pairs of sentences into one sentence. Delete or rearrange words if necessary. Example:

                                   so
I had finished studying for the test/, I went to bed.
                                 ^

1. The chef did not want to serve a heavy dessert. She was planning to have a rich
   stew for the main course.

2. My mother rarely allowed us to eat sweets. Halloween was a special exception.

3. Scientists have mapped the human genome. They learn more every day about how genes affect an individual's health.

4. Perhaps I will change my name when I get married. Maybe I will keep my maiden name.

5. Penguins cannot fly. They cannot walk the way other birds do.

---

bedfordstmartins.com/smhandbook
Exercise Central > Punctuation > Commas

44c Commas to set off nonrestrictive elements

Nonrestrictive clauses, phrases, and words are not essential to the meaning of a sentence because they do *not* limit, or restrict, the meaning of the words they modify. They should be set off with commas. Restrictive elements, on the other hand, *do* limit meaning and should *not* be set off with commas.

RESTRICTIVE   Drivers *who have been convicted of drunken driving* should lose their licenses.

In the preceding sentence, the clause *who have been convicted of drunken driving* is essential to the meaning because it limits the word it modifies, *Drivers*, to those drivers who have been convicted of drunken driving. Therefore, it is *not* set off by commas.

NONRESTRICTIVE   The two drivers involved in the accident, *who have been convicted of drunken driving*, should lose their licenses.

Here, the clause *who have been convicted of drunken driving* is not essential to the meaning of the sentence because it does not limit what it modifies, *The two drivers involved in the accident*, but merely provides additional information about them. Therefore, the clause is set off with commas.

Notice how using or not using commas to set off such an element can change the meaning of a sentence.

○ **The bus drivers rejecting the management offer remained on strike.**

○ **The bus drivers, rejecting the management offer, remained on strike.**

The first sentence says that only some bus drivers, the ones who rejected the offer, remained on strike, implying that other drivers went back to work. The second sentence suggests that all the drivers remained on strike.

To decide whether an element is restrictive or nonrestrictive, mentally delete the element. Does the deletion change the meaning of the rest of the sentence or make it unclear? If so, the element is probably restrictive, and you should not set it off with commas. If it does not change the meaning, the element is probably nonrestrictive and requires commas.

1 Adjective and adverb clauses

Adjective clauses (29c4) that begin with *that* are always restrictive; do not set them off with commas. Adjective clauses beginning with *which* may be either restrictive or nonrestrictive. (Some writers prefer to use *which* only for nonrestrictive clauses, which they set off with commas.)

NONRESTRICTIVE CLAUSES

○ **I borrowed books from the rental library of Shakespeare and Company,** *which was the library and bookstore of Sylvia Beach at 12 rue de l'Odeon.*   —ERNEST HEMINGWAY, *A Moveable Feast*

The adjective clause describing Shakespeare and Company is not necessary to the meaning of the sentence, so it is set off with a comma.

In general, set off an adverb clause (29c4) that follows a main clause only if it begins with *although, even though, while,* or another subordinating conjunction expressing the idea of contrast. (For a list of subordinating conjunctions, see 29b7.)

○ **He uses semicolons frequently, while she prefers periods and short sentences.**

The adverb clause *while she prefers periods and short sentences* expresses the idea of contrast; therefore, it is set off with a comma.

RESTRICTIVE CLAUSES

○ **The claim *that men like seriously to battle one another to some sort of finish* is a myth.** —JOHN MCMURTRY, "Kill 'Em! Crush 'Em! Eat 'Em Raw!"

The adjective clause is necessary to the meaning of the sentence because it explains which claim is a myth; therefore, the clause is not set off with commas.

○ **The man/ who rescued Jana's puppy/ won her eternal gratitude.**

The clause *who rescued Jana's puppy* is necessary to the meaning because only the rescuer won the gratitude; therefore, the clause takes no commas.

Do not set off an adverb clause that follows a main clause unless the adverb clause begins with *although, even though, while,* or another subordinating conjuction indicating contrast.

○ **Remember to check your calculations/ before you submit the form.**

2 Participles and phrases

Participles and participial phrases (29c3) may be either restrictive or nonrestrictive. Prepositional phrases are usually restrictive, but if they are not essential to the meaning, set them off with commas.

NONRESTRICTIVE PHRASES

○ **Stephanie, amazed, stared at the strange vehicle.**

The participle *amazed* does not limit the meaning of *Stephanie.*

○ **Many baby boomers, fearing that Social Security funds will be insufficient, are saving for their retirement through company investment plans.**

The participial phrase beginning with *fearing* does not limit the meaning of *Many baby boomers* or change the central meaning of the sentence.

○ **The bodyguards, in dark suits and matching ties, looked quite intimidating.**

The prepositional phrase *in dark suits and matching ties* does not limit the meaning of *The bodyguards.*

RESTRICTIVE PHRASES

▶ A bird *in the hand* is worth two *in the bush*.

The prepositional phrases *in the hand* and *in the bush* are essential to the meaning.

▶ Wood *cut from living trees* does not burn as well as dead wood.

The participial phrase *cut from living trees* is essential to the meaning.

▶ The bodyguards were the men *in dark suits and matching ties*.

The prepositional phrase *in dark suits and matching ties* is essential to the meaning.

3 Appositives

An appositive is a noun or noun phrase that renames a nearby noun (29c3). When an appositive is not essential to identify what it renames, set it off with commas.

NONRESTRICTIVE APPOSITIVES

▶ Jon Stewart, the irreverent news commentator, often pokes fun at

political leaders.

Mr. Stewart's name identifies him; the appositive simply provides extra information.

▶ Ralph Ellison's only completed novel, *Invisible Man*, won the

National Book Award in 1953.

Ellison completed only one novel, so its name is not essential.

RESTRICTIVE APPOSITIVES

▶ The news commentator/ Jon Stewart/ often pokes fun at political

leaders.

The appositive *Jon Stewart* identifies the specific commentator.

▶ Mozart's opera/ *The Marriage of Figaro*/ was considered revolutionary.

The appositive is restrictive because Mozart wrote more than one opera.

EXERCISE 44.3

Use commas to set off nonrestrictive clauses, phrases, and appositives in any of the following sentences that contain such elements.

1. What can you buy for the person who has everything?
2. Embalming is a technique that preserves a cadaver.
3. The enormous new house which was the largest in the neighborhood had replaced a much smaller old home.
4. The rescue workers exhausted and discouraged stared ahead without speaking.
5. The new mall has the same stores and restaurants as all the other malls in town.
6. Viruses unlike bacteria can reproduce only by infecting live cells.
7. Napoléon was imprisoned after his defeat at the battle of Waterloo.
8. Hammurabi an ancient Babylonian king created laws that were carved on a stone for public display.
9. Birds' hearts have four chambers whereas reptiles' have three.
10. A female cheetah hisses and swats if another animal gets too close to her young.

> bedfordstmartins.com/smhandbook
> **Exercise Central > Punctuation > Commas**

44d Commas to separate items in a series

Except in journalism writing, use a comma between items in a series of three or more words, phrases, or clauses.

▶ **I bumped into professors, horizontal bars, agricultural students, and swinging iron rings.** —JAMES THURBER, "University Days"

▶ **He has plundered our seas, ravaged our coasts, burnt our towns, and destroyed the lives of our people.**

—THOMAS JEFFERSON, Declaration of Independence

You may see a series with no comma after the next-to-last item, particularly in newspaper writing. Occasionally, however, omitting the comma can cause confusion.

▶ **All the vegetables in the cafeteria—broccoli, green beans, peas, and carrots—were cooked to an unrecognizable mush.**

Without the comma after *peas*, you wouldn't know if the cafeteria offered three vegetables (the third being a *mixture* of peas and carrots) or four.

When the items in a series contain commas of their own or other punctuation, separate them with semicolons rather than commas (45b).

Coordinate adjectives, those that relate equally to the noun they modify, should be separated by commas.

- The *long, twisting, muddy* road led to a shack in the woods.

In a sentence like *The cracked bathroom mirror reflected his face,* however, *cracked* and *bathroom* are not coordinate because *bathroom mirror* is the equivalent of a single word, which is modified by *cracked.* Hence, they are *not* separated by commas.

You can usually determine whether adjectives are coordinate by inserting the word *and* between them. If the sentence still makes sense with the *and*, the adjectives are coordinate and should be separated by commas.

- They are sincere *and* talented *and* inquisitive researchers.

The sentence makes sense with the *ands*, so the adjectives should be separated by commas: *They are sincere, talented, inquisitive researchers.*

- Byron carried an elegant *and* gold *and* pocket watch.

The sentence does not make sense with the *ands*, so the adjectives should not be separated by commas: *Byron carried an elegant gold pocket watch.*

EXERCISE 44.4

Revise any of the following sentences that require commas to set off words, phrases, or clauses in a series.

1. The students donated clothing school supplies and nonperishable food.
2. The hot humid weather did not stop the fans from flocking to the free outdoor concert.
3. The ball sailed over the fence across the yard and through the Wilsons' window
4. Several art historians inspected the Chinese terra-cotta figures.
5. The young athletes' parents insist on calling every play judging every move and telling everyone within earshot exactly what is wrong with the team.

> bedfordstmartins.com/smhandbook
> Exercise Central > Punctuation > Commas

44e Commas to set off parenthetical and transitional expressions

Parenthetical and transitional expressions often interrupt the flow of a sentence or digress, so they are usually set off with commas. Parenthetical expressions (*in fact, by the way*) add comments. Transitional expressions (5d and e), including conjunctive adverbs (29b7) such as *however* and *furthermore,* clarify how parts of sentences relate to what has come before them.

- Roald Dahl's stories, *it turns out,* were often inspired by his own childhood.
- Ceiling fans are, *moreover,* less expensive than air conditioners.
- Shark attacks, *for example,* happen extremely rarely.

44f Commas to set off contrasting elements, interjections, direct address, and tag questions

CONTRASTING ELEMENTS

- On official business it was she, *not my father,* one would usually hear on the phone or in stores.

  —RICHARD RODRIGUEZ, "Aria: A Memoir of a Bilingual Childhood"

INTERJECTIONS

- *My God,* who wouldn't want a wife?   —JUDY BRADY, "I Want a Wife"

DIRECT ADDRESS

- Remember, *sir,* that you are under oath.

TAG QUESTIONS

- The governor did not veto the unemployment bill, *did she?*

EXERCISE 44.5

Revise each of the following sentences, using commas to set off parenthetical and transitional expressions, contrasting elements, interjections, words used in direct address, and tag questions.

1. One must consider the society as a whole not just its parts.
2. Drinking caffeinated beverages can in fact be good for your health.
3. You don't expect me to read this speech do you?
4. Coming in ahead of schedule and under budget it appears is the only way to keep this client happy.
5. Believe me Jenna I had no idea things would turn out this way.

⊘ bedfordstmartins.com/smhandbook
Exercise Central > Punctuation > Commas

44g Commas with dates, addresses, titles, and numbers

Dates

Use a comma between the day of the week and the month, between the day of the month and the year, and between the year and the rest of the sentence, if any.

▶ **On Wednesday, November 26, 2008, gunmen arrived in Mumbai**

   by boat.

Do not use commas with dates in inverted order or with dates consisting of only the month and the year.

▶ **She dated the letter *18 October 2010*.**

▶ **Thousands of Germans swarmed over the Berlin Wall in *November 1989*.**

Addresses and place-names

Use a comma after each part of an address or place-name, including the state if no zip code is given. Do not precede a zip code with a comma.

○ Forward my mail to the Department of English, The Ohio State University, Columbus, Ohio 43210.

○ Portland, Oregon, is much larger than Portland, Maine.

Titles

Use commas to set off a title such as *MD* or *PhD* from the name preceding it and from the rest of the sentence. The titles *Jr.* and *Sr.*, however, often appear without commas.

○ Jaime Mejía, *PhD*, will speak about his anthropological research.

○ Martin Luther King *Jr.* was one of the twentieth century's greatest orators.

Numbers

In numerals of five digits or more, use a comma between each group of three digits, starting from the right.

○ The city's population rose to *158,000* in the 2000 census.

The comma is optional in four-digit numerals but is never used in years.

○ The college had an enrollment of *1,789* [or *1789*] in the fall of *2006*.

Do not use a comma in building numbers, zip codes, or page numbers.

○ My parents live at *11311* Wimberly Drive, Richmond, Virginia *23233*.

○ Turn to page *1566*.

EXERCISE 44.6

Revise each of the following sentences, using commas appropriately with dates, addresses, place-names, titles, and numbers.

1. The city of Dublin Ireland has a population of over 500000.

2. I rode a total of almost 1200 miles on my bike in 2009.
3. New Delhi India and Islamabad Pakistan became the capitals of two independent nations at midnight on August 15 1947.
4. MLA headquarters are at 26 Broadway New York New York 10004.
5. I was convinced that the nameplate I. M. Well MD was one of my sister's pranks.

bedfordstmartins.com/smhandbook
Exercise Central > Punctuation > Commas

44h Commas with quotations

Commas set off a quotation from words used to introduce or identify the source of the quotation. A comma following a quotation goes inside the closing quotation mark.

▷ A German proverb warns, "Go to law for a sheep, and lose your cow."
▷ "All I know about grammar," said Joan Didion, "is its infinite power."

Do not use a comma after a question mark or exclamation point.

▷ "What's a thousand dollars?/" asks Groucho Marx in *The Cocoanuts*.

"Mere chicken feed. A poultry matter."

▷ "Out, damned spot!/" cries Lady Macbeth.

Do not use a comma to introduce a quotation with *that*.

▷ The writer of Ecclesiastes concludes that/ "all is vanity."

Do not use a comma with a quotation when the rest of the sentence does more than introduce or identify the source of the quotation.

▷ People who say/ "Have a nice day" irritate me.

▷ He put off military service because he had/ "other priorities."

Do not use a comma before an indirect quotation—one that does not use the speaker's exact words.

○ Patrick Henry declared/ that he wanted either liberty or death.

EXERCISE 44.7

Insert a comma in any of the following sentences that require one.

1. "The public be damned!" William Henry Vanderbilt was reported to have said. "I'm working for my stockholders."

2. My mother was fond of telling me "You'd make coffee nervous!"

3. I refuse to believe the old saying that "nice guys finish last."

4. "Learning without thought is labor lost; thought without learning is perilous" Confucius argued.

5. "Do you have any idea who I am?" the well-dressed man asked belligerently.

---

bedfordstmartins.com/smhandbook
Exercise Central > Punctuation > Commas

44i Commas for understanding

Use a comma if it will make a sentence easier to read or understand.

○ The members of the dance troupe strutted in, in matching tuxedos
  ^
and top hats.

○ Before, I had planned to major in biology.
  ^

44j Unnecessary commas

Excessive use of commas can spoil an otherwise fine sentence.

Around restrictive elements

Do not use commas to set off restrictive elements—elements that limit, or define, the meaning of the words they modify or refer to (44c).

▷ **My mother dislikes films,/ that include foul language.**

▷ **A law,/ reforming campaign financing,/ was passed in 2002.**

▷ **My only defense,/ against my allergies,/ is to stay indoors.**

▷ **The actress,/ Sandra Bullock,/ won an Oscar in 2010.**

Between subjects and verbs, verbs and objects or complements, and prepositions and objects

Do not use a comma between a subject and its verb, a verb and its object or complement, or a preposition and its object—not even if the subject, object, or complement is a long phrase or clause.

▷ **Watching old movies late at night,/ is a way for me to relax.**

▷ **Parents must decide,/ how much television their children should watch.**

▷ **The winner of,/ the community-service award stepped forward.**

In compound constructions

In compound constructions (other than compound sentences—see 44b), do not use a comma before or after a coordinating conjunction that joins the two parts.

▷ **Donald Trump was born rich,/ and has used his money to make money.**

> The *and* here joins parts of the compound predicate *was born* and *has used*, which should not be separated by a comma.

○ Ellen Johnson-Sirleaf,/ and George Weah both claimed to have won the election.

The *and* here joins parts of a compound subject, which should not be separated by a comma.

In a series

Do not use a comma before the first or after the last item in a series (44d).

○ The auction included,/ furniture, paintings, and china.

○ The swimmer took slow, powerful,/ strokes.

THINKING CRITICALLY ABOUT COMMAS

Reading with an Eye for Commas

The following poem uses commas to create rhythm and guide readers. Read the poem aloud, listening especially to the effect of the commas at the end of the first and fifth lines. Then read it again as if those commas were omitted, noting the difference. What is the effect of the poet's decision not to use a comma at the end of the third line?

> Some say the world will end in fire,
> Some say in ice.
> From what I've tasted of desire
> I hold with those who favor fire.
> But if it had to perish twice,
> I think I know enough of hate
> To say that for destruction ice
> Is also great
> And would suffice.
> —ROBERT FROST, "Fire and Ice"

Thinking about Your Own Use of Commas

Choose a paragraph that you have written. Remove all of the commas, and read it aloud. What is the effect of leaving out the commas? Now, punctuate the passage with commas, consulting this chapter. Did you replace all of your original commas? Did you add any new ones? Explain why you added the commas you did.

Semicolons

Semicolons, which create a pause stronger than that of a comma but not as strong as the full pause of a period, show close connections between related ideas.

45a Semicolons with independent clauses

You can join independent clauses in several ways: with a comma and a coordinating conjunction (44b), with a colon (49d), with a dash (49c), or with a semicolon. Semicolons provide writers with subtle ways of signaling closely related clauses. The clause following a semicolon often restates an idea expressed in the first clause; it can also expand on or present a contrast to the first.

▷ **Immigration acts were passed; newcomers had to prove, besides moral correctness and financial solvency, their ability to read.**

> —MARY GORDON, "More Than Just a Shrine"

Gordon uses a semicolon to lead to a clause that expands on the first one. The semicolon also gives the sentence an abrupt rhythm that suits the topic: laws that imposed strict requirements.

A semicolon should link independent clauses joined by conjunctive adverbs such as *therefore*,

The following public service announcement, posted in New York City subway cars, reminds commuters what to do with a used newspaper at the end of the ride:

Please put it in a trash can; that's good news for everyone.

A *New York Times* article praised the writer of the announcement for choosing to use a semicolon, "that distinct division between statements that are closely related but require a separation more prolonged than a conjunction and more emphatic than a comma."

however, and *indeed* or transitional expressions such as *in fact, in addition,* and *for example* (36c).

○ **The circus comes as close to being the world in microcosm as anything I know; in a way, it puts all the rest of show business in the shade.**

—E. B. WHITE, "The Ring of Time"

If two independent clauses joined by a coordinating conjunction contain commas, you may use a semicolon instead of a comma before the conjunction to make the sentence easier to read.

○ **Every year, whether the Republican or the Democratic Party is in office, more and more power drains away from the individual to feed vast reservoirs in far-off places; and we have less and less say about the shape of events which shape our future.**

—WILLIAM F. BUCKLEY JR., "Why Don't We Complain?"

EXERCISE 45.1

Combine each of the following pairs of sentences into one sentence by using a semicolon. Example:

meet
Take the bus to Henderson Street/; ~~Meet~~ me under the clock.

1. Abalone fishing in California is strictly regulated. A person is allowed to harvest only twenty-four of these large mollusks per year.
2. City life offers many advantages. In many ways, however, life in a small town is much more pleasant.
3. The door contains an inflatable slide to be used in an emergency. In addition, each seat can become a flotation device.
4. Most car accidents occur within twenty-five miles of the home. Therefore, you should wear a seat belt on every trip.
5. Involvement in team sports provides more than just health benefits for young girls. It also increases their self-confidence.

> **QUICK HELP**
>
> ## Editing for semicolons
>
> - Use semicolons only between independent clauses—groups of words that can stand alone as sentences (45a)—or between items in a series. (45b)
>
> - If you find few or no semicolons in your writing, ask yourself whether closely related ideas in two sentences might be better expressed in one sentence with a semicolon. (45a)
>
> - If you find too many semicolons in your writing, try deleting some of them. Would making some clauses into separate sentences make your writing smoother or less monotonous? (45c)

45b Semicolons to separate items in a series

Ordinarily, commas separate items in a series (44d). But when the items themselves contain commas or other punctuation, using semicolons to separate the items will make the sentence clearer and easier to read.

◯ **Anthropology encompasses archaeology, the study of ancient civilizations through artifacts; linguistics, the study of the structure and development of language; and cultural anthropology, the study of customs, language, and behavior.**

45c Misused or overused semicolons

A comma, not a semicolon, should separate an independent clause from a dependent clause or a phrase.

◯ **The police found a set of fingerprints; which they used to identify**
        the thief.

A colon, not a semicolon, should introduce a series.

◯ **The reunion tour includes the following bands; Urban Waste,**
        Murphy's Law, Rapid Deployment, and Ism.

Be careful not to use semicolons too often. Sentence upon sentence punctuated with semicolons may sound monotonous and jerky.

> ○ Like many people in public life, he spoke with confidence, perhaps he even ~~spoke~~ with arrogance; yet I noted a certain anxiety; it that
> touched and puzzled me. he seemed too eager to demonstrate his He
> control of a situation.

EXERCISE 45.2

Revise the following passage, eliminating any misused or overused semicolons and, if necessary, replacing them with other punctuation.

Hosting your first dinner party can be very stressful; but careful planning and preparation can make it a success. The guest list must contain the right mix of people; everyone should feel comfortable; good talkers and good listeners are both important; while they don't need to agree on everything, you don't want them to have fistfights, either. Then you need to plan the menu; which should steer clear of problem areas; for vegans; no pork chops; for guests with shellfish allergies, no lobster; for teetotallers; no tequila. In addition; make sure your home is clean and neat, and check that you have enough chairs; dishes; glasses; napkins; and silverware. Leave enough time to socialize with your guests; and save a little energy to clean up when it's over!

> ○ bedfordstmartins.com/smhandbook
> Exercise Central > Punctuation > Semicolons

45d Semicolons with quotation marks

A semicolon goes *outside* closing quotation marks (48e).

> ○ Shirley Jackson's most famous story is "The Lottery"; its horrifying ending depicts a result of relying too heavily on tradition.

THINKING CRITICALLY ABOUT SEMICOLONS

Reading with an Eye for Semicolons

Read the following paragraph, which describes a solar eclipse, with attention to the use of semicolons. What different effect would the paragraph have if the author had used periods instead of semicolons? What if she had used commas and coordinating conjunctions? What is the effect of all the semicolons?

You see the wide world swaddled in darkness; you see a vast breadth of hilly land, and an enormous, distant, blackened valley; you see towns' lights, a river's path, and blurred portions of your hat and scarf; you see your husband's face looking like an early black-and-white film; and you see a sprawl of black sky and blue sky together, with unfamiliar stars in it, some barely visible bands of cloud, and over there, a small white ring. The ring is as small as one goose in a flock of migrating geese—if you happen to notice a flock of migrating geese. It is one 360th part of the visible sky. The sun we see is less than half the diameter of a dime held at arms' length.   —ANNIE DILLARD, "Solar Eclipse"

Thinking about Your Own Use of Semicolons

Think of something you might take five or ten minutes to observe—a football game, a brewing storm, an argument between friends—and write a paragraph describing your observations point by point and using semicolons to separate each point, as Annie Dillard does in the preceding paragraph. Then, look at the way you used semicolons. Are there places where a period or a comma and a coordinating conjunction would better serve your meaning? Revise appropriately. What can you conclude about effective ways of using semicolons?

46 End Punctuation

Periods, question marks, and exclamation points often appear in advertising to create special effects.

You have a choice to make.

Where can you turn for advice?

Talk to our experts today!

End punctuation tells us how to read each sentence—as a matter-of-fact statement, a query, or an emphatic request.

Making appropriate choices with end punctuation allows your readers to understand exactly what you mean.

46a Periods

Use a period to close sentences that make statements or give mild commands.

▷ **All books are either dreams or swords.**

—AMY LOWELL

▷ **Don't use a fancy word if a simpler word will do.**
—GEORGE ORWELL, "Politics and the English Language"

A period also closes indirect questions, which report rather than ask questions.

▷ **I asked how old the child was.**

▷ **We all wonder who will win the election.**

Until recently, periods have been used with most abbreviations (see Chapter 51) in American English. However, more and more abbreviations are appearing without periods.

Mr.	MD	BC *or* B.C.
Ms.	PhD	BCE *or* B.C.E.
Mrs.	MBA	AD *or* A.D.
Dr.	RN	AM *or* a.m.
Jr.	Sen.	PM *or* p.m.

QUICK HELP

Editing for end punctuation

- If you find that all or almost all of your sentences end with periods, see if any of them might be phrased more effectively as questions or exclamations. (46a, b, and c)

- Check to be sure you use question marks appropriately. (46b)

- Consider carefully whether any exclamation points are justified. Does the sentence call for extra emphasis? If in doubt, use a period instead. (46c)

Some abbreviations rarely if ever appear with periods. These include the postal abbreviations of state names, such as *FL* and *TN* (though the traditional abbreviations, such as *Fla.* and *Tenn.*, do call for periods), and most groups of initials (*MLA, CIA, AIDS, UNICEF*). If you are not sure whether a particular abbreviation should include periods, check a dictionary or follow the style guidelines (such as those of the Modern Language Association) you are using in a research paper.

46b Question marks

Use a question mark to close sentences that ask direct questions.

▶ **Have you finished the essay, or do you need more time?**

Question marks do not close *indirect* questions, which report rather than ask questions.

▶ **She asked whether I opposed his nomination?.**

Do not use a comma or a period immediately after a question mark that ends a direct quotation (48e).

▶ **"Am I my brother's keeper?/" Cain asked.**

▶ **Cain asked, "Am I my brother's keeper?"/**

Questions in a series may have question marks even when they are not separate sentences.

○ **I often confront a difficult choice: should I go to practice? finish my homework? spend time with my friends?**

A question mark in parentheses can be used to indicate that a writer is unsure of a date, a figure, or a word.

○ **Quintilian died in 96 CE (?).**

46c Exclamation points

Use an exclamation point to show surprise or strong emotion.

○ **In those few moments of geologic time will be the story of all that has happened since we became a nation. And what a story it will be!**
　　　　　　　　　　　　　　　—JAMES RETTIE, "But a Watch in the Night"

○ **Look out!**

Use exclamation points very sparingly because they can distract your readers or suggest that you are exaggerating. In general, try to create emphasis through diction and sentence structure rather than with exclamation points (43a).

○ **This university is so large, so varied, that attempting to tell someone everything about it would take three years!.**

Do not use a comma or a period after an exclamation point that ends a direct quotation.

○ **On my last visit, I looked out the sliding glass doors and ran breathlessly to Connor in the kitchen: "There's a *huge* black pig in the backyard!"/**
　　　　　　　　　　　　　　　—ELLEN ASHDOWN, "Living by the Dead"

EXERCISE 46.1

Revise each of the following sentences, adding appropriate punctuation and deleting any unnecessary punctuation you find. Example:

She asked the travel agent, "What is the air fare to Greece?"~~/~~

1. Social scientists face difficult questions: should they use their knowledge to shape society, merely describe human behavior, or try to do both.

2. The court denied a New Jersey woman's petition to continue raising tigers in her backyard!

3. I screamed at Jamie, "You rat. You tricked me."

4. The reporter wondered whether anything more could have been done to save lives?

5. Zane called every store within fifty miles and asked if they had the Wii game he wanted

6. "Have you seen the new George Clooney film?," Mia asked.

---

bedfordstmartins.com/smhandbook
Exercise Central > Punctuation > End Punctuation

THINKING CRITICALLY ABOUT END PUNCTUATION

Reading with an Eye for End Punctuation

Consider the use of end punctuation in the following paragraph. Then experiment with the end punctuation. What would be the effect of deleting the exclamation point from the quotation by Cicero or of changing it to a question mark? What would be the effect of changing Cicero's question to a statement?

> To be admired and praised, especially by the young, is an autumnal pleasure enjoyed by the lucky ones (who are not always the most deserving). "What is more charming," Cicero observes in his famous essay *De Senectute*, "than an old age surrounded by the enthusiasm of youth! . . . Attentions which seem trivial and conventional are marks of honor—the morning call, being sought after, precedence, having people rise for you, being escorted to and from the forum. . . . What pleasures of the body can be compared to the prerogatives of influence?" But there are also pleasures of the body, or the mind, that are enjoyed by a greater number of older persons.
>
> —MALCOLM COWLEY, *The View from 80*

Thinking about Your Own Use of End Punctuation

Look through something you have written recently, noting its end punctuation. Using the guidelines in this chapter, see if your use of end punctuation follows any patterns. Try revising the end punctuation in a paragraph or two to emphasize (or de-emphasize) some point. What conclusions can you draw about ways of using end punctuation to draw attention to (or away from) a sentence?

Apostrophes

The little apostrophe can make a big difference in meaning. The following sign at a neighborhood swimming pool, for instance, says something different from what the writer probably intended:

Please deposit your garbage (and your guests) in the trash receptacles before leaving the pool area.

The sign indicates that guests should be deposited in trash receptacles. Adding a single apostrophe would offer a more neighborly statement: *Please deposit your garbage (and your guests') in the trash receptacles before leaving the pool area* asks that the guests' garbage, not the guests themselves, be thrown away.

Apostrophes are used for two main purposes: they can indicate the possessive case, and they can show where a letter has been omitted from a contraction. Apostrophe placement can be confusing, but considering the purpose an apostrophe serves in a particular word can help you make appropriate choices.

47a Apostrophes to signal possessive case

The possessive case denotes ownership or possession of one thing by another (32a3).

Singular nouns and indefinite pronouns

Add an apostrophe and *-s* to form the possessive of most singular nouns, including those that end in *-s*, and of indefinite pronouns (31e).

- The *bus's* fumes overpowered her.
- *Star Wars* made George *Lucas's* fortune.
- *Anyone's* guess is as good as mine.

Apostrophes are not used with the possessive forms of personal pronouns: *yours, his, hers, its, ours, theirs.*

- His favorite movies have nothing in common with her/s.

Plural nouns

For plural nouns that do not end in -s, add an apostrophe and -s.

> men's
> ○ Most suits in the ~~mens'~~ department are appropriate
>   ^
>
> business attire.

For plural nouns ending in -s, add only the apostrophe.

> clowns'
> ○ The three ~~clowns's~~ costumes were bright green and orange.
>   ^

Compound words

For compound words, make the last word in the group possessive.

- ○ The *secretary of state's* speech was televised.
- ○ Both her *daughters-in-law's* birthdays fall in July.
- ○ My *in-laws'* disapproval dampened our enthusiasm.

Two or more nouns

To signal individual possession by two or more owners, make each noun possessive.

> ○ The differences between Ridley Scott's and Jerry Bruckheimer's films are enormous.
>
> Scott and Bruckheimer make different films.

To signal joint possession, make only the last noun possessive.

> ○ Wallace and Gromit's creator is Nick Park.
>
> Wallace and Gromit have the same creator.

EXERCISE 47.1

Complete each of the following sentences by inserting 's or an apostrophe alone to form the possessive case of the italicized words. Example:

> A. J.'s older *brother's* name is Griffin.
>   ^   ^

1. Grammar is not *everybody* favorite subject.
2. An *ibis* wingspan is about half as long as a *flamingo*.
3. *Charles and Camilla* first visit to the United States as a married couple included a stop at the White House.
4. The long debate over *states* rights culminated in the Civil War.
5. *Kobe Bryant and Tiger Woods* personal crises have threatened to overshadow their athletic careers.
6. She insists that her personal life is *nobody* business.
7. Parents often question their *children* choice of friends.
8. This dog has a *beagle* ears and a *St. Bernard* face.
9. The sidewalk smokers disregarded the *surgeon generals* warnings.
10. *Anna and Tobias* income dropped dramatically after Anna lost her job.

bedfordstmartins.com/smhandbook
Exercise Central > Punctuation > Apostrophes

QUICK HELP

Editing for apostrophes

- Check each noun that ends in *-s* and shows ownership or possession. Verify that the apostrophe is in the right place, either before or after the *-s*. (47a)

- Check the possessive form of each indefinite pronoun, such as *someone's*. Be sure an apostrophe comes before the *-s*. (47a)

- Check each possessive personal pronoun ending in *-s* (*yours, hers, his, its, ours, theirs*) and make sure that it does not include an apostrophe. (47a)

- Check each *its*. Does it show possession? If not, add an apostrophe before the *-s*. (47b)

- Check each *it's*. Does it mean "it is" or "it has"? If not, remove the apostrophe. (47b)

47b Apostrophes to signal contractions and other omissions

Contractions are two-word combinations formed by leaving out certain letters, which are indicated by an apostrophe.

it is, it has/it's	I would, I had/I'd	will not/won't
was not/wasn't	he would, he had/he'd	let us/let's
I am/I'm	would not/wouldn't	who is, who has/who's
he is, he has/he's	do not/don't	cannot/can't
you will/you'll	does not/doesn't	

Contractions are common in conversation and informal writing. Some academic and professional work, however, calls for greater formality.

Distinguishing *its* and *it's*

Its is the possessive form of *it*. *It's* is a contraction for *it is* or *it has*.

○ This disease is unusual; it's symptoms vary from person to person.

○ It's a difficult disease to diagnose.

Signaling omissions

An apostrophe signals omissions in some common phrases:

ten of the clock	rock and roll	class of 2003
ten o'clock	rock 'n' roll	class of '03

In addition, writers can use an apostrophe to signal omitted letters in approximating the sound of speech or a specific dialect.

○ You should'a seen 'em playin' together.

47c Apostrophes to form certain plurals

Many style guides advise against apostrophes for any plurals.

○ The gymnasts need marks of *8*s and *9*s to qualify for the finals.

Others use an apostrophe and *-s* to form the plural of numbers, letters, symbols, and words referred to as terms.

○ **The five *Shakespeare*'s in the essay were spelled five different ways.**

Check your instructor's preference. In any case, italicize numbers, letters, symbols, and terms but not the plural ending.

EXERCISE 47.2

The following sentences, from which all apostrophes have been deleted, appear in Langston Hughes's "Salvation." Insert apostrophes where appropriate. Example:

"Sister Reed, what is this child᾽s name?"

1. There was a big revival at my Auntie Reeds church.
2. I heard the songs and the minister saying: "Why dont you come?"
3. Finally Westley said to me in a whisper: . . . "Im tired o sitting here. Lets get up and be saved."
4. So I decided that maybe to save further trouble, Id better lie. . . .
5. That night . . . I cried, in bed alone, and couldnt stop.

bedfordstmartins.com/smhandbook
Exercise Central > Punctuation > Apostrophes

THINKING CRITICALLY ABOUT APOSTROPHES

Write a brief paragraph, beginning "I've always been amused by my neighbor's (or roommate's) _____." Then note every use of an apostrophe. Use the guidelines in this chapter to check that you have used apostrophes correctly.

Quotation Marks

48

Quotation marks, which always come in pairs, identify where the exact words of others begin and end. You use quotation marks when you quote sources in a research project, dialogue you've overheard, lines of poetry, or a passage from a novel. You should also set off certain titles—and language that is used ironically—with quotation marks.

48a Quotation marks to signal direct quotations

Use double quotation marks to signal a direct quotation.

- ▶ **President Obama asked Congress to "try common sense."**
- ▶ **She smiled and said, "Son, this is one incident I will never forget."**

Single quotation marks enclose a quotation within a quotation. Open and close the quoted passage with double quotation marks, and change any quotation marks that appear *within* the quotation to single quotation marks.

- ▶ **James Baldwin says, "The title 'The Uses of the Blues' does not refer to music; I don't know anything about music."**

As a way of bringing other people's words into our own, quotation can be a powerful writing tool.

Mrs. Macken urges parents to get books for their children, to read to them when they are "li'l," and when they start school to make certain they attend regularly. She holds herself up as an example of a "millhand's daughter who wanted to be a schoolteacher and did it through sheer hard work."

—SHIRLEY BRICE HEATH, *Ways with Words*

The writer could have paraphrased, but by quoting, she lets her subject speak for herself—and lets readers hear that person's voice.

1 Longer passages

If the prose passage you wish to quote exceeds four typed lines, set it off from the rest of the text by starting it on a new line and indenting it one inch from the left margin. This format, known as block quotation, does not require quotation marks.

> In *Winged Words: American Indian Writers Speak*, Leslie Marmon Silko describes her early education:
>
> > I learned to love reading, and love books, and the printed page, and therefore was motivated to learn to write. The best thing . . . you can have in life is to have someone tell you a story . . . but in lieu of that . . . I learned at an early age to find comfort in a book, that a book would talk to me when no one else would. (145)

This block quotation, including the ellipses and the page number in parentheses at the end, follows the style of the Modern Language Association (MLA). Other organizations, such as the American Psychological Association (APA) and the University of Chicago Press, have different guidelines for ellipses and block quotations. (See Chapters 16–19.)

2 Poetry

If the quotation is fewer than four lines, include it within your text, enclosed in double quotation marks. Separate the lines of the poem with slashes, each preceded and followed by a space, to tell the reader where one line of the poem ends and the next begins.

> In one of his best-known poems, Robert Frost remarks, "Two roads diverged in a wood, and I— / I took the one less traveled by, / And that has made all the difference."

Editing for quotation marks

- Use quotation marks around direct quotations and titles of short works. (48a and b)
- Do not use quotation marks around set-off quotations of more than four lines of prose or three lines of poetry or around titles of long works. (48a and b)
- Use quotation marks to signal irony and invented words, but do so sparingly. (48c)
- Never use quotation marks around indirect quotations. (48d)
- Do not use quotation marks to add emphasis to words. (48d)
- Check other punctuation used with closing quotation marks. (48e)
  Periods and commas should be *inside* the quotation marks.
  Colons, semicolons, and footnote numbers should be *outside*.
  Question marks, exclamation points, and dashes should be *inside* if they are part of the quoted material, *outside* if they are not.

To quote four or more lines of poetry, indent the block one inch from the left margin, and do not use quotation marks.

> The duke in Robert Browning's "My Last Duchess" is clearly a jealous, vain person, whose own words illustrate his arrogance:
>
> > She thanked men — good! but thanked
> > Somehow — I know not how — as if she ranked
> > My gift of a nine-hundred-years-old name
> > With anybody's gift. (lines 31 – 34)

When you quote poetry, take care to follow the indention, spacing, capitalization, punctuation, and other features of the original poem.

FOR MULTILINGUAL WRITERS

Quotation marks

Remember that the way you mark quotations in English (" ") may not be the same as in other languages. In French, for example, quotations are marked with *guillemets* (« »), while in German, quotations take split-level marks („ ").

3 Dialogue

When you write dialogue or quote a conversation, enclose the words of each speaker in quotation marks, and mark each shift in speaker by beginning a new paragraph.

○ "I want no proof of their affection," said Elinor, "but of their engagement I do."
  "I am perfectly satisfied of both."
  "Yet not a syllable has been said to you on the subject, by either of them." —JANE AUSTEN, *Sense and Sensibility*

Because of the paragraph breaks in the preceding example, we know when Elinor is speaking and when her mother is speaking without the author's having to repeat *said Elinor, her mother said,* and so on.

48b Quotation marks to signal titles and definitions

Quotation marks are used to enclose the titles of short poems, short stories, articles, essays, songs, sections of books, and episodes of television and radio programs.

○ "Dover Beach" moves from calm to sadness. [poem]

○ Walker's "Everyday Use" is not just about quilts. [short story]

○ The White Stripes released ten different versions of "The Denial Twist." [song]

○ The *Atlantic* published an article titled "Illiberal Education." [article]

○ In the chapter called "Complexion," Richard Rodriguez describes his sensitivity about his skin color. [section of book]

○ The *Nature* episode "Echo of the Elephants" denounces ivory hunters. [television series episode]

Use italics rather than quotation marks for the titles of television series, books, magazines, and other longer works (52a).

Definitions are sometimes set off with quotation marks.

○ The French phrase *idée fixe* means literally "fixed idea."

48c   Quotation marks to signal irony and invented words

To show readers that you are using a word or phrase ironically, or that you invented it, enclose it in quotation marks.

▶ **The "banquet" consisted of dried-out chicken and canned vegetables.**

The quotation marks suggest that the meal was anything but a banquet.

▶ **Your whole first paragraph or first page may have to be guillotined in any case after your piece is finished: it is a kind of "forebirth."**
    —JACQUES BARZUN, "A Writer's Discipline"

The writer made up the term *forebirth.*

EXERCISE 48.1

Revise each of the following sentences, using quotation marks appropriately to signal titles, definitions, irony, or invented terms.

1. Stephen Colbert introduced Americans to the concept he calls truthiness on the first episode of *The Colbert Report*.

2. Margaret Talbot's article A Risky Proposal examines the constitutionality of state laws that ban gay marriage.

3. "The little that is known about gorillas certainly makes you want to know more," writes Alan Moorehead in his essay A Most Forgiving Ape.

4. My father's way of helping usually meant doing the whole project for me.

5. Should America the Beautiful replace The Star-Spangled Banner as the national anthem?

6. In the chapter called The Last to See Them Alive, Truman Capote shows the utterly ordinary life of the Kansas family.

7. The *30 Rock* episode Reunion won an Emmy for outstanding comedy writing.

8. Several popular films, including *Mamma Mia!* and *Muriel's Wedding*, have used Abba hits such as Dancing Queen and Take a Chance on Me.

9. My dictionary defines *isolation* as the quality or state of being alone.

10. In his poem The Shield of Achilles, W. H. Auden depicts the horror of modern warfare.

`48d` Misused quotation marks

Do not use quotation marks for *indirect* quotations—those that do not use someone's exact words.

○ The teacher warned us that /"we could be expelled./"

Do not use quotation marks just to emphasize particular words or phrases.

○ Julia said that her views might not be /"politically correct/" but that she wasn't going to change them for anything.

○ Much time was spent speculating about their /"relationship./"

Do not use quotation marks around slang or colloquial language; they create the impression that you are apologizing for using those words. Instead, try to express the idea in formal language. If you have a good reason to use a slang or colloquial term, use it without quotation marks (27a1).

○ After our twenty-mile hike, we were ready to /"turn in./"

`48e` Quotation marks with other punctuation

Periods and commas go *inside* closing quotation marks.

○ "Don't compromise yourself," said Janis Joplin. "You are all you've got."

EXCEPTION

When you use parenthetical documentation with a short quotation, place the period after the parentheses with source information (16b, 17b).

○ In places, de Beauvoir "sees Marxists as believing in subjectivity" (Whitmarsh 63).

Colons, semicolons, and footnote numbers go *outside* closing quotation marks.

○ I felt only one emotion after reading "Eveline": sorrow.

○ Everything is dark, and "a visionary light settles in her eyes"; this light is her salvation.

○ *Tragedy* is defined by Aristotle as "an imitation of an action that is serious and of a certain magnitude."[1]

Question marks, exclamation points, and dashes go *inside* closing quotation marks if they are part of the quotation, *outside* if they are not.

PART OF THE QUOTATION

○ The cashier asked, "Would you like to super-size that?"

○ "Jump!" one of the firefighters shouted.

NOT PART OF THE QUOTATION

○ What is the theme of "A Good Man Is Hard to Find"?

○ "Break a leg"—that phrase is supposed to bring good luck to a performer.

For help using quotation marks in various documentation styles, see Chapters 16–19.

THINKING CRITICALLY ABOUT QUOTATION MARKS

Reading with an Eye for Quotation Marks

Read the following passage about the painter Georgia O'Keeffe, and pay particular attention to the use of quotation marks. What effect is created by the author's use of quotation marks with *hardness*, *crustiness*, and *crusty*? How do the quotations by O'Keeffe help support the author's description of her?

"Hardness" has not been in our century a quality much admired in women, nor in the past twenty years has it even been in official favor for men. When hardness surfaces in the very old we tend to transform it into "crustiness" or eccentricity, some tonic pepperiness to be indulged at a distance. On the evidence of her work and what she has said about it, Georgia O'Keeffe is neither "crusty" nor eccentric. She is simply hard, a straight shooter, a woman clean of received wisdom and open to what she sees. This is a woman who could early on dismiss most of her contemporaries as "dreamy," and would later single out one she liked as "a very poor painter." (And then add, apparently by way of softening the judgment: "I guess he wasn't a painter at all. He had no courage and I believe that to create one's own world in any of the arts takes courage.") This is a woman who in 1939 could advise her admirers that they were missing her point, that their appreciation of her famous flowers was merely sentimental. "When I paint a red hill," she observed coolly in the catalogue for an exhibition that year, "you say it is too bad that I don't always paint flowers. A flower touches almost everyone's heart. A red hill doesn't touch everyone's heart."

—JOAN DIDION, "Georgia O'Keeffe"

Thinking about Your Own Use of Quotation Marks

Choose a topic that is of interest on your campus, and interview one of your friends about it. On the basis of your notes from the interview, write two or three paragraphs about your friend's views, using several direct quotations that support the points you are making. Then see how closely you followed the conventions for quotation marks explained in this chapter. Note any usages that caused you problems.

Other Punctuation Marks

49

You can use parentheses, brackets, dashes, colons, slashes, and ellipses to signal relationships among sentence parts, to create particular rhythms, and to help readers follow your thoughts.

49a Parentheses

Parentheses enclose material that is of minor or secondary importance in a sentence — material that supplements, clarifies, comments on, or illustrates what precedes or follows it. Parentheses also enclose numbers or letters that precede items in a list, and sometimes they enclose source citations or publication information.

Enclosing less important material

▷ Inventors and men of genius have almost always been regarded as fools at the beginning (and very often at the end) of their careers.

—FYODOR DOSTOYEVSKY

▷ During my research, I found problems with the flat-rate income tax (a single-rate tax with no deductions).

A period may be placed either inside or outside a closing parenthesis, depending on whether the parenthetical text is part of a larger sentence. A comma,

Parentheses, brackets, dashes, colons, slashes, and ellipses are all around us. Pick up the television listings, for instance, and you will find these punctuation marks in abundance, helping viewers preview programs in a clear and efficient way.

❼⑧ College Football
3:30 501019 / 592361—
Northwestern Wildcats at Ohio State Buckeyes. The Buckeyes are looking for their 20th straight win over Northwestern. (Live) [Time approximate.]

if needed, is always placed *outside* a closing parenthesis (and never before an opening one).

◯ **Gene Tunney's single defeat in an eleven-year career was to a flamboyant and dangerous fighter named Harry Greb ("The Human Windmill"), who seems to have been, judging from boxing literature, the dirtiest fighter in history.**

—JOYCE CAROL OATES, "On Boxing"

If the material in parentheses is a question or an exclamation, use a question mark or exclamation point inside the closing parenthesis.

◯ **Our laughing (so deep was the pleasure!) became screaming.**

—RICHARD RODRIGUEZ, "Aria: A Memoir of a Bilingual Childhood"

In general, parentheses create more of an interruption than commas (Chapter 44) but less of an interruption than dashes (49c).

Enclosing numbers or letters in a list

◯ **Five distinct styles can be distinguished: (1) Old New England, (2) Deep South, (3) Middle American, (4) Wild West, and (5) Far West or Californian.**   —ALISON LURIE, *The Language of Clothes*

Enclosing textual citations

The first of the following in-text citations shows the style of the American Psychological Association (see Chapter 17); the second shows the style of the Modern Language Association (see Chapter 16).

A later study resulted in somewhat different conclusions (Murphy & Orkow, 1985).

Zamora notes that Kahlo referred to her first self-portrait, given to a close friend, as "your Botticelli" (110).

49b Brackets

Use brackets to enclose parenthetical elements in material that is itself within parentheses and to enclose explanatory words or comments that you are inserting into a quotation.

> **QUICK HELP**

Editing for effective use of punctuation

- Be sure that any material enclosed in parentheses or set off with dashes requires special treatment—and that the punctuation doesn't make the sentence difficult to follow. Use parentheses to de-emphasize the material they enclose and dashes to add emphasis. (49a and c)

- Use brackets to enclose parenthetical elements in material that is already within parentheses and to enclose words or comments inserted into a quotation. (49b)

- Be sure that you have *not* used a colon between a verb and its object or complement, between a preposition and its object, or after such expressions as *such as*, *especially*, and *including*. (49d)

- Use slashes to mark line divisions in poetry you are quoting, unless you are setting the lines off as a block quotation. (48a2, 49e)

- Use ellipses (three dots) to indicate omissions from quoted passages. (49f)

Setting off material within parentheses

○ **Eventually the investigation examined the major agencies (including the National Security Agency [NSA]) that were conducting covert operations.**

Inserting material within quotations

○ **Massing notes that "on average, it [Fox News] attracts more than eight million people daily—more than double the number who watch CNN."**

The bracketed words clarify *it* in the original quotation.

In the quotation in the following sentence, the artist Gauguin's name is misspelled. The bracketed Latin word *sic*, which means "so," tells readers that the person being quoted—not the writer using the quotation—made the mistake.

○ **One admirer wrote, "She was the most striking woman I'd ever seen—a sort of wonderful combination of Mia Farrow and one of Gaugin's [sic] Polynesian nymphs."**

EXERCISE 49.1

Revise the following sentences, using parentheses and brackets correctly. Example:

She was in fourth grade (or was it third?) when she became blind.

1. The committee was presented with three options to pay for the new park: 1 increase vehicle registration fees, 2 install parking meters downtown, or 3 borrow money from the reserve fund.

2. The FISA statute authorizes government wiretapping only under certain circumstances for instance, the government has to obtain a warrant.

3. The health care expert informed readers that "as we progress through middle age, we experience intimations of our own morality *sic*."

4. Some hospitals train nurses in a pseudoscientific technique called therapeutic touch TT that has been discredited by many rigorous studies.

5. Because I was carrying an umbrella, which, as it turned out, wasn't even necessary, I was required to enter the stadium through the high-security gate.

bedfordstmartins.com/smhandbook
Exercise Central > Punctuation > Other Punctuation

49c Dashes

In contrast to parentheses, dashes give more rather than less emphasis to the material they enclose. A typed dash is made with two hyphens (- -) with *no* spaces before, between, or after. Many word-processing programs will automatically convert two typed hyphens into a solid dash (—).

Inserting a comment

▷ Leeches—yuck—turn out to have valuable medical uses.

Emphasizing explanatory material

▷ Indeed, several of modern India's greatest scholars—such as the Mughal historian Muzaffar Alam of the University of Chicago—are madrasa graduates.   —WILLIAM DALRYMPLE

A single dash toward the *end* of a sentence may serve to emphasize the material at the end, to mark a shift in tone or a hesitation in speech, or to summarize or explain what has come before.

Emphasizing material at the end of a sentence

▶ **In the twentieth century it has become almost impossible to moralize about epidemics—except those which are transmitted sexually.**

—SUSAN SONTAG, "AIDS and Its Metaphors"

Marking a sudden change in tone

▶ **New York is a catastrophe—but a magnificent catastrophe.**

—LE CORBUSIER

Indicating a hesitation in speech

▶ **As the officer approached his car, the driver stammered, "What—what have I done?"**

Introducing a summary or explanation

▶ **In walking, the average adult person employs a motor mechanism that weighs about eighty pounds—sixty pounds of muscle and twenty pounds of bone.**   —EDWIN WAY TEALE

EXERCISE 49.2

Punctuate the following sentences with dashes where appropriate. Example:

He is quick, violent, and mean — they don't call him Dirty Harry for nothing — but

appealing nonetheless.

1. Most people would say that Labradors are easy dogs to train but they never met our Millie.
2. Even if marijuana is dangerous an assertion disputed by many studies it is certainly no more harmful to human health than alcohol and cigarettes, which remain legal.
3. If too much exposure to negative news stories makes you feel depressed or anxious and why wouldn't it? try going on a media fast.
4. Union Carbide's plant in Bhopal, India, sprang a leak that killed more than 2,000 people and injured an additional 200,000.

5. Refrigerators especially side-by-side models use up more energy than most people realize.

bedfordstmartins.com/smhandbook
Exercise Central > Punctuation > Other Punctuation

49d Colons

Use a colon to introduce something (such as an explanation) and to separate some elements (such as titles and subtitles) from one another.

Introducing an explanation, an example, or an appositive

○ The men may also wear the getup known as Sun Belt Cool: a pale beige suit, open-collared shirt (often in a darker shade than the suit), cream-colored loafers and aviator sunglasses.

—ALISON LURIE, *The Language of Clothes*

Introducing a series, a list, or a quotation

○ At the baby's one-month birthday party, Ah Po gave him the Four Valuable Things: ink, inkslab, paper, and brush.

—MAXINE HONG KINGSTON, *China Men*

○ The teachers wondered: "Do boys and girls really learn differently? Do behavioral differences reflect socialization or biology?"

The preceding example could have used a comma instead of a colon before the quotation (44h). You should use a colon rather than a comma to introduce a quotation when the lead-in is a complete sentence on its own.

○ The State of the Union address contained one surprising statement: "America is addicted to oil."

Separating elements

SALUTATIONS IN FORMAL LETTERS
○ Dear Dr. Mahiri:

TITLES AND SUBTITLES
○ *Better: A Surgeon's Notes on Performance*

HOURS, MINUTES, AND SECONDS
- 4:59 PM
- 2:15:06

RATIOS
- a ratio of 5:1

BIBLICAL CHAPTERS AND VERSES
- I Corinthians 3:3–5

CITIES AND PUBLISHERS IN
BIBLIOGRAPHIC ENTRIES
- Boston: Bedford, 2010

Eliminating misused colons

Do not put a colon between a verb and its object or complement, unless the object is a quotation.

- Some natural fibers are: cotton, wool, silk, and linen.

Do not put a colon between a preposition and its object or after such expressions as *such as, especially,* or *including.*

- In poetry, additional power may come from devices such as: simile, metaphor, and alliteration.

EXERCISE 49.3

In the following items, insert a colon in any sentence that needs one and delete any unnecessary colons. Some sentences may be correct as written. Example:

Images: My Life in Film includes revealing material written by Ingmar Bergman.

1. After discussing the case study, the class reached one main conclusion in any business, the most important asset is the customer.
2. Another example is taken from Psalm 139 16.
3. Roberto tried to make healthier choices, such as: eating organic food, walking to work, and getting plenty of rest.
4. A number of quotable movie lines come from *Casablanca*, including "Round up the usual suspects."
5. Sofi rushed to catch the 5 45 express but had to wait for the 6 19.

49e Slashes

Use slashes to mark line divisions in poetry quoted within running text (48a2), to separate alternative terms, and to separate the parts of fractions and Internet addresses. When a slash separates lines of poetry, it should be preceded and followed by a space.

Marking line divisions in poetry

○ In "Digging," Seamus Heaney observes, "Between my finger and my thumb / The squat pen rests; snug as a gun."

Separating alternatives

○ Then there was Daryl, the cabdriver/bartender.

—JOHN L'HEUREUX, *The Handmaid of Desire*

Separating parts of fractions and Internet addresses

○ $138^1/_2$

○ bedfordstmartins.com/smhandbook

49f Ellipses

Ellipses are three equally spaced dots. Ellipses usually indicate that something has been omitted from a quoted passage, but they can also signal a pause or hesitation in speech in the same way that a dash can.

Indicating omissions

Just as you should carefully use quotation marks around any material that you quote directly from a source, so you should carefully use ellipses to indicate that you have left out part of a quotation that otherwise appears to be a complete sentence.

The ellipses in the following example indicate two omissions—one in the middle of the sentence and one at the end. When you omit the last part of a quoted sentence, add a period before the ellipses, for a total of four dots. Be sure a complete sentence comes before and after the four points. If you are adding your own ellipses to a quotation that already has other ellipses, enclose yours in brackets.

ORIGINAL TEXT

▷ The quasi-official division of the population into three economic classes called high-, middle-, and low-income groups rather misses the point, because as a class indicator the amount of money is not as important as the source.   —PAUL FUSSELL, "Notes on Class"

WITH ELLIPSES

▷ As Paul Fussell argues, "The quasi-official division of the population into three economic classes . . . rather misses the point. . . ."

If your shortened quotation ends with a source (such as a page number, a name, or a title), follow these steps:

1. Use three ellipsis points but no period after the quotation.

2. Add the closing quotation mark, closed up to the third ellipsis point.

3. Add the source documentation in parentheses.

4. Use a period to indicate the end of the sentence.

▷ Packer argues, "The Administration is right to reconsider its strategy . . ." (34).

Indicating a pause or a hesitation

▷ Then the voice, husky and familiar, came to wash over us—"The winnah, and still heavyweight champeen of the world . . . Joe Louis."
   —MAYA ANGELOU, *I Know Why the Caged Bird Sings*

EXERCISE 49.4

The following sentences use the punctuation marks presented in this chapter very effectively. Read the sentences carefully; then choose one, and use it as a model for writing a sentence of your own, making sure to use the punctuation marks in the same way in your sentence.

1. The dad was—how can you put this gracefully?—a real blimp, a wide load, and the white polyester stretch-pants only emphasized the cargo.
   —GARRISON KEILLOR, "Happy to Be Here"

2. Not only are the distinctions we draw between male nature and female nature largely arbitrary and often pure superstition: they are completely beside the point.   —BRIGID BROPHY, "Women"

3. If no one, including you, liked the soup the first time round (and that's why you've got so much left over), there is no point in freezing it for some hopeful future date when, miraculously, it will taste delicious. But bagging leftovers—say, stews—in single portions can be useful for those evenings when you're eating alone.

—NIGELLA LAWSON, *How to Eat*

THINKING CRITICALLY ABOUT PUNCTUATION

Reading with an Eye for Punctuation

In the following passage, Tom Wolfe uses dashes, parentheses, ellipses, and a colon to create rhythm and build momentum in a very long (178-word) sentence. The editorial comment inserted in brackets calls attention to the fact that the "right stuff" was, in the world Wolfe describes here, always male. Look carefully at how Wolfe and the editors use these punctuation marks, and then try writing a description of something that effectively uses as many of them as possible. Your description should be about the same length as Wolfe's passage, but it need not be all one sentence.

Likewise, "hassling"—mock dogfighting—was strictly forbidden, and so naturally young fighter jocks could hardly wait to go up in, say, a pair of F-100s and start the duel by making a pass at each other at 800 miles an hour, the winner being the pilot who could slip in behind the other one and get locked in on his [never *her* or *his or her!*] tail ("wax his tail"), and it was not uncommon for some eager jock to try too tight an outside turn and have his engine flame out, whereupon, unable to restart it, he has to eject . . . and he shakes his fist at the victor as he floats down by parachute and his million-dollar aircraft goes *kaboom!* on the palmetto grass or the desert floor, and he starts thinking about how he can get together with the other guy back at the base in time for the two of them to get their stories straight before the investigation: "I don't know what happened, sir. I was pulling up after a target run, and it just flamed out on me."

—TOM WOLFE, *The Right Stuff*

Thinking about Your Own Use of Punctuation

Look through a draft you have recently written or are working on, and check your use of parentheses, brackets, dashes, colons, slashes, and ellipses. Do you follow the conventions presented in this chapter? If not, revise accordingly. Check the material in parentheses to see if it could use more emphasis and thus be set off instead with dashes. Then check any material in dashes to see if it could do with less emphasis and thus be punctuated with commas or parentheses.

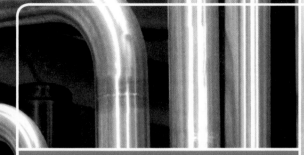

Part 10

MECHANICS

50 Capital Letters

Capital letters are a key signal in everyday life. Look around any store to see their importance: you can shop for Coca-Cola or *any* cola, for Levi's or *any* blue jeans, for Kleenex or *any* tissues. In each of these instances, the capital letter indicates the name of a particular brand.

One of the most common reasons for capitalizing a word is to indicate that it is part of a name or title—whether of a brand, a book, a newspaper, an article, a person, or something else.

Many writers struggle to determine which words should be capitalized and which should not—so many, in fact, that capitalization errors have become one of the most common problems facing student writers. As with other "mechanical" aspects of writing, following established conventions for capitalizing words can help you meet your readers' expectations.

50a The first word of a sentence or line of poetry

Capitalize the first word of a sentence.

○ **Posing relatives for photographs is a challenge.**

If you are quoting a full sentence, capitalize its first word.

○ **Kennedy said, "Let us never negotiate out of fear."**

Capitalizing a sentence following a colon is optional.

○ **Gould cites the work of Darwin: The [*or* the] theory of natural selection incorporates the principle of evolutionary ties between all animals.**

Capitalize a sentence within parentheses unless the parenthetical sentence is inserted into another sentence.

○ **Gould cites the work of Darwin. (Other researchers cite more recent evolutionary theorists.)**

○ **Gould cites the work of Darwin (see page 150).**

Editing for capitalization

- Capitalize the first word of each sentence. If you quote a poem, follow its original capitalization. (50a)

- Check to make sure you have appropriately capitalized proper nouns and proper adjectives. (50b)

- Review titles of people or of works to be sure you have capitalized them correctly. (50b and c)

- Double-check the capitalization of geographic directions (*north* or *North*?), family relationships (*dad* or *Dad*?), and seasons of the year (*winter*, not *Winter*). (50d)

When citing poetry, follow the capitalization of the original poem. Though most poets capitalize the first word of each line in a poem, some poets do not.

○ **Morning sun heats up the young beech tree
leaves and almost lights them into fireflies**

—JUNE JORDAN, "Aftermath"

50b Proper nouns and proper adjectives

Capitalize proper nouns (those naming specific persons, places, and things) and most proper adjectives (those formed from proper nouns). All other nouns are common nouns and are not capitalized unless they begin a sentence or are used as part of a proper noun: *the street where you live,* but *Elm Street.* Here, proper nouns and adjectives appear on the left and related common nouns and adjectives on the right.

PEOPLE

Ang Lee	the film's director
Nixonian	political

NATIONS, NATIONALITIES, ETHNIC GROUPS, AND LANGUAGES

Brazil, Brazilian	their native country, his citizenship
Italian American	an ethnic group
Cantonese	one of the nation's languages

PLACES

Pacific Ocean	an ocean
Hawaiian Islands	tropical islands

STRUCTURES AND MONUMENTS

the Lincoln Memorial	a monument
the Eiffel Tower	a landmark

SHIPS, TRAINS, AIRCRAFT, AND SPACECRAFT

the *Queen Mary*	a cruise ship
the *City of New Orleans*	the 6:00 train

ORGANIZATIONS, BUSINESSES, AND GOVERNMENT INSTITUTIONS

United Auto Workers	a trade union
Library of Congress	a federal agency
Desmond-Fish Library	the local library

ACADEMIC INSTITUTIONS AND COURSES

University of Maryland	a state university
Political Science 102	my political science course

HISTORICAL EVENTS AND ERAS

the Whiskey Rebellion	a revolt
the Renaissance	the fifteenth century

RELIGIONS AND RELIGIOUS TERMS

God	a deity
the Qur'an	a holy book
Catholicism, Catholic	a religion, their religious affiliation

TRADE NAMES

Nike	running shoes
Cheerios	cereal

Some companies use capitals in the middle of their own or their product's names. Follow the style you see in company advertising or on the product itself—*eBay*, *FedEx*, *iPod*.

Titles of individuals

Capitalize titles used before a proper name. When used alone or following a proper name, most titles are not capitalized. One common exception is the word *president*, which many writers capitalize whenever it refers to the President of the United States.

Chief Justice Roberts	John Roberts, the chief justice
Professor Lisa Ede	my English professor
Dr. Edward A. Davies	Edward A. Davies, our doctor

50c Titles of works

Capitalize most words in titles (of books, articles, plays, poems, songs, films, paintings, and so on). Do not capitalize an article (*a, an, the*), a preposition, a conjunction, or the *to* in an infinitive unless it is the first or last word in a title or subtitle.

Walt Whitman: A Life	"Where I'm Calling From"
"As Time Goes By"	Declaration of Independence
"Shooting an Elephant"	*Charlie and the Chocolate Factory*
The Producers	*Rebel without a Cause*

FOR MULTILINGUAL WRITERS

English capitalization

Capitalization systems vary considerably among languages, and some languages (Arabic, Chinese, Hindi, and Hebrew, for example) do not use capital letters at all. English may be the only language to capitalize the first-person singular pronoun (*I*), but Dutch and German capitalize some forms of the second-person pronoun (*you*). German capitalizes all nouns; English used to capitalize more nouns than it does now (see, for instance, the Declaration of Independence).

EXERCISE 50.1

Capitalize words as needed in the following sentences. Example:

> T. S. Eliot,   The Waste Land,   Faber   Faber.
> ~~t.s. eliot,~~ who wrote ~~the waste land,~~ was an editor at ~~faber~~ and ~~faber.~~
>   ^   ^   ^   ^

1. the town in the south where i was raised had a statue of a civil war soldier in the center of main street.

2. sarah palin, the former governor, frequently complained that the press had treated her harshly before she accepted a position as an analyst for fox news.

3. the corporation for public broadcasting relies on donations as well as on grants from the national endowment for the arts.

4. during the economic recession, companies such as starbucks had to close some of their stores; others, such as circuit city, went completely out of business.

5. most americans remember where they were when they heard about the 9/11 disaster.

6. accepting an award for his score for the john wayne film *the high and the mighty*, dmitri tiomkin thanked beethoven, brahms, wagner, and strauss.

50d Unnecessary capitalization

Do not capitalize a compass direction unless the word designates a specific geographic region.

○ **Voters in the South and much of the West tend to favor socially conservative candidates.**

○ **John Muir headed ~~West,~~ motivated by the need to explore.**
    west,

Do not capitalize a word indicating a family relationship unless the word is used as part of the name or as a substitute for the name.

○ **I could always tell when Mother was annoyed with Aunt Rose.**

○ **When she was a child, my ~~Mother~~ shared a room with my ~~Aunt.~~**
    mother   *aunt.*

Do not capitalize seasons of the year and parts of the academic or financial year.

spring	fall semester
winter	winter term
autumn	third-quarter earnings

Capitalizing whole words or phrases for emphasis may come across to readers as SHOUTING. Use italics, underlining, or asterisks to add emphasis.

○ **Sorry for the abrupt response, but I am *very* busy.**

EXERCISE 50.2

Correct any unnecessary or missing capitalization in the following sentences. Some sentences may be correct as written. Example:

southern governors   *Washington,*
A group of ~~Southern Governors~~ meets annually in ~~washington,~~ DC.

1. The Columbine School Shootings in 1999 prompted a debate about Gun Control Laws in the United States.
2. Every Professor in the department of english has a degree in literature.
3. The Cast included several children, but only two of them had Speaking Roles.
4. Airport checkpoints are the responsibility of the Transportation Security Administration.
5. The price of oil has fluctuated this Winter.

→ **bedfordstmartins.com/smhandbook**
Exercise Central > **Mechanics** > **Capital Letters**

THINKING CRITICALLY ABOUT CAPITALIZATION

The following poem uses unconventional capitalization. Read it over a few times, at least once aloud. What effect does the capitalization have? Why do you think the poet chose to use capitals as she did?

A little Madness in the Spring
Is wholesome even for the King,
But God be with the Clown—
Who ponders this tremendous scene—
This whole Experiment of Green—
As if it were his own!

—EMILY DICKINSON

51 Abbreviations and Numbers

Anytime you look up an address, you see an abundance of abbreviations and numbers, as in the following movie theater listing from a Google map of Berkeley, California:

Oaks Theater, 1875 Solano Ave, Berkeley, CA

Abbreviations and numbers allow writers to present detailed information in a small amount of space.

In academic writing, abbreviations and numbers follow conventions that vary from field to field. (See Chapter 27 for a discussion of using abbreviations and numbers in highly informal writing, such as texting, where conventions differ from those in academic writing.)

51a Abbreviations for titles and academic degrees

When used before or after a name, some personal and professional titles and academic degrees are abbreviated, even in academic writing.

Ms. Susanna Moller	Henry Louis Gates Jr.
Mr. Aaron Oforlea	Gina Tartaglia, MD
Dr. Edward Davies	Jamie Barlow Kayes, PhD

Other titles—including religious, military, academic, and government titles—should be spelled out in academic writing. In other writing, they may be abbreviated when they appear before a full name but should be spelled out when used with only a last name.

Rev. Franklin Graham	Reverend Graham
Prof. Beverly Moss	Professor Moss
Gen. Colin Powell	General Powell

Academic degrees may be abbreviated when used alone, but other titles used alone are never abbreviated.

▶ She received her *PhD* this year.

▶ He was a demanding ~~prof.,~~ *professor,* and we worked hard.

> **QUICK HELP**
>
> ## Editing abbreviations and numbers
>
> - Use abbreviations and numbers according to the conventions of a specific field (see p. 769): for example, *57%* might be acceptable in a math paper, but *57 percent* may be more appropriate in a sociology essay. (51g)
> - If you use an abbreviation readers might not understand, spell out the term the first time you use it, and give the abbreviation in parentheses. (51c)
> - If you use an abbreviation more than once, use it consistently.

Use either a title or an academic degree, but not both, with a person's name. Instead of *Dr. James Dillon, PhD*, write *Dr. James Dillon* or *James Dillon, PhD*. (Note that academic degrees such as *PhD* and *RN* often appear without periods; see 46a.)

51b Abbreviations with years and hours

You can use the following abbreviations with numerals. Notice that AD precedes the numeral; all other abbreviations follow the numeral. Today, BCE and CE are generally preferred over BC and AD, and periods in all four of these abbreviations are optional.

399 BCE ("before the common era") or 399 BC ("before Christ")

49 CE ("common era") or AD 49 (*anno Domini*, Latin for "year of our Lord")

11:15 AM (*or* a.m.)

9:00 PM (*or* p.m.)

For abbreviations, you may use full-size capital letters or small caps, a typographical option in word-processing programs.

51c Acronyms and initial abbreviations

Acronyms are abbreviations that can be pronounced as words: OPEC, for example, is the acronym for the Organization of Petroleum Exporting Countries. Initial abbreviations, on the other hand, are pronounced as separate initials: NRA for National Rifle Association, for instance. Many of these abbreviations come from business, government, and science: NASA, PBS, DNA, GE, UNICEF, AIDS, SAT.

As long as you are sure your readers will understand them, use such abbreviations in your college writing. If the abbreviation may be unfamiliar to your readers, however, spell out the term the first time you use it, and give the abbreviation in parentheses. After that, you can use the abbreviation by itself.

○ **The International Atomic Energy Agency (IAEA) is the central intergovernmental forum for cooperation in the nuclear arena.**

51d Abbreviations in company names

Use such abbreviations as *Co.*, *Inc.*, *Corp.*, and *&* if they are part of a company's official name. Do not, however, use these abbreviations in most other contexts.

○ **Sears, Roebuck & Co. was the only large ~~corp.~~ in town.**
corporation

51e Latin abbreviations

In general, avoid these Latin abbreviations except when citing sources:

cf.	compare (*confer*)	etc.	and so forth (*et cetera*)
e.g.	for example (*exempli gratia*)	i.e.	that is (*id est*)
et al.	and others (*et alia*)	N.B.	note well (*nota bene*)

○ **Many firms have policies to help working parents—~~e.g.,~~ flexible hours, parental leave, and day care.**
for example,

○ **Before the conference began, Haivan unpacked the name tags, programs, pens, ~~etc.~~**
and so forth.

51f Abbreviations for reference information, geographic terms, and months

Though abbreviations for such words as *chapter* (ch.), *edition* (ed.), *page* (p.), or *pages* (pp.) are common in source citations, they are not appropriate in the body of your text.

> edition
> ○ The 1851 ~~ed.~~ of *Twice-Told Tales* is now a valuable collectible.
>   ^

Place-names and months of the year are often abbreviated in source citations, but they should almost always be written out within sentences.

> August,   California, Los Angeles.
> ○ In ~~Aug.,~~ I moved from Lodi, ~~Calif.,~~ to ~~L.A.~~
>   ^   ^   ^

Common exceptions are *Washington*, *DC*, and *U.S.* The latter is acceptable as an adjective but not as a noun.

> ○ The *U.S. delegation* negotiated the treaty.

>   United States.
> ○ The exchange student enjoyed the ~~U.S.~~
>   ^

51g Symbols and units of measurement

In English and the other humanities, symbols such as %, +, $, and = are acceptable in charts and graphs. Dollar signs are acceptable with figures: *$11* (but not with words: *eleven dollars*). Units of measurement can be abbreviated in charts and graphs (*4 in.*) but not in the body of a formal text (*four inches*). Check with your instructor about using a word or a figure with the word *percent*: some documentation styles, such as MLA, require a word (*ten percent*), while others, such as *Chicago*, require a figure whether the word (*10 percent*) or the symbol (*10%*) is used.

> feet
> ○ The ball sailed 425 ~~ft.~~ over the fence.
>   ^

EXERCISE 51.1

Revise each of the following sentences to eliminate any abbreviations that would be inappropriate in most academic writing. Example:

United States
The population of the U.S. grew considerably in the 1980s.

1. Every Fri., my grandmother would walk a mi. to the P.O. and send a care package to her brother in Tenn.
2. The blue whale can grow to be 180 ft. long and can weigh up to 380,000 lbs.
3. Many a Mich.-based auto co., incl. GM, requested financial aid from the govt.
4. A large corp. like AT&T may help finance an employee's M.B.A.
5. Rosie began by saying, "If you want my two ¢," but she did not wait to see if listeners wanted it or not.

bedfordstmartins.com/smhandbook
Exercise Central > Mechanics > Abbreviations

51h Numbers within sentences

If you can write out the number in one or two words, do so. Use figures for longer numbers.

thirty-eight
▸ Her screams were heard by 38 people, but no one called the police.

216
▸ A baseball is held together by two hundred sixteen red stitches.

If one of several numbers *of the same kind* in the same sentence requires a figure, use figures for all the numbers in that sentence.

$100
▸ Our audio systems range in cost from one hundred dollars to $2,599.

TALKING THE TALK

Abbreviations and numbers in different fields

Use of abbreviations and numbers varies in different fields. See a typical example from a biochemistry textbook:

> The energy of a green photon . . . is 57 kilocalories per mole (kcal/mol). An alternative unit of energy is the joule (J), which is equal to 0.239 calorie; 1 kcal/mol is equal to 4.184 kJ/mol.   **—LUBERT STRYER,** *Biochemistry*

These two sentences demonstrate how useful figures and abbreviations can be; reading the same sentences would be very difficult if the numbers and units of measurement had to be written out.

Be sure to use the appropriate system of measurement for the field you are discussing and for the audience you are addressing. Scientific fields generally use metric measurements, which are the standard in most nations other than the United States.

Become familiar with the conventions governing abbreviations and numbers in your field. The following reference books provide guidelines:

MLA Handbook for Writers of Research Papers for literature and the humanities

Publication Manual of the American Psychological Association for the social sciences

Scientific Style and Format: The CSE Manual for Authors, Editors, and Publishers for the natural sciences

The Chicago Manual of Style for the humanities

AIP Style Manual for physics and the applied sciences

51i Numbers that begin sentences

When a sentence begins with a number, either spell out the number or rewrite the sentence.

One hundred nineteen
◗ ~~119~~ years of CIA labor cost taxpayers sixteen million dollars.
  ^

Most readers find it easier to read figures than three-word numbers; thus the best solution may be to rewrite this sentence: *Taxpayers spent sixteen million dollars for 119 years of CIA labor.*

51j Conventions with figures

ADDRESSES	23 Main Street; 175 Fifth Avenue
DATES	September 17, 1951; 6 June 1983; 4 BCE; the 1860s
DECIMALS AND FRACTIONS	65.34; 8½
PERCENTAGES	77 percent (*or* 77%)
EXACT AMOUNTS OF MONEY	$7,348; $1.46 trillion; $2.50; thirty-five (*or* 35) cents
SCORES AND STATISTICS	an 8–3 Red Sox victory; a verbal score of 600; an average age of 22; a mean of 53
TIME OF DAY	6:00 AM (*or* a.m.)

FOR MULTILINGUAL WRITERS

The term *hundred*

The term *hundred* is used idiomatically in English. When it is linked with numbers like two, eight, and so on, the word *hundred* remains singular: *Eight hundred years have passed, and still old animosities run deep.* Add the plural -s to *hundred* only when no number precedes the term: Hundreds *of priceless books were lost in the fire.*

EXERCISE 51.2

Revise the numbers in the following sentences as necessary for correctness and consistency. Some sentences may be correct as written. Example:

> twenty-first
> Did the ~~21st~~ century begin in 2000 or 2001?

1. Al Gore won the popular vote with 50,996,116 votes, but he was still short by 5 electoral votes.

2. 200,000 people may have perished in the 2010 Haitian earthquake.

3. The senator who voted against the measure received 6817 angry emails and only twelve in support of her decision.

4. Walker signed a three-year, $4.5-million contract.

5. In that age group, the risk is estimated to be about one in 2,500.

bedfordstmartins.com/smhandbook
Exercise Central > Mechanics > Numbers

THINKING CRITICALLY ABOUT ABBREVIATIONS AND NUMBERS

Reading with an Eye for Abbreviations and Numbers

The paragraph by Roger Angell at the end of Chapter 53 follows the style of the *New Yorker* magazine, which often spells out numbers in situations where this chapter recommends using figures. Read the paragraph carefully, and then consider whether it would have been easier to read if figures had been used for some of the numbers. If so, which ones? Then consider how the paragraph would have been different if Angell had used *semi-professional* instead of *semi-pro*. What effect does the abbreviated form create?

Thinking about Your Own Use of Abbreviations and Numbers

Look over an essay that you have written, noting all abbreviations and numbers. Check your usage for correctness, consistency, and appropriateness. If you discover a problem with abbreviations or numbers, make a note of it so that you can avoid the error in the future.

52 Italics

Italics give words special meaning or emphasis. But remember not to overuse italics to emphasize important words: doing so will get *very boring* to readers *very quickly.*

The slanted type known as *italics* is more than just a pretty typeface. In the sentence "Many people read *People* on the subway every day," the italics (and the capital letter) tell us that *People* is a publication.

It's easy to produce italic type on a computer, but you can also use underlining to indicate italics.

52a Italics for titles

In general, use italics for titles of long works; use quotation marks for shorter works (48b and 50c).

BOOKS	*Fun Home: A Family Tragicomic*
CHOREOGRAPHIC WORKS	Agnes de Mille's *Rodeo*
FILMS AND VIDEOS	*Avatar*
LONG MUSICAL WORKS	*Brandenburg Concertos*
LONG POEMS	*Bhagavad Gita*
MAGAZINES AND JOURNALS	*Ebony,* the *New England Journal of Medicine*
NEWSPAPERS	the *Cleveland Plain Dealer*
PAINTINGS AND SCULPTURE	Georgia O'Keeffe's *Black Iris*
PAMPHLETS	Thomas Paine's *Common Sense*
PLAYS	*Sweeney Todd*
RADIO SERIES	*All Things Considered*
RECORDINGS	*Slade Alive!*

| SOFTWARE | *Dreamweaver* |
| TELEVISION SERIES | *American Idol* |

Do not use italics for sacred books, such as the Bible and the Qur'an; for public documents, such as the Constitution and the Magna Carta; or for the titles of your own papers. With magazines and newspapers, do not italicize or capitalize an initial *the*, even if part of the official name.

QUICK HELP

Editing for italics

- Check that all titles of long works are italicized. (52a)

- If you use any words, letters, or numbers as terms, make sure they are in italics. (52b)

- Italicize any non-English words or phrases that are not in an English dictionary. (52c)

- If you use italics to emphasize words, be sure you use the italics sparingly. (52e)

52b Italics for words, letters, and numbers referred to as terms

Italicize words, letters, and numbers referred to as terms.

○ **One characteristic of some New York speech is the absence of post-vocalic *r*, with some New Yorkers pronouncing *four* as "fouh."**

○ **The first four orbitals are represented by the letters *s*, *p*, *d*, and *f*.**

○ **On the back of his jersey was the famous *24*.**

52c Italics for non-English words and phrases

Italicize words and phrases from other languages unless they have become part of English, such as the French word "bourgeois" and the Italian "pasta." If a word is in an English dictionary, it does not need italics.

○ **At last one of the phantom sleighs gliding along the street would come to a stop, and with gawky haste Mr. Burness in his fox-furred *shapka* would make for our door.**

—VLADIMIR NABOKOV, *Speak, Memory*

Always italicize Latin genus and species names.

○ **The caterpillars of *Hapalia*, when attacked by the wasp *Apanteles machaeralis*, drop suddenly from their leaves and suspend themselves in air by a silken thread.**

—STEPHEN JAY GOULD, "Nonmoral Nature"

52d Italics for names of vehicles

Italicize names of specific aircraft, spacecraft, ships, and trains. Do not italicize types and classes, such as Learjet and space shuttle.

AIRCRAFT AND SPACECRAFT	the *Spirit of St. Louis*, the *Discovery*
SHIPS	the *Santa Maria*, the USS *Iowa*
TRAINS	the *Orient Express*, Amtrak's *Lakeshore Limited*

52e Italics for special emphasis

Italics can help create emphasis in writing, but use them sparingly for this purpose. It is usually better to create emphasis with sentence structure and word choice.

○ **Great literature and a class of literate readers are nothing new in India. What is new is the emergence of a gifted generation of Indian writers *working in English*.**
—SALMAN RUSHDIE

EXERCISE 52.1

In each of the following sentences, underline any words that should be italicized, and circle any italicized words that should not be. Example:

The film Good Night, and Good Luck tells the story of a CBS newsman

who helped to end the career of Senator Joseph McCarthy.

1. One critic claimed that few people listened to *The Velvet Underground* and *Nico* when the record was issued but that everyone who did formed a band.

2. Homemade *sushi* can be dangerous, but so can deviled eggs kept too long in a picnic basket.

3. The Web site Poisonous Plants and Animals lists tobacco (Nicotiana tobacum) as one of the most popular poisons in the world.

4. The monster in the Old English epic Beowulf got to tell his own side of the story in John Gardner's novel Grendel.

5. The 2009 film Star Trek imagines the youthful life of James T. Kirk and the crew of the Enterprise.

> bedfordstmartins.com/smhandbook
> **Exercise Central > Mechanics > Italics**

THINKING CRITICALLY ABOUT ITALICS

Reading with an Eye for Italics

Read the following passage about a graduate English seminar carefully, particularly noting the effects created by the italics. How would it differ without any italic emphasis? What other words or phrases might the author have italicized?

> There were four big tables arranged in a square, with everyone's feet sticking out into the open middle of the square. You could tell who was nervous, and how much, by watching the pairs of feet twist around each other. The Great Man presided awesomely from the high bar of the square. His head was a majestic granite-gray, like a centurion in command; he *looked* famous. His clean shoes twitched only slightly, and only when he was angry.
>
> It turned out he was angry at me a lot of the time. He was angry because he thought me a disrupter, a rioter, a provocateur, and a fool; also crazy. And this was twenty years ago, before these things were *de rigueur* in the universities. Everything was very quiet in those days: there were only the Cold War and Korea and Joe McCarthy and the Old Old Nixon, and the only revolutionaries around were in Henry James's *The Princess Casamassima*.
>
> —CYNTHIA OZICK, "We Are the Crazy Lady"

Thinking about Your Own Use of Italics

Write a paragraph or two describing the most eccentric person you know, italicizing some words for special emphasis. Read your passage aloud to hear the effect of the italics. Now explain each use of italics. If you find yourself unable to give a reason, ask yourself whether the word should be italicized at all.

Then revise the passage to eliminate *all but one* use of italics. Try revising sentences and choosing more precise words to convey emphasis. Decide which version is more effective. Can you reach any conclusions about using italics for emphasis?

53 Hyphens

As Hall of Fame pitcher Jim Palmer once said, "The difference between *re-sign* and *resign* is a hyphen." Hyphens are supposed to make writing clearer, but for many writers, the decision about whether or not to use a hyphen can itself be a puzzling one.

Hyphen problems are now one of the twenty most common surface errors in student writing. The confusion is understandable. Over time, the conventions for hyphen use in a given word can change (*tomorrow* was once spelled *to-morrow*). New words, even compounds such as *firewall*, generally don't use hyphens, but controversy continues to rage over whether to hyphenate *email* (or is it *e-mail*?). And some words are hyphenated when they serve one kind of purpose in a sentence and not when they serve another.

53a Hyphens with compound words

Some compounds are one word (*rowboat*), some are separate words (*hard drive*), and some require hyphens (*sister-in-law*). You should consult a dictionary to be sure. However, the following conventions can help you decide when to use hyphens with compound words.

Compound adjectives

Hyphenate most compound adjectives that precede a noun but not those that follow a noun.

a *well-liked* boss	My boss is *well liked*.
a *six-foot* plank	The plank is *six feet long*.

In general, the reason for hyphenating compound adjectives is to facilitate reading.

○ Designers often use potted plants as living-room dividers.

Without the hyphen, *living* may seem to modify *room dividers*.

Commonly used compound adjectives do not usually need to be hyphenated for clarity—*income tax reform* or *first class mail* would seldom if ever be misunderstood.

Never hyphenate an *-ly* adverb and an adjective.

○ They used a widely⁄distributed mailing list.

Compound adjectives formed from compound proper nouns are hyphenated if the noun is hyphenated: *Austro-Hungarian history* but *Latin American literature*.

Coined compounds

You may need hyphens to link coined compounds, combinations of words that you are using in an unexpected way, especially as an adjective.

○ She gave me her *I-told-you-so* look before leaving the party.

Fractions and compound numbers

Use a hyphen to write out fractions and to spell out compound numbers from twenty-one to ninety-nine, both when they stand alone and when they are part of larger numbers. (Usually such larger numbers should be written as numerals. See Chapter 51.)

one-seventh	thirty-seven
two and seven-sixteenths	three hundred fifty-four thousand

Suspended hyphens

A series of compound words that share the same base word can be shortened by the use of suspended hyphens.

○ Each student should do the work *him-* or *herself*.

QUICK HELP

Editing for hyphens

- Double-check compound words to be sure they are properly closed up, separated, or hyphenated. If in doubt, consult a dictionary. (53a)

- Check all terms that have prefixes or suffixes to see whether you need hyphens. (53b)

- Do not hyphenate two-word verbs or word groups that serve as subject complements. (53c)

53b Hyphens with prefixes and suffixes

Most words containing prefixes or suffixes are written without hyphens: *antiwar, Romanesque.* Here are some exceptions:

BEFORE CAPITALIZED BASE WORDS	un-American, non-Catholic
WITH FIGURES	pre-1960, post-1945
WITH CERTAIN PREFIXES AND SUFFIXES	all-state, ex-partner, self-possessed, quasi-legislative, mayor-elect, fifty-odd
WITH COMPOUND BASE WORDS	pre-high school, post-cold war
FOR CLARITY OR EASE OF READING	re-cover, anti-inflation, un-ionized

Re-cover means "cover again"; the hyphen distinguishes it from *recover*, meaning "get well." In *anti-inflation* and *un-ionized*, the hyphens separate confusing clusters of vowels and consonants.

53c Unnecessary hyphens

Unnecessary hyphens are at least as common a problem as omitted ones. Do not hyphenate the parts of a two-word verb such as *depend on, turn off,* or *tune out* (58b).

- **Players must pick/up a medical form before football tryouts.**

The words *pick up* act as a verb and should not be hyphenated.

However, be careful to check that the two words do indeed function as a verb in the sentence; if they function as an adjective, a hyphen may be needed (29b1, b4).

▶ **Let's sign up for the early class.**

The verb *sign up* should not have a hyphen.

▶ **Where is the sign-up sheet?**

The compound adjective *sign-up*, which modifies the noun *sheet*, needs a hyphen.

Do not hyphenate a subject complement — a word group that follows a linking verb (such as a form of *be* or *seem*) and describes the subject (29c).

▶ **Audrey is almost three⁄years⁄old.**

EXERCISE 53.1

Insert or delete hyphens as necessary in the following sentences. Use your dictionary if you are not sure whether or where to hyphenate a word. Example:

The governor-elect joked about the polls.

1. The group seeks volunteers to set-up chairs in the meeting room before the event.
2. Despite concerns about reliability, police line-ups are still frequently used to identify suspects.
3. I was ill-prepared for my first calculus exam, but I managed to pass anyway.
4. Some passengers were bumped from the over-sold flight.
5. Having an ignore the customer attitude may actually make a service-industry job less pleasant.
6. Both pro and antiState Department groups registered complaints.
7. At a yard sale, I found a 1964 pre CBS Fender Stratocaster in mint condition.
8. Applicants who are over fifty-years-old may face age discrimination.
9. Neil Armstrong, a selfproclaimed "nerdy engineer," was the first person to set foot on the moon.
10. Carefully-marketed children's safety products suggest to new parents that the more they spend, the safer their kids will be.

→ bedfordstmartins.com/smhandbook
Exercise Central > Mechanics > Hyphens

THINKING CRITICALLY ABOUT HYPHENATION

The following paragraph uses many hyphens. Read it carefully, and note how the hyphens make the paragraph easier to read. Why do you think *semi-pro* is hyphenated? Why is *junior-college* hyphenated in the last sentence?

All semi-pro leagues, it should be understood, are self-sustaining, and have no farm affiliation or other connection with the twenty-six major-league clubs, or with the seventeen leagues and hundred and fifty-two teams . . . that make up the National Association—the minors, that is. There is no central body of semi-pro teams, and semi-pro players are not included among the six hundred and fifty major-leaguers, the twenty-five-hundred-odd minor-leaguers, plus all the managers, coaches, presidents, commissioners, front-office people, and scouts, who, taken together, constitute the great tent called organized ball. (A much diminished tent, at that; back in 1949, the minors included fifty-nine leagues, about four hundred and forty-eight teams, and perhaps ten thousand players.) Also outside the tent, but perhaps within its shade, are five college leagues, ranging across the country from Cape Cod to Alaska, where the most promising freshman, sophomore, and junior-college ballplayers . . . compete against each other. . . .   —ROGER ANGELL, "In the Country"

ARGENTINA

FOR
MULTILINGUAL
WRITERS

Part 11

54 Writing in U.S. Academic Contexts

Writing for college presents many challenges; such writing differs in many ways from high school writing as well as from informal writing like texting. If you grew up speaking and writing in other languages, however, the transition to producing effective college writing can be even more complicated. Not only will you have to learn new information and new ways of thinking and arguing, but you also have to do it in a language that may not come naturally to you—especially in unfamiliar rhetorical situations.

You already know that writing differs from one context to another. Right now, learning what counts as effective writing in the context of college should be one of your major goals.

54a Meeting expectations for U.S. academic writing

Xiaoming Li, now a college English teacher, says that before she came to the United States as a graduate student, she had been a "good writer" in China—in both English and Chinese. Once in the United States, however, she struggled to grasp what her teachers expected of her college writing. While she could easily use grammar books and dictionaries, her instructors' unstated expectations seemed to call for her to write in a way that was new to her.

The expectations for college writing are often taken for granted by instructors. To complicate the matter further, there is no single "correct" style of communication in any country, including the United States. Effective oral styles differ from effective written styles, and what is considered good writing in one field of study is not necessarily appropriate in another. Within a field, different rhetorical situations and genres may require different ways of writing. In business, for example, memos are usually short and simple, while a market analysis report may require complex paragraphs with tables, graphs, and diagrams. Even the variety of English often referred to as "standard" covers a wide range of styles (see

Chapter 26). In spite of this wide variation, several features are often associated with U.S. academic English in general:

- conventional grammar, spelling, punctuation, and mechanics
- organization that links ideas explicitly (Chapter 4g)
- an easy-to-read type size and typeface, conventional margins, and double spacing
- explicitly stated claims supported by evidence (Chapter 9)
- careful documentation of all sources (Chapters 16–19)
- consistent use of an appropriate level of formality (24c and 27a)
- conventional use of idioms (Chapter 58)
- the use of conventional academic formats, such as literature reviews, research essays, lab reports, and research proposals

This brief list suggests features of the genre often described as U.S. academic writing. Yet these characteristics can lead to even more questions: What does *conventional* mean? How can a writer determine what is appropriate in any given rhetorical situation? Most students can benefit from some instruction in how new contexts require the use of different sets of conventions, strategies, and resources. This is especially the case for multilingual writers.

54b Understanding genre conventions

Those who read your college writing—your teachers and peers—will hold some expectations about the texts you produce and about the features of those texts. Many writers learn these expectations through practice rather than through instruction. But if you have had limited exposure to various types, or *genres*, of academic writing in English, it may be helpful to think about these conventions explicitly. (For more on genres, see 2e.)

Genres of texts

At some point in your writing process, you should consider the genre or kind of text the instructor expects you to write. The expectation may be clear from the assignment, especially when the instructor is explicit about the purpose, audience, possible methods of organization, and

QUICK HELP

Strategies for analyzing genre features

Find some examples of the kind of text the assignment requires, and study them carefully for various features. Here are some questions to consider:

- What does the genre look like? How is the text laid out on the page? How are any visual features—such as headings, bylines, sidebars, and footnotes—incorporated into the main text? (23d)

- How are visuals or images (photographs, charts, graphs, maps, and so on) incorporated into the text, and how are they labeled?

- How long is the whole text, each section, each paragraph, and each sentence?

- How does the text introduce the topic? How and where does it present the main point? Is the main point stated explicitly or implicitly?

- What are the major divisions of the text? Are they marked with transitions or headings? (5d and 23c)

- How does each section contribute to the main point? How is the main point of each section supported?

- How are the key terms defined? How much and what kind of background information is provided?

- What is the level of formality? Does the text use technical terms, contractions (such as *I'm* and *isn't* instead of *I am* and *is not*), or many dependent or subordinate clauses? (41b)

- Does the text take a personal stance (*I*, *we*), address the audience directly (*you*), or talk about the subject without explicitly referring to the writer or the reader?

- How many sources are used in the text? How are they introduced? Are sources mentioned in the text, cited in parentheses, or both? Which documentation style—such as MLA or APA—is followed? (Chapters 16–19)

- How are the characteristics of the text similar to or different from similar genres in your native language?

criteria for assessment. In many cases, however, the assignment is not explicit about what the text should look like or accomplish. For example, if the instructor asks for a five-page essay about efforts to conserve the environment, can the essay take the form of a personal narrative or reflection on your frustrating experience with recycling? Is it sup-

QUICK HELP

Strategies for in-class writing tasks

For many multilingual students, the major problem presented by in-class writing is running out of time. You can overcome this problem by preparing carefully in advance.

- Review all the material carefully.

- Create a list of key terms and their definitions.

- Anticipate the questions, and write practice answers to them. (Do not, however, memorize answers to questions you think might be on the exam, since doing so might lead you to rely on answers that don't fit the questions on the actual test.)

- Explain the material you will be tested on—either orally or in writing—to someone unfamiliar with it.

- Do some timed writing right before class to get your writing muscles warmed up.

Here are some strategies you can use during the exam to minimize the risk of running out of time:

- Create a brief outline at the beginning of the exam to organize your thoughts and to keep you on track.

- State your answer or main point at the beginning before providing the background information or explanation.

- Save a few minutes at the end to read over your answer and make any corrections.

posed to examine a problem related to conservation and pose a solution? Or does it need to be an academic essay that presents new knowledge or insight about a specific aspect of conservation efforts supported by original data, secondary sources, or both?

If you are not sure what kind of text you are supposed to write, ask your instructor for clarification and examples. (Some examples may also be available at your school's writing center.) You may want to find multiple examples so that you can develop a sense of how different writers approach the same writing task. Another strategy is to discuss the assignment with a few classmates or a writing center tutor. You may find the help you need, and you may see that you are not the only one struggling to understand the assignment.

QUICK HELP

Strategies for borrowing without plagiarizing

To avoid plagiarism:

- Try not to reproduce the whole sentence; instead, borrow phrases that are not central to the author's idea and that are commonly used in academic writing, such as "drawing on" (see 54c).

- Find sample pieces of sentence structure from similar genres but on different topics so that you will be borrowing a typical structure (which does not belong to anyone), not the idea or the particular way the idea is phrased.

- Write your own sentence first, and look at other people's sentences to guide your revision.

Although the genres of writing required in college vary among fields of study and even among courses, research shows that the most common out-of-class writing assignments in college include the following: research-based papers that draw on sources from your library and online searches (Chapters 10–19); reports that include some interpretation (17e); summaries (7c), which may or may not call for analysis (12f4); proposals (19d); reviews or critiques (8g); and close readings or explications of a text (7e, 60c). This handbook provides basic information on all these kinds of writing.

One of the most common writing tasks for college students happens in class, in the form of short-answer questions and very brief essays on exams (Chapter 64). For this kind of writing, you will almost always be expected to display knowledge that you have learned in the course. In this setting, demonstrating that you know the material may be more important than developing new or original ideas about the topic—unless the assignment specifically asks you to synthesize or present your own perspective.

54c Adapting structures and phrases from a genre

If English is not your strongest language, you may find it useful to borrow and adapt transitional devices and pieces of sentence structure from other people's writing in the genre you are working in. You

Original Abstract from a Social Science Paper	Effective Borrowing of Structures from a Genre
Using the interpersonal communications research of J. K. Brilhart and G. J. Galanes, and W. Wilmot and J. Hocker, along with T. Hartman's personality assessment, I observed and analyzed the leadership roles and group dynamics of my project collaborators in a communications course. Based on results of the Hartman personality assessment, I predicted that a single leader would emerge. However, complementary individual strengths and gender differences encouraged a distributed leadership style, in which the group experienced little confrontation and conflict. Conflict, because it was handled positively, was crucial to the group's progress.	Drawing on the research of Deborah Tannen on men's and women's conversational styles, I analyzed the conversational styles of six first-year students at DePaul University. Based on Tannen's research, I expected that the three men I observed would use features typical of male conversational style and the three women would use features typical of female conversational style. In general, these predictions were accurate; however, some exceptions were also apparent.

should not copy the whole sentence or sentence structure verbatim, however, or your borrowed sentences may seem plagiarized (Chapter 14 and 16c).

The first example above illustrates effective borrowing. The student writer borrows phrases (such as "drawing on" and "based on") that are commonly used in academic writing in the social sciences to perform particular functions. Notice how the student also modifies these phrases to suit his or her needs.

The example on p. 788 illustrates poor borrowing practices. The student plagiarizes both ideas and whole sentences from the original text.

54d Strategies for learning from search engines

To multilingual writers, Internet search engines such as Google offer more than a tool for finding information. They also provide a useful way

Original Abstract from a Social Science Paper	Inappropriate Borrowing of Ideas and Sentences
Using the interpersonal communications research of J. K. Brilhart and G. J. Galanes, and W. Wilmot and J. Hocker, along with T. Hartman's personality assessment, I observed and analyzed the leadership roles and group dynamics of my project collaborators in a communications course. Based on results of the Hartman personality assessment, I predicted that a single leader would emerge. However, complementary individual strengths and gender differences encouraged a distributed leadership style, in which the group experienced little confrontation and conflict. Conflict, because it was handled positively, was crucial to the group's progress.	Using the interpersonal communications research of J. K. Brilhart and G. J. Galanes, and W. Wilmot and J. Hocker, along with T. Hartman's personality assessment, I observed and analyzed the leadership roles and group dynamics of my peers in a communications course. Based on findings of the Hartman personality assessment, I predicted that one leader of the group would appear. However, complementary individual strengths and differences in gender resulted in a distributed leadership style, in which there was little confrontation and conflict. Because it was handled positively, conflict was crucial to the group's progress.

of developing vocabulary or checking sentence structure and word usage. A number of common strategies can help. For example, you can include a wildcard in a keyword search to find all the forms of a word; a wildcard search using *reciproc** will yield *reciprocate, reciprocating, reciprocated, reciprocal,* and *reciprocity.* Most search engines use an asterisk (*) as a wildcard, though some use a question mark or other wildcard symbol. You can use *define:* to look up the definition of a word or a phrase (such as *define:social science*) or enclose a phrase in quotation marks to find Web pages that include it (such as "*language in society*").

In addition, you can use search engines to check your use of common expressions. For example, if you are not sure whether you should use an infinitive form (*to* + verb) or a gerund (*-ing*) for the verb *confirm* after the main verb *expect* (55d), you can search for both "*expected confirming*" and "*expected to confirm*" in quotation marks to see which search term yields more results. A Google search for "*expected confirming*" yields many entries with a comma between the two words, indicating that one phrase ends with *expected* and another begins with *confirming.*

"expected confirming"   ✕   Search

About 19,300 results (0.17 seconds)   Advanced search

▶ Fiona Ortiz | Journalist Profile | ☆
... their capital by 3.5 billion euros ($4.5 billion), much less than **expected, confirming** fears
the continent's long-awaited stress test was too soft. ...
blogs.reuters.com/fiona-ortiz/ - Cached - Similar

Bad GDP numbers **expected, confirming** recession in SA ☆
May 13, 2009 ... Bad GDP numbers **expected, confirming** recession in SA. Gross domestic
product (GDP) for the first quarter of the year will probably be worse ...
www.polity.org.za/.../bad-gdp-numbers-**expected-confirming**-recession-in-sa-2009-05-13 -
Cached

Islam's Way to Freedom - Religious Freedom News and Comment ☆
... their capital by 3.5 Billion Euros ($4.5 Billion), much less than **expected, confirming** fears
the continent's long-awaited Stress Test was too soft. ...
politifi.com/news/Islams-Way-to-Freedom-1158004.html - Cached

Search results for "expected confirming."

"expected to confirm"   Search

About 3,670,000 results (0.40 seconds)   Advanced search

FOXNews.com - Senate **Expected to Confirm** Gen. Petraeus
Wednesday ... ☆
Jun 29, 2010 ... A Senate panel on Tuesday backed Gen. David Petraeus to lead US and
NATO forces in Afghanistan even as he warned that that the US will need ...
www.foxnews.com/politics/.../gen-petraeus-face-congress-war-plan/ - Cached

IOC **expected to confirm** all 3 bid cities as finalists in race for ... ☆
Jun 21, 2010 ... 3 cities set to make final list for 2018 Olympics.
blog.taragana.com/.../ioc-**expected-to-confirm**-all-3-bid-cities-as-finalists-in-race-for-
2018-winter-olympics-113795/ - Cached

Clegg **expected to confirm** AV referendum date - Yahoo! News UK ☆
Jul 5, 2010 ... Nick Clegg is **expected to confirm** the date of the referendum on AV today.
uk.news.yahoo.com/.../tpl-clegg-**expected-to-confirm**-av-referen-81c5b50_2.html - United
Kingdom - Cached

Search results for "expected to confirm."

On the other hand, a search for "*expected to confirm*" yields many more
hits than a search for "*expected confirming*" —3,670,000 instead of 19,300, for
example, in the searches shown above. These results indicate that *expected to
confirm* is the more commonly used expression.

But you should also note that in the search above, some of the entries
shown are news headlines, which means that they may not use the same

construction used in ordinary English sentences (newspaper headlines, for example, often omit *be* verbs). To check whether ordinary sentences also use *expected to confirm* rather than *expected confirming*, you would want to click through a few more pages of search results, seeking out examples that do not come from headlines.

Clauses and Sentences

55

The requirements for forming sentences can differ across languages, and English has its own sets of rules. Among the more difficult features of English sentence formation are explicit subjects and objects, word order, noun clauses, infinitives and gerunds, adjective clauses, and conditional sentences.

55a Including explicit subjects and objects

English sentences consist of a subject and a predicate. While many languages can omit a sentence subject, English very rarely allows this. Though you might write *Responsible for analyzing data* on a résumé, in most varieties of spoken and written English, you must state the subject explicitly. In fact, with only a few exceptions, all clauses in English must have an explicit subject.

> it
▷ **They took the Acela Express to Boston because** ^
>
> **was fast.**

English even requires a kind of "dummy" subject to fill the subject position in certain kinds of sentences.

▷ *It* **is raining.**
▷ *There* **is a strong wind.**

Transitive verbs typically require that objects—and sometimes other information—also be explicitly stated (29c2). For example, you cannot just tell someone *Give!* even if it is clear what is to be given

Short phrases, or sound bites, surround us—from Taco Bell's "Think Outside the Bun" to Volkswagen's "Drivers Wanted." These short, simple slogans may be memorable, but they don't tell us very much. Particularly in writing, we usually need complete sentences, and sometimes fairly complicated sentences, to convey meaning.

to whom. You must say *Give it to me* or *Give her the passport* or some other such sentence. Similarly, saying *Put!* or *Put it!* is insufficient when you mean *Put it on the table*; however, *Put it down!* is fine because it includes the required destination.

Many dictionaries identify whether a verb is transitive (requiring an object) or intransitive (not followed by an object).

55b Using English word order

In general, subjects, verbs, and objects must be placed in specific positions within a sentence (29c).

SUBJECT VERB OBJECT   ADVERB
▻ **Mario left Venice reluctantly.**

The only word in this sentence that you can move to different locations is the adverb *reluctantly* (*Mario reluctantly left Venice* or *Reluctantly, Mario left Venice*). The three key elements of subject, verb, and object rarely move out of their normal order.

55c Using noun clauses

Examine the following sentence:

> In my last year in high school, my adviser urged that I apply to several colleges.

This complex sentence is built out of two sentences, one of them (B) embedded in the other (A):

> A. In my last year in high school, my adviser urged B.
> B. I (should) apply to several colleges.

When these are combined as in the original sentence, sentence B becomes a noun clause introduced by *that* and takes on the role of object of the verb *urged* in sentence A. Now look at the following sentence:

> It made a big difference that she wrote a strong letter of recommendation.

Here the two component sentences are C and D:

> C. D made a big difference.
> D. She wrote a strong letter of recommendation.

In this case, the noun clause formed from sentence D functions as the subject of sentence C so that the combination reads as follows:

> That she wrote a strong letter of recommendation made a big difference.

This sentence is gramatically acceptable but not typical. When a lengthy noun clause is the subject, it is usually moved to the end of the sentence. The result is *It made a big difference that she wrote a strong letter of recommendation,* which inserts the dummy subject *It* to fill the slot of the subject.

55d Choosing between infinitives and gerunds

Infinitives are verbs in the *to* + verb form (*to write, to read, to go*); gerunds are verbs that end in *-ing* and act as subjects or objects within a sentence. In general, infinitives tend to indicate intentions, desires, or expectations, and gerunds tend to indicate facts. Knowing whether to use an infinitive or a gerund in a particular sentence can be a challenge. Though no simple explanation will make it an easy task, some hints might be helpful (see 54d for another strategy).

▷ My adviser urged me *to apply* to several colleges.

▷ *Applying* took a great deal of time.

In the first sentence, the infinitive conveys the message that the act of applying was something wanted, not yet a fact. In the second sentence, the gerund calls attention to the fact that the application process was actually carried out.

Using infinitives to state intentions

▷ Kumar *expected to get* a good job after graduation.

▷ Last year, Fatima *decided to become* a math major.

▷ The strikers have *agreed to go* back to work.

At the moment indicated by the verbs *expect, decide,* and *agree* in these sentences, those actions or events were merely intentions. These three verbs, as well as many others that specify intentions (or negative intentions, such as *refuse*), must always be followed by an infinitive, never by a gerund. Many learner dictionaries provide information about which verbs must be followed by an infinitive instead of a gerund.

Using gerunds to state facts

- Jerzy enjoys *going* to the theater.
- We resumed *working* after our coffee break.
- Kim appreciated *getting* a card from Sean.

In all of these cases, the gerund indicates that the action or event that it expresses has actually occurred. Verbs like *enjoy, resume*, and *appreciate* can be followed only by gerunds, not by infinitives. In fact, even when these verbs do not convey clear facts, the verb form that follows must still be a gerund. Again, many dictionaries provide this information.

- Kim would appreciate *getting* a card from Sean, but he hardly knows her.

Understanding other rules and guidelines

A few verbs can be followed by either an infinitive or a gerund. With some, such as *begin* and *continue*, the choice makes little difference in meaning. With others, however, the difference in meaning is striking.

- Carlos was working as a medical technician, but he *stopped to study* English.

  The infinitive indicates that Carlos intended to study English when he left his job. We are not told whether he actually did study English.

- Carlos *stopped studying* English when he left the United States.

  The gerund indicates that Carlos actually did study English but then stopped doing so when he left.

The distinction between fact and intention is not a rule but only a tendency, and it can be outweighed by other rules. For example, use a gerund—never an infinitive—directly following a preposition.

- This fruit is safe for ~~to eat.~~ *eating.*

- This fruit is safe ~~for~~ to eat.

> **This fruit is safe for ~~to~~ eat.**
> us ⌃

For a full list of verbs that can be followed by an infinitive and verbs that can be followed by a gerund, see *Grammar Troublespots*, Third Edition, by Ann Raimes (Cambridge UP, 2004), or *Cambridge International Dictionary of English* (Cambridge UP, 1999).

55e Using adjective clauses

An adjective clause provides more information about a preceding noun.

> **The company *Yossi's uncle invested in* went bankrupt.**

The subject is a noun phrase in which the noun *company* is modified by the article *the* and the adjective clause *Yossi's uncle invested in*. The sentence as a whole says that a certain company went bankrupt, and the adjective clause identifies the company more specifically by saying that Yossi's uncle had invested in it.

One way of seeing how the adjective clause fits into the sentence is to rewrite it like this: *The company (Yossi's uncle had invested in it) went bankrupt*. This is not a normal English sentence, but it helps demonstrate a process that leads to the sentence we started with. Note the following steps:

1. Change the personal pronoun *it* to the relative pronoun *which*: *The company (Yossi's uncle had invested in which) went bankrupt*.

2. Move either the whole prepositional phrase *in which* to the beginning of the adjective clause, or move just the relative pronoun: *The company in which Yossi's uncle had invested went bankrupt* or *The company which Yossi's uncle had invested in went bankrupt*. While both of these are correct English sentences, the first version is somewhat more formal than the second.

3. If no preposition precedes the relative pronoun, substitute *that* for *which*, or omit the relative pronoun entirely: *The company that Yossi's uncle had invested in went bankrupt* or *The company Yossi's uncle had invested in went bankrupt*. Both of these are correct English sentences. While they are less formal than the forms in step 2, they are still acceptable in much formal writing.

55f Forming conditional sentences

English pays special attention to the degree of confidence we have in the truth or likelihood of an assertion. Therefore, English distinguishes among many different types of conditional sentences — that is, sentences that focus on questions of truth and that are introduced by *if* or its equivalent. The following examples illustrate a range of different conditional sentences. Each of these sentences makes different assumptions about the likelihood that what is stated in the *if* clause is true.

▷ **If you *practice* (or *have practiced*) writing frequently, you *know* (or *have learned*) what your chief problems are.**

This sentence assumes that what is stated in the *if* clause may very well be true; the alternatives in parentheses indicate that any tense that is appropriate in a simple sentence may be used in both the *if* clause and the main clause.

▷ **If you *practice* writing for the rest of this term, you *will* (or *may*) *understand* the process better.**

This sentence makes a prediction about the future and assumes that what is stated may turn out to be true. Only the main clause uses the future tense (*will understand*) or some other modal that can indicate future time (*may understand*). The *if* clause must use the present tense.

▷ **If you *practiced* (or *were to practice*) writing every single day, it *would* eventually *seem* much easier to you.**

This sentence indicates doubt that what is stated will happen. In the *if* clause, the verb is either past tense — actually, past subjunctive (30h) — or *were to* + the base form, even though it refers to future time. The main clause contains *would* + the base form of the main verb.

▷ **If you *practiced* writing on Mars, you *would find* no one to read your work.**

This sentence imagines an impossible situation. As with the preceding sentence, the past subjunctive is used in the *if* clause, although past time is not being referred to, and *would* + the base form is used in the main clause.

> If you *had practiced* writing in ancient Egypt, you *would have used* hieroglyphics.

This sentence shifts the impossibility back to the past; obviously, you aren't going to find yourself in ancient Egypt. But a past impossibility demands a form that is "more past": the past perfect in the *if* clause and *would* + the perfect form of the main verb in the main clause.

EXERCISE 55.1

Revise the following sentences as necessary. Not all sentences contain an error.

1. In the 1870s, a group of New York City dog owners formed officially the Westminster Kennel Club.

2. Members of the club enjoyed to tell stories about their dogs' talents.

3. Soon the group began hosting an annual dog show which dogs were judged and awarded prizes in it.

4. Was this show that eventually became the Westminster Dog Show, a popular event still held every January.

5. The Westminster Kennel Club contributes to charities that help many dogs and pet owners.

6. If you want to know more about purebred dogs, you have enjoyed watching the Westminster Dog Show.

bedfordstmartins.com/smhandbook
Exercise Central > For Multilingual Writers > Clauses

56 Nouns and Noun Phrases

Since all human languages are built on the same foundation, there are similarities between English and other languages. For example, even though the structure of sentences can vary greatly from one language to another, sentences in every language are built out of two primary components—nouns and verbs. Thus, you can bring your understanding of nouns and verbs in other languages to your study of nouns and verbs in English.

Although all languages have nouns, English nouns differ from those in some other languages in various ways, such as their division into count and noncount nouns and the use of plural forms, articles, and other modifiers.

56a Using count and noncount nouns

Look at the following sentences:

- ▷ **Research** shows that this chemical can be dangerous.
- ▷ **Studies** show that this chemical can be dangerous.

Studies is a count noun, and *research* is a noncount noun. Count nouns (also called countable nouns) refer to separate individuals or things that you can count: *a study, a doctor, a book, a tree; studies, doctors*, three *books*, ten *trees*. Noncount nouns (also called mass nouns or uncountable nouns) refer to masses or collections without distinctly separate parts: *research, milk, ice, blood, grass*. You cannot count noncount nouns unless you use a quantifier: *one blade of grass, two glasses of milk, three pints of blood*.

Count and noncount nouns also differ in their use of plural forms. Count nouns generally have both singular and plural forms: *study, studies*. Noncount nouns generally have only a singular form: *research*.

COUNT	NONCOUNT
facts	information
suggestions	advice
people (plural of *person*)	humanity
tables, chairs, beds	furniture
letters	mail
pebbles	gravel
beans	rice

Some nouns can be either count or noncount, depending on the meaning.

COUNT   Before there were video games, children played with *marbles*.

NONCOUNT   The floor of the palace was made of *marble*.

When you learn a noun in English, it is useful to know whether it is count, noncount, or both. Many dictionaries provide this information.

56b Using proper nouns

In addition to count and noncount nouns, English has proper nouns. These nouns include names of people, places, objects, and institutions — for example, *California, Yolanda, IBM,* and *First National Bank.* Proper nouns are always capitalized and generally cannot vary in number, so they are either singular (*John, the* New York Times) or plural (*the Netherlands, the Rocky Mountains*).

56c Using determiners

Determiners are words that identify or quantify a noun, such as *this study, all people, his suggestions.*

COMMON DETERMINERS
- the articles *a / an, the*
- *this, these, that, those*
- *my, our, your, his, her, its, their*
- possessive nouns and noun phrases (*Sheila's* paper, *my friend's* book)
- *whose, which, what*

- *all, both, each, every, some, any, either, no, neither, many, much, (a) few, (a) little, several, enough*

- the numerals *one, two,* etc.

Some determiners, such as *a, an, this, that, one,* and *each,* can only be used with singular nouns; others, such as *these, those, all, both, many, several,* and *two,* can only be used with plural nouns. Still other determiners — *my, the,* and *which,* for example — can be used with singular or plural nouns. See the chart on the next page for additional examples.

Determiners with singular count nouns

Every singular count noun must be preceded by a determiner. Place any adjectives between the determiner and the noun.

▷ my
    sister
    ^

▷ the
    growing population
    ^

▷ that
    old neighborhood
    ^

Determiners with plural count nouns or with noncount nouns

Noncount and plural count nouns sometimes have determiners and sometimes do not. For example, *This research is important* and *Research is important* are both acceptable but have different meanings.

Remembering which determiners go with which types of noun

The chart following describes which determiners can be used with which types of nouns.

56d Using articles

Articles (*a, an,* and *the*) are a type of determiner. In English, choosing which article to use — or whether to use an article at all — can be challenging. Although there are exceptions, the following general guidelines can help.

These determiners . . .	. . . can precede these noun types	Examples
a, an, every, each	singular count nouns some proper nouns	*a* book, *an* American *each* word *every* Buddhist
this, that	singular count nouns noncount nouns	*this* book *that* milk
(a) little, much	noncount nouns	*a little* milk *much* affection
some, enough	noncount nouns plural count nouns	*some* milk, *enough* trouble *some* books *enough* problems
the	singular count nouns plural count nouns noncount nouns	*the* doctor *the* doctors *the* information
these, those, (a) few, many, both, several	plural count nouns	*these* books, *those* plans *a few* ideas *many* students *both* hands, *several* trees

Using *a* or *an*

Use *a* and *an*, indefinite articles, with singular count nouns. Use *a* before a consonant sound (*a car*) and *an* before a vowel sound (*an uncle*). Consider sound rather than spelling: *a house, an hour*. Do not use indefinite articles with plural count nouns or with noncount nouns.

A or *an* tells readers they do not have enough information to identify specifically what the noun refers to (in other words, it's an unspecified, or indefinite, noun). The writer may or may not have a particular thing in mind but in either case will use *a* or *an* if the reader lacks the information necessary for identification. Compare these sentences:

▶ I need *a* new coat for the winter.

▶ I saw *a coat* that I liked at Dayton's, but it wasn't heavy enough.

The coat mentioned in the first sentence is hypothetical rather than actual. Since it is indefinite to the writer and the reader, it is used with *a*, not *the*. The second sentence refers to an actual coat, but since the writer cannot expect the reader to know which one, it is used with *a* rather than *the*.

If you want to speak of some indefinite quantity rather than just one indefinite thing, use *some* or *any* with a noncount noun or a plural count noun. Note that *any* is used in negative sentences.

- This stew needs *some* more *salt*.
- I saw *some plates* that I liked at Gump's.
- This stew doesn't need *any* more salt.
- I didn't see *any* plates that I liked at Gump's.

Using the

The definite article *the* is used with both count and noncount nouns whose identity is already known or is about to be made known to readers. The necessary information for identification can come from the noun phrase itself, from elsewhere in the text, from context, from general knowledge, or from a superlative.

- Let's meet at _∧fountain in front of Dwinelle Hall.
          the

  The phrase *in front of Dwinelle Hall* identifies the specific fountain. We know from the use of *the* that there is only one fountain in front of Dwinelle Hall.

- Last Saturday, a fire that started in a restaurant spread to a neighboring clothing store. ~~Store~~ was saved, although it suffered
         The store
  water damage.

  The word *store* is preceded by *the*, which directs our attention to the information in the previous sentence, where the store is first identified.

- She asked him to shut _∧door when he left her office.
          the

  She expects him to understand that she is referring to the door in her office.

The Pope
○ ~~Pope~~ is expected to visit Africa in October.
   ^

There is only one living pope, and *the* before *pope* signals that this sentence refers to him. Similar examples include *the president* (*of the United States*), *the earth*, and *the moon*.

        the
○ Bill is now best singer in the choir.
          ^

The superlative *best* identifies the noun *singer*.

Using the zero article

If a noun appears without *the*, *a* or *an*, or any other determiner (even if it is preceded by other adjectives), it is said to have a zero article. The zero article can be used with plural count nouns (*plans*, *assignments*), noncount nouns (*homework*, *information*), and proper nouns (*Carmen*, *New York*). With plural count nouns and noncount nouns, the zero article is used to make generalizations.

○ In this world nothing is certain but death and taxes.
                                              —BENJAMIN FRANKLIN

The zero article indicates that Franklin refers not to a particular death or specific taxes but to death and taxes in general.

Here English differs from many other languages that would use the definite article to make generalizations. In English, a sentence like *The snakes are dangerous* can refer only to particular, identifiable snakes, not to snakes in general.

It is sometimes possible to make general statements with *the* or *a/an* and singular count nouns.

○ *First-year college students* are confronted with many new experiences.
○ *A first-year student* is confronted with many new experiences.
○ *The first-year student* is confronted with many new experiences.

These sentences all make the same general statement, but the emphasis of each sentence is different. The first sentence refers to first-year college students as a group, the second focuses on a hypothetical

Modifier Type	Arrangement	Examples
determiners	at the beginning of the noun phrase	*these* old-fashioned tiles
all or *both*	before any other determiners	*all* these tiles
numbers	after any other determiners	these *six* tiles
noun modifiers	directly before the noun	these *kitchen* tiles
adjectives	between determiners and noun modifiers	these *old-fashioned* kitchen tiles
phrases or clauses	after the noun	the tiles *on the wall* the tiles *that we bought*

student taken at random, and the third sentence, which is characteristic of formal written style, projects the image of a typical student as representative of the whole class.

56e Arranging modifiers

Modifiers are words that give more information about a noun; that is, they *modify* the meaning of the noun in some way. Some modifiers precede the noun, and others follow it, as indicated in the chart above.

If there are two or more adjectives, their order is variable, but English has strong preferences, described below.

- Subjective adjectives (those that show the writer's opinion) go before objective adjectives (those that merely describe): *these beautiful old-fashioned kitchen tiles.*

- Adjectives of size generally come early: *these beautiful large old-fashioned kitchen tiles.*

- Adjectives of color generally come late: *these beautiful large old-fashioned blue kitchen tiles.*

- Adjectives derived from proper nouns or from nouns that refer to materials generally come after color terms and right before noun modifiers: *these beautiful large old-fashioned blue Portuguese ceramic kitchen tiles.*

- All other objective adjectives go in the middle, and adjectives for which no order is preferred are separated by commas: *these beautiful large decorative, heat-resistant, old-fashioned blue Portuguese ceramic kitchen tiles.*

Of course, the very long noun phrases presented as illustrations above would be out of place in most kinds of writing. Academic and professional types of writing tend to avoid long strings of adjectives.

EXERCISE 56.1

Each of the following sentences contains an error. Rewrite each sentence correctly.

1. Before a middle of the nineteenth century, surgery was usually a terrifying, painful ordeal.
2. Because anesthesia did not exist yet, only painkiller available for surgical patients was whiskey.
3. The pain of surgical procedures could be so severe that much people were willing to die rather than have surgery.
4. In 1846, one of the hospital in Boston gave ether to a patient before he had surgery.
5. The patient, who had a large on his neck tumor, slept peacefully as doctors removed it.

EXERCISE 56.2

Insert articles as necessary in the following passage from *The Silent Language*, by Edward T. Hall. Some blanks may not need an article.

Hollywood is famous for hiring _____ various experts to teach _____ people technically what most of us learn informally. _____ case in point is _____ story about _____ children of one movie couple who noticed _____ new child in _____ neighborhood climbing _____ tree. _____ children immediately wanted to be given _____ name of his instructor in _____ tree climbing.

57 Verbs and Verb Phrases

Verbs can be called the heartbeat of every language, but in English the metaphor is especially meaningful: in most cases, you cannot leave the verb out of an English sentence without killing it. Aside from a few stylistic exceptions, all written English sentences must include a verb. For more discussion of form and tense, see Chapter 30; for help making verbs agree with subjects, see Chapter 31.

Some of the distinctive features of English verbs include modals, perfect tenses, and progressive forms.

57a Forming verb phrases

Verb phrases can be built up out of a main verb and one or more auxiliaries (30b).

- **Immigration figures *rise* every year.**
- **Immigration figures *are rising* every year.**
- **Immigration figures *have risen* every year.**
- **Immigration figures *have been rising* every year.**

Verb phrases have strict rules of order. If you try to rearrange the words in any of these sentences, you will find that most alternatives are impossible. You cannot say *Immigration figures rising are every year* or *Immigration figures been have rising every year*. The only permissible change to word order is to form a question, moving the first auxiliary to the beginning of the sentence: *Have immigration figures been rising every year?*

1 Order of auxiliary verbs

In the sentence *Immigration figures may have been rising*, the main verb *rising* follows three auxiliaries: *may*, *have*, and *been*. Together these auxiliaries and main verb make up a verb phrase.

- *May* is a modal (57b) that indicates possibility; it is followed by the base form of a verb.

- *Have* is an auxiliary verb (30b) that in this case indicates the perfect tense (30e); it must be followed by a past participle (*been*).

- Any form of *be*, when it is followed by a present participle ending in -*ing* (such as *rising*), indicates the progressive tense (30a and e).

- *Be* followed by a past participle, as in *New immigration policies have been passed in recent years*, indicates the passive voice (43b).

As shown in the following chart, when two or more auxiliaries appear in a verb phrase, they must follow a particular order based on the type of auxiliary: (1) modal, (2) a form of *have* used to indicate a perfect tense, (3) a form of *be* used to indicate a progressive tense, and (4) a form of *be* used to indicate the passive voice. (Very few sentences include all four kinds of auxiliaries.)

	Modal	Perfect *Have*	Progressive *Be*	Passive *Be*	Main Verb	
Sonia	—	has	—	been	invited	to visit a family in Prague.
She	should	—	—	be	finished	with school soon.
The invitation	must	have	—	been	sent	in the spring.
She	—	has	been	—	studying	Czech.
She	may	—	be	—	feeling	nervous.
She	might	have	been	—	expecting	to travel elsewhere.
The trip	will	have	been		planned	for a month by the time she leaves.

Only one modal is permitted in a verb phrase.

> *be able to*
> ○ She will ~~can~~ speak Czech much better soon.
>   ^

2 Auxiliary verb forms

Whenever you use an auxiliary, check the form of the word that follows. The guidelines that follow describe the appropriate forms.

Modal + base form

Use the base form of a verb after *can, could, will, would, shall, should, may, might,* and *must.*

○ Alice *can read* Latin.

○ Sanjay *should have* studied for the test.

○ They *must be* going to a fine school.

In many other languages, modals such as *can* and *must* are followed by an infinitive (*to* + base form). In English, only the base form follows a modal.

○ Alice can ~~to~~ read Latin.

Notice that a modal auxiliary can express tense (for example, *can* or *could*), but it never changes form to agree with the subject.

Perfect have + past participle

To form the perfect tenses, use *have, has,* or *had* with a past participle.

○ Everyone *has gone* home.

○ They *have been* working all day.

Progressive be + present participle

A progressive form of a verb is signaled by two elements, a form of the auxiliary *be* (*am, is, are, was, were, be,* or *been*) and the *-ing* form of the next word: *The children are studying.*

> *are*
> ○ The children studying in school.
>   ^

> studying
> ◯ The children are ~~study~~ in school.
>   ^

Some verbs are rarely used in progressive forms. These verbs express unchanging conditions or mental states rather than deliberate actions: *believe, belong, hate, know, like, love, need, own, resemble, understand.*

Passive be + past participle

Use *am, is, are, was, were, being, be,* or *been* with a past participle to form the passive voice.

◯ Tagalog *is spoken* in the Philippines.

Notice that with the progressive *be* the following word (the present participle) ends in *-ing,* but with the passive *be* the following word (the past participle) never ends in *-ing.*

◯ Meredith *is studying* music.
◯ Natasha *was taught* by a famous violinist.

If the first auxiliary in a verb phrase is *be* or *have,* it must show either present or past tense, and it must agree with the subject: *Meredith has played in an orchestra* or *Meredith had played in an orchestra before she joined the band.*

57b Using modals

The nine basic modal auxiliaries are *can, could, will, would, shall, should, may, might,* and *must.* There are a few others as well, in particular *ought to,* which is close in meaning to *should.* Occasionally *need* can be a modal rather than a main verb.

The nine basic modals fall into the pairs *can/could, will/would, shall/should, may/might,* and the loner *must.* In earlier English, the second member of each pair was the past tense of the first. To a limited degree, the second form still functions as a past tense, especially in the case of *could.*

◯ Ingrid *can* ski.
◯ Ingrid *could* ski when she was five.

But, for the most part, in present-day English, all nine modals typically refer to present or future time. When you want to use a modal to refer to the past, you follow the modal with a perfect auxiliary.

▶ If you have a fever, you *should see* a doctor.

▶ If you had a fever, you *should have seen* a doctor.

In the case of *must*, refer to the past by using *had to*.

▶ You *must* renew your visa by the end of this week.

▶ You *had to* renew your visa by the end of last week.

Using modals to make requests or to give instructions

Modals are often used in requests and instructions. Imagine making the following request of a flight attendant:

▶ *Will* you bring me a pillow?

This request may appear demanding or rude. Using a modal makes the request more polite by acknowledging that fulfilling the request may not be possible.

▶ *Can* you bring me a pillow?

Another way of softening the request is to use the past form of *will*, and the most discreet choice is the past form of *can*.

▶ *Would* you bring me a pillow?

▶ *Could* you bring me a pillow?

Using the past tense of modals is considered more polite than using their present forms because it makes any statement or question less assertive.

Consider the meanings of each of the following instructions:

1. You *can* submit your report electronically.

2. You *may* submit your report electronically.

3. You *should* submit your report electronically.

4. You *must* submit your report electronically.

5. You *will* submit your report electronically.

Instructions 1 and 2 give permission to submit the report electronically but do not require it; of these, 2 is more formal. Instruction 3 adds a strong recommendation; 4 allows no alternative; and 5 implies, "Don't even think of doing otherwise."

Using modals to indicate doubt or certainty

Modals can also indicate how confident the writer is about his or her claims. Look at the following set of examples, which starts with a tentative suggestion and ends with an indication of complete confidence:

▶ The study *might* help explain the findings of previous research.

▶ The study *may* help explain the findings of previous research.

▶ The study *will* help explain the findings of previous research.

57c   Indicating tenses

Every English sentence must have at least one verb or verb phrase that is not an infinitive (*to write*), a gerund (*writing*), or a participle (*written*) without any auxiliaries. Furthermore, every such verb or verb phrase must have a tense (30e).

In some languages, such as Chinese and Vietnamese, the verb form never changes regardless of when the action takes place. In English, the time of the action must be clearly indicated by the tense form of every verb, even if the time is obvious or it is indicated elsewhere in the sentence.

▶ During the Cultural Revolution, millions of young people ~~cannot~~ go [could not] to school and ~~are~~ sent to the countryside. [were]

▶ Last night I ~~call~~ my aunt who ~~live~~ in Santo Domingo. [called] [lives]

Direct and indirect quotations

Changing direct quotations to indirect quotations can sometimes lead to tense shifts.

DIRECT	She said, "My work *is* now complete."
INDIRECT	She *told* me that her work *was* now complete.
INDIRECT	She *tells* me that her work *is* now complete.

In general, the verb introducing the indirect quotation (sometimes called the reporting verb) will agree in tense with the verb in the indirect quotation; there are, however, some exceptions. For example, if the reporting verb is in the past tense but the information that follows holds true in the present, shifting to a present-tense verb is acceptable.

▷ She *told* me that her work *is* as exciting as ever.

In academic writing, reporting verbs are used regularly to refer to ideas from other texts or authors. Depending on the documentation style you use, you will probably use the present tense, the present perfect tense, or the simple past for these verbs.

Lee *claims* that . . .
Lee *writes* . . .
Lee *has argued* that . . .
Lee *found* that . . .

57d Forming perfect and progressive verb phrases

The perfect and progressive auxiliaries combine with the present or past tense, or with modals, to form complex verb phrases with special meanings (30f).

Distinguishing the simple present and the present perfect

▷ My sister *drives* a bus.

The simple present (*drives*) merely tells us about the sister's current occupation. But if you were to add the phrase *for three years*, it would be incorrect to say *My sister drives a bus for three years*. Instead, you need a time frame that goes from the past up to the present. The present perfect or present perfect progressive expresses this time frame.

▷ My sister *has driven* a bus for three years.

▷ My sister *has been driving* a bus for three years.

Distinguishing the simple past and the present perfect

◯ Since she started working, she *has bought* a car and a DVD player.

The clause introduced by *since* sets up a time frame that runs from past to present and requires the present perfect (*has bought*) in the subsequent clause. Furthermore, the sentence does not say exactly when she bought the car or the DVD player, and that indefiniteness also calls for the perfect. It would be less correct to say *Since she started working, she bought a car and a DVD player.* But if you say when she bought the car, you should use the simple past tense.

◯ She *bought* the car two years ago.

It would be incorrect to say *She has bought the car two years ago* because the perfect cannot be used with definite expressions of time. In this case, use the simple past (*bought*).

Distinguishing the simple present and the present progressive

Use the present progressive tense when an action is in progress at the present moment. In contrast, use the simple present for actions that frequently occur during a period of time that might include the present moment (though the simple present does not necessarily indicate that the action is taking place now).

◯ My sister *drives* a bus, but she *is taking* a vacation now.
◯ My sister *drives* a bus, but she *takes* a vacation every year.

Many languages use the simple present (*drives, takes*) for both types of sentences. In English, however, the first sentence would be incorrect if it said *but she takes a vacation now.*

Distinguishing the simple past and the past progressive

◯ Sally *spent* the summer in Ecuador.

The simple past tense is used in this case because the action occurred in the past and is now finished.

The past progressive tense is used relatively infrequently in English. It is used to focus on duration or continuousness and especially to call attention to past action that went on at the same time as something else.

○ Sally *was spending* the summer in Ecuador when she *met* her future husband.

57e Using participial adjectives

Many verbs refer to feelings—for example, *bore, confuse, excite, fascinate, frighten, interest.* The present and past participles of such verbs can be used as ordinary adjectives (see 29c3). Use the past participle to describe a person having the feeling.

○ The *frightened* boy started to cry.

Use the present participle to describe the thing (or person) causing the feeling.

○ The *frightening* dinosaur movie gave him nightmares.

Be careful not to confuse the two types of adjectives.

                    interested
○ I am ~~interesting~~ in African literature.
      ^

                              interesting.
○ African literature seems ~~interested.~~
                          ^

EXERCISE 57.1

Each of the following sentences contains an error. Rewrite each sentence correctly.

1. Over the past forty years, average temperatures in the Arctic increase by several degrees.

2. A few years ago, a robin was observe in Inuit territory in northern Canada.

3. Inuit people in previous generations will never have seen a robin near their homes.

4. The Inuit language, which called *Inuktitut*, has no word for *robin*.

5. Many Inuits are concerning that warmer temperatures may change their way of life.

EXERCISE 57.2

Rewrite the following passage, adapted from "Cold Comfort" by Atul Gawande (*New Yorker*, March 11, 2002), adding appropriate auxiliaries and verb endings where necessary. The total number of words required in each case is indicated in parentheses.

The notion that a chill _____ (*put*—1) you at risk of catching a

cold is nearly universal. Yet science _____ (*find*—2) no evidence

for it. One of the first studies on the matter _____ (*lead*—2) by Sir

Christopher Andrewes. He _____ (*take*—1) a group of volunteers and

_____ (*inoculate*—1) them with a cold virus; previously, half of the

group _____ (*keep*—3) warm, and the other half _____

(*make*—3) to take a bath and then to stand for half an hour without a towel

while the wind _____ (*blow*—2) on them. The chilled group

_____ (*get*—1) no more colds than the warm group.

bedfordstmartins.com/smhandbook
Exercise Central > For Multilingual Writers > Verbs

58 Prepositions and Prepositional Phrases

You will need to decide which preposition to use for your intended meaning and understand how to use verbs that include prepositions, such as *take off*, *pick up*, and *put up with*.

58a Using prepositions idiomatically

Even if you know where to use a preposition in a sentence, it can be difficult to determine which preposition to use. Each of the most common prepositions has a wide range of applications, and this range never coincides exactly from one language to another. See, for example, how *in* and *on* are used in English.

- The peaches are *in* the refrigerator.
- The peaches are *on* the table.
- Is that a diamond ring *on* your finger?

If you speak Spanish

The Spanish translations of these sentences all use the same preposition (*en*), a fact that might lead you astray in English.

- Is that a ruby ring ~~in~~ your finger?

  on

There is no easy solution to the challenge of using English prepositions idiomatically, but the following strategies can make it less troublesome.

QUICK HELP

Strategies for using prepositions idiomatically

1. **Keep in mind typical examples of each preposition.**

   IN
   The peaches are *in* the refrigerator.
   There are still some pickles *in* the jar.
   The book you are looking for is *in* the bookcase.

   Here the object of the preposition *in* is a container that encloses something.

   ON
   The peaches are *on* the table.
   There are still some pickles *on* the plate.
   The book you are looking for is *on* the top shelf.

   Here the object of the preposition *on* is a horizontal surface that supports something with which it is in direct contact.

2. **Learn other examples that show some similarities and some differences in meaning.**

   IN
   You shouldn't drive *in* a snowstorm.

   Here there is no container, but like a container, the falling snow surrounds the driver. The preposition *in* is used for other weather-related expressions as well: *in a tornado*, *in the sun*, *in the rain*.

   ON
   Is that a diamond ring *on* your finger?

   The preposition *on* is used to describe things we wear: *the hat on his head*, *the shoes on her feet*, *the tattoo on his back*.

3. **Use your imagination to create mental images that can help you remember figurative uses of prepositions.**

   IN
   Michael is *in* love.

   The preposition *in* is often used to describe a state of being: *in love*, *in pain*, *in a panic*. As a way to remember this, you might imagine the person immersed *in* this state of being.

4. **Try to learn prepositions not in isolation but as part of a system.** For example, in identifying the location of a place or an event, you can use the three prepositions *at*, *in*, and *on*.

   At specifies the exact point in space or time.

   AT
   There will be a meeting tomorrow *at* 9:30 AM *at* 160 Main Street.

(continued on p. 818)

(continued from p. 817)

Expanses of space or time within which a place is located or an event takes place might be seen as containers and so require *in*.

IN   I arrived *in* the United States *in* January.

On must be used in two cases: with the names of streets (but not the exact address) and with days of the week or month.

ON   The airline's office is *on* Fifth Avenue.
           I'll be moving to my new apartment *on* September 30.

EXERCISE 58.1

Insert prepositions as necessary in the following paragraph.

The children's soccer game happened _____ 10:00 _____ Saturday morning. The families sat _____ blankets to watch the game. Everyone was _____ a good mood. When the game ended, both teams stood _____ a circle to cheer.

58b Using two-word verbs idiomatically

Some words that look like prepositions do not always function as prepositions. Consider the following two sentences:

◯ **The balloon rose *off* the ground.**
◯ **The plane took *off* without difficulty.**

In the first sentence, *off* is a preposition that introduces the prepositional phrase *off the ground*. In the second sentence, *off* does not function as a preposition. Instead, it combines with *took* to form a two-word verb with its own meaning. Such a verb is called a phrasal verb, and the word *off*, when used in this way, is called an adverbial particle. Many prepositions can function as particles to form phrasal verbs.

The verb + particle combination that makes up a phrasal verb is a single entity that usually cannot be torn apart.

off
◯ **The plane took without difficulty.~~off.~~**
        ^   ^

The exceptions are the many phrasal verbs that are transitive, meaning that they take a direct object (29c2). Some transitive phrasal verbs have particles that may be separated from the verb by the object.

- I *picked up my baggage* at the terminal.
- I *picked my baggage up* at the terminal.

If a personal pronoun (such as *it*, *her*, or *him*) is used as the direct object, it must separate the verb from its particle.

- I *picked it up* at the terminal.

Some idiomatic two-word verbs, however, are not phrasal verbs.

- We *ran into* our neighbor on the train.

In such verbs, the second word is a preposition, which cannot be separated from the verb. For example, it is not correct to say *We ran our neighbor into on the train*. Verbs like *run into* are called prepositional verbs, which are another kind of two-word verb.

In this sample sentence, *ran into* consists of the verb *ran* followed by the preposition *into*, which introduces the prepositional phrase *into our neighbor*. Yet *to run into our neighbor* is different from a normal verb + prepositional phrase, such as *to run into the room*. If you know the typical meanings of *run* and *into*, you can interpret *to run into the room*. Not so with *to run into our neighbor*; the combination *run + into* has a special meaning ("find by chance") that could not be determined from the typical meanings of *run* and *into*.

Prepositional verbs include such idiomatic two-word verbs as *take after*, meaning "resemble" (usually a parent or other older relative); *get over*, meaning "recover from"; and *count on*, meaning "trust." They also include verb + preposition combinations in which the meaning is predictable, but the specific preposition that is required is less predictable and must be learned together with the verb (for example, *depend on, look at, listen to, approve of*). There are also phrasal-prepositional verbs, which are verb + adverbial particle + preposition sequences (for example, *put up with, look forward to, give up on, get away with*).

EXERCISE 58.2

Each of the following sentences contains a two-word verb. In some sentences, the verb is used correctly; in others, it is used incorrectly. Identify each two-word verb, indicate whether it is a phrasal or prepositional verb, and rewrite any incorrect sentences correctly.

1. Soon after I was hired for my last job, I learned that the company might lay off me.

2. I was counting on the job to pay my way through school, so I was upset.

3. I decided to pick up a newspaper and see what other jobs were available.

4. As I looked the newspaper at, I was surprised to see that I was qualified for a job that paid much better than mine.

5. I gave my old job up and took the new one, which made attending school much easier.

---

bedfordstmartins.com/smhandbook
Exercise Central > For Multilingual Writers > Prepositions

ACADEMIC AND
PROFESSIONAL
WRITING

Part 12

59 Academic Work in Any Discipline

As you prepare essays or other written assignments for various courses, you will need to become familiar with the discourse — the expectations, vocabularies, styles, methods of proof, and conventional formats — used in each field.

59a Writing in any discipline

Students in the humanities tend to expect that writing will play a central role in their education; students in other areas sometimes imagine that writing will be of secondary importance to them. Yet faculty working in engineering, the sciences, social sciences, business, and other areas have a different understanding:

> Is writing important in chemistry? Don't chemists spend their time turning knobs, mixing reagents, and collecting data? They still get to do those things, but professional scientists also make presentations, prepare reports, publish results, and submit proposals. Each of these activities involves writing. If you remain skeptical about the need for writing skills, then ask your favorite professor, or any other scientist, to track the fraction of one workday spent using a word-processing program. You (and they) may be surprised at the answer.
>
> —OREGON STATE UNIVERSITY, *Writing Guide for Chemistry*

A student pursuing an education major agrees: "Writing is the key to just about everything I do, from constructing lesson plans to writing reviews of literature to learning to respond — in writing — to the students I will eventually teach."

As these statements suggest, writing is central to learning regardless of the discipline; in addition, writing plays a major role in the life of every working professional. So whether you are preparing a lab report for biology, conducting a case study for anthropology, or applying for an internship, writing well will help you achieve your goals.

59b Reading in any discipline

As you move through your college years, your ability to read and comprehend texts will be central to your success. As you already know, reading isn't a "one size fits all" activity: you will need to adjust your reading strategies to fit the task at hand. Most of the time, your instructors probably won't give you specific instruction in how to read these texts; they will simply assume that you know how.

The more you read in a discipline, the easier you will find it to understand. So read a lot, and pay attention to the texts you are reading. To get started, choose an article in an important journal in the field you plan to major in and then answer the following questions:

- How does a journal article in this discipline begin?

- How is the article organized? Does it have specific sections with subheads?

- What sources are cited, and how are they used — as backup support, as counter-examples, or as an argument to refute?

- What audience does the text seem to address? Is it a narrow technical or disciplinary audience, or is it aimed at a broader reading public? Is it addressed to readers of a specific journal? Is it published electronically and intended for an international readership?

- How is the text formatted, and what citation style does it use?

- How are visuals such as charts or graphs used?

Finally, make sure you know whether articles you are reading are from juried or nonjuried journals (11a2). Juried journals use panels of expert readers to analyze proposed articles and recommend publication (or not) to the journal editor, so articles in juried journals have been examined and accepted by experts in the field. Nonjuried journals can also offer valuable information, but they may bear the stamp of the editor and that person's biases more strongly than a juried journal would.

For additional guidelines on reading critically, see Chapter 7.

59c Understanding academic assignments

Since academic assignments vary widely from course to course and even from professor to professor, the tips this section offers can only be general. For any discipline, make sure you are in control of the assignment rather than letting the assignment be in control of you. To take control, you need to understand the assignment fully and to understand what professors in the particular discipline expect in response.

When you receive an assignment, make sure you understand what that assignment is asking you to do. Some assignments may be as vague as "Write a five-page essay on one aspect of the Civil War" or "Write an analysis of the group dynamics at play in your recent collaborative project for this course." Others may be fairly specific: "Collect, summarize, and interpret data drawn from a sample of letters to the editor published in two newspapers, one in a small rural community and one in an urban community, over a period of three months. Organize your research report according to APA requirements." Whatever the assignment, you must take charge of analyzing it.

QUICK HELP

Analyzing an assignment

- *What is the purpose of the assignment?*

- *Who is the audience?* The instructor will be one audience, but are there others? If so, who are they?

- *What does the assignment ask of you?* Look for key terms such as *summarize*, *explain*, *evaluate*, *interpret*, *illustrate*, and *define*.

- *Do you need clarification of any terms?* If so, ask your instructor.

- *What do you need to know or find out to complete the assignment?* You may need to do background reading, develop a procedure for analyzing or categorizing information, or carry out some other kind of preparation.

- *What does the instructor expect in a written response?* How will you use sources (both written and visual)? How should you organize and develop the assignment? What is the expected format and length?

- *Can you find a model of an effective response to a similar assignment?*

- *What do other students think the assignment requires?* Talking over an assignment with classmates is one good way to test your understanding.

EXERCISE 59.1

Analyze the following assignment from a communications course using the questions in 59c.

Assignment: Distribute a questionnaire to twenty people (ten male, ten female) asking these four questions: (1) What do you expect to say and do when you meet a stranger? (2) What don't you expect to say and do when you meet a stranger? (3) What do you expect to say and do when you meet a very close friend? (4) What don't you expect to say and do when you meet a very close friend?

When you have collected your twenty questionnaires, read them over and answer the following questions:

- What, if any, descriptions were common to all respondents' answers?
- How do male and female responses compare?
- What similarities and differences did you find between the responses to the stranger and to the very close friend?
- What factors (environment, time, status, gender, and so on) do you think had an impact on these responses?

Discuss your findings, using concepts and theories explained in your text.

59d Learning specialized vocabulary

Entering into an academic discipline or a profession is like going to a party where you do not know anyone. At first you feel like an outsider, and you may not understand much of what you hear or see. Before you enter the conversation, you have to listen and observe carefully. Eventually, however, you will be able to join in — and if you stay long enough, participating in the conversation becomes easy and natural.

To learn the routines, practices, and ways of knowing in a new field, you must also make an effort to enter into the conversation, and that means taking action. One good way to get started is to study the vocabulary of the field you are most interested in.

Highlight the key terms in your reading or notes to learn how much specialized or technical vocabulary you will be expected to know. If you find only a small amount of specialized vocabulary, try to master the new terms quickly by reading your textbook carefully, looking up key words or phrases, and asking questions. If you find a great deal of specialized vocabulary, however, you may want to familiarize yourself with it methodically. Any of the following procedures may help:

- Keep a log of unfamiliar or confusing words *in context*. Check definitions in your textbook's glossary or index, or consult a specialized dictionary.

- Review your class notes each day. Underline important terms, review definitions, and identify anything that is unclear. Use your textbook or ask questions to clarify anything confusing before the class moves on to a new topic.

- See if your textbook has a glossary of terms or sets off definitions. Study pertinent sections to master the terms.

- Try to use and work with key concepts. Even if they are not yet entirely clear to you, working with them will help you understand them. For example, in a statistics class, try to work out (in words) how to do an analysis of *covariance*, step by step, even if you are not sure of the precise definition of the term. Or try to plot the narrative progression in a story even if you are still not entirely sure of the definition of *narrative progression*.

- Find the standard dictionaries or handbooks of terms for your field. Ask your instructor or a librarian for help.

- Take special note of the ways technical language or disciplinary vocabulary are used in online information related to a particular field.

Whatever your techniques for learning a specialized vocabulary, begin to use the new terms whenever you can—in class, in discussions with instructors and other students, and in your assignments. This ability to use what you learn in speaking and writing is crucial to your full understanding of and participation in the discipline.

59e Following disciplinary style

Another important way to learn about a discipline is to identify its stylistic features. Study some pieces of writing in the field with the following in mind:

- *Overall tone.* How would you describe it? (See 4i)

- *Title.* Are titles generally descriptive ("Findings from a Double-Blind Study of the Effect of Antioxidants"), persuasive ("Antioxidants Proven Effective"), or something else? How does the title shape your expectations?

TALKING THE TALK

The first person

"Is it true that I should never use *I* in college writing?" In much writing in college, using the first-person *I* is perfectly acceptable to most instructors. As always, think about the context—if your own experience is relevant to the topic, you are better off saying *I* than trying too hard not to. But don't overdo it, especially if the writing isn't just autobiographical. And check with your instructor if you aren't sure: in certain academic disciplines, such as the natural sciences, using *I* may be seen as inappropriate.

- *Stance.* To what extent do writers in the field strive for distance and objectivity? What strategies help them to achieve this stance? (See 2c2.)

- *Sentence length.* Are sentences long and complex? Simple and direct?

- *Voice.* Are verbs generally active or passive? Why? (See 30g.)

- *Person.* Do writers use the first-person *I* or third-person terms such as *the investigator*? What is the effect of this choice? (See the box above.)

- *Visuals.* Do writers typically use elements such as graphs, tables, maps, or photographs? How are visuals integrated into the text? How are they labeled? What role, if any, do headings and other formatting elements play in the writing?

- *Documentation style.* Do writers use MLA, APA, *Chicago*, or CSE style? (See Chapters 16–19.)

Of course, writings within a single discipline may have different purposes and different styles. A chemist may write a grant proposal, a lab notebook, a literature review, a research report, and a lab report, each with a different purpose and style.

59f Using appropriate evidence

What is acceptable and persuasive evidence in one discipline may be less so in another. Observable, quantifiable data may constitute the best evidence in experimental psychology, but the same kind of data may be less appropriate — or impossible to come by — in a historical study. An engineering proposal will be backed up with drawings, maps, and detailed calculations. A case study in cultural anthropology, on the other hand, may depend almost entirely on interview data. As you grow familiar with an area of study, you will develop a sense of what it takes to prove a point in that field. You can speed up this process, however, by investigating and questioning. The following questions will help you think about the use of evidence in materials you read:

- How do writers in the field use precedent and authority? What or who counts as an authority in this field? How are the credentials of an authority established? (See 9e.)

- What kinds of quantitative data (countable or measurable items) are used, and for what purposes? How are the data gathered and presented?

- How are qualitative data (systematically observed items) used?

- How are statistics used and presented? Are tables, charts, graphs, or other visuals important, and why?

- How is logical reasoning used? How are definition, cause and effect, analogy, and example used?

- How does the field use primary and secondary sources? (See 11a1.) What are the primary and secondary materials? How is each type of source presented?

- What kinds of textual evidence are cited?

- How are quotations and other references to sources used and integrated into the text? (See Chapter 13.)

In addition to carrying out your own investigation, ask your instructor how you can best go about making a case in this field.

EXERCISE 59.2

Read a few journals associated with your prospective major or a discipline of particular interest to you, using the preceding questions to study the use of evidence in that discipline. If you are keeping a writing log, make an entry summarizing what you have learned.

59g   Using conventional patterns and formats

To produce effective writing in a discipline, you need to know the field's generally accepted formats for organizing and presenting evidence. A typical laboratory report, for instance, follows a fairly standard organizational framework and usually has a certain look (see 62c for an example). A case study in sociology or education or anthropology likewise follows a typical organizational plan.

Ask your instructor to recommend some excellent examples of the kind of writing you will do in the course. Then analyze these examples in terms of format and organization. You might also look at major scholarly journals in the field to see what types of formats seem most common and how each is organized. Consider the following questions about organization and format:

- What types of articles, reports, or documents are common in this field? What is the purpose of each?

- What can a reader expect to find in each type of writing? What does each type assume about its readers?

- Do articles or other documents typically begin with an abstract? If so, does the abstract describe the parts of the article to come, or does it provide substantive information such as findings or conclusions? (For an example of an abstract from a professional journal, see p. 831; for a student's abstract, see 17e.)

- How is each type of text organized? What are its main parts? How are they labeled?

- How does a particular type of essay, report, or document show the connections among ideas? What assumptions does it take for granted? What points does it emphasize?

Remember that there is a close connection between the writing patterns and formats a particular area of study uses and the work that scholars in that field undertake.

59h   Making ethical decisions

Writers in all disciplines face ethical questions. Those who plan and carry out research on living people, for example, must be careful to avoid harming their subjects. Researchers in all fields must be scrupulous in presenting data to make sure that others can replicate research and test claims. And although writers in any discipline should take into consideration their own interests, those of their collaborators, and those of their employers, they must also responsibly safeguard the interests of the general public.

Fortunately, a growing number of disciplines have adopted guidelines for ethics. The American Psychological Association has been a pioneer in this area, and many other professional organizations and companies have their own codes or standards of ethics. These guidelines can help you make decisions about day-to-day writing. Even so, you will no doubt encounter situations where the right or ethical decision is murky at best. In such situations, consult your own conscience first and then talk your choices over with colleagues you respect before coming to a decision on how to proceed.

59i Collaborating and communicating

In contemporary academic and business environments, working with others is a highly valued skill. Such collaboration happens when classmates divide research and writing duties to create a multimedia presentation, when peer reviewers share advice on a draft, or when colleagues in an office offer their views on appropriate revisions for a company-wide document.

Because people all over the world now have the ability to research, study, write, and work together, you must be able to communicate effectively within and across cultures. Conventions for academic writing (or for forms of online communication) can vary from culture to culture, from discipline to discipline, and from one form of English to another. What is considered polite in one culture may seem rude in another, so those who communicate globally must take care to avoid giving offense — or taking it where none was intended. (For more information on writing across cultures, see Chapter 24.)

THINKING CRITICALLY ABOUT READING AND WRITING IN A DISCIPLINE

Reading with an Eye for Disciplinary Discourse

The following abstract introduces an article titled "Development of the Appearance-Reality Distinction." This article appeared in *Cognitive Psychology*, a specialized academic journal for researchers in the subfield of psychology that focuses on human cognition. Read this abstract carefully to see what you can infer about the discourse of cognitive psychology—about its characteristic vocabulary, style, use of evidence, and so on.

Young children can express conceptual difficulties with the appearance-reality distinction in two different ways: (1) by incorrectly reporting appearance when asked to report reality ("phenomenism"); (2) by incorrectly reporting reality when asked to report appearance ("intellectual realism"). Although both phenomenism errors and intellectual realism errors have been observed in previous studies of young children's cognition, the two have not been seen as conceptually related and only the former errors have been taken as a symptom of difficulties with the appearance-reality distinction. Three experiments investigated 3- to 5-year-old children's ability to distinguish between and correctly identify real versus apparent object properties (color, size, and shape), object identities, object presence-absence, and action identities. Even the 3-year-olds appeared to have some ability to make correct appearance-reality discriminations and this ability increased with age. Errors were frequent, however, and almost all children who erred made both kinds. Phenomenism errors predominated on tasks where the appearance versus reality of the three object properties was in question; intellectual realism errors predominated on the other three types of tasks. Possible reasons for this curious error pattern were advanced. It was also suggested that young children's problems with the appearance-reality distinction may be partly due to a specific metacognitive limitation, namely, a difficulty in analyzing the nature and source of their own mental representations.
                —JOHN H. FLAVELL, ELEANOR R. FLAVELL, AND FRANCES L. GREEN,
                                                        Cognitive Psychology

Thinking about Your Own Writing in a Discipline

Choose a piece of writing you have produced for a class in a particular discipline—a blog or other posting, a laboratory report, a review of the literature, or any other written assignment. Examine your writing closely for its use of that discipline's vocabulary, style, methods of proof, and conventional formats. How comfortable are you writing a piece of this kind? In what ways are you using the conventions of the discipline easily and well? What conventions give you difficulty, and why? You might talk to an instructor in this field about the conventions and requirements for writing in the discipline. Make notes about what you learn about being a better writer in the field.

60 Writing for the Humanities

Disciplines in the humanities are concerned with what it means to be *human*. Historians study and reconstruct the past. Literary critics analyze and interpret texts, often to help others explore a text's meaning. Philosophers raise questions about truth, knowledge, beauty, and justice. Scholars of other languages learn not just to speak but to inhabit other cultures. In these and other ways, those in the humanities strive to explore, interpret, and reconstruct the human experience.

In humanities disciplines, the interpretation and creation of texts are central. The nature of texts can vary widely, from poems and plays to novels, articles, philosophical treatises, films, advertisements, paintings, and so on. But whether the text being studied is ancient or modern, literary or historical, verbal or visual, textual analysis plays a critical role in the reading and writing that people in the humanities undertake.

60a Reading texts in the humanities

To read critically in the humanities, you will need to pose questions and construct hypotheses as you read. You may ask, for instance, why a writer might make some points or develop some examples but omit others. Rather than finding meaning only in the surface information that texts or artifacts convey, you should use your own questions and hypotheses to create fuller meanings—to construct the significance of what you read.

Critical reading and interpretation

To successfully engage texts, you must recognize that you are not a neutral observer, not an empty cup into which the meaning of a work is poured. If such were the case, writing would have exactly the same meanings for all of us, and reading would be a fairly boring affair. If you have ever gone to a movie with a friend and each come away with a completely different understanding or response, you already have ample evidence that a text never has just one meaning.

Nevertheless, you may in the past have been willing to accept the first meaning to occur to you—to take a text at face value. Most humanities courses, however, will expect you to exercise your interpretive powers. The following guidelines can help you build your strengths as a close reader of humanities texts.

QUICK HELP

Guidelines for reading texts in the humanities

1. *Be clear about the purpose of the text.* The two most common purposes for works in the humanities are to provide information and to argue for a particular interpretation. Pay attention to whether the text presents opinions or facts, to what is included and omitted, and to how facts are presented to the audience. (12c)

2. *Get an overall impression.* What does the work make you think about—and why? What is most remarkable or memorable? What confuses you?

3. *Annotate the text.* Be prepared to "talk back," ask questions, note emerging patterns or themes, and point out anything out of place or ineffective. (See Chapter 7.)

4. *Look at the context.* Consider the time and place represented in the work as well as when and where the writer lived. You may also consider social, political, or personal forces that may have affected the writer.

5. *Think about the audience.* Who are the readers or viewers the writer seems to address? Do they include you?

6. *Pay attention to genre.* What category does the work fall into (graphic novel, diary, political cartoon, sermon, argumentative essay, Hollywood western)? What is noteworthy about the form? How does it conform to or subvert your expectations about the genre? (2e)

7. *Note the point of view.* Whose point of view is represented? How does it affect your response?

8. *Notice the major themes.* Are specific claims being advanced? How are these claims supported?

9. *Understand the difference between primary and secondary sources.* Primary sources provide firsthand knowledge, while secondary sources report on or analyze the research of others. (11a1)

60b Writing texts in the humanities

Strong writers in the humanities use the findings from their close examination of a text or artifact to develop an argument or to construct an analysis.

Assignments

Common assignments that make use of these skills of close reading, analysis, and argument include summaries, response pieces, position papers, critical analyses of primary and secondary sources, and research-based projects. A philosophy student, for example, might need to summarize an argument, critique a text's logic and effectiveness, or discuss a moral issue from a particular philosophical perspective. A literature assignment may ask a reader to look very closely at a particular text ("Examine the role of chocolate in Toni Morrison's *Tar Baby*") or to go well beyond a primary text ("Discuss the impact of agribusiness on modernist novels"). History students often write books or articles ("Write a critical review of Jane Addams's *Twenty Years at Hull-House*, paying special attention to the writer's purpose and goals and relating these to the larger settlement house movement in America") along with primary source analyses or research papers.

For papers in literature, modern languages, and philosophy, writers often use the documentation style of the Modern Language Association; see Chapter 16 for advice on using MLA style. For papers in history and other areas of the humanities, writers often use the documentation style of the University of Chicago Press; see Chapter 18 for advice on using *Chicago* style.

Analysis and critical stance

To analyze a text, you need to develop a critical stance—the approach you will take to the work—that can help you develop a thesis or major claim (see 3c and 9c). To evaluate the text and present a critical response to it, you should look closely at the text itself, including its style; at the context in which it was produced; and at the audience the text aims to reach, which may or may not include yourself.

A close look at the text itself includes considering its genre, form, point of view, and themes, and looking at the stylistic features, such as word choice, use of imagery, visuals, and design. Considering context means asking why the text was created—thinking about the original (and current) context and about how attitudes and ideas of its era may have influenced it. Considering audience means thinking about who the intended audience might be, and about how people outside this intended group might respond. Think about your personal response to the text as well. (See also Chapters 7 and 8.)

Carrying out these steps should provide you with plenty of material to work with as you begin to shape a critical thesis and write your analysis. You can begin by grounding your analysis in one or more important questions you have about the work.

Writing a literary analysis

When you analyze or interpret a literary work, think of your thesis as answering a question about some aspect of the work. The guiding question you bring to the literary work will help you decide on a critical stance toward the work. For example, a student writing about Shakespeare's *Macbeth* might find her curiosity piqued by the many comic moments that appear in this tragedy. She might turn the question of why Shakespeare uses so much comedy in *Macbeth* into the following thesis statement, which proposes an answer to the question: "The many unexpected comic moments in *Macbeth* emphasize how disordered the world becomes for murderers like Macbeth and his wife."

bedfordstmartins.com/smhandbook
Writing Resources > Writing about Literature

60c A student's close reading of poetry

Student Writer

The following paper, a close reading of two poems by E. E. Cummings, was written by Bonnie Sillay, a student at the University of Georgia. This essay follows MLA style (see Chapter 16). Bonnie is creating her own interpretation, so the only works she cites are the poems she analyzes. Note that this essay has been reproduced in a narrow format to allow for annotation.

Bonnie Sillay

bedfordstmartins.com/smhandbook
Student Writing > Writing in the Disciplines

1" Sillay 1

Bonnie Sillay

Instructor Angela Mitchell

English 1102

December 4, 2010

"Life's Not a Paragraph"

Throughout his poetry, E. E. Cummings leads readers deep into a

thicket of scrambled words, missing punctuation, and unconventional
structure. Within Cummings's poetic bramble, ambiguity leads the reader
through what seems at first a confusing and winding maze. However, this
confusion actually transforms into a path that leads the reader to the
center of the thicket where Cummings's message lies: readers should not
allow their experience to be limited by reason and rationality. In order to
communicate his belief that emotional experience should triumph over

reason, Cummings employs odd juxtapositions, outlandish metaphors,
and inversions of traditional grammatical structures that reveal the illogic
of reason. Indeed, by breaking down such formal boundaries, Cummings's

poems "since feeling is first" and "as freedom is a breakfastfood" suggest
that emotion, which provides the compositional fabric for our experience
of life, should never be defined or controlled.

In "since feeling is first," Cummings urges his reader to reject
attempts to control emotion, using English grammar as one example of

the restrictive conventions present in society. Stating that "since feeling
is first / who pays any attention / to the syntax of things" (lines 1-3),
Cummings suggests that emotion should not be forced to fit into some
preconceived framework or mold. He carries this message throughout the
poem by juxtaposing images of the abstract and the concrete — images

of emotion and of English grammar. Cummings's word choice enhances
his intentionally strange juxtapositions, with the poet using grammatical
terms that suggest regulation or confinement. For example, in the line

"And death i think is no parenthesis" (16), Cummings uses the idea that parentheses confine the words they surround in order to warn the reader not to let death confine life or emotions.

Header on each page

The structure of the poem also rejects traditional conventions. Instead of the final stanzas making the main point, Cummings opens his poem with his primary message, that "feeling is first" (1). Again, Cummings shows that emotion rejects order and structure. How can emotion be bottled in sentences and interrupted by commas, colons, and spaces? To Cummings, emotion is a never-ending run-on sentence that should not be diagrammed or dissected.

Transition sentence connects the previous paragraph to this one

In the third stanza of "since feeling is first," Cummings states his point outright, noting "my blood approves, / and kisses are a better fate / than wisdom" (7-9). Here, Cummings argues for reveling in the feeling during a fleeting moment such as a kiss. He continues, "the best gesture of my brain is less than / your eyelids' flutter" (11-12). Cummings wants the reader to focus on a pure emotive response (the flutter of an eyelash) — on the emotional, not the logical — on the meanings of words instead of punctuation and grammar.

Quotation introduced effectively

Metaphor captures the spirit of Cummings's point

Cummings's use of words such as *kisses* and *blood* (8, 7) adds to the focus on the emotional. The ideas behind these words are difficult to confine or restrict to a single definition: kisses mean different things to different people, blood flows through the body freely and continually. The words are not expansive or free enough to encompass all that they suggest. Cummings ultimately paints language as more restrictive than the flowing, powerful force of emotion.

The poet's use of two grammatical terms in the last lines, "for life's not a paragraph / And death i think is no parenthesis," warns against attempts to format lives and feelings into conventional and rule-bound segments (15-16). Attempts to control, rather than feel, are rejected

Paragraph reiterates Cummings's claim and sums up his argument

Sillay 3

throughout "since feeling is first." Emotion should be limitless, free from
any restrictions or rules.

Clear and
explicit
transition from
discussion of
first poem

While "since feeling is first" argues that emotions should not be
controlled or analyzed, "as freedom is a breakfastfood" suggests the
difficulty of defining emotion. In this poem, Cummings uses deliberately
far-fetched metaphors such as "freedom is a breakfastfood" and "time
is a tree" (1, 26). These metaphors seem arbitrary: Cummings is not
attempting to make profound statements on time or freedom. Instead,
he suggests that freedom and time are subjective, and attempts at
narrow definition are ridiculous. Inversions of nature, such as "robins
never welcome spring" and "water most encourage flame" (16, 7),
underscore emotion's ability to defy reason. These inversions suggest the
arbitrariness of "the syntax of things" (3).

Although most of "as freedom is a breakfastfood" defies logic,
Cummings shifts the tone at the end to deliver one last metaphor: "but
love is the sky" (27). The word *but* separates this definition from the
rest of the poem and subtly implies that, unlike the metaphors that have
come before it, "love is the sky" is an accurate comparison. In order to
reach this final conclusion, however, Cummings has taken his readers on
a long and often ambiguous journey.

Writer returns
to thicket
image from
introduction

Nevertheless, the confusion has been deliberate. Cummings wants
his readers to follow him through the winding path through the thicket
because he believes the path of the straight and narrow limits the
possibilities of experience. Through the unconventionality of his poetic
structures, Cummings urges his readers to question order and tradition.
He wants his readers to realize that reason and rationality are always
secondary to emotion and that emotional experience is a free-flowing
force that should not be constrained. Cummings's poetry suggests that
in order to get at the true essence of something, one must look past the
commonsensical definition and not be limited by "the syntax of things."

Sillay 4

Works Cited

Cummings, E. E. "as freedom is a breakfastfood." *E. E. Cummings: Complete Poems 1904-1962*. Ed. George J. Firmage. New York: Liveright, 1991. 511. Print.

---. "since feeling is first." *E. E. Cummings: Complete Poems 1904-1962*. Ed. George J. Firmage. New York: Liveright, 1991. 291. Print.

Second work by same author uses three hyphens in place of name

since feeling is first

since feeling is first
who pays any attention
to the syntax of things
will never wholly kiss you;

wholly to be a fool
while Spring is in the world

my blood approves,
and kisses are a better fate
than wisdom

lady i swear by all flowers. Don't
    cry
—the best gesture of my brain
    is less than
your eyelids' flutter which says

we are for each other: then
laugh, leaning back in my arms
for life's not a paragraph

And death i think is no
    parenthesis

as freedom is a breakfastfood

as freedom is a breakfastfood
or truth can live with right and
    wrong
or molehills are from mountains
    made
—long enough and just so long
will being pay the rent of seem
and genius please the talentgang
and water most encourage flame

as hatracks into peachtrees grow
or hopes dance best on bald
    men's hair
and every finger is a toe
and any courage is a fear
—long enough and just so long
will the impure think all things
    pure
and hornets wail by children
    stung

or as the seeing are the blind
and robins never welcome spring
nor flatfolk prove their world is
    round
nor dingsters die at break of dong
and common's rare and
    millstones float
—long enough and just so long
tomorrow will not be too late

worms are the words but joy's the
    voice
down shall go which and up come
    who
breasts will be breasts and thighs
    will be thighs
deeds cannot dream what dreams
    can do
—time is a tree (this life one leaf)
but love is the sky and i am for
    you

just so long and long enough

THINKING CRITICALLY ABOUT WRITING IN THE HUMANITIES

Choose at least two projects or assignments you have written for different disciplines in the humanities—say, history and film. Reread these papers with an eye to their similarities. What features do they have in common? Do they use similar methods of analysis and value similar kinds of evidence, for instance? In what ways do they differ? Based on your analysis, what conclusions can you draw about these two disciplines?

61

Writing for the Social Sciences

When do most workers begin to save toward retirement? What role do television ads play in the decision-making process of potential voters? How do children learn to read?

The social sciences — which include psychology, anthropology, political science, speech, communication, sociology, economics, and education — try to answer such questions by looking both to the humanities and to the sciences.

The social sciences share with the humanities an interest in what it means to be human. But the social sciences also share with the sciences the goal of engaging in a systematic, observable study of human behavior. Whatever their focus, all the social sciences attempt to identify, understand, and explain patterns of human behavior.

61a Reading texts in the social sciences

Strong readers in the social sciences — as in any subject — ask questions, analyze, and interpret as they read, whether they are reading an academic paper that sets forth a theoretical premise or overall theory and defends it, a case study that describes a particular case and draws out inferences and implications from it, or a research report that presents the results of an investigation into an important question in the field. Most of what students read in the social sciences is trying to prove a point, and readers need to evaluate whether that point is supported.

The social sciences, like other disciplines, often use specialized vocabulary as shorthand for complex ideas that otherwise would take paragraphs to explain.

Qualitative and quantitative studies

Different texts in the social and natural sciences may call for different methods and strategies. Texts that report the results of *quantitative* studies collect data represented with numerical measurements drawn from surveys, polls, experiments, and tests. For example, a study of voting patterns in southern states might rely on quantitative data such as statistics. Texts that report the results of *qualitative* studies rely on non-numerical methods such as interviews and observations to reveal social patterns. A study of the way children in one kindergarten class develop rules of play, for instance, would draw on qualitative data—observations of social interaction, interviews with students and teachers, and so on. Of course, some work in the social and behavioral sciences combines quantitative and qualitative data and methods: an educational report might begin with statistical data related to a problem and then move to a qualitative case study to exemplify what the statistics reveal.

In the social sciences, both quantitative and qualitative researchers must determine what they are examining and measuring in order to get answers to research questions. A researcher who studies childhood aggression must first define and measure *aggression*. If the research is qualitative, a researcher may describe types of behavior that indicate aggression and then discuss observations of children and interviews with teachers and peers about those behaviors. A quantitative researcher, on the other hand, might design an experiment that notes how often children hit a punching bag or that asks children to rate their peers' aggression on a scale of one to ten.

It's important to recognize that both quantitative and qualitative studies have points of view, and that researchers' opinions influence everything from the hypothesis and the design of the research study to the interpretation of findings. Readers must consider whether the researchers' views are sensible and solidly supported by evidence, and they must pay close attention to the kind of data the writer is using and what those data can—and cannot—prove. For example, if researchers of childhood aggression define *aggression* in a way that readers find unpersuasive, or if they observe behaviors that readers consider playful rather than aggressive, then the readers will likely not accept their interpretation of the findings.

Conventional formats

Make use of conventional disciplinary formats to help guide your reading in the social sciences. Many such texts conform to the format and documentation style of the American Psychological Association (APA).

In addition, articles often include standard features — an abstract that gives an overview of the findings, followed by an introduction, review of literature, methods, results, discussion, and references. Readers who become familiar with such a format can easily find the information they need. (For more on APA style, see Chapter 17.)

61b Writing texts in the social sciences

Perhaps because the social sciences share concerns with both the humanities and the sciences, the forms of writing within the social sciences are particularly varied, including summaries, abstracts, literature reviews, reaction pieces, position papers, radio scripts, briefing notes, book reviews, briefs, research papers, quantitative research reports, case studies, ethnographic analyses, and meta-analyses. Such an array of writing assignments could seem overwhelming, but in fact these assignments can be organized under five main categories:

Writing that encourages student learning — reaction pieces, position papers

Writing that demonstrates student learning — summaries, abstracts, research papers

Writing that reflects common on-the-job communication tasks undertaken by members of a discipline — radio scripts, briefing notes, informational reports

Writing that requires students to analyze and evaluate the writings of others — literature reviews, book reviews, briefs

Writing that asks students to replicate the work of others or to engage in original research — quantitative research reports, case studies, ethnographic analyses

Many forms of writing in the social sciences call either explicitly or implicitly for argument (see Chapter 9). If you write an essay reporting on the results of a survey you developed about attitudes toward physician-assisted suicide among students on your campus, you will make an explicit argument about the significance of your data. But even in other forms of writing, such as summaries and book reports, you will implicitly argue that your description and analysis provide a clear, thorough overview of the text(s) you have read.

The literature review

Students of the social sciences carry out literature reviews to find out the most current thinking about a topic, to learn what research has already been carried out on that topic, to evaluate the work that has been done, and to set any research they will do in context. The following guidelines are designed to help you explore and question sources, looking for flaws or gaps. Such a critical review could then lead to a discussion of how your own research will avoid such flaws and advance knowledge.

For a student's literature review in psychology, see 17e.

- What is your topic of interest or dependent variable (the item or characteristic being studied)?

- What is already known about this topic? What characteristics does the topic or dependent variable have? How have other researchers measured the item or characteristic being studied? What other factors are involved, and how are they related to each other and to your topic or variable? What theories are used to explain the way things are now?

- How has research been done so far? Who or what has been studied? How have measurements been taken?

- Has there been change over time? What has caused any changes?

- What problems do you identify in the current research? What questions have not been answered yet? What conclusions have researchers drawn that might not be warranted?

- What gaps will your research fill? How is it new? What problems do you want to correct?

Style in the social sciences

Writing in the social sciences need not be dry and filled with jargon. While you need to understand the conventions, concepts, and habits of mind typical of a particular discipline, you can still write clear prose that engages readers.

When discussing research sources in a paper conforming to APA style, use past or present perfect tenses for the verbs (*Raditch showed* or *Raditch has shown*). Finally, make sure that any writing you do is as clear and grammatically correct as possible to ensure that readers see you as capable and credible.

EXERCISE 61.1

Identify a literature review in a social-science field you are interested in (ask your instructor or a librarian for help in finding one), and read it carefully, noting how it addresses the questions on p. 845. Bring your notes to class for discussion.

61c A student's brief psychology report

Student Writer

Katie Paarlberg

Following is an example of effective writing in the social sciences, a brief report by Katie Paarlberg requiring a series of short responses to questions about a telephone survey that she and her classmates at Hope College conducted among fellow students. (For a sample research paper in APA style, see 17e.)

bedfordstmartins.com/smhandbook
Student Writing > **Writing in the Disciplines**

K. Paarlberg
Psych 100-01
February 24, 2006

Centered title
identifies the
assignment
clearly

Report #2 — Response to Questions about Attitude Survey

1. How could the construction of the survey and the ways in which the questions were phrased have influenced the students' responses?

One way in which the construction of the survey could have influenced the results is that many of the statements that respondents were asked to agree or disagree with centered not just on *gender* issues but on *women's* issues as well. For example, one statement read, "Women are just as capable as men when it comes to holding positions of responsibility and authority" instead of "Women and men are *equally* capable. . . ." Spotlighting women as the gender in question may have suggested to certain respondents that a particular answer was expected. This may well have been the point of the survey, but the wording of certain statements could have influenced the results.

Passive voice
(*were asked*)
used
appropriately
to put the
emphasis on
the respondent
rather than the
person
conducting the
survey

Another factor that may have had an effect on people's answers was the fact that demographic questions appeared in the survey. For example, students were asked whether they were male or female and whether their mothers worked while they were growing up. Some may have felt that they were in some way expected to represent their groups. For example, a survey responder who felt that his answers had to represent the "male / mother did not work" column might alter responses to fit this perception.

Cautious tone
and qualifiers
such as *may*
and *could have*
used for
reporting more
tentative
results

The topic of the survey was somewhat controversial; this also may have influenced students' responses. If the survey had asked about favorite colors instead of about gender attitudes, the respondents might not have felt the need to avoid offending the surveyor. If students had

Student Writing

Shortened title and page number on every page after the first

ATTITUDE SURVEY   2

been asked to give their names on this survey, which they were not asked to do, their answers might have been even less truthful.

2. What effect could the identity of the surveyor have had on the students' responses? Would the survey results have been different if the surveyor had been a faculty member?

Writer acknowledges effect of her participation on the responses elicited

The results of the survey were most likely somewhat influenced by the fact that students were reporting their attitudes to their peers and classmates, not to their instructors. If they had been surveyed by the faculty, respondents might have been more likely to search their minds for the "right" answers on which they were being "tested" rather than expressing genuine opinions.

3. How did you select the respondents for your survey? Was your sample population representative of the larger college community? Why or why not? What about the national population of college students? Was your sample population representative of that larger group?

Explains methods clearly

In order to obtain a representative sample of Hope students, we selected numbers at random from the Hope telephone directory. We used a random number chart to choose page and listing numbers, and then switched numbers with others in order to avoid knowing subjects' names.

Our sample might not be representative of the Hope community because many Hope students do not have on-campus numbers in the directory. Many commute from surrounding areas, and we did not ask those students to participate. Juniors and seniors are also more likely to live off-campus; their views as a group on this topic might differ from those of freshmen and sophomores.

These survey results probably do not represent the views of the American college population as a whole. Attitudes of students vary widely. Students from a school in western Michigan, the majority of whose

ATTITUDE SURVEY 3

students come from western Michigan, cannot be used as a representative sample of all American college students.

4. Did anything about the results of your survey surprise you? Why?

The results I found most unexpected were that 64% of all students, and 58% of men, said that they would sacrifice their careers to raise a family. I was surprised that so many students — who are presumably preparing for a career — were willing to put family obligations first. The fact that men and women were closely aligned on this issue was also surprising; men are traditionally less likely to devote time to family over careers. Perhaps students felt obligated to give politically correct responses, or perhaps attitudes really are changing more than I had known.

Avoids making sweeping or unjustified claims

5. What about the results did you find most interesting? Why do you think students responded the way they did?

I was interested to see that the population was split almost evenly among students whose mothers did not work when they were growing up, students whose mothers worked part-time, and students whose mothers worked full-time. Many students grew up during the 1980s, a time of developing economic freedom for women, when more mothers were entering the workforce. It was also interesting to note that while no women disagreed with the statement that women are as capable as men when it comes to holding positions of authority and responsibility, 13% of the men did disagree. Women are more likely to defend the ability of their sex and take such a statement personally, while men need not defend personal ability by agreeing with this statement. The men who disagreed may also have taken the fact that women do hold fewer powerful positions in the United States than men as evidence that women are less capable.

Maintains a neutral, objective tone throughout

THINKING CRITICALLY ABOUT WRITING IN THE SOCIAL SCIENCES

Reading with an Eye for Writing in the Social Sciences

Choose two readings from a social-science discipline, and read them with an eye toward issues of style. Does the use of disciplinary terms and concepts seem appropriate? In what ways do the texts attempt to engage readers? If the texts are not clear and understandable, how might they be improved?

Thinking about Your Own Writing in the Social Sciences

Choose a text you like that you have written for a social-science discipline. Then examine your style in this paper to see how well you have engaged your readers. Note variation in sentence length and type (do you, for example, use any questions?), number of active and passive verbs, use of concrete examples and everyday language, and so on. How would you rate your writing as a social scientist?

Writing for the Natural and Applied Sciences

62

More than many other scholars, scientists are likely to leave the privacy of their office or lab to engage in fieldwork and experimentation. Whether done in the lab or the field, however, writing—from the first grant proposal to the final report or scientific paper—plays a key role in the natural and applied sciences.

62a Reading texts in the natural and applied sciences

Scientists and engineers work with evidence that can be observed, verified, and controlled. Though they cannot avoid interpretation, they strive for objectivity by using the scientific method—observing or studying phenomena, formulating a hypothesis about the phenomena, and testing that hypothesis through controlled experiments and observations. Scientists and engineers aim to generate precise, replicable data; they develop experiments to account for extraneous factors. In this careful, precise way, scientists and engineers identify, test, and write persuasively about theoretical and real-world problems.

Identifying argument

As you read in the sciences, try to become familiar with disciplinary terms, concepts, and formats as soon as possible, and practice reading—and listening—for detail. If you are reading a first-year biology textbook, you can draw upon general critical-reading strategies. In addition, charts, graphs, illustrations, models, and other visuals

Whether they are studying geological faults or developing a stronger support structure for suspension bridges, scientists in the natural and applied sciences want to understand how the physical and natural worlds work. Natural sciences such as biology, chemistry, and physics study the natural world and its phenomena; applied sciences such as nanotechnology and the various fields of engineering apply knowledge from the natural sciences to practical problems.

often play an important role in scientific writing, so your ability to read and comprehend these visual displays of knowledge is particularly important. (See Chapter 7.)

When you read a science or engineering textbook, you can assume that the information presented there is authoritative and as objective as possible. When you read specialized materials, however, recognize that although scholarly reports undergo significant peer review, they nevertheless represent arguments (see Chapter 8). The connection between facts and claims in the sciences, as in all subject areas, is created by the author rather than simply revealed by the data. So read both facts and claims with a questioning eye: Did the scientist choose the best method to test the hypothesis? Are there other reasonable interpretations of the experiment's results? Do other studies contradict the conclusions of this experiment? When you read specialized texts in the sciences with questions like these in mind, you are reading—and thinking—like a scientist. (For additional information on assessing a source's credibility, see 12c.)

Conventional formats

As you advance in your course work, you will need to develop reading strategies for increasingly specialized texts. Many scientific texts conform to the format and documentation style of the Council of Science Editors (CSE); for more on CSE style, see Chapter 19. (However, you should be prepared to follow an instructor's guidelines for citation and references if another style is used in your discipline or in a particular course.) In addition, articles often include standard features—an abstract that gives an overview of the findings, followed by an introduction, literature review, materials and methods, results, discussion, and references.

You might expect to read a journal article for a science or engineering course from start to finish, giving equal weight to each section. However, an experienced reader in sciences and engineering might skim an abstract to see if an article warrants further reading. If it does—and this judgment is based on the reader's own research interest—he or she might then read the introduction to understand the rationale for the experiment and then skip to the results. A reader with a specific interest in the methods will read that section with particular care.

EXERCISE 62.1

Choose a respected journal in a discipline in the natural or applied sciences that interests you. (Ask your instructor or a reference librarian if you need help identifying a journal.) Then read quickly through two articles, taking notes on the author's use of any headings and subheadings, specialized vocabulary, visuals, and evidence. Bring the results of your investigation to class for discussion.

62b Writing texts in the natural and applied sciences

Students in the sciences and engineering must be able to respond to a diverse range of writing and speaking tasks. Often, they must maintain lab or engineering notebooks that include careful records of experiments. They also write memos, papers, project proposals and reports, literature reviews, and progress reports; in addition, they may develop print and Web-based presentations for both technical and lay audiences (see 22c–e). Particularly common writing assignments in the sciences are the literature review, research proposal, and research report.

Scientists undertake literature reviews to keep up with and evaluate developments in their field. Literature reviews are an essential first step in any research effort, for they enable scientists to discover what research has already been completed and how they might build on earlier efforts. Successful literature reviews demonstrate a student's ability to identify relevant research on a topic and to summarize and in some instances evaluate that research.

Most scientists spend a great deal of time writing research or grant proposals aimed at securing funds to support their research. Undergraduate writers often have an opportunity to make similar proposals—to an office of undergraduate research or to a science-based firm that supports student research, for instance. Funding agencies often have guidelines for preparing a proposal. Proposals for research funding generally include the following sections: title page, introduction, purpose(s) and significance of the study, methods, timeline, budget, and references. You may also need to submit an abstract.

> For a student research proposal, see 19d.

Research reports, another common writing form in the sciences, may include both literature reviews and discussions of primary research, most often experiments. Like journal articles, research reports generally follow this form: title, author(s), abstract, introduction, literature review, materials and methods, results, discussion, and references. Many instructors ask students to write lab reports (62c), which are briefer versions of research reports and may not include a literature review.

Today, a great deal of scientific writing is collaborative. As students move from introductory to advanced courses and then to the workplace, they increasingly find themselves working as part of teams or groups. Indeed, in such areas as engineering, collaborative projects are often the norm (see Chapter 6).

Style in the natural and applied sciences

In general, use the present tense for most writing you do in the natural and applied sciences. Use the past tense, however, when you are describing research already carried out (by you or others) or published in the past.

Writers in the sciences need to produce complex figures, tables, images, and models and use software designed to analyze data or run computer simulations. In addition, they need to present data carefully. If you create a graph, you should provide headings for columns, label axes with numbers or units, and identify data points. Caption figures and tables with a number and descriptive title. And avoid orphan data—data that you present in a figure or table but don't comment on in your text.

Finally, make sure that any writing you do is as clear, concise, and grammatically correct as possible to ensure that readers see you as capable and credible.

62c A student's chemistry lab report

Student Writer

Allyson Goldberg

The following piece of student writing is a lab report on a chemistry experiment by student Allyson Goldberg. Note that this report has been reproduced in a narrow format to allow for annotation.

bedfordstmartins.com/smhandbook
Student Writing > **Writing in the Disciplines**

Chemistry 119L Laboratory Report

Title page
includes name
of class, title of
the lab report,
student's
name, and
date of the
experiment
reported on

Evaluation of the Value of the Gas Constant R

Allyson Goldberg

Date of Experiment: Monday, September 27, 2010

Student Writing

Introduction explains purpose of lab and gives overview of results

Introduction

The purpose of this investigation was to experimentally determine the value of the universal gas constant, R. To accomplish this goal, a measured sample of magnesium (Mg) was allowed to react with an excess of hydrochloric acid (HCl) at room temperature and pressure so that the precise amount and volume of the product hydrogen gas (H_2) could be determined and the value of R could be calculated using the ideal gas equation, PV=nRT.

Materials and methods section explains lab setup and procedure

Materials & Methods

Two samples of room temperature water, one about 250mL and the other about 400mL, were measured into a smaller and larger beaker respectively. 15.0mL of HCl was then transferred into a side arm flask that was connected to the top of a buret (clamped to a ringstand) through a 5/16" diameter flexible tube. (This "gas buret" was connected to an adjacent "open buret," clamped to the other side of the ringstand and left open to the atmosphere of the laboratory at its wide end, by a 1/4" diameter flexible tube. These two burets were adjusted on the ringstand so that they were vertically parallel and close together.) The HCl sample was transferred to the flask such that none came in contact with the inner surface of the neck of the flask. The flask was then allowed to rest, in an almost horizontal position, in the smaller beaker.

The open buret was adjusted on the ringstand such that its 20mL mark was horizontally aligned with the 35mL mark on the gas buret. Room temperature water was added to the open buret until the water level of the gas buret was at about 34.00mL.

Goldberg 3

A piece of magnesium ribbon was obtained, weighed on an analytical balance, and placed in the neck of the horizontal side arm flask. Next, a screw cap was used to cap the flask and form an airtight seal. This setup was then allowed to sit for 5 minutes in order to reach thermal equilibrium.

After 5 minutes, the open buret was adjusted so that the menisci on both burets were level with each other; the side arm flask was then tilted vertically to let the magnesium ribbon react with the HCl. After the brisk reaction, the flask was placed into the larger beaker and allowed to sit for another 5 minutes.

Next, the flask was placed back into the smaller beaker, and the open buret was adjusted on the ringstand such that its meniscus was level with that of the gas buret. After the system sat for an additional 30 minutes, the open buret was again adjusted so that the menisci on both burets were level.

This procedure was repeated two more times, with the exception that HCl was not again added to the side arm flask, as it was already present in enough excess for all reactions from the first trial.

Passive voice throughout is typical of writing in natural sciences

Results and Calculations

Trial #	Lab Temp. (°C)	Lab Pressure (mbar)	Mass of Mg Ribbon Used (g)	Initial Buret Reading (mL)	Final Buret Reading (mL)
1	24.4	1013	0.0147	32.66	19.60
2	24.3	1013	0.0155	33.59	N/A*
3	25.0	1013	0.0153	34.35	19.80

*See note in Discussion section.

Results and calculations show measurements and calculations of final value of R

Goldberg 4

Trial #	Volume of H_2 (L)	Moles of H_2 Gas Produced	Lab Temp. (K)	Partial Pressure of H_2 (atm)	Value of R (L atm/ mol K)	Mean Value of R (L atm/ mol K)
1	0.01306	6.05×10^{-4}	298	0.970	0.0704	0.0728
2	N/A	N/A	N/A	N/A	N/A	
3	0.01455	6.30×10^{-4}	298	0.968	0.0751	

Table 1 Experimental results

(Sample Calculations — see Table 1)

Volume of H_2 gas = final buret reading − initial buret reading

Volume of H_2 gas = 32.66mL − 19.60mL = 13.06mL = 0.01306 L

Moles of H_2 gas produced = mass of Mg used/molar mass of Mg

Moles of H_2 gas produced = $0.0147g/24.305g$ mol^{-1} = 6.05×10^{-4} mol

Kelvin temperature = Celsius temperature + 273.15 = 24.3°C + 273.15

$$= 298 \text{ K}$$

Partial Pressure of H_2 gas in the gas buret = $P_{atmosphere}$ − pressure due to water vapor at the temperature of interest

$P_{atmosphere}$ = 1013 mbar

(unit conversion of $P_{atmosphere}$) $\dfrac{1013.25 \text{ mbar}}{1 \text{ atm}} = \dfrac{1013 \text{ mbar}}{x \text{ atm}}$ (conversion value taken from Ganapathi [2004])

$x = 0.9998$ atm

(unit conversion of pressure due to water vapor) $\dfrac{22.4 \text{ mm Hg}}{x \text{ atm}} = \dfrac{760 \text{ mm}}{1 \text{ atm}}$ (values taken from Ganapathi [2004])

$x = 0.0295$ atm

Partial Pressure of H_2 gas in the gas buret = 0.9998 atm

− 0.0295 atm = 0.9703 atm

Goldberg 5

Value of R:

$R = PV/nT$

$R = [(0.9703 \text{ atm}) (0.01306 \text{ L})]/[(6.05 \times 10^{-4} \text{ mol}) (297.5 \text{ K})]$

$R = 0.01267 \text{ L atm}/0.180 \text{ mol K}$

$R = 0.0704 \text{ L atm/mol K}$

Mean Value of $R = (R\text{-value}_1 + R\text{-value}_3)/2$

Mean Value of $R = (0.0704 \text{ L atm/mol K} + 0.0751 \text{ L atm/mol K})/2$

Mean Value of $R = 0.0728 \text{ L atm/mol K}$

Percent Error = [(measured value − accepted value)/accepted value]

      $\times$ 100

Percent Error = absolute value of [(0.0728 L atm/mol K

      − 0.08206 L atm/mol K)/0.08206 L atm/mol K]

      $\times$ 100

Percent Error = 11.3%

Discussion

Discussion
section
analyzes
results and
possible
sources of
inaccuracy

Despite the adherence to the experimental procedure, the mean value of
R determined in this investigation deviated slightly from the accepted
value, 0.08206 L atm/mol K. This deviation was most likely due to the
leakage of some H_2 gas through the screw cap of the side arm flask during
the reaction. Though this could have been better avoided, the tightening
of the screw cap onto the side arm flask was necessarily a compromise
between an extremely tight seal and a seal too strong to be later
removed; thus, any error during experimentation was difficult both to
judge and to avoid. In this way, the buret reading after the reaction in
Trial 2 was read at 30.80mL. With only a 2.79mL change in the volume of
the gas in the buret, it was evident (from comparison with the previous
trial) that not all of the hydrogen gas produced in the reaction was
captured in the gas buret. Thus, upon recognition of this error, the

Goldberg 6

experimental procedure for that trial was suspended, and data from Trial 2 was disregarded in analyses.

However, detailed attention to pressure was paid during the experiment, such that the position of the open buret was adjusted several times in order to equilibrate its water level with that of the gas buret. This was done to equalize the pressure of the hydrogen gas with that of the atmospheric pressure in the laboratory, as the pressure of the hydrogen gas itself was impossible to measure inside the gas buret. Subsequently, because the atmospheric pressure in the laboratory remained constant throughout the procedure, it was differences in other components of the ideal gas equation (volume, number of moles, and temperature) that made for the varying R-values calculated.

Additionally regarding pressure was the need to account for the contribution of the partial pressure of water vapor when determining the pressure of the H_2 gas produced. Because the ideal gas equation was used to calculate R-values, it was necessary to use the purest values possible relating to the hydrogen gas when substituting values into the equation. Though the hydrogen gas produced was not quite an ideal gas, the light weight of and weak attractive forces between its molecules rendered it close enough to one that it was suitable for this experiment. The water vapor molecules, on the other hand, had much larger masses, and the electronegativity of the oxygen atoms added an attractive force that would have added more deviation from the accepted value for R.

Accuracy in this experiment could have been compromised by a number of factors. Regarding pressure, more accurate values could have been obtained if the digital barometer used was allowed to have been taken to each workstation, rather than remaining in the front desk; atmospheric pressure likely varied a little bit around the room. Regarding volume, the ruler technique used to confirm that the water level in

Goldberg 7

each buret was horizontally equivalent was helpful, but could have been more effective had the tool used been a level. (Additionally, it was important to note at the beginning of the experiment that both burets were not only close enough together to judge equivalent water levels, but that the two were vertically parallel as well.) Further, the accuracy of temperature measurements could have been improved had there been an apparatus to hold the bulb of the thermometer in midair; resting the thermometer on, or even too near to, the surface of the lab table gave temperature readings that were lower than that of the air surrounding the experimental system.

Conclusions

Conceptually, this experiment was fairly simple to grasp. Experimentally, however, it provided the opportunity to become more intimate with common laboratory equipment, as well as provided a hands-on explanation of the ideal gas equation. For example, the previously learned technique of using a glass stirring rod to channel a liquid into a narrow opening proved to be useful in this procedure when it was necessary to pour HCl into the side arm flask without getting any of the acid inside the neck of the flask. Additionally, the need to account for the partial pressure of water vapor provided a tangible example of what it means to be an ideal gas versus a real gas, and how the concept of the ideal gas equation applies in the real world.

Conclusions section analyzes purpose of experiment: to teach concept and lab technique

Student
Writing

Goldberg 8

References

References
section follows
CSE style for
citing books

Ganapathi N. Chemistry 119L laboratory manual. New Haven (CT): Yale
     University Press; 2004.

Oxtoby DW, Gillis HP, Nachtrieb NH. Principles of modern chemistry. 5th
     ed. Farmington Hills (MI): Thompson Learning; 2002.

THINKING CRITICALLY ABOUT WRITING FOR THE SCIENCES

Reading with an Eye for Writing in the Sciences

Identify one or more features of scientific texts, and consider their usefulness. Why, for instance, does an abstract precede the actual article? How do scientific nomenclatures, classification systems, and other features of scientific writing aid the work of scientists? Try to identify the functions that textual elements such as these play in the ongoing work of science. Finally, research the scientific method to see how it is served by the features of scientific writing discussed in this chapter.

Thinking about Your Own Writing in the Sciences

Choose a piece of writing you did for a natural or applied science class—a lab report, a research report, a proposal—and read it carefully. Note the format and headings you used, how you presented visual data, what kinds of evidence you used, and what citation system you used. Compare your piece of writing with a similar piece of writing published in a journal in the field. How well does your writing compare? What differences are most noticeable between your writing and that of the published piece?

Writing for Business 63

To succeed in business, you need to know how to manage many kinds of writing—from negotiating an ever-increasing number of digital messages to communicating effectively with readers from Manhattan, Montgomery, Mexico City, and Mumbai.

63a Reading texts for business

A team of businesspeople today has almost unlimited access to information and to people whose expertise can be of use in the business world. Somehow, the members of this team need to negotiate a huge stream of information and to evaluate that information.

To meet these demands, you can draw on general strategies for effective reading (Chapter 7). One such strategy — keeping a clear purpose in mind when you read—is particularly important for work-related reading. Are you reading to solve a problem? to gather and synthesize information? to make a recommendation? Knowing why you are reading will increase your productivity. Time constraints and deadlines will also affect your decisions about what and how to read; the ability to identify important information quickly is a skill to cultivate as a business reader.

63b Writing texts for business

Writing assignments in business classes serve two related functions. While their immediate goal is to help you master the theory and practice of business, these assignments also prepare you for the kinds of writing you will face in the world of work. For this reason,

In today's business world, the global economy is now a commonplace concept, and both corporate giants and home-office eBay operations conduct business worldwide. Yet in the midst of these changes, one constant remains: written communication is still essential in identifying and solving the complex problems of today's companies.

students in *every* discipline need to know how to write effective business memos, emails, letters, résumés, and reports.

1 Memo

Memos are a common form of print or electronic correspondence sent within and between organizations. Memos tend to be brief, internal documents, often dealing with only one subject.

QUICK HELP

Guidelines for writing effective memos

- Write the name of the recipient, your name, the subject, and the date on separate lines at the top.

- Begin with the most important information: depending on the memo's purpose, you may have to provide background information, define the task or problem, or clarify the memo's goal.

- Use your opening paragraph to focus on how the information you convey affects your readers.

- Focus each subsequent paragraph on one idea pertaining to the subject.

- Present information concisely and from the readers' perspective.

- Emphasize exactly what you want readers to do and when.

- Use attachments for detailed supporting information.

- For print memos, initial your memo next to your name.

- Adjust your style and tone to fit your audience.

- Attempt to build goodwill in your conclusion.

Student Writer

Michelle Abbott

Student Writer

Carina Abernathy

Following is a memo, written by student writers Michelle Abbott and Carina Abernathy, that presents an analysis and recommendation to help an employer make a decision.

MEMO

❖ *Jenco* ❖

INTEROFFICE MEMORANDUM

TO: ROSA DONAHUE, SALES MANAGER

FROM: MICHELLE ABBOTT & CARINA ABERNATHY   *MA CA*

SUBJECT: TAYLOR NURSERY BID

DATE: 1/30/2010

CC:

Initials of senders added in ink (for print memo)

Paragraphs not indented

As you know, Taylor Nursery has requested bids on a 25,000-pound order of private-label fertilizer. Taylor Nursery is one of the largest distributors of our Fertikil product. The following is our analysis of Jenco's costs to fill this special order and a recommendation for the bidding price.

Opening paragraph provides background and states purpose

The total cost for manufacturing 25,000 pounds of the private-label brand for Taylor Nursery is $44,075. This cost includes direct material, direct labor, and variable manufacturing overhead. Although our current equipment and facilities provide adequate capacity for processing this special order, the job will involve an excess in labor hours. The overtime labor rate has been factored into our costs.

Most important information put in bold

Double-spaced between paragraphs

The absolute minimum price that Jenco could bid for this product without losing money is $44,075 (our cost). Applying our standard markup of 40% results in a price of $61,705. Thus, you could reasonably establish a price anywhere within that range.

Options presented

In making the final assessment, we advise you to consider factors relevant to this decision. Taylor Nursery has stated that this is a one-time order. Therefore, the effort to fill this special order will not bring long-term benefits.

Relevant factors explained

Finally, Taylor Nursery has requested bids from several competitors. One rival, Eclipse Fertilizers, is submitting a bid of $60,000 on this order. Therefore, our recommendation is to slightly underbid Eclipse with a price of $58,000, representing a markup of approximately 32%.

Final recommendation

Please let us know if we can be of further assistance in your decision on the Taylor Nursery bid.

Closing builds goodwill by offering further help

2 Email

Business email can be formatted much like a print memo but is easier to create and store and faster to distribute. Remember, however, that email is essentially public and that employers have easy access to email written by employees. As always, it's best to use discretion and caution in email, especially on the job. (For more about email see 20a.)

3 Letter of application

Despite the popularity of email, letters remain an important form of communication. When you send a business or professional letter, you are writing either as an individual or as a representative of an organization. In either case, and regardless of your purpose, a business letter should follow certain conventions.

One particular type of letter, the letter of application or cover letter (see opposite page), often accompanies a résumé. The purpose of a letter of application is to demonstrate how the experiences and skills you outline in your résumé have prepared you for a particular job. In a letter of application, then, it is important to focus on how you can benefit the company, not how the company can help you. If you are responding to a particular advertisement, mention it in the opening paragraph. Finally, be sure to indicate how you can be reached for an interview.

Student Writer

Nastassia Lopez

The following application letter for a summer internship was written by student Nastassia Lopez. Note that the letter has been reproduced in a narrow format to allow for annotation.

bedfordstmartins.com/smhandbook
Student Writing > Business Writing

LETTER OF APPLICATION

▼ 1"

Nastassia Rose Lopez

523 Brown Avenue
Stanford, CA 94305
650-326-6790 / nrl87@hotmail.com

Contact
information

February 1, 2010

Mr. Price Hicks
Director of Educational Programs and Services
Academy of Arts and Sciences
5220 Lankersheim Blvd.
North Hollywood, CA 91601

Inside address
with full name,
title, and
address

Dear Mr. Hicks:

Salutation to
specific person

I am an enthusiastic student who believes that a Development Internship at
the Academy of Arts and Sciences would greatly benefit both the Academy
and me. A Los Angeles native in my first year at Stanford, I'm a serious student
who is a hard worker. My current goal is to comprehend the full scope of the
entertainment industry and to learn the ropes of the craft.

Opening
provides
information
and lists major
goals

As an experienced writer, I am attracted to the Development Department
because I am curious to learn the process of television production from paper
to screen. In high school, I was enrolled in Advanced Placement Writing, and
I voluntarily took a creative writing class. At Stanford, I received High Honors
for maintaining an excellent grade-point average across all my classes, including several writing-intensive courses.

My passion for writing, producing, directing, and learning is real. If my application is accepted, I will bring my strong work ethic, proficiency, and creativity to the Academy.

Background
information
illustrates
skills and
strength of
interest

Thank you very much for your time and consideration. My résumé is enclosed,
and I look forward to hearing from you.

Sincerely yours,

Nastassia Rose Lopez

Four line
spaces for
signature

QUICK HELP

Guidelines for writing effective letters

- Use a conventional format. (See p. 867.)

- Whenever possible, write to a specific person (*Dear Tom Robinson* or *Dear Ms. Otuteye*) rather than to a general *Dear Sir or Madam*.

- Open cordially and be polite—even if you have a complaint.

- State the reason for your letter clearly. Include whatever details will help your reader see your point and respond.

- If appropriate, make clear what you hope your reader will do.

- Express appreciation for your reader's attention.

- Make it easy for your reader to respond by including your contact information and, if appropriate, a self-addressed, stamped envelope.

4 Résumé

While a letter of application usually emphasizes specific parts of the résumé, telling how your background is suited to a particular job, a résumé summarizes your experience and qualifications and provides support for your letter. An effective resume is brief, usually one or two pages.

Research shows that employers generally spend less than a minute reading a résumé. Remember that they are interested not in what they can do for you but what you can do for them. They expect a résumé to be formatted neatly, and your aim is to use clear headings and adequate spacing that will make it easy to read. Although you may be tempted to use colored paper or unusual type styles, avoid such temptations. A well-written résumé with a standard format and typefaces is the best way to distinguish yourself.

Your résumé may be arranged chronologically (from most to least recent) or functionally (based on skill or expertise). Include the following information:

1. *Name, address, phone and fax numbers, and email address.*

2. *Career objective(s).* List immediate or short-term goals and specific jobs for which you realistically qualify.

3. *Educational background.* Include degrees, diplomas, majors, and special programs or courses that pertain to your field of interest. List honors and scholarships and your grade-point average if it is high.

4. *Work experience.* Identify each job — whether a paying job, an internship, or military experience — with dates and names of organizations. Describe your duties by carefully selecting strong action verbs.

5. *Skills, personal interests, activities, awards, and honors.*

6. *References.* List two or three people who know your work well, first asking their permission. Give their titles, addresses, and phone or fax numbers. Or simply say that your references are available on request.

7. *Keywords* (for a scannable résumé). In general, nouns function as keywords for résumés that are scanned by Web search engines and organized in databases. Look for places where you can convert verbs (*performed laboratory tests*) to nouns (*laboratory technologist*). Place the most important keywords toward the beginning of the résumé.

Increasingly, job seekers are composing online résumés as hypertext screen documents, which make keywords more visible to search engines and thus tend to produce more hits. In addition, some businesses ask applicants to fill out résumé forms on company Web sites. In such cases, take special care to make sure that you have caught any errors or typos before submitting the form.

Student Writer

The following pages show student Dennis Tyler's résumé in two formats, one in conventional print style, the other formatted for scanning.

Dennis Tyler Jr.

bedfordstmartins.com/smhandbook
Student Writing > Business Writing

RÉSUMÉ

DENNIS TYLER JR.

Name in bold-
face and larger
type size

CURRENT ADDRESS	PERMANENT ADDRESS
P.O. Box 12345	506 Chanelle Court
Stanford, CA 94309	Baton Rouge, LA 70128
Phone: (650) 498-4731	Phone: (504) 246-9847
Email: dtyler@yahoo.com	

Position being
sought

CAREER OBJECTIVE Position on editorial staff of a major newspaper

EDUCATION

Educational
background

9/00–6/04	**Stanford University,** Stanford, CA
	BA, ENGLISH AND AMERICAN STUDIES, June 2004
9/02–12/02	**Morehouse College,** Atlanta, GA
	STANFORD STUDY EXCHANGE PROGRAM

EXPERIENCE

Work experi-
ence relevant
to position
being sought

6/03–9/03	**Business Scholar Intern,** Finance, AOL Time Warner, New York, NY
	Responsible for analyzing data for strategic marketing plans. Researched the mergers and acquisitions of companies to which Time Inc. sells advertising space.
1/02–6/03	**Editor-in-Chief,** *Enigma* (a literary journal), Stanford University, CA
	Oversaw the entire process of *Enigma*. Edited numerous creative works: short stories, poems, essays, and interviews. Selected appropriate material for the journal. Responsible for designing cover and for publicity to the greater community.
8/02–12/02	**Community Development Intern,** University Center Development Corporation (UCDC), Atlanta, GA
	Facilitated workshops and meetings on the importance of home buying and neighborhood preservation. Created UCDC brochure and assisted in the publication of the center's newsletter.
6/02–8/02	**News Editor,** *Stanford Daily,* Stanford University, CA
	Responsible for editing stories and creating story ideas for the newspaper. Assisted with the layout for the newspaper and designs for the cover.

SKILLS AND HONORS

Talents and
honors not
listed above

- Computer Skills: MS Word, Excel, PageMaker, Microsoft Publisher; Internet research
- Language: Proficient in Spanish
- Trained in making presentations, conducting research, acting, and singing
- Mellon Fellow, Gates Millennium Scholar, Public Service Scholar, National Collegiate Scholar
- Black Community Service Arts Award, 2003–2004

REFERENCES Available upon request

SCANNABLE RÉSUMÉ

Dennis Tyler Jr.

Current Address
P.O. Box 12345
Stanford, CA 94309
Phone: (650) 498-4731
Email: dtyler@yahoo.com

Permanent Address
506 Chanelle Court
Baton Rouge, LA 70128
Phone: (504) 246-9847

Keywords: journalist; journal editor; literary publishing; finance; community development; design; leadership; newspaper writer; PageMaker; Spanish; editor-in-chief

Education
BA in English and American Studies, June 2004, Stanford University, Stanford, CA
Morehouse College Study Exchange, fall 2002, Atlanta, GA

Experience
Business Scholar Intern, fall 2003
Finance, AOL Time Warner, New York, NY
Data analyst for strategic marketing plans. Researcher for the mergers and acquisitions of companies to which Time Inc. sells advertising.

Editor-in-Chief, 2002–2003, Enigma (a literary journal), Stanford University, CA
Oversaw the entire process of Enigma. Editor for numerous works: short stories, poems, essays, and interviews. Content selection for the journal. Cover design and publicity to the greater community.

Community Development Intern, fall 2002
University Center Development Corporation (UCDC), Atlanta, GA
Workshops on the importance of home buying and neighborhood preservation. Publication responsibility for UCDC brochure and the center's newsletter.

News Editor, summer 2002, Stanford Daily, Stanford University, CA
Story editor for the newspaper. Layout and cover design for the newspaper.

Skills and Honors
Computer skills: MS Word, Excel, PageMaker, Microsoft Publisher; Internet research
Language: Proficient in Spanish
Trained presenter, researcher, actor, singer
Mellon Fellow, Gates Millennium Scholar, Public Service Scholar, National Collegiate Scholar
Black Community Service Arts Award, 2003–2004

References
Available upon request

Marginal annotations:

Each number, email address on a separate line

Standard typeface (Times Roman) and type size

Keywords to aid in computer searches

White space separates sections

No underlining, italics, boxes, borders, or columns

Verbs converted to nouns where possible

Keywords used in body of résumé wherever possible

THINKING CRITICALLY ABOUT BUSINESS WRITING

Reading with an Eye for Writing in Business

Monitor your mail and email for a few days, saving everything that tries to sell a product, provide a service, or solicit information or money. Then go through these pieces of business writing and advertising, and choose the one you find most effective. What about the writing appeals to you or gets and holds your attention? What might lead you to buy the product, choose the service, or make a contribution? What might make the piece of writing even more effective? Bring the results of your investigation to class for discussion.

Thinking about Your Own Business Writing

Chances are, you have written a letter of application for a job, completed a résumé, or sent some business-related letters or email messages. Choose a piece of business-related writing that is important to you or that represents your best work, and then analyze it carefully. How clear is the writing? How well do you represent yourself in the writing? Do you follow the conventions for business letters, résumés, memos, and so on? Make notes on what you could do to improve this piece of writing.

Essay Examinations

Preparing for an essay examination will help you produce your best work in a timed-writing situation.

64a Preparing for an essay examination

Nothing can take the place of knowing the subject well, so you can start preparing for an essay examination by taking careful notes on lectures and readings. You may want to outline a reading assignment, list its main points, list and define its key terms, or briefly summarize its argument. A particularly effective method is to divide your notes into two categories, labeling the left-hand side *Summaries and Quotations* and the right-hand side *Questions and Comments*. Then, as you read, use the left side to record summaries of major points and note worthy quotations. On the right, record questions that your reading has not answered, puzzling ideas, and your own comments. This note-taking encourages active, critical reading and, combined with careful class notes, will do much to prepare you. Here are one student's notes:

The skills you need to perform well on a written exam are skills that can serve you in your nonacademic life. Being prepared to present information effectively is always useful—for example, when you are asked to submit a personal statement to accompany an application for insurance, an internship, or a loan.

SUMMARIES AND QUOTATIONS

Rhetoric—"the art of discovering, in any particular case, all available means of persuasion." (Aristotle, on p. 3)

All language is argumentative—purpose is to persuade

QUESTIONS AND COMMENTS

Maybe all language is persuasive, but if I greet people warmly, I don't consciously try to persuade them that I'm glad to see them. I just respond naturally.

In addition to taking careful, detailed notes, you can prepare by writing out essay answers to questions you think are likely to appear on the exam. Practicing ahead of time is much more effective than last-minute cramming. On the day of the exam, do ten to fifteen minutes of writing just before you go into the examination to warm up your thinking muscles.

EXERCISE 64.1

Create a question you think you might be likely to encounter on an essay examination in a class you are currently taking. Then write a paragraph or two about what you would need to know in order to write an A+ answer.

Analyzing essay questions

Before you begin writing, read the question carefully several times, and analyze what it asks you to do. Most essay examination questions contain two kinds of terms, strategy terms that describe your task in writing the essay and content terms that define the scope and limits of the topic.

STRATEGY	CONTENT
Analyze	Jesus's Sermon on the Mount.
STRATEGY	CONTENT
Describe	the major effects of Reconstruction.
STRATEGY	CONTENT
Explain	the advantages of investing in government securities.

Words like *analyze, describe,* and *explain* tell what logical strategy to use and often set the form your answer takes. Since not all terms mean the same thing in every discipline, be sure you understand exactly what the term means in context of the material covered on the examination. In general, however, the most commonly used strategy terms have standard meanings, as shown in the box on the opposite page. Do not hesitate to ask your instructor to clarify terms you're unsure of.

If strategy terms are not explicitly stated in an essay question, you need to infer a strategy from the content terms. For example, a question that mentions two groups working toward the same goal may imply comparison and contrast, and a question referring to events in a given time period may imply summary.

QUICK HELP

Common strategy terms

- *Analyze*: Divide an event, idea, or theory into its component elements, and examine each one in turn.

  Analyze Milton Friedman's theory of permanent income.

- *Compare and / or contrast*: Demonstrate similarities or dissimilarities between two or more events or topics.

  Compare the portrayal of women in *Beloved* with that in *Their Eyes Were Watching God*.

- *Define*: Identify and state the essential traits or characteristics of something, differentiating it clearly from other things.

  Define *osmosis*.

- *Describe*: Tell about an event, person, or process in detail, creating a clear and vivid image of it.

  Describe the dress of a medieval knight.

- *Evaluate*: Assess the value or significance of the topic.

  Evaluate the contributions of jazz musicians to American music.

- *Explain*: Make a topic as clear and understandable as possible by offering reasons, examples, and so on.

  Explain the functioning of the circulatory system.

- *Summarize*: State the major points concisely and comprehensively (7c).

  Summarize the major arguments against using animals in laboratory research.

Thinking through your answer

You may be tempted to begin writing an essay examination at once. Time is precious—but so, too, are organizing and planning. So spend some time (about 10 percent of the allotted time is a good rule of thumb) thinking through your answer.

Begin by deciding which major points you need to make and in what order to present them. Jot down support for each point. Craft a clear, succinct thesis that satisfies the strategy term of the exam question. In most writing situations, you start from a working thesis, but when writing under pressure you will probably find it more efficient to outline (or simply jot down) your ideas and craft your thesis from your outline. For example, if you were asked to define the three major components of personality according to Freud, you could write a brief informal outline as a framework for your answer.

Id

basic definition—what it is and is not
major characteristics
functions

Ego

basic definition—what it is and is not
major characteristics
functions

Superego

basic definition—what it is and is not
major characteristics
functions

From this outline, you can develop a thesis: *According to Freud, the human personality consists of three major and interconnected elements: the id, the ego, and the superego.*

64b **Writing an essay examination response**

Your goal in producing an essay examination answer is twofold: to demonstrate that you have mastered the course material and to communicate your ideas and information clearly, directly, and logically.

Writing notes in your own language

Before writing an essay answer in English, consider making some notes in whatever language you are most comfortable writing in. Writing down key words and main points in your native language may help you organize your answer more quickly and ensure that you don't leave out something important.

Drafting

During the drafting stage, follow your outline as closely as you can. If you depart from it, you will lose time and perhaps have trouble returning to the main discussion. As a general rule, develop each major point into at least one paragraph. Be sure to make clear the connections among your main points by using transitions. <u>The last element</u> *of the human personality, according to Freud, is the superego.*

Besides referring to your outline for guidance, pause and read what you have written before going on to a new point. Rereading may remind you of other ideas while you still have time to include them and should also help you establish a clear connection with whatever follows. If you are writing on paper, write neatly, skip lines, and leave ample margins so that you have space for changes or additions when you revise. If you are writing your essay exam on a computer, use double spacing and paragraph indentations.

Revising and editing

Leave enough time (at least five to ten minutes) to read through your essay answer carefully. Consider the following questions:

- Is the thesis clearly stated? Does it answer the question?
- Are all the major points covered?
- Are the major points adequately developed and supported?
- Is each sentence complete?
- Are spelling, punctuation, and syntax as correct as you can make them? Have you checked for missing words?
- Is the handwriting legible? If you are using a computer, take time to run your spell checker.

64c Writing take-home exams

You may sometimes be asked to do your essay exam at home. If so, make sure to clarify any guidelines about how much time you should spend working on the exam, how long your answer should be, and how you should submit the exam (for example, through email or to the instructor's campus mailbox).

In general, remember that you will not have as much time on a take-home essay exam as you would for a regular academic essay, so follow the same procedures you would for an in-class exam. In addition, be direct in your response, starting right in with your thesis, and use a straightforward beginning-middle-conclusion organizational sequence. Most important, as you plan for your take-home exam, bring in ways to show that you know the subject matter of the course and that you can provide concrete, detailed examples to support the main points you are making. As with any essay exam, look closely at the question itself and make sure that you are responding to the question in appropriate ways.

64d A student's essay exam response

See how one student handled an essay and short-answer examination in a first-year American history course. She had fifty-five minutes to answer two of three essay questions and three of five short-answer questions. She chose to answer the following question first.

> Between 1870 and 1920, African Americans and women both struggled to establish certain rights. What did each group want? Briefly analyze the strategies each group used, and indicate how successful they were.

This student began her exam with this question because she knew the most about this topic. With another essay and three short answers to write, she decided to devote no more than twenty minutes to this essay.

First, she analyzed what the question asked her to do, noting the strategy terms. She decided that the first sentence of the question strongly implied comparison and contrast of the two struggles. The second sentence asked for an explanation of the goals of each group, and in the third sentence, she took *analyze* and *indicate* to mean "explain what each group did and how well it succeeded." (As it turned out, this was a very shrewd reading of the question; the instructor later remarked that those who had included a comparison and contrast produced better answers than those who did not.) Note that, in this instance, the strategy the instructor expected is not stated explicitly in the question. Instead, class members were expected to read between the lines to infer the strategy.

The student then identified content terms around which to develop her answer: the groups—African Americans and women—and their actions, goals, strategies, and degrees of success. Using these terms, she spent about three minutes producing the following informal outline:

Introduction

goals, strategies, degree of success

African Americans

want equality
two opposing strategies: DuBois and Washington
even with vote, great opposition

Women

many goals (economic, political, educational), but focus on vote
use men's arguments against them
use vote to achieve other goals

Conclusion

educational and economic differences between groups

From this outline, the student crafted the following thesis: *In the years between 1870 and 1920, African Americans and women were both fighting for equal rights but in significantly different ways.* She then wrote the following answer:

> The years between 1870 and 1920 saw two major groups—African Americans and women—demanding more rights, but the two groups approached the problem of inequality in different ways. Initially, women wanted the vote, equality within the family, and equal job and education opportunities. Their attempts to achieve all these goals at once were unsuccessful, as men countered by accusing them of attacking

Thesis

Section on women and their goals

the sanctity of the family institution. (Demanding equality in the family meant confronting Christianity, which subordinated women to men.) With the lead of Carrie Chapman Catt, women narrowed their goal to a focus on the vote. They emphasized that they would vote to benefit middle-class Americans (like themselves), reduced the stridency of their rhetoric, and said that they would clean up an often corrupt government (they turned the men's strategy against them here by emphasizing their own purity and virtue). They also invited Wilson to talk at their conventions and won him to their side. Because of their specific focus and reorganization, women did finally receive the vote, which then gave them the power to work toward their other reform goals.

Strategy used to achieve goal

Degree of success

Less well organized and less formally educated than middle-class white women, African Americans often were unable to dedicate their full effort to the cause of equality because of severe economic problems. In addition, their leaders disagreed over strategy. Washington told them to work hard and earn the vote and equality, while DuBois maintained that they, like all other Americans, deserved it already. African Americans also had to overcome fierce racial prejudice. Even after they finally won the vote, whites passed laws (literacy tests and grandfather clauses) and used force (particularly through the Ku Klux Klan) to keep African Americans from voting. Therefore, even after African Americans got the vote in name, they had to fight to keep and use it.

Section on African Americans and their goals

Dual strategy used to achieve goals

Degree of success

Thus both women and African Americans fought for (and are still fighting for) equal rights, but women were more successful than African Americans in late nineteenth-century America. Educated, organized, and financially secure, they concentrated their efforts on getting the vote as a means to higher political objectives, and they got it. African Americans, on the other hand, had to overcome great financial barriers that reduced access to education and worked against strong organization. Even after they received the vote, these Americans were kept subjugated by prejudicial laws and practices.

Two groups contrasted

THINKING CRITICALLY ABOUT ESSAY EXAMINATIONS

Choose an essay exam that you have recently written. Use the guidelines in 64a to analyze what the exam question asked you to do. Then reread your answer carefully. Did you do what the question asked? If not, how should you have responded? Then, referring to 64b, reconstruct how you answered the question. How could you improve the content and presentation of your answer? Note any new strategies that might help you improve your success in taking essay exams.

65 Portfolios

Putting together a portfolio is another academic opportunity that can help you develop real-world skills. Applicants for jobs and internships in many fields can make an impact with a carefully chosen portfolio of work that shows off relevant expertise or training.

A portfolio is a selection of your work—whether for class, for a job, or for some other purpose—that you think shows off your skills to best advantage. Many college writing classes require portfolios from students at the end of the course.

65a Planning a portfolio

Depending on your purpose, audience, and the type of work you plan to include, you may want to create a traditional paper portfolio in a folder or binder, an electronic portfolio online, or some other specialized kind of portfolio. Your concept of what the portfolio should accomplish will affect the form it takes.

1 Purpose

Some possible purposes for a writing portfolio include fulfilling course requirements, showing work to a prospective employer, entering a competition, and keeping a record of your college (or artistic) work. Each of these purposes will lead to different decisions about what to include, how to arrange the material, and whether to make work available online, in print, or in some other format.

2 Audience

Your audience will also affect what materials you include. If, for example, your audience is a writing instructor, you will need to demonstrate what you've learned; if it is a prospective employer, you may need to focus on what you can do. In some cases, the primary audience for a portfolio may be yourself.

3 Organization

Your audience and purpose should guide you in deciding how to organize the material. If you are presenting a portfolio as the final component of a course, your instructor may designate an organizational arrangement. If not, you may decide to arrange the portfolio in chronological order and comment on your progress throughout the course. Other methods of organization include arranging material by theme, by importance, or by some other category that makes sense for your work.

4 Design

Think carefully about how you want your portfolio to look. What impression do you want to give? Choose color, fonts, typefaces, images, and other graphic elements that will enhance the appeal of your portfolio and enhance the content. Make sure the design is helpful for your audience, too, with clear navigation such as a table of contents. For more on design, see Chapter 23.

5 Selection

How many entries should you include in a portfolio? The answer depends on your purpose. If you are developing an electronic portfolio, you may include a variety of materials in several categories — essays, problem sets, photos, Web texts, multimedia presentations, a résumé, or anything else that seems relevant — because those reviewing your portfolio will click on only those items that interest them. If you are developing a print portfolio for a writing class, however, you should probably limit yourself to five to seven examples of your writing. Here are some kinds of writing you might include in a portfolio:

- an academic essay demonstrating your ability to argue a claim
- a personal essay that shows self-insight and demonstrates your ability to paint vivid pictures with words
- a piece of writing that reflects on your learning over the college years
- a brief report for a class or community project

- a writing project (print or multimedia) showing your ability to analyze and solve a problem
- your favorite piece of writing
- writing based on field research, library research, or both
- a piece of writing for a group, club, or campus publication
- an example of a collaboratively written document, accompanied by a description of how the team worked and what you contributed
- an example of your best writing on an essay examination
- correspondence, such as a letter of inquiry, an email, or a job application

You should also include the assignments for your work, whenever applicable. If your portfolio is for a writing course, you may be expected to include examples of your notes and early drafts as well as any responses you got from other readers.

One student who had done spoken-word performances throughout his college years decided to assemble a portfolio of those performances. To do so, he digitized the videotapes he had of his work and compiled a DVD that he could distribute when applying for scholarships and for admission to graduate school—and that he could keep as a record of his writing and performing. Given his purpose and potential audiences, he organized the portfolio chronologically and made each piece easily accessible for future use.

EXERCISE 65.1

Make a list of the times you have organized some of your work—to apply for a job, to create a record of your writing from middle through high school, or for some other reason. What spurred you on to carry out these tasks? Did you have an audience other than yourself in mind? What criteria did you use in choosing pieces? Bring your list to class to compare with those of other students.

65b Completing a portfolio

To complete a portfolio, you will need to prepare a written statement, assemble your material, obtain feedback from others, and prepare the final revised copy.

1 Written statement

You should introduce a portfolio with a written statement that explains and reflects on your work. This statement might be in the form of a memo, cover letter, personal essay, or home page, depending on the format your portfolio takes. Think carefully about the overall impression you want the portfolio to create, and make sure that the tone and style of your statement set the stage for the entire portfolio. The statement should include the following:

- *a description of what is in the portfolio*: what was the purpose of each work (or of the portfolio as a whole)?

- *an explanation of your choices*: how did you decide that these pieces represent your best work?

- *a reflection on your strengths and abilities*: What have you learned by completing the work for the portfolio? What problems have you encountered, and how have you solved them?

2 Final assembly

For a print portfolio, number all pages in consecutive order, and prepare a table of contents. Label and date each piece of writing if you haven't done so previously. Put a cover sheet on top with your name and the date; if the portfolio is for a class, include the course title and number. Assemble everything in a folder.

For an electronic portfolio, prepare navigation that identifies your work to its best advantage, and check the links to each piece.

3 Responses

Once you have assembled your portfolio, seek responses to it from several classmates or friends and, if possible, from at least one instructor. (You may want to refer your reviewers to the guidelines on reviewing a draft in 4b.) Revise accordingly.

If this portfolio is part of your work in a course, ask your instructor whether a few handwritten corrections are acceptable. If you intend to use it as part of a job search, however, you will want to print out clean copies. Either way, the time and effort you spend revising and editing the contents of your portfolio will be time well spent.

65c A student's portfolio cover letter

Student Writer

James Kung

Here is the cover letter that James Kung wrote to introduce the portfolio he submitted at the conclusion of his first-year writing course. His instructor had asked for print documents only. Note that in his cover letter James does not simply describe the portfolio but also analyzes the works included — and his strengths, weaknesses, and development as a writer — in some detail.

December 6, 2008

Dear Professor Ashdown:

"Writing is difficult and takes a long time." This simple yet powerful statement has been uttered so many times in our class that it has essentially become our motto. In just ten weeks, my persuasive writing skills have improved dramatically, thanks to many hours spent writing, revising, polishing, and thinking about my topic. The various drafts, revisions, and other materials in my course portfolio show this improvement.

Addresses audience directly

Reflects on improvement

I entered this first-quarter Writing and Rhetoric class with both strengths and weaknesses. I was strong in the fundamentals of writing: logic and grammar. I have always written fairly well-organized essays. However, despite this strength, I struggled throughout the term to narrow and define the various aspects of my research-based argument.

Analyzes overall strengths and weaknesses

The first aspect of my essay that I had trouble narrowing and defining was my major claim, or my thesis statement. In my "Proposal for Research-Based Argument," I proposed to argue about the case of Wen Ho Lee, the Los Alamos scientist accused of copying restricted government documents. I stated, "The Wen Ho Lee incident deals with the persecution of not only one man, but of a whole ethnic group." You commented that the statement was a "sweeping claim" that would be "hard to support."

Analyzes first piece included

I spent weeks trying to rework that claim. Finally, as seen in my "Writer's Notebook 10/16/08," I realized that I had chosen the Lee case because of my belief that the political inactivity of Asian Americans contributed to the case against Lee. Later, I once again

Explains revision process

revised my claim, stating that the political inactivity did not cause but rather contributed to racial profiling in the Wen Ho Lee case.

I also had trouble defining my audience. I briefly alluded to the fact that my audience was a "typical American reader." However, I later decided to address my paper to an Asian American audience for two reasons. First, it would establish a greater ethos for myself as a Chinese American. Second, it would enable me to target the people the Wen Ho Lee case most directly affects: Asian Americans. As a result, in my final research-based argument, I was much more sensitive to the needs and concerns of my audience, and my audience trusted me more.

Concludes with
future plans

I hope to continue to improve my writing of research-based arguments.

Sincerely,

Signature

James Kung

James Kung

65d A student's portfolio home page

Jenny Ming composed the following home page for her electronic portfolio in her senior year, as she was preparing to look for a job. She wanted to get her work out for others to see, and so she created an eye-catching graphic as background for her name along with a menu of her work on the left side of the page. Her welcome text introduces herself clearly and simply and invites viewers to take a look at her work and to contact her with comments or questions. Note that she includes a link to her résumé at the bottom of the page.

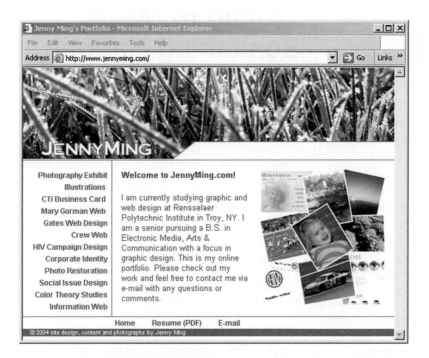

THINKING CRITICALLY ABOUT PORTFOLIOS

Choose a portfolio cover letter or home page that you have recently created. Ask first how your portfolio introduces your work to readers. How does the cover letter or home page represent your strengths as a communicator? How well do you present the portfolio physically? What could you change, add, or delete to make your portfolio more effective?

66 Writing to Make Something Happen in the World

What kinds of writing make something happen in the world? College students in a six-year research study felt particular pride in the writing they did for family, friends, and community groups—and for many extracurricular activities that were meaningful to them. They produced flyers for fundraising campaigns, newsletters for community action groups, nature guides for local parks, press releases for campus events, and Web sites for local emergency services. Furthermore, once these students graduated from college, they continued to create—and to value—these kinds of public writing.

A large group of college students participating in a research study were asked, "What is good writing?" The researchers expected fairly straightforward answers like "writing that gets its message across," but the students kept coming back to one central idea: good writing "makes something happen in the world."

At some point during your college years or soon after, you are highly likely to create writing that is not just something that you turn in for a grade, but writing that you do because you want to make a difference. The writing that matters most to many students and citizens, then, is writing that has an effect in the world: writing that gets up off the page or screen, puts on its working boots, and marches out to get something done!

66a Identifying your audience

When you decide to write to make something happen, you'll generally have some idea of what effect you want that writing to have. Clarify what actions you want your readers to take in response to your writing, and then think about what people you most want to reach—audiences today can be as close as your immediate neighbors or as dispersed as global netizens. Who will be interested in the topic you are writing about? For example, if you are trying to encourage your elementary school to plant a garden, you might try to interest parents, teachers, and PTA members; if you are planning a voter registration drive, you might start with eighteen-year-olds on your campus.

> **QUICK HELP**
>
> ## Characteristics of writing that makes something happen
>
> - Public writing has a very clear *purpose* (to promote a local cause or event; to inform or explain an issue or problem; to persuade others to act; sometimes even to entertain).
>
> - It is intended for a specific *audience* and addresses those people directly.
>
> - It uses the *genre* most suited to its purpose and audience (a poster to alert people to an upcoming fund drive, a newsletter to inform members of a group, a brochure to describe the activities of a group, a letter to the editor to argue for a candidate or an issue), and it appears in a *medium* (print, online, or both) where the intended audience will see it.
>
> - It generally uses straightforward, everyday *language*.

66b   Connecting with your audience

Once you have a target audience in mind, you'll need to think carefully about where and how you are likely to find them, how you can get their attention so they will read what you write, and what you can say to get them to achieve your purpose.

If you want to convince your neighbors to pool time, effort, and resources to build a local playground, then you have a head start: you know something about what they value and about what appeals would get their attention and convince them to join in this project. If you want to create a flash mob to publicize ineffective security at chemical plants near your city, on the other hand, you will need to reach as many people as possible, most of whom you will not know.

Genre and media

Even if you know the members of your audience, you still need to think about the genre and medium that will be most likely to reach them. To get neighbors involved in the playground project mentioned above, you might decide that a colorful print flyer delivered door to door and posted at neighborhood gathering places would work best. For a flash mob, however, an easily forwarded message—text, Twitter, or email—will probably work best.

Appropriate language

For all public writing, think carefully about the audience you want to reach—as well as *unintended* audiences your message might reach. Doing so can help you craft writing that will be persuasive without being offensive.

Timing

Making sure your text will appear in a timely manner is crucial to the success of your project. If you want people to plan to attend an event, present your text to them at least two weeks ahead of time. If you are issuing a newsletter or blog, make sure that you create posts or issues often enough to keep people interested (but not so often that readers can't or won't keep up). If you are reporting information based on something that has already happened, make it available as soon as possible so that your audience won't consider your report "old news."

66c Sample writing that makes something happen in the world

On the following pages are some examples of the forms public writing can take.

POSTER

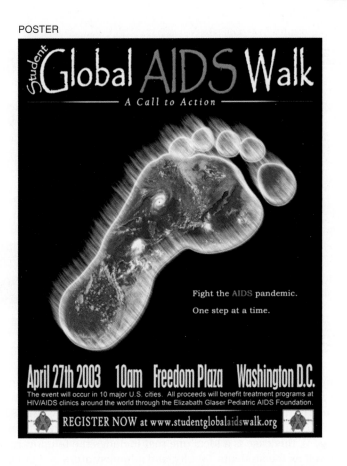

This poster, created by student Amrit Rao, has a very clear purpose: to attract participants to a walk aimed at raising money in support of AIDS research. In this case, Rao wanted to reach college students in the DC area; students, he felt, would be particularly aware of the need for such research and likely to respond by showing up for the walk. To reach as many students as possible, he decided to distribute the poster in both print and digital forms. He called on friends in the area to help place the poster in key locations on a dozen college campuses, and he emailed PDF versions of the poster to student body presidents on each campus, asking them to help spread the word.

FLYER

Local 715 SEIU

El Boletín de Trabajadores Temporales

Volume 1: Issue 3

Servicios educativos para sus hijos:

Necesitan mas ayuda sus niños con la tarea? o Quieren hacer algo despues de la escuela para divertirse? Informece sobre los varios programas que ofrece Stanford para niños que viven en la area cercana. Hay programas para niños de todos años desde la escuela primaria hasta la preparatoria. Ofrecen apoyo academico como ayuda con la tarea y tambien actividades Los programes son durante y despues de la escuela. Para aprender como puede inscribir sus hijos en uno de estos programas, llame a Leticia Rodriguez en la oficina de SEIU Local 715 al (650) 723-3680.

Preocupado por dinero?

Esta endeudado con tarjetas de credito? Quiere saber como obtener su reporte de credito? Nosotros podemos ayudarle a crear un presupuesto mensual, mejorar su puntuacion en su reporte de credito, reducir los intereses que paga en tarjetas de credito, y ahorrar dinero. Para citas gratuitas comuniquese con Araceli Rodriguez o Nancy Villareal a la oficina de SEIU, Local 715 al (650) 723-3680.

OPORTUNIDADES PARA TRABAJOS PERMANENTES

Según el acuerdo en el nuevo contracto de la union, Stanford va a crear 40 posiciones permanentes en los próximos 4 años. Adicionalmente, trabajadores temporales que han trabajado 20 horas por semana por más de cuatro

CUENTO PERSONAL

Student Anna Mumford created and posted copies of this flyer advocating for pay raises for campus workers. Again, her purpose is clear: she wants to raise awareness on her campus of what she views as highly inequitable salaries and working conditions for temporary workers. Her audience in this case is a local one that includes the temporary workers as well as the students, faculty, and administrators on her campus. Mumford did not have an easy way to distribute the information electronically to temporary workers, nor was she certain that all of them had access to computers, so she chose to produce a print flyer that would be easy to distribute across campus. She wrote in Spanish (on an English-speaking campus), the home language of most of the temporary workers, to reach her target audience more effectively.

NEWSLETTER

As with the writers of the poster and flyer, yoga teacher Joelle Hann has a clear purpose in mind for her e-newsletter: to provide information to her audience—students and others interested in her yoga classes and developments in the yoga community. Emailing the newsletter to her subscribers allows Hann to reach an interested audience quickly and to provide links to more of the content she's discussing, and it also means that she can include photos, illustrations, and color to enhance her document's design impact.

Band promoter Bryan Swirsky used Facebook, where he has many friends who share his interest in punk rock, to reach an audience interested in seeing a reunion show by an all-black punk band that had a cult following in the 1970s. Those invited by Bryan could also invite their own interested friends, allowing news of the event to spread virally.

EVENT INVITATION ON SOCIAL NETWORKING SITE

+ Select Guests to Invite

Pure Hell / The Bad Luck Charms / TV Tramps
• Share • Public Event

Time:	Saturday, October 16 · 6:00pm - 9:30pm
Location:	Europa
Created By:	Scenic Nyc, Bryan Swirsky
More Info:	All Ages (16+ with government issued ID, under 16 w/ parent, guardian) $8 adv, $10 day of. !!! Early show.

Pure Hell, one of the earliest all-black American punk-rock bands, formed in Philadelphia, Pennsylvania, in 1974, as punk rock was taking off and developing a following in nearby New York City. Discovered by Johnny Thunders during the heyday of the New York Dolls, the band moved to New York. In 1978, they toured Europe and released their only single ("These Boots are Made for Walking" b/w "No Rules"). Live performances by Pure Hell have been compared to the MC5, Sex Pistols, Dead Boys, Germs, and fellow Afropunks the Bad Brains, who identified Pure Hell as an influence. Their album (Noise Addiction), recorded in the late 1970s, was finally released this year. Pure Hell also has an unreleased album (The Black Box) produced in the mid 1990's by former members of L.A. Guns, Nine Inch Nails, and Lemmy Kilmister of Motorhead. Recent performances by Pure Hell in NYC showed that they still have what it takes!

ONLINE REPORT

Less Trash, More Compost!
A report on a community partnership to reduce trash and promote composting and recycling at a summer camp

Funded in part by the New England Grassroots Environmental Fund

...When campers have something in their hand, they are very likely to ask where is the compost, where is the recycling...and that is exciting...
                                    Counselor, Athol Area YMCA Day Camp

---

Deb Habib and Kaitlin Doherty
Seeds of Solidarity
November, 2007

Project Background and Goals
"Gross, but fun!" exclaims an eight-year old compost enthusiast, one of over 200 campers, plus counselors and staff at the Athol Area YMCA day camp in Orange, Massachusetts who worked together to successfully divert over one ton of their breakfast and lunch waste from the landfill to compost. And they won't mind telling you that they had fun doing it.

Seeds of Solidarity, a non-profit organization based in Orange, partnered with the summer food service director, the Athol Area YMCA, and a local hauler to implement a composting and recycling initiative, diverting the waste from approximately 3,600 meals at two sites over an eight-week period in the summer of 2007. This pilot project was inspired by success using biodegradable and compostable utensils and plates at the annual North Quabbin Garlic and Arts Festival, also sponsored by Seeds of Solidarity, which results in only two bags of trash for 10,000 people.

Athol and Orange are located in the North Quabbin region, where 20% of the children live below the federal poverty line. Food service director Sherry Fiske runs a state and federally funded summer food service program at 11 sites in Orange and Athol, providing free breakfast and lunch to children and families during the summer months. The YMCA camps based both at the Y site in Athol and Lake Selah in North Orange are among these summer food service sites. While school year lunch programs in the area utilize washable dishes and utensils, the summer food service program is held at temporary sites, resulting in heaping dumpsters of paper, plastic and polystyrene waste.

This report, created by Deb Habib and Kaitlin Doherty of the non-profit group Seeds of Solidarity, provides information about a successful experimental recycling and composting program at a Massachusetts camp. (Only the first page of the twenty-six-page PDF is shown.) Other sections include "Project Description," "Voices of Campers," "Successes and Challenges," "Summary of Key Considerations," and an appendix with additional documents (interviews with campers, letters to campers' parents before the program began, and graphs quantifying the outcomes). The report appears on the organization's Web site, which notes that Seeds of Solidarity "provid[es] people of all ages with the inspiration and practical tools to use renewable energy and grow food in their communities." While the report offers information about an experiment that has already taken place, the document also serves to encourage and inform others who might want to create a similar program.

THINKING CRITICALLY ABOUT WRITING THAT MAKES SOMETHING HAPPEN IN THE WORLD

You have probably done quite a bit of writing to make something happen in the world, though you might not have thought of it as official "writing." Yet as this chapter shows, such writing is important to those who do it—and to those affected by it. Think about the groups you belong to—informal or formal, home- or community- or school-based—and choose a piece of writing you have done for the group, whether on your own or with others. Then take a careful look at it: looking at it with a critical eye, is its purpose clear? What audience does it address, and how well does it connect to that audience? Are the genre (newsletter, poster, flyer, brochure, report, etc.) and the medium (print, electronic) appropriate to achieving the purpose and reaching the audience? How might you revise this text to make it even more effective?

GLOSSARIES

Glossary of Terms

absolute phrase See *phrase*.

active voice The form of a verb when the subject performs the action: *Lata <u>sang</u> the chorus again.* See also *voice*.

adjective A word that modifies, quantifies, identifies, or describes a noun or a word or words acting as a noun. Most adjectives precede the noun or other word(s) they modify (*a <u>good</u> book*), but a **predicate adjective** follows the noun or pronoun it modifies (*the book is <u>good</u>*). A **proper adjective** is formed from a proper noun (*Egyptian*) and is capitalized.

adjective clause See *clause*.

adjective forms Changes in an adjective from the **positive** degree (*tall*, *good*) to the **comparative** (comparing two — *taller*, *better*) or the **superlative** (comparing more than two — *tallest*, *best*). Short regular adjectives (*tall*) add *-er* and *-est*, but most adjectives of two syllables or more form the comparative by adding *more* (*more beautiful*) and the superlative by adding *most* (*most beautiful*). A few adjectives have irregular forms (*good*, *better*, *best*), and some (*only*, *forty*) do not change form.

adverb A word that qualifies, modifies, limits, or defines a verb, an adjective, another adverb, or a clause, frequently answering the questions *where? when? how? why? to what extent?* or *under what conditions?* Adverbs derived from adjectives and nouns commonly end in the suffix *-ly*. *She will <u>soon</u> travel <u>south</u> and will <u>probably</u> visit her <u>very</u> favorite sister.* See also *conjunction*.

adverb clause See *clause*.

adverb forms Changes in an adverb from the **positive** degree (*eagerly*) to the **comparative** (comparing two — *more eagerly*) or the **superlative** (comparing more than two — *most eagerly*). Most adverbs add *more* to form the comparative and *most* to form the superlative, but a few add *-er* and *-est* or have irregular forms (*fast, faster, fastest; little, less, least*).

adverbial particle A preposition combined with a verb to create a phrasal verb.

agreement The correspondence of a pronoun with the word it refers to (its antecedent) in person, number, and gender or of a verb with its subject in person and number. See also *antecedent, gender, number, person.*

antecedent The specific noun that a pronoun replaces and to which it refers. A pronoun and its antecedent must agree in person, number, and gender. *<u>Ginger Rogers</u> moved <u>her</u> feet as no one else has.*

antithesis The use of parallel structures to highlight contrast or opposition.

appositive A noun or noun phrase that identifies or adds identifying information to a preceding noun phrase. *Zimbardo, <u>an innovative researcher</u>, designed the Stanford Prison Experiment. My sister <u>Janet</u> has twin boys.*

appositive phrase See *appositive*.

argument A text that makes and supports a **claim**. See also *evidence, warrant*.

article *A, an,* or *the*. Articles are the most common adjectives. *A* and *an* are **indefinite**;

they do not specifically identify the nouns they modify. *I bought an apple and a peach.* *The* is **definite**, or specific. *The peach was not ripe.*

auxiliary verb A verb that combines with the base form or with the present or past participle of a main verb to form a verb phrase. The primary auxiliaries are forms of *do, have,* and *be. Did he arrive? We have eaten. She is writing.* **Modal** auxiliaries such as *can, may, shall, will, could, might, should, would,* and *ought* [*to*] have only one form and show possibility, necessity, obligation, and so on.

base form The form of a verb that is listed in dictionaries, such as *go* or *listen.* For all verbs except *be,* it is the same as the first-person singular form in the present tense.

case The form of a noun or pronoun that reflects its grammatical role in a sentence. Nouns and indefinite pronouns can be **subjective, possessive,** or **objective,** but they change form only in the possessive case. *The dog* (subjective) *barked. The dog's* (possessive) *tail wagged. The mail carrier called the dog* (objective). The personal pronouns *I, he, she, we,* and *they,* as well as the relative or interrogative pronoun *who,* have different forms for all three cases. *We* (subjective) *took the train to Chicago. Our* (possessive) *trip lasted a week. Maria met us* (objective) *at the station.* See also *person, pronoun.*

claim An arguable statement.

clause A group of words containing a subject and a predicate. An **independent clause** can stand alone as a sentence. *The car hit the tree.* A **dependent clause,** as the name suggests, is grammatically subordinate to an independent clause, linked to it by a subordinating conjunction or a relative pronoun. A dependent clause can function as an adjective, an adverb, or a noun. *The car hit the tree that stood at the edge of the road* (**adjective clause**). *The car hit the tree when it went out of control* (**adverb clause**). *The car hit*

whatever grew at the side of the road (**noun clause**). See also *nonrestrictive element, restrictive element.*

climactic order Arranging ideas in order of increasing importance or power.

collective noun A noun that refers to a group or collection (*herd, mob*).

comma splice An error resulting from joining two independent clauses with only a comma.

common noun See *noun.*

comparative or **comparative degree** The form of an adjective or adverb used to compare two things (*happier, more quickly*). See also *adjective forms, adverb forms.*

complement A word or group of words completing the predicate in a sentence. A **subject complement** follows a linking verb and renames or describes the subject. It can be a **predicate noun** (*Anorexia is an illness*) or a **predicate adjective** (*Karen Carpenter was anorexic*). An **object complement** renames or describes a direct object (*We considered her a prodigy and her behavior extraordinary*).

complete predicate See *predicate.*

complete subject See *subject.*

complex sentence See *sentence.*

compound adjective A combination of words that functions as a single adjective (*blue-green sea, ten-story building, get-tough policy, high school outing, north-by-northwest journey*). Most, but not all, compound adjectives need hyphens to separate their individual elements.

compound-complex sentence See *sentence.*

compound noun A combination of words that functions as a single noun (*go-getter, in-law, Johnny-on-the-spot, oil well, southeast*).

compound predicate See *predicate.*

compound sentence See *sentence.*

compound subject See *subject.*

conciseness Using the fewest possible words to make a point effectively.

conditional sentence A sentence that focuses on a question of truth or fact, introduced by *if* or its equivalent. *If we married, our parents would be happy.*

conjunction A word or words that join words, phrases, clauses, or sentences. **Coordinating conjunctions** (*and, but, for, nor, or, so,* or *yet*) join grammatically equivalent elements (*Marx and Engels* [two nouns]; *Marx wrote one essay, but Engels wrote the other* [two independent clauses]). **Correlative conjunctions** (such as *both . . . and, either . . . or,* or *not only . . . but also*) are used in pairs to connect grammatically equivalent elements (*neither Marx nor Engels; Marx not only studied the world but also changed it*). A **subordinating conjunction** (such as *although, because, if, that,* or *when*) introduces a dependent clause and connects it to an independent clause. *Marx moved to London, where he did most of his work. Marx argued that religion was an "opiate."* A **conjunctive adverb** (such as *consequently, moreover,* or *nevertheless*) modifies an independent clause following another independent clause. A conjunctive adverb generally follows a semicolon and is followed by a comma. *Thoreau lived simply at Walden; however, he regularly joined his aunt for tea in Concord.*

conjunctive adverb See *conjunction.*

coordinate adjective Adjectives in a sequence that relate equally to the noun they modify and are separated by commas: *the long, twisting, muddy road.*

coordinating conjunction See *conjunction.*

coordination Relating separate but equal ideas or clauses in a sentence and clarifying the emphasis given to each, usually using a coordinating conjunction or semicolon. *The report was short, but it was persuasive.*

correlative conjunction See *conjunction.*

count noun See *noun.*

cumulative sentence A sentence that adds details, in phrases and dependent clauses, to an independent clause. *Sarah waited, anxious and concerned that the class had been canceled.*

dangling modifier A word, phrase, or clause that does not logically modify any element in the sentence to which it is attached. *Studying Freud, the meaning of my dream became clear* is incorrect because *the meaning* could not have been studying Freud. *Studying Freud, I began to understand the meaning of my dream* is correct because *I* was studying.

declarative sentence See *sentence.*

definite article The word *the.* See also *article.*

degree See *adjective forms, adverb forms.*

demonstrative pronoun See *pronoun.*

dependent clause A word group containing a subject and a predicate but unable to stand alone as a sentence; usually beginning with a subordinating conjunction (*because, although*) or a relative pronoun (*that, which*). See also *clause.*

determiner In a noun phrase, a word used to identify or quantify the noun, including articles (*a, an, the*), possessive nouns (*Bob's*), numbers, and pronouns such as *my, our,* and *this.*

direct address Using a noun or pronoun to name the person or thing spoken to. *Hey, Jack. You, get moving.*

direct discourse A quotation reproducing a speaker's exact words, marked with quotation marks.

direct object A noun or pronoun receiving the action of a transitive verb. *We mixed paints.* See also *indirect object.*

elliptical construction or **elliptical structure** A construction in which some words are left out but understood. *Josh is more* *aggressive than Jake* [*is*]. *The service was good, but the food* [*was*] *average.*

evidence Support for an argument's claim.

exclamatory sentence See *sentence.*

expletive A construction that introduces a sentence with *there* or *it,* usually followed by a form of *be. There are four candidates in the race. It was a dark and stormy night.*

faulty predication A mixed structure in which a subject and predicate do not fit together grammatically or logically.

faulty sentence structure An error in which a sentence begins with one grammatical pattern and switches to another.

first person See *person.*

font The typeface or style and size of text characters.

fragment A group of words that is not a grammatically complete sentence but is punctuated as one. See also *sentence fragment.*

fused sentence A sentence in which two independent clauses are run together without a conjunction or punctuation between them. Also known as a **run-on sentence**.

future tense See *simple tense.*

gender The classification of a noun or pronoun as masculine (*god, he*), feminine (*goddess, she*), or neuter (*godliness, it*).

gerund A verbal form ending in *-ing* and functioning as a noun. *Sleeping is a bore.*

helping verb See *auxiliary verb.*

imperative mood The form of a verb used to express a command or a request. An imperative uses the base form of the verb and may or may not have a stated subject. *Leave. You be quiet. Let's go.* See also *mood.*

imperative sentence See *sentence.*

indefinite article The words *a* and *an.* See also *article.*

indefinite pronoun A word such as *each, everyone,* or *nobody* that does not refer to a specific person or thing. See also *pronoun.*

independent clause A word group containing a subject and a predicate that can stand alone as a sentence. See also *clause.*

indicative mood The form of a verb used to state a fact or an opinion or to ask a question. *Washington crossed the Delaware. Did he defeat the Hessians?* See also *mood.*

indirect discourse A paraphrased quotation that does not repeat another's exact words and hence is not enclosed in quotation marks. *Coolidge said that if nominated he would not run.*

indirect object A noun or pronoun identifying to whom or to what or for whom or for what a transitive verb's action is performed. The indirect object almost always precedes the direct object. *I handed the dean my application and told her that I needed financial aid.* See also *direct object.*

indirect question A sentence pattern in which a question is the basis of a subordinate clause. An indirect question should end with a period, not a question mark. *Everyone wonders why young people start smoking.* (The question, phrased directly, is "Why do young people start smoking?")

indirect quotation See *indirect discourse.*

infinitive The base form of a verb, preceded by *to* (*to go, to run, to hit*). An infinitive can serve as a noun, an adverb, or an adjective. *To go would be unthinkable* (noun). *We stopped to rest* (adverb). *The company needs space to grow* (adjective). An infinitive can be in either the active (*to hit*) or passive (*to be hit*) voice and in either the present (*to* [*be*] *hit*) or perfect (*to have* [*been*] *hit*) tense. An **infinitive phrase** consists of an infinitive together with its modifiers, objects, or complements. See *phrase.*

intensifier A modifier that increases the emphasis of the word or words it modifies. *I would very much like to go. I'm so happy.*

Despite their name, intensifiers are stylistically weak; they are best avoided in academic and professional writing.

intensive pronoun See *pronoun*.

interjection A grammatically independent word or group of words that is usually an exclamation of surprise, shock, dismay, or the like. *Ouch! For heaven's sake, what do you think you're doing?*

interrogative pronoun See *pronoun*.

interrogative sentence See *sentence*.

intransitive verb A verb that does not need a direct object to complete its meaning. *The children laughed.*

inversion Changing the usual order of a sentence to create surprise or emphasis.

irregular verb A verb whose past tense and past participle are not formed by adding *-ed* or *-d* to the base form, such as *see, saw, seen*.

keyword A word or phrase used to search a computer database.

linking verb A verb that joins a subject with a subject complement or complements. Common linking verbs are *appear, be, become, feel,* and *seem. The argument appeared sound. It was actually a trick.* See also *verb*.

main clause An independent clause. See *clause*.

main verb The verb that carries the central meaning in a verb phrase, such as *given* in the phrase *could be given*.

mechanical error An error in the use of capitalization, italics, or punctuation.

misplaced modifier A word, phrase, or clause positioned so that it appears to modify a word other than the one the writer intended. *With a credit card, the traveler paid for the motel room and opened the door.* Unless the writer intended to indicate that the traveler used the credit card to open the door, *with a credit card* should follow *paid* or *room*.

mixed structure A sentence that begins with one grammatical pattern and switches to another.

modal See *auxiliary verb*.

modifier A word, phrase, or clause that acts as an adjective or an adverb and qualifies the meaning of another word, phrase, or clause. See also *adjective, adverb, clause, phrase*.

mood The form of a verb that indicates the writer's or speaker's attitude toward the idea expressed by the verb. Different moods are used to state a fact or an opinion or to ask a question (**indicative**); to give a command or request (**imperative**); and to express a wish, a suggestion, a request or requirement, or a condition that does not exist (**subjunctive**). *The sea is turbulent* (indicative). *Stay out of the water* (imperative). *I wish the water were calm enough for swimming* (subjunctive). See also *imperative mood, indicative mood, subjunctive mood*.

noncount noun See *noun*.

nonrestrictive element A word, phrase, or clause that modifies but does not change the essential meaning of a sentence element. A nonrestrictive element is set off from the rest of the sentence with commas, dashes, or parentheses. *Quantum physics, which is a difficult subject, is fascinating.* See also *restrictive element*.

noun A word that names a person, place, object, concept, action, or the like. Nouns serve as subjects, objects, complements, and appositives. Most nouns form the plural with the addition of *-s* or *-es* and the possessive with the addition of *'s* (see *number, case*). **Common nouns** (*president, state, month*) name classes or general groups. **Proper nouns** (*Barack Obama, Florida, July*) name particular persons or things and are capitalized. **Collective nouns** (*family, committee, jury*) refer to a group of related elements. **Count nouns** (*women, trees*) refer to things that can be directly counted. **Noncount**

nouns (*sand, rain, violence*) refer to collections of things or to ideas that cannot be directly counted.

noun clause See *clause.*

noun phrase See *phrase.*

number The form of a noun or pronoun that indicates whether it is singular (*book, I, he, her, it*) or plural (*books, we, they, them, their*).

object A word or words, usually a noun or pronoun, influenced by a transitive verb, a verbal, or a preposition. See also *direct object, indirect object, object of a preposition.*

object complement See *complement.*

objective case See *case.*

object of a preposition A noun or pronoun connected to a sentence by a preposition. The preposition, the object, and any modifiers make up a **prepositional phrase**. *I went to the party without her.*

participial phrase A phrase consisting of a participle and any modifiers, objects, and complements and acting as an adjective. See also *participle, phrase.*

participle A verbal with properties of both an adjective and a verb. Like an adjective, a participle can modify a noun or pronoun; like a verb, it has present and past forms and can take an object. The **present participle** of a verb always ends in *-ing* (*going, being*). The **past participle** usually ends in *-ed* (*ruined, injured*), but many verbs have irregular forms (*gone, been, brought*). Present participles are used with the auxiliary verb *be* to form the **progressive tenses** (*I am making, I will be making, I have been making*). Past participles are used with the auxiliary verb *have* to form the **perfect tenses** (*I have made, I had made, I will have made*) and with *be* to form the passive voice (*I am seen, I was seen*). These combinations of auxiliary verbs and participles are known as **verb phrases**. See also *adjective, phrase, tense, verbal, voice.*

particle A preposition or adverb that combines with a verb in a two-part verb: *the plane took off.*

parts of speech The eight grammatical categories into which words can be grouped depending on how they function in a sentence. Many words act as different parts of speech in different sentences. The parts of speech are *adjectives, adverbs, conjunctions, interjections, nouns, prepositions, pronouns,* and *verbs.*

passive voice The form of a verb when the subject is being acted on rather than performing the action. *The batter was hit by a pitch.* See also *voice.*

past participle See *participle.*

past perfect or **past perfect tense** The form a verb takes to show that an action or a condition was completed before another event in the past (*The virus had killed six people before investigators learned of its existence*). See also *tense.*

past subjunctive See *subjunctive mood.*

past tense See *simple tense.*

perfect progressive or **perfect progressive tense** The form a verb takes to show an action or a condition that continues up to some point in the past, present, or future (*The workers had been striking for a month before they signed the contract; She has been complaining for days; The experiment will have been continuing for a year next May*). See also *tense.*

perfect tense The form a verb takes to show a completed action in the past, present, or future (*They had hoped to see the parade but ended up stuck in traffic; I have never understood this equation; By tomorrow, the governor will have vetoed the bill*). See also *tense.*

periodic sentence A sentence that builds to a climactic ending by postponing the main idea until the very end.

person The relation between a subject and its verb, indicating whether the subject is speaking about itself (**first person**—*I* or *we*), being spoken to (**second person**—*you*), or being spoken about (**third person**—*he, she, it,* or *they*). *Be* has several forms depending on the person (*am, is,* and *are* in the present tense and *was* and *were* in the past tense). Other verbs change form only in the present tense with a third-person singular subject (*I fall, you fall, she falls, we fall, they fall*).

personal pronoun See *pronoun.*

phrasal-prepositional verb A verb phrase made up of a verb, particle, and preposition: *put up with, made up of.*

phrasal verb A verb that combines with a preposition. *The plane took off.*

phrase A group of words that functions as a single unit but lacks a subject, verb, or both. An **absolute phrase** modifies an entire sentence. It usually includes a noun or pronoun followed by a participle (sometimes implied) or participial phrase. *The party having ended, everyone left.* A **gerund phrase** includes a gerund and its objects, complements, and modifiers. It functions as a noun, acting as a subject, a complement, or an object. *Exercising regularly and sensibly is a key to good health* (subject). An **infinitive phrase** includes an infinitive and its objects, complements, and modifiers. It functions as an adjective, an adverb, or a noun. *The Pacific Coast is the place to be* (adjective). *She went to pay her taxes* (adverb). *To be young again is all I want* (noun). A **noun phrase** includes a noun and its modifiers. *A long, rough road crossed the barren desert.* A **participial phrase** includes a present or past participle and its objects, complements, and modifiers. It functions as an adjective. *Absentmindedly climbing the stairs, he stumbled. They bought a house built in 1895.* A **prepositional phrase** is introduced by a preposition and ends with a noun or pronoun, called the object of the preposition. It

functions as an adjective, an adverb, or a noun. *The gas in the laboratory was leaking* (adjective). *The firefighters went to the lab to check* (adverb). *The smell came from inside a wall* (noun). A **verb phrase** is composed of a main verb and one or more auxiliaries, acting as a single verb in the sentence predicate. *I should have come to the review session.*

plural The form of a noun, pronoun, or adjective that refers to more than one person or thing, such as *books, we,* or *those.*

positive or **positive degree** The basic form of an adjective or adverb (*cold, quick*). See also *adjective forms, adverb forms.*

possessive or **possessive case** The form of a noun or pronoun that shows possession. Nouns and indefinite pronouns in the possessive case use apostrophes (*Harold's, the children's, everyone's, your parents'*), while personal pronouns in the possessive case do not (*my, mine, its, yours, hers*). See also *case.*

possessive pronoun A word used in place of a noun that shows possession. See also *possessive, pronoun.*

predicate The verb and related words in a clause or sentence. The predicate expresses what the subject does, experiences, or is. The **simple predicate** is the verb or verb phrase. *For years the YMHA has been a cultural center in New York City.* The **complete predicate** includes the simple predicate and any modifiers, objects, or complements. *Jose gave Cristina an engagement ring.* A **compound predicate** has more than one simple predicate. *The athletes swam in a relay and ran in a marathon.*

predicate adjective See *complement.*

predicate noun See *complement.*

prefix An addition to the beginning of a word that alters its meaning (*anti-French, suburban*).

preposition A word or group of words that indicates the relationship of a noun or pronoun, called the object of the preposition, to another part of the sentence. *He was at the top of the ladder before the others had climbed to the fourth rung.* See also *phrase.*

prepositional phrase A group of words beginning with a preposition and ending with its object. A prepositional phrase can function as an adjective, an adverb, or a noun. See also *phrase.*

present participle See *participle.*

present perfect or **present perfect tense** The form a verb takes to show that an action or a condition has been completed before the present (*The team has worked together well*). See also *tense.*

present progressive The form a verb takes to show an action or a condition that is ongoing in the present (*He is planning a sales presentation*). See also *tense.*

present tense See *simple tense.*

primary source A research source that offers firsthand knowledge of its subject.

progressive tense The form a verb takes to show an action or a condition that is continuing in the past, present, or future (*He was singing too loudly to hear the telephone; The economy is surging; Business schools will be competing for this student*). See also *tense.*

pronoun A word used in place of a noun, called the antecedent of the pronoun. **Demonstrative pronouns** (*this, that, these, those*) identify or point to specific nouns. *These are Peter's books.* **Indefinite pronouns** (*any, each, everybody, some,* and similar words) do not refer to specific nouns. *Many are called, but few are chosen.* **Intensive pronouns** (such as *myself* and *themselves*) emphasize their antecedents and have the same form as reflexive pronouns. *She wanted to make dinner herself.* **Interrogative pronouns** (*who, which, that*) ask questions. *Who will attend?* **Personal pronouns** (*I, you, he, she, it, we,* and *they*)

refer to particular people or things. They have different forms (*I, me, my, mine*) depending on their case. **Possessive pronouns** (*my, your, her, hers,* and similar words) show ownership. **Reciprocal pronouns** (*each other, one another*) refer to individual parts of a plural antecedent. *The partners helped each other.* **Reflexive pronouns** (such as *yourselves* and *himself*) end in *-self* or *-selves* and refer to the subject of the clause in which they appear. *We taught ourselves to type.* **Relative pronouns** (*who, whose, that, whatever,* and similar words) connect a dependent clause to a sentence. *I don't care what happens.*

proper adjective See *adjective.*

proper noun See *noun.*

reciprocal pronoun See *pronoun.*

reflexive pronoun See *pronoun.*

regular verb A verb whose past tense and past participle are formed by adding *-d* or *-ed* to the base form (*care, cared, cared; look, looked, looked*). See also *irregular verb.*

relative pronoun See *pronoun.*

restrictive element A word, phrase, or clause that limits the essential meaning of the sentence element it modifies or provides necessary identifying information about it. A restrictive element is not set off from the rest of the sentence with commas, dashes, or parentheses. *The tree that I hit was an oak.* See also *nonrestrictive element.*

root A word from which other words grow, usually through the addition of prefixes or suffixes.

run-on sentence See *fused sentence.*

secondary source A research source that reports information from research done by others. See also *primary source.*

second person See *person.*

sentence A group of words containing a subject and a predicate and expressing a complete thought. In writing, a sentence begins with a capital letter and ends with a period, a question mark, or an exclamation point. A sentence may be **declarative**, making a statement (*The sun rose*); **interrogative**, asking a question (*Did the sun rise?*); **exclamatory**, indicating surprise or other strong emotion (*The earth moved!*); or **imperative**, expressing a command (*Get here at six*). Sentences are also classified grammatically. A **simple sentence** consists of a single independent clause without dependent clauses. *I left the house.* Its subject, predicate, or both may be compound. *Jorge and Tim designed and programmed the site.* A **compound sentence** contains two or more independent clauses linked with a coordinating conjunction, a correlative conjunction, or a semicolon. *I did not go, but she did.* A **complex sentence** contains an independent clause and one or more dependent clauses. *After he cleaned the kitchen, he went to bed.* A **compound-complex sentence** contains at least two independent clauses and at least one dependent clause. *We had planned to hike, but we did not go because it rained all day.* See also *clause.*

sentence fragment A group of words that is not a grammatically complete sentence but is punctuated as one. Usually a fragment lacks a subject, a verb, or both or is a dependent clause that is not attached to an independent clause. In academic and professional writing, fragments should be revised to be complete sentences.

sequence of tenses See *tense.*

simple past tense See *tense.*

simple predicate See *predicate.*

simple subject See *subject.*

simple tense Past (*It happened*), present (*Things fall apart*), or future (*You will succeed*) forms of verbs. See also *tense.*

singular The form of a noun, a pronoun, or an adjective that refers to one person or thing, such as *book, it,* or *this.*

split infinitive The often awkward intrusion of an adverb between *to* and the base form of the verb in an infinitive (*to better serve* rather than *to serve better*).

squinting modifier A misplaced word, phrase, or clause that could refer equally, but with different meanings, to words either preceding or following it. For example, in *Playing poker often is dangerous,* the position of *often* fails to indicate whether the writer meant that frequent poker playing is dangerous or that poker playing is often dangerous.

subject The noun or pronoun and related words that indicate who or what a sentence is about. The **simple subject** is the noun or pronoun. The **complete subject** is the simple subject and its modifiers. In *The timid gray mouse fled from the owl, mouse* is the simple subject; *The timid gray mouse* is the complete subject. A **compound subject** includes two or more simple subjects. *The mouse and the owl* heard the fox.

subject complement See *complement.*

subjective case See *case.*

subjunctive mood The form of a verb used to express a wish, a suggestion, a request or requirement, or a condition that does not exist. The present subjunctive uses the base form of the verb. *I asked that he be present. Long live the Queen!* The past subjunctive uses the same verb form as the past tense except for the verb *be,* which uses *were* for all subjects. *If I were president, I would change things.* See also *mood.*

subordinate clause A dependent clause. See *clause.*

subordinating conjunction A word or phrase such as *although, because,* or *even* *though* that introduces a dependent clause and joins it to an independent clause. See also *conjunction*.

subordination A way of distinguishing major points from minor ones. Minor points are often placed in dependent clauses.

suffix An addition to the end of a word that alters the word's meaning or part of speech, as in *migrate* (verb) and *migration* (noun) or *late* (adjective or adverb) and *lateness* (noun).

superlative The form of an adjective or adverb used in a comparison of three or more items (*happiest, most gladly*). See also *adjective forms, adverb forms*.

syntax The arrangement of words in a sentence in order to reveal the relation of each to the whole sentence and to one another.

tense The form of a verb that indicates the time at which an action takes place or a condition exists. The times expressed by tense are basically **present**, **past**, and **future**. Each tense has **simple** (*I enjoy*), **perfect** (*I have enjoyed*), **progressive** (*I am enjoying*), and **perfect progressive** (*I have been enjoying*) forms. The relationship of a verb with other verbs in the same sentence or surrounding sentences is called the **sequence of tenses**.

third person See *person*.

transition A word or phrase that signals a progression from one sentence or part of a sentence to another.

transitive verb A verb that takes a direct object, which receives the action expressed by the verb. A transitive verb may be in the active or passive voice. *The artist drew the sketch. The sketch was drawn by the artist.* See also *verb*.

verb A word or group of words, essential to a sentence, that expresses what action a subject takes or receives or what the subject's state of being is. *Edison invented the incandescent bulb. Gas lighting was becoming obsolete.* Verbs change form to show tense, number, voice, and mood. See also *auxiliary verb, intransitive verb, irregular verb, linking verb, mood, person, regular verb, tense, transitive verb, verbal, voice*.

verbal A verb form that functions as a noun, an adjective, or an adverb. The three kinds of verbals are gerunds, infinitives, and participles. See also *gerund, infinitive, participle*.

verbal phrase A phrase using a gerund, a participle, or an infinitive. See *phrase*.

verb phrase See *phrase*.

verb tense See *tense*.

voice The form of a verb that indicates whether the subject is acting or being acted on. When a verb is in the **active voice**, the subject performs the action. *Parker played the saxophone fantastically.* When a verb is in the **passive voice**, the subject receives the action. *The saxophone was played by Parker.* The passive voice is formed with the appropriate tense of the verb *be* and the past participle of the transitive verb. See also *verb*.

warrant Assumptions, sometimes unstated, that connect an argument's claims to the reasons for making the claims.

Glossary of Usage

Conventions of usage might be called the "good manners" of discourse. And just as manners vary from culture to culture and time to time, so do conventions of usage. Matters of usage, like other language choices you must make, depend on what your purpose is and on what is appropriate for a particular audience at a particular time.

a, an Use *a* with a word that begins with a consonant (*a book*), a consonant sound such as "y" or "w" (*a euphoric moment*, *a one-sided match*), or a sounded *h* (*a hemisphere*). Use *an* with a word that begins with a vowel (*an umbrella*), a vowel sound (*an X-ray*), or a silent *h* (*an honor*).

accept, except The verb *accept* means "receive" or "agree to." *Except* is usually a preposition that means "aside from" or "excluding." *All the plaintiffs except Mr. Kim decided to accept the settlement.*

advice, advise The noun *advice* means "opinion" or "suggestion"; the verb *advise* means "offer advice." *Charlotte's mother advised her to dress warmly, but Charlotte ignored the advice.*

affect, effect As a verb, *affect* means "influence" or "move the emotions of"; as a noun, it means "emotions" or "feelings." *Effect* is a noun meaning "result"; less commonly, it is a verb meaning "bring about." *The storm affected a large area. Its effects included widespread power failures. The drug effected a major change in the patient's affect.*

aggravate The formal meaning is "make worse." *Having another mouth to feed aggravated their poverty.* In academic and professional writing, avoid using *aggravate* to mean "irritate" or "annoy."

all ready, already *All ready* means "fully prepared." *Already* means "previously." *We were all ready for Lucy's party when we learned that she had already left.*

all right, alright Avoid the spelling *alright*.

all together, altogether *All together* means "all in a group" or "gathered in one place." *Altogether* means "completely" or "everything considered." *When the board members were all together, their mutual distrust was altogether obvious.*

allude, elude *Allude* means "refer indirectly." *Elude* means "avoid" or "escape from." *The candidate did not even allude to her opponent. The suspect eluded the police for several days.*

allusion, illusion An *allusion* is an indirect reference. An *illusion* is a false or misleading appearance. *The speaker's allusion to the Bible created an illusion of piety.*

a lot Avoid the spelling *alot*.

already See *all ready, already.*

alright See *all right, alright.*

altogether See *all together, altogether.*

among, between In referring to two things or people, use *between*. In referring to three or more, use *among*. *The relationship between the twins is different from that among the other three children.*

amount, number Use *amount* with quantities you cannot count; use *number* for quantities you can count. *A small number of volunteers cleared a large amount of brush.*

an See *a, an.*

and/or Avoid this term except in business or legal writing. Instead of *fat and/or protein*, write *fat, protein, or both.*

any body, anybody, any one, anyone *Anybody* and *anyone* are pronouns meaning "any person." *Anyone* [or *anybody*] *would enjoy this film. Any body* is an adjective modifying a noun. *Any body of water has its own ecology. Any one* is two adjectives or a pronoun modified by an adjective. *Customers could buy only two sale items at any one time. The winner could choose any one of the prizes.*

anyplace In academic and professional discourse, use *anywhere* instead.

anyway, anyways In writing, use *anyway*, not *anyways*.

apt, liable, likely *Likely to* means "probably will," and *apt to* means "inclines or tends to." In many instances, they are interchangeable. *Liable* often carries a more negative sense and is also a legal term meaning "obligated" or "responsible."

as Avoid sentences in which it is not clear if *as* means "when" or "because." For example, does *Carl left town as his father was arriving* mean "at the same time as his father was arriving" or "because his father was arriving"?

as, as if, like In academic and professional writing, use *as* or *as if* instead of *like* to introduce a clause. *The dog howled as if* [not *like*] *it were in pain. She did as* [not *like*] *I suggested.*

assure, ensure, insure *Assure* means "convince" or "promise"; its direct object is usually a person or persons. *She assured voters she would not raise taxes. Ensure* and *insure* both mean "make certain," but *insure* usually refers specifically to protection against financial loss. *When the city rationed water to ensure that the supply would last, the Browns could no longer afford to insure their car-wash business.*

as to Do not use *as to* as a substitute for *about. Karen was unsure about* [not *as to*] *Bruce's intentions.*

at, where See *where.*

awful, awfully *Awful* and *awfully* mean "awe-inspiring" and "in an awe-inspiring way." In academic and professional writing, avoid using *awful* to mean "bad" (*I had an awful day*) and *awfully* to mean "very" (*It was awfully cold*).

awhile, a while Always use *a while* after a preposition such as *for, in,* or *after. We drove awhile and then stopped for a while.*

bad, badly Use *bad* after a linking verb such as *be, feel,* or *seem.* Use *badly* to modify an action verb, an adjective, or another verb. *The hostess felt bad because the dinner was badly prepared.*

because of, due to Use *due to* when the effect, stated as a noun, appears before the verb *be. His illness was due to malnutrition.* (*Illness*, a noun, is the effect.) Use *because of* when the effect is stated as a clause. *He was sick because of malnutrition.* (*He was sick*, a clause, is the effect.)

being as, being that In academic or professional writing, use *because* or *since* instead of these expressions. *Because* [not *being as*] *Romeo killed Tybalt, he was banished to Padua.*

beside, besides *Beside* is a preposition meaning "next to." *Besides* can be a preposition meaning "other than" or an adverb meaning "in addition." *No one besides Francesca would sit beside him.*

between See *among, between.*

breath, breathe *Breath* is a noun; *breathe*, a verb. *"Breathe," said the nurse*, so June took a deep *breath.*

bring, take Use *bring* when an object is moved from a farther to a nearer place; use *take* when the opposite is true. *Take the box to the post office; bring back my mail.*

but, yet Do not use these words together. *He is strong but* [not *but yet*] *gentle.*

but that, but what Avoid using these as substitutes for *that* in expressions of doubt.

Hercule Poirot never doubted <u>that</u> [not *but that*] *he would solve the case.*

can, may *Can* refers to ability and *may* to possibility or permission. *Since I <u>can</u> ski the slalom well, I <u>may</u> win the race.*

can't hardly *Hardly* has a negative meaning; therefore, *can't hardly* is a double negative. This expression is commonly used in some varieties of English but is not used in academic English. *Tim <u>can</u>* [not *<u>can't</u>*] *<u>hardly</u> wait.*

can't help but This expression is redundant. Use the more formal *I cannot but go* or less formal *I can't help going* rather than *I can't help but go.*

censor, censure *Censor* means "remove that which is considered offensive." *Censure* means "formally reprimand." *The newspaper <u>censored</u> stories that offended advertisers. The legislature <u>censured</u> the official for misconduct.*

compare to, compare with *Compare to* means "regard as similar." *Jamie <u>compared</u> the loss <u>to</u> a kick in the head. Compare with* means "examine to find differences or similarities." *<u>Compare</u> Tim Burton's films <u>with</u> David Lynch's.*

complement, compliment *Complement* means "go well with." *Compliment* means "praise." *Guests <u>complimented</u> her on how her earrings <u>complemented</u> her gown.*

comprise, compose *Comprise* means "contain." *Compose* means "make up." *The class <u>comprises</u> twenty students. Twenty students <u>compose</u> the class.*

conscience, conscious *Conscience* means "a sense of right and wrong." *Conscious* means "awake" or "aware." *Lisa was <u>conscious</u> of a guilty <u>conscience</u>.*

consensus of opinion Use *consensus* instead of this redundant phrase. *The family <u>consensus</u> was to sell the old house.*

consequently, subsequently *Consequently* means "as a result"; *subsequently* means "then." *He quit, and <u>subsequently</u> his wife lost her job; <u>consequently</u>, they had to sell their house.*

continual, continuous *Continual* means "repeated at regular or frequent intervals." *Continuous* means "continuing or connected without a break." *The damage done by <u>continuous</u> erosion was increased by the <u>continual</u> storms.*

could of *Have,* not *of,* should follow *could, would, should,* or *might. We could <u>have</u>* [not *<u>of</u>*] *invited them.*

criteria, criterion *Criterion* means "standard of judgment" or "necessary qualification." *Criteria* is the plural form. *Image is the wrong <u>criterion</u> for choosing a president.*

data *Data* is the plural form of the Latin word *datum,* meaning "fact." Although *data* is used informally as either singular or plural, in academic or professional writing, treat *data* as plural. *These <u>data</u> indicate that fewer people are smoking.*

different from, different than *Different from* is generally preferred in academic and professional writing, although both phrases are widely used. *Her lab results were no <u>different from</u>* [not *<u>than</u>*] *his.*

discreet, discrete *Discreet* means "tactful" or "prudent." *Discrete* means "separate" or "distinct." *The leader's <u>discreet</u> efforts kept all the <u>discrete</u> factions unified.*

disinterested, uninterested *Disinterested* means "unbiased." *Uninterested* means "indifferent." *Finding <u>disinterested</u> jurors was difficult. She was <u>uninterested</u> in the verdict.*

distinct, distinctive *Distinct* means "separate" or "well defined." *Distinctive* means "characteristic." *Germany includes many <u>distinct</u> regions, each with a <u>distinctive</u> accent.*

doesn't, don't *Doesn't* is the contraction for *does not.* Use it with *he, she, it,* and singular nouns. *Don't* stands for *do not*; use it with *I, you, we, they,* and plural nouns.

due to See *because of, due to.*

each other, one another Use *each other* in sentences involving two subjects and *one another* in sentences involving more than two.

effect See *affect, effect.*

elicit, illicit The verb *elicit* means "draw out." The adjective *illicit* means "illegal." *The police elicited from the criminal the names of others involved in illicit activities.*

elude See *allude, elude.*

emigrate from, immigrate to *Emigrate from* means "move away from one's country." *Immigrate to* means "move to another country." *We emigrated from Norway in 1999. We immigrated to the United States.*

ensure See *assure, ensure, insure.*

enthused, enthusiastic Use *enthusiastic* rather than *enthused* in academic and professional writing.

equally as good Replace this redundant phrase with *equally good* or *as good.*

every day, everyday *Everyday* is an adjective meaning "ordinary." *Every day* is an adjective and a noun, meaning "each day." *I wore everyday clothes almost every day.*

every one, everyone *Everyone* is a pronoun. *Every one* is an adjective and a pronoun, referring to each member of a group. *Because he began after everyone else, David could not finish every one of the problems.*

except See *accept, except.*

explicit, implicit *Explicit* means "directly or openly expressed." *Implicit* means "indirectly expressed or implied." *The explicit message of the ad urged consumers to buy the product, while the implicit message promised popularity if they did so.*

farther, further *Farther* refers to physical distance. *How much farther is it to Munich? Further* refers to time or degree. *I want to avoid further delays.*

fewer, less Use *fewer* with nouns that can be counted. Use *less* with general amounts that you cannot count. *The world needs fewer bombs and less hostility.*

finalize *Finalize* is a pretentious way of saying "end" or "make final." *We closed* [not *finalized*] *the deal.*

firstly, secondly, etc. *First, second,* etc., are more common in U.S. English.

flaunt, flout *Flaunt* means to "show off." *Flout* means to "mock" or "scorn." *The drug dealers flouted authority by flaunting their wealth.*

former, latter *Former* refers to the first and *latter* to the second of two things previously mentioned. *Kathy and Anna are athletes; the former plays tennis, and the latter runs.*

further See *farther, further.*

good, well *Good* is an adjective and should not be used as a substitute for the adverb *well. Gabriel is a good host who cooks well.*

good and *Good and* is colloquial for "very"; avoid it in academic and professional writing.

hanged, hung *Hanged* refers to executions; *hung* is used for all other meanings.

hardly See *can't hardly.*

herself, himself, myself, yourself Do not use these reflexive pronouns as subjects or as objects unless they are necessary. *Jane and I* [not *myself*] *agree. They invited John and me* [not *myself*].

he/she, his/her Better solutions for avoiding sexist language are to write out *he or she,* to eliminate pronouns entirely, or to make the subject plural. Instead of writing *Everyone should carry his/her driver's license,* try *Drivers should carry their licenses* or *People should carry their driver's licenses.*

himself See *herself, himself, myself, yourself.*

hisself Use *himself* instead in academic or professional writing.

hopefully *Hopefully* is often misused to mean "it is hoped," but its correct meaning is "with hope." *Sam watched the roulette wheel hopefully* [not *Hopefully, Sam will win*].

hung See *hanged, hung.*

illicit See *elicit, illicit.*

illusion See *allusion, illusion.*

immigrate to See *emigrate from, immigrate to.*

impact Avoid the colloquial use of *impact* or *impact on* as a verb meaning "affect." *Population control may reduce* [not *impact*] *world hunger.*

implicit See *explicit, implicit.*

imply, infer To *imply* is to suggest indirectly. To *infer* is to guess or conclude on the basis of an indirect suggestion. *The note implied they were planning a small wedding; we inferred we would not be invited.*

inside of, outside of Use *inside* and *outside* instead. *The class regularly met outside* [not *outside of*] *the building.*

insure See *assure, ensure, insure.*

interact, interface *Interact* is a vague word meaning "do something that somehow involves another person." *Interface* is computer jargon; when used as a verb, it means "discuss" or "communicate." Avoid both verbs in academic and professional writing.

irregardless, regardless *Irregardless* is a double negative. Use *regardless.*

is when, is where These vague expressions are often used incorrectly in definitions. *Schizophrenia is a psychotic condition in which* [not *is when* or *is where*] *a person withdraws from reality.*

its, it's *Its* is the possessive form of *it. It's* is a contraction for *it is* or *it has. It's important to observe the rat before it eats its meal.*

kind, sort, type These singular nouns should be modified with *this* or *that*, not *these* or *those*, and followed by other singular nouns, not plural nouns. *Wear this kind of dress* [not *those kind of dresses*].

kind of, sort of Avoid these colloquialisms in formal writing. *Amy was somewhat* [not *kind of*] *tired.*

later, latter *Later* means "after some time." *Latter* refers to the second of two items named. *Juan and Chad won all their early matches, but the latter was injured later in the season.*

latter See *former, latter* and *later, latter.*

lay, lie *Lay* means "place" or "put." Its main forms are *lay, laid, laid.* It generally has a direct object, specifying what has been placed. *She laid her books on the desk. Lie* means "recline" or "be positioned" and does not take a direct object. Its main forms are *lie, lay, lain. She lay awake until two.*

leave, let *Leave* means "go away." *Let* means "allow." *Leave alone* and *let alone* are interchangeable. *Let me leave now, and leave* [or *let*] *me alone from now on!*

lend, loan In academic and professional writing, do not use *loan* as a verb; use *lend* instead. *Please lend me your pen so that I may fill out this application for a loan.*

less See *fewer, less.*

let See *leave, let.*

liable See *apt, liable, likely.*

lie See *lay, lie.*

like See *as, as if, like.*

likely See *apt, liable, likely.*

literally *Literally* means "actually" or "exactly as stated." Use it to stress the truth of a statement that might otherwise be understood as figurative. Do not use *literally* as an intensifier in a figurative statement. *Mirna was literally at the edge of her seat* may be accurate, but *Mirna is so hungry that she could literally eat a horse* is not.

loan See *lend, loan.*

loose, lose *Lose* is a verb meaning "misplace." *Loose* is an adjective that means "not securely attached." *Sew on that loose button before you lose it.*

lots, lots of Avoid these informal expressions meaning "much" or "many" in academic or professional discourse.

man, mankind Replace these terms with *people, humans, humankind, men and women,* or similar wording.

may See *can, may.*

may be, maybe *May be* is a verb phrase. *Maybe* is an adverb that means "perhaps." *He may be the head of the organization, but maybe someone else would handle a crisis better.*

media *Media* is the plural form of the noun *medium* and takes a plural verb in formal writing. *The media are obsessed with scandals.*

might of See *could of.*

moral, morale A *moral* is a succinct lesson. *The moral of the story is that generosity is rewarded. Morale* means "spirit" or "mood." *Office morale was low.*

myself See *herself, himself, myself, yourself.*

nor, or Use *either* with *or* and *neither* with *nor.*

number See *amount, number.*

off of Use *off* without *of. The spaghetti slipped off [not off of] the plate.*

OK, O.K., okay All are acceptable spellings, but avoid the term in academic and professional discourse.

on account of Use this substitute for *because of* sparingly or not at all.

one another See *each other, one another.*

or See *nor, or.*

outside of See *inside of, outside of.*

owing to the fact that Avoid this and other wordy expressions for *because.*

per Use the Latin *per* only in standard technical phrases such as *miles per hour.* Otherwise, find English equivalents. *As mentioned in* [not *As per*] *the latest report, the country's average food consumption each day* [not *per day*] *is only 2,000 calories.*

percent, percentage Use *percent* with a specific number; use *percentage* with an adjective such as *large* or *small. Last year, 80 percent of the members were female. A large percentage of the members are women.*

plenty *Plenty* means "enough" or "a great abundance." *They told us America was a land of plenty.* Colloquially, it is used to mean "very," a usage you should avoid in academic and professional writing. *He was very* [not *plenty*] *tired.*

plus *Plus* means "in addition to." *Your salary plus mine will cover our expenses.* Do not use *plus* to mean "besides" or "moreover." *That dress does not fit me. Besides* [not *Plus*], *it is the wrong color.*

precede, proceed *Precede* means "come before"; *proceed* means "go forward." *Despite the storm that preceded the ceremony, the wedding proceeded on schedule.*

pretty Avoid using *pretty* as a substitute for "rather," "somewhat," or "quite." *Bill was quite* [not *pretty*] *disagreeable.*

principal, principle When used as a noun, *principal* refers to a head official or an amount of money; when used as an adjective, it means "most significant." *Principle* means "fundamental law or belief." *Albert went to the principal and defended himself with the principle of free speech.*

proceed See *precede, proceed.*

quotation, quote *Quote* is a verb, and *quotation* is a noun. *He quoted the president, and the quotation* [not *quote*] *was preserved in history books.*

raise, rise *Raise* means "lift" or "move upward." (Referring to children, it means "bring up.") It takes a direct object; someone raises something. *The guests raised their glasses to toast. Rise* means "go upward." It does not take a direct object; something rises by itself. *She saw the steam rise from the pan.*

rarely ever Use *rarely* by itself, or use *hardly ever. When we were poor, we rarely went to the movies.*

real, really *Real* is an adjective, and *really* is an adverb. Do not substitute *real* for *really*. In academic and professional writing, do not use *real* or *really* to mean "very." *The old man walked very* [not *real* or *really*] *slowly.*

reason is because Use either *the reason is that* or *because*—not both. *The reason the copier stopped is that* [not *is because*] *the paper jammed.*

reason why This expression is redundant. *The reason* [not *reason why*] *this book is short is market demand.*

regardless See *irregardless, regardless.*

respectfully, respectively *Respectfully* means "with respect." *Respectively* means "in the order given." *Karen and David are, respectively, a juggler and an acrobat. The children treated their grandparents respectfully.*

rise See *raise, rise.*

set, sit *Set* usually means "put" or "place" and takes a direct object. *Sit* refers to taking a seat and does not take an object. *Set your cup on the table, and sit down.*

should of See *could of.*

since Be careful not to use *since* ambiguously. In *Since I broke my leg, I've stayed home*, the word *since* might be understood to mean either "because" or "ever since."

sit See *set, sit.*

so In academic and professional writing, avoid using *so* alone to mean "very." Instead, follow *so* with *that* to show how the intensified condition leads to a result. *Aaron was so tired that he fell asleep at the wheel.*

someplace Use *somewhere* instead in academic and professional writing.

some time, sometime, sometimes *Some time* refers to a length of time. *Please leave me some time to dress. Sometime* means "at some indefinite later time." *Sometime I will take you to London. Sometimes* means "occasionally." *Sometimes I eat sushi.*

sort See *kind, sort, type.*

sort of See *kind of, sort of.*

stationary, stationery *Stationary* means "standing still"; *stationery* means "writing paper." *When the bus was stationary, Pat took out stationery and wrote a note.*

subsequently See *consequently, subsequently.*

supposed to, used to Be careful to include the final -*d* in these expressions. *He is supposed to attend.*

sure, surely Avoid using *sure* as an intensifier in formal situations. Instead, use *surely* (or *certainly* or *without a doubt*). *I was surely glad to see you.*

take See *bring, take.*

than, then Use *than* in comparative statements. *The cat was bigger than the dog.* Use *then* when referring to a sequence of events. *I won, and then I cried.*

that, which A clause beginning with *that* singles out the item being described. *The book that is on the table is a good one* specifies the book on the table as opposed to some other book. A clause beginning with *which* may or may not single out the item, although some writers use *which* clauses only to add more information about an item being described. *The book, which is on the table, is a good one* contains a *which* clause between the commas. The clause simply adds extra, nonessential information about the book; it does not specify which book.

theirselves Use *themselves* instead in academic and professional writing.

then See *than, then.*

to, too, two *To* generally shows direction. *Too* means "also." *Two* is the number. *We, too, are going to the meeting in two hours.* Avoid using *to* after *where. Where are you flying* [not *flying to*]?

two See *to, too, two.*

type See *kind, sort, type.*

uninterested See *disinterested, uninterested.*

unique Some people argue that *unique* means "one and only" and object to usage that suggests that it can mean merely "unusual." In formal writing, you may want to avoid constructions such as *quite unique.*

used to See *supposed to, used to.*

very Avoid using *very* to intensify a weak adjective or adverb; instead, replace the adjective or adverb with a stronger, more precise, or more colorful word. Instead of *very nice*, for example, use *kind, warm, sensitive, endearing*, or *friendly.*

way, ways When referring to distance, use *way. Graduation was a long way* [not *ways*] *off.*

well See *good, well.*

where Use *where* alone, not with words such as *at* and *to. Where are you going* [not *going to*]?

which See *that, which.*

who, whom Use *who* if the word is the subject of the clause and *whom* if the word is the object of the clause. *Monica, who smokes incessantly, is my godmother.* (*Who* is the subject of the clause; the verb is *smokes.*) *Monica, whom I saw last winter, lives in Tucson.* (*Whom* is the object of the verb *saw.*)

who's, whose *Who's* is a contraction for *who is* or *who has. Who's on the patio? Whose* is a possessive form. *Whose sculpture is in the garden? Whose is on the patio?*

would of See *could of.*

yet See *but, yet.*

your, you're *Your* shows possession. *Bring your sleeping bag along. You're* is the contraction for *you are. You're in the wrong sleeping bag.*

yourself See *herself, himself, myself, yourself.*

Derek Bok. "Protecting Freedom of Expression at Harvard." From *The Boston Globe*, March 25, 1991. Reprinted by permission of the author.

E. E. Cummings. "since feeling is first." Copyright 1926, 1954, © 1991 by the Trustees for the E. E. Cummings Trust. Copyright © 1985 by George James Firmage. "as freedom is a breakfastfood." Copyright 1940, © 1968, 1991 by the Trustees for the E. E. Cummings Trust, from *Complete Poems: 1904–1962* by E. E. Cummings, edited by George J. Firmage. Used by permission of Liveright Publishing Corporation.

Emily Dickinson. "A Little Madness in the Spring." From *The Poems of Emily Dickinson*, Thomas H. Johnson, ed., Cambridge, Mass.: The Belknap Press of Harvard University Press. Copyright © 1951, 1955, 1979, 1983 by the President and Fellows of Harvard College. Reprinted by permission of the publishers and the Trustees of Amherst College.

Langston Hughes. "A Dream Deferred — Harlem [2]." From *The Collected Poems of Langston Hughes* by Langston Hughes, edited by Arnold Rampersad with David Roessel, Associate Editor. Copyright © 1994 by The Estate of Langston Hughes. Used by permission of Alfred A. Knopf, a division of Random House, Inc. and Harold Ober Associates Incorporated.

James Hunter. "Outlaw Classics." From *Rolling Stone*, March 9, 2006. Copyright © Rolling Stone LLC 2006. All rights reserved. Reprinted by permission.

Richard Wright. Eight lines (p. 250) from *Black Boy* by Richard Wright. Copyright © 1937, 1942, 1944, 1945 by Richard Wright: renewed © 1973 by Ellen Wright. Reprinted by permission of HarperCollins Publishers.

ART

Part-opening illustrations: Part 1, p. 13, Veer; **Part 2, p. 143,** © Image Source/Corbis; **Part 3, p. 219,** © Eva Wernlid/Nordicphotos/Corbis; **Part 4, p. 445,** Veer; **Part 5, p. 501,** © Steve Dunwell/Photolibrary; **Part 6, p. 559,** Veer; **Part 7, p. 643,** Veer; **Part 8, p. 679,** © Nathalie Darbellay/Sygma/Corbis; **Part 9, p. 707,** © Chris Cheadle/All Canada Photos/Corbis; **Part 10, p. 757,** © Lester Lefkowitz/CORBIS; **Part 11, p. 781,** Veer; **Part 12, p. 821,** Veer; **Glossaries, p. 899,** Veer.

Other illustrations: p. 18, Jupiter Images/Getty; **p. 33,** Peter Steiner/The New Yorker Collection/www.cartoonbank.com; **p. 34,** Michael Enright/www.menright.com; **p. 40,** Jupiter Images/Getty; **p. 42,** (upper) Rick Wilking/Landov;

(lower left) Bettman/Corbis; (lower right) Bettman/Corbis; **p. 56,** Michael Enright/www.menright.com; **p. 57,** Animal Locomotion/Bridgeman Art; **p. 58,** © 2010 Woters Kluwer Health, Lippincott Williams and Wilkins; **p. 60,** Royalty Free/Getty Images; **p. 91,** Peter Souza/White House/Corbis; **p. 113,** Royalty Free/Getty Images; **p. 114,** (upper and lower) Michael Enright/www.menright.com; **p. 115,** Royalty Free/Corbis; **p. 116,** Royalty Free/Corbis; **p. 118,** RF/Getty Images; **p. 119,** Bettmann/Corbis; **p. 121,** RF/Getty; **p. 146,** Library of Congress; **p. 147,** Library of Congress; **p. 149,** From The New York Times © 2010 The New York Times. All rights reserved. Used by permission and protected by the Copyright Laws of the United States. The printing, copying, redistribution or retransmission of the material without express permission from The New York Times is prohibited; **p. 153,** Craig F. Walker/The Denver Post; **p. 157,** © 2010 C. Herscovici, London/Artists Rights Society (ARS), NY; **pp. 158–61,** From *Fun Home: A Family Tragicomic* by Alison Bechdel. Reprinted by Permission of Houghton Mifflin Harcourt Publishing Company. All rights reserved; **p. 163,** Katja Heinemaan/Aurora Photos; **p. 167,** AP Images; **p. 170,** Spur Design; **p. 174,** Adbusters Media Foundation; **p. 178,** (both images) David King Collection; **p. 185,** Michael Ochs Archive; **p. 194,** Sustainable Foods; **p. 196,** Sustainable Foods; **p. 197,** Jan Weber/As We Sow; **p. 203,** Bloomberg/Businessweek; **p. 204,** AP Images; **p. 206,** Tom Tomorrow; **p. 207,** Getty Images; **p. 231,** (upper left) *Michigan Quarterly Review*; (lower left) Berkeley Electronic Press; (upper right) *Scientific American*; (lower right) Salon.com; **p. 237,** University of North Carolina; **p. 238,** University of North Carolina; **p. 239,** University of North Carolina; **p. 240,** (upper and lower) EBSCOhost; **p. 257,** Harvard University/Nieman Reports; **p. 259,** Ungar, Mark. "Prisons and Politics in Contemporary Latin America," *Human Rights Quarterly* 25:4 (2003): 909–10. © 2003 The Johns Hopkins University Press. Reprinted with permission of The Johns Hopkins University Press; **p. 317,** (upper) Book cover and copyright and title pages from *Small Wonder: Essays* by Barbara Kingsolver. Copyright © 2002 by Barbara Kingsolver. Reprinted by permission of HarperCollins Publishers; (middle) Douglas Conway, Lucas Marcoplos; (lower) Nobelprize.org; **p. 318,** (upper) Michael Enright/www.menright.com; (lower) Library of Congress; **p. 323,** Book cover and copyright and title pages from *Small Wonder: Essays* by Barbara Kingsolver. Copyright © 2002 by Barbara Kingsolver. Reprinted by permission of HarperCollins Publishers; **p. 329,**

Douglas Conway, Lucas Marcoplos; **p. 330,** *Columbia Journalism Review*; **p. 335,** EBSCOhost; **p. 339,** Nobelprize.org; **p. 366,** Palgrave Macmillan; **p. 367,** (upper) *The American Scholar*; (middle) Alexander, Meredith. "Thirty Years Later, Stanford Prison Experiment Lives On," Stanford Report (online), August 22, 2001, http://news.stanford.education/2001/prison2--822.html. Photo: Chuck Painter/Stanford News Service; (lower) Everett Collection; **p. 373,** Palgrave Macmillan; **p. 377,** *The American Scholar*; **p. 381,** EBSCOhost; **p. 383,** Alexander, Meredith. "Thirty Years Later, Stanford Prison Experiment Lives On," Stanford Report (online), August 22, 2001, http://news.stanford.education/2001/prison2--822.html. Photo: Chuck Painter/Stanford News Service; **p. 399,** (upper) Jacket design by Susan Mitchell. Copyright and title page from *The Metaphysical Club* by Louis Menand. Jacket design © 2001 by Susan Mitchell. Jacket photo of the Fort Sumter Flag courtesy of the National Park Service. Copyright and title pages copyright © 2001 by Farrar, Straus and Giroux, LLC. Reprinted by permission of Farrar, Straus and Giroux, LLC; (lower) Granger Collection, NorthWind Picture Archive; **p. 403,** Jacket design by Susan Mitchell. Copyright and title page from *The Metaphysical Club* by Louis Menand. Jacket design © 2001 by Susan Mitchell. Jacket photo of the Fort Sumter Flag courtesy of the National Park Service. Copyright and title pages copyright © 2001 by Farrar, Straus and Giroux, LLC. Reprinted by permission of Farrar, Straus and Giroux, LLC; **p. 409,** EBSCOhost; **p. 411,** Granger Collection, NorthWind Picture Archive; **p. 419,** Courtesy College of Architecture and the Arts, University of Illinois at Chicago; **p. 421,** Courtesy College of Architecture and the Arts, University of Illinois at Chicago; **p. 429,** (upper) Reprinted by permission of the publisher from *The Diversity of Life* by Edward O. Wilson, Cambridge, Mass.: The Belknap Press of Harvard University Press, Copyright © 1992 by Edward O. Wilson; (lower) EBSCOhost;

p. 433, Reprinted by permission of the publisher from *The Diversity of Life* by Edward O. Wilson, Cambridge, Mass.: The Belknap Press of Harvard University Press, Copyright © 1992 by Edward O. Wilson; **p. 437,** EBSCOhost; **p. 458,** Michael Enright/www.menright.com; **p. 460,** Typewriter © 1923 Corona, Courtesy the Albuquerque Museum, gift of Harry E. Chrisman and Don Bell in memory of Ernie Pyle, PC 1990 10.1a&b; **p. 471,** © 2010 C. Herscovici, London/Artists Rights Society (ARS), New York; **p. 474,** From *Fun Home: A Family Tragicomic* by Alison Bechdel. Reprinted by Permission of Houghton Mifflin Harcourt Publishing Company. All rights reserved; **pp. 481–84,** From *Persepolis: The Story of a Childhood* by Marjane Satrapi, translated by Mattias Ripa and Blake Ferris, translation copyright © 2003 by L'Association, Paris, France. Used by permission of Pantheon Books, a division of Random House, Inc.; **p. 489,** National Geographic; **p. 490,** Google; **p. 497,** (cartoon) Doug Fowler; (photo) Michael Enright/www.menright.com; **p. 498,** (middle) Charles Maxwell/Underwater Video Services; (right) U.S. Air Force photo by Tech. Sgt. Lance Cheung; **p. 499,** (upper and lower) Michael Enright/www.menright.com; **p. 511,** Royalty Free/Getty Images; **p. 512,** Reprinted with permission of Simon and Schuster Inc. Cover of *The Pocket Book of Baby and Child Care* by Benjamin Spock, MD. Copyright © 1946 edition of *The Pocket Book of Baby and Child Care* by Benjamin Spock, MD (NY Pocketbooks an imprint of Simon and Schuster Inc.). All rights reserved; **p. 521,** (upper) From "Today's Demon: Lost Worlds," *One! Hundred! Demons!* by Lynda Barry, Copyright © 2002 by Lynda Barry, published by Sasquatch Books and used courtesy of Darhansoff, Verrill, Feldman Literary Agents; (lower) SPL/Photo Researchers; **p. 523,** Karl Smitak/Photo Researchers; **p. 545,** Bridgeman Art/Getty Images; **p. 623,** Peanuts © 2010 Peanuts Worldwide LLC dist by UFS, Inc.

Index

presentations, oral and multimedia
  accessibility, 469
  assignment, purpose, and audience, 466–68
  collaborating on, 140–41
  guidelines for presentation software, 480–82
  practicing and delivering, 478–80
  Quick Help, 467
  student examples, 467–78, 482–85
  thinking critically about, 487
  translating between media, 40, 41
  visuals and, 194–95, 474–78
  webcasts, 486–87
  writing to be heard, 470–74
present participles, 589–90, 905
  as adjectives, 814
  with auxiliary verbs, 808–9
present perfect progressive tense, 601
present perfect tense, 812, 813, 907
present progressive tense, 600, 813, 907
present subjunctive, 607
present tense, 599–601, 909
  of *be*, 591
pretty, 915
previewing texts, 144–47
primary sources, 230–31, 907
principal, principle, 915
print vs. electronic text, 488
problem/solution
  organizing by, 59
  for paragraph development, 121
proceed, precede, 915
process, for paragraph development, 120–21
process model of collaboration, 138–40
progressive tenses, 599–601, 905, 907, 909
pronoun-antecedent agreement, 9–10, 626–28
pronouns, 566–67, 630–31, 907
  antecedents: collective nouns as, 627; compound, 627; indefinite pronouns as, 627–28; lack of agreement with, 9–10; Quick Help, 628; reciprocal pronouns as, 568
  pronoun case: in compound and elliptical structures, 624–25; pronouns as subjects, objects, and possessives, 619–22; Quick

Help, 620; *we* and *us* before a noun, 625–26
pronoun reference: ambiguous, 4, 630; editing for, 633
  sexist, avoiding, 510, 511, 628–29
  thinking critically about, 633–34
  types of: indefinite, 567, 903, 907; personal, 562, 566, 734, 907; reciprocal, 568, 907; relative, 567–68, 907
proofreading, 83, 100–101, 306, 551–53
proper adjectives, 565, 904
  capitalization of, 6, 759–61
proper nouns, 565, 904
  capitalization of, 6, 759–61
  multilingual writers and, 799
  spell checkers and, 5, 551
proposals
  emotional appeals in, 206–7
  student sample, 440–44
proximity, 463, 490, 491
public writing, 891–97
publishers/sponsors, credibility of, 254, 256, 258
punctuation
  apostrophes: contractions and omissions, 737; errors with, 8; forming plurals with, 737–38; possessive case and, 734–36; Quick Help, 736; thinking critically about, 738
  brackets, 268, 279–81, 748–50
  colons, 752–53: to introduce a series, 727; quotation marks and, 744–45
  commas: and absolute phrases, 582; in compound sentences, 8, 710–12; with contrasting elements, interjections, direct address, tag questions, 718; with dates, addresses, titles, numbers, 719–20; with introductory elements, 3, 708–9; with items in a series, 716–17; with nonrestrictive elements, 712–15; with parenthetical and transitional expressions, 718; Quick Help, 710; with quotation marks, 721–22, 744; for understanding, 722; unnecessary, 5–6, 722–24

T

U

unarguable statements, 188–89
understanding academic assignments, 24, 26–28
unified paragraphs
academic expectation of, 108–9
positioning topic sentences, 109–11
relating each sentence to the main idea, 111–12
uninterested, disinterested, 912
unique, 640, 917
us, we, 625–26. *See also* first person
usage labels, dictionary, 542
used to, supposed to, 916
usefulness of sources, 253–55

V

vague pronoun reference, 4
vague use of *it, this, that,* and *which,* 630–31
values, appeals to, 23–24
varieties of language. *See* language variety
veiled threat, 176
verbal fallacies, 175–77
verbal phrases, 580–82, 909
verbals, 909
pronouns as objects of, 621
in sentence fragments, 662
vs. verbs, 589
verb phrases, 580, 905, 906
verbs, 564–65, 909
auxiliary, 564, 901: errors with, 603; forming, 592, 808–9; order of, 806–8
forms of: *be,* 591; overview, 589–90; Quick Help, 590; regular and irregular, 592–97
mood, 904: confusing shifts in, 644; subjunctive, 607, 608; verbs and, 564
participial adjectives, 814
pronouns as objects of, 621
Quick Help, 605
sentence fragments and, 11
signal verbs, 279
strong, 702–3

tenses, 598–99, 811–12, 909: confusing shifts in, 7–8, 644; future, 601–2; past, 601; present, 599–601
thinking critically about, 609
transitive, 578, 579, 909
two-word verbs: hyphens and, 11, 778–79; using, 818–20
voice, active and passive, 605–6, 909: concise writing and, 683–84; confusing shifts in, 645; disciplinary style and, 827; forming passive with auxiliary verbs, 592; overuse of passive, 98
See also subject-verb agreement; verb tenses
very, 917
videos, translating from text-based works, 41
videotaping presentations, 140
visual arguments
analyzing appeals in, 169–71
analyzing elements of, 173–74
visual fallacies, 177–79
visual rhetoric, 488
visuals
acknowledging sources of, 289, 290
analyzing for critical reading, 166
in cross-cultural communication, 504
details in, 113–14
formatting: APA style, 360; CSE style, 427; MLA style, 309, 314–15, 345–46
integrating, 283–85
making appeals with: emotional appeals, 207–8; ethical appeals, 194–95; logical appeals, 202–3
misleading, 177–79
organizing, 56
for presentations, 141, 474–78
revision process and, 74–75, 99
rhetorical situations and, 30, 42
writing design and: analyzing and altering, 498–99; for arguments, 213; identifying in writing, 496; selecting, 496; types of, 497
visual structure of texts, 489–91
visual texts, 153

Directory of Student Writing

Advice for Multilingual Writers

Advice for "Talking the Talk" in College

Advice for Considering Disabilities